C000273723

UP TO THEIR NECKS

THE STORY OF A
NATIONAL SERVICEMAN

Richard

Joe Plant

Nov 2016

JOE P. PLANT

Acknowledgements.

In memory of my wife Annette, who was the inspiration in writing this book. I also extend my thanks to: Marlene Burridge who set me on the right road, Graham Reeves a fellow R.E.M.E. N/S who spent his time attached to the Royal Scots Fusiliers residing in Colombo Barracks Ipoh, who supplied some of the photos taken in Ipoh Town. To 'Jacko' Alan Jakeman for his contribution and photos, to all my comrades in arms of 3 Coy R.E.M.E. LAD whose exploits provided me with such great memories of past times. My grandson Charlie who helped with the cover layout. St. Anne's Club, the Lambeth Archives, the Honiton Museum, the Army Museum ...... all other materials and in particular photographs used to illustrate the text are the author's collection except for a few obtained from the Internet. Not forgetting my old pal John Parkinson who I recently rekindled a friendship of all those years ago who provided some of the photos taken when we were at No. 9 Battalion R.E.M.E Malvern 9/Elect/7.
Also in remembrance of all those National Servicemen buried in Malayan Military Cemeteries that never again will grace the shores of England.

Also Plublished by the Author.
'Cornwall First Town in the Front Line' Torpoints War Diaries 1939 -1946.

Published by Joe Plant
Publishing partner: Paragon Publishing
© 2012 Joe Plant

The rights of Joe Plant to be identified as the author of this work have been asserted by him in accordance with the Copyright, Designs and Patents Act of 1988.
All rights reserved; no part of this publication may be reproduced, stored in a retrieval system, or transmitted in any form or by any means, electronic, mechanical, photocopying, recording or otherwise without the prior written consent of the publisher or a licence permitting copying in the UK issued by the Copyright Licensing Agency Ltd, www.cla.co.uk

ISBN 978-1-78222-054-1

Book design, layout and production management by Into Print
www.intoprint.net
+44 (0)1604 832149

Printed and bound in UK, USA and Australia by Lightning Source

'UP TO THEIR NECKS'
THE STORY OF A NATIONAL SERVICEMAN

Chapters

Prologue.

PART ONE - THE BEGINNING

PART TWO - DURING

PART THREE - AFTER

PROLOGUE

Many books and articles written about the war, record what had happened in different battles fought on Land, Sea and Air. However, very few record the endurance and hardships to the civilians, throughout the years of the war who were on the receiving end of the bombs that fell from the skies but also the following fourteen years of rationing. In August 1945. The dropping of the Atom Bombs on Hiroshima and Nagasaki ended World War II and so, began a New Era, which would change the world into two distinctive ideologies. Democracy and Communism. We the youngsters and youth of that period had all experienced the instability and mental strife that the war brought with it, but it did not go away. What quickly followed in its wake was the beginning of the 'COLD WAR 'and the continuation of Conscription.

My story based on facts from my earliest memory during the war, the transformation of living standards that gradually became better in the early post war era, only to be faced with the prospect of forced enlistment. The generation of young lads born between the years of 1930 and 1942, were destined to become a Conscript (later defined as National Serviceman). Particularly those from cities that bore the blunt of wartime bombing also those other forgotten civilians of the war who suffered, were the thousands of Mothers who were to endure the anguish and worry of their young lads, being sent away to fight in further conflicts in defence of a shrinking British Empire, many never to return home. I feel no doubt in various ways and under different circumstances that my story relates to many comrades in arms, who experienced the same way of life all went through the hardships of growing up during the war years followed by a few years of freedom and then to face an enforced culture shock period of two years as Conscripts/National Servicemen under the then present National Service and Employment Act 1939 plus amendments, whose conception and history date back to World War One.

In 1914. The numbers of volunteers eager to join the forces was unprecedented, however as the War trundled on and the list of casualties grew, volunteers became rare and by **January 1916,** they had drastically fallen. The Government of the day had to do something about it. Over a period of two days, an intense debate took place in the House of Commons, discussing the results of a previous National Survey to determine the number of men willing to volunteer. The results indicated that half a million unmarried men were not, yet an equivalent number of married men were. The outcome, as judged by the Government, was compulsory enlistment that became an act of Parliament. The National Service Act passed was for; the call up of eligible single men followed by those eligible married men. The implications of this act caused great unrest amongst the population and particularly by a majority of young men in Ireland; the postponement of further discussions on the Home Rule for the Ireland Bill caused much grievance amongst many eligible Irish men who disagreed with fighting for the British with the outbreak of War. That enhanced their case of being anti British, resulting in the formation of the Irish Volunteer Movement and in April 1916 the Easter Rebellion. Although this Rebellion, was put down by British Troops. Within the Irish community, it created a great deal of sympathy in favour of the Irish Volunteer Movement. The rest is history.

November 1918. The cessation of the National Service Act was passed until. Its reintroduction of the Act **in 1939.**

April 1939. Heading the list of the British Government's "Planned Agenda". Was the armed forces. "IF", in the event of an outbreak of war, the Territorial Army would be doubled in strength to 340,000 men. The strength of the Naval fleet to be increased. More aircraft to be manufactured and in addition. The National Service (Armed Forces) Act 1939. Became an Act of Parliament. Compulsory Military Service for men, between the ages of 20 to 41. And the specified term of Service stated within that document.

Quote:

"The said start date until the end of the present emergency"?

Unquote.

(During the subsequent years of 1941, 1942, 1944 and 1947, the same Act of Parliament. Had readings in the House of Commons. All were repealed).

March 12th 1947. The National Service Bill was presented to the House of Commons by the Minister of Labour Mr. Isaacs and published on **March 13th.**

(For further reading refer to Hansard 1947).

March 31st. Moving the second reading in the House of Commons. Mr. Isaacs stated. The continuation of Compulsory Service, furthermore an increase in the period of service to 18 months, to come into effective on **Jan. 1st. 1949.**

The Bill was chiefly necessitated by the fact, owing to the interruption by the war of regular recruitment, the Services had become seriously depleted. The number of men serving regular terms of enlistment (including men who would shortly be finishing their engagements). The Army had reduced to just over 200,000, the R.A.F. and Royal Navy, 70,000 though better, being also unsatisfactory. Although the Government's recruiting campaign had produced an increase in the voluntary intake, during the period April – June 1946: from 13,298 to 22,348. This increase was not sufficient to build up the Forces to even pre-war strength, and unless the then present arrangements for calling-up men were continued, the regular element in the Services was likely to be, "insufficient to meet even a fraction of our minimum defence needs". The Government considered that to enable the gap to be filled, not only was compulsory military service essential, but efficient and well-trained reserve and military forces be built up and sustained at an adequate level in the Defence Forces that by spreading responsibility for the defence of the country amongst all of our young men, irrespective of class or, occupation, was the most democratic way of providing the forces required. Until **Jan. 1st. 1949** men would be called up under the present arrangements, those called-up this year serving for 2 years and the period of service being gradually reduced from Jan. 1st. 1948 to 18 months, for those called-up at the end of the year. In the past; in other countries that power had been reserved, to shorten the service period, in case of an increase in voluntary recruitment or, of a possibility of reducing our foreign commitments. Doctors or Dentist, unless taking specialist courses, would normally be called up at 25 years of age; apart from deferment for underground coal miners. No deferments, would be granted on industrial grounds; furthermore application for postponement on hardship grounds would continue to be dealt with by the Hardship Committees. Explaining the provision of the Bill. Mr. Isaac said the Government, disliked the connotation of:

"CONSCRIPTION"

"therefore adapted the term "

"NATIONAL SERVICE "

That very statement, made by the Government of the day. changed the terminology from.

"CONSCRIPT" TO NATIONAL SERVICEMAN".

The transition had been made. Nevertheless, we were still 'CONSCRIPTS.' As were our Grandfathers and fathers conscripted during and at the beginning of two World Wars.

July18th. 1947. Royal assent was given to the
Employment and National Service Act. 1947.
(For further reading, refer to Hansard. 1948).

November 24th. It was announced in the House of Commons that the Government had decided to raise the time of compulsory whole time service under the National Service Act, from 12 to 18 months. To this effect, the National Service (Amendment Bill) was introduced by the Minister of Labour in the House of Commons.

November 26th. The provisions of the bill was published

(For further reading refer Hansard 1948).

The debate continued and on the same day. The third reading of the Bill was passed.

December 18th. 1948. After a unanimous second reading in the House of Lords. The Bill was enacted on.

(For further reading refer to Hansard 1949).

30th. August. 1950. In a broadcast to the nation, The Prime Minister Mr. Clement Attlee announced the Government's decision, to extend the period of National Service from, 18 months to 2 years. Stating that the Government's full defence plans will be laid before Parliament when it reassembles on September 12th. Adding that a short bill would be introduced for the extension of the period of National Service.

August 31st. The White Papers dealing respectively, with the extensions of the period of National Service and with the increases in forces pay, was published. (For further reading refer to Hansard 1950).

From then on. Due to the political state of world affairs. There was little of any further debate or, amendment that affected the Bill until 1957 when a new amendment was passed in Parliament. Mr. Duncan Sandys, the Conservative Defence Minister issued a White Paper, published on April 5th. Outlining the Government's future defence policy, stating sweeping changes affecting all three Services. Officially described as "the biggest change in defence policy ever made in normal times".

The main point in the new policy. Directly, affected National Service:

**A progressive reduction in National Service Intake.
With no further call -up after the end of 1960**

PART ONE

THE BEGINNING.

'YOU'RE CONSCRIPTED LADDIE'

CHAPTER ONE
DESTINED FOR TWO

Thursday February 3rd. 1955. What we young eighteen year olds were about to be
introduced to:
Was a mandatory period of two years Conscription. Serving Queen and Country.
Unfortunately. There was no way out!
Were we deterred by our initial introduction of all becoming bastards?
However, my story begins long before that date.

In **1938**, the Government reintroduced. The National Service Act of Parliament. Those
Servicemen listed as category 'E' reservist were recalled to the colours; amongst those
recalled was my father, who in 1935 had completed twenty-one years service in the Army.
Another Government plan was for the protection and safety of the population. Air raid
shelters would be issued to all family owned dwellings. In the cities, deep shelters were to
be constructed and under the code name. "Pied Piper". 2,500,000 Children were to be
evacuated out of London to places of safety. Of course, **there** were other plans to be
instigated. During the month of **August 1939**. The signs of war became inevitable.
August 31st. Operation PIED PIPER began. The mass evacuation of London children.
September 3rd. Prime Minister Neville Chamberlain announced.
'Britain. Was at War against Germany.'
The beginning of World War Two.
The following passage of history, relates to the events that took place over the next
two years, until **November 1941.** When, an amendment to the National Service Act 1939.
Was introduced to reduce the then current age of men, eligible for conscription, from 19
to 18 ½. Whilst the age limit was raised from 40 to 50 years of age. At the same time, the
Act also introduced the Conscription of eligible unmarried women between the ages of 20
to 30 and the introduction of Registration for both married and single women up to 50
and for boys and girls, between 16 to 18 years of age.
December 7th. The Japanese attacked Pearl Harbour forcing the Americans to declare
war on Japan. The Japanese Task Force simultaneously bombed Hong Kong, Singapore
and continued onto an amphibious invasion of North Malaya. Immediately Britain
Declared War on Japan.
- "It was going to be a very long war"-
1944. A new crisis had developed, due to manpower shortages in the Coal mines,
there was a desperate need for men to work down "The Pit's". The eligible age for
conscription into the armed forces was still 18 ½. By Act of Parliament, the National
Service Act of 1939. Was again amended. Young men between the ages of 18 and 25
would be conscripted as. "Coalminer's". So began the age of the 'Bevan Boys.' Those
eligible men upon reaching the age of 18 were faced with an alternative. They could be
conscripted either as Coalminer's or, Volunteer for military service. Rather than work down
the coalmines, many 18 year old lads, chose to volunteer for military service? As did my
brother, who served in Burma.
Throughout the passage of the war, both sides developed armaments and weaponry,
none more significant than rocket propulsion. The Germans had secretly developed two
weapons of mass destruction in the form of: The VI. Pilotless bomb (Doodlebug) and the
VII Rocket. The physically discovered of the so-called Vengeance Weapons did not occur
until **June 1944** during the period of the D-Day invasion and as the Allies advanced, they
discovered and captured more sites but unfortunately not before the Germans did unleash

and aim them at the population of London and the South Eastern Home Counties. This brought about the third mass evacuation of Londoners. Under the Code name of "Operation Rivulet".

The launching of these Weapons of Mass Destruction continued from **June 1944** until **March 27th. 1945.** When the last VII landed on British soil. Throughout that short period the number of V I's launched was 9,251 of which 4,261 were intercepted or, destroyed by Ack -Ack, the R.A.F, the Navy and the passive Barrage Balloons. The remainder of 4,990 landed on target, causing severe damage fatalities and injuries whereas only 1,115. VII rockets landed on the mainland of Britain. "They where unstoppable". The Allies, had no answer to these latter weapons? Their only cause of action was to destroy the launching sites. Gradually over the following months, they advanced against the retreating German Army and destroyed those sites.

30th. April 1945. Adolf Hitler committed suicide.

8th. May. The German's surrendered. Thus ending the war in Europe.

Nevertheless, the Allies had created the Atomic bomb.

June 26th. The formation of a new International Peace keeping body called "The United Nations". Delegates from 50 countries around the world signed the World Security Charter. One month later a General Election in England swept the Labour Party into power, headed by Prime Minister Clement Attlee.

July 31st. At a conference in Potsdam. Attlee, Truman and Stalin the three leaders of the occupying forces, met to agree the fate of the occupied territories of Europe. Stalin disagreed. Winston Churchill complained.

'That an Iron Curtain was being slammed down against the west.'

However, the war in the Far East continued until:

August 6th. The first Atomic Bomb was dropped on the city of Hiroshima.

August 9th. Three days later. The second atomic bomb was dropped on the shipbuilding city of Nagasaki. Totally obliterating it. The sheer impact of its destructive power, forced the Japanese to surrender.

August 14th. Victory over Japan was declared and the end of the Second World War

The end of World War II brought Peace nevertheless an unstable period of uncertainty, mistrust, allied occupation and a fight for supremacy in the race for armaments and technology driven specifically by two inventions of the war. The Rocket and Atomic Bomb. Both caused the beginning of the Cold War. However unlike 1918. The National Service Act remained in force.

The bombing and atrocities had ceased but at what price? 55,000,000. Killed Military and Civilians alike. "Yes Peace". In effect, the laying down of arms the lives lost could not be replaced or forgotten. The ravages of the war had left many European countries occupied, particularly by the Germans who during the thirties had invaded and ravaged, nearly all of the countries spread across the continent of Europe together with, the Italian and Japanese, whose forces had also occupied other countries. Those countries left exposed to any internal elements that could cause disruption and anarchy. The allied liberating forces in those countries, divided each into sectors so called "The spoils of war". Britain, America, Russia, France and Poland each took over sections of the liberated countries. Germany divided into two sectors, East and West. Its capital Berlin divided into five sectors. The Russians, controlled East Germany and those other countries occupied during the thirties by the Germans. Leaving West Germany under the control of the English, Americans, French and Polish. In the Far East, Britain along with France and Holland returned to control those countries held under Japanese occupation, whilst the Americans, took control of Japan. Russia along with America partitioned Korea. Russia controlled the North. America controlled the South. With all these agreements between the five major powers ratified, this required workforce on the ground. Who better than the existing military forces! Soldiers supported by the Air Force and Navy.

World War II ended. The fighting had ceased and so the process of de-mobilisation began.

Throughout the world, Countries were seeking their own independence from the previous Colonial rule or, forced rule imposed by the events prior to and during the war. Political turmoil was common in various countries. Those personnel of the armed forces still engaged were very willing to return to civilian life and permitted to pick up the pieces of their own lives interrupted by the war. The urgency of "Conscription". Had waned. The numbers of forces being demobed drastically fell. Some were kept on whilst others eligible for Call-Up, had the task of carrying out the mopping up operations throughout the various countries. In Europe, the Middle and Far East. Mainly the Army undertook these tasks. So began the marshaling policing and the investigations of atrocities inflicted, the commissioning of war graves, the rehabilitation of the remnants of the infamous death and concentration camps and the war trials, a thankless task. Since the end of the war, the political events in Europe and the Far East had drastically changed. The increasing threat of Communism, the "Red Peril" (Russia) and the "Yellow Peril" (China). As they came to be known. Those threats were never very far away. Moreover, was the uppermost thought of all western society?

What emerged from the Second World War, were two different ideological super powers. In the West "Democracy" and in the East "Communism". So divided, what followed in its wake, in less than one month, on **October 9th. 1945. The Cold War began.**

It was then that Conscription. Took on a new face and meaning.

Winston Churchill had declared:

Quote.

*"We *will be ready for any other conflicts"*.*

'Unquote.

Demobilisation continued at a rate of approximately 17,100 per month. Nevertheless, what did continue under The Ministry of Labour and National Service Act of 1944 was the conscription of eligible males.

1946/47. During that very bad winter there was coal and transport strikes. Due to power cuts, frozen Britain worked by candle light. Rationing returned to the conditions enforced during 1942. Conscripted Soldiers had to assist in the transportation of various commodities. Likewise, during the Dock strikes of **1947/48**, the soldiers were called upon to manhandle incoming cargo off the ships at various ports. Whilst in Cairo, India and Palestine riots occurred furthermore, it was a period of time when the exodus of European Jews left their previous countries of birth en-route to a new Jewish country of Palestine. The riots in India resulted in the Independence of India and possibly the beginning of the breakup of the British Empire nevertheless, India's Independence did not solve the problem of religious hatred. After the British troops left India, the migration of people with different religious beliefs began, devided Moslems settled in the East (Bangladesh) and in the West (Pakistan) whilst the Hindus and other various religions stayed within the new borders of India that sparked off more riots causing the death of thousands and resulted in the Partition of India. With the British departure from India completed, other countries within the British Empire still had deployments of British Forces. Many Conscripts were sent to these countries to be engaged in peacekeeping activities, until the Cold War intensified.

April 1st.1948 The Russians began checking all traffic in and out of Berlin. This escalated into a Blockade stopping all supplies in and out of BERLIN.

June 16th 1948. The Emergency in MALAYA was declared and rapidly progressed; ensuring that more Armed Forces were required to cope with the insurgency of the Communist led Malayan Peoples Anti Japanese Army (MPAJA). A force the British had reluctantly armed and formed into a regimented Army during the period 1942-1945. Only to reform take up arms and declare war against the British Government and then became the renamed Malayan Peoples Anti British Army. (MPABA).

June 30th. 1948. The Western Powers reacted against the Berlin blockade. So began the Berlin Air Lift. Thousands of tons of food and supplies were flown in through previously agreed air corridors.

May 12th.1949. After a year, the Air Lift ended with agreement in New York between the United Nations and Russia. The Army drove lorry loads of food and supplies into the streets of Berlin.

July 30th. 1949. The River Yangtze Incident became headlines when H.M.S. Amethyst made a dash for freedom down the River Yangtze after being held captive by the Chinese.

June 25th 1950. The North Korean Army, trained by the Communists stormed across the 38th Parallel and invaded South Korea. In an attempt to repel and force back the North Korean Army instigated the first armed involvement by the United Nations. With Great Britain and all the members of the Commonwealth Countries committed to the United Nations. Many National Servicemen were engaged in the fighting. Many killed, wounded or, taken prisoner to spend the rest of their time in captivity, until the agreement on **25 July 1963.**

February 1952. His Majesty King George the VI died. Many National Servicemen, were to line the funeral route as the King's coffin mounted on a gun carriage was pulled through the streets of London by the Royal Navy.

The enforced military employment of two years service became a thorn in the side of millions of young eligible men that left a stigma on all. Even now only, a minority wish to be associated too or, to remember their period of National Service. As individuals, they had not chosen to follow a military career in any of the services. During their initial period of basic training every National Serviceman in the armed forces was so occupied and drilled by the authoritative ways of Service life, they did not have time for a shit. Even that was at the double. After the initial period of indoctrination, quickly followed by the cultural shock of the stringent basic training that normally lasted a minimum of six to eight weeks. Then if, selected? Up to three months at a Trade Training Battalion then to serve the rest of your time posted at your final service unit.

A majority of National Servicemen wasted their time employed in orderly rooms, carrying out menial desk type tasks shifting mountains of paper forms or, just skiving. Others spent their time square bashing parade grounds or, being involved in military exercises all over the country, in Germany and other so called 'home postings'. Whilst others were dispatched to all parts of the world, to serve their time showing the flag fighting for King /Queen and Country in defence of the ever decreasing Empire. In some instances a life of boredom, for many others excitement a chance to see the world in many instances many unfortunate ones were not to return to the shores of England however, it was not long before the creation of a simple chart or calendar with numbers in decreasing order. Its sole purpose, the crossing out of each individual day as they passed by into the setting sun! Some made notes on what happened on such and such a day:

"Days to do 365. God another bloody year of this crap.
Roll on death. Demob's too far away".

Unable to break the shackles that held them in their current state of employment or, had the balls to go Absent Without Leave (AWOL) get caught and suffer the rigors and discipline of the "Glasshouse". All were in the same boat, even the three-year short term

11

regular, attracted by the bait of a few shillings increase per week. Had signed on for an additional years period just to get that little extra money that added to his weekly pay. They were doing the same as any two-year National Serviceman. All taking orders performed without question, the shit, grime and humility that came from meaningless or, senseless tasks.

Those so-called Short Term Regulars inferred a stigma upon all National Servicemen making comments that the National Servicemen were not really a Serviceman unless one had signed on for an extra year as a Reg. They themselves being the biggest bigot's of all. What did the three year Reg, with his little extra pay spend it on? Not much? He too had the same restrictions imposed upon him. Nevertheless, one thing was certain. The National Serviceman was glad to get out be re-employed in his civilian trade or profession, earn a much higher wage and become free once again.

After the National Serviceman had finished his time and gratefully received his demob papers, the three-year regular would still have to spend a further year crossing out his daily calendar:

Nevertheless, some National Servicemen having completed their mandatory two-year period did decide to sign on and make it their chosen career, serving in one of the branches of the armed forces. Good Luck to them however, it would be unfair to class all the three year Regs as bigots; I met quite a few that were good comrades in arms. Even now, the stigma of being a National Serviceman still lives on whether they served in any of the three services:

Royal Navy: Most N/S Naval Ratings were more confined to shore bases.
Army: Infantry, Armoured or Corps.
Royal Air Force Ground crews and supports unit's
Nowadays in conversation, any person maybe asked:
Questioner.   'Were you in the Services?'
Person.   'Yes! I was a National Serviceman.'
Questioner.   'Oh. Only a National Serviceman! Not like us Regulars.'

Implying, that the National Serviceman had never served for any length of time? Nevertheless, two years or 730 days (731 Leap year included). Was indeed-

'A Very Very Long Time.'

Throughout the period of their Conscription. The National Servicemen was the backbone of the Armed Forces specifically the Army. A majority of National Servicemen achieved and, did more during their two years service than some of the short-term regulars. Many National Servicemen were to receive commissions or, were awarded a rank outranking the regulars. A majority of the much suffering Poor Old National Serviceman were engaged On Active Service in conflicts such as Aden, Cyprus, Egypt, Kenya, Korea and Malaya. Much more can be said for those National Servicemen, who were unfortunately killed in action or died through disease never to return and grace the shores of their homeland. Unlike those who had never been out of the country, never saw anything or, were active in nothing. Records of brave acts of courage with appropriate medals awarded, including battle honours won such as, the Glouster Regiments four day engagement at the Imjin River in Korea that earned them the title of "The Glorious Gloucester's".

Nevertheless, how did we "individuals" Become involved in its process & procedures?
Any young lad who was born between 1930 and 1942.
Were destined to be conscripted.

CHAPTER TWO
A FUTURE CONSCRIPTED /NATIONAL SERVICEMAN

Before the Second World War if a family could afford it, food and clothing were in adequate supply their biggest problem was employment. With the outbreak of war in 1939. Conscription was re-introduced; therefore somewhat resolving the problem of employment. Nevertheless, what the war brought was rationing and hardships that all civilians were to endure, in a fight for family survival, which continued into the early fifties, nevertheless it all began on:-

Thursday August 31ˢᵗ. The Governments plan for the evacuation of children began at the ungodly hour of 5.30 am for transportation to nominated safe areas. All London terminus stations became crowded with thousands of evacuees leaving by the trainload. Yet there were others being entrained to their ports of departure, there to board various ships sailing to Canada and Australia thousands of miles away from any involvement. The Children suitably identified with named labels pinned to their coats carrying their possessions in a small suitcase or parcel, a cardboard box containing their gas mask was draped around their shoulders some were crying, others laughing whilst swinging their body to move their cardboard box around in an arc, obviously eagerly looking forward to the possibility of the beginning of a great holiday in the country. A high percentage of the London evacuees had never seen a cow or any other farmyard animal nevertheless, soon to be introduced to the rudiments and delights of rural living. However, a majority of rural families, although they were paid monies towards the evacuees lodging cost, did not welcome the intrusion of their new charges. Many evacuees were subjected to ill treatment and unable to cope in their new environment, spent every night crying their hearts out until exhausted they fell asleep. Subsequently throughout their unwelcome and miserable stay was repeated.

A period, many future Conscripts / National Servicemen lived through.

During the early war years, a majority of us young kids were too young to understand the necessity of air-raid precautions. The surrounding edges of windowpanes painted black; strips of sticky tape criss- crossed each pane of glass. Drawn every night thick heavy black- drapes replaced normal curtains. To erect an Anderson Shelter in the back garden required digging a big hole, fixing the kit together then covering the shelter with earth. During the hours of darkness, street lamps remained switched off. Roadside trees had white rings painted around the trunks, all forms of road transport had the edges of mudguards and running boards painted white, the headlamps covered with a cardboard disc with narrow slits, the internal lights of buses and trams remained switched off. Everyone had to carry a gas mask in a brown cardboard box secured and hung by a length of string over the shoulder, ready for the expected gas bombing that never occurred. The imminent threat of bombing passed, a period of what the Americans called. 'The Phoney War.' People's attitudes became less cautious, many evacuees did return to be with the rest of the family but it all changed after the evacuation of Dunkirk. Within a month, air raids and bombings became a reality.

Throughout the daytime, the warning wail of the air-raid siren had everyone running for cover into the so-called security of an air raid shelter. High above the large silver barrage balloons floating serenely overhead appeared to be inadequate and useless. As the steady drone of the bombers approached, dropping their bombs loads to whistle down onto those unfortunate enough to be on the receiving end. Many watched with mixed emotions as high above in the evolving dogfights, the chattering of machine guns and the sound of the fighter planes engines rising and falling as they dived, twisted and turned to weave intricate white vapor trails in the skies above. The darkness of the night provided no let up. Gone was the fighter planes as the constant drone of the night bombers continued for hours on end, instead the black sky was criss- crossed with the beams of searchlights in their quest to illuminate a German bomber for the Ack-Ack gunners to shoot them down. Gun flashes lit up the sky instantly followed by the crack of their guns as they blazed away and with luck shot the plane down in flames. Whilst down below, the whistle and intermittent crash and thuds as a stick of bombs landed, causing destruction mayhem and fire. The screams and shouts for help, the clanging bells of fire tenders and shrill ring of ambulance bells. Firemen pumping endless gallons of water into huge buildings, some blazing out of control. Throughout the Blitz in London and elsewhere, families who experienced being bombed out and witnessed the mayhem caused, cannot erase it from their memory.

March 1941. During the height of the Blitz our family suffering the anguish of being bombed out were relocated to the Lancashire Town of Bamber Bridge, where within a year an American camp became operational. We youngsters never took much notice of their presence nevertheless, were extremely pleased to take their chewing gum, candies, along with all the other goodies they would hand out copies of American comics and Geographical Magazines. In the latter, pictures published in vivid colours illustrated the might of the American fighting machine; in places, we had never heard of or could hardly pronounce Guadalcanal, Iwo Jima and Guam. Many pairs of young eyes were to see these pictures of the American soldiers, fighting on the land and in the air, the side gunners of their Flying Fortress's surrounded by piles of empty cartridge shells. Those images captivated our imagination and became part of our everyday life.

Innocent lads that we were, all happy in our environment and oblivious to the circumstances or, casualties that the real world was enduring, The ever presence of Bren Gun Carriers, Field Artillery, Aeroplane Trailers and American lorries that constantly rumbled through the streets of the town; triggered our imagination and, we were not alone . Others like us were playing at war games. Strange as it may seem, we never went into jungles. Year by year the battles we had heard about on the steam radio, the North African Desert, Sicily, Crete, Italy, we amidst the safety of the trees and foliage of the local wood, re- enacted those battles, my cousin Tommy, Freddie Peacock, Jack Slater and others. We the British soldiers and the Germans, imaginary ghosts were in range of our weapons, wooden makeshift guns. 'Bang bang. I've got one, he's dead.' Grasping a shoulder or leg would cry out.

'Aah! I've been hit. Kill that one over there.'

Stuka dive-bombers screaming down towards us, with one single accurate rifle shot blown out of the sky. Inevitably, we won the battle; in front of us, thousands of Germans lay in heaps.

London, 1945. Before the end of the war, we returned to our roots in London to pick up the pieces of our interrupted lives. The nightly bombing raids carried out by the German Luftwaffe, over the period of five years had left behind total devastation and, a mass of bombsites. Many areas where a Doodlebug (V.I) or Rocket (V.II) had landed, had completely wiped out terraced houses along streets and roads. Other cities and towns were in a similar condition. Roadways that led to nowhere, were cleared of tons and tons of rubble that was piled up high on either side, still standing halfway down was a lone gas lamp standard waiting for a gas man riding past with his pole to switch it on. Nevertheless, there was no gas supply and possibly no gasman? Scarred trees stood burnt and lifeless, in between rows of terraced houses gaps appeared, where a solitary bomb had wiped out a house or two, visible to see was the party wall with the torn wallpaper flapping in the breeze. Cut into the walls were the remains of stairways, chimneybreasts revealed the blackened mouths of fireplaces, which once burnt bright casting flickering glows of red within the room. Perched on the top of a pile of rubble was a lavatory pan, placed there by some labourer with a sense of humour. In some streets, only the shell of a house remained its roof a mass of gaping holes and broken tiles. All windows laid open to the elements and a front door hanging on by one hinge. Identified by their black painted walls embossed with a large white painted cross at various sites, one could see the precious wartime brick water holding tanks used by the fire brigade crews, within its empty confines were piles of rubble unwanted remnants of household effects, prams, tin baths, even doors floating aimlessly about in shallow waters in the middle. The open spaces of Parks, previously a scene of many allotments laid out in military lines, scarred by bomb craters then left unattended without flowers but plenty of weeds, which soon grew in abundance to cover other bombsites.

Herne Hill. The area we moved into, had been badly bombed and was typical of many of the bombed areas of London. We had been re-housed in a patched up terraced house in Heron Road, a turning off Milkwood Road running alongside the railway tracks between Herne Hill and Loughborough Junction. The German Bombers, aiming for the railway lines had missed them hitting many houses within its vicinity, with devastating

 consequences killing many people and seriously injuring others. Out of the sixty or more houses in Heron Road, twenty remained on one side and eighteen on the other; the houses in between had been demolished creating three large bombsites.

Aerial View of Pre-Fabs in Heron and Lowden Road.
Photos by kind permission of the Lambeth Archives

Subsequently, we grew up in an environment that created a sense of opposition and rivalry. During the Labour / Conservative elections, the wearing of either a red or blue rosette was a sign of family support. We had no idea what it was all about even later, the wearing a rosette of either a dark blue Oxford or light blue Cambridge for the boat race, but of course there were others.

To us youngsters, these bombsites amongst the shells of house and piles of rubble became the battle areas for many street gangs playing war games. However, as the Councils rebuilding programme proceeded the erection of Pre-Fabricated house began on the largest bombsite in Heron Road. To keep us out, up went the fences and in what seemed like no time fourteen Prefab's had been erected complete with surrounding gardens. Very posh, shortly afterwards they were occupied by small families. Upon completion, work began on the opposite side of the road and to add insult to injury the third remaining site was fenced off. The next available bombsite was the large one occupied by the Lowden Road gang. Something had to be done? The Heron Road gang took over the Lowden Road bombsite; setting up camp with old doors and timbers, this intrusion caused a problem of territorial ownership. The two opposing gangs began to fight, hurling half bricks as grenades charging across the open space around water-filled craters, to engage in hand tussles. The frantic activity caused cuts, bruises, bloody noses, until the Heron Road gang won the day. The defeated moved to a smaller site down the other end of the road. All was at peace until workers took possession of our site, we moved on until a serious accident occurred, falling from a roof Jimmy was killed. An inquest was held and the Police not only warned us of the dangers, but also notified our mothers and fathers. Threatened, with a cuff around the ear we were banned from bombsites nevertheless; we still had scores to settle over Jimmy; it was not long before street fights began.

One gang called the other, a load of Germans or Itie's bleeders. A big insult between the street rivals a gauntlet was offered and accepted. Armed with sticks and dustbin lids, like screaming banshees charged towards each other, meeting in the center of the road beating tom tit out of each other in an attempt to gain supremacy, until along came the Number 48 tram the driver frantically clanging its bell in an attempt to swathe a path through the two stick wielding gangs. On occasions, the tram driver would have to stop. Climb down pick up a rather battered dustbin lid and toss it like a giant Scooby-do onto the pavements, he shouting.

'Get out of the bleedin' road, yer little bleeder's. Yer 'll get yourselves killed.'

In turn, he would receive a torrid of abuse from the stationary gangs joined together in protest over his stopping that tussle. The leaders would agree to resume it the following week after school that for some reason, always occurred the day before the dust carts came around when the householders put out their dustbins. 'Charge!' Until we all were tired of it or, all had received clouts from our fathers for mangling up the dustbin lids all of which had the house number painted on it. The inter-road rivalry never was settled.

It was back to Cowboys and Indians or, Robin Hood against the Sheriff of Nottingham. Even more dangerous were the bows made out of long bamboo canes, bent into a bow shape tied by string at either end, the arrows were short bamboo sticks. Swords made from a stave of wood, the hand guard was a small piece of wood nailed in place, the shield again the dustbin lid. Aimed with no concern for injuries the two opposing sides would fire off their arrows, charging to meet in the middle of the road smashing swords on dustbins lids slashing and thrusting, knocking fingers dropped swords bruised and battered, nobody knew who won. Until an arrow hit Peter in the eye, the meat wagon (Ambulance) arrived ringing its bell loud enough to deafen the dead. At the hospital the doctors removed Peter's eye, that put paid to that game.

By this time, we had discovered the wide-open space of the wartime allotments of Ruskin Park. We made camps out of old pieces of wood and doors, fires were lit. For at least two or three weeks we had a wonderful time, before the baddies arrived. The PKs (Park Keepers) dressed in their tweedy brown uniforms, brown leather gaiters and cowboy hats adorned not with a star but a large bronze badge with the letters P. K. We were chased off never to return. Games changed, but always finished up with two sides opposing each other it.

Other street games played: Ally gobs, Fag cards, Cannon, Knock down Ginger, Tin Can Tommy, Ball Tag. Cricket and Football were seasonal. A glut of ball bearing races became available; scooters and go-carts were constructed from odd planks of wood and

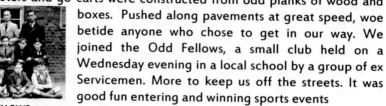 boxes. Pushed along pavements at great speed, woe betide anyone who chose to get in our way. We joined the Odd Fellows, a small club held on a Wednesday evening in a local school by a group of ex Servicemen. More to keep us off the streets. It was good fun entering and winning sports events

Members of the ODD F'ELLOWS
The Heron Road Gang (all Potential Conscripts)

Apart from outdoor games, our social side of life was reading books from the local library, swopping the glut of American comics and listen to the wireless programs: Children's Hour, Just William, Valentine Dial (The Man in Black, Tales of horror). Boxing matches. Our local hero Freddie Mills winning the world boxing championship also Dick Turpin against Sugar Ray Robinson. Bunking in (Not paying) to watch Dulwich Hamlet play football. Another attraction, the Saturday morning pictures. We all became members of the two main cinemas. The Odeon and ABC. Queues began forming about an hour before the start of the picture show. At nine fifteen, the doors would open, in an attempt to pay their money and get the best seats; hundreds of kids would push and shove their way to the front. Until a "Children's Attendant" appeared. His badge of authority was his armband, any act of unruly manner fighting etc., unceremoniously the culprit would be dragged out marched to the rear if, his misdemeanor was bad refused entry. The culprit together with the rest of his gang would head for the other cinema. Nothing deterred one from getting in to see the Saturday morning pictures. The seating area inside was awash with kids, clambering over the rows of tip up seats, sitting down popping up again, fed up with that out came the pea shooters, with deadly aim the sudden stinging force of a hard pea hitting someone three rows down, a yell of:

'OW! Who dun that?' Standing up, looked around in a vain attempt to find who was responsible? Impossible! He would sit down to receive another two for his trouble. Fights did break out and were not uncommon.

The lights would dim and with the mechanical sound of "Clackety-clack-clackety-clack" to the cheering patrons the curtains drew apart revealing the silver screen, followed by the showing of the Odeoner's song as the famous bouncing ball picked out each word. Sung with gusto by the then attentive audience, those with peashooters would try to hit the ball the stage in front became littered with hard peas. The films would roll, a cartoon, the weekly cowboy episode followed by another film of some sorts. With gaping gob's the audience engrossed by the passage of the film until it broke down, immediately Boo-ing, Whistling, Cat calls and chanting,

'We want our money back.' Until the picture was flashed back onto the screen.

At the end of the show, the playing of the National Anthem caused pandemonium, everyone wanted to avoid standing up therefore if, you were not quick enough you would be trampled to death by the hordes behind.

October 7th 1946. Broadcast on the steam radio at quarter to seven from Monday to Friday night a new program began. Dick Barton Special Agent. Captured every kid's imagination. Fifteen minutes of sheer action packed breath-taking excitement! The streets became silent; those kids who did not have a steam radio, their mates invited them in. With ears glued to the speaker area, if one attempted to turn up the sound he would receive a swift clout and scolding.

'I told you not to turn that thing up.'

At precisely seven 'o' clock, the streets became alive with Kids punching the air, re-enacting what had happened to Dick, Jock and Snowy, 'Will they, won't they. Get out of their immediate danger?

Yet, in the confines of a demolished single house our attraction to girls, led to a new game "kiss chase". Such was our life in post war London.

The political situation in the real world did not concern us. Nevertheless, I did know that my uncle Dick, a Captain in the Royal Artillery was in Germany helping with the War Graves Commissions. Whilst in pubs our Dads possibly would discuss the events going on, such as the Nuremberg War trials. We lads eager for a packet of crisps, would slightly open the Pub door, peeping around into the smoke laden atmosphere with the heavy smell of beer wafting around, trying to interrupt our Dad's flow of conversation by quietly calling out a plaintive cry. 'Dad! Dad! Can I 'ave a packet of Smith's Crisps?' Gradually raising the level of our voice until, after about five of those plees you gained a packet of crisps plus a cuff around the ear and a warning.

'I don't want to hear another word out of you, do you hear? Wait until I get home?' The cuff around the ear was worth the treat. By the time Dad got home he had forgotten all about it.

With everything on ration and money scarce, to earn pocket money for Saturday morning pictures, we had to work doing household shopping. On one bombsite I found an old pram, its four wheels were void of rubber tyres with a few spokes missing nevertheless that pram became my Chariot. Every week there and back I pushed it to shop at Herne Hill, to Brixton for wooden crates piled high tied on by bits of string used for firewood and during the bad winters every week to Vauxhall, to queue up for two hundred weight of Coke. That Chariot carried everything and with all the miles, I pushed it, the four rims of the metal wheels became so worn and flat the spokes ends were quite visible. I ran errands for other Ladies too and if they came out asking.

'Would anyone like to earn some pocket money?'

Just to get a couple of coppers out of the change she would be surrounded by a mob of kids yelling.

'I'll go Missus.'

1946-1947. That winter was extremely cold. Heavy falls of snow caused more chaos than the struggling economic recovery could cope with. Strikes caused Power cuts, which meant the return to wartime lighted candles. Coal Strikes, caused shortage of Coal. Had kids queuing for hours shivering with snotty noses red hands and chapped legs for a "Rationed one hundred weight bag of coke per week". That is when my Chariot came in handy. Burst water mains meant queuing up at standpipes down the road to fill up buckets, large jugs or basins full of water. Still we had to attend school with chapped legs, soaking wet shoes and socks. That was the winter my brother Jackie arrived home from the Far East who to avoid becoming a Bevin Boy, had volunteered in 1943 as a RAF Pilot. Instead, became a Royal Fusilier and was shipped out to fight in Burma, Malaya, Singapore finally, the Dutch East Indies. After a short leave at home, was posted to Germany.

January 1948. The Indian Leader Gandhi was assassinated. I remember the newspaper photos of his burning funeral pyre. It amazed me to understand, that was what they did in foreign lands. However, India's problems were no longer the responsibility of the British but unbeknown to us. The Cold War was still an ever-increasing threat to our very own existence.

As we grew older, our street games ceased football and cricket became the main attraction, yet the older lads had adopted another sport craze. Motorbike Speedway at New Cross- Wimbledon, Harringey plus some others. Their bike handlebar was replaced with a Motorbike handlebar to resemble a speedway bike. Once again, any remaining bombsites large enough to create an elliptical cycle track was cleared of all rubble, the dips and holes filled in, old canvas fire hose's formed the inner and outer track perimeters the start and finish line was chalk marked ready for the race. Six cyclists three from each team, handkerchiefs covering their mouths, stood in line arms outstretched hands gripped the handlebars. At the start pedaling like fury down the straight, at the first corner throwing the rear wheel into a skid inevitably a crash, amidst a shower of dust goaded on by cheering kids, the injured riders would get up to complete four laps of the circuit, the usual victor was Johnny.

Our introduction to Conscription happened in 1948. My brother Mike, together with my mate Maurice's brother Bert were called-up, followed a few months later by my cousin Pat Thomas. Weeks later dressed in uniforms they arrived home for a weekend leave, extremely eager to change into civvies and, taste the freedom of the good life. Grumbling about a Sergeant or, some bastard they could not abide. 'Wait until I meet up with him in civvy street. I'll teach him a lesson or two.' In their own way, they were confiding in us not our Dads, who had seen it, done it and forgotten it. If they did complain to them, all they would get back was.

'Get on with it, service life will do you good, it never did me any harm.'

On Sundays, they would change into uniform and return. After a few months overseas postings took Mike to West Africa and Bert to Germany, a few months later Pat was posted to Egypt. Many many months later they came home to be demobed.

Johnny the speedway bike rider, who lived next door to Maurice got his marching orders and was posted overseas. Much later, his family received the sad news of his death in Malaya. About that time, the average age of the Heron Road gang was 13. Realised that Conscription, was not a game and for us it was not too far away, before we would be conscripted. After a week or so the event of Johnny's death forgotten.

Still at Secondary School. To further our education and future careers, we had two choices either remain at the Secondary School or, sit exams for either a Grammar or Technical College Education. Fortunately, I passed and chose to go to a Technical Engineering College where the mode of dress was uniforms. Blazer with school badge, cap, scarves, included long trousers (no more chapped knees) all was a mark of distinction. Apart from the three 'R's', the college syllabus was specifically linked to engineering with previously unheard of tons of homework that we despised. Discipline was not by the prior rule of the cane, instead after lessons detention. A healthy code of competition existed between the Houses of Bailey, Chaucer and Faraday. Placed in Bailey, became great friends with my new mate Taffy Davies, quickly we joined the Air Training Corps Unit and were togged out with ATC uniforms. Twice a week after the lessons, there was free tea and rolls provided before we went on parade in the playground. The Wing Commander in charge of the unit was our English Master Mr. Pond. (Affectionately called. Old' Pondiculas). He claimed during the war, he was a Group Captain in fighter command somewhere in Kent. He would relate stories about his war experiences that had us open mouthed, holding onto his every word. In his uniform, he looked like a sack of potatoes he was old, withery and did not stand up straight. Shouting out orders in his squeaky voice, he drilled us and had us all in tears with laughter as we tried to keep in step. It must have been hilarious to watch. He arranged an outing to Horse Guards Parade, where the R.A.F displayed their new jet fighters. The De' Havilland 'Meteor,' a twin jet engine plane and a 'Vampire.' The latter, a twin boomed tailed jobbie not unlike the American 'Lockheed Lightning.' Apart from the fact, it had a jet engine that the Pilot sat on. Anyway Taffy and I did not learn much from the ATC and to tax Old' Pondiculas patience we were always larking about. Finally, one afternoon, he had enough of us and we were drummed out of the ATC. Not that we really cared anyway, pity about the free bread rolls. I do not think it prepared us in any way for our future term of service. Our environment had changed, so had the world events. Inevitably so did the Act of Parliament that would affect our future as Conscripted National Servicemen.

June 1950. The war in Korea erupted, North against South. To assist the South Koreans, America deployed its forces to Korea and Mr. Shinwell, Britain's Minister for Defence committed British Forces to fight under the Flag of the United Nations. He also made a statement in the House of Commons that, legislation had been passed to increase the period of National Service, from twelve to eighteen months.

August 1950. With the Royal Navy already on "A war footing, the first British Infantry Battalions to see action was the Middlesex Regiment and the Argyles, followed in November by Regiments of the Gloucester's and Black Watch. Whose ranks consisted of many National Servicemen? Amongst whom serving with the Black Watch was Private. Bill Speakman later awarded the Victoria Cross. At that time, 15 years old I watched the war unfold on the Pathe News. A stark reminded of our own experiences during the blitz. Then we had been on the receiving end and I certainly did not like the thought of another war!

In 1949, going back a bit. When I was thirteen, my brother Mike a good football player had encouraged me to join the St. Anne's Club where he was a member of their football team. It was also the club where all my cousins were members, for me it was quite a hike to walk from Heron Road to Vauxhall.

The club was open every night from seven until ten 'o.' clock. For all those caring to join, it became a very popular venue for Catholic youths to meet, make new friends and chat up birds (not the feathered kind). However, its principle activity was to encourage youths to take up sporting and indoor activities, such as Netball. Football, Cricket, Athletics, Fencing, Ballroom Dancing, Table tennis, Snooker & Darts. Affiliated to the NFBC (National Federation of Boys Clubs) Competing for Shields, Cups and medals whose football league system was based on those of the Football Association. The Club had two football teams; the under 18's played on Saturday and over 18's on Sunday afternoon. They would attract big crowds wherever they played, on the local Commons of Clapham, Wandsworth, Mitcham, Blackheath, Hackney Marshes, Wormwood Scrubs, Boston Manor, plus others. Nobody liked playing at Hackney Marshes with its 100 pitches side-by-side, end-to-end, stretching for miles and you had to carry the goal posts to the allotted pitch. Sometimes a football from another game would land on your pitch; and be swiftly kicked into another games play, much to the irate shouting of players. With the game over, caked in mud soaking wet carried the goal post back and then change to go home muddy. It was the same elsewhere, but never like Hackney! To get to the above-mentioned Commons, we travelled by bus tube or tram. As I grew older, was to play in both teams along sides Johnnie, Derek, Brian, Maurice, Mike, Roy.

At the club, I became great pals of Derek Beamish, Kenny Richardson, Brian (Ginger) Jenkins and Tom (Junior) O'Neill. Derek, about nine months older than me, Junior the same age, Kenny a year younger and Brian the youngest, all lived within a few miles radius of the club. All were employed in different types of work; I was employed as a Trainee Draughtsman earning £ 2-10/- per week, which I gave mum £1 for my bed and board, the rest was spent on paying for a bike and the odd drink or two in the Beehive (over 18 of course). I was the only one amongst them did not smoke; the others could only afford a packet of five Weights or Woodbines and if, flush a packet of Turf and five Spangles. As soon as they lit up started coughing their lungs up, it was pitiful to watch the tears in their eyes as they spluttered. 'It's gone down the wrong way.' We walked everywhere; a favorite walk after Sunday Mass, was to the Doughnut makers underneath Waterloo Bridge, to buy and gorge ourselves with fresh Ring Do-nuts before Sunday dinner at home. We all owned racing cycles for our weekly race to Reigate Hill and back to the Stockwell Clock tower. Longer rides were to Brighton, Southend, Virginia Waters, and long weekend trips to the Isle of Wight.

Gradually the older members of the Club became conscripts. One week Harry was there then gone followed by Arthur and my cousin Tommy. Not seen for eight weeks until they returned on weekend leave. The evidence surrounded us; they stuck out like sore thumbs. Ruddy weather beaten faces a ring of white skin above the collar indicating long hours spent in the open. "Bags of fresh air". Hair scalped white to the rim of a beret, any hair above had been hacked and was either heavily Brylcreamed or Brillianteened and combed to make a parting. At the dance on Saturday night, Arthur dressed in his civvies, with gleaming eyes the picture of health, his haircut completely out of character with his mode of dress, whilst on Sunday would turn up dressed in his Army uniform, smartly turned out, gleaming brasses, sharp creases in his trousers and boots like mirrors. All for a quick dance around the floor (although barred from dancing in his hob-nailed boots). Maybe he would stay for half an hour and then depart to catch his train back to wherever his camp was. Others would do the same. Higgins and Skinner members of the football team played Sunday afternoon that night they would return to their respective unit's. Chi-acking with enlisted members about their Army and RAF. 'Term of Office.' Their stories were varied, similar and funny that made us laugh nevertheless, we were all conscious of our pending fate. Because of his stomach ulcers, (which did not stop him smoking)? Junior was very blasé about the possibility of not being accepted.

There were plenty of girls at the Club: Betty, Jean, Joyce, Marion, Maureen, Nina, Pat, Sheila. Oh, a host of them to enjoy dancing to records with, however due to shortage of cash, nothing progressed. The Club organised trips to Southend for a day in the Kersal, just to spend your money on the fairground rides, eat winkles, shrimps, candyfloss and buy the usual Kiss Me Quick hat without success. On Saturday nights, we had a choice to visit other dance halls that featured live bands at Lambeth: The London School of Dancing (LSD), the Peckham CO-OP, the Locarno Streatham and the Lyceum in the Strand. Take your pick of girls to dance and jive and maybe chat up a girl. Earned by the sweat of our brows, our meager amount of money provided a complete new lease on life. Derek, Junior and I were into the Jazz scene and became members of Jazz clubs in Soho. The Flamingo, the 51 and Star Clubs. The scene of post war social activity in London was changing fast. The West End was vibrant, big motion pictures to see it was a world of freedom, which we lavished upon and enjoyed to the fullest. Nevertheless, within a short period was to cease.

The Government really had you by the short and curlies. Once you were 18, your Employer informed the Labour Exchange. Who set the paperwork in motion? A Brown envelope came fluttering through the letterbox. However, if you were an apprentice studying for a profession at university you were deferred until aged 21 years. The procedure repeated however if, you could prove to the Medical Examination Board that you had a legitimate ailment or, disability. You either were missing an arm, a leg, or turned up blind or, dead. Only then were you graded. Unfit for National Service. Alternatively. You joined the Merchant Navy for 12 years. Not a likely choice. I like everyone else did not want to go! Thoroughly enjoying my freedom and life style. Thank you very much!

Out of the five of us mates, Derek was the first to receive his Brown envelope. He had to report to a Medical Center on Blackheath. He thinking, because of flat feet and the state of his lungs? Would fail so two weeks before his M.E. Derek decided to cultivate his cough and chain-smoked until when he lit his fag with the first drag he retched at will coughing like mad eyes streaming. I thought it was. "Bleedin' silly". He promised he would delay opening his results until we all met in the Beehive two weeks later.

Every Thursday the Club was open mainly for the over Twenty-one's therefore on a Thursday night we used to meet early in the Beehive, due to the fact it was empty and could get a beer. Two weeks later, we met to listen to Derek's medical experience. He was at the bar waiting for us to arrive and bought us a round of drinks before he started his tale of woe. He had us in fits of laughter with particular emphasis on his cough.

'I did it so well, I nearly died; they had to give me oxygen to save me. I asked the Doctor. Have I failed?' The Doctor told me.

'Your results will be posted to you within two weeks. Until then you wait.' Brian exclaimed.

'Blimey! Another two weeks before they declare you dead. '

'Hoi! I'm not bleedin' dead; I'm only trying to get out of the Kate. Wait until it's your bleedin' turn. Look two weeks from now we will meet in here, then I'll open the results okay? C'mon Brian. Stop yer chatting it is your round.' Brian not happy responded,

'Don't 'ave any dosh. I'm broke.' Derek accusing responded.

'When it's your turn. Your always. Bleedin broke.' Kenny interrupted.

'Bet yer ain't got any fags iver?' Conveniently, at that moment Junior began a fit of coughing, whereas I suggested.

'Right! Jews march past. Get yer shrapnel out.'

Halfpennies, pennies, three-penny bits, tanners, and a couple of shillings, landed on the table. Derek counted it all out.

'Enuf for half each. Junior get em in. Who's chalking then? Nearest Bull.' Five separate darts were thrown. Brian was chalking.

Two weeks later in the Beehive apart from Junior ordering a round at the bar and Brian and I finishing a game of bar billiards, the Saloon bar was empty when in walks Derek and Kenny. Derek called out.

'Just in time. Junior another two light ales please.' Junior not very happy replied 'Bleedin' cheek.'

As we gathered around a table Junior brought over the beers then; Derek with a fag stuck out of his mouth produced the Brown envelope and waved it in our faces. Merrily coughing away through a haze of smoke, grinning he slowly thumbed it open removing the sheet of paper, quickly scanning the words his face gradually turned pale the same colour as the froth on his beer, his jaw dropped his fag fell from his mouth onto the floor, with a strangled cry.

'I've been graded A1. Aw Shit.'

Picking up his fag took a drag, causing another fit of coughing physically shattered; he sat down at the nearest chair before taking a quick swig of beer. Placing my hand on his shoulder with compassion asked.

'Anything else in the letter, about when you gotta go in?' Shaking his head, he forlornly replied.

'Nah. Just wait for further information. Aw bleedin' 'ell.'

The four of us stood there watching his dejected form, hunched shoulders arms resting on his knees, his fag lightly held between his fingers as he mournfully looked into the half-drunk glass of beer in front of him. The inevitable had happened. The beginning of our immediate involvement with National Service. I looked at Junior, he rolled his eyes upwards and I knew what he meant. Junior and I were the next to receive our Brown envelopes. So began a night of commiseration and reflection. Brian changing the subject exclaimed!

'Anyone for a game of Bar Billiards?' Kenny replied.

'Yer alright I'll play yer.'

Unconcerned those two sods set up the Bar Billiards game; they still had a couple of years to wait!

The Christmas before Derek left, we all had a good piss up and as Derek was the only male amongst about fifty females. For moral support, he invited all of us to his employers Christmas Dance. Somewhere up the west end, we met in a Pub about seven 'o'clock. Derek was already plastered then, his drunken excuse was he had set up the bar with his boss. At the dance there was a great choice of females, unfortunately Derek could not stand the pace, threw up and slept under a chair. Eventually we left at nine to take him home. An evening's opportunity wasted. Within a month. Derek received his call up papers and reported to The Royal Signals Training Camp at Catterick.

Six weeks later, he arrived home on a weekend pass having completed his basic training. Looked very smart in his uniform his face glowing from outside exposure, he was not coughing. Drinking beer in the Beehive, he related his experience of his past six weeks.

'Our bleedin' feet. Didn't touch the floor. Double here; double there, everything done at the bleedin' double.'

Of course, he was winding us up. Derek returned on the Sunday to start his trade training as a Wireless Operator. Since Derek had left school he had trained as a Tailor's Cutter give him a piece of cloth and he could tell you who wove it and where woven.

Nevertheless, sparks, forget it! Absolutely no knowledge of electrics. How the Army ever sorted out service trades with similar careers, was beyond everybody's comprehension. During his Trade Training, he would come home on weekend leaves. All we ever got out of him was. 'Da Dit Dit Da Dit Da.' whatever that meant? He was hooked on it. We thought he was trying to take part in the Goon show. At that time, nearly everyone was trying to imitate the characters broadcast by Spike Milligan, Harry Seacombe, Peter Sellers, etc. However, his call-up had happened about six months earlier. Just a month before me Junior got his Brown Envelope. We met down the Beehive for the opening of his results. Downgraded. 'Unfit for National Service.' Something to do with his bleedin' ulcers. He was cock o' hoop but he still carried on smoking? Such was our days of carefree abandonment.

I, too was conscripted and the following chapters, relate to the.
Process that we all were too experience.

CHAPTER THREE
MAY 1954. THE BROWN ENVELOPE

One sunny May morning, having washed dressed and completed my toiletries, was on my way downstairs into the misshapen area of the hall, laid on the doormat below was the dreaded Brown Envelope. Separated from the other letters its bold, black printed letters glared up at me.

"ON HER MAJESTY'S SERVICE"

Knowing it was addressed to me thought, "Chr...ist not already. It's not my birthday for another six weeks". That really pissed me off. Only two weeks before down the Beehive, Junior had produced his results and was passed unfit due to Ulcers. Ignoring the envelope, continued down into the hall walked into the kitchen towards the gas stove where mum, had left a pot of tea warming over a low flame on the back gas ring. Placed on the side unit was a cup and saucer, opening the fridge taking out a bottle of milk poured a measure into the cup, then spooned in two sugars from the sugar bowl before pouring in the tea. Whilst stirring the tea very aware of that ghastly envelope lying in the hallway, taking the cup to the table sat down on the stool.

On the tabletop in front of me, lay evidence of Margaret and Michael's haste before they departed for work. Used cups, saucers and a couple of plates, one had a discarded piece of partially eaten toast on the other a few uneaten slices picking one up, about to take a bite heard the sound of mum coming downstairs, a pause... followed by the soft pad of her slippers on the lino floor, entering the kitchen, she placed the Brown envelope on the corner of the table, quietly murmured.

'Here you are son. Your call up envelope. You must have walked past it.'

Mum aware of its contents, having seen plenty of those Brown envelopes during her life, what with Dad a regular soldier of twenty-eight years, my elder brother Jackie called up in 1944 and Mike my other brother called up in 1947, and all three in the army. With my mouth full of toast reluctantly looked down at the address. Mr. J. P. P. Plant. Esq.

Picking it up, with trembling fingers, pounding heart pulled open the flap, removed the neatly folded wad of pages, the contents of which were about to change my whole life? Flattening out the wad, read the heading of the first sheet:

MINISTRY OF LABOUR AND NATIONAL SERVICE.

NATIONAL SERVICE ACTS 1948 TO 1950.

Still munching toast laid the wad on the table; one by one turned each page over, trying to understand the contents and details of information about National Service.

(1) Registration. (2) Medical examination. (3) Call-up.

Pages and Pages of Bla Bla Bla.

The Registration Card instructed me to. Fill in the Reverse side and bring the card with you.

To   The Medical Center for Medical Examination
No 1 .Montague St.
London W1.
Report by. 08:30 hrs Thursday 3rd. June.
Turning the card over revealed; Fill in your chosen branch of the Armed Forces
Royal Navy/ Army/ Royal Air Force.
Typed below was,
If Army, Identify, three Regiments or Corps. of your choice (a) (b) & (c).

Simple enough! On all three counts it was the Army and Royal Electrical Mechanical Engineers. Stuffing the remainder of the toast into my mouth thought, "Only a weeks' notice. God! What if I failed the medical? Fearful of not wanting to be labeled. "Unfit for Service". How bleedin' ironic. It was the same with all of us blokes, full of courage about how to make oneself ill or, doing anything to avoid the call-up. However the truth was, we were all shit scared of being found to have something nasty about our body. Mum interrupting my thoughts casually asked

'What day is your medical?'

Taking a sip of tea, glanced in her direction, mum was almost inside the pantry cupboard noisily sorting out the cooking utensils. First the frying pan, placing it on the gas ring striking a match lit the gas, returning to the cupboard extracted a box of eggs and a bowl of dripping. With a mouthful of partially chewed toast and quite near to choking, swallowed the remainder of the tea before with lack of interest mumbled.

'Next Thursday.'

Refolding the pages, eased the wad back inside the envelope and placed it on the edge of the table, returned my gaze towards the stove where mum stood in her woolen edged slippers was about four feet ten in height, her graying hair was swept up tidily on top of her head, her rimless glasses were propped up by her funny little nose and she permanently wore an apron, holding the frying pan over the heat asked.

Mum at the stove

'Any news from Derek?' Stretching up yawning replied.

'No. Not since he was last home.' Relaxing, leant on the table to watch as mum cracked an egg on the edge of the frying pan, it spluttered and spat as it slipped into the hot dripping quickly lifting the pan away from the heat, she asked.

'Do you want anything to eat while I'm cooking myself an egg?'

'No thanks. It's getting on for quarter to nine.' Shifting my gaze to the menacing Brown envelope, found myself wishing it would miraculously vanish before my eyes, shaking my head thought, " No such luck". Above the side unit was a serving hatch to the dining room, through its wide open doors drifted the sound of Frankie Laine belting out the end of "Jezebel". The Disc Jockey announced. 'The time now. Is exactly twenty minutes to nine.' Time for me to be moving.

Leaving the egg spluttering in the frying pan, mum crossed to the table to clear away the dirty crockery into the sink. Had me thinking, "What a dull life she must lead in the house, maybe should ask her to take my place, but knew she would say. "Get on with it; it will do you a power of good". Picking up the envelope got up, leaving the kitchen grabbed my jacket off the coat hook in the hallway, slipping it on slotted the envelope into the inside pocket, sitting down on the second stair tread fitted my cycle clips around my ankles. Opening the front door shouted.

'I'm off now Mum.' Banged the door shut behind me.

Although sunny outside, the dampness of the previous night's rain was still evident on the sparse area of grass. From my pocket took out the cycling gloves eased fingers into them as I walked across the narrow service road to the sixteen lockup pram sheds a most curious setup, as both Evans and Johnston House had seventeen dwellings, sixteen flats and the addition of our masionette built on the end. From my pocket took out the keys ; inserting one opened the door, wheeling out the flamboyant green coloured racing bike, relocked the door wheeled the bike to the roadway and got on. Just then emerging from the entrance to the flats was our next-door neighbour Mrs. Elbows, holding the hands of her two young daughters. She was a pleasant and rather attractive person; you would not think she had two teenage sons. David sixteen and Mickey fourteen, her husband was a cook in the Merchant Navy, she called out.

'Morning Joe. Off to work are you?'

'Yes. Morning Mrs. Elbows.'

The local firm who employed me, was less than five minutes away by bike. That morning oblivious to the short ride, turned off the main road down into the yard and as I freewheel up to the workshop heard the screech of a tool against metal, getting off leant it up against the door. Just inside the doorway against the wall was a lathe, total unaware of my presence the machinist Ron, short and stocky with a square jaw a flat nose that had felt many a thump from a leather glove, he had a thick mop of curly gingery blonde hair; tattoos covered his arms his mementoes of service life in the Navy. Not wanting to talk entered, inside the doorway located on the sidewall was the time clock, from its pigeonhole took out my time card and clocked in replacing it, wheeled the bike back across the yard and parked it under the concrete staircase leading up to the Drawing Office. (DO.) Bounding up the stairs opened the office door wide entered; the office reeked of the smell of stale pipe smoke even before removing bike clips and gloves, quickly crossed to the opposite wall and opened up all the windows to get some fresh air circulating. Come hail, rain or shine did that every working day.

In comparison to the main group of offices, our DO was quite a spacious room, covering the area of the double doored rear entrance below, where the firm garaged their lorry. Placed close to the windows, were two drawing boards, mine was directly opposite the doorway whilst the DO. Manager John's, a lever operated drawing unit including his office table, both conveniently positioned away from any draughts. Neatly laid out on the top of his table, was his smelly pipe stand with four different pipes and a dirty bleedin' ashtray. Placed on either side of the desk, was a telephone and his correspondence. (Copies of the Amateur Photographer [AP]). Against the sidewall, stood his ornate coat stand with curved antlers that he had purchased in a junk shop and he claimed. 'It once belonged to a Scottish Laird.' It was a lie; it was a piece of junk. John was a keen photographer, not a hobby of mine but did scan his A.P's to ogle the black and white photos of nudes. Yet another of his hobbies was smoking pipe tobacco.

Setting about my chores, filled up the print machine with the smelly liquid developer (It didn't arf pen and ink). Switching on the power, the twin bulbs pinged flickered then lit, their bright lights shining through the green canvass shield casting a greenish hue within the room. Removing the dustsheet off my Drawing board, sat down on the stool with the offending Brown envelope burning a hole inside my jacket pocket waited.

Soon in the street outside, the noisy roar of John's Velocette motorbike entering the confined space of the void below was briefly amplified to a roar, before cutting to a spluttering chuff as it freewheeled to the far end of the yard where he parked it. A couple of minutes later the clump, clump, of his footsteps ascending the stairway announced John's arrival. Entering through the wide open door, he shut it firmly behind him. Looking like Mr. Toad of Toad Hall his outfit made up of war surplus oddments from the three services. A Dispatch riders heavy beige coloured waterproof topcoat, a pair of Dispatch Rider's gloves, a pair of Air Force Pilot's goggles kept his beret on. Slung over one shoulder was a battered Army gas mask case that contained his lunch, fish paste sandwiches a diet that had never changed all the time I had worked there. In a pair of Navy issue wellies, he plodded across the room uttered a cheery. 'Morning.' Removing his beret and goggles hung them on one of the antlers; his partly balding head of blonde hair was an untidy mess and around his eyes were round indents made from the rims and tightness of his goggles. Slipping the strap of his gas mask case over his head dropped it down next to his desk. I moaned.

'Morning.'

'Blimey! What's up with you then?'

Getting down off the stool, walking across removing the Brown envelope from my

Jacket pocket handed it to him. John still popping open the studs of his greatcoat, grasped it with his free hand, glancing briefly exclaimed.

'Aah. What is this then? On Her Majesty's Service! Why has the Queen invited you to her annual garden party? What have you done to deserve that Eh?' Then uninterested, tossed it onto his desk. Despondent with his attitude urged.

'Read it. Need time off.'

'Oh that time off? Don't you worry about a little thing like that? You're as fit as a fiddle and I'm sure. More than eager to be called up...laughing adding insult to injury... Before you know it. You'll be in the Kate Carney (Army).' Immediately thought, "You bastard". Hastily asked.

'Can I get an apprenticeship?' Shaking his head.

'Nope! You know we cannot do that.'

With my hopes dashed. John begun his early morning ritual. At the coat stand kicked off his wellies, sitting down slipped on a pair of shoes he kept underneath his desk, from out of his breast pocket took out a comb to rearrange his hair, returning it swiveled his chair to position himself at the desk, so began phase two. Out of his pocket removed a tin of St. Bruno's Shag tobacco and a box of Swan Vesta matches, placing them on the table selected a pipe from the rack, removing the lid proceeded to fill the bowl with shag. Gripping the pipe firmly between his teeth, took out a match striking it held the flaring end close to the bowl, sucked and puffed until the tobacco was glowing red, tossed the match into the ashtray. With clouds of blue smoke engulfing his head, he began rubbing the palms of his hands together, exclaimed.

'Bloody cold in here! Shut the windows.' John's morning ritual ended. Ignoring him watched as he picked up the Brown envelope. Opening the flap removed the wad, clenching his pipe between his teeth gabbled.

'Get me a cup of tea from Eileen.'

Knowing that John had done his National Service about 1947. Thought, "Sod him! He could not care a shit about my concern". Out of spite left the office with the windows wide open. On the way to the main office, made up my mind not to mention anything about my enforced invitation. Entering through the basement door of the renovated old bombed out house, climbed the short flight of stairs leading up to the corridor and the General Office upon approaching it heard the faint sounds of girl's voices. Opened the door and entered. Immediately their conversation ceased, sat at their desks all three chorused.

'Morning Joe.'

'Morning Girls! Eileen. You got a cuppa Rosie Lee (tea) for John?' She snapped back.

'No. You are a pest. Go away.'

There was no sign of Harry the Office Manager. A jolly type of bloke with a strange resemblance to an older version of Billy Bunter. Rather rotund, his receding hair was swept back off his partially balding head; red chubby cheeks supported a pair of thick horn-rimmed spectacles, whichever tie he chose to wear was always splattered with soup or dinner stains. Ex Merchant Navy, always cracking jokes and taking the piss. Unlike John Harry, was not the tidiest of managers? In the far corner, his desk was littered with correspondence and the hand piece of his telephone was off its rest. (No doubt on purpose). Behind his desk was the cupboard where office stationary and tea making items were stored. Harry was in charge of the three local girls Eileen, Veronica and Pauline. Eileen was the telephonist and bookkeeper. Veronica and Pauline the typist and filing clerks.

Surveying the scene before me. Eileen sat at the desk with her elbows rested on top; her two white pillars of arms raised level to her mouth as she sipped tea from the cup cradled in her hands. Not quite in line with the Teddy Girl trend of those days, she always dressed in a light charcoal grey suit a jacket top, white cotton blouse and a pencil slim skirt. Laid open in front of her, was a ledger book with invoices or, payment slips secured by rubber bands. To one side was a typewriter, waiting for its keys to be touched. Fixed to the wall behind her was the small switchboard she was in charge of. No plugs were in that too was silent. Eileen was always early for work, primarily to take incoming calls and make tea. If you asked her nicely, she could produce an extra cuppa from the teapot.

The eldest girl Veronica, had dark curly hair thick eyelashes, brown eyes (that peeped at you through her glasses) a small nose and a gash of a mouth, with a figure similar to Eileen's was more into frocks and to emphasize her figure, wore a wide plastic belt around her waist. Open in front of her, was a make-up bag and perched precariously on the keys of her typewriter, was a small hand mirror. With her mouth agape and eyes fixed on the mirror, applied mascara to her eyelashes. Rather comical, as without her glasses she could not see a thing. Possibly later in the day with her war paint on, she might turn her hand to typing.

Now Pauline. Quietest of the three and another frock girl, was sat at her desk, she was plump, well endowed with straight mousy coloured hair, rosy cheeks, bright blue piercing eyes, a podgy nose and full lips. She, could be very offish and aloof, cannot remember ever hearing her laugh? Her typewriter, was still covered as she stared out of the window oblivious to everything. Nevertheless, according to Harry – she was the hardest worker of them all, once she started typing she did not stop.

Out of the three of them, I fancied Eileen. A bit of all right! A blue-eyed blonde with long wavy hair down to her shoulders, an attractive face with a sharp featured nose and small pert mouth, similar to the film star Gloria Graham's. Her voice was husky and in a bad mood could be cutting but the sound of her chuckling laughter was better. Without her stiletto high- heeled shoes she was about the same height as me five feet five, rather slim not much up in the tit area, but her rear view! What an attractive sight as she minced around the office, nice hips and a well rounded behind! Half way up her thighs, the tightness of her skirt revealed little moulds where concealed suspender clips were attached to the top of her silk stockings. Enough to get one's imagination going. Impatiently I asked.

'Eileen. Have you got a spare cup of Rosie lee for your mate John. Please.' Not attempting to move replied.

'Maybe. Tell him he's a nuisance.'

I stood there, patiently waiting to see which one of them was going to start work first. Could have stood there all bleedin' day! Repeating my question demanded.

'Eileen. Do you have a cuppa or not?' Angrily she snapped back.

'You're a pest. Do you know that?' Putting down her cup, got up and minced her way across towards the cupboard where the tea making items were stored together with the big teapot covered by its floral tea cosy. Lifting off the cosy held it limply in her hand and extended one leg to rest on the point of her stiletto heel, revealing a shapely calf. Totally distracted by this instant peep show, forgot about the Brown envelope. Eileen pouring out the tea, huskily asked.

'Hoi. Pest. Do you want one as well?' Being caught out letching, spluttered.

'No. No ta very much. Just finished a cuppa at home.' Not bothered she answered.

'Suit yerself.' Continued with filling three cups, two for the girls, deliberately taking her time replaced the cosy over the teapot, added milk and one by one spoonfuls of sugar into the cups noisily she stirred the tea. Picking up two cups, minced across to Veronica and Pauline whom gratefully received the tea. Just then the switchboard buzzer sang out, neither of the girls moved. Eileen mincing back to the switchboard leant over the back of the seat, to present a well rounded backside and enforced the widening of the tailored split at the hemline of her skirt, revealing a lacy petticoat. Captured by this spectacle thought, "Now. Things are really cooking". In her attempt to stop the buzzing; had to stretch even further over the seat to put a plug in the appropriate socket, so much so, her blouse became detached from the skirt waistband, exposing an expanse of white flesh. Totally engrossed with the lecherous sight of bare flesh, gulped.

'Good morning. Can I help you?...Oh it's you!...No! Sorry John. He's not in yet...Yes! I'll get him to speak to you the minute he comes in...Tea...Yes! I've just finished making it... He'll be over in a minute...All right?' Pulling out the plug, she muttered something to herself, turned towards the other girls said.

'Damn nuisance. Cheek of him! mimicked, "Is my tea ready yet"? With one arm behind her back, she swayed across the room tucking the blouse back into the top of her skirt, picking up the cup, lazily minced back to hand it over, she snapped.

'There you are Pest. Take it to him. Hope he drowns in it. 'Having partially recovered from the spectacle murmured.

'Ta. About bleedin' time.' Placing her hands on her hips glared at me and snapped.

'Don't you start?' I was not going to, turning to leave; the door was flung open nearly knocking the cup out of my hand. Harry late as usual, came bursting in.

'Sorry...Oh...It's you! Get out of my way...Morning all... Any messages?' Lifting up the counter flap went through the gap in a mad panic; let the flap go with a resounding bang, whereas I grab the door to leave. Taking care not to spill any tea, made my way back to our office still thinking about petticoats bare flesh and given the chance, what I would do? Opening the door entered into a thick haze of smoke. Noting the windows shut, spotted John standing at my Drawing Board gently tapping the drawing slide with the Brown envelope. Immediately, images of petticoats and bare flesh vanished, asked.

'John. Where dyer want yer cuppa? On yer table?' With pipe firmly clenched between his teeth gabbled.

'No... Bring it over here.' Crossing the room offered the cup, removing his pipe took hold of it, taking a sip said.

'You took your time. Where's the biscuit's?' Knowing Eileen did not like giving John Biscuits lied.

'She didn't have any left.' Unconcerned, studied the drawing before remarking.

'That pipe work there. Can you re-route it along that back wall?' Indicating to the appropriate point replied.

'Already tried that. But, it crosses that doorway.'

'Mmm! Did not see that. Okay that looks fine. Here...handing over my envelope...That's all right take the morning off. Your medical should not take that long.' He returned back to his desk, sat down picked up a copy of his A.P, began sipping his tea.

Shoving the envelope into the inside jacket pocket. Settled down to start work thinking. "Bleedin' 'ell. Only a week before I go". Time drifted by until John called out.

'When you're down at Bill's. Get me a cheese roll.'

'Blimey! Is it that time already?' Putting down the pencil, approaching his desk he handed over some money.

Leaving the office, en-route to the workshop to collect their orders and money. Decided. Not to mention anything about the Brown envelope, keep it a secret. Entering through the open doorway was immediately confronted by Ron and Dougie the firm's Chief Engineer. A big bloke, with a baldhead and a thick black bushy beard, he was holding a burner nozzle between his fingers, obviously they were discussing the finer points of machine turning? Dougie greeted me with a question.

'Heh Joe! What are we going to do, when you join up then?'

Baffled thought, "Oh shit! They all know about it. Now I'm in for it"?

Ron laughing responded, 'Join the wavy Navy.' From the depths of the workshop Fred shouted. 'Nah. He don't want to do that. He wants to join the A.T.S. You'll like that mob. Get as much crumpet as you can lay yer 'ands on.'

Fred, the store man and keeper of the keys, wearing a long light brown coat with a flat hat stuck on the back of his head walked around as if he owned the bleedin' place. Nothing seemed to worry him, he had a fat cheerful face and was a dirty old bugger. Very crude, always asking to see the palms of my hands? During the War he was a Gunner and according to him. 'Seen a lot of action.' He had a squint in one eye that he claimed. "Got looking through the keyholes of the brothels in Naples". "Looking through keyholes?" I reckoned he was a bleedin' liar! Angrily shouted back.

'Who wants' wot?' Fred keeping up the memento shouted.

'Hoi. Keep yer shirt on. You won't say that to the Sergeant Major.'

His latest remark, brought roars of laughter from the others. Quickly collecting their orders and money, hurriedly made my exit back to the General Office to see if Harry and the girls wanted anything? Upon entering, Harry sat at his desk looked up, seeing it was me, addressed all.

'Heh girls! Did you hear that Joe's about to join the WAAFs. Ha Ha.' My face beginning to redden up replied.

'Harry. Don't be bleedin' silly...demanded... Wot do you all want?' Looking straight at me with a smile on her face, Eileen stated

'I wanna nice man.' At that moment, could have offered myself but all I wanted was to get the hell out of there, thinking." That earlier phone call made by John, was to inform Harry of the Brown envelope". With his ability for diplomacy had informed everyone else? Cringing at the thought. "Bleedin' 'ell. I've got about another six weeks of this ribbing to face. Why couldn't John keep his big mouth shut"?

Being the youngest employee, it was expected of me to purchase various bread rolls for all of the firm's staff at. "Bill's Café". A short walk away from the main office down at Wandsworth Road Station. It was not really a café where you could sit down, just a tiny kitchen built into the corner of the supporting wall of the overhead railway bridge. Amid the noisy clattering of the trains above and the roar of traffic thundering past. If raining, you could shelter under the bridge and drink a cup of Rosie Lee. The owner Bill had been there for years and years and made the best ham or cheese rolls I had ever tasted. On the way down, was in an angry mood for biting at their bait thinking. "No doubt that day I was not the only poor bastard to receive his Brown envelope. An irrevocable invitation from Her Majesty the Queen. To become one of millions of her National Servicemen.

Throughout the following week, the ribbing from members of the workshop continued until the day before the medical, when they all wished me Good Luck.

CHAPTER FOUR
P.U.L.L.H.H.E.E.M.S.

'Come along son. Wakey wakey...The sound of mum's voice penetrated my deep sleep... She urged. Here's a cup of tea for you. It's time you were up and out on your way.'

Rubbing the sleep out of my eyes peered at the watch, Twenty to seven. "Chr...ist! That early". Propping myself up saw the cup on the side table. Casting aside the bedclothes swung out my legs and headed for the bathroom. The two bedroom doors on either side were closed, therefore Mike and Margaret were still asleep and by the sound of snoring, definitely Mike. Dressing, taking the cup went downstairs into the kitchen, handing it too Mum asked for a refill. Sitting down at the table where a plateful of buttered toast lay waiting to be eaten picking one up took a bite. Mum, about to leave the kitchen on her tea rounds gave me another refill, said.

'When your father left for work. He wished you Good Luck.'

'Ta.' Sipping the tea thought. "Good Luck? Needed that like a hole in my head". Full of apprehension at my future prospects and hopeful they would find something wrong with me too be sufficiently downgraded not to be called up. Mum re-entering urged.

'C'mon Son, its twenty past seven, you should have left by now.'

Reluctantly, got up. In the hallway putting on my coat opened the front door. Mike passing bye, muttered.

'Watch out for those Doctors. Feign you only have one leg. Make out your Long John Silver?' Thinking, "How the hell was I going to get away with that"? Quietly responded.

'Shut up. Don't be so bleedin' daft. See you later.'

That day. The 3rd. of June was a lovely summer's day. The walk to Stockwell tube station was through an area that appeared to be one big building site. Stretching from Wandsworth Road through to Stockwell and Clapham North. It was all part of Lambeth Councils redevelopment program that included the new Stockwell Bus Garage. During the months before the firm had moved to Wandsworth Road. I had watched with interest the progress of its construction and thought. "It was a great piece of structural engineering". It was about two hundred feet long with nine forty to fifty foot high archways, only supported by sidewalls all built out of reinforced concrete. Even at that ungodly hour of the morning, there was plenty of activity going on.

Commuting in London by Tube was the easiest and quickest mode of transport. The morning rush hour, began about seven thirty until nine thirty and the afternoon exodus began from four thirty until six thirty. Due to its locality. Stockwell on the Northern Line was a very busy station, serving both the West End and City. All workers, South of Stockwell would start their journey either walking; catch a tram or, bus to the tube station. During the rush hours, all trains were packed solid. To get on you had to fight your way into a heaving mass of humanity only to be crushed into the smallest space available and then, fight your way off. A very good indication of where a commuter worked was by their mode of dress. The city gentry. Bankers, Solicitors, Stock Exchange etc were well known as the. "Bowler Hat Brigade". Their mode of dress was Bowler hats or, Homburgers, pinstriped suit black polished shoes, carrying a brief case in one hand and tucked under the arm was a neatly folded newspaper of either the Telegraph or, Pink edition of the FT. In the other hand, held like a sword in its scabbard a carefully furled umbrella. Even the girls were somberly dressed. Whereas the "West- End Mob". Employed by the big stores or offices within the vicinity, were dressed entirely different. Italian style suit's, flashy coloured ties, gaudy waistcoats brogue shoes or, various coloured Teddy Boy outfits with brothel creepers. Whereas the girls, wearing pretty dresses with many layers of petticoats, their skirts billowing out like a ballroom dancer. Of course their shoes were winkle pickers with stiletto heels. It was not until they got off, you had a chance to look at their pins, as they swished and tottered past on their stiletto heels.

Joining the end of the long ticket queue, moved slowly forward into the station vestibule. The rush of warm air ruffled papers and provided the girls trying to hold down their skirts with a bit of morning exercise, which had me thinking, "Thank Christ. The Firm was just up the road". Passing a ten bob note through to the ticket man, shouted.

'Return, Russell Square mate.'

With the ticket and change, followed others onto the downward escalator passing many lazy people taking a rest from their previous strenuous journeys. The Northbound platform was packed and the indicator board displayed. - 1st. train. "Via the Bank". - 2nd. "Charring Cross". Okay for me, change at Leicester Square onto the Piccadilly Line then three stops to Russell Square.

In the tunnel, the rumbling noise gradually increased to produce a flow of warm air that ruffled all skirts and hair-do. Bursting out of the tunnel, the Bank train came to a grinding halt; its automatic doors slid open, no one got out. From the rear the Bowler Hat Brigade pushing forward fought like alley cats to get on, ever hopeful to grab a hanging strap. As the pushing and shoving subsided the doors slid closed, reopened, someone or something, a briefcase a coat or, someone's leg, was stuck in between the rubber edges of the doors they closed and the train left. Within two minutes, the rush of warm air predicted the noisy arrival of the Charring Cross train. This time, the late comers of the "Bowler Hat Brigade" remained at the rear girding their loins for the next Bank train. Whilst I, en-route to attend a medical, possibly to be accepted to fight for Queen and Country was caught in the melee of pushing, shoving, grunting that was all part of the early morning exercise. Victoriously, fought my way on that had me thinking, "What the hell was it all about? If, I changed my job to somewhere in the City or, the West End. Twice a day would be in a fight, with the added danger of either being trampled to death or even worse, thrown under a train"? The doors slid closed, we were off.

Inside the confined carriage the tinged atmosphere of a variety of smells; cigarette smoke, sweat, different perfumes powder and war paint, if anyone happened to fart; the change in smell caused suspicious glances around. Next stop Oval. (Similar to Stockwell). As soon as the doors opened, nobody got out exit the smells, yet masses forced their way on. Forcibly shoved into the center and squeezed in amongst the three "B's". (Bums, Bellies and Breast). The worst! A face-to-face encounter, where both parties avoided. "The eye contact stares". Pinned in, arms by your side unable to move even scratch your nose. Fatal! If an itch did occur and you even attempted to raise your arm, you might engage some birds skirt line or touch a tit, therefore risk an indignant. 'Keep yer filthy 'ands to yer sel' yer dirty bleeder. ' It was best to stay pinned in and twitch. The doors closed, wafts of new smells would circulate until the next stop. Kennington. Even more people got on. At Waterloo. A connecting station to the overhead railway. A few passengers fought like lunatics to get out whilst fifty more took their place, again at Charring Cross another overhead terminus, a repeat performance the crush was unbearable. Leicester Square. My chance to fight my way out, to be swept along with the tide of humanity down to the Eastbound Piccadilly train already under siege. Along with the other passengers forced our way on, wedged by the doors face squashed against the curvature of the glass, thinking, "Thank Christ. Only three stops to go". The events of the journey had taken my mind off the pending M. E. At Russell Square, was ready to fight a way through the mass of humanity yelled.

'Coming through. This is my stop.' Forcing my tiny frame through the mass of bodies, to be popped out like a pea from a pod. The doors shut; the train continued on its, crush and be crushed routine.

At street level to revive myself, took deep breaths of the smelly air of London. Taking my life in my hands crossed the main road avoiding Taxi's whose drivers thought they owned the roads and streets of London. Walking around Russell Square, the birds in the trees were singing their hearts out. That morning, they did not have to attend an M.E. Arriving at number 1. Montague Street, found nobody. Decided to walk around the British Museum, an impressive but miserable looking building. It's brickwork blackened by London's grime and smoky atmosphere, its Greek styled fascia with dirt encrusted colonnades streaked with rivulets of grey caused by many spells of rainfall over the years. Completing the circuit, returned back down Montague Street, where the grimy houses of the same elegant style with their large doors painted black. Architectural period? Possibly Georgian, anyway at that moment could not have cared a shit. Outside number 1. Joined the group of blokes all puffing away at fags waiting for the doors of doom to open. Gradually more arrived, Teddy Boys, Mods, City Slickers, nobody spoke, and only a hacking cough broke the silence.

As the distant chimes of Big Ben herald eight thirty. The big black door of Number 1 opened, out walked a beanpole. A tall skinny civvy chap dressed in a black pin striped suit, his head held up by a starched collar and a tie with the smallest knot I had ever seen? His dark hair parted on one side, exposed a straight white scalp line, his spectacles, were round black wire rimmed like the Nips wore. In one hand he held a clipboard, in his other a pencil. His attire and attitude announced he was a "Civil Servant". Stopping on the edge of the top step, surveyed the mob in front of him. To attract our attention, turned over the board and tapped it with his pencil. He need not have bothered; all eyes were focused on the beanpole. From his thin-lipped mouth, came the sound of a squeaky voice.

'Ahem! Gentlemen. May I have your attention please? When I call out your name, please answer. HERE. Step forward and enter the building through the door behind me. Proceed to the table at the far end of the hallway and register... a pause... I trust everyone has brought their cards with them? ...Appleby'...

'EAR.' A bloke moved up the steps, passing the beanpole.

'Baker.' No answer...Is Baker not here?'...'Belcher.'

'Here' someone else moved. 'Butcher.'

'YES.' Another moved, so the register went on then. 'Plant.'

'Ear.' Following behind a Ginger headed bloke dressed in a sandy checked patterned jacket, his black tapered trousers and big brothel creepers emphasized his skinny legs. Entered into a spacious hallway with a high ceiling, at the far end Ginger came to a halt at a table, being eye level with his neckline noted his well-worn but dirty white shirt collar, after a few seconds he moved away to his right. Behind the table sat another. "Civil Servant" in similar attire. Was it their badge of office? However, his large bulbous nose supported his thick horn rimmed spectacles, his hairstyle was not unlike the advert for Brylcream, but certainly nothing like Dennis Compton's dark well-groomed locks, he demanded.

'Name and registration card?'

'Plant.' Handing over the card. He quickly scanned the register ticked it, from out of a box file took a white card and handed it to me ordered.

'Go through that doorway there. Get undressed down to your underpants. Do not. Use the toilets. Hand this card over to each Doctor.' Nice? No Please or Thank you?

Pushing open the door directly in front at eye level, pinned to a black partition was a card with a large feathered arrow indicating right, down at the next corner a similar card pointed left. Rounding the corner, down at the far end some blokes were already in various stages of undress, their discarded clothes placed on top of long bench seats.

Joining Ginger, stripped off down to my 'Y' fronts, stood waiting with card in hand. Observing the black partition, it had openings at various intervals, obviously Doctors cubicles. At the far end, noticed another card its feathered arrow indicating left maybe more cubicles down that way. Above us, the high white painted ceiling displayed ornate cornices. Glancing at the card, turning it over revealed the letters P. U. L. L. H. H. E. E. M. S. Thinking, "What do those stand for"? About to ask Ginger did he know? When a noisy explosion shattered the silence, somebody down the line farted followed by a yell.

'Yer dirty bastard.' The obvious culprit replied.

'Betta out than in mate! Anyway ain't 'ad me tomtit yet.'

'Phoor! Yer can say that again. Dirty bastard.' To which the guilty culprit managed another long explosive fart. Brought further ribald comments and all began laughing; fortunately, we were out of range.

Dennis Compton decided to make his appearance, as he walked past all heads followed his progress down to the far end coming to a halt turned around. Where he stood, his head was dead centre of the sign with the feathered arrow, which appeared to enter through one ear and out the other. In a stage whisper, somebody muttered. 'Din't nah they 'ad bleedin' red injuns in 'ere as well?' Dennis Compton called out.

'Can you hear me down at the far end? Nobody answered...Please. Turn to your right facing me. Have your cards ready. First one follows me.' Whilst everyone turned to their right, he disappeared out of sight. Slowly in line, we moved forward then came to a halt. Waited until the first bloke returned, moved again, near the corner, Ginger who was next, asked the bloke returning.

'Ear Mate. Wot's going on then?' A disinterested reply

'Not much. Just measuring yer, that's all.'

As Ginger returned, I padded down towards Dennis Compton, standing beside a playing card table its green beige top had seen better days, he demanded.

'Card.' about to say to him. "You told me. Only hand it to a Doctor". Snatching it, he placed it on top of the table. From around his neck, whipped down a tape measure. 'Arms outward stretch.' With the ease and practice of a professional tailor flicked the tape around my chest, catching it adjusted it...'Arms down. Thirty-six and a half. Breathe in...Hold it...Forty.' Whilst scribbling on the card ordered. 'Right breathe out.' The tape, was whipped from around my chest, its friction burnt the skin. Grabbing hold of my arm, dragged me around the table pushing me up against a wooden measuring strip, stuck to the wall. 'Stand. With your back against the wall.' Lowering a peg onto my head muttered. 'Five feet five inches.' Marking the card gave another curt order. 'Get on those scales there.' Standing on its cold metal platform, he adjusted the weights on the bar. 'Eight stone seven pounds.' Scribbling on the card, handed it back. 'As your name is called out, give this to the Doctor. Get back to your place.'

That procedure took about two minutes. We were like cattle. No time to waste. Rejoining the line of 'Y' fronts, waited until the last bloke had been done. By that time, it must have been nine thirty, only then did the real medical start. At different entrances of various cubicles. Doctors appeared, each calling out names. Hearing my name called did not know by which Doctor?

'Plant...PLANT. Are you here or, are you deaf?' Three entrances further up a tall bald headed Doctor with a grey goatee beard, was waving a card above his head mouthing something? Approaching him muttered.

'Plant Sir.'

'Oh! So you are here. You are not Deaf. He snatched the card from my hand. Come in here.' Following behind him. Cocking his head to one side enquired.

'How's your hearing Plant?'

'Eh?' Cocking his head again as if he had a nervous twitch asked

'Did you not hear me the first time?'

'Er. When sir?'

'Outside Plant.' Again the twitch.

'Er. Yes sir. But...Interrupting he said.

'I am Doctor Prendergast and amongst other duties. I am the Ear Nose and Throat specialist. Now. I am going to give you a series of hearing tests and. Want you. To tell me if, you can hear what I am saying?' Again, he cocked his head to one side as if attempting to listen to my reply asked.

'What is your name Plant?'

'Plant. Sir.'

'Good...A tick or something on the card...What is your...?' Again the twitch.

'Pardon Sir. Did not hear you sir.'

'Hmm. Your address Plant?' Rattled it off. Another tick or something on the card.

'Now Plant. What is...' Again the twitch.

'Pardon sir?'...

'Date of birth!'...

'Oh! Date of birth. Twenty-second sir.'....

'Hmm?' Again that twitch...

'Pardon Sir?' Again the twitch.

'Month...Month!' Dr Prendergast, the twit was having a game with me and it was catching. Cocking my head sideways answered.

'Pardon. I didn't hear sir.'

'Month and Year. Plant.... exasperation creeping into his voice. MONTH and YEAR.'

'Oh. June nineteen thirty-six. Sir.'

'Now then Plant. I want you to go over there. Turn to face me and tell me if. You can hear what I am saying.'

Dutifully moved into the corner, turned to face him. Reflecting on his baldhead the lights above temporarily diverted my attention. Looking upwards saw a very ornate rose with a spray of chandelier lights. Admiring its beauty gazed at it. He shouted.

'PLANT. YOU ARE NOT PAYING ANY ATTENTION TO ME.'

His sudden outburst startled me. Therefore concentrating my gaze on his goatee beard, through its stubble his lips made exaggerated movements as he spoke words. Moreover, with the entire hubbub going on outside, did not think anyone could have heard what he was saying thinking, "Two can play at this game". Cocking my head to one side shouted.

'IT'S A NICE DAY TODAY.'

'Very good Plant.' I could not believe had answered him correctly. Maybe. He was deaf? Extracting a wicked looking instrument from his coat pocket ordered.

'Plant come over here.' Full of apprehension slowly walked towards him, he grabbed hold of my right ear.

'Now let me look into your ears...Pulling back the lobe, thrust the cold thing into my ear ole....murmured Mmm. Now the other one...Hmm...Head back.' He forced my head backwards down to the base of my spine, just so this twit, could look up my nose...Hmm ... Now let's look at your throat...Open wide...opening my mouth wide; he rammed a wooden spatula onto my tongue and forced it down my throat he said. Now say Aagh.' Gagging.

'ARRaagh.' Without removing the wooden stick he enquired...Do you clean your teeth regularly?' With the spatula stuck down my throat, managed a strangled reply,

'Aagh. Yaaah. Raahgaalaar.' From half way down my throat he dragged out the spatula, which brought tears to my eyes forcing me to swallow hard. With a flourish as if aiming a dart, he threw the wooden implement of torture into a wide-open mouthed wicker wastebasket conveniently located in the corner. That I'm sure. Gagged as well. Cocking his head said.

'Hmm. Very well Plant...Scribbled something on the card, handing it back ordered. Wait outside.'

I left Dr. Prendergast twitching alone. Outside, did not have long to wait; someone was calling out my name.

'Plant.' In the confines of the corridor just to visit a Doctor, a mad scramble ensued like many rats scurrying from one cubicle to the next, blokes bumping into each other were cursing and swearing, there was no time to apologise.

'Sorry Mate.' It was more of. 'Git out' me f.....g way.'

'PLANT.' Two cubicles away spotted another white-coated Doctor wearing a monocle. In fact, they all wore white coats. This Doctor, had a headband with a silvered disc stuck in the air, possibly his badge of office? To keep the monocle in position, the right side of his face was screwed up tight thinking, "He must be the eye Doctor". Passing one cubicle, a loud cough rent the air. I shuddered and thought, "Christ. They're killing that poor Bastard". Arriving at the Silver Disc saloon the Doctor enquired,

'You're name Plant?' Nodding, he too snatched the card out of my hand...Good. Follow me.' Scurrying in behind him noticed the black steel band securing the silver disc conveniently parted his grey hair in two. Turning around revealed he also had a squint in his left eye, possibly from the contortion of wearing the monocle?

'Good. Now you are here... covering my left eye with the card ordered.'

'From the bottom line on that card on the wall. Read upwards.'

'AFOJ.... TUVXY'

'Good...Switching the card from left to right...Read upwards.' Remembering the letters, spoke them aloud.

'Good...Writing something on the card he enquired...Any problems seeing?'

'No sir. Not that I know of.'

'Good... Do you wear glasses for anything? Reading or?'

'No sir.'

'Good...Now read this passage for me.' Handing me a card revealed a verse or poem printed in tiny script read it out aloud... Good. Producing a large pack of playing card, he asked. Can you see anything different on these cards?' Maybe, he wanted to play three-card brag. No such luck. Holding up the first one covered in coloured dots. Derek had told me about this test. "The Colour Blind Test. Within the coloured dots. Look for the hidden numbers". Doctor Good began playing cards.

'Now. Read each one in turn.' As presented, each had a different number.

'10.... 3.... 8.... 4... 6...'

'Good...scribbling something on the card continued...Good...Right that is it. You are done. Wait outside until your name is called again.' However, never once did he look into my eyes with that silvered disc. What did he have it stuck to his head for? I think his name was Dr. Good.

Outside it was pandemonium. Blokes rushing around in 'Y' fronts with a couple of dung hampers thrown in. Bumping into one bloke coming out of a cubicle, he still heaving his 'Y' fronts up over his arse, muttering. 'Bleedin' 'ell.'

It all appeared like organised chaos. Amidst the shouting by the various Doctors? 'Barker.' - 'Proctor.' - 'Smith.' – I heard. 'Plant. ' Down at the far end cubicle noticed a Doctor shouting. 'Anyone here by the name of PLANT?'

Dodging around one bloke sidestepped another as I got near him noticed the look of boredom on his face. Standing with both hands deep in the pockets of his white coat, his stethoscope hung loosely around his neck thinking, "This must be for the Chest Examination". Cautiously announced. 'Plant sir.' With a sigh of resignation took the card.

'Right...Come on inside.' Padding in behind him, he asked.

'How's your breathing?'

'It's all right sir. At this moment. I'm breathing in short pants sir.'

'Ha. Bloody. Ha. I suppose you think that's funny?' Without hesitation slapped the cold end of the stethoscope against my chest. Staring at his round face showed signs of a blue beard, his eyes were closed hairs protruded from his nostrils and his ears matching the scraggly mop on top. He was a hairy bugger, he urged.

'Breathe. Innn...Out...Pah...Innn...Hold it...Out... 'Paah...Innnn...Hold it......Out...Paah.' Grabbing my shoulders spun me around. Felt the then warm end of the stethoscope slapped against my back. Again the same procedure. "In- Out- Shake it all about". Then with his fingers, began a drum roll, just like Gene Krupa. Thump, Thumpety, Thump. First on the back, spun me around to face him, once again played the drums. Thump, Thumpety, Thump. With urgency in his voice asked

'Had any problems?' Detecting a serious tone in his voice, immediately my heart began racing. Banging away inside the cavity of my chest. Had he found only one lung? Christ! Unfit for service?

'Er. N.n.no.'

'Oh...Right...Once again. Breathe.Innn...Holdit.......(Five minutes passed)... Out...Paaaaaah. A rush of hot air fanned his head of hair out straight. Once again... Breathe. Innn...Hold it... (Another five minutes passed and I was close to passing out)...Out...Paaaaaaah.'

Red in the face, another rush of hot air belched from the depths of my inner chest, this time he avoided it. Rather worried gasped,

'I have got two. Ain't I Doc?' Quizzically looking at me said

'Okay...scribbled something on the Card...Wait outside.'

Shaken! Left his cubicle the last in the row, saw Dennis Compton pointing at me beckoning he said.

'You. Follow me.' He turned and disappeared down the corridor. Padding past the weighing scales, found him stood in a darkened corner, he urged

'Come here. Hurry up.' On the floor beside him was a white enameled bucket with a blue-rimmed top, behind him was a small square white sink with a single tap however, he was not alone. Close to the sink stood another bloke. Dennis Compton demanded.

'Card...Handing him the card, in part exchange he thrust a bottle into my hand...Sample of your (He emphasized) URINE In the bottle please. Not water from the tap. Like that idiot in the corner provided. If you overrun, urinate in that. ' Pointing to the white bucket he left.

The other bloke stood by the sink whispered...

'Ear mate. When he gave me the bottle. He just told me to fill it up. So's, I fills it with water from that tap. Din I? An gives it back to im. He stuck some paper init and told me. It weren't a sample of my urine. It is tap water...Making some straining noises...urmm continued...Then he tells me. Piss in the bottle. You can't fool those sods. can yer? Now I can't piss a bleedin' drop. I've been here ten bleedin' minutes. He keeps on givin' me bleedin' water to drink. I've drunk a gallon. I can't take anymore...I'll burst.'

Letting him strain by himself, whilst I squeezed and pulled. First a dribble then, with the thought and fear of drinking a gallon of water it flowed. As it quickly filled up, the gurgling noise in the sample bottle was quite audible.

'Ooooh...Chriiist.' Gasped the other bloke, as he started pissing possibly a reaction to the noise of my piddling. Whilst I moved away from him to wait for Dennis Compton to arrive back. During which time the other bloke exclaimed,

'I can't...bleedin'...stop.' Turning his hosepipe in the direction of the bucket. As urine hit metal, it created a tinny sound. The sound of music attracted Dennis Compton, who came running back. Proudly. I handed over my hot pint of pale yellow urine, he ignoring the other bloke demanded. 'Name?'

'Plant.' Writing it down on some tape or paper plunged into the sample bottle. After a couple of seconds, it changed colour. Pouring it down the sink, scribbled something on the card, handed it back.

'Right you're done. Return and wait for your name to be called.' Disregarding me Dennis Compton yelled at the other bloke.

'Stop urinating. Watch out! Don't wet my feet.' Leaving him with the other bloke still pissing into the bucket. Returned into a melee of blokes. A Doctor stood in the doorway of a cubicle wheezed. 'Is your name Plant?'

'Yes sir.'

'Where have you been? I've called out your name a few times.' Truthfully, I replied.

'Been for a piss sir.' Snatching the card from me.

'Come on. Quickly in here.' Padding in behind him, he turned around. He was short rather fat, his open white coat revealed, a pinstriped waistcoat; the two lower buttons were undone. A large polka dot bow tie covered his neck, stuck out of his fat forehead was a lump of something or other? A mass of meticulously combed black wavy hair covered his head, in one hand held a pair of large horn-rimmed spectacles. He presented a picture more in keeping with a bleedin' politician than a doctor. He ordered.

'Stand up straight. Arms by your sides.' Scrutinizing my person, from tip of head to tip of toes. Probably counting if, there was two of everything... Holding one arm of his spectacles twirled them around, indicated...'Walk over there...Right...Now back...murmured...No flat feet...marking the card...Any problems with your water works?'

'No sir.' Thinking, "Not like that poor bleeder around the corner".

'Bowel movement?'

'No. Sir. Er. Yes Sir. That is to say....'Drop your underpants...doing so, the Doctor moved in close, his cold fat hand grabbed hold of my balls resulting in an instant shriveling of scrotum and a quick intake of breath. Instinctively pulled away, he hung on tight... Cough...he muttered so, coughing a little louder produced a muffled Cough...he was not satisfied squeezing tighter ...I said. COUGH.' That made me cough and my eyes water... 'AGAIN. LOUDER... this time loudly coughed. Thank Christ he let go and putting on his spectacles ordered...Turn around stand with your legs apart, bend over and touch your toes.' Thinking, "Oih. Oih. Here we go". Making no comments abruptly said...Stand up. Pull your underpants up, turn around and face me.' After that embarrassing experience, pulled them up sharpish before turning around to see hm busy scribbling notes on the card. 'Plant. Isn't it? Any history of venereal diseases?'

'No?'

'Do you. Masturbate?' Taken aback by his question.

'Do I what Sir.'

'Wank. Is the common word for it.' Mumbled.

'Who me sir? No sir.' Handing back the card he sarcastically commented.

'Well. You will not. Do it in the services. Wait outside.'

The melee of blokes continued. Padding from one cubicle to another, whilst above the drone of the busy bees. Doctors were still shouting out surnames of those still to be examined. Dodging out of the way returned to where my clothes were stacked to wait for the next appointment, it never happened. Standing there glanced at the card, scrawled below the letters of P.U.L.L.H.H.E.E.M.S. was a lot on unintelligible scribble? Hieroglyphics and doctor's signatures? Maybe, all the Doctors suffered from the same illness? Just then,

Ginger arrived back so enquired.

'Ear mate. Know what these mean?' His intelligent reply was

'Nah! It's all f..... g rubbish ain't it?'

None the wiser and still baffled studied the card for inspiration. After the intense exertion of scrambling about, we stood there sweating until the last loud cough rent the air, someone in the line loudly called out. 'COUGH LOUDER.' This comment raised a few laughs. A few minutes later, a red-faced bloke emerged from one of the cubicles. The very last one for Kit Inspection. Passing along the line of the grinning 'Y' fronted blokes he walked the gauntlet. The hue of his red face quickly spread downwards to his chest. We waited. Silence descended. Then a fart ripped through the air that had everyone gaffing, as the culprit's besieged neighbour cried out.

'Bleedin' 'ell. Not you again?'

'Cor. I've got t'ave a pony.' Came the culprits strained reply.

'Yer dirty bastard. Can't yer bleedin' well wait til yer get outside.' At that moment, the original beanpole orderly arrived and loudly squeaked.

'You can all get dressed. As you leave. Please return your card to the orderly at the desk in the hallway outside. Within the next two weeks. Notice of your medical grading. Will be posted to you.'

Yet another long fart rent the air. Ignoring the outburst of language, everyone rapidly dressed and ran on our hurried exit, throwing cards at Dennis Compton we fought to get out the front door, bumping into Ginger he went one way I the other, never did see him again.

So pleased to get away from that ordeal, taking my life in my hands ran crossing main roads all the way back to the tube station, straight through the vestibule down the escalator onto the completely empty westbound platform. Falling against the wall, with heart pounding and lungs bursting knew just how much Roger Bannister must have felt a week before, after running the mile in less than four minutes. The flow of warm air gently fanned me, as the rumble of an approaching train grew louder. With a noisy roar, it erupted from the tunnel, coming to a screeching stop the doors opened. Boarding the empty carriage slumped down in the comfort of a seat, sweating, breathing freely had plenty of time to reflect on my recent M. E. It was more hilarious than arduous. Judging by its regular pace my heart was all right but when the Quack asked me. 'Breathe in again.' It started beating nineteen to the dozen; it really frightened the shit out of me.

Changing trains at Leicester Square another couple got on; at the next stop, they got off leaving me thinking. "How bleedin' silly. Three hours before you had to fight your way into a carriage, now you could hold a dance in any of them". Still puzzled about PULLHHEEMS. Somewhere, I had heard that expression. Then laughing aloud it dawned on me who exactly did that during our first and last lesson of the school year. It was our college PT master "Dusty Miller".

What a character he was. Ex-Army Physical Training Sergeant. About five feet seven in height, with cropped iron grey hair; his matching moustache was tinged yellow from constantly smoking Woodbines. Rippling with muscles, had one shoulder tattooed with a Crown and Crossed Sabers, stripped to the waist reeking of sweat his barrel chest was covered in a mass of grey hairs. An army belt held up his gym trousers and the leg ends secured by cycle clips and wore enormous brown plimsolls on his feet. His bright beady blue eyes watched all that went on. Unfortunately, for us although the college had every other facility available for teaching Engineering, it did not have a gym. Dusty's classes were held in another local school hall. Regardless of the elements hail, rain or sunshine Dusty dressed in the same uniform, would march between the two schools. For our first lesson, our class left the main school and proceeded about 500 yards further down the road to the other school. Unaware of what to expect, most of us dawdled before climbing the four flights of stairs to the second floor into the hall where Dusty was waiting. As we entered each received a whack on our behind with a rather large slipper and ordered.

'You're late. Line up. – You're late. Line up.' He went on as we...formed a long line in the hall. He then stood in front of us and with beady eyes scanning the line, began his first brief but very instructive introduction that took exactly fifteen seconds.

'My name. Is Mr. Miller. Some people call me. 'Dusty.' I warn all of you. DO NOT. I repeat. DO NOT EVER; let me catch anyone calling me by that name. UNDERSTAND?' Now. You have two minutes to change into your PT Kit and be outside in the Gymnasium.' We were pushed and shoved into an empty classroom to change. As we came out he gave each one of us another whack on the bum with his lethal looking slipper. Standing around, rubbing our behinds, he informed us.

'You lot are all too slow. I will change that. Your first lesson, I am going to take your PULLHHEEMS. To see if you are alive or not.'

Lining us up into four teams. A, B, C, D. He made each team get out the apparatus, Pomeroy and Box horses, springboards and mats, Bench Forms, untying ceiling ropes from the wall bars it became a Gymnasium. Setting exercise for each team whilst the others did exercises, the 'A' team would form a line outside his little office, until we changed over. One by one, we would enter to be scrutinized: Height, weight, chest measurements all jotted down, our eyesight and hearing ability, placing one ear against our chest he would listen to our heart. Dusty was an articulate person and was only interested in our physical development. However, that was only the first lesson, after that our weekly lessons were just Physical Torture moreover, to get there on time we would race down the road undoing ties, belts and removing jackets scramble up the stairway knackered just to avoid a whack from his slipper. Now that is discipline. As proof of our physical development, that first and last lesson he dedicated to measurements, entering all details into a dog-eared school exercise book, making audible comments in a voice tinged with disappointment, as if he had failed in his efforts. 'You. Have not grown a smidgen over the past year. Half an inch on your chest measurement. Although. You can see and still hear.' The details he handed to the Headmaster for the annual report.

By the time, the train had reached Stockwell. Still none the wiser thought, "I'll ask Dad, if anyone would know he would". Bursting for a piss galloped up the escalator into the vestibule and out into bright sunlight. Glancing across to the white clock tower on the island, its hands showed five to twelve. The Swan Pub opposite looked inviting, maybe could have a quick drink and use their toilets, in desperation chose the public convenience. Descending the steps two at a time, entered the world of the attendant below the streets of London tinged with the heavy smell of carbolic drifting around. At the urinals rather than pissing into a bottle, with an air of abandonment, could relieve myself and inspect the polished brass copper tubes and fittings done with loving care by the attendant, thinking, "Someone has to do it, better him than me". Back at street level, walking home passed the building site. As it was lunchtime the workers, had downed tools and were down either the betting shop or swilling beer in the Angel Pub opposite. Arriving home, opening the door met Dad coming out of the kitchen, he greeting me with a big grin asked.

'How did you get on Son?'

'Oh. All right s'pose. At least they know I've got two of everything. Ear. Dad. What are PULLHHEEMS?' Placing his hands on his hips replied.

'PULLHHEEMS. Now there is music to my ears. It is the Armies medical way of using the first letter for various parts of the body. P. is for Physical Capacity, U. Upper Limbs; L. Lower Right Limb; L. Lower Left Limb; H. Right Ear; H. Left Ear; E. Right Eyesight; E. Left

Eyesight; M. Mental Aptitude; S. Stability. You Okay?'

'Spose so. It was just as Derek had explained it. Hilarious.' Mum, calling from the kitchen.

'Now you're back early, I'll cook your dinner then you can get back to work. While you wait. Make yourself some tea.' Knowing the answer would be yes, I asked

'You and Dad, like one as well?'

'You might as well fill up the pot.'

With the kettle filled and on the lighted gas went into the other room to play an Earl Bostic record. "Moonglow" Just as the sounds of the last bars of the tune finished the kettle whistled, making the tea poured out three cups taking mine back into the room, played a recording of the Modern Jazz Quartet's. 'Django.' The music would take my mind off my recent ordeal. Increasing the volume was lost in the mood of the music, until Dad entering the room demanded.

'Turn that Heebie Jeebie noise down.' Unless it was military music, he always called any music. Heebie Jeebie's. However, military music had him stomping around the house blowing an imaginary trombone or, whistling a tuneless note. From the depths of the kitchen mum called.

'Joe your dinners ready. C'mon or you'll be late for work.'

Leaving the confines of my world of music, entered the kitchen where laid on the table was a plateful of double egg and chips just waiting to be eaten. Stood at the gas stove, mum was cooking another pan of chips for Dad. Pouring myself out another cuppa, cut and buttered two slices of new crusty bread and sat down to eat. Mum placing another plate of chips at the far end of the table, called out.

'Jack. Dinners ready.' Dad coming in sat down, shaking salt all over the chips enquired

'How many were at the medical center?'

'Don't really know? But there must have been a least fifty or so? The Doctors. Went through us like a dose of salts.' Grinning like a Cheshire cat replied.

'No! I must admit. They don't take long once they get going. It's just like. Lambs to the slaughter.' Not very happy with his last remark retorted.

'Pack it in Dad. It ain't funny.'

'G'wan. It will do you good. Get some discipline into you.' He was enjoying my present dilemma, that of not wanting to do something, but being forced into doing it. Not prepared to start an argument, quickly finished my dinner and was ready for work, so left them eating in the kitchen.

At one o' clock entering the workshops to clock in. Immediately the blokes ribbed me rotten. Dirty 'ole Fred yelled out.

'Did they find out how many balls yer got? I bet the 'ole Quack 'ad a good feel around din he?'Helpless in defence shouted back

'Shut up. Dirty 'ole bastard.' But he continued...

'Hoi. Ow is yer piles? 'Anging free are they? Ere. I bet your piss was just lemonade.'

His last remark, brought howls of laughter, with that ringing in my ears quickly departed heading back to the office. Entering the smoky atmosphere began coughing. John puffing out a cloud of smoke.

'Oh your back then. Look. Harry has some drawings to be taken up to St. Thomas's Hospital. They have to be there tonight. You can take them up on your bike. Okay?'

That was all he cared. Bugger all about how I got on? With John engulfed in smoke, left the office thinking. "It would not take me long to do that trip. Maybe an hour there and back. Entering the General office leant up against the reception counter asked.

'Where's these Drawings for St Thomas's then?' Harry glancing up quipped.

'Oh Joe. Thought you had gone to join up and, we wouldn't see you anymore.'

41

Avoiding any further conversation on the subject replied.

'Nope just me medical. John said yer got a parcel ready for St. Thomas's.' But Harry continued... 'I bet. You had to cough a lot, for the Quack's then. The girls began to titter. Eileen has them ready parceled up on her table. Be quick. It has to be there by four. Give them to the Chief Engineer Mr. Meluish. Okay.' Eileen smiling asked in a husky whisper.

'How did you get on then Joe?' Seeking sympathy, which they all fell for.

'It was 'Orrible. Lots of Quacks grabbing and poking at me.' The girl's chorused.

'Aah! That was not very nice. Was it?' Harry urged.

'C'mon, C'mon. Less of the chat. Get yourself out of here.' Approaching the counter with the parcel, Eileen huskily whispered.

'When you get back, I'll make you a nice cuppa. All right?'

'Okay. I'll be as quick as I can.' With the parcel left the office down the stairs two at a time to collect my bike.

St. Thomas's Hospital was not that far away. Basically, a straight run towards the crossroads at Vauxhall Bridge, along the Embankment to Lambeth Bridge and just beyond Lambeth Palace was the hospital. Knowing where to go, entered their office dropped the parcel on top of the table, called out. 'Auto's Drawings for Mr. Meluish.'

By the time I got back was sweating like a pig, there and back in less than the hour. Heading straight back to the General office to see Eileen and her promise of a cuppa tea. There was no sign of Harry, possibly he was telling jokes down in the workshop. Eileen surprised upon my arrival back exclaimed.

'Bloody hell. You were quick.'

'Well. It was. The promise of your cuppa tea. Anyway, at this time of the afternoon, the roads weren't that busy.'

Getting up, minced her way across to the cupboard pouring out the tea, carried it back gave it to me, cupping her free hand over mine coyly smiling said.

'There you are. Three biscuit's mind you don't tell John.' I watched, as she minced back to her table. Then madly in love with Eileen. Dunking the biscuits drank the tea before heading back to the office to sit at the drawing board and for the rest of the day, daydream about her. I went to night school and later met Kenny, Brian and Junior in the Beehive. To relate the happenings of my most exciting day at the medical center and, the possibility of failing?

CHAPTER FIVE
DOOMED - THE LONG WAIT.

A fortnight later on my way down to the kitchen lying on the doormat was a Brown envelope. Not ignoring that one quickly picked it up thumbing open the flap took out the document walking towards the kitchen reading stopped, was mortified with the result. Passed A1 Fit for Active Service. Further information and instruction will follow, loudly exclaimed.

'Aw shit!' Mum called out from the kitchen.

'What's that Son? Your results?' Entering the kitchen mournfully muttered.

'Sorry Mum. Yeah. Passed A1.'

Oh. Never mind at least your fit that is the main point. Anyway, two years is not a long time. Cup of tea?'

'Yes please...sitting down at the table continued...Well if the Government has anything to do with it. They will increase it to three years just like Michael, he had to do a year and then they added an extra six months. It's not fair. Don't want to go in anyway.'

'Here you are Son have a cup of tea calm your nerves. I'll make some fresh toast for you.' Whilst she made the toast I sat there oblivious to all around me just thinking, "In a couple of weeks time will not be here but in some bleedin' barracks miles from anywhere. Aw shit"! Stirring the tea ate some toast oozing with butter, satisfied picking up the envelope left for work. At work advised John of my results, he being as cheerful as ever responded.

'Well. That was inevitable wasn't it? Not long now just a couple of weeks and you'll be off. I'll have to get someone to take your place. The Employment Exchange might have someone suitable? I'll get Harry to sort it out.'

Very disenchanted settled down to begin work. Later, doing my rounds to collect the orders for Bill's upon entering the workshop there was no slagging off. Obviously, they already knew.

'Good luck mate. Not long now.' Even the girls and Harry avoided the situation.

That Thursday night, upon entering the Beehive saloon bar Junior was stood watching Kenny and Brian playing Bar Billiards. Flipped the Brown envelope onto the snooker table in the process knocked over a peg. Kenny about to make a shot exclaimed.

'Hoi! Watch wot yer doing.' To which I blurted out.

'Yer know what? Bleedin' passed A1. Need a beer.' Junior said.

'Ard luck mate.' Kenny mumbled.

'Aw I'm sorry. Bleedin' ell. I'm next. With a grin, Brian said.

'Well. Glad it's not me.' We had a Jews march past and a game of darts before going over the club. For the next two weeks checked every delivery of the post, nothing came. Another two weeks passed bye, still nothing. One Thursday night in the Beehive, Kenny informed us.

'Heh! The week after next. I've got two weeks holiday. Heard about a cheap holiday camp down near Bracklesham Bay. Anyone fancy a week down there?' Brian and Junior refused, on the other hand I agreed. Although we did not have the money by begging borrowing and stealing, we could just about raise enough to pay for it.

Two weeks later, early Saturday morning each carrying a small hand case containing holiday clothes arrived at Victoria Coach Station. Locating the right coach found an irate driver pacing up and down waiting for us, he was the spitting image of the comedian Arthur English, gruffly he greeted us.

'You two for Bracklesham?' A dual reply.

'Yes.' An equally gruff response.

'You're late. Give me your luggage and climb aboard. 'Urry up.'

He certainly was no comedian. Handing over our cases, pushing Kenny in front climbed aboard then to be confronted by a sea of staring eyes leering at us for being late. With red faces, made our way to the only two seats left about half way down the coach. Guiltily we sat down, as the driver slammed down the luggage door the coach shook with a resounding thud, he appeared at the doorway purposely glaring at us apologised for the delay in departure. Sliding the door shut, climbed up into his cab started the engine slipping in the gears. Slowly the coach left the Station turning onto the main road outside Kenny ignoring all stared out of the window, digging an elbow into his ribs muttered.

'It's your bleedin' fault that we're late.'

'We're 'ear nah ain't we? I need a fag.' His answer to everything. Fishing out of his pocket a packet of fags and matches lights up. Having regained our composure casually looked at the other passengers. Families with young kids of varying ages but there was two pairs of girls, one sat up the front the other sat three behind. The journey was uneventful until the coach made a scheduled stop at Hindhead overlooking the Devil's Punchbowl. A natural deep depression in the land visited by many? Even by us on our various weekend cycling trips to the Isle of Wight. Carrying tents and various scrounged camping

Me at the Punchbowl

equipment. The previous year before Derek was called up the pair of us had cycled down to Sandown on the Isle of White to spend a week camping. That very week a group of his friends from the same flats turned up at the campsite. That turned into a hilarious week's adventure but that is another story.

Me, Brian & Derek

The driver, getting out of his cab came around to slide open the door. Standing on the steps pointedly glaring at us informed all.

'We are stopping here only for a half hour. The coach will leave. Promptly at eleven forty-five. The next stop will be Chichester.'

Immediately everyone got up. Time was of the essence as they pushed their way to the exit, once on *terra firma* started running like demented things dragging their kid's hell bent on being the first in the queue for either, the cafeteria or, the toilets. On the other hand, Kenny had already lit up yet another fag and was coughing heavily into his clenched fist we were the last to get off. First to the toilet then to the café to buy a tea and some rolls, gulping down the tea scoffed the rolls. There was no way we were going to be last on board. Retreating to the coach a few families had already returned, as we reoccupied our seats Kenny immediately lit up another fag. Gradually as others arrived back, the two girls sat behind came towards us. Having ogled them, Kenny nudging me whispered.

'I fancy Blondie the first one. You can 'ave the second?' Not that the first one really drew my attention; the second as a potential was even lower. A couple of minutes before our departure, the driver boarded the bus and made a head count satisfied we were on board slid the door shut. Once again, we were on our way bouncing along in the uncomfortable coach seats down the leafy lanes of Sussex towards Chichester. Stopped there, half the passengers got off but not the girls to us the horizon was looking good. Onto Bracklesham Bay, stopped at the holiday camp this time there was no mad panic the passengers appeared somewhat reluctant and resigned to their fate for the next week, whatever it might be.

Getting off was a pleasure. Out of a cloudless sky, the sun was beating down; it was hot and looked as if we were going to have a good time albeit only a week. Collecting our cases at the rear, out of sheer spite the driver had already flung them further away from all the rest of the cases. Whilst picking them up noticed the other two girls. One was a cracker. Briefly, our eyes met, something inside me stirred and had me thinking. "Oh yeah! Let's see what develops over the next week".

Entering through the double doors of the main building. A girl in a yellow blazer welcomed us. Her long black hair cascaded down over her shoulders; a big beam creased her face flashing a set of tombstones she directed us to the reception desk. Where another blonde girl in similar attire, took our names and registered us in. Handing over a key festooned with a hut number together with an itinerary of times of meals and such like. With the appropriate directions, passed about twenty huts all facing the sea we found ours was the very last one.

The hut. Was an 'L' shaped double apartment. Our abode was to the right. Unlocking the door entered the room. In between two small beds was a small set of drawers with the exception of a Tannoy speaker mounted high on the wall. That was all. Whilst we were unpacking, the occupying family next door arrived a married couple with one boy about twelve and a girl about thirteen. Obviously, of no interest to us young stags. Anyway leaving the hut made our way to the main building to find out what other facilities the holiday camp had. A dance floor with a stage, a lounge area with a sort of Bar/café and the eating hall where they were already serving meals. It was very basic but to us great. The bar was open, so we indulged ourselves with two halves. Having drunk our beers we went into the eating hall and sat down at a table, soon to be served with a meal and a pudding. Having finished that decided to walk around the camp to see what it was like. A few marked out areas for sports, a football pitch with netball post the swimming pool was the sea. With the tide on the ebb, the sea was flat and calm with just a hint of white on the tip of a wave; with a shushing sound, it gently moved the pebbles serene to say the least.

 Having been on outings to Bracklesham Bay with St. Anne's club, we knew when the tide was out, after the treacherous walk across the pebbles onto a vast amount of flat sandy beach that we had played

St. Anne's Outing 1954

Bracklesham Bay beach

football or cricket. In our opinion not much to do so decided to go for a swim. Back in the hut changed into our cossies. On our way out bumped into the next-door family. The blonde thirteen-year-old girl was too eager for my liking and wanted to join us for a swim as did her brother. However, managed to wriggle out of it by saying,

'You know, the sea is rather choppy and very deep.' What a load of codswallop. Anyway, we got away and headed for the sea, had a good frolic in the extremely cold but calm sea, drying ourselves Kenny lit up a fag. A few hours later after laying in the sun on the pebbles we were, red raw and burnt like toast. Very hot and bewildered made our way back to the hut to get ready for the evening meal and the so-called dance.

The meal, was adequate for our needs, having had our fill departed the dining room en-route to the bar, ordered a couple of beers sat down at one of the round tables close to the dance floor to discuss the possibilities of the next week. We laughed about Derek in the Kate; he would have lapped it up here. Other families arrived to occupy the tables, quickly the bar filled up and being overworked the lone barman became frantic. At about seven thirty, the bandsmen dressed in Tuxedos with bow ties arrived on stage - Piano, Base, Trumpet/Sax and drums began tuning up before playing some current tunes. Appearing on stage a woman, the singer of the Band very fetching in her long blue dress attempted to sing an out of tune version of "Fly me to the moon". When she finished, outlandish applause broke out; we joined in with a slow handclap that she appreciated and started to sing again. There was no sign of the girls? Another drink was the order of the day, it was my round. At the bar, families were ordering masses of drinks the barman was run off his feet when he asked.

'What's yours?' Quickly realising the waiting time ordered.

'Four light ales please.'

With the drinks clutched tightly between my extended fingers returned to our table. Kenny, with a side nod of his head motioned my gaze towards the dance floor. In the middle and far end, the girls were dancing together Kenny asked

'Why? Double order?'

'That's so. You. Don't have to get up next time. There's a gigantic queue for bleedin' drinks. They're all going barmy buying em. Anyway, most of the time you are a lazy git, just interested in fags.'

'I fancy that little blonde one.' Thinking. "Aw sod it. Apart from fags, he's sex mad".

Sat down to watch the girls dancing. The two sat behind us on the coach both dressed in pencil slim grey skirts, white blouses and slip-on shoes, whilst the other two girls dancing at the far end, wore floral coloured dresses and similar style shoes. With a crash of cymbals, the tune came to a finale. Immediately the band livened things up with a rather jazzy number. Hesitating, the two floral dressed girls moving in time with the music began jiving. This was more interesting. The one that smiled at me was quite a mover; her partner was not bad either? They jived away spinning and turning their dresses flared out and upwards showing more of their legs. The band continued with another swingy tune. "Mr. Sandman". The singer joined in and an old couple got onto the dance floor to do the quickstep, but the rhythm of the music was too fast for them so after another circuit retired gracefully.

'Ear Kenny. Fancy a jive?'

'Sod off. Not with you.'

'Okay. Which one do you fancy?'

'The little blonde one.'

'C'mon then let's go.'

With a quick swig of beer, we ventured out into the unknown. What we were about to do was break up two girlie relationship's, but hell who cared? You could not fancy two at once or, could you? Kenny made for the little blonde bird whilst I made for the tall blonde-haired one. All was amicable, whilst the spare girls joined up as partners. Therefore, there were three jiving couples and no one else on the floor nevertheless, it was early evening and the last waltz was nowhere in sight. We had temporally scored. The band rapped up for the interval. Thanking her for the jive, invited her and her friend to join us, she accepted. Leaving her to sort out her friend; walked back to the table. Kenny already taking a swig of beer said.

'Ear Joe. She's a cracker. So. I've invited those two back to our table.'

'Blimey. So have I. Dig deep, we got a long way to go.'

Four grinning girls arrived, with only four chairs available like a pair of gentlemen offered our seats and stood. Introductions were in order, although cannot remember the other girl's names, certainly remembered Cecilia's. She was about five foot eight, short wavy blonde hair with a fringe, blue eyes very attractive face a generous mouth, which gave way to an enormous smile.

That night we danced too all different types of dances, she was a good dancer and we did dance with the other girls. We had a good evening and as the last waltz began, we invited our fancy bits to dance. Doing the correct thing took up the Ballroom stance, with one sweaty paw holding her hand the other was snug tight in the small of her back we began to waltz. Clearly, a distance apart but she was not having any of that, moving in closer her right breast was tight under my left armpit, as we danced our thighs rubbed together after a few graceful steps turns and how's yer father, was not thinking properly and cautiously drew away. Thankfully, the music ground to a finale. With salutations all around dispersed to our respective abodes. By the look on his face, Kenny was smitten but what about me? To -morrow was another day. Kenny lighting up another fag suggested.

'Blimey. Could do with another beer, want one?'

'Yeah. Why not.' At the bar, ordered a couple of drinks from the shattered barman, his hair in disarray as he looked at the array of dirty glasses lined up on the bar top. Whilst we talked about the girls he continued with his chore. Finishing off our beers added another two glasses to his pile and retired for the night's sleep.

With a blast, from a trumpet or something else? The Tannoy system came alive. An irritating voice cackled.

'Wakey. Wakey. Good morning campers. Outside it is a glorious day. First serving for breakfast eight o'clock'. Kenny shrieked.

'Aw shit. What time is it? I need a fag.' Turning over replied.

'Too bleedin' early. Not ready to get up I'm on holiday.' Dozed off, but not for long.

The family next door was up, the two youngsters were having a fight and the parents were yelling and shouting.

'KEEP QUITE. WE'VE GOT NEIGHBOURS NEXT DOOR.'

Pulling the pillow over my head did not help to dampen the sound of those wretched kids. Next, the whiff of cigarette smoke wafting up my nostrils. That was it! The hands of my watch showed 7.15. Did not even get up this early at home. Lay there thinking. "Some bleedin' rest I'll get on this holiday", retorted.

'Kenny do you have to light up? Bleedin' smokes woke me up.' He began coughing.

'Well... it bleedin...cough... splutter...wakes me up.'

Taking no notice needing a pee, swung my legs out grabbing my trousers pulled them on and zipped up, taking my towel said. 'I'm off to the wash house. Where are the keys?...In the early morning sunshine noticed the light was still on switching it off, retorted.

'Hoi. Kenny. Next time. You. Turn out the light.'

'Yeah. Okay. Sod off. Yer didn't do it last night.' Impatiently asked.

'Where's the bleedin' key?' Coughing again spluttered.

'Where I...cough...left em...cough... In the door '

'Well. It ain't there now. Where dyer put it?'

'How the hell should I know? I was tired.' Sitting up in bed with his fag dangling out of his mouth, grabbed hold of his trousers fished around in his pockets found it and lobbed it towards me.

'Ear catch. Aw shit! Wait for me. Bleedin' row next door can't even have a fag in peace. Some bleedin' holiday this is turning out to be.' Swinging his legs off the bed stood up, stretched beneath the fabric of his Y fronts was something of a swelling. I remarked.

'What's matter Kenny. Fruity?'

'Nah. Need a piss.'

'Well Bleedin' 'urry up or you'll swamp us out of the room.' Unlocking the door pulled it open to be confronted by the family next door. Fully dressed and ready for breckers they all chorused. 'Morning.'

'Morning.' Thinking, "Sod it. Do we have a week of this ahead of us"?

Following behind them, down the four steps they went one way; we went the other towards the washhouses. Very basic, wash stands with basins, mirrors, and cubicles, heading for them relieved ourselves, had a quick wash. Kenny gasped as he splashed the cold water into his face he did not need to shave, not that mine was very aggressive.

Outside in the early morning sunshine it was warm, fanned by a slight breeze blowing off the sea if, it stayed like that for a week I was not going to complain to anyone.

'C'mon. Urry up or we'll get no breckers, whatever that consist of?' Turning the handle of the door it opened, exclaimed.

'Hoi. You didn't lock up when yer left?'

'Nope.'

'Well. That's bleedin' daft ain't it?'

'We ain't got anything to steal. Unless yer got the crown jewels under yer bed?'...he laughed... I'm hungry. Let's get a move on.'

'Christ Kenny. You couldn't get a move on even if someone stuck a squib up yer arse. Yer a lazy git. Dyer know that?' A curt reply.

'Sod off.'

Arriving at the food hall, joined the empty queue to be faced with a choice of: Cornflakes, Shredded wheat, bread, butter and jam with tea thrown in. Take your pick. Nice breakfast! As most of the other campers had scoffed their lot and left there were ample tables full of dirty crockery to sit at; we chose a table near where the four girls were sat they obviously had teamed up. Kenny's fancy bit chirped up.

'Your late you two. If you turned up any later. You might be first in the queue for dinner.' They all laughed. Quickly I answered.

'Nope. We've already bin for a swim. Bit cold but good.' She snapped back at me.

'Get on. Bet you didn't.' Kenny intervening spoke up in my defence.

'Nah. He's right. The water was bleedin' cold. Took my breath away.' Little did they know that was true albeit a cat's lick of a face wash, but not in the sea? We sat down to enjoy our sumptuous brekkers of cornflakes. Kenny addressing his fancy bit.

'Wot they got planned for us today?'

'Don't really know? Something about a netball match or something else. It's on a notice board in the reception area. Do you fancy coming then?' Thinking. "Christ Kenny. You're in there mate and, only after a few dances last night lucky bugger". Kenny continued with conversing with his fancy bit then having finished his brekkers, lit up a fag his fancy bit retorted.

'Hey. You're a tight one. What about me?'

'Oh sorry. Didn't know yer smoked.' Offering them around, much to his relief she was the only one to take one. Kenny did not like sharing out his fags. As the two of them puffed away and chatted across the tables the blue clouds of smoke wafted over us. Being not one for conversation when indulging in food kept quiet until finished. Getting up asked.

'While I'm up anyone want more tea?' A spontaneous response from everyone.

'Yes.' I retorted.

'Hold on a minute. I've only got one pair of hands.' Cecilia offered.

'I'll help.'

'Okay. Thanks. At least you're willing. That lazy lot don't want to know. C'mon then let us get the teas in.' Thinking, "Hey maybe I'll be all right here"? Having filled the cups with me carrying the tray she walked in front and could not help noticing her shapely legs and the tight yellow coloured shorts revealing a nice rounded behind. Having been in contact with her well-formed frontage, thought. "Well that's a pleasing sight, let's wait and see what transpires"? Rearranging seats handed out the teas, sitting together the main topic of conversation was what we all thought of it so far. 'Not much?' It was mundane chatter and obvious all thought the same, dancing every night.

The days of sunbathing and swimming flew past and then it was Friday. It was packing up time and the last time for dancing together in the evening. We jived to the quickies danced to the slower beat stuff. The woman singer called Alison Stoop or something like that, dressed in a long purple dress crooned her versions that were not very good of Frank Sinatra's. "Strangers in the Night- 'Falling In Love with You.' and 'All the Things You Are.' After her final words had died wild applause broke out. Someone must have appreciated her singing. The end of the nights snogging session became more prolonged before we finally broke up to return to our own habitats.

Saturday morning. The coach arrived and who was there to greet us? "Arfur English". As we climbed back onboard his coach, he muttered.

'You two. Hurry up.'

The trip back was rather subdued. At the coach station after retrieving our cases, we swopped addresses and telephone numbers. With a quick peck on the cheek we all went our different ways via the tube or, like us the bus. On the bus Kenny muttered.

'When I get home. I'll call her (fancy pants) and take her to the pictures. What dyer reckon?'

'Bleedin' hell Kenny! You've only just left her. Your bleedin' eager aren't you? I don't know about Cecilia. I'll think about it.'

Parting company at Vauxhall, arranged to meet in the Beehive that night nevertheless, walking home deep in thought was in the same frame of mind as Kenny. At least his 'fancy pants' lived in Peckham. For me to make a trip to Wanstead was out of the question. It was on the other side of London but she had mentioned worked in an office near Trafalgar Square, at least we could meet half way in the West-end. Maybe later, would give it a go and see if she would like to go to the pictures one night? Back indoors my first question.

'Mum. Has my Brown envelope arrived yet?'

'No son. Nothing for you yet...Thinking. "That's a relief"...Did you and Kenny have a good time?'

'Yes. It wasn't bad. Not much to do though, but the weather was good.'

'Well. I can see that. You're quite brown. Going out tonight?'

'Yep. Going to meet Kenny and go to the dance at St. Anne's.' Mum offered.

'I suppose, you would like a fry up for your tea?'

'Aw yes please Mum. The grub there was not too good. Anyway I'm starving. Where is everybody?'

'Margaret is at Lily's; Michael is out Bowling and your Dads seeing Alec. He should be home shortly.'

Upstairs in the bedroom, unpacking the dirty clobber left them in a pile ready for the Monday washing session. Had a bath, shaved the two bristles on my face putting on a clean shirt and another pair of slacks, went downstairs to see what was on the television stopped in the hallway before picking up the telephone, saw Mum cooking at the stove then dialed Cecilia's number. A woman's voice stated.

'Wanstead ???? Who's calling?' Assuming it was her mother replied.

'Can I speak to Cecilia? Please?'

'Who? Shall I say is calling?'

'Joe.' Heard her call out.

'Cecilia! It is for you. Someone called Joe. Come and take the call.' A clunk, silence, then Cecilia's voice.

'Hello. What do you want? I didn't expect you to call so soon?'

'Well. I thought we might go to the pictures at the Tivoli on Wednesday. I'll meet you up there.' Silence then.

'Erm. Yes! I suuuppose that will be Okay. I finish work at five thirty.'

'So do I. But can't meet you that early. What will you do? Go home then come back?'

'No. Take too long. I'll stay there have a coffee and something to eat.'

'Okay. What about meeting you at the Embankment tube station say about six thirty?' Eagerly she replied.

'Yes. Okay. See you Wednesday. '

Pleased with myself, quietly replaced the receiver on its rest and walked into the front room settled down in front of the television to watch the wrestling, with nothing else on changed Channels to watch another episode of William Tell just as Mum brought in the fry up. A big plateful of goodies chips the lot, finishing off the last chip. Took my empty plate into the kitchen to wash up. Mum enquired.

'You had enough?'

'Phew! Yes thank you. I'm bloated. It was smashing. I'm off to meet Kenny, see you later.'

Having a fair way to walk, set off at a quick pace passing the Granada met Dad coming the other way we stopped, had a few words about the holiday then parted. Stood outside the Beehive smoking a fag was Kenny. Going inside at the bar he blurted out.

'Ear Joe. I rang her. Taking her to the flicks tomorrow night. Meeting her outside the Metropole.' Eagerly informed him.

'Guess what? I'm meeting Cecilia on Wednesday. Taking her to see the flicks at the Tivoli.'

Jubilant with our success's started a game of Bar Billiards, when Brian arrived we told him all about our Holiday Camp outing. "Our final decision. Never again". That in my case was true; instead was soon to spend the next two years in Army Camps.

Monday back at work, my thoughts were not on Eileen but my newfound love. Wednesday dinnertime at home, put on a clean shirt, pressed pants, polished shoes, about to leave wearing a blazer. Mum queried.

'You taking your bike. Dressed like that?'

'No Mum. I'm walking. Won't be in for dinner see you later this evening.' I'm sure Mum knew? The first thing John said was.

'Hello you. Out on the tiles to night? You dirty little bugger.'

'Nah. Just meeting my mate Kenny.' I lied.

'What! Dressed up like that? Pull the other leg. It's got bell's on.'

At five thirty. I was out of the door like a scalded cat running to catch the 77 bus that would take me as far as Waterloo then a tube to the Embankment. Getting off, ascending the stairs two at a time up to the booking hall and out through the Embankment entrance. There was no sign of her. Waited for about ten minutes thinking, "You're crazy. It wasn't really on". Disillusioned, decided to catch the tube home going back inside heard.

'Joe'...turning around saw Cecilia coming in through the opposite Villiers Street entrance added...Sorry I was late. Thought I'd missed you.'

'No. I was waiting outside. Thought you would come out that way.' Politely I queried

'Have you been waiting long?'

'No. Not really. Had a cup of coffee with my friend from the office who was willing to keep me company after we left work.' Knowing the reason of our meeting stupidly asked.

'You, ready for the flicks then?' Enthusiastically she replied.

'Yes.'

'Do you know what's on?'

'Some film called. "The Thing". I think it's something about space.'

Leaving the station began walking up Villiers Street thinking. "Maybe, she might not like that kind of film." So suggested.

'Do you want to see it or, go somewhere else?' Hesitating she replied.

'Wait a minute. I'll show you the offices where I work is that all right?' Not answering my question went along with her suggestion.

'It's okay by me.' Pointing to the arches beneath the Charring Cross railway line, she said.

'It's quicker if we go through the tunnel there.' Well aware that it led through to Northumberland Avenue as before had visited that tunnel many times to see the paintings that Artist exhibited there, answered.

'Yeah okay.'

Crossing over entered, at that time of the evening it was empty apart from of few pedestrians like us. With only sufficient light seeping from both ends we progressed into the partial darkness, about half way through we stopped chemistry kicked in; fell into each other's arms and began to snog. After about five minutes, we broke clean; holding sweaty hands with big smirks on our faces emerging from the tunnel continued walking up the Avenue, nearing the top she stopped outside a doorway with a big wooden polished double door said.

'This is where I work. On the second floor.' As far as I was concerned, the building had been there for centuries but then knew where she worked thought. "It would be convenient for any future rendezvous". Then she goes and says.

'Oh. I forgot to ask you? Have you received your call-up papers yet?' Thinking. "Oh Shit. Did not want to be reminded of those right then".

'No. Thank Christ. Nothing to report.' She squeezed my hand, which gave me goose pimples then said.

'That's good. We just need to go up to the top and turn to the right into the Strand the Tivoli is further down on the right.'

'Heh. You're telling me about London. I know it backwards. I've been to the Tivoli many times and to the Lyceum dance hall. You can say that the West-end is part of our haunts. Don't worry about it.'

Having decided that she still wanted to see "The Thing". At the Tivoli I bought the tickets and we ventured into its dark interior. The Usherette's flashlight illuminated our faces as she directed us to our seats in amidst other patrons. The film being shown was a second rate sleuth tale. In the interval asked.

'Like an Ice cream?'

'That would be nice. I'll pay for it.'

"The Thing". Was a science fiction film that we spent snogging all the way through? Three weeks later, one Wednesday night saying our goodnights at the Embankment tube station, Cecilia said.

'Joe. I want you to come home and meet my mum and dad; they have suggested you come on Saturday?'

Taken aback by her suggestion, something I said would never do, travel over to their house in Wanstead had to think of something quick.

'Next. Saturday! Dunno! Playing football...Trying to get out of it suggested...Look, it's a bit early ennit? Don't know em?'

'Well. I. Would like them to meet you. After your football. I will meet you seven thirty at Wanstead Tube station. Don't. Say. No.'

With a quick kiss, we parted. I caught the tube to Waterloo then the bus home all the way sat thinking. "What the bleedin' 'ell have I let myself in for? Do not want to travel right across London it's a real drag, take me bleedin' hours there and back.

Saturday I was late and about quarter to eight, Cecilia met me at Wanstead station. According to her, we took the short cut; it was a long way it took about a quarter of an hour walking most of the way with me meekly protesting, it was wrong. Nevertheless, she holding my hand guided me up the garden path. Her Mum and Dad were nice both tall in stature. He was Ex RAF Type. He said to me.

'You are waiting to be called up. Aren't you Joe?' Being polite answered.

'Er. Yes. Don't know when though?'

'Well. Suggest you join the RAF.' However, responding to his suggestion stated.

Er. No. I'm for the Army.' That went down like a lead balloon. Her Mum had made rolls and gave me some Orange juice. I appeared to be accepted before they left in their car. A car! To visit someone.

For the next four months on a Saturday night travelled across London to her house. To eat rolls drink Orange juice and tear up the front room carpet jiving, then a snog before her parents came home, followed by the long walk to the tube station to catch the last tube home arriving close to midnight. Three nights a week, I attended night school. Every Wednesday night the pictures on Saturday and Sunday played football. In-between times visited the club and, getting more agitated about the fact had not received my call-up papers? Having spent his penny and she had smoked all his fags Kenny had packed up seeing Miss Fancy pants and, was eager to be one of the boys again. When Derek was home on a weekend, leave did not meet Cecilia. On those isolated weekends, the four of us pals had a great time, listening to Derek's chatter about army life. He convinced me. 'Once you were called-up there was no way to keep a relationship going?' However, with the cold winter nights drawing in I could not get her out of my mind realised I was being sucked into getting too involved with Cecilia. What was I to do about our relationship had to do something drastic, tell her. That was it.

Taking courage in my conviction on the last Saturday night I spent the whole journey on the tube to Wanstead thinking about how I was going to tell her the bad news. Finally, decided to leave it until the end and do a runner. Arriving at their front door her Mum and Dad were about to get into the car. Polite hellos were passed they unaware of my mission and I would be gone before they came back? We did the usual jiving; eat rolls, drunk orange juice followed by a long snog. Just about to depart her mum and dad arrived back early that stopped any further discussion. However, in our last embrace she in turn did something. It surprised me. I went along with her demands nothing serious moreover; it was her action warned me off. At the doorway, we kissed again. On the tube ride home called myself all the idiots imaginable and with the latest incident was convinced. Earmarked for a very long relationship furthermore with the current circumstances hanging over my head. Certainly did not want to become deeply involved.

The next day before going to football, telephoned her and told her. I did not want to go out with her. My reason being before receiving my call-up papers wanted to go out and have a good time with the lads. That was true however, she argued her case; everything would be all right even after I had been called-up nevertheless, my mind was made up. Declined her suggestions whereupon she cried. Feeling bad, but as far as I was concerned that was it however, it did not end there.

A couple of nights later, just about to leave for night school was putting on my coat when the phone rang, thinking it was for Margaret picked up the receiver, automatically said.

'Hold on Pat. I'll get Margaret.' To my surprise, an unknown girl's voice asked.

'Is that Joe? Baffled, answered.

'Yes. This is Joe. What do you want?'

'You don't know me. I am a friend of Cecilia. I work with her. Cecilia is terribly upset. She told me what happened. She wants to meet you again.'

This girl cannot even remember her name; as she tried to talk sense into me I could not get a word in anywhere. However, when I did, fully explained my reasons for giving her up. It was my pending call-up, not wanting to continue the way it was. Besides, was finding it increasingly difficult to carry on with all my commitments, football, night school Bla Bla. It went on until I said.

'Look I'm sorry. But right now I do have to leave I'm on my way to night school.' Hung up. That chat with someone I did not even know was so embarrassing it made me feel even worse.

A development at work, brought things to a head. One day a bloke by the name of Roy turned up demobed. Wanting his old job back. John accepted him as my replacement. The Labour Exchange was informed. With only a few weeks away from Christmas I was on the wanted list and scared of getting my marching orders and miss the festive season. Christmas came, as did New Year. Dad suggested just in case. 'Invite some of your mates to a farewell Party Son.' The party was arranged; even Derek got a weekend leave. It was a riotous occasion I think, we all got drunk?

Third week in January. The Brown envelope fluttered through the letterbox.
'YOU'RE CONSCRIPTED LADDIE'.

Taking it to work presented it to John to show him his handiwork? Leaving work the following Friday with many wishes from the engineers of. Good Luck, a few smackaroos from the girls and with me back in love with Eileen she gave me a special one. Then I was away.

My last Saturday. The four of us had a few farewell drinks in the Beehive. On Sunday night invited Joyce to the pictures.

Wednesday night with Joyce saw. "The Bridges at Toko Ree". Had a snog with her, she wishing me.

'Good luck, see you when you get a leave?'

Thursday. I was already up when mum brought me an early morning cup of tea.

'C'mon son it's your big day. You have to catch that early train from Waterloo. So you had better get a move on. Your Dad wishes you good luck and will see you in eight weeks time?' Reluctantly left the confines of our house to catch a 77 bus to Waterloo.

Off to join the Army.

PART 2.

-DURING -

'B' Platoon Intake Honiton February 1955
Royal Electrical and Mechanical Engineers

CHAPTER SIX
HOW TO BECOME A BASTARD

As the brake shoes of the Waterloo-Exeter train bit against the wheels, it came to a shuddering halt with a screech. Above the last hiss and gasp of steam from the engine, you could hear the Station Porter further down the platform shouting.

'HONITON. HONITON. ALL PASSENGERS FOR HEATHFIELD CAMP. ALIGHT HERE.'

At Waterloo station on purpose along with another couple of blokes, we had got into the last compartment of the rear carriage, silly! But when you are about to embark on a journey to the unexpected your instincts tell you to be very cautious. Finally, we had arrived at our destination; smearing away the condensation on the window pensively looked out onto a bleak deserted tiny platform, just wide enough for two people walking abreast. Getting up exclaimed.

'This is it!' Someone behind said

'Don't like the look of this place.' Full of uncertainty replied.

'No mate. Neither do I.' Reaching up to the luggage rack, collected the little brown paper parcel containing my possessions, with my free hand opened the carriage door. Leaving the sanctity of the train jumped down onto the platform. Further up the train as a last desperate act of defiance. Other blokes leaving the carriages were slamming doors behind them. Little did any of us realise that within fifteen minutes we would all be marching towards our home for the next six weeks: Heathfield Camp. The residence of:

No. 2. Basic Training Camp. Royal Electrical and Mechanical Engineers and the beginning of our conscription into National Service. The bloke behind enquired.

'Where do we go now?' Just as inquisitive and not knowing replied.

'Don't bleedin' know mate. Make our way outside.' Hopefully he suggested.

'They might take us in a lorry to the Camp.'

One thing was certain! None knew what was in store for us, as we followed others walking ahead towards a station Canopy covering the width of the platform, giving the appearance that Honiton was the back of beyond? In front a few had stopped to drag on fags, one of them a Teddy Boy dressed in full drape velvet collared coat drainpipe trousers and brothel creepers, his Tony Curtis hair do a mop of black greasy hair meticulously combed back into a DA (Duck's Arse). With a flash of a match into cupped hands lit the fag dangling from his lips. Drawing deeply before emitting a puff of blue smoke, rapidly followed by a fit of coughing up his lungs, which had him bent double with hands on knees and very audible above the hissing and periodic chuff of the train, red in the face from the exertion of his coughing the quiff of hair in front had fallen out of place. Firmly clenching the fag between his teeth produced a comb out of the velvet edged coat pocket and with an expert flourish, no doubt practiced over many months or perhaps years of grooming, carefully combed his hair back into place. As we came level with him he broke into another fit of coughing, trying to talk at the same time. 'Roight bleedin'...cough...carry on this... Cough...Ain't it mate? I'm going sick...cough... as soon as I get into this bleedin' camp...cough and a splutter...wherever it bleedin' well is?' Blinking his watering eyes his pasty face cracked open with a knowing smile. Somebody? Must have told him about going sick. Clearing his throat, he directed a question at me.

'Where yer from mate?'

'Vauxhall. Where you from?'

'Ighbry. Where the bleedin' 'ell is Voxall? It ain't in London is it?' I retorted.

'Course it bleedin' well is! South of the river near the Oval.'

'Yer a bleedin' souvener then? Eared of the Oval, Charlton n' Millwall. Not bleedin' Voxall.'

'Yer must 'ave? Wot abowt cricket then? Bowlin' from the Vauxhall end.'

'Oh yerse o'caws. Nah's I no's. Is that where it is?' A knowledgeable reply.

Gradually we had moved along the platform towards the shelter of the station canopy, when our conversation came to an abrupt halt. A bullnecked bastard dressed in Army uniform was pointing at us shouting.

'YOU LOT! OVER HERE. AT THE DOUBLE.' We carried on strolling then he yelled.

'YES. YOU LOT MOOOVE.'

Diverting his attention away from us, began shouting at a young lad as he leisurely leant out of the train window wondering what all the shouting was. He oblivious to the urgency of his task. To get out.

'THAT MAN. HANGING OUT OF THE WINDOW. YES YOU. WHERE DO YOU THINK YOU ARE GOING? EXETER? GET OUT NOW. JUMP TO IT.'

With an ear-piercing screech the engine whistle blew, signaling the train to start and continue on its scheduled journey. Motivated by the whistle, the Soldier leapt into action two leaps across the platform lunging at the carriage door handle yanking it down pulled open the door. The Lad, falling out landed on the platform his small parcel dropped in front of him. The soldier kicking it away slammed the moving carriage door with a resounding bang, yelled.

'YOU. THIS IS YOUR STOP. GET FELL IN OUTSIDE. MOOOVE.'

The red-faced young lad scrambling to his feet retrieved his parcel and scampered towards the exit. This minor incident was just the start of the rude awakening that lay in store for us. By this time the train had gradually gathered speed and as the wheels of its last carriage clattered by to reveal its rear end blackened by smoke, soot and dust from decades of hauling unfortunates like us to our fate, the single rear red lamp, winked at us mockingly in farewell.

The narrow platform was crowded with young raw recruits. Dressed in various mixtures of clothing fit for the fashion era of that time. 1955. Depending on where they came from, one could tell whether they were City, Townie or Country wise; Drainpipe trousers, draped jackets, brothel creepers or brogue shoes (City of course). A more formal suit or sports jacket and trouser somber shoes (Townie's). Tweeds and the like (For Country boys). All wore some form of overcoat; Velvet collared, Crombie style, Trench or Rain Mac... The infamous brown call-up letter. "On Her Majesties Service". Had invited the (so-called) named person (stated) with the enclosed Travel Warrant, to report to and bring only as (per) stated on the enclosed list of specified items, mainly toiletries. The invitation also included our first day's pay a four-shilling postal order. It appeared that all carried their meager possessions in a brown paper parcel, tied up with string.

Standing at the exit doors the uniformed soldier suddenly emitted a roaring shout loud enough to blast the eardrums of us poor unfortunates.

'THE LOT OF YOU. MOOOVE OUTSIDE.' Exaggerating the word move like a moo-ing cow. He disappeared through the exit doors.

As a body, all at once we headed for the exit like bees around a jam pot all trying at the same time to get through the doors. No such luck. Just a mass of struggling bodies. Another roar from inside stopped the frenzied actions of all.

'YOU IDIOTS. GET BACK IN THERE.' A single voice piped up.

'Make up yer bleedin' mind mate.'

'WHO SAID THAT? I'LL KILL HIM?' The Soldier, forcing his way back through the doors pushing and shoving the mass of bodies out of his way to get at whoever had. "The audacity and balls to query an authoritative order". He let out another roar.

'WHO WAS IT?'... His piggy eyes quickly scanned the mob, nobody owned up...Right you lot. Your days are numbered. Follow me in single file through the doors. If you please.'

As ordered, we in an equally courteous fashion followed him through the doorway into a small booking hall. No wonder he was polite. On our way through passed a small group of passengers queuing at the tiny window of the Ticket office, who had observed this charade by the Bullnecked Bastard?

Early in the afternoon on the third of February, it was a bitterly cold and windy day when we gathered on the forecourt outside. Blown up against ridges some evidence of snow was visible however, nobody was taking any notice of the immediate surroundings; all eyes then focused on the Bastard standing across and away from the station entrance. He was tall, stockily built and immaculately dressed in his Khaki uniform; a gleaming REME cap badge centered in his black beret that was at least three sizes too small for his head. His piggy red face and bloodshot but watchful eyes glared at all. His bull sized neck disappeared into a khaki shirt collar, secured by a tie neatly tucked into the top of his open necked tunic. The belt around his waist secured by a set of gleaming buckles, with two brass strips on either side, his trousers neatly tucked into a pair of gaiters had creases that stood out like the edge of a well-honed knife and with boots polished like mirrors stood like a ramrod, his figure presenting the image of what he really was, a menace to all. Opening his mouth wide, he emitted a roar.

'FACING ME. FORM UP. IN RANKS OF THREE...Spreading out one arm...TALLEST AT THIS END...then the other... SHORTEST AT THE OTHER END.'

With absolutely no understanding of who was the longest or shortest of the mob. Each looking at others regarding height, all began shuffling around everyone desperately trying to form the back row away from the menace. As we stopped, dancing together managed to fall in. The Bastard eyeing up the shambles of three ranks muttering to himself moved pacing up and down the front rank, circling around the assembled mob came to a halt in front of us. Began picking out specific individuals.

'You. At the back. Move up here into the front rank. You. Move to your right. You in the front. Move into the middle rank.' After most had been moved, he began circling around the mob again, eventually stopped at me.

'You and You. Fall out. Follow me.' He marched over to a green bike leant against the steel railings, alongside were two sticks. Picking them up, attached to each one was a notice board. Turning around roared.

'YOU TWO. DOUBLE OVER HERE.' I and the bloke next to me sauntered over and stood in front of him. In turn he thrust a stick into our hands.

'NOW YOU TWO IDIOTS. TAKE NOTE. YOUR FRONT AND REAR MARKERS SAVVY? YOU ARE GOING TO CARRY THESE NOTICES. Pointing at me. YOU. IN THE FRONT. AND YOU. (The other bloke) AT THE REAR. NOW BACK INTO LINE. MOOOVE.'

Carrying these sticks scampered back to rejoin the motley formation of three ranks moving upto the front stood beside the tallest bloke. With my brown paper parcel in one hand and clutching the stick in my other sweaty one glanced at its notice. "TROOPS MARCHING" This tickled my sense of humour. I cracked to the tall bloke.

'We ain't in the bleedin' army yet.' Who with a Brommie accent curtly replied.

'According to that bastard there we are.' A spontaneous yell from the Bastard stopped any further conversation.

'NO TALKING IN THE RANKS... Now. For those that do not know me...My name is Lance Corporal King and I. Am going to march YOU LOT. Back to Camp. I take it. Everyone knows what is their left from their right? A pregnant silence filled the air...WELL ... SPEAK UP... YES OR NO?' "Mumble Mumble ". Echoes from within the mob...WAS... THAT A YES! ON THE OTHER HAND...I DO NOT KNOW. WHERE IS THAT RECRUIT I YANKED OFF

THE TRAIN? (A marked man already). A strangled cry from within the depths of the ranks called out.

'Here Sergeant.' The Bastard roared back.

'SERGEANT! So. You. Have promoted me already. HAVE YOU? (Laughter from the ranks). SILENCE IN THE RANKS...I LIKE YOU... WHAT'S YOUR NAME?' An unsure reply.

'Green Serg...Lance Corporal.' He roared back.

'GREEN EH...YOU ARE CHUFFING GREEN. I HAVE JUST TOLD YOU...I AM A LANCE CORPORAL...DOUBLE OUT HERE GREEN. MOOOVE.' This wretch came out from within the confines of the ranks his brown paper parcel bumping against his leg, walking towards the Bastard stood in front of him. The Bastard looking down at Green placed his hands on his hips and spoke.

'Now then Green. See this? Pointing to the white chevron on his tunic sleeve. That chuffing Green. Signifies. I am a Lance Corporal. Two of them mean. I would be a full Corporal and with three. I would be a Sergeant and if, I was a Sergeant...proceeded to yell in Greens ear. I MIGHT PUT YOU. CHUFFING GREEN. ON A CHUFFING CHARGE. SAVVY? IF I WERE YOU GREEN. I WOULD REMEMBER THIS FIRST LESSON. MOOOVE BACK INTO LINE. THAT GOES FOR ALL YOU MISERABLE BUNCH OF BASTARDS.' Apparently, from then on.

"We Were All Related".

A red-faced Green scurried back into line to join us lot stood shivering with the icy wind blowing into our faces, thinking about the remark someone had made. "Getting a lift back to this camp". No such luck, we would be marched to it, wherever it was? The Bastard, having made his point roared.

'NOW YOU MISERABLE BUNCH OF BASTARDS. WHEN I GIVE THE ORDER ATTENTION. I WANT YOU ALL TO BRING YOUR RIGHT FOOT NEXT TO YOUR LEFT FOOT. AND THEN...WHEN I SHOUT LEFT TURN. ALL TURN TO YOUR LEFT...PLA...TOOONA. ATTEN...HA. With unco-ordinated stamping of feet, he roared....LEEEF TURR.' Turning to my left dragged the stick across the ground. He roared...RIII...TAR TURR.. Turning to my right, again dragged the stick across the ground. He roared. 'NO.NO.NO. WHEN I SAID LEFT THE FIRST TIME. I MEANT LEFT. SIX OF YOU BASTARDS TURNED TO THE RIGHT INCLUDING YOU CHUFFING GREEN. YOU THAT CHUFFING IDIOT IN THE FRONT HOLDING THAT NOTICE. ARE YOU AWARE THAT WHAT YOU HOLD IN YOUR SWEATY HAND IS GOVERNMENT PROPERTY. PICK THE CHUFFING THING UP. DO NOT DRAG IT. OTHERWISE YOU. WILL BE ON A CHUFFING CHARGE FOR DAMAGING GOVERNMENT PROPERTY. SAVVY.' Had me thinking, "What Government Property"? He continued... Now let us try it again. LEEEF TUUR.' He roared, I think everyone got his message, as he did not say anymore the next thing he was alongside me roaring in my ear. 'YOU CHUFFING IDIOT START MARCHING UNTIL I TELL YOU TO HALT. THEN STAND STILL. KERWICK MA...ACH.' Immediately thinking back to my ATC days at school tightly gripping the notice full of importance stepped out, until he roared.

'HALT...THAT WAS 'ORRIBLE...STAND STILL...ABOooOUT TURR.'

Turning saw the Bastard was down alongside the other stick carrying Bastard roaring into his ear. 'KERWICK...MA...ARCH.' Marching him away from the rest of the mob. Realising it was not me he was roaring at quickly turned to face the other way. Then addressing all he said.

'Right...You 'Orrible. Lot of Bastards. This is your first lesson in marching. Heathfield Camp is about a mile away. As you march through Honiton Town, I want bags of swank. Savvy?' Echoes from the ranks of. 'Mumble Mumble.'

'On my word of command...AT...TEN - Wait for It - HAA' More intermittent stamping, then silence. By the RIII...TAR KERWICK MA...ARCH. He clung onto his words, as we clung on to the seats of our trouser. The overbearing tones of the Bastard cut through the wind. LEF.RIGH.LEF...LEF....LEF.RIGH.LEF...LEF.LEF...LEF...RIGH...LEF.' We were off to join the Army.

I was about ten paces ahead of the others and about to enter the roadway when the Bastard riding his bike passed me. Obviously, he was not going to march the mile like us. Stopping in the middle of the road checked to see if any cars were about to mow us down, he roared.

'LEF. WEE...OL...MOVE INTO THE CENTER OF THE ROAD... CHUFFING IDIOT.'

Away from his immediate attention as I fought to keep the notice upright against the buffeting wind, which through the funnel of the railway bridge had increased in strength whilst behind he roared...'LEF WEEE...OL. LEF...LEF...LEF...RIGH...LEF;,,, The muffled sound of marching shoes was far from rhythmic, thinking. "I was the only one in step." Carried on until he riding up, roared in my ear

'YOU. IDIOT. HALT. STAND STILL. LOOK BEHIND YOU.'

Glancing back at the rest of the. "Troops Marching". We're a good forty paces behind like dots on the horizon. He roared in my ear

'NOW YOU CHUFFING IDIOT...DO NOT...MARCH SO QUICKLY... YOU'RE NOT IN THE CHUFFING INFANTRY.'

Unaware of what that really meant. In the middle of the main road we waited, as he sat astride his bike judging the right distance between us until he rather quietly said.

'Right. Start marching. Lef...Righ...Lef...Leaving him he began shouting again.

'LEF...LEF...LEF...RIGH...LEF.' Slowing down to keep in pace with his bellowing. Feeling a right f......g idiot marching through a shopping center with this stick waving about in the wind. The small groups of locals stood chatting took no notice of us. Apparently this "Troops Marching " lark was a common occurrence down this high street? An old chap leaning on a rail touched his cap called out.

'Hoi.Yungun. Doon't ye be letting em beet ye. Giv em 'ell.' Bemused, did not understand his dialect. Leaving the town the road sloped up and out into the countryside along barren windswept hedgerows, passing a quaint church. The Bastard rode up alongside. 'YOU. IDIOT. Take note. About another quarter of a mile away. You will come to the camp entrance. Upon my command. You. Will turn to your LEFT. Savvy?'

'Yes. Lance Corporal.' He continued shouting. 'LEF. LEF. LEF...RIGH...LEF.'

Marching along the staggered white painted line. Behind the hedgerow on my left were some wooden huts; further on was a large shed and in the distance a flagpole with the flag blown horizontal by the strength of the wind. Emerging from out of the hedgerow an army lorry turned right, drove towards us going past, the driver sarcastically shouted.

Heathfield Camp Entrance.
Photos by kind permission of Honiton Archive

'You'll be sorry.' Taking no notice of his remark continued on, before reaching an area of pavement that curved left into the camp entrance. On the opposite side, a large coloured board painted in three coloured bands. Red, Blue and Yellow, with white letters –
ROYAL ELECTRICAL MECHANICAL ENGINEERS.
No. 2 BASIC TRAINING BATTALION.
HEATHFIELD CAMP.
A sudden roar from behind. 'FRONT MARKER...LEF...WEEE.OL.'
Turning smartly left, continued marched up an incline along the white painted line.

How he knew exactly when to make me turn LEFT. I will never know. Carrying on up the incline towards a white pole about four feet above the ground, in the centre was a red disc with 'HALT' painted in white. Behind that stood, a Soldier, of similar attire as the bastard, except his belt cross-strap and gaiters were white. Behind him on a parade ground saw groups of soldiers marching. The soldier, springing smartly to attention right turned, lifting his leg waist high with a quick downward movement crashed his big polished boot onto the ground, being sideways towards me on the sleeve of his tunic displayed a single white stripe and wore a black armband with red letters. R.P. (Regimental Police). With a crunching of studs marched smartly to the counterweighted end of the pole. Halting, left turned, placed his khaki gloved hand on the counterweight forced it down, up swung the pole. Standing at attention, he glared at the gaggle of civilians entering.

A roar from L/Cpl. King. 'PLA..TOONAA... ALT...We came to an ungainly halt. RIGH TURN...STAND STILL... NO TALKING.'

Turning to our right faced a block of buildings resembling a cricket pavilion, above the centre door was a big notice. "GUARD HOUSE".

The sound of a dull thud ensured the white pole was back in its resting position. TO STOP anyone trying to ESCAPE. We were now in the confines of Heathfield Camp.

Holding the other notice, the Bastard crunched his way towards me and took mine. Taking both, crunched his way up a pathway leading to four steps up onto a long veranda and entered the doorway into the building. On one side of the doorway was a very long vertical mirror, along both sides of the veranda was a rail about four feet high with crossed timbers, all the walls window frames and doors were painted green, whilst all the other timbers were painted white. Everything was equal and symmetrical. Within our ranks, murmurings broke out a roar from the RP...'QUIET IN THE RANKS.'... Brought immediate silence. He then proceeded to strut around us like a bleedin' peacock. The only sound was the howl of the wind the rapid flapping of the flag and creaking flagpole. L/Cpl. King, reappearing in the doorway, crunched his way back to stand in front of us then bellowed.

'FRONT UN REAR MARKERS...FALL IN.' Once in the rear rank he continued.

'Welcome to Number Two Basic Training Camp of the Royal Electrical and Mechanical Engineers. I am sure. You. 'Orrible lot of bastards. Will enjoy your stay with us. Now if you all look to your left. On the far side of the square. You will see some buildings. Those buildings are the Admin Block. Where. You. Will receive your official signing up papers together with all necessary documentation. Savvy?...'Mutter Mutter.' A resigned response, he ignoring it carried on... AND. As you, all did so well. Marching from the station? I am going to march you. 'Orrible lot of bastards. All the way around the square to your left....On my word of Command. PLA... TOONAA. ATTEN...HAA. LEF TURR.' Shuffle, bang, bump went the synchronized feet. 'By the LEF...QWI.... IK MARRCH.' We were off to sign on.

In an unsynchronised fashion we marched up the incline towards the square; a right wheel took us to the end left wheeled up another incline. Halfway up on our left we viewed the activity-taking place on the big square. Squads of soldier's were marching in different directions. All the Sgts. and Cpls were bawling out orders trying their level best to outdo each other. Close to the top of this incline. L/Cpl. King kindly informed us.

'On your right, that building below. Is the Naafi. LEF...LEF.' All taking note looked down to our right unfortunately to our detriment, our marching tempo suffered greatly that brought, a roar of disapproval from L/Cpl. King.

'PLA TOONA...ALT.' some of us halted, others still looking down crashed into the men in front. Swearing and cursing broke out... 'YOU. 'ORRIBLE. LOT OF BASTARDS. GET BACK INTO THREE RANKS...NOW! All raise you're left arm, fingers out-stretched. Touch the other idiots left shoulder in front of you. That...You. 'Orrible lot is. The regulation distance.

You should be standing away from the idiot marching in front. MOOOVE.'... As left arms shot up to push or, shove the bloke in front with a lot of shuffling of feet we were once again reassembled into three ranks and to the bastard's satisfaction, he roared.

'PLA...TONAA...KERWI...IK...MARRCH.' We were off again. At the top of the rise, we took a. 'LEF WEOL'. Continued to march along the roadway until L/Cpl. King roared

'PLA...TOON. AA...ALT.' with most of the platoon still watching the ongoing activity on the square. Taken by surprise at his order blokes crashed into those in front, once again a shambles. We stood waiting, handbags at the ready a note of resignation crept into his next order.

'IDIOTS. RIGH. TURR.' We turned to face this Admin Block. It appeared all buildings were made out of wood! He continued...'Now. You. 'Orrible lot. In single file. I want you to go through that doorway and sit yourselves in the chairs provided. You. Lofty in the front rank. Lead off.'

Exceptionally pleased to get out of the cold biting wind, like a huge snake we followed Lofty inside. The rows of seats on our left were quickly occupied I sat down on one three rows from the front, on our right noticed a row of tables and sat behind each one was a soldier, stacked on the tabletop in front of them were piles of neatly stacked papers and Brown books? At the far end of the room, a couple of tables were piled high with sets of white crockery. Sitting in silence until someone quietly muttered.

'At least we've got rid of that bastard. What a fooking pig he was.' Murmurs of agreement ensured all were glad to see the back of him.

Behind us the door opened letting in a cold blast of wind along with it two soldiers entered coming to a halt in front of us. One had a long stick tucked under his arm; on the sleeve of his tunic was a large crest and judging by the grey stubble of hair beneath his beret, he looked as if he was near to retirement. His hard featured face similar to my Dad's showed years of experience in the Army. The second one over six feet tall and big with it maybe in his early twenties. Displayed on his sleeve were three white stripes obviously as Kingy's description a Sergeant. In comparison, his face was like babies with twinkling eyes and a ready smile. They stood there like ramrods spotless every crease pressed to a sharp razor point boots polished like mirrors. Talking quietly between themselves, they surveyed the magnificent body of men sat in front of them eagerly waiting. To join the army! After a few minutes, the senior one addressed us.

'Now. That we have you here. Stand up all those who would like to sign on for an extra year and become short term Regulars?' The question? Fell on deaf ears he had no volunteers. Surveying the mob in front of him with a curl of his upper lip, he said. 'Right...You lot are a shower of I do not know what? And...You...Will get what you deserve.' With his right hand he removed the stick from under his arm pointing it directly at me glared and said. 'You...You are Plant...Aren't you?'

'Er! Yes Sir.' This uncalled for introduction caught me unawares and worried me. Baffled? How the bleedin' 'ell did he pick me out from everyone else? In all my life had never seen him and certainly had not even mentioned my name. The bloke In front of me turns around enquired.

'Mate of yours?' Bemused and scared of his knowledge quietly said.

'Never clapped eyes on 'im in my life before. I swear it.' Nothing more was mentioned until the Sgt. muttered.

'Right...Let's get started.' He began a head count then stated.

'Sir. Two have not yet arrived. Pointing at the blokes on the front row instructed... Right! You Lot. First four. Up to the tables over there. Leave your worldly possessions behind. Mooove.'

Four enthusiastic bodies launched themselves into action ambling slowly across the room sat down at the tables.　After what seemed ages it was my turn. Along with three others took over the vacated seats the soldier sat behind the table demanded.

'Name and initials?'

'Plant. J. P. P.' checking the list.

'First name?'

'Joseph.'

'Address?' - Bla Bla. On it went he checking comments until he passed over a Brown Book. 'This is your AB 64 Part I. and part II. Do not lose it. At all times you will carry it in your left top breast pocket. Your Army number is 23112429. Learn that off by heart. Forget your name. From now on. You will be addressed by your number. You are assigned to hut Thirty-seven. Pushing a couple of forms towards me dipping a pen into an inkpot handed it to me.

'Right. Sign. Here Here and Here.' With the scratchy nib signed away my next two years and with equal reluctance, slowly slid the forms back towards him. He checked them then ordered.

'To your left on that table are eating utensils. Collect and sign for them. If, you break them. You will have to pay for them.'

Leaving him crossed to the other table to receive my eating utensils. The soldier stood beside the table demanded.

'Number?'

'Eh?'

'What's your Army number Soldier?' Looking at the brown book, pointed to the number muttered.

'Mmm. That one.'

'I can't. Chuffing well read. Tell me. Your army number.' Reading from the book.

'23112429.'

'Right 429. Take these.' He handed me one white plate, one soup bowl, a steel knife, fork and spoon a rather large white mug. By its size, you could just about have a bath in it. Thrusting a pen at me ordered.

'Sign. Here Here and Here.' With another blunt nib scratched my name.

'Right go and sit down.'

Rejoining the other 'New Soldiers' sitting down noticed the senior soldier had left the hut. Placing the eating utensils on my lap opened up the little Brown Book to see what its pages revealed. Number rank and name flicking over the pages on one of the pages the letters. P.U.L.L.H.H.E.E.M.S. drew my attention. Scratched below each letter were some hieroglyphics. The last page in the book read. 'FORM OF WILL.' Quickly closed it. Inspecting the steel eating utensils all stamped with a broad arrowhead marked "Government Issue". Just like convicts and through the glaze of the items of crockery printed in green "EIIR Nelson Ware Made in England 1952". Dong! Someone dropped a croc, looking round to see a red-faced bloke retrieving his mug from the floor immediately thought, "So thick and heavy. How could you possibly break them"? Somebody muttered.

'If they've given us these bloody plates when do we get fed? I'm starving?'

Whoever asked the question was right. It was the middle of the afternoon and I had not eaten anything since early that morning. Eventually, when the last four were done; the Sgt. approached the mob of starving soldiers and said.

'Now. You lot of idiots are officially in the Army. The next job is to take you to the Cookhouse and provide you with rations.... (All muttered a silent hooray)...Do not say! The Army does not feed you. Afterwards you will be marched to your assigned huts. Where. You will leave your personal effects therein. Then off to the Bedding Stores to draw bedding. So that you can get your sleepy heads down tonight. Right. Collect your personal effects, eating utensils. Move outside and form up in three ranks. Mooove'

Amid the noise of scraping chairs clink of steel against crockery, leaving the warmth of the room behind us we moved out into an icy wind that had increased in force. Forming up into three so-called ranks the Sgt. ordered.

'ATTEN...HOW...WIOT. TAR (Attention. Right turn) KWICK-- AARCH.' (Quick March)

The prospect of getting some grub inside us was an incentive to keep in step. 'EFT. HEEEL.' Totally out of step we Eft Heeled. 'WIOT. HEEEL...EFT.EFT...EFT. WIOT. EFT.' He yelled. His orders were shorter not easy to understand, but we knew what he meant. During the following days, we quickly adjusted to each individual command shouted out. Albeit, with different phonetic sounds. Out of step, we carried on marching up to the front entrance of a large red brick building, the Sgt. bawled

'PTOON... AAAAL.' (Platoon Halt) The blokes at the front stopped the ones at the rear cannoned into the ones in front taking no notice the Sergeant shouted.

'JUST. FORM UP IN SINGLE FILE. GO THROUGH THAT DOOR.'

The ravenous mob entered the mess hall to be greeted by a sight of splendor! Many light bulbs dangling from the steel roof struts above lit up the interior like a dance hall. The polished concrete floor was shining black spaced out in line were masses of tables with six chairs tucked under each one. A white painted line defined the dining area from the red painted walkway leading to the serving counter illuminated by a row of lights. There were three occupants in the mess hall. At the far end, a squaddie dressed in some sort of uniform stuck under his left epaulette was his beret. Grasping a very long pole attached to a heavy oblong block he swung it backwards and forwards with the motion of a pendulum; polishing the gleaming floor. Behind the serving counter stood two Cooks, dressed in white tunic tops perched on their heads were round forage caps displaying a gleaming badge. As the head of the queue reached them very quickly, they began serving each civvy. Arriving at the counter in a monotonous tone the first Cook demanded.

'Hold out your plate... offering it at arm's length the Cook ladled some foul looking stuff out of a Dixie and dumped it on the plate...Hurry up. Move along, Next.' From another Dixie, the second Cook provided what looked like mashed spuds, which landed with a heavy thud on the plate.... 'Hurry up. Move along. The tea urns over there! Next.'

Balancing plate's mug and personal possessions made my way to a table depositing the rations and baggage went to the urn to fill up the mug with tea to the brim. Some others had joined me at the table to digest the plate of Ritz style food. What was it? Digging at what appeared to be some form of mashed potato remnants of cabbage and carrots with bits of meat mashed together into a colorful speckled dish. At the Ritz. You would have had to pay at least five bob (shillings) for this delicacy. Too us. It was free!

At the table no one appeared very eager to eat, some stabbed at the heap of mangled mash someone with a sense of nostalgia, stated.

'This is like fooking school dinners.'

The boiling hot tea burnt your lips and tasted foul. Another bloke sipping the tea with his lips puckered out like a chimpanzee taking a breather suggested.

'This tea is made from sump water.' Everyone agreed but we did not have time to enjoy or, finish the delicacy set before us interrupted by a roar.

'YOU LOT. OUTSIDE...PICK UP YOUR PERSONAL EFFECTS AND EATING UTENSILS...ANY GRUB LEFT ON THE PLATES. EMPTY IT INTO THE SWILL-BINS. BY THE SERVING COUNTER...WASH YOUR PLATES. IN THE WATER BINS ALONG SIDE...MOOOVE.'

We did move a mad stampede ensued to the swill-bins to get rid of the delicate mound of grub on everyone's plates. After the last person had finished scraping away the

63

glaze off his plate the dustbin was three-quarters full of a speckled mush. The water in the huge square water holders was disgusting nevertheless, whilst swirling the crocs around in the greasy water. The comments came thick and fast to the instant dislike of the food just served...'That was a pile of shite' - 'I'm still fooking 'ungry. When do we get some good grub like bangers and mash?'- 'Wot aboot fooking fish and chip?' Still starving collecting our personal effects left the confines of the Ritz behind and formed up outside in three ranks. Now. That is discipline and, only after being told a couple of times? The Sgt. shouted.

'PTOON...ATTEN...HOW...EFT TAR...BY THE WIOT...KWICK...AARCH.'

As our Platoon rambled back along the road overlooking the square, the bawling and unintelligible shouting at the groups of Squaddies marching backwards and forwards continued. At the end we 'EFT WEOL.' Up an incline towards two huts...'WIOT WEOL' ...onto a pathway up to them, the Sgt. bawled...'PTOON. AAAAL. EFT...TARR...

Right listen up! The two huts behind me; will be your accommodation during your stay at Honiton. The first one is hut thirty-seven the one behind, hut thirty-nine. Those allocated to hut thirty-seven move to the right. Those for hut thirty-nine stand fast...as we separated...he continued. Inside those huts you will find empty beds. Choose any unoccupied one and leave your personal effects on the bed. Immediately return outside and fall in three ranks at the double. Mooove.'

Like scalded cats, the two sections dispersed to the two huts. Our group hot on the heels of the first bloke crashed through the doorway to enter into our new accommodation. What a wonderful sight met our eyes? Wooden planked floors, in the center of the room was a big black pot bellied stove, behind that was an upturned small tin bath and a set of brushes. On either side of the room against the walls were rows of green painted iron bedsteads, the diamond patterned wired springs beckoned a warm welcome to its next recipient. Beneath each bed, was a green painted wooden box, whilst above was a wide shelf. There were no curtains! A few unlit light bulbs hung from the 'A.' framed struts supporting the roof. Turning to my left, walked away from the doorway past some empty beds towards the end where three beds faced inwards. The center bed was already made up; the bloke sitting on it was busy polishing his brogue style shoes. He hailed me.

'Ee. Cum 'ere lad. Tak ter spur bed thur.' Indicated to the bed on his right. Having lived in Lancashire recognised his dialect. Throwing my personal effects on top of the empty bedsprings he questioned.

'Whir ta froom?'

'London mate.' Glancing at his smiling face with hair cut short like mine, he still polishing his brogue shoes exclaimed.

'Ee eck. Entit a reet pickle. Entit?'

'Bleedin' say that again.'

'Ee. Did ter Lance Jack. A reet Bastard by ter neem o' King meet yur at ter station?' Surprised at his question replied.

'Yeah. Wot of it?'

'Well. He sleeps en'ter rooom et tother en' o' huit.' Looking towards the other end of the room saw a closed door hiding whatever lurked behind it. Outside the Sgt. roared.

'COME ON. YOU 'ORRIBLE LOT OF BASTARDS. MOOOVE. WE HAVEN'T GOT ALL NIGHT TO PONCE ABOUT.'

The latest inhabitants of Hut 37 rushed to the doorway, spilling out in a dash to join the other running bodies eager to form up once again in three ranks. Impatiently waiting the Sgt. spoke.

'Because you. 'Orrible lot of bastards. Are idle on parade. I am going to double you to and from the Bedding Stores. On my word of command at the double. 'PTOON. EFT

WIOT EFT WIOT EFT. C'MON. MOOOVE. FRONT RANK. GET ORGANISED. MOOOVE.'

At a gallop, we returned the way we came but this time took a left down past the NAAFI a right wheel at the bottom and half way along the roadway, he shouted.

'PTOON. AAAAAL.' Shambles! A sandwich of blokes all puffing and gasping for breath and we had only run about four hundred yards most of that was downhill. We had stopped outside some wooden huts. A notice beside a doorway proudly announced. BEDDING STORE. The Sgt. ordered.

'In single file. You in front lead off Into the bedding store.'

It was very warm inside possibly due to the amount of bedding. A row of bare light bulbs hanging from the 'A' frames above provided some means of light. Leant on the top of a long counter were two store men, behind them stacked on the racks was the bedding. The Sgt. called out.

There's twenty-one for bedding.' One store man drawled.

'Form a line up along the front of the counter.' The Sgt. urging us on.

'MOOOVE...YU IDLE BASTARDS. As if we had been practicing it for weeks. As one, the line physically jumped against the counter. One store man turning around began removing sets of biscuit shaped blankets from the racks, placing each set on the counter top added two white sheets and a black Zebra striped pillow with all sets lined up. The other store man moved further along the counter to stand in front of a pile of mattresses, he called out.

'Ready Sarge.' The Sgt. ordered.

'Right. You idle bastards, first one lead off collect you're bedding.'

Moving quickly along the counter, each was issued with a set of blankets sheets and pillow with one arm wrapped around them the mattress was unceremoniously draped over one shoulder and if you were, a short arse like me trying to hold up the mattress was a problem, on such occasions you would be better off being an octopus. Still in line, we went out through another door at the end of the store out into the twilight with the exception of a few distance shouts, all was quiet and the Square was empty. With our pile of bedding, we formed up. The Sgt. Not changing his tune said.

'Now. You idle shower of bastards. Double back to the huts.'

At the double, interrupted by a few stops to pick up an item of bedding, which gained torrid words of abuse from the Sgt. roaring at the "Idle Bastard". Staggering up the incline towards the huts then he kept us doubling on the spot, gasping for breath each clutching disheveled bedding, before he took pity and dismissed us.

Inside the four light bulbs provided meager lighting to the interior. The original occupants sat on their beds, watched with interest as the tangled mess of bedding entered and headed towards our very own bed spaces. Still polishing his shoes, the grinning face of the Lancashire lad greeted me.

'Ee tis a reet rum do tis is Eh?' Followed by a chuckle.

'Yeah! Yer can bleedin' well say that again mate.' Heaving the bedding onto the bedspring caused my brown paper parcel to bounce off onto the floor, leaving it there sat down. enquired.

'Wot's yer name mate?'

'John Parkinson. I'm fray Bolton in Lancashire, wet's yours?'

'Joe Plant from Vauxhall London.' We shook hands. So began an instant friendship.

'Ear. Wot's that you were saying earlier about that bastard King?' Once again, we were interrupted by the entrance of the Sgt. followed by the familiar figure of. The Bastard. L/Cpl. King. John whispered.

'Telter din't I?' Instant panic. The pit of my stomach opened up, thinking, "Aw. Shit. Not him in here"?

'Right. Hut thirty-seven listen up. My name is Sergeant Barnes. I am your Platoon Sergeant. I believe. Everyone has met Lance Corporal King. He is the senior Rank in charge of hut thirty-seven and. YOU. Will take orders from him. (At the last piece of information, L/Cpl. King physically swelled another six feet). The time now is sixteen forty. Tea is served in the Mess hall between seventeen hundred and eighteen hundred hours. After you have eaten your fill. You. Will return to this hut learn all about bed making kit layout and hut inspection routines? For your guidance photograph's of which are hanging on the wall. You will memorize them. If there are any questions. Lance Corporal King, will provide you with the answers. Lights out at twenty-two hundred hours. For those with Mickey Mouse watches that is. Ten o'clock sharp. I suggest everyone get good nights kip. Tomorrow morning. Reveille is at o' six hundred hours. Nobody. I repeat nobody. Will remain in his pit. Ablutions: shaving washing and shitting will be completed by o' seven hundred hours. Breakfast is served between o' seven hundred and o' seven-thirty hours. At o'eight hundred hours, you will muster outside hut thirty-seven. Any questions?'...Nobody responded...Right...I will leave you in the capable hands of Lance Corporal King. And I suggest you all get to know each other tonight as after reveille tomorrow morning you will not have the time?' The pair of them walked to the end room entered and closed the door shut...Silence. A thunderbolt had hit the occupants of hut thirty-seven. John whispered.

'Fooking 'ell?' I looked at him he looked at me and we both grinned.

'Ain't no f.......g laughing matter mate?'

'Lits git ouit of err.' Surprised at his suggestion responded.

'We can't do that. Were in the f.......g Army.'

'No. Yo' daft bugger. Oouter ter huit. C'mon. I'll show ter washhooses ant quick way ter coookhoose.'

Outside it was pitch black. 'This way ter tother yon huit with ter light on.' Following him blindly, thought. "This bloke John seems to know his way around the camp".

Inside the empty washhouse, three light bulbs providing inadequate light. In the middle of the hut, there were two rows of tin troughs the water supply a single length of pipe with water taps at regular spacing's on either side, above the taps was a wooden shelf for toiletries etc. The wastewater dispersed through holes in the trough ran into a gulley that disappeared somewhere into the floor. Against the rear wall an open metal urinal similar to the ones in football stadiums, needing a piss watered it. John informed me.

'Thurs only coold water.'

'Wot about shaving then?'

'Dunno. Spose yoose ter cold.' He had moved away and was exploring some cubicles that proved to be the toilet pans. At the other end, fitted to the wall were four shower roses. I exclaimed.

'Bleedin' 'ell, this ain't on.' He laughed...

'Taint mooch yer cun do aboot it.' I suggested.

'Living up in Bolton. I bet yer use to it. They ain't got hot water up there 'ave they?'

'Doon't bae fooking silly. Cors we have, on Fridie nites mi wife runs ta bath for me and scrubs mi back.' Taken aback by his last remark exclaimed.

'Soddin 'ell! Yer married?'

'Yeah got babbie as well.' Another shock remark enquired.

'How old are yer?'

'Eighteen. Married when I wer' near seventeen. Put mi missus in ter puddin club did reet thing tho'got married. But I luv her, reely miss her now.'

'Well. It's only fer two years ain't it?' I pointed out thinking to myself. "This bloke's a bleedin' idiot. Who wants to get married at seventeen? I had not even dipped me wick". A couple of blokes entered dressed in some sort of army uniforms busy chatting to each other took no notice of us. John suggested.

'C'mon I show ter coookhoose.' Leaving the coziness of the washhouse moved out into the blackness and bitter cold wind. John said.

'It's time ter eet. On tway, collect our eating utensils,'

Back inside the hut it was obvious that Sgt. Barnes and L/Cpl. King had left as a few of the blokes were talking together; collecting our eating utensils at the doorway John shouted.

'Groob up. Follow mi. I noos ta shoort cuit way.' An open invitation.

With the pangs of hunger, gnawing at their stomachs en-masse grabbed eating utensils and like a load of lost sheep, the mob followed John outside into the darkness. Leading the way he crossed a roadway walking between some huts then alongside a wall rounding a corner found a number of squaddies illuminated by the light above the entrance. Joining the queue, the squaddies in front displaying the trademark of raw recruits, short back and side's and red weather beaten faces compared to us dressed in civvies we were the outcast. Entering the mess hall the noisy chatter of squaddies mingled with the audible chipping scraping of knives and forks against crockery filled the air as we swiftly moved along, I asked.

'John. How long were you in camp before we turned up?'

'Earlay tis morn'n. Cum dun on ter neet train wit tother blookes fra Scotland. We dun our signing in afore t'midday meal. Twere so fooking 'oorful, trew it away an et the reemeender of ter sandwiches int'huit.' By this time, we had arrived at the serving counter shoving me forward, John remarked.

'You go first.' Thought, "What a gentleman"!

Behind the serving counter stood four cooks dressed in their regulation uniforms. White tunics wearing round styled caps their gleaming badge of trade pinned on the front looked like a brass button in a sea of white snow. A Cook Sgt. in similar uniform, his white top gleaming like the advert for Persil white his sleeves were buttoned at the wrist half way up his arm he displayed a Khaki armband with three stripes his tall white chef's hat extenuating his height, which I'm sure had been starched using a whole bag of Robin's starch? He roamed around; taking note of what had to be replenished in the big Dixie's placed in front of the four cooks dishing out the food they serving the individuals with the panache of a butcher. The first cook invited.

'Hold out yer plate...Doing as told he like a Savoy chef delicately wacked a ladle full of smashed potatoes on the edge of the Dixie. as it landed on the plate was surprised by its force, quickly followed by a load of stewed carrots thrown in a heap on top...Move along. Next.'...Moving along served stewed greens, their smell reeked of school dinners then surprise surprise! Minced meat and onions finally sprayed over the top a ladle full of gravy. Well! Coloured dishwater and to give it more flavor spots of oil that was swirled around on the surface by the disinterested cook. 'Move along, Next.'...Finally. Rice pudding so sticky and lumpy the cook using another spoon had to scrape it off the ladle. A rather large dollop landed in the middle of the soup plate. I was then about to become a juggler, in one hand holding the knife fork spoon and the plate of specially prepared Hungarian Goulash whilst in the other the plate of rice pudding and dangling from my little finger the mug. About to leave the carvery, a Sgt. Wearing a bright red sash diagonally across his broad expanse of chest and tied together by a bunch of tassels level with the left cheek of his arse, confronted me in a gruff voice urged.

'Chuffing mooove. You're holding the queue up.'

Unaware of any hold up? The speed we had been served was seconds not minutes! Heading for an empty table placing the exotic meal down went to the urn to get some tea. Returning found a further five plates of food on the table sat down there was no salt or pepper. One by one, John and the others returned as we poked at the mound of food in front of us, a lad at the other end of the table remarked.

'I'm never ever coming to this café again.' Like him was not interested in eating the mess of food in front of me, looking around noticed other squaddies were scoffing everything in sight, gaping mouths waited impatiently for the next shovel full of shite. Amazed at the sight remarked.

'Ear John. They must like this shit.' John displaying a face of imaginary sickness remarked.

'I'd swar ta God, tiss ter sam as ter midday meal. Oonly re'eated.' He took up his spoon and tried to tackle the rice pudding after three jabs at it picking up his knife and fork began to carve it up, jabbing his fork into a load of congealed rice remarked.

'Tis tar bloody best reece cake. I've ever eaten.' Shoving it into his mouth moving his jaws in an exaggerated fashion rolled his eyes in delight at the texture and no doubt, flavour of this delectable morsel. Had us in fits of laughter.

'Any complaints at this table?' The Duty Sgt. Stood at the end of the table. Instantly we froze a pregnant silence.

'You. Eating the rice pudding. Any complaints? Speak up.'

With his mouth full of the congealed rice pudding, John attempted to utter something but the mouthful of rice pudding prevented him doing so. The Sgt, growled.

'I'M. WAITING.' We waited as John was forced to swallow the remains. A few gulps and down it went a strangled cry emitted from his now empty mouth.

'No-o-o. Sergeant.'

'Good. I do not want to hear any complaints whatsoever. This is good army grub the army is feeding you and it cost a lot of money. YOU. Will get used to it.' With that last comment he turned and moved to the next table. 'Any complaints?'

We all kept silent until he was out of earshot. A bloke at the end of our table muttered.

'Good Army grub. It might have started out as but it has been cooked for hours. It's only fit for fooking pigs.' He too was stabbing at his rice pudding. I asked

'Heh John. How was your rice pud?'

'Doon't fooking ask. Nairly hooped uup over tis booits.' More suppressed laughter followed his remark. Yet another lesson was learnt. "Do not say anything, suffer in silence". We were all still hungry and did not care to eat instead drank the bitter tasting tea. Thinking about what Derek had said, commented.

'Do not drink too much of that bilge. It has bromide init.' A bloke asked.

'Wots fooking bromide. Poison?'

'Nah. It's to stop yer getting an 'ard on. Wanking is not allowed in the army. It interrupts yer performance or summat so I hear.'

Behind us the squaddies leaving their table broke up our conversation. It was time we left the Ritz. Carrying platefuls of partially eaten pigswill to the much larger swill bins. Scraping the food off our plates proceeded to the wash bins, a quick swish and twirl of the eating utensils and a quick dip into the equally greasy second water bin. With dripping crocs departed into the cold darkness. It was lashing down with sleet; we all galloped for the shelter of the hut crashing through the doorway full of laughter. The roar of L/Cpl. King greeted us.

'STAND BY YOUR BEDS.' Had us running like scared chickens to our bedsides.

'Fooking 'ell he's started alreedy.' Chuckled John. He did not chuckle any more. The striding figure of L/Cpl. King made his way down to our end of the hut. Pointing to John.

'You. What's your name?'

'Parkinson. Lance Corporal.'

'Parkinson. Your beds not made.' John looking at his made up bed answered.

'It tis. Lance Corporal.'

Quick as a flash L/Cpl. King moved past him ripped off all the bedding tossed it as a heap on the floor.

'Parkinson. Nobody told you to speak. When I say your bed is not made. IT IS NOT. CHUFFING MADE. SAVVY?...pointing at me he roared. You. What's your name?'

'Plant. Lance Corporal.'

'Plant. Oh! You were the one trying to damage government property down at the station. Weren't you?'

'No. Lance Corporal.' Going rigid, scared shit at what his next move would be; his piggy eyes glared at me and haltingly said.

'If. I say. You. Were. Then. You. Were. Savvy?'

'Yes. Lance Corporal.'   With venom in his voice.

'What? Were you doing down at the station?' My arseole tweaked mumbled.

'Trying to destroy government property. Lance Corporal.'

'Why? Haven't you made up your bed?' Just then, the next bloke to John arrived.

'You. What's your name?'

'Pilkington. Lance Corporal.'

'Well. Well. Well! Three 'P's in a pod Eh? Get your bed straightened out.' Pilkinton moved to do his bed a further roar from the bastard stopped him.

'Not. Now. You Chuffing Idiot. When I tell you too. WHERE'S CHUFFING GREEN? ...No answer... IS THERE A GREEN IN HERE...Still no answer, he moved along to the next bloke...YOU. WHAT'S YOUR NAME? YOUR BED IS HALF MADE. YOU. ARE AN IDLE BASTARD. WHAT ARE YOU?'

'Idle. Lance Corporal.'

'Idle. What?'

'Idle bastard. Lance Corporal.' L/Cpl. King visited each individual in the hut stopping shouted. What's your name? If their bed was made up he quickly threw it on the floor. If it was not made up the individual got a bollicking. Nobody was going to get off the hook. We all stood there speechless the hut was a shambles with bedding everywhere, outside the force of the wind and rain was beating shit out of the window panes. Inside it was decidedly getting colder, completing his tour down at our end he started on the little lad stood close to me I had not noticed before, he bawled.

'WHAT'S YOUR NAME?'

'Wilkins.'

'Wilkins. What?'

'Ernest Wilkins.' Intimidating the little lad in front of him L/Cpl King placed his hands on hips and shouted.

'SO. YOU. HAVE TWO NAMES. HAVE YOU? WHAT'S MINE THEN?' At that precise moment I am sure if we all had the guts to shout out. 'BASTARD.' We would all be given a medal for courage nevertheless, silence is golden so they say.

'Wilkins. Lance Corporal.'

'Ernest. Wilkins. Idle. Bastard. Now. You have four names. As your bed has not been made. YOU. Will demonstrate how all the beds in hut thirty-seven are to be made up. Have you seen the picture on the wall?'

'Yes. Lance Corporal.'

'Okay. While I watch. YOU. Ernest. Wilkins. Idle. Bastard get started. You can go and study the photo if you want. You Idle Little Melt. ALL YOU OTHER BASTARDS. DOWN HERE. MOOOVE.'

"Melt". A new word? Certainly, did not understand it and I doubt if anyone else did?

L/Cpl. King sat down on the next bedsprings to watch Wilkins perform. Quietly we stood watching this poor little melt struggling to make a bed the Army way. Once or twice, he ventured to the photo to check until, finally making the last tuck of the blanket under the corner of the mattress. Wilkins obviously pleased with his efforts stood up. L/Cpl. King, looking at his watch got up, moved forward surveyed the finished article.

'Wilkins. What do you make of it? Is it good?   Well look at it.' A long pause while Wilkins inspected his handy work, answered positively.

'Yes. Tis alreet.'

'Wilkins. Go and study the photo again and explain to me. What is wrong with your chuffing bed?'

Wilkins moved, while studying the photo glanced back towards his bed then at the photo, coming back murmured.

'Tis alreet accordin' ta photoe. Lance Corporal.'

'Wilkins. Where do you come from?' A proud smile enlightened his face as he stated 'Manchester Lance Corporal.'

'Well Wilkins. It might be. Alreet for Manchester. But.   IT'S. NO CHUFFING GOOD. DOWN HERE IN THIS HUT.' Stripping the bed clean of everything roared.

'START AGAIN WILKINS. THIS TIME I WANT YOU TO DO IT IN FIVE MINUTES. NOT FIFTEEN. MOOOVE.' Amidst the watching bodies someone coughed. L/Cpl. King cried out.

'Who said that?' The next one who says anything. Will be on jankers?' Everybody stopped breathing where we stood and concentrated on Wilkins frantic bed making activity. L/Cpl. Kingy spoke.

'Times up Wilkins. Stand away.' Began inspecting Wilkins bed, at the top end the edge of a sheet was hanging down the top blanket with three woven stripes down its middle was not central, pointing to a corner of the bed he stated.

'Wilkins. You haven't finished making your bed have you?' Poor little melt was the picture of misery.

'No. Lance Corporal.'

'At least...You have the blankets in the right order of lay...NOW YOU CHUFFING IDLE BASTARDS. TAKE NOTE OF WHAT I SAY. Then the lesson begineth...This bed is far from being correct the photo is your guide. Note the position of the three lines. They should run exactly down the center of the bed. Wilkins where do yours run?'

'Center. Lance Corporal.'

'No. THEY CHUFFING WELL DON'T... L/Cpl. King. Pointed out his error. Once again. Wilkins bed was stripped naked then he roared. ALL OF YOU MAKE UP YOUR BEDS. IN STRICT ACCORDANCE WITH THE PHOTO. YOU HAVE FIVE MINUTES. MOOOVE.'

Like scalded cats, the ensemble of the new occupants of hut thirty-seven scrambled over heaps of bedding to busy themselves making beds. Glancing at my 'Mickey Mouse' watch an eighteenth birthday present from mum and dad, its hands pointed to half past seven. Not concerned about making beds, as at home it was a weekly chore for each of us along with cleaning out our bedrooms. With mattress, spread over the bedsprings one by one spread the sheets tucking them in, passing John he muttered in a hushed tone.

'I tilled thee wot. I've funny feeling. Fra noo on, tis is gooin' ta 'appen evra neet seeing e's 'sponsible fir ter hut. Ter Bastards. Going te ave us daeing summat?' In response I suggested.

'Let us put in for a transfer. To the other hut.' Had him in fits of suppressed laughter.

'Ee belt up. Te daft bugger...He chuckled...Hoose dis blook Green?'

'I don't bleedin' know. He just called that bastard a sergeant. that's all.'

'Tha's all? Fooking 'ell ee's a marked man and yoo. Wit guvernment propity weren't tha damaging?'

'Oh that. I had a pole with a notice troops marching. Just dragged it across the surface of road that's all. But he heard it.' John laughed again.

'Yoor int fer it as well...concluded with...Wach ouit for him ee's a reet bastard.'

That was a remark he did not need to remind me about. As out of his room strode L/Cpl. King. Glancing at my watch its hands pointed to exactly five and twenty to eight. The beginning of the serious stuff. He started at the other end of the hut without exception going past each bed space ripped everything off. By the time he had completed his round bedding littered the floor of the hut and we had to start all over again. By half past nine, we were experts in bed making. Finally. He gave us the thumbs up with a warning... 'Beds are for sleeping on and laying out kit or. If one is sick. Which is forbidden? The sick bay is where one reports sick. If sick, you go on sick parade. Returning all...Your bedding to the bedding store. On no account will anyone SIT on his bed. The bed box under your bed. Is your only seat. Now at twenty-two hundred hours. The lights will be switched out. Those of you, that want to go for a piss or a shit. I suggest. Go. Now.'

Over the past three hours everyone fed up with making beds decided to go for some form of relief. When we got there, it was crowded with squaddies shoving and jostling each other to gain space, some holding small mirrors at arm's length to catch the light from the dim glow of the incandescent light bulbs as they shaved and scratched away at lathered faces. John was bold enough to ask one of the blokes.

'Wit yu, sheeving so late fer?'

'You're the new intake.'

'Yeah.'

'Well. You wait and see? Come tomorrow night. You'll be doing the same. Aah shit. I've nicked myself. That's your fooking fault talking to you. Silly bastard.'

'Sorra mate. Doont cal mi ah bastard. Oonly Lance Corporal King can cal mi thit.'

'Look mate! Everyone in this Army is a bastard and if. You have him. Fook your 'Orrible luck that's all I'm going to say.' Obviously. L/Cpl. King, Had a very good reputation?

We did what we had to and made our way back through the rain to hut thirty-seven. Inside it was freezing cold. Undoing my parcel of personal effects got ready for the morning. Having done that stripped down to my underpants and vest climbed in between the crisp cold white sheets, shivering with my teeth chattering nineteen to the dozen for extra warmth got out of bed grabbed hold of my overcoat spread it over the top of the blankets. John. Already in bed, watching me asked.

'Dun't ter ware jarmas.' Unabashed by his question replied.

'No. Never 'ave done. What's the point of dressing up to get into bed?'

The sound of a Bugle, somewhere out in the square or beyond drifted along with the wind. 'Lights Out.' It was ten o'clock. Oops! Twenty-two hundred hours. Laying there thinking, "What have I done to deserve this? According to the sergeant that evening, we were supposed to get to know each other. Hardly knew this married bloke John and only a few other surnames Pilkington and Wilkins who was sniveling in his bed". Down the other end of the hut, a door creaked open. A roar of.

'LIGHTS OUT HUT THIRTY-SEVEN. YOU. NEXT TO THE LIGHT SWITCH. GET OUT OF YOUR PIT AND. TURN THE CHUFFING LIGHTS OUT.' A good night signal from L/Cpl. King. That no doubt could be heard in the local pubs at Honiton. Then his door banged shut. From underneath one of the blankets. Came a muffled shout.

'Fooking 'ell. Do we have to put up with that bastard. It's bad enough being in the fooking Army?'

Someone spoke on behalf of all of us. Our exact sentiments in a nutshell.

So ended. Our first day in the Kate.

CHAPTER SEVEN
WHAT HAVE WE DONE TO DESERVE THIS?

BOOM. BOOM. BOOM...The banging on a drum shattered the snoring bodies of Hut 37. A rude awakening to our second day in the Kate. As I lay curled up nice and warm under the blankets in a daze muttered. 'What the shit's that?' Then heard the muffled sound of someone shouting. 'Who the fooking 'ells that?' Peering at the luminous dial of the watch, according to the Sgt. its Mickey Mouse hands pointed to 5:30. The bleedin' middle of the night! Groaning uncovering my head to see it was pitch black, the beating of the drum briefly ceased, as the lights were switch on BOOM. BOOM it continued accompanied by the booming voice of L/Cpl. King yelling.

'YOU IDLE LOT OF BASTARDS. TIME TO GET UP. HANDS OFF COCK'S. ON SOCKS.'

In amazement, gazed around at covered up figures some still in a heap others trying to focus on. "What the shite was happening". Next to me John was sat up in bed with his pajama top still on whilst pulling his shirt over his head to keep the cold out. He muttered.

'C'mon. We'd bitter ger washed tet bastard King has decided we have ter get up early.' Concerned replied.

'Soding 'ell! It's only half past five!... uncovering one arm from under the blankets immediately felt the biting cold on my skin exclaimed...Bleedin' 'ell it's freezing in here.' Seeing L/Cpl. King bearing down towards our beds wielding his drumstick. What an awesome sight for anyone to see first thing in the middle of the night. BOOM. BOOM. BOOM. Leaping out of bed groping for clothes he roared.

'THAT MAN. PLANT. YOU'RE A DIRTY BASTARD. SLEEPING IN YOUR UNDERWEAR. YOU DO THAT AGAIN AND I WILL CHARGE YOU. ANYONE ELSE LIKE PLANT. WILL GET THE SAME TREATMENT.' BOOM. BOOM. BOOM. Doing another circuit trying to catch anyone else not in pyjamas.

By that time the hut was heaving with fully awake bodies, all frantically dressing, trying not to incur the wrath of the menace as he continued to parade up and down, beating his f.....g drum. Minus a sock, yet another item was wearing in bed, dived back under the blankets to retrieve it, fumbling around without success. Tying up his polished brogues John urged,

'C'mon. I'm gitt'ng tae fook oit of 'ere.' Finding a sock pulled it on slipped into shoes only to discover did not have my trousers on panicking yelled.

'Bleedin' 'ell. Hang about John I'm coming with you...Kicking off the shoes pulled up my trousers tucked in the shirt then slipped feet into shoes...I'm ready lead the way.' Wilkins alarm bells ringing he almost dressed was sorting out his washing kit muttered.

'Sudin el.' I had forgotten all about him, not bothering about a coat as the washhouse was just a dash away meanwhile John nearing the doorway was held up by the crush to get out, with Wilkins close behind me we caught up with him as the infernal BOOM. BOOM. BOOM reverberated around the hut glancing at the watch its hands pointing to nearly 20 to 6, almost eight minutes of sheer panic. Just to get a bleedin' wake up wash.

Outside, the bitter cold took our breath away as we dashed through the darkness; other dark shapes emerged in front and alongside us all running in the same direction. What the sodin 'ell was going on? This was a race in the middle of the night. Arriving at the washhouse we joined in behind the swarm of dark shapes that had beaten us to the door; behind us others added their weight and pushed us through the doorway. Inside partially illuminated by the meager lighting hordes of squaddies were gathered around the trough. Having relieved myself tried to worm my way into the rugby scrum then someone's elbow made contact with my head. 'Sorry mate.' Came a response from above looking up into the dim light saw a half-shaved Squaddie about seven foot tall looking down at me. He was very lucky being so tall he was closer to a light bulb and could see what he was doing whilst around the trough, others in a frenzy felt around their chins to find some bristles to scrape away. As three bodies wormed their way out I managed to worm my way in once there was hemmed in by the crush of the others, shoulders, elbows, the pushing and shoving going on was unreal. With the towel gripped between my knees and new bar of soap in hands let the icy water run over them, lathering up placed it on the shelf washed face next then came the real test! With head down cupped hands sploosh! The sudden icy coldness rapidly spread throughout my body and had me gasping for air another couple had me thinking. "That is enough; Sod this for a game of soldiers". Not shaving today anyway yesterdays shave would do me until tomorrow'. Dried myself with the towel, cleaning teeth reached for the soap. It was gone! In its place was a well-used bar of Lifebuoy soap? Yelled.

'Who's pinched my new bar of Knights Castile soap?' A few gawfs came from the surrounding mob as they splashed scraped and scrubbed. Nobody owned up but someone gave me an informative answer.

'Ear mate. Don't leave anything new lying around it will be swopped.'

Seeing no point in arguing or searching for it, maybe next time someone else will be on the receiving end of my new exchange policy. Collecting my toiletries forcing my way out of the scrum as more squaddies entered they in various stages of dress, shirt collars tucked inside the neckband, big wide braces supported their trousers a few wore a green jumper, nearly everyone wore Brown plimsolls. Back inside the hut it was freezing cold; the temperature was maybe half a degree lower than outside and in the dim light revealed John and Wilkins were already back from the washhouse, nearing my bed space John commented.

'Reet fook up oot yonder.'

'Yer can say that again. Some bastard swiped my soap and left his own bit behind. Now I know why those squaddies were out there shaving last night, to miss the f.. k up in the morning.'

The three of us readily agreed, particularly Wilkins who was showing signs of more than a few spots of blood on his face, asked.

'Wits te teem?' My Mickey Mouse watch hands indicated 3 minutes past 6. Exclaimed. 'Christ. It's just gone six and it's taken half an hour to get a bleedin' wash. No wonder Kingy got us up so bleedin' early beating shit out of that soding drum. Is that what he'll do every morning? We had better get beds made up the Kingy way.' Wilkins added.

'At leest te goit reet las' neet.' Responding stated.

'Gerra way. It was all you're bleedin' fault.' Wilkins in defence of his previous repetitive exercise said.

'Aw coom off it. Evrione gi it wrong. You wert first ter get bed thrown on'ter groond.'

We began bed making, shaking sheets and blankets laying up the beds the way we had practiced. Gradually others returned shivering from the cold and muttering obscenities, after their recent escapades in the washroom Pilkington arrived back at his bed space, throwing his washing kit on his bed exasperated exclaimed.

'Da no's tis crazy oot tint ta waashrooom, me sooap wer swiped un nearli lost ma toweel in'ter panic. I'm fooking sick of ter shite all reedy.' John laughed.

'Ee. Dus tha think it ter get better. Yoove only bin in Kate less than twinty-four hours.'

L/Cpl. King carrying his toiletries entered as he disappeared into his room a strange hush descended upon all, quietly the bed making continued. Within two minutes Kingy opened his door fully dressed and spotless marched down the center of the hut surveying each bed if, anything was wrong with a quick tug the bedding was on the floor.

Neverthelessm whilst he stood alongside the cold potboiler all had to remake beds until the last offender had finished, then Kingy roared.

'STAND BY YOUR BEDS.' Had everyone jumping to attention twitching as slowly he inspected each bed; somehow all beds passed and he returned to his previous position by the potboiler and started bellowing.

'THIS CHUFFING HUT'S A DISGRACE. IF. YOU 'ORRIBLE LOT OF BASTARDS. DO NOT START MAKING AN IMPROVEMENT. I WILL BE ON TOP OF ALL OF YOU. LIKE A TON OF BRICKS FALLING OUT OF THE SKY. YOU'RE AN IDLE BUNCH OF BASTARDS. WHAT ARE YOU?...Nobody dare say anything... He let out another roar. WHAT ARE YOU?' We the girls chorus replied.

'AN IDLE BUNCH OF BASTARDS LANCE CORPORAL.'

'NOW. BREAKFAST IS IN TEN MINUTES TIME. I WANT YOU ALL. TO BE BACK IN THE HUT SHARP AT O' SEVEN THIRTY HOURS TO CLEAN UP THIS SHIT HEAP OF A HUT. I WANT IT SPOTLESS FOR MY INSPECTION BEFORE. YOUR PLATOON OFFICER INSPECTS IT. SAVVY? NOW MOVE TO THE COOKHOUSE FOR BREAKFAST.' In unison the girl's chorus replied.

'YES LANCE CORPORAL.'

En-mass all moved, eating utensils were grabbed and a mad rush for the door ensued. Outside it was still pitch black we took the short route and arrived to join the queue of squaddies; we waited for about three minutes until there was movement in the queue it was precisely 0700 hrs. It was quite warm inside as the queue progressed quickly towards the serving counter. What was on the menu? Cornflakes, Eggs, Bacon, Sausage, Beans, Fried bread? Not on Your Nellie! Porridge. Bleedin' heaps of it.

The Duty Cook Sgt. with his four cooks was making sure everyone received his rations. He instructed them to dump the ladle of gunge on the recipient's plates resulting with the Cooks smashing hell out of the rims of the Dixie with their ladles trying to shift the unyielding shite they were serving. When it did drop it nearly broke the plate in half. Milk, one ladle full per person; the only other thing on the menu was. Hard Tack Biscuit's, designed to be so hard that they lasted all day, just to make them soft you had to suck them for hours and of course the mug of tea. Having received this delight, one retreated to the restaurant area to partake of the flavour afforded from such a meal. None of us ate the porridge even dunking the Hard Tack biscuits in the tea did not soften them and you can imagine the remarks that were made. Gazing around, other squaddies were tucking into this gunge with gusto they had been brainwashed. With just a mug of tea inside us there was no point in lingering about having other things to concern ourselves with, we had work to do. Leaving the warmth of the mess hall behind departed outside it was still dark and sleeting down. Soaking wet we entered the hut, peering at the photograph to understand its detail, checked our beds thinking we had them right. Our personal stuff was thrown into bed-boxes and correctly positioned under the bed. With only two brooms available ssing a bit of common sense Pilkington upon re-entering had picked one up; therefore, we began our next chore sweeping the floor. The floorboards looked spotless you could eat off them but soon the hut was enveloped in clouds of dust. Outside it was just beginning to get light and we were ready for Kingy's hut inspection. At 0745 hours. L/Cpl. King made his entrance, coughing and spluttering thundered into his room; within seconds he came out like a raging bull roaring his head off.

'WHAT CHUFFING IDIOT. WITHOUT MY PERMISSION CAUSED THIS DUST.?' He vented his rage on two unfortunate bastards holding brooms about to push more grime and dust into the atmosphere. John began to laugh.

'WHO'S LAUGHING?...nobody answered least of all John...YOU TWO BASTARDS. AND ALL THE REST OF YOU BASTARDS. HAVE EXACTLY A QUARTER OF AN HOUR TO

CLEAN THIS SHIT HEAP UP. AND DAMPEN DOWN THE DUST. YOUR PLATOON OFFICER IS HERE AT O' EIGHT HUNDRED HOURS SHARP.'

He stomped back into his room banging the door firmly behind him. Having done what we thought was right the broom sweeping ceased and were put back whence they came from. At precisely two minutes to eight the menace reappeared immaculately dressed his piggy eyes ablaze with fire roaring his head off.

'RIGHT. STAND BY YOUR BEDS. KEEP QUITE. THE OFFICER. WILL BE HERE IN TWO MINUTES TIME.'

In the few hours we had been in the camp had not seen sight of an officer. As we stood by our beds L/Cpl. King stood at attention outside the open door to his room. At 0800 hrs the door opened. Kingy bellowed out an ear shattering order.

'HUT THIRTY-SEVEN ATTENTION. HUT THIRTY-SEVEN. READY FOR OFFICER'S INSPECTION. SAR.'

In came the Officer wearing a peak cap with a short stick stuck under his left arm, his brown boots had mirror polished toecaps and heels. He was young maybe the same age as us, about my height five feet five however more on the chubby side. Accompanied by the Sgt, whom we had already had the pleasure of meeting, plus two other unknown L/Cpl's? They were about the same age both with weather beaten faces, one of them about the same height as the Officer was broad in the shoulders whereas the other, head and shoulders above them and definitely on the lean side. The four stood in the middle of the hut surveying the apparitions stood before them. The bottoms of their trousers tucked into their gaiters were all exactly the same height off the floor. If you put a tape measure up against each one all would measure six inches. Sgt. Barnes introduced the officer.

'For the next six weeks. Until you pass through your basic training period. Second Lieutenant Holmes will be your Platoon officer. Behind me are Lance Corporals Gabe and Smethers. They are your Drill Instructors (DI's) In charge of instructing you all in the rights and wrongs of performing drill movements. Second Lieutenant Holmes will now inspect the hut. Remain standing and if, the Officer asks any questions. You will answer accordingly and address the officer with a Sir. STAND STILL.'

Removing his swagger stick Second Lieutenant Holmes held it in his right hand and followed by his entourage, he stopped at each individual bed too cast a cursory inspection until he came to Wilkins. Pointing his stick questioned.

'What have you done to your face?' Wilkins face spotted with dried blood replied.

'Coot it sheaving Sarge- Sir.'

'What's your name?'

'Wilkins. Sir.'

'Did you know Wilkins? You could be on a charge for that. It is called. Self-inflicting wounds?' A hint of panic in Wilkins voice.

'N-No No. Sir.' The officer moved and stand in front of me asked.

'What's your Army Number?' Truthfully I answered.

'Don't know sir.'

'Do you know your Name?' Instantly Thought, "Wot a daft bleedin' question to ask"?

'Yes sir.'

'Why. Don't you know your number then?'

'Don't know sir. Haven't thought about it sir.'

'Have not thought about it? You. Are in the Army now. Not in civvy street.' Pointing his stick at John.

'You. What's your number?'

'I thin' tis 2311 sommat or tother. Sir.'

'Something or other what?'

'Some tother noombers I can't remeeber.'

'Don't you address me with. Sir?'

'Yes. Sir'

'Well. YOU. Do so in future...Sergeant...These two here. Watch them?' He turned around and addressed the rest of the hut.

'How many do know their army Number?'... Silence and judging by the contortions of facial expressions movement of lips closed or squeezed eyes pulled back grins glances at the rafters, proved that mental concentrating on numbers was whizzing around within the grey matter of everybody's brains. Mentally I was trying to remember what came after 2311 or was it 3211? Could not remember them and even if we had any time to study them, what with the bed-making saga the night before.

'Right. Sergeant Barnes. By ten thirty hours Immediately after Naafi break. This shower. Will know their army number.' Continuing with his inspection entered L/Cpl. King's room. Turning my head slightly towards John, with a smile he mouthed 'NAAFI.' In return winked maybe, some decent food was on the horizon at last? The officer finished with his inspection came back to the doorway and addressed us.

'This hut. Is a mess. You are a shower. Get a grip. After I have finished inspecting Hut thirty-nine. I will be back in ten minutes time.' They left.

To me? It looked perfectly clean but not to L/Cpl. King who came around shouting.

'THIS HUT. IS A SHIT HEAP. EVERYONE CLEAN IT UP. NOW.'

God alone knows what could we do to improve its cleanliness? However, L/Cpl. King knew different.

'LOOK AT THOSE BEDS. THEY ARE OUT OF LINE. STRAIGHTEN THEM UP. THOSE BED BOXES. ARE ALL OUT OF LINE. GET THEM MOVED IN LINE. YOU HAVE FOUR MINUTES TO DO IT.' L/Cpl. King returned to his room and shut the door with a bang.

Everyone looked at their bed and bed-box I could not see anything wrong with mine. Someone looking at the photo called out.

'Fooking look's all right to me.' John went down and looked at the photo, coming back said.

'Ter booxes 'ave ter face ouitwards fra oonder te reet seed o' ter bed.'

Glancing at the box, noticed it was at an angle halfway under the bed maneuvered it about until the box was straight and facing outwards. My bed appeared in line with John's and Pilkington's. L/Cpl. King's door opened, he stood there his piggy eyes glared at every bed space until he found something he could bawl and shout about.

'YOU. WHAT'S THAT HANGING FROM YOUR BED?' The individual looked at his bed, obviously could not see anything hanging questioned.

'What? Lance Corporal.'

'YOUR. CHUFFING COAT. STUPID BASTARD.'

Hanging from a nail on the shelf above the 'Stupid Bastards' bed was his overcoat. It looked tidy but not to Kingy. The civilian soldier walking around his bed unhooked the offending coat pulled out his bed box, opened it dumped his coat inside closed the lid then lined it up. A pair of piggy eyes carried on searching for the lost pin, until one of the DI's entering bawled out.

'EVERYONE OUTSIDE...FORM UP INTO THREE RANKS...MOOOVE.'

Like bees round an open jam pot en-masse we gathered at the doorway, pushing and shoving to get outside and away from Kingy. Stumbling outside on the pathway in front of us were the occupants of Hut 39 stood in three ranks. Hurriedly we joined them like many misfits the long the short and the tall, dressed in various types of civvies without overcoats hut's 37 and 39 had become one Platoon. On our left stood the Officer, the Sgt and two DI's. The two DI's moved from their positions and began to march around the gaggle of bodies, eyeing up the uneven mess before them until they came to a halt in front of us. The shortest DI, bellowed out an order.

'RIGHT...YOU SHOWER. FORM UP IN A SINGLE LINE...TALLEST AT THAT END. SHORTEST AT THE OTHER END.'

Following yesterday's episode down at the station. We all began to dance again with a lot of too-ing and fro-ing a couple of Barn dance Dozie Dozes, until somehow a single line was formed the two DI's stood back to survey the line in front of them.

'You. Number three in line; take up positions one, close up in the rank. Number five. Yes. You. Move into number three position.' They began moving one person from his position to maybe three or four down or up the line until we were arranged into what appeared to be. The final solution? Addressing all the Sgt. spoke.

'Now. Recognize the person on both sides of you. In future, when ordered to fall into single file. This will be your position.' Glancing to either side everyone making certain they knew who was standing next to them. Either side of me were two blokes from hut 39. The shortest DI bellowed out.

'PLATOoooN...FROM THE LEFT...NUMBER?' Immediately thinking. "Number? Oh shit. This is it. The test. They wanted everyone to recite his army number from the tallest down to the shortest. What the soddin 'ell was mine"?

The first bloke blurted out 231...silence. The DI shouted

'NO! NO! NOT. YOUR ARMY NUMBER. YOUR NUMBER IN THE LINE...YOU ARE NUMBER ONE...HE IS NUMBER TWO...HE IS NUMBER THREE AND SO ON. SAVVY?' Much relieved we all understood.

'NOW. FROM THE LEFT NUMBER.'

'One...Two.Three...Long pause...Four Five...longpause....Six........silence. The DI bawled.

'YOU. NUMBER SEVEN. CALL OUT YOUR NUMBER. NO! DO NOT LOOK UP AND DOWN THE LINE. YOU ARE NUMBER SEVEN. REMEMBER THAT. NOW NUMBER.'

'Seven.' Etc, etc. Definite hesitation between each call until the bloke next to me called out. 'Twenty-six...anticipating called out Twenty-seven...Twenty-eight...Twenty-nine. Thirty...Thirty-one, finally little Wilkins. Thirty-two. The DI shouted.

'THAT. WAS CHUFFING AWFUL. NOW. START AGAIN. FROM THE LEFT NUMBER.'

Time and time again it was repeated until we were bawling out our number as loud as we could. Our throats were sore and in a most ungainly fashion, our uvulas extending to the front of our mouths were wobbling about. Finally, the exercise was completed to their satisfaction. Ordered into three ranks the first row one behind the other, numbers 1, 2 and 3, the second row 4, 5 and 6. etc. etc, until the last two. Wilkins and another short arse the DI bawled.

'LAST TWO RANKS. MOVE TWO PACES SIDEWAYS...LAST RANK. MOVE IN BETWEEN THE LAST TWO RANKS...YOU TWO. WHEN ORDERED INTO THREE RANKS...ALWAYS TAKE UP THAT POSITION. SAVVY?'

Then he ordered all back into single file then back in three ranks, repeating the movement many times until the senior NCOs were satisfied that we had. "The hang of it". Finally back into single file again. We were freezing cold with red noses, unable to use hankies sniffing the dripping snot providing a pleasant picture of how cold we were. There was certainly. 'NO' going back inside for a warm up. The Sgt. taking pity ordered us to run on the spot, accompanied by encouraging shouts from the DI's. Urging us on and upward with our knees.

'GET THOSE KNEES UP TO YOUR SHOULDERS. HUP HUP HUP.' We carried on for five knackering minutes until the Sgt. Ordered. 'PTOON... A AAA LT.'

We hung onto our lives by a thread; there was more barking and coughing than in any Doctors waiting room. Those puffing and wheezing (no doubt the smokers) had collapsed on the ground; others bent double by their exertion grasped their knees. Our exhaled breath created clouds of vapour above our heads the Officer, who had not said a word since we had joined his party?   Seeing the state, we were in some dying hanging onto each other for support, suddenly he came to life and spoke.

'Stand easy men.   Now while you are getting your breath back. I would like to welcome you to Heathfield Camp. Huts thirty-seven and thirty-nine will now be known as A Platoon and will remain as that for a period of two weeks. After which you will become B Platoon until your passing out parade in six weeks time. With a lot of hard work you will soon become a fighting fit machine ready for anything that could come your way... Had me thinking. "Christ! Were all knackered before we start never mind passing in six weeks, half of us were about to pass out then"... After Naafi break. You will be marched to the equipment store. There to be kitted out with your uniforms and equipment....You have a busy time ahead of you. Carry on Sergeant Barnes.'

Glancing at my watch its hands showed nearly 1000 hours. Thinking. "Bleedin' 'ell. We've been outside for nearly two hours just learning to form up and count by numbers". The Sgt. turning smartly towards the Officer, raising one knee until it was horizontal then smashed his foot three feet into the ground, whilst with his right arm he threw up a salute that nearly knocked his head off, returning his right arm straight down to his side. The officer acknowledging the compliment returned a snappy salute before retreating. He too must have been bleeding cold. The Sgt. spoke.

'Now. You 'Orrible lot. Its Naafi break.' Ordered us to atention, about turn, quick marched us to the NAAFI. We were brought to a stumbling halt on the roadway alongside the square ordered. 'A' PIT OON. DISsssMISS.'

The NAAFI. A long wooden building about the same length as the square, where the whole of the camp internees had formed a queue along its side. Due to the incline of the road the only means of access to its entrance was down twelve concrete steps, stumbling down them joined the queue. John turned to me and remarked.

'Dus da nos'. I din't think I'd ever remeember ter army noombers!'

From the time we had arrived there had been no time available to learn numbers always doing something else. The pattern of our training had already been set; everything done for a purpose. We moved along at a quick pace, whilst out of our pockets we took out our AB 64 Part. I. Comparing our numbers discovered the only difference was the last three. In my case 429, John's 540. Moving rapidly forward I began reciting my number and by the time had reached the doorway. "Got em".

Inside, with all the chattering going on it was very noisy. Along its full length all the tables were occupied, whilst by the window wall other squaddies stood holding mugs of tea and stuffing something in their mouths their eyes glazed with glutinous delight. It was help yourself from the trays of goodies laid out along the counter. A variety of cakes, Kit Kats Mars's bars and other brands of chocolate and packaged sweets. On the wall behind, cabinets displayed other items for sale. Boot polish, Brasso, all cleaning stuff. In attendance were three Waitresses, dressed in white coats their small NAAFI hats secured to their hair with hairpins. One waitress holding a steaming jug of tea frantically poured tea into dozens of cups on a tray, which was quickly replenished by the second waitress. Taking a cake from one tray and a cup of tea moved along the counter to pay my money to the third waitress, the quickness of her eyes was amazing.

'Four pence halfpenny. Thank you. Next.'

The service was like a conveyor belt, no sooner had we settled into a free space in a corner than with a resounding rattle down went the shutters. My watch hands indicated. 1025. Thinking, "Must be closing time"?

Those not served, began shouting.

'Hoi. Open up. I want some tea.' The shutters remained down.

Ravenously, took a bite out of the Eccles cake held in my hand half of it disappeared into my mouth; you could only sip the scalding hot tea blowing it to make it cool. Nevertheless, another roar disturbed our Naafi break. Our very own Sgt. standing in the doorway was shouting.

'HUTS. THIRTYSEVEN AND THIRTYNINE. AT THE DOUBLE OUTSIDE NOW. LEAVE EVERYTHING BEHIND.' About to take another bite of the Eccles cake, exclaimed.

'Christ. Can't even have something to eat?'

'Fooking "ell. Mi teas ta hot ta drink. Dust ta noo yoors numbers?' John mumbled through a mouthful of cake. I too mumbling.

'Yeah. 23..1..12 ,,,429.' Gradually moving towards the doorway attempting to drink my scalding tea gave up, placed it on the counter immediately someone else snatched it.

'Ta mate din get served.'

It appeared that was the order of play. Another lesson learned. If you were not served drink someone else's. Shoving the remnants of the cake into my mouth unfortunately it became stuck to the roof of my mouth, trying with my tongue to force it away continued towards the exit, glancing at my watch it was exactly 1030. Outside, Sgt. Barnes was bellowing.

'A PLATOON. GET YOUR ARSES UP HERE AT ONCE. MOOOVE. YOU IDLE BUNCH OF BASTARDS.'

Sgt. Barnes was not the only one. Other Platoon Sgt's. were bawling out to their. 'Idle bunch of bastards.'

So began the mass exodus from the Naafi. A mad scramble up the concrete steps onto the roadway falling in with other members of Hut 37 and 39. Unfortunately A Platoon assembled in the wrong order. Most had forgotten whom they should have been standing beside behind or in front of. Another bawling session emitted from the DI's. Shoving and dragging bodies about until we were back into our proper order and were the last Platoon to leave. Sgt. Barnes Roared.

'A. PITOON. ATTEN. HOW...EFT TAR...KW ICK AARCH....EFT. EFT...EFT.WIOT.EFT.'

Back down the roadway we Wiot Weoled at the bottom passing the Bedding Stores towards the Guardroom, then a shout of. 'A' PTOON. AAAA L.' Come to a respectable halt. ' EFT. TAR.' We were then facing the EQUIPMENT STORES.

Sgt. Barnes addressed us.

'NOW. YOU. 'ORRIBLE SHOWER YOU. ARE A PILE OF SHIT. YOU ARE UNDRESSED. We want to get YOU out of your civilian clothing into khaki so that YOU will be all nice and warm and be able to start. YOUR ARMY LIFE. Through that door there in front of you. You will receive all the necessary clothing and equipment to stand up in. Complete with all that nice new webbing provided for all your needs, not forgetting kit inspections. This will require. Work to be done on. I am sure that as the days and week's go by. You will all come to enjoy and like. THE ARMY WAY OF LIFE. Won't they Lance Corporals?'

'Yes. Sergeant.' Gleeful replies came from, Messrs Gabe and Smethers.

'A PITOON...SINGULL RANK...MOOOVE....The three ranks broke up into a single line... pointing to Wilkins. YOU. SHORT ARSE. LEAD OFF DOWN INTO THE STORES.'

Off stepped Wilkins followed by the crocodile down a couple of steps into the confines of the stores. Inside it was a repeat of the Bedding store however not two, but six store men waiting to shell out the bits of clothing plus equipment. Forming up at the counter we stood waiting for further instructions. The first store man holding out a folded piece of olive green canvas spoke up.

'This. Is your Universal Kit bag. Unfold your Uni; open it up, as you proceed along the counter. You will be handed over two sets of everything. Stuff it in the Uni. Next.'

Moving to the next store man who casting his expert eye at the person in front of him, depending on your height and stature, called out. 'Number Four's, two sets.' You were issued with two sets of everything: Pyjamas; BD (Battle dress); Denims; Cellular Underwear; V necked long sleeved jersey (Green); Khaki knitted ties (Light brown); PT Vest (White); PT shorts (Blue); the store man enquired.

'Collar size?'

'Fourteen and 'arf...Two hairy khaki shirts were passed over, another question. Shoe size?' I replied.

'Small six.' He retorted.

'Where do you think this is? Freeman Hardy & Willis? SIX.'

Thrown across the counter; two pairs of heavy duty black pimply boots, followed by two pairs of plimsolls (Brown); Laces four pairs (Black and Brown); Socks thick woolen (Grey) Identity disc (Steel) with leather thong, Towels (White), Beret's (Deep navy blue), Braces (singular) Helmet (Tin) was placed on the top of one's head. Net Camouflage, Gas Respirator and canvas bag. Then the webbing issue: Water bottle, Water bottle carrier, Belt, Brasses, Gaiters, Large pack, Small pack, Cross straps, Ammunition pouches; Groundsheet /cape, Bayonet with scabbard, Bayonet holder (Frog), Rifle strap, Housewife, Mess tins, Brushes boot (for the use of), Brushes clothes, Button stick, Jack-knife with white lanyard, Badges R.E.M.E, Epaulette flashes (Yellow four of), plus extra bits and pieces. At rapid speed all items stuffed into the Uni. With tin helmets plonked on heads at rakish angles some could not see where they were going. The last item of issue. A Khaki Greatcoat, straight from the London Tailors. "Cecil Gees". As it was flung across the counter you were instructed.

'Put on a BD tunic. Then try on this Greatcoat.'

The length of mine reached down to my ankles, tall blokes had short ones, short blokes the opposite, was this done on purpose? The funniest was a Light-Green Greatcoat. Issued to the tallest bloke, the bottom of which flared out and was about an inch from the floor you could not see his feet. With the rim of his tin helmet covering his eyes he looked a right "Goon". Everyone cracked up at this sight; even the NCOs and Store men. Wearing the overcoat, BD, tin helmet with the packed Uni full of kit struggling outside to form up in three ranks, right in the front rank was the "Goon". Sgt. Barnes unable to control his mirth ordered.

'You. Leave your uni on the floor. Button up your overcoat. Go up those steps there onto the square.'

As ordered. The Goon hitching up the bottom of the greatcoat like a dancer climbed the step up onto the square, followed by Sgt. Barnes who ordered.

'QWIK MAR-RRCH. SWING THOSE ARMS SOLDIER...As this "Goon" marched the greatcoat simulated a walking green bell tent...in between fits of laughter Sgt Barnes instructed. ABOOUT. TERN. EFT WIOT.'

This pantomime had everyone in fits of laughter including other NCOs drilling on the square. I'm sure that. 'The Coat.' was a 1914 Issue. This 'comedy act 'must have been played on any unfortunate idiot of a new intake at every kit issue. After the frivolity had died down the "Goon" returned to the stores, soon to come out wearing a greatcoat the right fit and colour for his size. Back at the huts ordered to dismiss.

'Leave your kit on your beds collect eating utensils. And get to the Mess hall.' Having not eaten a good meal for the past twenty-four hours, like the rest of the ravenous bunch was looking forward to some good food.

In Civvy Street, a traditional meal on Friday was "Fish and Chips". Upon entering the mess hall, the odour of cooked fish filled the air. At the service counter, the same four cooks served the meals from flat dishes and big round Dixie's. The first cook wielding a large flat serving implement onto the offered plate landed a portion of boiled Haddock. The second cook poured over the fish a ladle full of white gunge coloured with bits of green. The third cook who with a flourish of a spoon a ritual that must have been taught at the catering establishment forcibly crashed it against the rim of the Dixie. The lump of smashed potato hit the plate with a "Splurge" resulting in some of the white gunge slopping onto the counter top, which by then had more on it than was in the Dixie ordered. 'Move along your holding up the rest. 'The last cook forced Rice pudding off the ladle that dropped like a ten-ton weight into the offered soup plate 'Dong.' With a mug of tea to wash it all down, was about to eat my first mouthful when Pilkington wretched at the sight of what was on his plate exclaimed.

'Blooody Hell! What dit te cat brung up?'

As it happens, regardless of its smell I like fish and thought this meal would be quite tasty? How wrong can one be? Taking a mouthful spat it out along with masses of little bones. It was foul, prodding and poked at it trying to find some edible flesh, gave up and chewed on the smashed potatoes. Beginning to be brainwashed into eating. If I did not eat would starve to death, it had to be a mouthful of smashed spuds with a mouthful of tea.

Over the following weeks, one became used to the quality and variety of so-called "Edible" food. It was very basic, a staple diet produced to feed the constant flow of National Servicemen during their period of basic training. When the raw food was delivered, if prepared and cooked properly it was most likely in a fit state to eat. Not butchered, stewed, boiled, buggered and baked to make the most unappetizing dishes ever to be served. You either ate the shite or starved to death. In other words, it was what it was. "Bilge". Left over's from lunchtime were recycled reheated combined or, added too and changed into for example. "Brown Windsor Soup". A lunchtime starter, with the addition of stewing beef finished up on the evening menu as. "Brown Windsor Stew". (Probably a rare Delicacy at the Ritz). From our lunchtime menu the left over boiled fish, was recycled into fish cakes or, fish pie the latter with the same white gungy sauce poured over it added a bit of moisture to the inside of the pie. The crust was so hard it must have been made out of the hard tack biscuit's. What they did with the rice pudding? I am not sure, probably made up breezeblocks for use on building sites. Eggs, now there is a story. The treat of the week, always served up as square rubber objects, which when stabbed with the fork if not quick enough to dodge out of the way, the fork stabbed you in the eye. They were the "Delights of Sunday morning breakfast", served with charred bacon pieces, sections of burnt fried bread soaked in fat and as hard as bleedin' iron, I am sure were to get rid of rotten teeth?

Like all National Servicemen, the Catering Corps cooks could not give a shit about the gastronomic ways of cooking a decent meal. One thing can be said for them, they were spotlessly clean extremely generous with their helpings and the latter of course, was pure and simple. Their orders were. 'Feed em, give 'em all what is on the menu.' I can honestly say that I never ever finished a meal served up during my period of basic training. Like everyone else did not have the stomach for it. Having left our lunch in its rightful place, "The swill bin", made our way back to the hut for the afternoon's dress rehearsal of becoming soldiers.

The hut was in disarray, beds were littered with BD tops, greatcoats, all sorts of equipment. Adding my crocs and eating irons to the mess on my bed sat down on the bed-box to survey others returning. There was no chatting all were miserable; it was the time of reckoning. No doubt, all had the same thoughts racing around in their brains. Our individuality was about to be taken from us, our civvies disposed of and replaced by an army uniform and we, would be known as just a number. Still hungry sat there thinking, At home in the comfort of the kitchen would be tucking into Mum's home cooked fish and chips, then back to work to get a cuppa from Eileen still very fresh in my mind, when leaving work, she had got her teeth into me gave me a sincere Smakaroo. Placing my arms around her to hold onto her slim body. It could have lasted longer but she had resisted my advances, the smell of her unmistakable. 'Evening in Paris' perfume lingered on me for hours after. At the sheer memory of two days ago, squeezing my eyelids shut wiped the back of my hand against lips trying to recapture that kiss. John interrupting my train of thoughts asked.

'Penny for ter thooughts Joe.' Miserably I replied.

'Oh. I was just thinking about n tucking into a big plate of fish and chips Mum used to cook on Fridays. I am so bleedin' hungry could eat three platefuls right now.' His equally miserable reply.

'I noos hoos yus fel. I teld te missus...t'woon't be fur long. Two years will soon goo. We've only been in fer two fooking days tat seems like two fooking years. Ee' w'at dust ter think of ter idiots greetcoit then?' We burst out laughing. A few bed spaces away from us, sat on his bed-box was the "Goon". His beret stuck on the back of his head hearing our outburst looked up.

'Wot's thee pair of idiots tinks funny?'

'Yu. Yer daft bugger. Wit greetcoit on. What's ta name.'

'Albert. ...Der meet well laugh aboot it, elsewise I would fooking cry. Bit of eh fooking silly idiot poncing aboot on ter parade groond.' His long lean face broke into grin. Pilkington interrupted.

'Ouit thur. Yur looked lik a fooking bell tent.' Wilkins added.

'Ee Albert. Ter tin 'elmet needs a bit of teetning up.' More howls of laughter. Albert responded.

'Goo on. Yoou's git thees out. Stick it on ter head. List 'ave laugh at yus.'

'Ee. I din mind.' Wilkins got his 'elmet, placed it on his head it fell down over his eyes to rest on his nose. Albert pointing at Wilkins.

'Fooking 'ell. Ets woorst then meen.' More howls of laughter.

Our moment of nostalgia quickly disappeared as one by one, we began to take our free issue out of the Uni. Out came the different garments, laying them over the bed some fell on the floor the most intriguing puzzle was, with the different straps and various sized canvas bags. How did all the webbing fix together? Where did one start? In an attempt to emulate Kingy's tiny Beret. The beret was placed on the head pulled down over the right ear, as big as they were they stuck out like large dark blue flat plates however you tried to smooth it down, gently it returned to its former shape that caused much merriment and piss taking, as each individual tried on his beret. Nevertheless, everyone was wearing some item of uniform and the frivolity came to an abrupt halt, when in stomped Sgt. Barnes and the two DIs, all wearing webbing. Sgt. Barnes shouted.

'Right. Hut thirty-seven pay attention. As you can see. We three are dressed in our F.S.M.O. To you ignorant bastards that means full service marching order. It is about time. You got rid of your civvies. Dress up in your army uniforms and join the army. To-day is Friday. The rest of the afternoon will be spent changing into uniform and being instructed on how to assemble your webbing. Once you are kitted out. I will inspect every one of you. Lance Corporal Gabe is your tailor's dummy. Lance Corporal Gabe. Take over.' Sgt. Barnes and L/Cpl Smethers left.

L/Cpl. Gabe's BD had razor sharp creases, immaculate blanco-ed webbing with gleaming brasses, a shining example of what we would look like in a matter of hours. Stopping at Albert wearing his BD top ordered.

'You. Button up your battle dress (BD) including the belt strap.'

Albert fumbling with the buttons, pulling in the waistband secured it. The lower part of his BD sagged well over covering the waistband. L/Cpl. Gabe remarked.

'Um-m-m. Definitely needs tailoring.' Unlike Kingy, he did not bawl or shout but spoke with a rather croaky voice as if he had a cold, he continued... I want every piece of clothing and webbing off the beds and dumped on the floor. Mooove.' Standing beside Albert making sure that all beds were clear he croaked.

'Now. As I call out each article of clothing or, item of equipment. I want everyone to place it on the bed like 374 is about to do. So watch carefully. BD trouser bottoms.' Albert sorting out both pairs lay them out on his bed. Two BD tops; Denim bottom two; Denim tops two; Beret two; and so he went on until all the inhabitants beds were covered with neat piles of clothing plus webbing.

'Right. Now everyone is familiar with your Army issue! I want everyone to open up your bed boxes. And as you will no longer need your civvies. I want all to strip off place each item of your civvies in your bed-boxes until you are naked, and then close them. You have two minutes to change into your cellular underwear, socks, boots, denim trousers with braces, shirt and tie take note, Windsor knots are not permitted finally your denim jacket and beret, Mooove.'

Panic bells rang. The inhabitants of Hut 37. Began another race to change into Army uniform. Nobody had time to stand to gawk or feel shy about their persons, undressing discarded them into the open bed-box, whilst changing my thoughts went back to. "Dusty Miller's PT lessons". Two minutes to get changed". L/Cpl. Gabe ordered.

'Right as you are. Stand by your beds.'

My denim jacket was still undone, wearing no boots stood on the leg ends of the miles too long trousers even the crotch hung below my knees. John was trying not to laugh, then I noticed his boots were brown. We stood in various stages of undress, looking like green coloured tailor's dummies much in need of a needle and cotton to put things right. With his hands behind his back a huge smile on his face. L/Cpl. Gabe moved slowly from one tailors dummy to the next. With a tug here a push there slowly progressed down towards us, stopping at John demanded.

'How did. You. Get them boots?'

'Ter blooke in ter stoorer 'anded t'over Sergeant. Er. Sorry. Lance Corporal.'

'Not. Anded em over. Issued them. They are officer's boots. Get them dyed black.' Turning to me a huge smile split his face.

'Got something wrong with your crotch? Where's your braces. Soldier?'

'Holding up my trousers. Lance Corporal.'

'Show me.' Undoing the buttons of my top tunic revealed my much-shortened braces. He croaked.

'Adjust them properly.' Indignantly retorted.

'I did Lance Corporal. As far as they would go.' He laughed.

'It did not improve the hanging though. What size are they?'

'What the braces Lance Corporal?' He croaked.

'No. Idiot. Your chuffing denim bottoms.'

'Too big Lance Corporal.'

'I know that. Idiot. What is the size on the label...pointing at John. You. Help him find the label.'

Removing my Denim top with a bit of twisting and turning, from an inappropriate position behind me. John answered.

'Size Tribil Oh. Lance Corporal.'

'Treble O. Umm. Well. You. Will have to use them or, swop with a taller squaddie. In the mean time idiot. Tie a chuffing knot in your braces.' He moved away and left me thinking. "Tie knots in my braces? Was he serious"?

83

As I unbuttoned the braces the trousers fell in a heap around my ankles, left exposed must have looked a right bleedin' idiot stood in a heap of green material, two spindly legs disappeared under a rather itchy khaki shirt. Adjusting the braces, managed to tie a knot in each length pulling up my trousers re-attached them to the buttons, pulled both straps over my shoulders, slipped my feet into the boots minus laces and pulled on my jacket. By this time, John and Wilkins were in fits of laughter. L/Cpl. Gabe shouted out.

'WHAT'S ALL THAT LAUGHTER DOWN AT THE END FOR?' Striding back towards us caught sight of me. Stopped exclaimed.

'What the Shite. Do you look like?'

'Don't know Lance Corporal. Ain't got a mirror.' Shaking his head chuckling away to himself, called out.

'Did any of you notice amongst you? There is a two humped camel in this hut.' ...advancing towards me placed both hands on my shoulder continued...On second thoughts. You. Should have joined the ATS. Some of them have tits slung over their shoulders...ordered. Feel your shoulders soldier. Touching both shoulders felt large lumps... Chuffing Hell. What a sight. Open up your jacket.'

Undoing the buttons revealed the trouser waistband was above nipple level, acting as a built in waistcoat thinking, "At least I will be warm". Nevertheless, beginning to itch the hairy shirt was nothing like the poplin shirt just thrown in the bed-box. Still grinning he exclaimed.

'That will do. You will have to swop or exchange them later... Grinning, he turned and strode away calling out...Now everyone has got the right uniform on. Unless ordered otherwise. Your denims are your working dress. You will wear them at all times. Who has gaiters on? Nobody!...pointing to Albert...You. Get a set and put them on.'

Albert picking up a set unsure of what he had to do with them, for guidance looked at L/Cpl. Gabe who pointing down at his ankles said..

'They are worn around your ankles.'

Albert kneeling down began putting the gaiters on when adjusted stood up.

'No. You idiot that is not the right way. Look at mine. Adjust them properly.'

Albert bending down twisted them around then stood up. L/Cpl. Gabe questioned.

'Now what's wrong with them?' The Squaddie immediately opposite Albert spoke out.

'They're back to front."

'Correct. Gaiters are handed. Left and right for each leg. Now. All of you. Over your trouser bottoms. Fit your gaiters.'

Picking a set up sorted out the left from right, folding the trousers bottoms around my ankles, wrapped each gaiter around doing up the two straps, standing up looked at John's. He had them on right but his brown boots stood out like sore thumbs. Looked at Wilkins who asked.

'Ee. Art meen al reet?'

'No. Change 'em round?' Hurriedly he changed them, before L/Cpl. Gabe arrived back to inspect us.

'Now. You all know how gaiters go on. Two minutes to change into a set of your B D uniforms. Mooove.' immediately I thought. "Here we go again! The ghost of Dusty Miller was back to haunt me"? Once more, the occupants of the hut sprang into intense activity; undressing exchanging the braces, quickly pulled up the trousers legs slipped the braces over my shoulders nearly castrated myself. The crotch piece was cutting me in two, slipping off the braces readjusted them pulled them over my shoulders put on my BD blouse bent down to fit the gaiters, standing up stared directly into the eyes of L/Cpl. Gabe who loudly spoke out.

'Oh. I am ever so pleased you could join us. What took. YOU. So chuffing long?...He bleedin' well knew pulling at my BD remarked. That needs to be taken in... going behind me felt some tugging...That needs to be boxed. How's your crotch area?' Without waiting for my answer he moved to Wilkins, then all the others pulling tugging advising what had to be done to the BD. Picking up Albert's webbing belt, held it above his head.

'Now Belts! Everyone take hold of your webbing belt and take note of what I say. This belt has two functions. Number one. It is part of your uniform and number two. Most important. You hang items from it and attach items to it. In its present state just a long strip of webbing with at both ends, brass tabs with little hooks at the top and bottom. Set at an angle in the centre of the belt are two brass buckles that you lace webbing straps through. On the reverse side of the belt, there are two rows of equally spaced fabric loops woven into the webbing; their sole purpose so you can individually adjust the belt to your waist measurement. Now. Lay the belt on the bed with the loops facing you. From each end, count the same number of loops in then fold over the ends, slip the little brass hooks into the loops, when turning over the belt both brass buckles will be central. Savvy...Any questions...Nobody responded...Quickly. All movedown here and gather around this bed here...pointing at Wilkins...You. Bring your belt here lay it out flat on that bed top and follow exactly what I have just instructed.'

Watched by many pairs of eyes eager to see how he made up his belt. Wilkins reluctantly approached the bed holding his belt in both hands like a peace offering, laying it down counted the loops in folded over the belt ends and hooked them in place. L/Cpl Gabe commented.

'Now. That is a good effort, put it around your waist...They do not meet, readjust them. Wilky worked out where to put the hooks and wrapped the belt around his waist this time they met. A big grin creased his face. Words of encouragement poured forth.

'There you are. See. It is easy. Isn't it? Now. Idiot. Are you going to walk around all day long, holding up your belt with your hands?'

'No-o. Lance Corporal.'

'Well. What's missing?'

'Bookles. Lance Corporal.'

'Yes. Buckles. When I said. Assemble the belt exactly like mine. I meant. With all the chuffing brasses?'

Wilkins doubled to his bed, sorting out a set of buckles returned and began reassembling the belt, slipping it around his waist clipped the clasp together; unfortunately it sagged in the middle.

'That's much better. With further adjustment it will fit. Leaving you with a pair of hands free. Won't it?'

'Yes Lance Corporal.'

'Now. Look at my belt. Tell me. What's missing from yours?' Wilkins muttered.

'Ee. Eck. Te brasss strips Lance Corporal.'

'Correct Idiot. Now fit them. Do not forget. It was very loose around your waist.'

Wilkins collected the missing brasses, with a cautious glance at the Cpl's belt worked out which piece went on first, reassembling the belt slipped it around his waist and coupled up, this time it was much tighter.

'Well. Well. Well. Do we have success? Let us see. Adjustment Okay. Clasp right. Brasses on but not correct. They should be pulled over the folded belt ends. Anyway, that was a good effort. Now. You all have two minutes to assemble your belts. Mooove.'

Apart from the belt being as stiff as a board, it was not that complicated. Quickly finished the exercise, wrapped the belt around my waist clipping the clasp tight. Whilst waiting I began to understand why he let Wilkins make the mistakes. The more mistakes he made veryone noted his errors thinking, "There was method in their madness". L/Cpl.

Gabe having checked all stated.

'Good effort by all. Now every item of webbing will be blanc-oed and before applying blanco to your belt. Remove the buckles and brass strips. There will be. No blanco visible on any piece of attached brass. Another attachment. The bayonet frog, slip it on and move it around to the left rear buttock. Always line up the belt buckle with the button seam of your BD. Next. Berets. Back to your bed space put on one beret... Berets adorning heads were pancakes of various sizes and dangling from different positions around everyone's head were two black draw tapes... he continued. You have been issued with two Berets, when you have shrunk and shaped them pick out the best one for Parades and inspections... Removing his beret placed it on the palm of his hand, as he spoke displayed it by moving his arm from side to side...Both berets, should be like mine and to achieve this you shrink both of them by plunging them first in hot water, obtainable from the cookhouse, then into cold. You all know where the cold water is! Do this a couple of times and put the wet beret on your head pulling the right side down over your right ear. Those two draw tapes dangling down should be at the rear of your head. Take hold of each end pull them tight, remove the beret and tie them neatly into a knot then ease each loose end into the leather rim. Inside the front of the beret, you will see a small leather strip, on the outside a little slot to insert your cap badge and when cleaning that, both sides are to be polished. To position your beret correctly the leather rim should be one inch above the eyebrow and the cap badge position above your left eye. Get your berets sorted out.'

Fitting the beret on my head, pulled at the draw tapes until tight tied a knot replaced it on my head. Lined up the belt and bayonet frog, glancing sideways saw John lining up his badge then at Wilkins, his Beret was at a silly angle across his forehead. I began to laugh looking at me quizzically he remarked.

'Pull ter beret dun on ter reet side.' Feeling the edge of my beret it was horizontal, palmed it down.

'RIGHT EVERYBODY READY?' At the far end, L/Cpl. Gabe began his inspection. Belts and berets were removed for adjustment until all appeared in order said.

'Now having got that far. Turn inwards and face the next idiot. Check each other's uniforms for undone buttons anything not lined up correctly or missing. Every time you leave the hut, carry out that procedure either on parade or hut inspections. Savvy? Otherwise. Bollockings. Will be dished out. With Jankers? The Officer. Will bollock the Sergeant. He in turn. Will bollock me for having a sloppy platoon and I. Do not like bollockings. So. I will bollock you. Then you can give a good bollicking to the idiot who checked you. Savvy? And. As a bonus. I'm sure Lance Corporal King will have the last word. That everyone will appreciate. Right! Gather around. 374. (Albert) Remove your belt. Now as I instruct him. He will demonstrate. The correct way to assemble all the webbing.'

Removing his belt, Albert reversed it face down on the bed. L/Cpl. Gabe told him, what item was attached to the belt. Ammunition pouches on either side, water bottle carrier on right side, slipped the two long webbing straps through the rear brass clips.

'Put your belt back on. Pull those two long straps through your epaulettes and lace them through the buckle on each ammunition pouch then slip the loose ends under the belt. Attaching two shoulder straps to the big pack and with the small pack underneath; secured the tin helmet onto the big pack with two straps. Slipping his arms through the shoulder straps had the assembled webbing positioned at neck level on his back. When all this was done L/Cpl. Gabe ordered.

'Take a good look at this mess? Help each other to assemble your webbing in the correct order Moove.' This was a big puzzle, which had everyone scratching their heads. In small groups managed to assemble the webbing and in the correct order. Within a short period everyone was ready for his inspection.

'Now. You lot of idiots. This is the moment of truth. Inspection will be carried out by. Sergeant Barnes. I am going across to hut thirty-nine and whilst I am gone. Nobody moves...pointing to Albert...You. Are in charge. I want you. To report to me anyone who speaks.' Albert mumbled.

'Ee. Eck. Yes Lance Corporal. With that curt assurance, L/Cpl. Gabe left a silent hut whereas Albert was the first to speak.

'Wit te fook wer doing herr? I cood be ate fooking hoom in Doncaster wi me girl friend Gladys. I'll kep te watch untel es coom'g bac.' Everyone cracked up. There was plenty of talking and conversing until Albert called out.

'Queet ter Sergeants on't tway bac.' Everyone stopped chatting. Entering a silent hut. L/ Cpl. Gabe asked Albert.

'You. Someone was talking. Who was it?'

'Nae Lance Corporal. Naeboody says enythin', whil yer t'wer goone.' Albert had set the pattern. Nobody would split on anyone. Sgt. Barnes roared.

'HUT THIRTY-SEVEN. STAND BY YOUR BEDS.' So, began his tour of inspection. He pulled shoved heaved and tugged at every piece of equipment on the individual in front of him. Some bit's fell off straps became unattached from another piece of webbing; big packs hung by one strap helmets littered the floor. The only items that remained stable were those attached on the belt. Everyone got a bollocking, the hut was a shambles and so were we standing petrified with our webbing hanging on one's body or, littered around our feet on the floor. Taking stance in the middle of the shambles shouted.

'YOU. SHOWER OF IDLE BASTARDS. WHAT A CHUFFING MESS. LOOK AROUND YOU. ALL YOUR WEBBING HAS BEEN DESIGNED. NOT TO COME UNDONE. AND. EACH PIECE. IS TO BE DONE UP TIGHT. SO THAT IT DOES NOT COME LOOSE. WHEN WE GO INTO BATTLE... His baby looking face had turned bluish red, the veins in his neck were so pronounced thought he was going to burst a blood vessel. The hairs at the back of my neck bristled thinking, "Bleedin' 'ell. Wot's he talking about? Going into battle. Has another war been declared? We've only been in the soddin army twenty-four hours". Still ranting...NOW. WHAT WE WILL DO. IS START ALL OVER AGAIN. AND. GET THE STRAPS DONE UP SECURELY. I WANT THEM SO TIGHT. THAT I CANNOT. GET MY HANDS BEHIND THE STRAPS. MOOOVE.'

Everyone began helping each other; with trembling fingers pulled webbing straps tight and adjusted clips. After a very frantic period all were so called. "Ready for his inspection". Beginning at the far end Sgt. Barnes grabbed hold of the first soldier's belt, flipped open the buckle leaving two ends dangling. The next one similar and all the way down something came off even Wilky's belt was flipped open. Moving to me, grabbing my buckle. Flip it held as he tried to slip the webbing off my shoulders I braced myself, he did not succeed. Looking straight into my eyes with a hint of. "Next time m'lad. I'll get you"? Moved to John who must have been smiling? He demanded.

'What. Are you smiling at?' John responded.

'Nuting. Sergeant.' the Sgt. haltingly stated.

'This. Is. No. Chuffing. Laughing Matter. Are. You A Funny Man Lad? Have You Come Here To Be A Comic?' John quietly said.

'No. Sergeant.' He then screamed in John's ear ole.

'YOUR. JUST AS BAD AS THE OTHER CHUFFING MELTS... a quick twist and John's belt was open... SEE WHAT I MEAN. YOU SILLY BASTARD.' The Sgt. carried on with his game of twisting belts. There might have been four without undone belts again a shambles. With hands on hips, Sgt. Barnes stood in the middle of the hut. Beside him stood L/Cpl. Gabe. In a raised audible voice sufficiently for all to hear.

'Gabe! What kind of shit have we here? That I see before my eyes. There is not one soldier amongst them. Look at them. They are. A bunch of wankers. Don't you agree? Now. When the battalion sergeant major and I. were looking them over yesterday. We both agreed. This intake was the best-looking bunch of bastards we had seen this year. Now. I have to go back and inform him. We. Were both wrong and these bastards are a right bunch of chuffing idiots. Just like the other wankers in hut thirty-nine, they are just as bad. Where is that man Plant? The battalion sergeant major had cause to point out yesterday. One pace forward march.' The hairs on the back of my neck stiffened, fear overcome me having forgotten all about the incident and still did not have a clue how. I had been singled out, unable to move stood rigid thinking, "Bleedin' 'ell. He remembers me". The Sgt. bellowed.

'COME ON OUT.' Taking one-step forward stood there a disheveled sack of shit, webbing just about hanging onto my frail body quaking in my boots waiting for the onslaught. John mumbled.

'Noow ye furr it.'

'THAT MAN. WHO GAVE YOU PERMISSION TO TALK? YOU. ONE STEP FORWARD.' As he came along side me John whispered. 'Fooking 'ell.'

The pair of them one large and one small monsters, came striding down towards us about three feet in front of us stopped. Glaring through smoldering eyes the large monster spoke.

'Aah! You are the pair. Second lieutenant Holmes told me to keep an eye on. Well. You both have come to the right place....glaring at me...You. What is your last three?' Paused recalling my number to the end.

'Er... 429 Sergeant.'

'Took you long enough. Where have you been down to Honiton for it?'

'Er. No Sergeant.'

'Speak. When you are spoken to and not before.' Thought, "He asked a question all I said was. No".

Addressing John he asked. 'You. What's your number?'

'540 Sergeant.' The Sergeant haltingly roared.

'DID. YOU. NOT HEAR. WHAT I SAID?'

'Yes Sergeant.' Who roared back in Johns ear.

'SPEAK. WHEN YOU ARE SPOKEN TO. NOT BEFORE. I ASKED YOU FOR YOUR NUMBER. NOT YOUR LAST THREE.' John quickly responded.

'23112540 Sergeant.'

'That is better. There is quite a difference between your number and. Your last three. Isn't there?

'Yes Sergeant.' In a menacing manner he leant forward glaring down at John.

'I did not. Tell you to answer me. Did I 540?' You. Are just as bad. As that bag of shit standing next to you ... Not flinching I stared straight ahead aware that every pair of eyes was watching us...Now. You two little piles of shit. I suppose. You want warming up. Don't you? Well. I have news for you two. We will warm. You. And the rest of hut thirty-seven. You two are on. Fire duty. Located amongst the rest of the cleaning implements there is a small bath.. You will use that small bath. To collect the huts ration of selected coal lumps from the coal stores. But. Not today...429...Where is the coal ration store located?...'Don't know Sergeant.' He bawled.

'WELL! FIND OUT. OTHERWISE OVER THE WEEKEND. YOU. ALONG WITH THE REST OF HUT THIRTY-SEVEN. WILL BE VERY COLD. I DO NOT THINK THE REST OF THE PILES OF SHITE IN HERE. WILL LIKE YOU. WILL THEY?'

'No Sergeant.'

'540. Go and pick up the small bath. Bring it here. Mooove.'

John, with his beret about to take off his brown boots still unlaced clumped away, his webbing making a rustling sound as it moved easily about his person. With both hands picked up the small bath, clumping back revealed half his webbing was hanging from one arm coming to a halt alongside of me. Sgt. Barnes ordered.

'429. Take hold of one handle.' Grabbing hold of the right handle.

'Now 429. What does it say on the front of the bath?' Peering down at the front could not see anything.

'Nothing Sergeant.'

'540. What does it say on the reverse side?'

'Reeting. Sommat lik huit thirty-seven. Sergeant.'

'Right. That coal bath. Is the property of hut thirty-seven. Turn around.' Looking at one another I went one-way John followed me. He roared.

'NO! NO! YOU PAIR OF BLOODY IDIOTS. THE BATH! THE BATH! NOT YOU TWO.'

We stopped in midstream swopped handles and turned the bath around to display written in smudged chalk. "Hut 37".

'That is better. Now 540. What! Was your occupation in civvy street?'

'Lectrician Sergeant.'

'Oh. A Sparkly. Eh? Well there is no sparks coming out of you then. Is there?   And you. 429?'

'Trainee Draughtsman Sergeant.'

'Draughtsman. Eh? Is that the type of job your trained to fill up holes to keep out draughts. If. That is so. You. Will be very useful in hut thirty-seven. It's full of them. Eh?' Was he asking me to respond? I carefully responded.

'Er. No.Sergeant. I draw up engineering drawings.'

'Oh. Engineering drawings Eh? So. You do printing as well do you?'

'Yes Sergeant.'

'Well. 429. In that case. Whilst you are in hut thirty-seven. It will be your job to inscribe with chalk. Hut thirty-seven on that bath the Pair of you idiots are holding. Savvy?' I asked a simple question.

'Yes Sergeant. Where's the chalk Sergeant?'

'Find some. Now. We have sorted that out. For the next week. You 540 and. You 429. Will be on fire duty. That means not only getting coal from the coal store. But also. cleaning out the ash, removing it to the rubbish dustbin outside and before lighting the fire. Cleaning the stove with Zebo to make it shine nice and bright. Ready for hut inspection. Any questions?' John spoke up.

'Yes Sergeant.'

'Well! 540?'

'When woore cleening ter stove. Wilt it be aleet? Sergeant.'

'Well questioned 540. It appears that there is a spark of light between them ears. No it will not be alight. Each day after Eleven hundred hours you will light the fire. Your huts ration of coal has to last throughout the full day. By the time reveille comes around the fire will be out. Therefore cleaning. Will be carried out before hut inspection at o'eight hundred hours. Does that answer your question 540? You may speak.' He prompted.

'Yes Sergeant...Anither question Sergeant...Wurre day we geet Zebo from?'

'540. Buy it at the Naafi.'

'HUT THIRTY-SEVEN. PAY ATTENTION. I AM GOING BACK TO HUT THIRTY-NINE. TO INSPECT THAT PILE OF SHIT. WHEN I RETURN. TO INSPECT YOUR WEBBING. I WANT TO SEE WEBBING. ATTACHED TO ONES PERSON. OTHERWISE? CARRY ON LANCE CORPORAL.'

'Right. You two. Return the coal bath to its place. On the double Mooove.'

We doubled there and back to restart on our kit again. John muttered.

'Fooking 'ell. Tis becoom'g ter pain in t'arse.'

'Your 'e bleedin' right there. When do we answer and when not?'

'Dun noo. Best te keeps gob shut.' Sound advice. L/Cpl Gabe shouted.

'Right hut thirty-seven. Start adjusting your webbing.' When it appeared that had been carried out L/Cpl. Gabe ordered.

'STAND BY YOUR BEDS.'

In the gloom of the hut the piles of shitty webbing stood by their beds for inspection. The same procedure happened however, this time everyone had their webbing so tight, they could not breathe. Sgt. Barnes entering the hut ordered.

'You. Next to the light switch. Turn the lights on.'

The few bare light bulbs created limited illuminations. Glancing at my watch its Mickey Mouse hands pointed to quarter to five. We had spent four sodin' hours dressing up. Interrupting my thoughts, Sgt. Barnes roared.

'STAND EASY. This weekend is your first in the Army. With effect from twelve hundred hours Saturday to o' six hundred hours Monday morning. Is your very own free time. However. The army. Does not want anyone to be lazing about. Therefore, everyone will spend their free time. Pressing uniforms, polishing brasses, blanco-ing webbing. For the benefit of all those that do not know. All webbing must be blanco-ed; all brasses will be cleaned with brasso. Boots. Are to be spit and polished, taking particular attention to the toecaps and heels. I want to see my face in them to shave. One pair of boots will become your best boots for parades, guard duties and hut inspections. Both uniforms pressed with single line creases. No tramlines. Greatcoats pressed and formed in dolly fashion. Berets shrunk and shaped to fit the wearer's head. Finally, your top kit placed on the shelf above your bed. The Naafi opens between the hours of nineteen hundred to twenty-one hundred hours. So. Have your money ready to pay for your cleaning material. The denim uniform you are wearing now is your everyday working dress. To-morrow morning. Dressed in that uniform. You will visit the barbers for a trim up as I have noticed. You. All need It. After Naafi break. A visit to the MRS (Medical Reception Center) for a medical. To answer any questions you may have. Lance Corporal King will be available. And if you ask him nicely. He will let you borrow his iron and ironing board. To enable you all to carry out pressing creases into your uniforms. Finally cleaning up the hut. Some of you will say. But sergeant. That is our free time? Let me tell you now. The only free time in the Army is. Between twenty-three fifty-nine. To. One minute past midnight. One minute before and one minute after midnight. Within those, two minutes. Providing it does not contravene military rules and regulation. You may do what you want.'

A deathly silence descended upon the occupants of the hut. Outside the wind appeared to whistle louder and rattle the windowpanes. I groaned John sucked on his teeth. Wilkins shoulders sank almost to waist level, Pilkington murmured. 'Blooody 'ell.' What others were thinking I dread to think? The Sgt. roared.

'429 – 540. AT THE DOUBLE. COME HERE.' That was our cue. As Albert muttered.

'Fooking ard look?' We doubled towards him to stand in front and look up at his grinning face as he spoke.

'To-morrow morning. At ten thirty hours. After your Naafi break. You two. Will double back to the hut. Take that coal bath lying at ease on the floor. Double to the coal store. Collect the huts rations. Double back. Light the fire. Then double all the way down to the MRS. For your medical. Right lance corporal. Take over.' As Sgt. Barnes left the hut. L/Cpl. King re-entered, knowing what had been going on roared.

'WHAT A CHUFFING MESS THIS HUTS IN.' Clumped off to his room slamming the door behind him, seconds later he came out with his eating utensils and left the hut. One good thing. Thank Christ. He was not one of our Drill Instructors. L/Cpl. Gabe, ordered.

'Hurry up. You chuffing idle bastards. Because of you lot I am missing my tea. Get your webbing off. Put it away. This evening besides buying all your cleaning items. Lance corporal King has in his possession, sets of stencils and metal punches that you will use to mark every piece of your clothing and equipment with your full army number including in addition on your two metal identity discs, your surname initials and religious denomination. For example C.E. Church of England. RC. Roman Catholic. If you do not have, a religion and you believe your Agnostic. Stamp your disc with CE. That covers a multitude of sins. To-morrow morning you will be up early. Muster parade is at o'eight hundred hours, Dress as you are now. You. ALL. Have said good-bye to your civvies. They will be parceled up and sent home within the next few days. Tomorrow's duties are Haircuts, Naafi Break and Medical in that order. When everyone has finished putting away his kit. I would suggest. You get along to the cookhouse. Any questions? John spoke.

'Yes Corporal.'

'Well 540.'

'Tis freeezin' inter hut. Can we get sum cooal foor ter fire?'

'No. The coal store is shut. As ordered. Tomorrow morning. Any more questions? Silence reigned...Right I am away to get out of my kit and get my meal.' He left.

No sooner had he gone than a squaddie close to L/Cpl. King's room stood up shouting loud enough so everyone could hear.

'I am. Fed up with this bloody army game. I did not want to be called up. I am not going to stand and listen to all the rudeness these jumped up soldiers is dishing out. I am certainly not going to be ordered about.' The squaddie opposite him asked.

'Hoi mate. You're in the same boat as all of us. We do not want to be here either. Hands up all those that volunteered?...nobody put up their hands...See. I told you so. Anyway. If you did not want to be called up. Why did you get this far without complaining? Are you a conshie then?'

'No, I am not a conscientious objector. It is just that it's interrupted my studies.'

'You can say that again. It's interrupting all our fooking lives. Anyway what you studying? I bet your one of those public school yobs. Who think they know it all.'

'As a matter of fact. I did go to a Public school.' A cheer from the rest of the squaddies greeted his answer. John said.

'Tis ess warming up. C'mon lits git soom grub.' As we grabbed our plates, I remarked.

'Who the soddin 'ell does he think he is?' Down at the far end they were still arguing, as we left, I called out.

'Hoi mate. Wot were you studying for then?'

'As a matter of fact. I worked in a solicitor's office.' Came back his reply. The other squaddie retorted.

'Oh yeah. Just a fooking office tea boy then.' We left them to argue amongst themselves.'

Outside the bitter wind took your breath away, although we had no fire in the hut at least it kept the wind out. Taking the short route arriving at the cookhouse joined the end of the queue then dressed the same as everyone. My new boots were killing me; the woolen socks were like a pair of jumpers on my feet I was itching all over and with the trouser legs resting on top of my boots hiding the gaiters. The squaddie in front of us with his beret stuck under his left epaulette that displayed a yellow flash turning around laughed.

'New intake. You lot are for it. Nodded at me asked...Hoi Mate! How did you get to have a pair of tits on your shoulders?' His companion a tall bloke turning around seeing the apparition began to laugh as he saw. "The Joke" standing behind him.

'Fooking 'ell mate. Let's have a feel of yer tits.' He went to grab my shoulder. I retaliated.

'Sod off. Or I'll smash yer one.'

'Ooh. Temper Temper... breaking into laughter...Come on mate it's only a joke. Can assure you you'll see funnier sights than that in the next two fooking weeks.' Pointing to the yellow flashes adorning his shoulders I questioned. 'How long you been in then?' he replied. 'Two long fooking weeks. 'B' Company...Noticing his knife fork and spoon, were sticking out of his top pocket that seemed sensible. Undoing my left top pocket button slipped them in, removing my beret tried to slip it under the epaulette. It would not go so stuck it in the letterbox opening of the voluminous pocket in my trouser leg. It disappeared down within its depths...as he continued... Done all our Admin shit. Now were into soldiering. Still. How did you get those pair of tits on your shoulders?' ...'It's me bleedin' trousers they're too long. I've had to tie a knot in the braces, just look at the trousers bottoms.' The two Squaddies peered down towards my feet the tall bloke said.

'Cannot see anything wrong. Yer just a short arse that's all.'

'Get some Army grub down yer. That will make you grow.' Howls of laughter followed his remarks. I responded.

'Not with the shite the cooks serve up.' The tall fellow remarked.

'Hoi mate. After a week you'll eat anything that's served up. You mark my words.' The other squaddie chipped in.

'No! What he wants is a dose of porridge to sole his boots with. You know. After two days, the porridge is so hard; they take it to the armory and make bullets out of it. Ask Cookie for some.' More laughter and to be sociable we joined in.

'Ear mate. Do you know where the coal store is on this camp?' The tall squaddie retorted.

'Bloody 'ell. They got you on that one already. What you done then?'

'Yeah. Him and me got picked out by Sergeant.'

'That's a bit of a skive. Fooking cold though standing around waiting. It's down at the end of the camp by the short firing range, turn right go past that right down to a barbed wire compound at the bottom. That's so nobody can pinch any coal.' I asked.

'Where's the firing range then?'

'What fooking hut you in?' John prompted.

'Hut thirty-seven.'

'In there! Kingy's hut. Right go past the ablutions to the end of the pathway. In front of you is the firing range, turn right down to the end you can't miss the barbed wire and the piles of coal all the lumps are painted white.' More gales of laughter.

'Cheers mate.' By this time, we had reached the counter the same four cooks were still there ready to serve us up more shite. Waving a long handled spatula over two trays, the first Cook asked. 'What would you prefer, Fish Cake or, Fish Cake?'

Having a choice. One tray partially filled with round burnt looking objects so-called fish cakes, whilst the other tray was full of the same offerings, pointing at the full tray said.

'Those Ones.'

'No. We have to get rid of these first...Two burnt fish cakes were scooped up and dropped with a dull thud onto my plate, the cook invited...Come back for seconds!' Thinking, "No. Thank you very much".

Moving along. The big oval pot looked the worst for wear; the dents around the rim had dents that had dents! The next cook was poised ready with a ladle full of. "Lumpy smashed Potatoes". I held out the plate as he kindly smashed a ladle full onto it, while waiting in anticipation the next cook held a soup ladle full of white gunge that he poured the white green spotted sauce all over the smashed potatoes. Looking at the most appetizing mess swimming around offered the soup plate to the next cook. Smack. Down came the lump of rice pudding into the middle of the plate, it appeared that meal to be the stable diet. Weighed down by the two plates of offerings moved away from the shite counter. Stood beside the tea urn was the Duty Sgt. A ruddy face chap, with a bristling mustache, his head shaved up to his beret no doubt all over, his giant size boots gleamed like mirrors not just heels and toes but uppers as well. Eyeing everyone up when he spotted something that was not quite correct he roared. Spotting me he did roar.

'YOU SOLDIER. WITH THE HUMPS ON YOUR SHOULDERS. WHAT ARE YOU A CHUFFING CAMEL? PULL YOUR TROUSERS UP. GET THEM SORTED OUT. YOUR UNDRESSED. DO YOUR TOP BREAST POCKET UP. WHERE'S YOUR BERET?'

Not caring to answer and dare not tell him my plight. Otherwise, he would have me parading up and down. Thank Christ. He diverted his attention to John just behind me.

'YOU. YOUR UNDRESSED AS WELL. GET YOURSELVES SORTED OUT.'

In my pantaloons, swished my way to an empty table putting down the plates, from the Denim breast pocket removed my eating irons doing up the button was then dressed. Glancing around saw the Sgt. had moved away from the tea urn so quickly swished my way to it. He shouted.

'YOU. AT THE TEA URN. WHERE'S YOUR CHUFFING BERET?' The bristles at the back of my head stood out like a porcupine, with mug in hand turned around.

'In my trouser pocket Sergeant.' He roared.

'GET IT OUT OF YOUR CHUFFING TROUSER POCKET. AND PUT IT. WHERE IT SHOULD CHUFFING WELL BE. NOW.'

The Beret was lost in the voluminous expanse of the pocket, feeling about found it close to my ankles dragging it out attempted to put it on my head again he roared.

'NO. YOU CHUFFING IDIOT. UNDER YOUR LEFT EPAULETTE. DON'T YOU DARE SPILL THAT TEA. I WILL HAVE YOU ON JANKERS IN THE COOKHOUSE. WHAT A CHUFFING LOAD OF IDIOTS WE HAVE TO PUT UP WITH.'

Obeying his command, whilst shoving the beret under the left epaulette and careful not to spill the tea from my swimming pool of a mug, swished my way back to the table, resigned too being picked upon sat down muttered.

'I wish they would f.....g tell yer. Wot to wear and where to f.....g wear it.'

'Yoou'd be'ter swop ter denims troosers. Yu din't arf loook fooking silly, when yoose were walking acrooss wit ter tea. Ter trooser botums were dragging on ter fluor. If ta dooty Sergeant catches yoose agin. Yoou'sll be doing moor than cooal heeving.' John grinning likes a Cheshire cat as he twirled his black burnt fish cakes around in the spotty white sauce, cutting into the fish cake jabbed his fork into it. Watching as he took a mouthful.

'Ugh! Te's fooking disgoosting.' Trying the smashed potatoes. 'Eet it weuit ter sauce.' Was his comment.

Trying the burnt fishcake. It was a masticated mixture of fish and bones covered in crumbled hard tack biscuits, apart from the burnt taste totally bland instead chewed at the smashed potatoes.

'Any complaints here?' The duty Sgt. Appeared at the end of our table. His mustache was bristling ready for anyone's complaint. 'No.' the girl's chorus from Hut 37answered. He moved to the next table. Not until he was out of earshot Albert moaned.

'Fooking shite. Me Gladys is noo coook. But cun mak bitter shite than tis shite.' John asked.

'Ar ter married then?' Albert quickly retorted.

'Doon't be fooking blooody silly. Wha doos I's want to get married furr. She luvs me.

That's all te needs. Givs err a goood ard'un and err's satisfied.' I exclaimed.

'Yer dirty bugger. Yer an animal. Should have some respect for her.'

'Cumming fray where's I cum's fray Doncaster. Tes al luv it.' I questioned.

'How long yer being going out with her?'

'Aboot a coouple munths.'

'What's she doing? While yer away then?'

'Staying int dooers we err mither. She promised mar.'

'What! She's goin to stay in for two whole bleedin' years? Waiting for you to come out of Kate?' With a glazed look creeping into his eyes he reminisced.

'Sher proomise mar neet twor I left.'

'Gerra way, If. Like you said. Their all like it up in Doncaster. She's out shagging next bloke.' Albert trying to changing the subject.

'Nay. Shers a reet goood un me Gladys. Sher luvs mar. Er. Who's married on tis table?'

'I'm married. John spoke up. Bin married for te year got baby son un all.' John's admission stopped the conversation.

'Buggering 'ell! Yu reely meen et. How old art turr?'

'Just gooin eighteen.'

We were all drinking the foul tasting tea, looking down at my plate it was almost empty like some of the others included Alberts. We were so intent on the conversation, we had eating the evening meal. John quick to notice quipped.

'Hey. Gladys wit'al thas talking. Yoove eaten al'ter shite onter plate. Yus gooing to complane ter Sergeant noow?'

'Ugh. It'wer yoose fallt. Gitting ma gooin on aboot. ma Gladys. I think I'm going te pewk.' With his slow northern drawl from that moment on. "Albert" became known as "Gladys". An apt nickname for Albert, a very slow character.

Leaving the table, disposed of the remnants of our dinner and foul tasting tea in its rightful place. The slush bins, washing our eating utensils left to face yet another cold night in the misery and confines of the hut. Nevertheless, a welcome sight was waiting for us. L/Cpl King did not look pleased. As we walked towards our beds I could feel his Piggy eye's boring into my back, John warned. 'Fooking 'ell. Were in for it.' Suddenly John spoke.

'Lance Corporal King. We've bin told te ask for yoor elp?'

'Well. What of it?'

'Sergeant Barnes said. We ha'ter spen' ter neet stencil'g our noombers on al ter equipment and cloothing. You have ter stencils could yus lettus 'ave um pleese?'

'Well. If Sergeant Barnes said I have them. I suppose better look for them in my room. Hadn't I?' Politely John replied.

'If turr deen't meed. Lance Corporal.'

'WHAT THE CHUFFING 'ELL? WHO ARE YOU TO TELL ME TO GET THEM. I AM A LANCE CORPORAL. NOT YOUR CHUFFING SERVANT. YOU GET THEM. THERE'RE IN A LARGE BOX ON MY SHELF. MOOOVE YOUR IDLE ARSE.'

John, moving his idle arse doubled up to Kingy's room. Soon returned carrying a large box, placing it on his bed began to sort out its contents. Two sets of wooden stencils, two inkpads two hammers some metal punches. By that time all occupants had returned and in the presence of Kingy all were very quiet then Kingy began his lesson.

'Right Listen up. After 540 and 429 have finished stenciling. You shower of bastards. Take it in turn to number all your clothing and webbing. If you're not numbering your kit. You can go down the Naafi to buy your cleaning requisites. The Naafi opens at o' seven hundred hours. All numbering will be complete by lights out. So. You had better get moving.' L/Cpl. King had spoken; returning to his room slammed the door shut.

'Ear John. Why did you say Barnes ordered us? It was Gabe.' Picking up a couple of stencil sets, John passing them over answered.

'I nose. But git less problem tersay twer Sergeant.'

'Wot's it like in his room then?'

'Nit mooch. Tis a bit pokey, he as a corner window. His bed's oop ageenst ter end wall inta corner. His bed's immacoolate all turrn'd down and square. Above his bed is te shelf, wit his kit all squared off, blanco-ed wit gleaming brasses. Noo wunder he din't complain aboot ter cold. He has little lectric fire in theer. Oh yeah. A cupboard and on top of it. His fooking drum!'

'Blimey. I had forgotten about that. Bet we'll get that soding noise first thing in the morning? Spose we'll have to start using these stencils before everyone else wants em.' From the box John took out two small hammers, handing one over enthusiastically said.

'Ere. Tweev'e each got t'ammer. Let's fix 'is drum.' Grasping the hammer urged.

'That. Would be bleedin' great. Tomorrow morning we would get a lie in. The only problem is he wouldn't arf take it out on us. Put us on a charge or summat. Damaging government property? Not sodin' worth it. Where's me identity disc? I will start on them, then someone else can do theirs, need something solid beneath these discs. John started

'Bang! 'Use ter flooor tis ard.'

Following his example, soon had the two discs appropriately stamped, passed the punches to Wilkins. Next job stenciling clothing. The stencils, square wooden pegs etched into one end were the numbers zero to nine, starting with the numbers set them up in a small wooden frame pressing them on the inkpad. First the pyjamas concentration camp issue, thick winciette jobs with thin blue stripy lines all over them did not fancy wearing them in bed. Then onto every item of clothing and webbing, stenciling was tedious taking ages to complete, fed up with stamping nevertheless with each imprint done my number became etched into my brain never to forget my number, finished until John reminded me.

'Dint forgit ter cloothes yu wooring.' Stripping off, it was freezing cold and was quick to get that job over. Amidst the chatting in the hut was the intermittent sound of 'bang bang' as metal hit metal. L/Cpl. King came out of his room shouting and bawling about, the noise before leaving said. I'll be back later to inspect every item of kit, to check that it had been done properly.' Then left the hut that had me wondered what that bastard Kingy did over the weekend. Hoping he would be out all the time.

Time seemed to be speeding past, glancing at my watch its Mickey Mouse hands showed five to seven the Naafi would be open soon, again my mind wandered thinking. "I would be on my way down to the Beehive to meet Derek as I had received a letter from him on Wednesday, saying he would be home on Friday that very day. A picture flashed before me. Derek drinking beer laughing his head off at my expense." Starting to get morbid began squaring off the kit, but it was doing nothing just collapsing. Going to scrutinise the picture passing by Gladys busy mutilating his identity disc smashing hell out of them. Did not bother to ask how he was getting on. My main concern was the kit assembly on the top shelves. In the photograph it looked so square; mine was just a heap of webbing decided that perhaps after applying this blanco stuff, it might stiffen up the webbing. Blanco was the answer and the Naafi is where to buy it. Returning noting the time quarter past seven said aloud. 'Aah sod it.' Gladys muttered.

'Nay Lad. Blasfeeming int ere, te woon't do ter any fooking good.'

'Nah maybe not. But wot piss's me off is we even have to buy our own soddin' cleaning gear.' Gladys did not reply as he stamped yet another number onto his disc. John was busy messing about with his webbing.

'Ear John. Fancy coming down Naafi buy some cleaning stuff?'

'Jist as well, te shooits at nine o'clock, Ee they dun hang about int Naafi dust they?

Dunn coom ter shootters and you have fooking 'ad it. Held un ter minute... Finished doing up a webbing strap stood up...Fooking neetmare o' puzzle, alter webbing dun ter thinks Eh?' I did not reply about to leave the hut half way towards the doorway. Wilky called out.

'Hoi. Yus two. Arts ter gooin wioout ter berets an ter belts?' John laughing.

'Ee fooking 'ell. If thit bastard Kingy caught uss like tis. He'd fooking shoot us.' About turned to retrieve our berets and belts. I said.

'Well-spotted Wilky. Do same for you someday mate.' With our berets and belts on, we inspected each other.

'Come on. We'll be here all bleedin' night flattening them down. We look like a pile of shit anyway.' John laughing asked.

'Whit ter gooin ter do with yore tit's then? Ere Wilky. Whit's he fooking loook lik Eh?' Wilky burst out laughing.

'Fooking Camel.'

'Okay you two stop taking the piss. I can't bleedin' 'elp it, it's wot I've bin issued with. C'mon lets git out of ear.' John still laughing followed behind me. Very conscious of my Army issued "pair of tit's". Somehow, if I could? Would have to swop my denim trousers with a taller bloke. Outside, it was blowing a hooley as we ran the almost horizontal rain stung your face. At the Naafi entrance, we were wet but thanks to our berets, our head and right shoulder were dry. Gasping for air entered the Naafi gone was morning mayhem there was no queue, instead a more relaxed atmosphere sat at various tables was a handful of squaddies, serving behind the counter were two different Naafi girls. The counter top void of cakes displayed large tins of different cleaning materials. Black Cherry Blossom boot polish, Blanco, Brasso, Zebo, Brushes, and Dusters yellow. The only thing not on sale? Was spit. Proceeding along the counter thinking. "Take a tin of each item that would easily last a fortnight". Picking them out with a couple of brushes two dusters, spotted a box containing sticks of white chalk took two. I asked.

'Ear John wot about sharing the cost of Zebo?'

'Al reet.' Further down was a tray of different bars of chocolate. Stacking the flat tins brushes and dusters on the palm of one hand picked up a Crunchy and Mars bar, approaching the wench serving out drinks instant recognition. "It's Eileen. But no". Similar hairstyle, broad nose large pair of lips plastered with red lipstick, black penciled eyebrows and enhanced by the tightness of her uniform she sported a big pair of tits. Adorned above her left one was the *NAAFI* logo. Flashing her eyelids at me, she smiled sweetly.

'Want anything to drink soldier?'

'Err. Light ale please.' Taking a bottle from under the counter with an expert flips of a bottle opener chained to her belt, snapped off the top poured some beer into a glass, smiling sweetly advised. 'Pay at the till please. Next. Want anything to drink soldier?'

'Orange Juice polease.'

Seriously disillusioned, it was all a con just to get you to have a drink. With both hands full and the drink stood on the counter with John in the same predicament, decided to leave the beer on the counter and do two trips. With that done the girl at the till of similar beauty. Had dark hair pulled tightly back and tied into a ponytail, a heavily powdered round face, a sharp pointed nose and a gash of a mouth plastered with red lipstick, the exact same colour as the blonde girl, maybe they shared it? She studying my requisites lifted up each tin, peering at me though a set of false eyelashes, asked.

'New Intake Soldier?'

'Yes. Does it show?' She giggled.

'What. Are those two lumps on your shoulders? Pips?'

'Er no. They are...' She not interested enquired.

'When did you arrive?'

'Yesterday. Why?'

'Tch, Tch, Tch...She waved a hand at my pile of tins...You will need a few more tins than that to clean your kit, adding...Only one brush for boots and blanco-ing! Well you take my advice you will need two of each. Double up on everything, treble up on the boot polish and blanco...adding...Um-m-m. Another duster will not go amiss.' Indignantly I retorted.

'Why? There's enough boot polish there to last me a fortnight.'

'Believe me Soldier. That tin, will not last this weekend...she questioned...You and your mate on fire duty then?. Beginning to get suspicious of her knowledge, took an instant dislike to this snotty cow...'Why?' ... Smiling sweetly retorted...'Anyone and everyone who buys zebo and chalk. Are always on fire duty.' Casting my eyes down on my tiny stack of tins thought. "This Cow. Seemed to know more about the soddin' army than we did. But there again she must have served thousands of new soldiers in more ways than one"?...She questioned...'Well. Do you want extra tins and brushes?'...'Yeah. Well you seem to know all about how much we need. Spose I'd better take another tin of each and some more brushes.'...'That's the ticket...she called out. Mavis. Would you please double up on this order.'

'What was it Dot?'

'One tin each of. Cherry. Brasso. Zebo. Two tins Blanco. One duster. Two boot and blanco brushes and four sticks of chalk.' Mavis collecting the requisites returned with them dropped them next to my meager pile of tins. Smiling she asked.

'There you are soldier. What about another couple of chockie bars then?'

'Err. No thanks.' Mavis turned her attention to John and pointing at my pile questioned.

'Same again soldier?' John enquired.

'Dust ter reelly think tis necessary?' Mavis laughing called out.

'Dot. Did you hear the cheek of this one. Is it necessary he asks?' I interrupted.

'Ear you two. Aren't 'aving a game with us are yers?' Dot spat back at me.

'No. Were not. But I bet. You and your mate will be back in here again within the week buying more tins and when you do. You will thank us for being so helpful... If you please. That will be five shillings and sixpence.' In the mean time Mavis had returned back with more tins to add to John's little pile. She chirped.

'There you are Soldier. Some more tins to add to your bill.'

Fishing out my money from the depts of my voluminous pocket did not have enough in cash. Handed her a ten bob note. With a grin creasing her face, she asked.

'Got anything smaller?'

'No. Sorry.'

'What about your mate then?'

'Hoi! I ain't bleedin' paying for his stuff.'

'No Soldier. I did not mean that. Maybe to make it up he can lend you some?' John enquired of Dot.

'How mooch dust mi lot cum to'?

'Five shillings and Two pence.' John studying his change exclaimed.

'Noo. Cun jist pay fer mine.' Dot deciding what to do said.

'Right. First I will take yours. Then change his ten bob note... John passed over his money. Dot hitting the right keys up popped 5- 2p on the glass money indicator, out flew the cash drawer. Separating the coins she dropped them into the cash compartments, closing the till rang up mine holding out her open palm...Right. If you please. Your ten bob note.' Reluctantly gave her the note, Dot scraping out the change from the drawer compartment laid out the change. Gathering it up and my requisites put them into pockets did not know I had? Finally picked up the glass of flat beer. Dot creased her lips in a false smile muttered.

'See you two very soon. Move along. Next please.' Behind us a long queue had formed waiting to pay for their purchases.

As we made our way to a table, my left thigh pocket bulging with tins was banging against my leg; my thoughts were about what the two girls had just said. "We would be back within the week for more cleaning stuff". To make things worse we had to pay for it and the nasty bleedin' thing about it, all came out of the grand sum of Twenty-eight shillings per week. The week before my weeks wage was three pounds ten shillings, even after having paid Mum one pound for my keep. I was a rich man. What did they think we were? Made of bleedin' money? Beginning to feel very pissed off, took a sip of beer said.

'I've just been thinking how much it's going to cost me in bleedin' cleaning stuff. If those two cows up at counter, knows what they are talking about. We'll be soddin' broke every week and they knew what the Zebo and chalk was for.'

'Yoose talking aboot thit. When tother one doubled up on my list, she gave me another tin or Zebo. Blooody Cow. So I din't oow yu iny muney for ter item.'

'That's all right. Then were quits. Didn't miss a bleedin' trick did they? Don't' you drink then?'

'Yeah. Nit mooch thou. Can't affoord te, wit babie'

'Where der live then?'

'Wi er mum. Wife and I, has ter bedroom twer yoose un everything else, except kitchen. We's eats it ter wit reest of famly.'

'Don't yer find it a bit strange then?'

'Noo not reely. Known famly fir bloody year's. She was mi girlfrien way back fro' schoooldays jist git carrie away one neet, an putt's eer int pudden club.'

'Wot yer reckon of it so far?'

'Fooking stinks. But mi Dad waarned mi afore I left. Not ter vulunteer for oout. Wit appened? Git blooody firre duti street way.' I laughed.

'Don't forget I were first bleeder to get it. You bleedin' laughing at me, got you into it. My Ole man said same thing to me. He knew I didn't want to go so, took me to his local boozer for a couple of pints and told me. Go and do your bit. Don't worry about it. Get stuck in. Have a good time and get out. Two years isn't a long time? Bleedin' lifetime to me. Anyway my ole man should know he was a regular for twenty-eight years or more.'

'Twenty-eight blooody years? Fooking hell thit is a leeftim?'

'Yeah. A sight bleedin' longer than two years. Wot yer do in civvy street then?'

'Lectrician worked fer ter local cumpny. Ome wiring tipe of work yer noose. Cudn't do prentiship cumpny weern't big enough.'

'Same as me. Firm I worked for wouldn't take me on as apprentice draughtsman.'

'When yer came in ter camp yisterday. Wet's tis abooit ter BSM?' Still mystified despondently replied.

'I dun know. Honest. Never clapped eyes on im before. Swear to it. Likewise never heard of him. How he picked on me I'll never know.'

'Well. Ter second looey and sergeant seems to ave goot uus tu inter sights. We'd bitter witch oorselves keep oor moouths shut and get on wi whit ever ter tell us to do.' While we had been talking. Gladys, Wilkins, Pilkington and a few of the others from hut 37. Entered the Naafi and joined the queue. Glancing at my Mickey Mouse watch, its hands pointed to quarter past eight.

'Bleedin' 'ell John. Look at time. Naafi will shut soon and we have to get kit and all that shit ready for morning.' We both drained our glasses. John suggested.

98

'I'm shaving t'neet'

'Good Idea.' I felt my chin not very much stubble thinking, "What's the point"?

Outside it was still raining and blowing a hooley. With the tins, banging against my leg had to drag it as we ran back to an almost empty hut. Two squaddies were doing their stenciling , looking up one asked with a Scotch accent.

'Hoo loong's dae quoo doon tae Naafi?' John remarked.

'Yer's bitter git dun quick. Totherwis te shuitters will coom down.' The other one, broad of build with ginger hair and eyebrows sporting a bit of a smashed nose, a wide grin creased his face from ear to ear responded.

'Och aye.' The first one, with stencil in one hand holding a sock in the other muttered.

'Wees neeley finished.' Looking at him thought. "Christ. Even sitting down he is tall must be over six foot, reasonably broad in the shoulder a ruddy coloured face with high cheekbones and a bulbous nose and dark eyes. If you gave him a claymore, he would become a fiery Scot. He stood up. He was tall. His trouser length appeared to be half way up his legs.

'Ear Mate. Wot's yer denim trousers like?'

'Shorrrt.'

'Dyer wanna swop.'

'Dinna ken.'

'Ear hold on. Lets 'ave a look then...With tins banging ran to the bed-box grabbed the other pair and ran back...Ear mate try these up against yer legs... They appeared to be his right size...Do a swop then. My two for your two pairs and I'll finish off yer stenciling.'

'Aye Soonds guid.' Swopping one pair each, at the bed removed the tins out of my pockets changing quickly into the new pair adjusted the braces although still a bit too long. 'There, that's the second pair Okay.' Jock having changed they fitted, he was happy and so was I.

As others were coming back in the Jocks left. All were moaning about buying double rations of cleaning material, those two cows down the Naafi had conned us all. With the swopped bottoms on lacing up the gaiters they became visible, with the beret and belt on, presented myself to John. 'Wot der think John?'

'Walk up ter huit.' Doing so walked back.

'Jacket's still ter big, lost ter tit's tho', trowsers moor bitter tan t'others. Loooked like fooking Arab wer pantaloons on, all ter needed was a cutlass not te fooking gun.' His comment caused laughter amongst others. Finishing off the stenciling for the two Jocks John asked

'Yer gooin ter shave then?'

'Hang on. I'll get me kit.' Sorting out toiletries followed him out into the driving rain. Inside the washhouse washing and shaving was in progress. Managing to squeeze in between two blokes placing my toiletries on the shelf kept a wide eye open, took out my new Gillette razor, lathered up with cold water to shave away half a dozen bristles from various areas around my chin. Satisfied that the bum fluff was gone, splashed water over face and neck gasping at the coldness quickly drying myself, noticed on the shelf. A new bar of Knights Castile that quickly disappeared into the folds of my towel rapidly departed. Approaching the doorway of the hut heard the roar of Kingy inside ranting and raving thought, "Oh bleedin' 'ell wot now"? Opening the door saw the two Scots lads stood to one side, sidling past them noticed Wilky was practically under his bed. Behind me Kingy roared.

'WHERE YOU TWO MELTS BEEN?'

'Doon tae naafi fer tae supplies.'

'YOU FINISHED STENCILING YOUR KIT?'

'Aye Lance Corporal.'

'SHOW ME.' By that time he was stood close to the tall Jocks bed and had the full attention of hut 37.

'Der ye arr. Lance Corporal.' Kingy bent down and began picking items up to see if he could find a piece not done. The tall Scot glanced down towards me and mouthed something. I suppose it was thanks? Sticking up my thumb he winked in response. Having not found apiece unmarked, Kingy shouted

'GET YOUR BED SPACE TIDY. IT'S A CHUFFING MESS.' He stormed away stomping past the Public schoolboy then stopped shouted. 'I HAVEN'T FINISHED WITH YOU.' Then carried on into his room slamming the door shut. Just then John entered. Muttered to me.

'Been stoood ouit seed listen'g wit's gooin on?'

'Dun know. When I came back in. Kingy was 'aving a go at the Jocks un 'ole Public up there. Wilky may know? Hey. Wilky. Wot's been going on?' From under his bed came Wiley's muffled cry.

'As he goone?'

'Wilky come on out. Tell us wots been going on hurry up.' Wilkins crawled out and stood up. His five-foot nothing frame trembling looked towards Kingy's room.

'He's goone as ae?' John laughing asked.

'Wot the fooks matter wit thee? Teld us wit 'appened c'mon.'

'Wen we got back fra Naafi. It twere all reet. Thin Kingy cum in un sturted raaving at ter blook down thure. Blook stoood up un told him wit ae cud doo wit tarmy. I thought thure meet be a reet feght o'summat. Went ter Jock's cum in, Kingy sturted on thim.' I remarked.

'Good for im. He's just saying what we all think anyway. I bet he'll be for it now. Storm in a bleedin' tea cup.'

'Not in te fooking mugs.' John said and we cracked up. The hut became strangely quiet as some of the others took their turn stenciling clothing, the familiar bang of a hammer on metal continued. Unraveling my towel to inspect the bar of soap, it was mine.

'Ear John. Got my soap back dyer no, it were a good thing we helped those two Jocks out. Kingy jumped at the big fella and inspected his kit. Din't find anything wrong though.' Looking up saw the two Jocks on their way towards us, the tall bloke spoke first.

'Ta fur yee elp, my nams Jock Anderson.'

'Aye. Thet ges fer me tae. Me nams McIntyre.'

'Joe Plant. He's John Parkinson.'

'Aye. We ken.' We all shook hands now we were getting to know other?

'Where yer from?' I asked.

'I'm fra Glasgie ee's fra Falkirk. A pissy wee place'

'Aye. It might ba te thee bit tas bitter boozers thae Glasgie.' McIntyre answered.

'Nah. London's got best boozers. Get any type of beer yer want there'

'We'd lak to knae. Werre yon matey Kingy es fra. Ye ken?' Thinking, "Hello these two buggers want to 'ave a go at Kingy"

'Dun know mate. One things fer certain it ain't London,trying to change the subject I inquired. Did yer manage to get yer tins and stuff down at Naafi?'

'Aye. An doooble o everthin.' Anderson said.

'Yer got dun. I think we all did. Those two Cows down there. Seem to know it all?' Just then, L/Cpl. King emerged from his inner sanctuary carrying his toiletries leaving the hut shouting.

'IN HALF AN HOURS TIME. IT'S LIGHTS OUT. SO GET CHUFFING MOVING AND DO. WHAT'S NECESSARY. IF YOU WANT A PISS.' As he turned and moved away Anderson muttered.

'Fooking bastard.'

'Right. If it's that time. It's like brass monkeys in here. I'll have to try out my pyjamas. Roll on tomorrow let's get a fire going and warm this soddin' place up.' Pilkington asked.

'Er dusts thee think we'd get the fooking drum int'mornin?' He was the quiet type. Most of the time kept himself to himself; he had a longish face extenuated by a high forehead, long jaw sharp pointed nose and sparkling blue eyes. Having noticed when he was undressing he was shy maybe he had something we did not have? John laughed.

'Fooking ope not. Scared shite oout termi tis'mornin.'

'Tell yer wot this Kingy. Ain't arf got a reputation. A couple of squaddies we were talking to-night in mess hall,f....d our luck. Maybe there's worst to come?' Wilkins moaned.

'Ee. Dist thee think so. I caan't stand bastard. An we oonly bin her two days.' John said.

'Well. Ta can't do fook all ta bout it.' Albert started shouting.

'Ooh. Gladys. Wert art thee Gladys? I luv yers.' John called out.

'He's off is rocker. Gee him a pill.' There was genuine burst of laughter from the others in the hut.

Putting away my kit into the bed-box was down to my army issue underpants. Wot the hell I will leave them on, sat on the bed and pulled up my very own winciette pajama bottoms tied up the cord around my waist slipped on the jacket buttoned it up, they too were at least two sizes too big? I laughed. 'If only me mum could see me now?' John exclaimed.

'I'll bet she'd 'ave a fit wit lafter. Loook at you yer a pile of shite. Thur just as bad as yur denims. Get inter fooking bed thur making huit loook unteedy.'

'Well. I don't want ter wear em anyway. But I 'ave to.' I squawked. But I did get into bed very sharpish. Kingy returning shouted. 'FIVE MINUTES.'

The sheets were cold. I got out and put my great coat over the rest of the blankets. Thinking, "That'll keep me warm". Slipping back between the cold sheets lay there shivering, miserable not even tired it was only ten o'clock and I could be down at the Beehive having a drink, instead I'm tucked up in bed in a bleedin' camp waiting for bleedin' lights out. Peeking over the top of the sheets saw most of the squaddies were in their beds, one or two were still putting things away Pilkington was kneeling down by his bed, must be pleading with God to take him back home? Shall I say a few prayers for myself? To be whisked away, back to the Beehive even if it was only for the last half-hour. At least it would be a little relief from this f.......g place. Giving up the thought, it would not work. Somewhere outside the strangled note of a trumpet echoed on the wind. Some lucky bastard was still up blowing his bleedin' brains out trying to get everyone to sleep. Little did he realise that he was keeping everyone awake with his soding din.

Lights Out, in the hut came quicker than you could blink out come Kingy.

'LIGHTS OUT. YOU MISERABLE LOT OF BASTARDS.' Someone shouted out.

'Same to you.'

'WHO SAID THAT? I WILL CHUFFING MURDER HIM. GET TO CHUFFING SLEEP. I WILL HAVE THE LOT OF YOU UP WELL BEFORE THE CRACK OF CHUFFING DAWN.'

Out went the lights. In new pyjamas curled up in a ball trying to get warm the end of my second day. To say the least, an eventful day and it had not changed my opinion. Did not like the soddin' Army. Under the confines of his blankets, the muffled sound of little Wilkins sobbing disturbed me. Poor little bastard he like us will have to get use to it. Switching my thoughts to Eileen trying to recapture her last passing farewell to me. Her perk little mouth puckered up trying to devour me or, was it the opposite way around. I felt a faint stirring in my loins but it did not last long. My pyjamas were making me itch.

CHAPTER EIGHT.
A FREE WEEK-END

Beneath the cover of the blankets, I heard the muffled beat of a drum. Boom. Boom. Boom. Exclaimed. 'Wot the hell?' Then realized it was f...g Kingy protector of Hut 37. Screwed up in a ball nice and warm within the comfort of my cocoon, the constant Boom. Boom. Boom became louder a violent jolt on the bed shook my body, about to tell whomever it was to sod off pulling back the blankets against the sudden glare of the lights screwed up my eyes. Kingy yelled.

'YOU. 'ORRIBLE MELT. GET YOUR HANDS OFF YOUR COCK AND GET ON YOUR SOCKS.' Kingy had spoken, followed by another BOOM. BOOM. The noise reverberating through my scull. Not moving just peered towards the end of the bed where Kingy's huge figure stood his arm raised, out of spite, he hit it BOOM then roared.

'YOU. GET OUT NOW' followed in quick succession by BOOM. BOOM. Still standing there a menacing figure with drum hanging by his side and arm raised about to swing down. Resigned to this rude awakening pulled back the covers and swung my legs down onto the cold floorboards.

'PYJAMAS ON I SEE.' Kingy had remembered purposefully he had come to see if I was wearing them. Satisfied he turned around made his way back up the hut beating shit out of his bleedin' drum. BOOM. BOOM. BOOM.

Through bleary eyes looked across to Wilkins, he rubbing his puffy eyes most likely from his previous nights sniveling. Taking a quick look around at the rest of them half in half out of bed, some stood up stretching and farting in unison. John was groveling around in his bed box, looking across towards the yawning face of Pilkington his mouth a great chasm displaying his uvula in his throat wobbling about as he noisily exhaled. Gladys had collapsed back down in a heap on his bed, pulling his legs up under him in an effort to keep warm. Having successfully got everyone up at the other end of the hut Kingy still beating shite out of his drum was on his way back down the other side. Spotting the form of Gladys laid on his bed immediately ran down with his big booted foot kicked the steel bed support with a crashing jar. The same treatment I had received just a few minutes before. Shouted.

'UP! YOU IDLE BASTARD. UP! YOU ARE IN THE ARMY NOW. NOT AT CHUFFING HOME. Gladys sprang up very much wide-awake stated.

'Its nae gitting oop tim yit.' Kingy mimicked.

'Its nae gitting oop tim yit. IN HUT THIRTYSEVEN. IT CHUFFING WELL IS. BOOM BOOM. GET CHUFFING DRESSED.'

So began our third day. The hands of the Mickey Mouse watch showed twenty-five to six. Aw bleedin' 'ell the middle of the night, a miserable start to Saturday. Slowly undoing the knot of the winciette bottoms, pondering on what was in store for us today, the prospects of shite for breakfast then haircuts, not a problem not much to cut off. Naafi breaks if you could get it down you. Fire duty a new venture the delights of which we would find out later followed by a Medical, then shite for lunch. A full free afternoon packed with excitement of pressing, cleaning and polishing. Normally Saturday at home was a day of sporting activity. Playing football in the afternoon, the soccer results at five followed by the fry-up mum cooked Michael and I before we went out on our separate Saturday evening binges. What is missing here? No radio, no newspapers. What is going on in the world outside? While we stuck here with Kingy embarking on a short army career. John interrupted my world of make believe.

'Yu cuming fer ter wash?' Coming back to reality, without realising it had changed into the Denims and khaki shirt and was in the process of tying up the bootlaces replied.

'Yeah. Spose so.' Quickly glancing at the Mickey Mouse watch its hands pointed to nearly twenty to six. In less than seven minutes, we had been rudely woken up changed into working clothes and were about to enter into a fight to get a soddin' cold wash. This was not justice! Grabbing my toiletries followed the rest of them out of the hut into the blackness outside. It was still pissing down and the howling wind forced the rain horizontal. The morning race had begun running along with all rest of the dark shadows in front besides and behind me; through the washhouse doorway, the dim light guided us like moths around a light bulb. When we got there a mass of heaving bodies, were all trying to get in at once to secure a prized place at the cold taps? It was not an orderly way to get in, but who the f..k cared. Once inside the mass of squaddies carried on milling around the water trough enticed by the cold-water eager to splash it on their faces. With exclamations of Ooh's. Aagh's and Fook as they gasped for breath. I headed for the pissoire had a slash and returned to the melee to sort out an entrance into the scrum. No way, looking up recognized the tall squaddie that yesterday morning had dug a hole in my head with his elbow he still in the same position head close to the light bulb busily doing his shaving routine. Was he still shaving from yesterday? I asked him.

'Hoi mate. Can I get in there fer a wash?' Looking down at me, he smirked.

'You'll be fooking lucky. Wait until I come out.'

If I waited for him, I would be there a week. Someone forced his way out three tried to get in. I won. The cold water was colder than yesterday, how could that be? Sluicing it around the back of my neck, its coldness astounded me and woke up parts I did not know had shuddered. Ooogh! Please God give me some hot water, finished doing my ablutions this time with my very own bar of soap fought my way out of the washhouse and back into the blackness and rain as I ran back, somewhere in the camp some idiot was blowing his bleedin' brains out trying to wake everyone up with renditions of REVEILLE. It was 0600 hours. Hadn't anyone informed him he was late! By courtesy of Kingy the camp had apparently been up since 0530 hours he beating his drum must have woken all within hearing distance as well as the inhabitants of Honiton.

Entering the hut the place looked as if a hurricane had been through it, Anderson and Gladys were the only others back, at least it was dry albeit freezing cold. Passing Gladys, he muttered.

'Sum baastard swopped mi soop,' Thought, "Tough! It happens to all of us". Putting the toiletries away hung up the greatcoat re-arranging and smoothing out the sheets and pillows remade the bed with blankets laid central and squared off. Hearing a movement behind me, expecting it to be Wilky or John looked around. It was Kingy roaring.

'THAT. SOLDIER! IS NO WAY TO MAKE UP A CHUFFING BED?' Walking past shoving me aside he got hold of the folded down sheet and blanket section. Zip off came the lot thrown in a heap on the floor, the under sheet was stripped off and thrown on top of the pile of blankets quickly followed by the pillow and mattress. He yelled so close to my ear, the wax came out the other side.

'NOW IN FUTURE. CHUFFING IDIOT. WHEN YOU MAKE UP YOUR BED. YOU START BY TURNING OVER THE MATTRESS FIRST. THEN REMAKE THE CHUFFING BED.' I stood there shitting myself muttered.

'Yes Lance Corporal.'

My bed space was just the beginning. He began to throw everything off each bed stopping at Gladys; decided that Gladys bed was far too tidy ripped that apart and, just for the sheer hell of it, carried on doing the same to all of them. Looking at Gladys rolling his eyes skywards, balled his fist made an uppercut I think he mouthed, "Fooking Bastard". As others entered they just stood at the entrance as Kingy did the works, he went past them like a steam train before returning to his room leaving the door ajar. The hut now looked as if a tornado had hit it. The group at the doorway began to pick their way back to their own bed space, taking care not to tread muddy wet boots onto any of the sheets or blankets amongst the debris of bedding. As I began to pick up the bedding John arrived back, looking at his spring-framed bed he enquired.

'Wit te fook 'appened here?' I explained what I was doing when Kingy crept up on me and started on me bed

'He need's is fooking 'ead eggsamined.' He said indignantly adding...I niver turrn ter mattress atome. Neether dust me mither, maybe once evera six weeks or mooer'

'Well according to Kingy. In this hut you have to do it three soding times a soding day, this is bleedin' stupid. No wonder they get you up so bleedin' early.' Having already hauled the mattress back onto the bed and started with the under sheets, when Wilky arrived back. John advised him.

'Kingy's on't woorpath wit bedding agin.' Poor old Wilky dejectedly sat down on the bedsprings, towel drooped around his neck and with a look of dismay on his face, moaned.

'I win't ter goo 'ome'. I encouraged him.

'C'mon Wilky. It's only your bleedin' bed mate.'

'No. Taint. Tis hole fooking lot. I'm sik ov it.' John offered.

'Twer all sick of it. Ant ter's nowt yu can do aboot it'.

'I'm goin ter reet ter my MP aboot it. I'm sik ov it.' Wilky replied sitting there on the bedsprings looking the picture of misery his toiletries still in his hand, adorning his face were a few dabs of white paper daubed with crimson. Self-inflicted wounds a chargeable offense. Gee-ing him up and lying said.

'C'mon Wilky. We got free time this afternoon and. We got eggs, bacon, sausage and mash fer breakfast.'

'Ow dyer noo that theen?' He enquired.

'I met a cook down Naafi last night, He told us. Ain't that right John?' John added.

'Yeah. An he said. Tomorro bean' te Sunday. Tis rooast bef yorkshire pud un tu veg.' Wilky seemed to brighten up at this idea.

'Well. I'm still sik ov it.' I suggested.

'Wilky. Were all sick of it? Particularly with that bastard down the end. If ever I see him in civvy street after I get out of Kate. I'll knock shit out of him.' Wilky retorted.

'Gerra way. Yus coodn't knock shite oot ter. piper bag. Ter half his heet.' I suggested.

'Well! We'll both do it together then. Wot der say to that. Eh Wilky?' Wilky swelling up replied.

'Ee eck! That urd be greet. Kicking shite outer im ter big bastard.' Wilky now back on a level plain was lifting up his mattress. Kingy coming out of his room roared.

'GET THIS CHUFFING HUT CLEANED UP READY FOR MY INSPECTION AT O' SEVENFIFTY HOURS.' Wilky tucking in his under sheet. Muttered.

'Fooking bastard.'

By 0645, the beds had been made and some idea of kit layout was in progress. Kingy came out of his room stormed out of the hut shouting.

'NOT STRAIGHT ACCORDING TO REGULATIONS. GET IT DONE PROPERLY. THAT GOES FOR ALL OF YOU CHUFFING BASTARDS.' Anderson livid at this new onslaught by Kingy muttered.

'I'll morder te bastard. Afore I leave here.' Someone else said.

'No ter won't mate, ter aboot fifth in ter queue.' In a jubilant manner, Wilky called out.

'Were't fist. Dun ere.'

The Kit Layout photograph was studied again, making the best attempt possible to get the webbing right, however you tried six times out of ten it lost its shape we gave up and went to get breakfast. That just turned out to be the same as Friday's menu. Lumpy porridge and hard tack biscuit's. We did not eat breakfast. Wilky hissed at us

'Use twos. Er fooking liars.'

Back in the hut we began the clean up. Kingy re-entered deposited his eating utensils in his room. At 0750 he came out roaring. 'STAND BY YOUR BEDS.'

We sprang to attention. Starting at the far end, he grunted and groaned at each bed space mentally making notes as he progressed right around the hut passing us, his piggy eyes boring into ours until he arrived in the middle of the hut where the cleaning kit was chucked in a heap. Brooms, coal bucket dustpans etc. whoever used them last just left them at ease! Kingy standing with hands on his hips went ballistic.

'WHO IS CHUFFING RESPONSIBLE FOR THIS PILE OF SHIT?...Nobody volunteered... WHO IS ON FIRE DUTY THIS MORNING?'

'Here Lance Corporal.' We chorused. He raved.

'GET YOUR ARSES UP HERE ON THE DOUBLE.'

We doubled towards him.

'YOU TWO. I MIGHT HAVE CHUFFING WELL GUESSED. WHO'S GOT THE CHALK?'

'I have Lance Corporal.'

'WHERE'S. THE HUT NUMBER ON THE COAL BUCKET?'

'Don't know Lance Corporal.'

'DON'T CHUFFING KNOW? AREN'T YOU. THE SIGN WRITER?' I suggested.

'No Lance Corporal. A Draughtsman.'

'SAME CHUFFING THING. YOU ARE SUPPOSED TO CHALK THE HUT NUMBER ON ITS SIDE. CHUFFING IDIOT.'

'Yes Lance Corporal.'

'WHY? ISN'T IT DONE THEN?'

'Didn't have time. Lance Corporal.' Going red in the face, he raved.

'TIME! YOU HAVE HAD PLENTY OF TIME. YOU HAVE BEEN UP SINCE O' FIVE THIRTY HOURS. I KNOW. BECAUSE. I GOT YOU UP. YOU CHUFFING IDIOT. GET STARTED NOW.'

Running back getting a stick of chalk on the way back saw Kingy running his finger around the top of the Pot Stove, looking at his finger turned around to face John showing the palm of his hand, he asked rather politely.

'Do you see any dust on my fingers?'

'Err. Yes Lance Corporal.'

'If. The stove has been cleaned. Should there be any dust on my fingers?'

'Er. No Lance Corporal.'

'Have you got any Zebo?'

'Yes Lance Corporal'

'Well. I suggest that you use some and when you do. You will polish it. So that no black smudges are left on, my fingers won't you 540? He roared. GET A DUSTER AND WIPE THE TOP OVER.

'Yes Lance Corporal.' John doubled away as I finished sign writing HUT 37 on the coal bin stood up. His attention was now on the tin bath and me.

'You finished 429. Let me see.' I stood to one side as he peered down at it.

'That is not very good for a Draughtsman is it 429?'

'I don't know Lance Corporal. It's first attempt.' He said menacingly.

'Well. You had better improve by your second attempt. Hadn't you 429?'

'Yes Lance Corporal.' At that moment, the door opened and in walked the Officer and his entourage. Kingy ordered.

'Get back to your bed space. Mooove.' We ran back and took up position beside our bed as Kingy bawled out.

'HUT THIRTYSEVEN. READY FOR INSPECTION. SIR.' The officer informed him.

'Right Lance Corporal King. I will start with your room first.' Heaving a sigh of relief as they walked away John muttered.

'Fooking 'ell. I din't know we had ter do it. Ter fire's not even bin fooking aleet yet.' Out of the corner of my mouth muttered.

'See Wilky. Were in the shit over summat else not just bleedin' beds.' Sgt. Barnes shouted.

'WHO'S TALKING DOWN THE END. NO TALKING DURING OFFICERS INSPECTION. ONLY SPEAK WHEN YOU'RE SPOKEN TO.'

The silence was audible as we all stood beside our beds to await his scrutiny of the motley mob under his command. After having been issued with our uniforms this was the first time, we had been inspected by 2nd. Lt. Holmes. Moreover, was gratefully conscious of the fact that my pair of shoulder tits had now disappeared. Leaving Kingy's room, the officer moved slowly around each bed, prodding with his stick at something or other he had noticed making comments to Sgt. Barnes. Who responded with some words or grunted. 'Yes Sir.' Slowly he moved down towards us, Wilky was clearly agitated by what was going on, the Officer looked at him moving past looked at his kit laid out on his bed. He prodded and poked made a comment about the top kit and came back to confront a Wilky blurted out.

'Sir.'

'Yes. What is it?'

'I shood noot be err. I've git ter sik mither at t'ome.'

'Oh. Have you brought this to the Sergeant's notice?'

'Ee eck. No. Sir.'

'Is she dying?'

'No. Sir.'

'You're Mother. What' ails her?'

'Ee. It's ter floo Sir. Proper poorly sha's.'

'Sergeant Barnes. Take a note of this soldier's details and get the PSO (Personnel Selection Officer) to make contact with his Mother. Cannot have someone like this fine specimen of manhood worried about his mother now. Can we?'

'No Sir. Right Sir.' Sgt. Barnes designated the chain of command.

'Lance Corporal Gabe. Take note of that man's details.' The matter finished, they moved onto me. He looked at me; he walked round to my bed and started poking about.

'Not very good this layout. When is the Platoon going to blanco their kit Sergeant?'

'After their midday meal Sir.' The officer stood in front of me eyed me up once more, and then moved onto John, walked behind him to inspect his bed and kit.

'This is not good enough Sergeant. This kit needs a lot more work than what has been put into it.'

'Yes. Sir.' Facing John he looked at me.

'I must say Sergeant. That the hut is rather cold in here. These two here put them on fire duty.' Sgt. Barnes commented.

'Yes Sir. Begging your pardon Sir. But they are already on fire duty for the next week Sir.' To which the officer responded.

'Oh right! Good. These two need a bit of extra duty.' Thinking, "Extra duty, soding cheek". He moved away and completed the rest of the hut in rapid time before he and his entourage were about to depart stopped.

'Who left the lights on in this hut? Waste of army money. Deduct it from their pay. Barrack room damages. Lance Corporal Gabe. Sort them out along with all their queries. Whilst I inspect hut thirty-nine.'

'Yes Sir.' L/Cpl. Gabe carried out his orders making a beeline straight for Wilky.

'What is this about your mother then? You trying the old trick then? Someone sick at home? Is there anyone else at home besides you?' An unsuspecting Wilky replied.

'Ee. Eck. Yes Lance Corporal. Me Da and two sisters.'

'Right. They can look after her. You. Are looking for extra duties. Aren't you? Take your mind off the subject. Won't it?'

'Ee. No-o. Lance Corporal. No-o-ot treeing anything on.' His face red with guilt and embarrassment.

'Right. Today and tomorrow is blanco time. After YOU have blanco-ed all your kit. YOU will. Tomorrow. At sixteen hundred hours. Be dressed in FSMO and ready for my inspection Savvy.' A very dejected Wilky replied.

'Yes Lance Corporal.' As he passed by us turned and with a smirk on his face said.

'You two. Fire duty. Ten thirty hours. Right has anyone else. Got a sick mother. Sick Dog. Cat. Rabbit or, anything they wish to inform me about?' No response, it was obvious to all. "Do Not Complain". He slowly walking past each squaddie he had a go at every one. Then ordered.

'EVERYONE OUTSIDE. LINE UP IN SINGLE FILE MOOOVE.' It was his way of saying he had finished with his comments. As the bees formed around the entrance asked John.

'Wot's this new thing about lights and barrack room damages then?'

'Dun noo. Moor cash te pay oot. Sommat else we'll find oot aboot.'

Outside the rain had stopped but it was bitterly cold. We lined up and stood facing the hut awaiting the arrival of the rest of the platoon from hut 39. However, the Army time was not going to be wasted? L/Cpl. Gabe busied himself inspecting us. I heard him yell at someone. 'Do up that Button on your left leg pocket.' It was not long before stood in front of me, with a smirk on his face he shouted.

'429. YOU GOT RID OF YOUR TIT'S?' Some laughter was heard from the far end. Very pleased with myself yelled.

'YES. LANCE CORPORAL.'

'GOOD! I AM GLAD YOU DECIDED TO LEAVE THE A.T.S. OR WAS IT THE CAMEL CORPS? AND TRANSFER TO A PROPER ARMY.... AREN'T YOU. 429?' More subdued laughter along the line.

'YES. LANCE CORPORAL.'

'STILL A PILE OF SHIT. AREN'T YOU 429?' Even more laughter.

'YES. LANCE CORPORAL. STILL A PILE OF SHIT. LANCE CORPORAL.' The only sensible answer was 'Yes' to everything; otherwise, further duties would be dished out. He moved to the next squaddie however, our attention was drawn away to a new feature; there still was civilisation outside the camp something none of us had time to notice before. At the top of the rise from our right appeared a train, its engine emitting plumes of black smoke and white steam as with a blast of its whistle it clanked past until the last coach clattered by. The sound of its whistle halted Cpl. Gabe's inspection of Wilky. Taking a few paces forward faced us.

'Now then. That train is the London bound train. But. None of you. Are getting on it. And for your added information. Anyone even trying to think of getting out of camp. Do remember that the only way out. Is past the guardhouse. With I might add. A Bona fide

Pass. That will not happen for the next four weeks.' So endeth his lesson, you could feel the dejection melt from our bodies, into the hard ground where we stood. Returning his attention to Wilky demanded.

'Take out. Your AB64 part one.' Wilky uttered a puzzled question.

'Me wit? Lance Corporal.'

'You're brown pay book soldier.' Wilky completely understanding what was required answered.

'Left it, in't tother pooket. Lance Corporal.' L/Cpl. Gabe yelled.

'Right. Everyone. Get out their AB64 part one. Hold it above your heads.' Buttons were undone those that had them held them aloft. Looking along the line, he spoke up.

'Those. WITHOUT their AB64's One pace forward.' About five stepped forward.

'You. 'Orrible lot of chuffing melts. Double to the hut and get them. Mooove. The rest of you clever bastards. Return your AB64's to its right and proper place. Button up. Stand still. Keep quiet.'

The defective five, quickly returned from hut 37 to take up their places in the line as running behind them the occupants of Hut 39 joined the line. Followed by the Officer, Sgt. and L/Cpl. Sgt. Barnes stood surveying the line roared.

'YOU 'ORRIBLE LOT. CAN'T YOU REMEMBER THE SOLDIER; YOU WERE STANDING NEXT TO YESTERDAY? GET SORTED OUT. YOUR ALL PILES OF SHIT.' A lot of shuffling, as about eight bodies danced around did a couple of dozy does too disrupt the formed line and changed places. Sgt. Barnes roared.

'FROM THE RIGHT, NUMBER.'

'One. Two....Three Four... Five ......six. ......seven............eight.....

'NO. NO. NO. I DO NOT WANT HESITATIONS. I WANT RAPIDITY. FROM THE RIGHT, NUMBER.' We did it again, he was satisfied...Fall in in three ranks. Mooove.' More shuffling, as we formed into three ranks.

'PITOON...ATTEN...HOW...EFT.TAR...KWICK...AARCH.'

We were off to get our haircut; it was precisely eight thirty by the hands of the Mickey Mouse watch. We clumped to the top of the square totally out of step along to the far end where a line of Cricket Pavilion styled buildings stood. Further on, we wiot wheeled up a slope, then an 'eft wheel took us past some more buildings that Sgt. Barnes Reverently informed us.

'If anyone wishes to have their sins forgiven? Those are the places you may visit. In your own time of course?' In other words never. Approaching some buildings on our left, just as we passed them Sgt. Barnes shouted.

'PITOON...AAAAL...WIOT...TAR...STAND EASY.' A lot of shuffling and banging we faced Sgt. Barnes, gleefully rubbing his gloved hands together haltingly said.

'Right. You. Lucky. Bastards. It is time. For your first Army haircut. For your information. The Barber is a civilian employed by the Army to cut hair. He. God bless him. Holds the rank of a. WO1. Warrant Officer Class One. In other words. You treat him the same as you treat senior NCOs. Only speak when you are spoken too. Savvy? Now just think of it. He is a civilian and, needs paying for his service. As all of you in civvy street paid for a haircut. So for each haircut, a sum of six-pence will be deducted each week out of your army pay, as I am sure YOU will all need one. Savvy? If you look down you will notice on either side of that doorway. Stood at ease are two dustbins. Through that doorway. You will enter into the barber's emporium. Now form up into single line MOOOVE... A quick shuffle and we were in single line...Mooove towards the curb.' More shuffling and scraping of boots until the curb lined us up Sgt.Barnes then ordered the tallest squaddie.

'Right. You Lofty, in the front... Lead off down to that door where Lance Corporal's Gabe and Smethers are stood. Then stand still.'

Going down the four steps by the door Lofty halted, those behind on the stairs almost toppled over onto the man in front. At precisely 0845, the door opened and in went L/Cpl. Gabe quickly followed by the first five squaddies, counted in by L/Cpl. Smethers who pulling the door shut remained outside. We shuffled forward five paces. In a matter of minutes out came Lofty rubbing the back of his shorn head, at the top of the steps. Sgt. Barnes muttered.

'Replace you beret and join the end of the queue.'

Doing as ordered Lofty's ears held up his beret, as he walked past me feeling the back of his scalped neck muttering, 'He's a fooking butcher, not a barber.'

In a matter of minutes the next tallest came out, ascending the steps walking past me swearing to himself. I thought. "It was a good thing that on Tuesday went for a trim up at Phil's the local hairdresser". Phil was a young Hairdresser who was into men's hair coiffure in a big way, taking advantage of the sudden demand for the new developing hairstyles. The Tony Curtis, DA's, Crew Cuts, Blow-waving was his specialty. As I reached the top of the steps seeing the two dustbins already full up with hair that was all forgotten as we descended one step at a time inching forward to where L/Cpl. Smethers was stood, as one shorn head came out he let another unshorn in. Entering through the doorway of the. Hall of Future Coiffure, inside stood a smiling Cpl. Gabe who ordered.

'Off beret. Take a seat.'

Against the wall were four chairs, sitting down in the vacant seat about to take note of the proceedings. The Barber with his back to us was a tall man, dressed in short white coat black trousers and black shoes, his shaved neck had a neatly trimmed hairline. With arms raised to the head of the seated squaddie, one hand held it forward as the other using a haircutting machine zzZZzz zzZZzz ed scalped the recipients head. Slipping the machine in his pocket produced a four-inch paintbrush, deftly he swept away the fallen locks of the shorn soldier, it was John getting up from the barber's chair (just an ordinary one). The Barber turning round, revealed he had several strands of black hair swept over the top of his shiny baldhead, having plastered them down in a misguided attempt to disguise his baldness. Wearing a pair of thick lens horn rimmed spectacles, maybe if he took them off he could see better and make a proper job of everyone's hair? His Roman nose did nothing to enhance his looks. With outstretched arms in one hand held a black comb in the other the brush and with a smile invited. 'Next one please.'

The squaddie at the end got up, by his haircut immediately recognized him as the Teddy boy from. 'Ighbry North London. His dark black locks still groomed the way he obviously liked it. He had not gone sick therefore must be in hut 39. Reluctantly he approached the chair; his face was ashen maybe from fear, as we three moved up one another sat down beside me. 'Ibury settled himself in the barber's chair, we in anticipation waited for the Barbers next move. The sheep shearer looking into the long mirror hanging on the wall reflecting 'Ibury's locks.' Gesticulated and preened over the magnificent head of hair sat in front of him he spoke loudly.

'Aah- ha. What have we here? What a wonderful head of hair. Mooost encouraging. How would you like it cut. Sir?'

This took us all by surprise. Obviously, he was very impressed at what he saw. The Teddy boy could not believe his luck this sheep shearer had recognized his hairstyle. The mirror in front of the barber's chair reflected the face of the loner. More colour had flushed his cheeks and was a picture of gratitude, in contrast to the scraggy baldhead of the leering sheep Shearer behind cupping his hands around the sides of the thick black mop of hair exclaimed.

109

'Wonderful head of hair.' The Teddy boy said.

'Hoi Mate. I'm real proud of me hair style. Can yer, just take enuf of the sides and the back, so that sargeant wot yer mer call im. Won't keep on shouting at me. Ter. Git yer haircut.'

'Certainly Sir.' Leered the sheep Shearer turning towards L/Cpl. Gabe.

'Lance Corporal. What do you think? Is that exceptable?'

'Yes. That is fine. But make sure it is short and tidy though. I don't want a bollocking.'

'Right Sir. Just tilt your head forward slightly. Yes. That's right. Good. Just a little further.'

The sheep Shearer placed his hand firmly on the crown of the head of hair, purposely forcing the head forward holding it. ZzZZzz. The electric haircutter came to life the sheep Shearer was about to attack. Zoom the haircutter swathed a path deep into the black DA up over the top to stop at the crown of the head leaving a white pathway, another swift movement took another wide slice out of the hair quickly followed by another. Before the Teddy boy knew what was going on? The back of his head was shorn white. Forcibly his head was pushed to one side and with a couple of quick zips, his sideburns disappeared; the same treatment was quickly applied on the other side. He had been shorn army style. Finished, the sheep Shearer removed his restraining hand. The Teddy boy lifting up his head looked into the mirror, seeing the devastation that had just taken place the whiteness of his scalp matched his protruding ears, his face seething with rage was scarlet.

'Hoi. Wot the F..K Yer playing at? Yer said. Yer'd just trim it up for sargeant. Me hair do's. F.......g butchered. As the Sheep Shearer stood there knee deep in black hair replied.

'In accordance with the sergeants instructions. I did trim it up my good man.' Adding insult to injury, as the Teddy boy staggered out towards the door he gave him a quick brush down. Noticed L/Cpl. Gabe smile as the defrocked Teddy boy fell out through the door. The sheep Shearer pointed to me.

'You there. Get that broom sweep up that pile of hair into that dustpan and take it outside to the dustbins.'

I got up, moved across to where a broom with an extra long brush head was propped up against the wall, beside it the large open jaws of the dustpan lay on the floor. Taking hold of the broom handle began to sweep away the evidence from around the sheep shearer's feet, the different coloured fallen chunks of hair mainly black into a big pile. Meanwhile the zzZZzz-ing of the haircutter continued as more chunks of hair fell to the floor. Finding it difficult to manhandle both the brush head and the large dustpan together using my foot to steady the dustpan somehow managed and carried the mass of hair towards the doorway. A grinning L/ Cpl. Gabe kindly opened the door for me.

Outside both dustbins were already full of hair, judging the left one to be the least full tipped the full dustpan onto the different coloured hair whilst in the process, had to stand aside to let the latest shorn head pass on his way out, which made me the next but one for the chop. With little time to spare returned to my seat to gaze around the room. It was very sparse and definitely not a Barbers shop. There was no sink, one mirror, a single light bulb dangled directly above the conveniently placed operating chair; the extra long broom head and dustpan propped up the sidewall. Clinging to a nail in the wall was the sheep shearer's black coat and a Homburger hat, lying on the floor below was his open empty brief case. Adding a touch of class to this Barber's emporium. Partly hidden from view by the figure of L/Cpl. Gabe, was a Picture of Dennis Compton advertising Brylcreem. There were no magazines. So you were forced to watch the humiliation of the unfortunate in the operating chair. Then it was my turn. Walking to the chair sat down looked into the mirror to wait for the buzz saw to do its bit. There was no thought of a barber's cloth to keep the falling hair off one's person, the principle being let it fall onto the person after all; it was his hair in the first place. Talking to me via the mirror the sheep shearer said.

'Oh. You've just recently had your hair cut then?'

'Er Yer. I thought it best too.'

'That was a sensible idea. Saves me sweeping up a lot? You will not take long. Head down please.'

His hand forced the back of my head forward. ZzZZzz zzZZzz went the shearing machine, digging into the back of my neck zipped over the back of my head, whatever bristles I had was gone then the side's five zips all finished. Looking into the mirror, saw a white scar mark like a round ring around the top of my head, above that was the remains of my crew cut standing up like a toilet brush thinking. "Soddin 'ell he couldn't 'ave done better with a razor". Standing up the sheep Shearer brushed away the little lumps of fluff before shoving me out, another satisfied customer done. 'Next please.'

Staggering out past the grinning face of L/Cpl. Gabe. The bitter wind swirling around my shorn head sent a cold shiver down my spine. The growl of Sgt. Barnes urged.

'You. Up here. Take your place at the rear.'

Pulling on the beret, which was then very loose on my head, ascended the steps to fall in with the rest of the long line of shorn sheep. I could not help but notice the other Squaddies berets, after the recent shearing job they were more than loose, some hung extremely low on the head almost covering their eyes headbands certainly needed more adjustment. Falling in line behind the last man stared at the back of his gleaming white shorn neck, lifting my hand up to the back of my head with fingertips felt no bristles; it was almost as if it was shaved thinking. "Bleedin' six-pence for that shave". The couple of blokes in front of me were in the same state; amongst them was the defrocked Teddy boy. From the rear he looked bleedin' ridiculous, the weight of his beret was held up by his horizontal ears forcing me to stifle a laugh. As we waited for the last few to return from the sheep Shearer, you could feel the strange silence amongst the ranks moreover it did not take very long. The last three shorn sheep one by one walking past me joined the file behind, the last one little Wilky the rim of his beret was below the level of his eyebrows, his lips quivering. I grinned, but got no response. Glancing down at the Mickey Mouse watch it was nearly ten o' clock. Bleedin' "ell, thirty-two blokes had been done in just about an hour; the Honiton Sheep Shearer was trying for a world record. The Sgt. interrupted my thoughts as he addressed us.

'Right you idle shower. Now you are all respectable. With your hair neat and tidy... Pause...I think, he was waiting for someone to pass a comment, but no one did...At all times. You. Will keep your hair cut like that. The Barber will be more than pleased to see you all again, FREQUENTLY (Deliberately emphasised) and by the sight of some of your berets. You will all need to adjust the headbands. However, that will be done this afternoon in your spare time...NOW. You 'Orrible lot. It is your well-earned Naafi break so, the quicker you march the more time you will have in the Naafi. 'A' PITOON Form into three ranks. Mooove.' Shuffle Shuffle Bang. 'A' PITOON...ATTE...HOW...QWICK. AARCH...EFT. EFT. EFT. WIOT EFT.'

We set off marching or stumbling partly running at break neck speed retracing our steps towards the square. Very quickly, the reason for the panic marching became evident. It was the Naafi break race every other platoon was under the same orders. You could see them advancing from all directions racing along nevertheless, they had been taught how to march at double quick time, short steps twenty to the dozen, arms pumping away outstretched in front of them shoulder high. Left Right Left Left Left Right... All with the same purpose to beat all other platoons and be first in the Naafi queue. This was not the first or indeed last time, we were entered for the daily Naafi break race. However we, all out of step trying to keep our berets from falling over our eyes, some with heads tilted backwards peeping under the rims as we galloped along the top roadway towards the end with a sharp right wheol came to a.... AAAALT. Right alongside the Naafi steps what a f...g shambles. We did not know how to march or do synchronised running that would come later. Sgt. Barnes ordered.

'Right. You idle lot. You are far too slow for Naafi break. I want everyone back up on the roadway in three ranks sharp at ten thirty hours and I mean ten thirty hours. PITOON. WIOT...TAR. FALL OUT.'

A quick right turn dispersed us to join the melee at the top of the steps. We went down the steps bumping and shoving eager to join the end of the queue that was already two miles long. If, we were lucky we might get a cup of scalding hot tea and a wad to bite into. By the time we eventually got inside the scene was the same as the previous morning's episode. A heaving mass of squaddies slurping mugs of tea and taking great bites out of wads and cakes as if they had never eaten before. By the skin of our teeth we managed to get served before the shutters came rattling down. Roars from angry squaddies shouting for blood, some trying to hold up the shutters. We stood in a corner mesmerised by the sheer pace of activity going on around us, hardly anyone of the newly sheep shorn mob spoke as they scalded their lips on the tea and joined in the ravenous way of eating wads and cakes. Most still shell shocked by the shearing job were rubbing the back of their scalped heads; as if that would encourage hairs to miraculously grow. Sgt. Barnes appeared at the doorway yelling.

'HUT THIRTYSEVEN. HUT THIRTYNINE. OUTSIDE ON THE ROADWAY NOW.'

We were conditioned when the word of command was issued to jump. Down went the tea, stuffing the remnants of cake into mouths we were off like scalded cats, scrambling up the steps behind the other heaving and struggling mass of squaddies that spilled out onto the road to form up into three ranks. Whilst the two DI's pushed and shoved us Sgt. Barnes screamed obscenities at us, for being idle on parade.

'PRIVATES. 429 - 540 - 623 - 654. THREE PACES FORWARD. MOOOVE.'

Our Que. Moving three paces forward stood still. The four of us well spaced out in line. Then he spoke.

'You four Idiots. NOW's your chance to make everyone happy by getting some fires lit. You four. Will double back to your huts; pick up the coal receptacle. Double to the coal store and collect your huts coal ration. Double back to your huts, where you will light the fire. By eleven hundred hours. You will return at the double to the MRS. that is located close to the Barbers. And I mean. Eleven hundred hours. Dismiss. We walked away. He roared.

'DOUBLE. I SAID DOUBLE. YOU IDLE BASTARDS.'

With those words of comfort ringing in our ears we crashed in through the hut door, grabbing the Coal Receptacle crashed out doubled down past the washhouse in the direction of the Rifle Range. We did not have a clue where we were heading hard on our heels behind us, were the two from Hut 39. At the Rifle Range John shouted.

'Cooal dumps down ter reet.' As we made our way down the gradient, spotted others carrying coal receptacles racing towards the coal dump breathless I cried out.

'C'mon John. This is another bleedin' race.' We arrived at the gateway third in line. The first pair was already being served their ration of coal. Gasping for breath I had a stitch, the next two were served and then it was our turn. The duty Coalman wearing a leather waistcoat and gloves prompted.

'New intake Eh? Hold on tight.' Three shovelfuls crashed into the bath. John asked.

'Git sumat te leet fire wit?'

'Over there. Take three sticks and some paper that's yer fooking ration.' Thinking. "Ration! Soddin' 'ell that lot will set the world alight". With our heavy load held between us, we doubled back to the hut. Knackered wheezing and gasping for breath looked at the watch its hands pointed to eight minutes to eleven, yelled.

'We got eight minutes to light this soding fire and get to the MRS. 'Urry up.' John put some paper and three sticks in, waving his outstretched hand about shouted.

'Matches.'

'I ain't got any. Don't bleedin' smoke.' Panic set in John screamed.

'Oh shite lits leeve it.'

'No Way. I am not being beaten up by that bunch of animals, just because of a fire. Find some.' We split up searching the bed spaces for a match to light the bleedin' fire or two boy scouts anything. John screamed out.

'Ee. I found one o' Te Joocks leeter's.'

'C'mon. Set it alight then.' Setting the paper alight threw in some coals within seconds the draft from the stovepipe did the rest, after a couple of minutes it was ablaze, John muttered.

'Leev it tis aleet.'

Running out of the hut continued all the way passing the Honiton Butchers Coiffure for men, towards the large figure of Sgt. Barnes standing outside the MRS.

'Where the shite. Have you two idle bastards been? Down a coalmine? Your are five minutes late. I told you to be here at eleven hundred hours sharp. Where the other two Idiots from hut thirty-nine?'

We stood there with chests heaving; the picture of Olympic heroes hearts banging away inside of our chest gasping to catch our breath, could not answer for ourselves never mind them. Soon the other two idiots came staggering up. Collapsing alongside of us, he was not impressed growled.

'Stand up. You chuffing idle bastards. Where do you think you are? On a picnic? The other two struggled up off their knees...Now you four. Double on the spot. LEF. LEF. LEF. GET THEM KNEEES UP.'

Shagged out and forced to do some extra running my boots weighing a ton were killing me and my legs felt like lead, as my beret had slipped over my eyes was unable to see tilting my head back saw Sgt. Barnes move off the road towards a door, opening it roared. 'FORWARD AT THE DOUBLE. IN SINGLE FILE. MOOOVE.' We doubled or, staggered into a large room, obviously the MRS. I did need a Doctor. 'HAAALT' he roared. We collapsed he yelled. 'STAND UP STRAIGHT. DO NOT MOVE.' LAST FOUR HERE DOC.' Our Platoon stood in single file stripped to the waist with braces holding up their denim bottoms, their AB 64's at the ready, three paces to one side lay discarded clothes in a regimental line. At the far end was a Doctor with his stethoscope glued to a private's chest. You were done where you stood. Sgt. Barnes roaring brought us back to life.

'YOU FOUR. STRIP OFF. DOWN TO YOUR WAIST. Remove your AB64 part ones from your breast pocket and have it ready for the Doctor. JOIN THE LINE IN THAT GAP.'

Panting and heaving we moved into the dividing gap of. "Done and Not Done". He came up alongside of us, ordered those done.

'Stand still do not move.' One at a time, we moved forward and then it was my turn. The Doctor was an army officer in disguise. His giveaway brown boots, silk shirt and gabardine tie clearly visible through his open white coat; he was tall and looked like Peter Lorre with his goldfish eyes, which squinted at you. Assisted by two orderlies both in short white coats, but identified by black shiny boots and hairy shirts they were of lower caste. One demanded. 'AB64.' Handed it over, the doctor asked.

'Last three?'

'429. Sir.'

'Right. 429. Let's see what shape you are in. Cover up your left eye and read the bottom line on that wall card behind me...I read out the appropriate line...Now the other....Okay now ears...using that nasty looking instrument checked my ears then quickly followed by the spatula job...Open wide. Sore throat?'

'No. Sir.'

'Good. Heart and lungs next.' Clamping the stethoscope to my chest enquired.

'Have you been running or something?'

'Coal duty Sir'

'Oh that! That is all right then. Turn around...Thump Thump...Turn around drop your trousers and underpants..."Kit inspection"...Cough...You are fit.' He said something to the assistant, who scribbled away in my AB64 handing it back stated.

'Back of line.' Behind me, the last three were done in double quick time. The disguised officer addressed all.

'Next TAB vaccinations and a Schick tests. Stand where you are in line. Place both hands on hips like this. (Demonstrated). Thus allowing the two orderlies here, to insert the needle easily and correctly.'

Armed with two giant sized hypodermic needles fit for elephants, the two orderlies approaching Lofty at the head of the line standing on either side of him...the disguised doctor ordered. 'GO'. In went the needles into both Lofty's upper arms a quick squirt and a dab of antiseptic onto next victims arm. The line of idiots were done at the double. No time to be squeamish or, pull one arm away it was done. The worst off, the last few in the line evidence of blood pouring out of the wounds inflicted, dribbling down the victims arm. Cause! Blunt needles. However, that was not the end of needles torture.

At the head of the line of idiots a table was placed. Armed with two fresh giant hypodermic needles, the two orderlies positioned themselves side by side on the opposite side of the table, one called out.

'First man forward...Lofty stepped forward and was quickly dealt with...Next.' And on it went until it was my turn at the table. One orderly advised.

'Reverse both arms lay them flat on the table with wrists exposed...What for? Did not have a clue. Having done as instructed soon found out. Both orderlies stuck a needle in each wrist. Horrified watched to see two small bubbles erupt beneath my skin, thinking "My God. Wots all this about"? You are done. Next.' Whatever it was for it was over, rejoining the rear of the line, sore and confused as to what had been pumped into me. Within a matter of minutes, the Medical was over. The disguised doctor instructed.

'Sergeant Barnes. Medical all completed. March them out.'

'Thank you Sir. Right you 'Orrible lot. Get dressed and get back outside in three ranks. Mooove.'

Somebody did, a very tall private collapsed in a heap. Sgt Barnes shouted.

'Leave him. The orderlies will sort him out.' The orderlies did attend the heap spread-eagled on the floor arms and legs everywhere. We dressing, watched as the two orderlies began fanning him with his AB64 Part I., a quick way to revive him. Coming too sat up the colour of a ghost, forcibly was helped into the standing position; he was deathly white from shock including the nipples on his torso. A few more fans from the book had him sufficiently fully recovered to get back to his pile of clothing. Learning something else, use your AB64. Pt. 1 as a fan. Outside it was sleeting again. The last one out was the tall Private, who encouraged by the Sgt. staggered back into his place.

'YOU. STAND STILL AND STOP SWAYING ABOUT, YOU ARE MAKING ME FEEL SEASICK.' Right, 'A' Platoon. YOU. Have had a busy morning. What with haircuts, a medical, with a few jabs thrown in. Now your arms are going to be sore. However, that

114

will not stop you from getting all your uniforms and equipment ready for Monday morning kit inspection. WILL IT? In fact, by pressing polishing and blanco-ing all your kit that will ease your soreness. Therefore. No need for any complaints. OR. WILL THERE?'

Nobody cared to answer. Possibly done on purpose so that nobody could object to the treatment. No warning of the jabs had been given. My stomach was rumbling and the watch hands showed it was nearly midday, had me wondering? What delights did the cooks have in store for us today? Interrupting my thoughts. Sgt. Barnes leaning down rudely shouted in my face felt the spittle emerged from his mouth.

'YOU. ARE YOU. WITH US OR. STILL IN THE M R S? I. CAN SOON PUT YOU BACK IN THERE. WHEN I. CALL OUT. 'A' PLATOON THAT INCLUDES. YOU. NOW WAKE UP. 'A' PI TOON...ATTEN.HOW. AAABOW...TAR. BY THE WIOT...KWICK... AARCH. EFT. EFT. EFT. WIOT. EFT. GET THEM ARMS SWINGING DO THE SORENESS GOOD. EFT. WIOT. EFT.

Retracing our steps back to the huts where he dismissed us to collect our eating utensils for lunch and enjoy the rest of the weekend off. It was going to be a long weekend. Thanks to the glimmer of a fire, the temperature inside the hut was slightly up from that outside; John added more coal to the fire. At the cookhouse, the chosen menu pleasantly surprised us. Battered Spam Fritters served in a sea of oil, together with the usual smashed potatoes and stewed carrots followed by Semolina and a splash of jam. The batter was soggy with oil the potatoes chewy and carrots tasteless, the semolina came in big lumps with a dash of some red stuff called jam. Nevertheless, eaten. By the time we had finished and started to make a move back to the hut, the muscles in my upper arms were beginning to stiffen up. Brushing shoulders with anyone at the dustbins indicated soreness and the rubbing of the hairy shirt on the needle punctures, made them itch.

The hut was empty; definitely unhappy of the prospects of the so-called free weekend, putting away the eating utensils pulled out the bed-box and sat down, trying to collect my thoughts on why I was there. Should not have bothered, we all were in the same bleedin' boat marooned in this hut, waiting for an iron to press some shapeless soding uniforms into a presentable item of clothing, followed by bulling- blanco-ing, polishing boots and brasses. John exclaimed.

'Ee. Fooking 'ell.' Turning saw him lying on his bed, his arms crossed over his chest holding his shoulders his face was white as a sheet.

'What's up mate? Sore arms?'

'I think. I'm gooin ter bay sik.' Not wanting him to chuck up next to me. Urged him.

'Go outside and get some fresh air.' He struggled up and made his way to the door and out. Others entered but not John. Wilky came walking down and sat down on his bed-box, holding his arms moaned.

'Twer fooking poison they injected inter ma. I kern ardly move t'arms. So fooking sore.' A mournful statement.

The hut began filling up with others all moaning and groaning about sore arms. Mine felt as if they were on fire and gradually I was getting warmer, certainly not from the heat of the fire thinking, "I'd better go and put some coal on and keep it going". Dragging the bath over, opened the fire door it was glowing bright red so added a few more lumps and dragged it back. The effort of just doing that shagged me out so flopped down onto the bed. John arrived back from his fresh air trip his face ashen, offered his diagnose.

'Bin sik! Twer fooking spaam freetters laayng on ter stoomach en ter big lump.' Personally, could not have cared a shit they too were lying on my stomach and did not feel so perky myself. Very hot, developing a headache maybe from the fire? Gladys was sat on his bed box his arms sprawled out across his bed moaning. Pilkington was pacing backwards and forwards beside his bed holding his arms. Wilky with a screwed up red face sat on his bed holding his upper arms, looked as if he was in agony and certainly not in the best of condition for the afternoons planned activities like many others. Quarter of an hour later L/Cpl. Gabe entered the hut going into Kingy's room came out with an ironing board and iron. Setting it up near the potboiler and doorway plugged the iron lead into the socket called out.

'Listen up! There is only one plug in this hut and this area is where all ironing will take place pointing at Jock Anderson... You. Give me your BD trousers... Jock promptly handed a pair to him...Now. You chuffing idle shower of Bastards. Gather around and watch me press this idiots BD.'

I think all of us could have just stayed where we were, but that was out of the question. L/Cpl Gabe had already laid out Jocks trousers flat on the ironing board.

'This weekend. Is. Your free time. Every one of you. Will press both BD's, your Greatcoat. Take turns at the iron. Whilst you are waiting your turn, you can be doing any one of the following jobs. Blanco all your webbing. Polish all brasses. Shrink berets. Boots. Pimples on toes and heels to be spooned away then spit and polished. ALL. I repeat ALL. Will be ready for inspection on Monday morning. Any questions?...silence just then, Kingy entered the hut...Aah. Lance Corporal King. I took the liberty of taking your iron and board so I can get this shower of idle bastards working. Any spare brown paper and maybe a coat hanger in your room?'

'Yes. I'll get them.' Returning handing over the items, retorting.

'This is the worst lot of bastards. I've had in this hut.'

'Well! You might be right there. When you are ready, you can show them how to blanco and clean brasses...'I. shall be most delighted to instruct them.' A joyful reply as he returned to his room...L/Cpl. Gabe continued...First. I will demonstrate how to iron using the brown paper spread it over the trouser leg and with your hand or whatever and apply water. You. Bring me over that fire bucket.' A reluctant squaddie muttering. 'Aah's & Ooh's' carried out the order taking no notice L/Cpl. Gabe proceeded...Wet the paper and with the iron. Firmly press front and rear trouser leg, turn them over repeat the press. (He laid them flat on the bed)...Next the BD jacket...draping it over the end of the ironing board, the pressing process was repeated the front, lapels, pockets, sleeves from shoulder to wrist produced two separate creases front and rear...Now. Let us see the difference. You. Put them on.' Jock quickly dressed in his uniform stood still as L/ Cpl. Gabe observed.

'Notice. No tramlines. I do not want to see any either. Next. Give me your greatcoat. This has to be folded into what we call dolly fashion.' Following the same procedure with care created two creases in the sleeves and removed all creases on the front, turning it over repeated the procedure then undoing the three buttons on the rear belt, taking both ends pulled the two belt ends around to the front, overlapped them buttoned up. Inserting the coat hanger walked to Jocks bed space and hung it from the shelf; its appearance was like an hourglass.

'Now. All greatcoats are to be pressed and hung dolly fashion like that. Savvy? I suggest you buy a few coat hangers down at the naafi and You...pointing to Jock... Return that coat hanger to Lance Corporal King...Next. Berets. Now you have all had haircuts! Your berets do not fit. Pull the two ends of the draw tapes to suit your true head size... pointing to Anderson...Now I have pressed half your uniform, take that other fire bucket to the cookhouse and bring it back full of boiling water... Jock grabbing the handle grunted in pain. 'Aw fook. Mi arrm.' Mumbling to himself, left on his way to the cookhouse... You can use this bucket or you can walk across to the washhouse and use the cold tap. So while we are waiting for that idiot let's get boots sorted out. Someone give me a pair of boots and a spoon....someone eagerly obliged...540. You will have to dye your brown boots black. Buy the dye at the naafi.' Out the corner of his mouth, John muttered.

'Ee. Fooking moor moony.' L/Cpl. Gabe. Quickly asked.

'540. Did you say something?'

'No. Lance Corporal. Jist clearing te throit. Lance Corporal.'

'Okay. I will continue. Both boots need to be done, select one pair as best and the second as working boots. Before applying boot polish all, the pimples have to be removed. Take note. No flat studs or worn heels are permitted. A boot mender is on the camp, so that is where you will take them for repair. There will be no. Dirt dust or, fluff on clothing on any hut or parade inspection. All dirty kit, bedding, sheets and pillowcases, every Monday morning will be collected and sent to the laundry. Whereas in return you will receive clean clothes and new replacement bedding...Anderson arrived back struggling in with the pail of hot water was greeted by...What took you so long? The water is probably cold; place it there on the floor. First, soak the beret in hot water, wring out and plunge into the cold water. Repeat a couple of times before fitting them on your head to shaping and drying. Back to boots! To remove pimples without burning any fingers heat the end of the spoon in the fire until red; apply the hot part to the pimpled area of toe and heel, burn off until all the pimples disappear. Then wrap the cloth around your finger; apply a good layer of polish then lots of spit, using the cloth with circular movements rub in the spit with the polish, applying layer after layer until they shine like a mirror as mine do...he demonstrated all this procedure on one boot...Now I will leave you in the capable hands of Lance Corporal King. Carry on.'

With a roster for the ironing board by 1500 hrs, everyone had stiff and aching arms and were engaged in any one of the several jobs to be performed, it was sheer purgatory to lift anything. Some went to tea; like me, others felt too ill to eat anything that might be edible? The chores seemed never ending. Later John accompanied by Wilky disappeared down to the Naafi to buy some black dye. Upon his return, he had purchased shoulder supports for both of us. More bleedin' money to shell out. By 1900 hrs, physically knackered was roasting hot had a blinding headache and ached all over so gave up. "Sod the lot of you". Changed into pyjamas and got into bed.

A massive jolt on the bed shocked me into life. It was Sunday. A day of rest. No booming of the drum going on instead, Kingy went around kicking the bed frames. If you stirred then it was all right you had not died during the night. I was red hot, sweat was pouring out of me my upper arms were on fire and so stiff. The lights were on, but little movement was happening. Peering at the Mickey Mouse watch its hands pointed to quarter past six. We had been allowed a lie in. Levering myself up with my arm tried to sit up but almost fell back in bed. Moans and groans, echoed from different beds. Wilky, was aah-ing ooo-ing, as he struggled to raise his aching body out of the swathe of blankets engulfing him and by the state of them he must have had nightmares, his kit was strewn all over the floor. John emitted a groan asked.

'Di te sleep well?'

'Dun know? I've just been woken up by Kingy, kicking shit out of the bed.'

'Yus must'ave dun. Yer passed out, snoring like two hundred pigs. Even Kingy tried to wake yer.'

'Christ. Was it that bad?'

'Twern't blooody' good. Aah... another groan. Still we got ter finish off alter kit and git fire aleet as well!' That was the last thing I wanted. To go out into the freezing cold to get bleedin' coal, asked.

'What time we got to be there?'

'Same as yisterday. Yoors gooin te Breakfast.'

'In my state. Sod Off.'

'Well. I's agrees wit yer, last neet chucked up agin. Makes me sik jus thinking aboot it.'

117

Further, down the hut, some of the others were trying to muster up the strength to struggle into their denims, gingerly sliding arms into jacket sleeves pulling them tight to button them up, groans and moans rent the air. There was nothing for it, we had to get up, it was freezing cold and my sweaty pyjamas were becoming like boards of ice. Looking at my upper arms, both flaming red very sore and hard as iron. Slowly got dressed and wondered, how I was going to finish all the polishing, ironing and blanco-ing, But was not alone, we were all close to deaths door thought, "Dear Mum please let me come home"? That weekend, was sheer bleedin' 'ell, getting coal, lighting the fire spending the rest of the day learning the art of bulling. Someone left their spoon in the fire far too long, the end dropped off. I had chosen a good Kangol beret as my best, it had shrunk well into shape, whilst drying it off by the heat of the pot-boiler left the beret hanging on Ernest's (an idiot from Bromwich) bed, only a foot away from the stove and requested him to turn it for me. He being just as bad as everyone else fell asleep on his bed. Retrieving my beret, found a big brown scorch mark on the top using boot polish covered up the mark.

Kingy, was getting on everyone's nerves, on his all too frequent rounds had been the most helpful person you could wish for. Passing words of encouragement, roaring obscenities in one's ear 'ole. Whilst watching ironing parade. His favorite expression was.

'CAN. I. DRIVE MY TRAM UP YOUR CREASES SOLDIER?'...'No Lance Corporal King.'... 'YES. I CHUFFING WELL CAN. LOOK AT THOSE DOUBLE LINES IN THE CREASES. DO THEM AGAIN. THIS TIME SINGLE.' The only peace we got was when he disappeared for meals or left the hut for some other reason. Then everyone would take the piss out of him until he arrived back.

By Sunday mid afternoon, from all the shelves above the beds hung a "Dolly Fashion" greatcoat. The hut reeked of blanco, brasso and boot polish. As Wilky had to dress up in all his webbing, we helped him sort it out and assemble it correct on him. At Sixteen-hundred hours in walked L/Cpl. Gabe. Briskly stomped down to where Wilky stood looking like a cabbage, half his webbing was still damp and had rubbed off on his denims, but at least he was dressed in FSMO. The hut became a time capsule, all eyes were glued to the proceedings most were poised in what they were doing, fingers adorned with a black tipped yellow duster or a hand holding a brush poised in mid air about to brush a boot, whilst others with green hands held wet blanc-coed webbing. L/Cpl. Gabe. Looked, not saying anything, moved behind a red-faced shivering Wilky waiting for the tirade of abuse. That we too expected. L/Cpl Gabe with a wicked smile stood in front of Wilky asked.

'Now. 772. Is. Your. Mither ill?'

'No-oo Lance Corporal. Mu-uch bitter Noow?' He exclaimed.

'Well. Well. Quick recovery. Eh?' Let this be a lesson to you. YOU. Can't. Pull the wool over our eyes. Mither's. Ill. Indeed! Carry on.' With that he stomped out.

The time capsule exploded into life, chattering broke out as all carried on with their individual chores. Not feeling hungry but did make tea, that serving was just as revolting: Brown Windsor Stew with uncooked lumpy potatoes to follow, semolina with a splash of red stuff. They knew what they could do with that! On the way back from the cookhouse, it began to snow that was all we needed? With all the blanco applied to the webbing, a substance that just did not dry, every time you picked it up a smudge of light green remained on your hands, the worst item was the belt and the attempts to square off top kit in varying shapes, became a pain in the arse. The only thing that was uniform was the helmet covered with a camouflage net perched haphazardly on the top of the kit. All had to be ready for the mornings kit inspection.

By 2130, fed up with ironing, blanco-ing, polishing brasses, shrinking berets, bulling boots, having used a full tin of polish, I had run out of spit and we had run out of coal keeping the fire alight, the temperature in the hut plummeted and it stank of blanco, polish and brasso. Just before lights out with the exception of one or two bodies, everyone had completed their bulling. All very happy to get into bed to get some sleep nevertheless, the winciette pyjamas had another trick up its sleeves. The sore parts of one's upper arms were itching, at the touch they were like furnaces never mind scratching.

Kingy came out and shouted. 'You. (Ernest) Next to the lights. LIGHTS OUT.'

A grunting Ernest muttered something inaudible. The lights were turned off. Amid grunts and groans the occupants of hut 37, were at last about to have their first bit of free time of their so-called free weekend. Only to be shattered by a bleedin' idiot somewhere out in the middle of the camp square blowing his bleedin' head off playing. "Lights Out". I am sure we could all have gone out and kicked out his soding lights.

CHAPTER NINE
BASIC TRAINING. 'A' PLATOON

BOOM. BOOM. BOOM. Monday morning 0530 hours. With no respite from the endless beat of the drum, unfinished dreams were shattered. Forced to get up and start the day right, pushing aside the blankets it was freezing cold. Soaked in sweat quickly dressed to join the outside race along the pathway to the ablutions, where many footprints had cleared away the thin layer of snow. In the mess hall PORRIGE! Was thrown at you unbelievably having been conditioned we ate the shite. Back in the hut, John and I had an idea to reduce any dust wet the bristles of the brush. The activities in the hut were carried out in silence at speed, everything lined up, top kit's haphazardly squared off, gleaming brasses, overcoats hung dolly fashion all resembled something of an army barrack room? Unfortunately, by the time the officer turned up for hut inspection, with our extra duty of stove and coal bath activities, we had not finished. Kingy roared.

'HUT THIRTYSEVEN. STAND BY YOUR BEDS. OFFICER PRESENT.'

Dropping everything ran to the side of the bed. The first thing the Officer saw was the so-called tidy heap of the cleaning utensils, crossed unevenly over the inverted coal bin lay the broom handles, the dustpan lay where it had been thrown. Notes were taken. Running a finger over the stove with a look of disgust surveyed his finger. Out of the corner of my mouth, muttered. 'Now were for it.'

Addressing all the Officer shouted.

'RIGHT. THIS HUT IS A PIGSTY. NOT FIT FOR HUMANS TO LIVE IN. THE WINDOWS ARE SO DIRTY, NO ONE CAN SEE OUT OF THEM. I WILL BE BACK IN FIVE MINUTES. LANCE CORPORAL KING. GET A GRIP OF THESE, THESE?' Lost for words, without swearing he with his entourage left. It was not even 0800 hours.

Kingy did get a grip, he too had been caught out and we were the ones to take the blame, he charged around like a bull in a china shop screaming and shouting at everyone, finding fault where there was no fault to find. Red in the face roared.

'THOSE BASTARDS NEXT TO WINDOWS. ITS YOUR JOB. TO CLEAN THEM? CHUFFING DO IT...He blared at me...CHALK. YOU CHUFFING IDIOT...Yelling at John....POLISH THE STOVE. He screamed. WHO'S IN CHARGE OF BROOMS?'

0805 hours. The entourage re-entered. A roar from Kingy had everyone stood quaking in their boots.

'HUT THIRTYSEVEN. STAND BY YOUR BEDS. OFFICER PRESENT.'

2nd./Lt. Holmes entering stood by the gleaming black stove, as he run his figure around the edge looked at the cleaning utensils where on the inverted coal bin proudly displayed in bold chalk marks was. "HUT 37". Half way up their handles the brooms were evenly crossed and together with the dustpan stood at attention. The officer nodding his approval said.

'Lance Corporal King. I will inspect your room next.' Looking into Kingy's room about turned and began his inspection of us. All stood rigid at attention straining to be straight, upright with shoulders pulled back chins jutting out almost vertical, as if about to take off. All equipment, berets and cap badges, belts brasses, boots, top-kit and bed layout, the lot was inspected. Chipped mugs cracked plates were easily disposed of smashed on the floor if a mug didn't smash it was violently kicked into smitherings. All with a warning bellowed in ones ear ole. 'DIRTY BASTARD GET A GRIP BUY ANOTHER.' More bleedin' money. The floor became littered with broken crockery. Comments made by the Officer were noted by Sgt. Barnes. By 0815, he had completed his rounds without making any further comments departed to the other hut. L/Cpl. Gabe ordered.

'ALL OUTSIDE WITH YOUR CAPES ON. STAND IN SINGLE FILE.'

At 0825. Wearing capes the occupants of Hut 39, joined the freezing miserable shower of Hut 37. A sharp order of.

'PIT—OON. SINGLE FILE MOOOVE.' Without music the dancing began, when everyone was in the right place ordered.

'FROM THE RIGHT NUMBER.' Completed without a pause the Officer addressed us.

'You shower! You are all total bags of shit. Not fit to wear the Queens uniform. You are all a disaster and possibly at home you live in a pigsty. However. In this man's Army. You will not. Woe betides anyone. Who has anything wrong with their person kit or during to-morrows hut inspection! Sergeant Barnes. Carry on.' With the usual arm waving conducted, Sgt. Barnes who appeared sorry at the bollicking we had just received, ordered.

'ON THE SPOT. DOOBLE.'

Urged on by the two DI's who threw more obscenities at us? We continued doubling on the spot for five minutes, then as a break changing course, ordered.

'PITOON. BY THE FRONT. QUICK DOOBLE.'

Down past the Naafi, a full circuit of the square before returning to the hut, coming to a scattered halt, gasping for air all heaving coughing and spluttering, soaked by our sweat the inside of our wet capes were stuck to our denims. Might not as well put them on in the first place. Sgt. Barnes addressed all.

'Now that you are all nice and warm. THAT. IS ONLY A TASTE. OF WHAT. YOU ARE IN FOR. As of now, you officially start your basic training. This week you will learn how to march. In quick time, slow time, double time and any other time. I feel, is appropriate for the occasion. Say waltz time. Savvy?... (That was a joke of course)....You will learn. How to form up from single file into two ranks then into three ranks and the reverse order. In three ranks the open and close order position. Whilst marching turning changing step, wheeling in slow and quick time, marking time double time. Number of paces forward or to the rear, the side pace, saluting whilst marching and at the halt, dismissing and falling out. All done. Without rifles. We cannot let you shower of bastards loose with rifles. Not. Until. You. Know how to march properly. As each order is given you will count by numbers.' His lecture seemed to go on for ages thinking, "There can't be that many maneuvers in marching? Just left, right, left".

'YOU. 429. WHAT WAS THE LAST THING I SAID?' He bellowed as he progressed very rapidly in my direction.

'Er. Lot about marching Sergeant.' Addressing the little fellow next to me bellowed.

'YOU. 'ORRIBLE LITTLE MELT. YOU TELL HIM WHAT I SAID?'

'Like he says about marching Sergeant.'

'NO I DID NOT. YOU 'ORRIBLE LITTLE MELT. YOU WERE NOT LISTENING EITHER. I REPEAT. ALL WILL BE CARRIED OUT, COUNTING BY NUMBERS SAVVY. THE PAIR OF YOU. ARE IDLE SHIT'S ON PARADE. DOUBLE AROUND THE HUTS TWICE. MOOOVE.'

At the double we raced twice around the huts, returning to our empty spaces puffing, panting, noting our knackered state Sgt. Barnes roared.

'YOU TWO STAND UP. NOW. YOU TWO IDLE BASTARDS. OPEN UP YOUR EARS. Pay attention to what I have to say, that goes for all of you shower of bastards. From time to time, I will ask someone to repeat. Exactly what I had just said. Now in basic training. Everyone will when executing a command, do it by numbers. As an example Lance Corporal Gabe will demonstrate. Upon my word of command,...wait for it. ATTN... HOW.' Lifting one knee horizontal L/Cpl Gabe, shouted out.

'ONE. TWO THREE. ONE.' Crashed his boot six feet into the ground and stood smartly at attention.

'Note. By all of you shouting out numbers. It ensures everyone gets it right first time. And most important. Together. Now all together, call out. One. Two Three. One.'

A lot of ones and two's went astray. Threes did not come into it. It was pathetic. Many times, we repeated the exercise with Sgt. Barnes shouting.

'LOUDER. WHAT I WANT TO SEE, IS YOUR UVULAS FLAPPING ABOUT IN WIDE-OPEN MOUTHS. DO YOU UNDERSTAND?' A unified shout.

'YES SERGEANT.'

'Now. The right dress. All raise your right arm and with fist clenched, touch the left shoulder of the man next to him, at the same time face your right. Making sure, you see only the rear of the head in front of you. If you see someone else's, you are out of line, therefore shuffle into line.' After repeating this a few times, the movement was completed to his satisfaction. Declared it was Naafi Break. We doubled to the Naafi. Last again. After the burnt lips routine, back up on the roadway he ordered the four of us to fall out, gave us half an hour to carry out fire lighting. Racing along to the coal compound, speaking to John through staggered breathes, said.

'After...that grinding...pace...we've just...had I...feel...much better.' He in staggered breathes replied.

'Maybi...thit's ter way...ter woork drugs...thro't ter seestem.'

Upon completion of that duty we stood waiting as the Platoon marched down the road from the perimeter fence. Coming to an uncoordinated halt with much bellowing and shouting from the two DI's. The platoon formed a single line. Of course with closed ranks there were no spaces for us to plonk ourselves. That caused more bellowing and shouting by the DI's.

'YOU 'ORRIBLE LITTLE MELTS. RECOGNISE THESE FOUR AND MOVE ONE STEP SIDEWAYS...with quick glances four spaces became available...YOU FOUR. FALL IN...BY THE RIGHT NUMBERS.'

Once again a shambles and it was raining horizontal. Our ground sheets square piece of waterproof, which buttoned up around the neck leaving the tail ends at knee level, anything below did not matter. Sgt. Barnes spoke.

'Now! You are going to form up into two ranks. On my word of command I want. All odd numbers to stand firm. Even numbers take one pace back. It is a simple as that. PITOON SHUN...On my word of command even numbers one pace back. MOOOVE.'

HUGE strides were made. Some evens stayed with the odds some odds went with the evens forming a ragged line. No one dared to move except one? One of the DI's, quickly advanced and gave him a tirade of abuse in his left ear.

'STAND STILL THAT MAN. NOBODY GAVE YOU ORDERS TO MOVE.' Sgt. Barnes bellowed.

'WHAT A SHOWER OF WET BASTARDS. Look at you. Number five. WHY are you in the front rank? Number eight. WHY are you in the rear rank. Number. TEN which rank are you supposed to be in?' He shouted a few more out before he had covered all the errors...FALL IN SINGLE FILE....With a lot of shuffling and shoving we reformed into a single line...'Pitoon Right Dress...Shuffling and pushing into a straight line...Eyes Front Now! On the word of command. Odd numbers remain firm. Even numbers one pace back. Mooove.' This time it worked.

'Rear rank. One pace to your left. Now. Number one in the rear rank, raise your right arm and with fist clenched touch the right shoulder of the man in front. Good. Now! Only the rear rank. Right dress'

With a lot of shuffling and scraping of boots formed two ranks. It was a procedure always followed in all future line-ups. We were marched up and down the sloping road. Swinging our arms at shoulder height. We learnt how to reverse on the march. All shouting out. 'ONE. TWO THREE. ONE.' Then back down the slope, the reverse order. 'ONE. TWO THREE. ONE.' Back up again. That first morning was nothing but marching at a pace of thirty inches shouting by numbers. By the time dinner break arrived, the platoon had some idea of marching in unison. A break for dinner, then back to marching, until about 1600 hrs, inside the hut we had a kit inspection. Well! Not really. Every piece of kit was manhandled and thrown on the floor, accompanied by verbal abuse shouted into the ear of the cringing squaddie.

'IT'S A MESS. IT IS PITIFUL. REDO IT. READY FOR TOMORROWS INSPECTION.' That meant bulling all night.

The next and following days regardless of the tins of blanco applied, we all got the same abuse and the webbing packs remained misshapen. Someone found out about shoving pieces of cardboard inside. Therefore, the hunt was on for cardboard boxes. "The Cookhouse". Using our Jack Knife has cut the pilfered boxes into squares, oblongs, and strips, gradually our kit started to take and stay in shape.

On Wednesday night. Kingy, handed out brown paper and string, instructing all.

'Make up a parcel with all your civilian clothing. Tie them securely and address them with your home address.'

Thursday. The following morning. We were marched down to the Army Post Office to deposit the parcels and pay for the postage. Then marched to the familiar empty admin office. Inside we formed up in three ranks in front of 2nd Lt. Holmes sat at a table beside him sat another soldier, on the tabletop in front of them neat piles of money was placed. It was our first Pay Parade. Sgt. Barnes stood us at ease before advising us of the pay parade procedures.

'When your last three and name is called out. Spring to attention. Shout out. Sir. Make a right turn and march smartly towards the Officer. Come to a regulation halt make a right turn, salute. Inform the Officer of your last three, name and. Rank of. Private. When offered take the money in your left hand. Check it. Address the Officer by saying. Pay and pay book correct. Sir. Salute. Right turn. Quick march back to your position in the ranks. Sir. Ready to begin pay parade. Sir.'

As instructed, we received the worldly sum of our first weeks pay! Fourteen shillings. Out of twenty-eight shillings, less first days pay, seven shillings to your mother, barrack room damages, haircuts and in some cases the cost of one or more pieces of crockery.

Our routine did not change. From the rude awakening in the morning until lights out at night. Marching at the regulation stride of thirty inches became a problem for the platoon. Some took giant strides others preferred shorter one, one or two of the platoon became. "Tick-tock men". Swinging left arm and leg together, then the right ones. So our marching became unsynchronized. Nevertheless, it was very quickly rectified by the DI's. Shouting out by numbers. Our voices became croaks. When not marching we doubled everywhere, when we were stood at the Open Order March formation, Sgt. Barnes walking around the rear of our line. Tapped everyone's shoulder speaking loudly murmured in our ear.

1'M STANDING ON YOUR HAIR PRIVATE. GET IT CUT AT THE BARBERS.'

Therefore, we were doubled to the Sheep Shearers Emporium, to make sure the hair bristle had not grown anymore. However, the dustbins outside remained upright with only a layer of bristles on the bottom?

With P.T, kit under our arms we doubled to the P.T. shed given two minutes to change into white singlet, blue draws and brown plimsolls emblazoned with the Squaddies number. Then a rigorous forty minutes of running, jumping, climbing ropes, pull-ups; lifting oneself above chin height at the high beam. With aching arms, twitching bodies legs kicking and wildly thrashing about. Whilst encouraging words of insults, were bellowed out by the Physical Training Instructors. Whose muscles rippled even as they breathed? By the time those sessions were over we were truly knackered, but no rest! A two-minute change, followed by a race around the square to be first in the Naafi queue. The pain of it all was too much, roll on the weekend. No such luck. Exactly the same as the previous one, without the pain of being stabbed.

Sunday was a lie in, with a swift kick by Kingy at your iron bed to get you up for breakfast. This one we all went to. It was delicious! Rubber eggs, burnt sausage, crispy burnt bacon, a mass of orange coloured hard lumps, representing baked beans and to even out the weight on the plate a piece of fried hard tack biscuit. All ravenously eaten, there was not a dirty plate left for washing up. Then back to bulling.

Monday morning, we were marched onto. "The Square. The holy sanctum of the Battalion Sgt. Major". Whereas the other Platoons were accustomed to the rigors of the battalion muster parade. We were not. It was a shock. Our platoon a shambles. Squaddies turning to the left not the right, the right dress was a wiggly line. Above the yelling and shouting of all the other Sgt's. Was the screaming voice of the B.S.M. Pointing his stick at 'A' Platoon.

'SERGEANT BARNES. GET A GRIP OF THAT BUNCH OF WANKERS. UNDER YOUR COMMAND. NOW.'

Sgt. Barnes did. He screamed at the DI's, who briskly marched about bawling at anyone out of line, or whatever else they spotted. It was not a pretty sight moreover; we were all quaking in our boots. When the BSM called for Muster, all the other platoon Sgt's. Began yelling out.

'All Present and correct. SAR. Two for sick parade SAR.' Finally, Sgt. Barnes roared out.

'A PLATOON. ALL PRESENT AND CORRECT SAR. NO SOLDIER FOR SICK PARADE SAR.' Thinking, "With the state of us, we were all on sick parade". We were the last to be marched off. Doubled back to the huts doubled on the spot with further abuse from the DI's for five minutes, halted and verbally abused in no uncertain terms by a raging Sgt. Barnes with a red face and bulging veins in his neck emitting spittle as he roared.

'YOU ARE AN IDLE BUNCH OF BASTARDS. THE WORST IDIOTS THAT HAVE EVER BEEN ON A PARADE GROUND. ON TO MORROW'S MUSTER PARADE. IT WILL NOT HAPPEN. SAVVY. ' as he stomped up and down the Platoon.

Once again, up to our necks we were put through the mangle. The single file, three ranks, right dress the full works with no Naafi break and the routine continued the only respite they allowed us was to march around the perimeter of the square. Our attempts to wear in the unfamiliar footwear of hob-nailed boots with leather so reluctant to soften produced blisters on our heels aching toes and the tightness at the top of the boots cut into skin. By dinner break we were knackered we ate ravenously. Back out for more marching followed by the dreaded kit inspection. Same routine. 'A pile of shit. Do it again.' More bulling. Down the Naafi to purchase more boot polish and Blanco, there to be met with the sarcasm of Dot and her mate.

'Hello soldiers. You two back already? That will be three shillings and sixpence each please.' Disillusioned felt like telling her to sod off silly cow, but restrained myself could only afford a mug of tea. On Muster parade the next morning's the B.S.M. waving his pace stick in our direction, yelled.

'A' PLATOON. YOU ARE AN UNTIDY MESS. ALL LOOK LIKE BAGS OF SHITE. SERGEANT BARNES. GET THOSE BUNCH OF WANKERS SORTED OUT BEFORE TOMORROW'S MUSTER PARADE.'

We got it in the neck again more drill no Naafi break instead doubled to the barbers for a quick trim of skin. That was number two even before payday. One whole shilling deducted. This was followed by dress inspection. Berets, correctly positioned on one's head, belts lined up, with all the rest of the bollocks that went with it. With my oversized denims bottoms and tops. I was a sure target for a bollicking for not swopping them.

'But Sergeant I.'

'Did I tell you to speak? About to say. 'No Sergeant.' But without getting more duties kept my lips firmly shut... Right. You bags of shite. Tomorrow at o' seven fifty hours. You will line up outside the huts, for dress inspection. Woe betides anyone I catch out.'

The pattern of our basic training was set in concrete. It did not matter what you did how hard you tried you were. 'AN 'ORRIBLE PILE OF SHITE.' You could not speak or reason about the state of one's person or kit. Nevertheless something was going on that we were not party too? After Thursdays Pay Parade. We doubled back to the roadway alongside the huts halted. Sgt. Barnes addressed us.

'To-morrow. Is the final passing out parade. For the platoon having completed their square bashing. The Colonel in chief of REME will inspect them. (CRÈME) In addition on Saturday. He will inspect a special OC's Parade. That includes. YOU. LOT OF IDLE BASTARDS. THEREFORE, EVERYONE WILL SCRUB THE HUTS FROM TOP TO BOTTOM AND I MEAN SCRUB. (He yelled) The following members of the Platoon have VOLUNTEERED to scrub clean the A frames. In hut thirty-seven. 429. 540. - In hut thirty-nine. 623, 654. All kit is to be blanco-oed, brasses spotless, boots gleaming BDs pressed and will be worn on Saturday's parade. Dismiss to your duties.'

Inside the hut it was busy busy. Kingy, ordering all to scrub this and scrub that. He had produced scrubbing brushes from somewhere. And was more than happy handing John and I one each ordered.

'YOU TWO. UP THERE ON THE A FRAMES. SCRUB THEM. AND. DO NOT LEAVE ANY DIRTY DRIBBLES.'

With me at one end and John at the other suspended like monkeys, we clung to the A frames scrubbing possibly our extra duty, was something to do with emptying out the fire ash? By mid afternoon, the hut was pristine. Then it was bulling time.

Friday Morning Muster. Being bollocked by all, more marching bulling and pressing, nothing changed.

Saturday morning. To put on a rather good show. 'Ole Boy.' Dressed in our number one BD. All smart and Bristol fashion we were marched on parade with the other platoons dressed in battle order webbing and carrying rifles. Whilst 'A' Platoon were only required to obey the orders of drill as called out. All went well; we were the last to march off the parade ground. In the hut stood at attention by our beds ready for the scheduled inspection by CRÈME. Along with many senior officers he appeared in the doorway stood, looked around retreated, apparently everything was A1.

After Naafi break. Sgt. Barnes advised all that.

'CRÈME. Has ordered a thirty-six hour pass. For all occupants of the camp. That includes. You shower of bastards, why I do not know. Coaches travelling to London, Manchester, Birmingham, Bristol, Southampton. Will leave camp at thirteen thirty hours. They will return on Sunday at sixteen thirty hours. Those that can afford the return cost of, seven shilling and sixpence. Can go. If anyone misses the return coach. They will have to travel back by train. AT THEIR OWN COST. Reporting in no later than twenty hundred hours, Sunday night. IF NOT. AWOL. Absent Without Leave. Those going give your number name and rank to Lance Corporal Gabe and Lance Corporal Smethers for issue of a pass. They will also advise you on your dress and other details. On Monday morning's muster parade, all will wear yellow flashes in their epaulets. Coal duty parties dismiss.'

The announcement was treated with misbelieve, but we jumped at the chance to get out of the place. Get home and have some good grub. By 1330 hrs, those boarding coaches were sat waiting in their seats itching to get going.

Our coach full of squaddies drove into the big open bombsite in the Cut close to Waterloo. For me very handy, catching the 77 bus from near the station. Arriving home well after six. A great surprise for mum and dad, who was well aware I had only been gone two weeks. Dad enquired.

'Have you gone AWOL?' Waving my pass satisfied him. Michael and Margaret were both out gallivanting somewhere so Mum gave dad his orders.

'While I get cooking. The pair of you out to the Nott, a couple of drinks and back.' That seemed a good idea to dad. The first question I asked him.

'Ear Dad. Has war broke out or summat?'

'No. Not to my knowledge. Why?'

'Well Sergeant Barnes ranted on about we were all going into battle. Dad roaring with laughter said.

'Look son. Get used to it. If it comes to it. You will be the first up the front.' Thinking, "There is no justice in this world." After a couple of pints and a good chat returned home.

Back home sat down to a massive plate of chips eggs bacon sausage and tomatoes. By the time the last morsel had been downed was blown out. After a few beers and a good night's rest woke up late next morning well refreshed, decided not to do anything and spent best part of the morning pressing and cleaning my kit. Michael showed me a few short cuts, about polishing boots, flattening brasses, and cleaning webbing, i.e. belt, gaiters and small pack. He also told me. 'Try to get out of camp and visit a Mrs. Birds café in Honiton. She cooks egg and chips and it's dirt-cheap.' That information. Did Not Go Amiss. After a smashing Sunday lunch set off back to Waterloo. Tomorrow our Platoon would become 'B' Platoon.

CHAPTER TEN
BASIC TRAINING 'B' PLATOON.

BOOM. BOOM. BOOM! An early morning reminder, our weekend of real freedom was over and the beginning of square bashing. Nevertheless, what followed everyday thereafter was regimented to time and the same routine would apply. Cleaning, double marching, drilling, back to bulling. On Muster Parade, all wore 'Yellow' flashes, but it made no difference. The BSM screamed at Sgt. Barnes who likewise screamed at the DI's, who screamed at us during another torturous session of drilling, interrupted by the Naafi break race. After the scoffing session we were marched at breakneck speed back to our huts, where outside hut 39 two more squaddies stood waiting. Sgt. Barnes bellowed out.

'PITOON...AAALT......BEESTON. MACKENZIE. AT THE DOUBLE. FALL IN.'

Beeston was a tall spindly person about six feet five; MacKenzie was five foot and built like a brick shit house. Strangely with their introduction, our position in the ranks remained the same. That first day the new 'B' platoon marched backwards and forwards, after three paces. Jock taking huge strides at the rear was out of step, whilst up the front Beeston was unable to swing his arms up to regulation shoulder height. It was bleedin' awful and we were again. " Getting it in the neck". The Sgt. and DI's screaming obscenities at all of us. No longer bastards we were. 'ORRIBLE PILES OF SHITE.'

The DI has extracted both of them from our ranks, to stand and watch us perform marching forward then reversing, all bellowing out. ONE TWO THREE ONE. Many many times we were marched up and down the incline unfortunately, when they rejoined our ranks, after two strides, Jock extended his step forcing everyone else out of step. It was a f...g shambles. We were dismissed for dinner after which we were marched up and down until it was getting dark; it made no difference until Sgt. Barnes gave up. He was getting nowhere. Dismissed the platoon. As Beeston and Jock were in the other hut, we did not have much to do with them however, during the evening meal Ian another Coal Duty compatriot informed us.

'Those two have been in the Kate five weeks, this was the second time they've been back squadded, couldn't fooking march in step. Jock's name is Cameron Mackenzie; he come from the Outer Hebrides only speaks Gaelic or summat? That big fella comes from somewhere in Norfolk. He's as thick as two planks.' His description of Beeston had us in fits of laughter until the Duty Sgt. arrived.

'Any complaints here?' John retorted.

'No Sergeant. Luvley gruub Sergeant.' Satisfied with the answer he suspiciously eyed all sat at the table wondering what the laughter was about, we did not flinch out of earshot, I muttered.

'Ear John. You're a lying bastard. Lovely grub in deed. Its Shite and you know it.' More laughter.

'Yeah. Buit wis I gooing te tel thit bastard wot I reelly thoouit?'

As we ate the shite amid the scrapimg of plates the conversation was about, those two they were different theirs was a physical abnormality, disability calls it what you like we could not help. In our hut, we all helped each other. Gladys stated.

'Therrr fooking poolin' ter woool orter iis. Seend Kingy ore ter sleep in ter ut. Thit bastard heel ort em oot.'

We laughed, but all believed Kingy was the man for the job. After three days of this revised basic training routine, we were totally pissed off; our marching remained a shambles. On the third day 2nd. Lt. Holmes, who used to appear and then disappear, spent a long time observing our marching. The following day Beeston and Jock were gone.

Later on the odd occasion, we saw the pair of them doing odd duties around the camp. They were just classed as General Duty (GD) wallahs; they must have remained a Honiton throughout their two years?

Thursday. It was bitterly cold with a heavy fall of snow stood at ease waiting to attend pay parade whilst dripping from the nostrils of our red noses; the dewdrops were almost becoming icicles. During the Pay Parade, inevitably Barrack room damages were deducted what for Christ knows we had not broken anything. After pay parade, we were marched to the armory. Upon entering all issued with a rifle and bayonet. The recipient had to shout out the rifle number engraved on the casing before signing for both items, the Armourer warned.

Rifle drill on the square
With kind permission of Honiton Archives

'This is your rifle and bayonet upon passing out. You will return it. If you lose it or, do damage with it, you will be charged and Court Martialed.' Outside the armory. Sgt. Barnes ordered.

'Place and hold the rifle between your knees. Quickly attach the bayonet to the frog on your belts.' Whilst we were doing this the DI's moved amongst us helping with placing the bayonet in the correct position, with all done he ordered.

'P'TOON SHO..OLDOR ARMS BY THE RIGHT KWIK MARCH.' Back outside the huts halted dismissed to collect our rifle slings and attached them to the butt and barrel end of the rifle. Outside received instructions on the rudiments of the rifle, the use of battle sight, regulated distance sight safety catch on/off, cocking the weapon taking aim firing, removing spent cartridges reloading and with safety catch on. All preliminary instructions without ammunition.

Friday morning. Informed that we were going to learn rifle drill. At attention, at ease, shoulder arms, slope arms, order arms, salute arms, present arms, trail arms, every movement you could perform with a rifle except shoot the bleedin' thing, on top of that, according to Sgt. Barnes.

'During the first three days of the week. YOU PILES OF SHITE. WERE 'ORRIBLE AT MARCHING? So now you will double everywhere with rifles. Savvy?'

In the howling wind, rain, sleet, and snow, we doubled everywhere such was our pace, apart from the Naafi race we did not know what time of day it was. The only rest we got was whilst visiting the Honiton Sheep Shearers Emporium. Within two weeks of becoming members of 'B' Platoon, we became very fit. The food! No one complained. We scoffed it. Naafi visits were made only to buy more cleaning materials and ogle the lips of Dot and Mavis. Not. That it did us any good drinking tea laden with bromide.

Our transformation from "Piles of shite". Was breathtaking our BD.s tailored with R.E.M.E., shoulder flashes stitched on applying soap inside of the trouser legs creating razor sharp creases? With all the spit and polish applied, you could see to shave in our number one boots. To produce a flat strip of gleaming brass on our belts like Kingy's, one side of the brass strip was beaten flat with a hammer borrowed from Kingy, then rubbed violently on a piece of cardboard soaked in brasso. Having mastered the application of blanco with top kits squared off and the tips of fingers and nails almost embedded with green. All became very conscious of our dress if, anything found wrong even a piece of stray cotton or fluff you received extra duties. Cookhouse fatigues or, any other fatigues they could dream up. When not drilling we were bulling, particularly Friday nights with OC's parade the following morning. It was whilst on that parade stood at attention with our rifles at the slope straining against in the bitter cold wind driving in our faces, when the order was shouted out.

'BATTALION. ORDER ARMS.' Unfortunately, for one of the Squaddies in hut 39, carrying out the order dropped his rifle with a very audible clatter. The BSM went ballistic.

'SERGEANT BARNES. TAKE THAT PRIVATES NAME. CHARGE HIM WITH. DAMAGING GOVERNMENT PROPERTY. PUT HIM ON DEFAULTERS IMMEDIATELY.'

In turn, Sgt Barnes went ballistic. The Culprit our compatriot coal heaver Ian, the poor bastard had to parade every day at 1630 dressed in FSMO. In addition clean out all the cooking tins in the cookhouse. At his expense, another lesson learnt. "Do not drop your rifle".

Our third weekend was a good one. With rifles at the trail we doubled to see the disguised doctor and his orderlies. Whom, without asking provided us with booster jabs to make us feel better? It was worse than the first lot, everyone left with real sore arms. Sgt. Barnes was very kind to us. Instead of doubling back with rifles at the trail. He ordered...

'SLOPE ARMS...EFT TURN...BY THE WIOT KWIK AARCH, EFT. EFT. EFT WIOT EFT.' We marched back along the top of the square, then he ordered PTOON...SLOOOW...AARCH.' We slow marched the full length of the square, did a wiot weol down to the bottom then he ordered. PITOON. KWIK...AARCH.' All along the bottom wiot weol up the incline then ordered. 'PTOON...SLOOOW...MARCH.' We did two complete circuits of the square with rifle at the slope, it was extreme agony I nearly died. Then it was back to our free weekend. Pressing, bulling as per normal. At some point I felt dizzy, lying down on my bed with the rafters doing somersaults until Kingy came along and bellowed.

'BEDS ARE FOR SLEEPING IN. NOT LYING ON. GET BULLING. YOU IDLE BASTARD.'

Wilky was almost crying holding both arms. John was as white as a sheet and Pilkington's face was red like a lobster, beside his bed Gladys was laid out on the floor moaning. We somehow scoffed the meal before we ventured down to the Naafi, for more supplies, to a rapturous welcome by Dot and her compatriot in arms. Mavis.

'My. Don't' you two look ill? What do you say Dot?' A very uninterested reply.

'Must have seen that doctor again.' I could have slapped her one, but could not raise me arm high enough. I fitfully slept through nightmares and received the usual free weekend wake-up call. A violent kick of the bed by Kingy. However, someone from hut 39 bursting through the door interrupted our Sunday afternoon bulling session yelling.

'Come and see Blackley, he's dying, come and look.'

Full of curiosity some of us dashed over to hut 39. Dying in bed was the bloke from "Ibury". He looked ghastly in a coma snoring and sounded very bad as he breathed green mucus bubbled out of his nose. John said.

Ee! Eck. Tel ter Lance Corporal. Te shud be int tospital.' Someone did, sometime later the meat wagon arrived and two orderlies carted him off on a stretcher never to return to our platoon. To make up our numbers someone else was introduced and slotted into his place. 'Ibury!' Was seen about a week later doing fatigues in the cookhouse. From that recent episode, no one desired to get sick. Otherwise. 'Back Squadded.'

After Monday morning muster parade we were marched back to the huts, Sgt. Barnes ordered.

'Two minutes to change into your PT kit. (However, with a change). Do not wear plimsolls wear socks and boots and make sure. You tie up your laces very tight and form up outside on the roadway in three ranks. Moove.' Outside cooled by a freezing cold easterly wind the warm early morning sun shone brightly upon the figures of two PTI's, dressed in singlet's long gym trousers and boots. Totally surprised by their presence formed up in three ranks unsure of what to expect until Sgt. Barnes advised his shivering Platoon.

'Now we do understand that none of you are familiar with the countryside around Honiton. So as a treat. You. Will be leaving camp to go on a five-mile jog around the frozen lanes and pastures of Honiton. "Whoopee. Like bleedin' 'ell." As there will be no stopping. You. Will take orders from the two PTI's in charge. Savvy. ATTE...HOW. They are all yours Corporals.'

The two grinning PTI's moved to the front ad rear of the Platoon, the one in front bawled out.

'PLATOON BY THE FRONT RUN.'

We ran, once around the square and out through the camp entrance, even the pole stood at attention to let us pass through. Turning left ran in the direction of Exeter when the road was clear of traffic crossed over and ran down a side lane. The start of our cross-country sightseeing tour over frozen hard furrows of previously ploughed fields where snow lay in the dips, through freezing cold brooks as we tried to tip toe through them the freezing running water splashed everyone. Cold shagged out and miserable, the PTI's did help them running backwards, urging us.

'PICK YOUR FEET UP. MOOOVE YOU IDLE SHOWER OF BASTARDS.'

After about two and a half miles, one of my bootlaces became loose and finally came undone. Through halting breaths shouting to the PTI.

' COOOR--ORAL! REE--QQUEST TO ST—O-OP. T-TIE UP MY BOO -OT LACE.' To which he still running backwards shouted.

'NO. WERE NOT STOPPING. RUN WITH IT UNTIED.'

Therefore, trying to keep my boot on ran dragging one leg. Having completed the circular tour of Honiton we finally returned to camp and just as an extra ran around the square twice before returning to the huts where our three NCO's stood waiting to take over. Sgt. Barnes yelled.

'THANK YOU CORPORALS. B. PITOON ON THE SPOT DOUBLE.'

Oh, Christ. I was in agony my leg had seized up, which made me hop rather than jog. Everyone was gasping panting wheezing and with all the coughing going on lungs were rung out, after about two minutes of this intense activity he bawled.

'B. PITOON ALT.'

Allowed or shall I say permitted the mandatory. 'Two Minutes' to change back into our Denims. Only to be re-entered for the Naafi race.

On Wednesday night we payed another visit to the Naafi to replenish our dwindling cleaning materials. Having run the gauntlet with Dot and her mate Mavis, whilst sat having a drink, suggested to John.

'Ear its payday tomorrow. Get some money in pockets. You know what? That weekend at home my brother Mike did his basic in this camp and told me about a Café in Honiton called Mrs. Bird's. Who does rgg and chips for one and sixpence. How about trying to get out. Say we were going to Mass at that Catholic Church we passed on the cross country run.'

'Ee. Eck, I cud doer wit summat lik thit. Geraway we'd neer git ouit.'

'Well. No harm in trying. Let us ask Gabby, he is all right he knows the ropes.' John retorted.

'Youse can ask him. Not mi.'

Next morning after Muster parade taking a chance asked L/Cpl Gabe.

'Excuse me Lance Corporal. Can we get a pass to leave camp on our free week-end?' In disbelief looked hard at me, smiling asked.

'Get out! What for? There's plenty to do in the hut bulling.'

'Well Lance Corporal. You did say. That it would be four weeks before we could get out with a pass and today its four weeks since we arrived. On Sunday, we would like to go to mass in the Catholic Church. Can we get a pass?'

'We? Whose we?'

'Me and 540 Parkinson. Lance Corporal.'

'I might have known. It was you two scheming bastards. 429. You are up to something. What is it?'

'Church Parade Lance Corporal. It is our free weekend. We would like to say a few prayers. Can we get a pass?' Shaking his head in disbelief smiled.

'You. Two. Want to say a few prayers? 429 I cannot believe what I am hearing. I will speak with Sergeant Barnes. See what he say's?'

We continued with drilling, bulling that included the Friday and Saturday Morning, after we had marched and drilled all morning, on the road alongside the huts the Platoon came to a halt. Sgt. Barnes called out.

'429. 540. Stand fast. Remainder of the Platoon fall out.'

Immediately the bristles on the back of my shorn head stood up thinking, "Oh shit. Now were for it". Sgt. Barnes and the two DI's remained in position until the Platoon had disappeared into the huts. Then he roared.

'540 STAND STILL. 429. RIGHT DRESS.' Shuffling into position alongside John, while he crunched his way in front of us so that we both could hear, he bent closer to our faces then questioned.

'429! What. Is this I hear? You two bastards. Want to leave this man's army and join a Church Army in Honiton. Eh? Speak up. 429.'

Gulping deeply and I am sure heard John do the same. Not really knowing how to answer his question. There was as he put it. No Way of transferring out of the Army. He yelled in my ear.

'WELL. SPEAK UP. 429.'

'Just wanted to go to Mass at the Catholic church Sergeant.' Bearing down at me, he growled in my ear.

'Church Parade indeed. I will tell you what you can do. I WANT. BOTH OF YOU. TO BE AT THE GUARDROOM DRESSED IN FSMO WITH RIFLES. FOR INSPECTION AT SIXTEENHUNDRED HOURS. SAVVY. NOW DISMISS.'

We scurried away to be met by others emerging with their eating irons. Collecting ours, on the way to the cookhouse said.

'Soding 'ell. Sorry mate. Bleedin' waste of time asking, should have kept me mouth shut.'

'Ee. Dun wurry it twerr wooth a tree.'

'Yeah. But we got to bull up our webbing for the bleedin' inspection, don't fancy that lot of bullshit.'

At 1555 hours. We arrived at the guardroom dressed as instructed. We had taken meticulous care to ensure that everything was spotless. The Duty Sergeant ordered.

'DEFAULTERS ATTENTION. FIVE PACES SIDEWAYS. MOOOVE. STAND AT EASE NO TALKING.'

At 1600 hours. Sgt. Barnes arrived to inspect us. Ordering us to attention, slope arms etc. Together with the Duty Sergeant tried to find something at fault with our dress, they could not. Without saying anything they entered the Guardroom. Ten minutes later, Sgt. Barnes came out stood in front of us his gloved hands behind his back said.

'Well. 429. 540. You want to go to Mass in Honiton. For your information. It starts at Eleven hundred hours. Be there. Here are your passes. Two hours only. Savvy. Walking out dress. Best BD, Berets, Belts, Boots, Gaiters and Gloves. Present yourself at the guardroom at. Ten hundred hours....429. Tell me. Where is it.'

'About quarter of a mile away Sergeant. Left hand side towards Honiton Sergeant.'

'SMART ARSE. WHAT ARE YOU. 429?'

'YES SERGEANT. SMART ARSE SERGEANT.'

'YOU ANSWERED THAT CORRECTLY. DIDN'T YOU. 429?
'YES SERGEANT.'
'NOW. YOU TWO BASTARDS. DOUBLE AWAY AND GET CHANGED.' We could not believe our luck, and neither could anyone else.

Next morning, an inch of snow covered the ground when we presented ourselves at the Guardroom; we looked into the long Mirror to see if we were pristine. The same Duty Sergeant inspected us. We were actually out of camp, free for two hours. In church we sat at the back John followed what I did until half way through thinking it was safe for us to leave, we left the choir singing the Angelus. We found Mrs. Bird's Café and entered, sat at a table and ordered egg and chips, two slices of bread and a cup of tea. The plate was full of crinkly chips with two eggs on top and, with salt pepper and sauce. It was delicious and well worth the effort of asking. Arriving back in the hut Wilky, Pilkinton and Gladys were just leaving for the midday meal. Glowing with pride at our achievement. Wilky muttered.

'Yu. Jaaamy pair o' bustards.' Pilkington chorused his comment. Whilst Gladys said aloud.

'Fooking 'ell. I'm gooing te chenge mi relgioon. I'll spake te Kingy.'

Full up, we did not go to the mess hall. During the afternoon L/Cpl. Gabe made his appearance in the hut. All were bulling kit, making straight for us roared.

'429, 540. STAND UP. Standing up John muttered.

'Wit te fooks oop?'

'NO TALKING. STAND TO ATTENTION. YOU TWO BASTARDS. I WANT TO HAVE WORDS WITH YOU TWO.' The hut descended into silence.

'NOW. YOU TWO. 429, 540. SCHEMEING PAIR OF BASTARDS THINK YOU HAVE GOT AWAY WITH IT. DON'T YOU? Quaking in my boots asked.

'Got away with what Lance Corporal?

'YOU 429. ARE THE INSTIGATOR OF THIS CHURCH PARADE LARK. ARE YOU NOT?

I honestly replied. 'Er. Well Lance Corporal. I wanted to say a few prayers in church and 540 thought the same.'

'WELL. WELL. WELL. ALL OF A SUDDEN YOU TWO HAVE BECOME HOLY. IF, THAT IS THE CASE. HOW WAS YOUR EGG AND CHIP MEAL. WAS IT TOO BOTH OF YOU'RE LIKINGS?

Stumped for words thinking. "Christ. how has he found out. Did not see anyone in Mrs. Birds too interested in eating good grub". replied.

'Very good Lance Corporal.

'VERY GOOD WAS IT? 540. WAS IT AN OFFERING FROM GOD?"

'Er. It twer alreet Lance Corporal.

'ALREET. I WILL TELL YOU WHAT IS ALREET. ALL NEXT WEEK. THE PAIR OF YOU ARE ON COOKHOUSE JANKERS. REPORT TO THE COOKHOUSE SERGEANT EIGHTEEN HUNDRED HOURS. THAT WILL TEACH YOU TWO BASTARDS A LESSON. DO NOT ABSCOND FROM CHURCH PARADE. NOW ALL THE REST OF YOU. THE DRESS FOR TOMORROW. NUMBER TWO BD AND FSMO. YOU ARE ALL GOING ON A ROUTE MARCH. UP GITTISHAM HILL.' With that he stomped out of the hut. Immediately Wilky burst out laughing.

'Blooody geeft fra Gods. Yoose two ont Jankers.' This brought howls of laughter from everyone. Smirking with pride replied.

'Hoi Wilky two hours ago you were calling us a jammy pair of sods. I tell yer what. We had a smashing meal, so stick that up yer bleedin' jumper.' John called out.

'Ear Gladys. Art te gooing ter change yer religion Eh? A very curt response.

'Fook off.'

Monday morning. Dressed in number two B.D. and FSMO order. We formed up outside with slung rifles. The snow was at least six inches deep and we were ready for a route march up Gitttisham Hill. Marching out of the camp towards Honiton at the bottom of the hill, Sgt. Barnes bellowed out.

'B. PITOON. ALT. FORM UP IN TWO RANKS. MOOOVE.'

In the snow, a lot of quiet shuffling went on followed by a muffled bang as two ranks were formed.

'B. PITOON. RIGHT FACE. ALL TAKE FOUR PACES SIDEWAYS TO YOUR RIGHT. MOOOVE.

Along the main road the two ranks stood four paces apart. Sgt. Barnes bellowed.

'FRONT RANK ONLY. CROSS OVER THE ROAD. MOOOVE.

With both ranks on either side of the road he bellowed.

'B. PITOON. EFT FACE.' A pause 'KWIK MARCH. WIOT WEOL.'

Unaccustomed to mountaineering we tackled the steep incline on its snow packed icy surface we slipped and slid, a few fell over the DI's yelled at them...'ON YOUR FEET. NOBODY GAVE THE ORDER TO CRAWL.'

How the DI's could march up and down the two lines they must have been sodding mountain goats. Yelling encouragement at us...'DIG YOUR HEELS IN. DIG, DIG.'

Finally knackered we reached the top. The area, flat as a pancake was covered in deep virgin snow only disturbed by the visible car tracks of a roadway. With the biting wind blowing straight into our faces we fanned out in a straight line. Above the roar of the wind, Sgt. Barnes began shouting out instructions, pointing to one of the Jocks.

'I WANT A VOLUNTEER. YOU. MARCH FORWARD UNTIL. YOU. HEAR ME SHOUT OUT. HALT. MOOOVE.'

As instructed, Jock marched on his journey to nowhere while Sgt. Barnes advised us. About using the rifles battle sight and judging distance.

'UPON THE RECEEDING FIGURE IN FRONT OF YOU. LOOK THROUGH THE REAR BATTLE SIGHT, LINE HIM UP WITH THE FORESIGHT. WHEN HIS FIGURE MATCHES THE SAME HEIGHT AS THE FORESIGHT. THAT. DISTANCE IS ONE THOUSAND YARDS.'

Whilst we aligned Jock's image against the horizon he became smaller and smaller than the foresight. Sgt. Barnes shouting his loudest against the prevailing wind could not stop him. 'HALT. HAAALLTTT.'

Meanwhile Jock disappeared. L/Cpl. Gabe was ordered to go and fetch him back. Whilst we returned, back to camp down the slippery slopes of Gittisham, the morning's route march over. In the hut the fire was out the pair on fire duty, had been out mountaineering still dressed in FSMO they were ordered to get the coal ration. Whilst they were out, we were informed of our afternoon activity. Dress up in our number ones. The purpose to have a platoon photo taken and as loudly instructed by Sgt. Barnes.

'YOU. ALL WILL. PURCHASE A COPY FOR MEMORIES SAKE. AS IN LATER YEARS. YOU. ALL WILL LOOK BACK AND SAY. THOSE WERE THE BEST YEARS OF OUR LIVES. WHAT A WONDERFUL TIME. WE HAD AT HONITON.'

I had a different opinion. "Who did he think he was kidding? It was just more sodding money to shell out". During the midday meal Jock joined us at the table, frozen like a turd still shivering and pissed off. After we had finished scoffing the shite in the cookhouse, we returned to the hut to be insulted by Kingy yelling his head off.

'YOU PILES OF SHITE. HAVING YOUR MUG SHOT. TAKEN FOR PROSPERITY. THAT IS A LAUGH. YOU'RE NOT WORTH A SHIT.'

The weather outside was overcast with just a hint of a breeze nevertheless, still a chilly day as we lined up to be inspected. Nay scrutinized by all three NCO's. If anyone had a Windsor knot in his tie ordered to redo. Someone did.

133

'YOU! FOR THE REST OF THE WEEK REPORT TO LANCE CORPORAL GABE, AT SIXTEEN FORTYFIVE, DRESSED IN FSMO.'

Moving amongst the three lines of smartly turned out soldiers Sgt. Barnes, picked out thirteen unsuspecting squaddies...'you...You...You...etc ... Because, YOU. Thirteen are the smartest looking in the platoon. YOU. Have volunteered. For to-nights Guard Duty.... Thought, "That can't be right? Kingy has just informed us that we were all piles of shite. Anyway, I don't want to be on guard, let some other sod do it". Sgt. Barnes was leering down at me, his eyes fixed to mine.

'429. WHAT. WAS THE LAST THING I SAID?' I yelled back.

'BOUT. GUARD DUTY TONIGHT SERGEANT.'

'YES. AND YOU'RE ON IT. SAVVY? KEEP YOUR EARS OPEN. Now I have 429's undivided attention. You thirteen will be dressed as you are and, because we think of you standing outside on a cold freezing winter's night. You will wear your greatcoats and parade without rifles. However. One of you volunteers. Shall be chosen as "Stickman". That is to say. That soldier. IF, he is the smartest on Guard inspection. Will be excused the duty. Therefore he. Will be allowed to return to his hut and tuck himself in his nice warm bed. Savvy?' With little or no conviction, we chorused.

'YES SERGEANT.' I called out.

'Question Sergeant.'

'Yes. 429. You may speak.'

'Request to be excused guard duty Sergeant? Sgt. Barnes rapidly crunched towards me roared.

'429. NOBODY IS EXCUSED GUARD DUTY. WHY ARE YOU SO SPECIAL? YOU MAY ANSWER.' Hoping to get out of guard duty .

'Lance Corporal Gabe. Has detailed us to Cookhouse Fatigues all this week Sergeant.' He questioned.

'429 who is us?'

'Myself and 540 Parkinson Sergeant.' Placing his gloved hands on his hips, he asked.

'What have you two done that requires Jankers?

'Went to Church Parade on Sunday Sergeant.'

'Yes that is correct. I gave you permission. Lance Corporal Gabe advice please. '

'Absconded from Church Parade. Sergeant. Teach them a Lesson. Sergeant.'

'Aah. Good. No you are not excused Guard Duty but tonight you and 540 will be excused cookhouse fatigues. Instead will do it on Saturday night. Does that answer your request 429? You may answer.

'Yes Sergeant. Thinking. "Can't get away with anything".

Satisfied, he ordered us into three ranks and marched us through the slush down towards the Naafi a wiot weol along the top, then lef weol onto the parade ground covered in slush. There stood waiting our arrival was 2nd. Lt. Holmes together with the photographer and his tripod, in front of a row of chairs with two rows of gym bench forms stacked behind. Coming to a halt Sgt. Barnes ordered.

'First Eleven, tallest first, form the back row use the forms as steps...Next ten, form the second row, stand on the forms...Next ten. Third row standing...Remainder take up the end seats.'

When all were in position 2nd. Lt. Holmes moved and sat down on the center seat, whilst Sgt. Barnes and the two DIs sat down on either side. The Photographer obviously not happy at the shape and size of his dummies in front of him. Told the ones on the top back form.

'You chappies on the top row. Squeeze your way inwards please.' Whereas, the one in the middle, falling backwards yelled.

'Fooking 'ell.' Immediately Sgt. Barnes sprang to his feet screaming obscenities at the unfortunate soldier.

'WHO TOLD YOU TO FALL OUT?' The fallen, limping around to the side about to clamber up again. Sgt. Barnes roared.

'STAND STILL. IDIOT.' Then began rearranging the line formation to accommodate the fall out. I was stood next to John and together with one other at the far end was swopped with two seated in the front. The fall out was moved to stand on the end of the standing row until Sgt. Barnes was happy and sat down. The photographer standing behind his camera with both arms outstretched in front of him, using his hands with both thumbs touching made an oblong shape. Disappearing under his black cape he came up for air, with a grin squawked.

'Is everybody ready? As this, is a very happy time for you all? When I say cheese. All together say cheese and hold it... At that moment in time, do not think anyone was very happy all freezing cold and thirteen of us were more than pissed off...Cheese... he cried...Hold. Disappearing under his black cape, a whirr a click. He popped up from under his cape...Just one more please men. ' Thinking, "Gentlemen, why like everyone else didn't he call us bastards"? Having finished taking the photo's the Photographer suggested...Gentlemen. A copy will cost two shillings and sixpence. If anyone would like their photos taken in uniform. Please come along to my Studio that is on the camp next to the Barbers and make it after 1800 hours.' Left me thinking, "Who's he kidding. In uniform. We do not have anything else to wear". With the photograph session over, ordered to disengage and form up in three ranks. Back outside the hut, Sgt. Barnes ordered the thirteen "Volunteers". To stand fast. Dismissing the others proceeded to explain the Duty of a Guard.

'With the exception of the Stickman. Who will get a tap on the shoulder from the Duty Officer? You will be provided with a whistle and pick axe handle. Taken to a specific area to guard, there in order to defend the camp in case of enemy attack. You will march around the perimeter fence. 'IF, in the event of an attack. The said guard will blow his whistle continuously, until someone arrives to assist him. Only then and not before. Would he be allowed to use his pickaxe handle and. Beat shit out of the intruder. After supper. At seventeen forty-five hours. You will be marched down to the guardhouse.' I soon found out John was another one of the "Volunteers" he said.

'Ee. Eck Joe. Gooid try ter git off Guard.'

'Yeah. But Gabbie didn't say anything about the meal did he? Just do soddin' jankers and keep quiet.

The pair of us was in an open competition, no holds barred. Our first chore was put on our greatcoats adjust the belt to suit, blanco the bit's that had been exposed to allow time to dry. We bulled and polished as no one else had ever done before. Nobody had volunteered for guard duty. But Stickman. Yes. Everyone wanted that duty. Kingy yelled out.

'STAND UP. THOSE DETAILED FOR GUARD DUTY. Along with four others we stood up. The beady eyes of Kingy noted the standing squaddies, some with brushes in their hands or dusters wrapped around a spit and polish finger...he continued shouting...

NOW. AT SEVENTEEN FORTY HOURS. I WANT YOU PILES OF SHITE. OUTSIDE. READY FOR ME TO MARCH YOU DOWN TO THE GUARDROOM.'

At 1735 hrs, all six of us were dressed ready to become. "The Stickman". We shone like pins minus our handbags and not a bristle out of place. SMART! We almost, got an ovation from the rest of the hut infortunately, it was more of jeering and sniggering; they did not have to do it. We assembled outside before Kingy came out and began to rant and rave getting us into two ranks of three. He marched us off whilst behind us, the guard from hut 39, followed with their L/Cpl. yelling his head off as well. At the guardroom we halted, the two small units became one. It was not long before the Guard Commander. The Sergeant we had first encountered in the mess hall still wearing his red sash came down the steps and dismissed the two NCO's. (Never did know his name. Certainly not as well known as Kingy). Before he began to roar.

'GUARD. OPEN ORDER MARCH. CLOSE ORDER MARCH. STAND EASY. ATTENTION.'

The Duty Officer arrived and together with the Sgt., did his tour of inspection as we stood like ramrods waiting for a tap on the shoulder. "Off you go Soldier to your bye byes". But NO! Stood in front of us he said.

'Well done. An excellent turnout...pointing his stick at John...Stickman dismiss.'

John, with all the pomp and ceremony of bullshit stamping and saluting marched off swinging his arms like windmills. It was favoritism. The officer recognised a fellow officer's boots. Whilst we the twelve "Volunteers", all pissed off were ordered into the Guard Room, stood silent as our time of duty and stag beats were read out. My duty began immediately outside the Guard Room. The Guard Sgt. ordered me.

'You. Stand outside at ease. Every five minutes spring to attention march smartly up and down the veranda and if any traffic, require to come in or, go out. It is your duty to raise that barrier. You must also check any authenticated pass and at all times salute any officer that walks past.'

I watched as the other section of the Volunteers was marched away swinging pickaxe handles, they had weapons. I had not been long at post when a lorry drove down the slope and stopped at the barrier. Springing to attention marched smartly down the steps towards the barrier. Doing the correct thing leant on the weighted end lifting the pole upwards as the lorry drove out. Taking my hand away from the weight the pole on its downward plunge missed its resting post and hit the ground with a crash. Shittng myself, scared about being banged up in the cells. Quickly leaned on the weighted end to guide it back into its resting place. The Sgt hearing the commotion came running out shouting.

'WHAT. WAS THAT SOLDIER?'

'Nothing Sergeant. Had a bit of difficulty guiding it into the 'ole.' Not saying anything, he retreated inside.

No one came in, but without further mishap let three more Lorries out. By the time we changed guard at 2000 hrs; my teeth were chattering and fingers were numb. The Guard Sgt. provided a hot mug of tea with two extra sugars murmured.

'To warm the cockles of your heart me lad.' At 2150hrs, the duty bugler arrived.

At 2158, wetting his lips went outside to blow. "Lights Out". So it all happened near the Guard Room. Re-entering had a few words with the Sgt. Then lucky sod, departed back to his warm bed. At 0000 hrs began my last stag, as the other Guards were marched into the interior darkness of the camp all swinging their pickaxe handles and for practice blew their whistles. What a lot of old bollocks. At 0200hrs was relieved totally frozen stiff retired into a guardhouse cell (not locked in) to sleep. At 0530 hrs was woken with a mug of tea and the distance sound of muffled drumbeats. The replacement R/Ps turned up for their daily chore, along with the duty bugler. Who did his late stuff with his rendition of "Reveille". He too disappeared. Just after 0600hrs the rest of the Guard returned with shouldered pick handles. As we formed up outside the wind had decided to whip itself into a howling gale. An R/P Cpl. marched us back to the huts inside it was the normal hive of activity. Knackered spoke to John.

'Yer know what John? You arranged being a Stickman with that soddin' Officer. Showing off yer bleedin' boots. Have good nights kip did yer? Yer lucky bastard.' Grinning he said.

'Nay. Nit me. He cuid ave choose yu.' Then laughed. Wilky asked.

'Wit's it leek on te guard dooty?' Politely told him.

'F..k Off.'

That evening we attended the cookhouse to be met by the Sergeant Cook who showed us a mountain of dirty tins and Dixie's to clean. We did clean all of them to his satisfaction and in reward were given a mug of tea. It was the same the rest of the week.

Our training programme included a session in the Gas Chamber. It was a hilarious experience. We along with the Sgt. two L/Cpl's were all dressed in FMSO with Gas Respirator strapped to our chest. The only difference between them and us was they wore berets whilst as ordered; we wore our tin helmets strapped tight. We marched down past the coal tip to the Gas Chamber. A Nissan hut with all its windows blacked out. In single file we entered its empty interior, a couple of light bulbs illuminated its darkness in its confined space there was no need for shouting so Sgt. Barnes politely ordered.

'Right . All form up in a large ring. Face to your left. Then upon my word of command. Start running... pause...Pitoon Run.'

We began running slowly at first then urged on by the L/Cpls turned the running into a gallop, after about five minutes of wild Indian running panting and wheezing we halted. Sgt. Barnes, standing in the center of our circle ordered.

'Remove helmets...Put on respirators...Replace helmets. Moove.' Whilst heaving trying to catch my breath noticed the L/Cpl's had put the respirators on. With ours on Sgt. Barnes shouted. 'BEGIN RUNNING.'

Pulling on his respirator, he placed a small canister on the ground and set it off. First, a wisp of smoke that rapidly developed into clouds of dense white smoke, for another five minutes we continued our galloping exercise. Everyone fearful of the swirling white smoke and due to the restriction of the mask, condensation quickly formed on the inside clear Perspex visor. Gasping for breath and unable to see through the swirling smoke the circle of Red Indians became ragged; someone fell over causing a pile up forcibly the DI's dragging them to their feet whilst the muffled shouting inside their mask was inaudible as they gesticulating to us to. 'STOP. REMOVE RESPIRATORS.'

Well! That was it, you had to take it off or, it would have forcibly been ripped off. Immediately inhaling great gulps of bleedin' gas coughing and retching broke out. Wearing their respirators the three bastards urged us to keep on running around like wild Indians, completely disoriented crashing into each other screaming to get out crawling up sloping walls, we endured this for another two minutes, until finally filtering through the white smoke a shaft of daylight showed the way out. En-masse we charged for the door. Everyone was in a panic clawing shouting coughing and spluttering obscenities at whoever was in their way. To ease the congestion in the doorway the DI's hauled some back in for another gassing.

Eventually I managed to stumble outside tears streaming down my face snot pouring out of my nose my lungs were bursting with hurt, reeling around gasping for air the helmet strap was cutting into my throat swinging freely by its rubber hose was my respirator mask and stood in front of me. The grinning face of L/Cpl, Gabe. His respirator swinging free, he pointing to a tree some distance away shouted.

'RUN DOWN. AROUND THAT TREE AND COME BACK.'

In a haze and through floods of tears, about 100 yards away saw the blurred image of tree thinking, "Run around that tree and back for some more gassing. That is the last thing I will do. Put me in clink but not that again". Staggering after the drunken mob of gassed men in front some taking detours to the right and left, one had collapsed on all fours noisily heaving his guts up all over the grass, thought. "Serves you right, taking more than his fair share". However, we did not get any more. It was explained to us that the gas was only. 'Tear Gas.' Its intended purpose was to disorientate soldiers and would do us no harm, but if under gas attack. Do not remove your gas respirator.' A well and truly valuable lesson was learnt.

Alarmingly our pace of training quickened, everything done at the double double time. Given ten rounds of live ammunition and taught how to load and unload a magazine using the thumb to push the bullets into the magazine. When Sgt. Barnes thought we were able to do it correctly, he galloped us to the twenty-five yard firing range. Conveniently placed out of the way of any huts. There to lie down in the slush and bang away ten rounds of ammunition at the target in front. With a perfect sight on the Bull's-eye as taught first pressure on the trigger. BANG. The bleeder next to me let off his round. Frightening the shit out of me jerked the trigger, up went the rifle; the bullet was last seen heading for the moon?

'THAT MAN 429.' Glancing sideways saw. Sgt. Barnes bearing down on me like a steam train.

'YES. YOU IDIOT. WHAT THE CHUFFING 'ELL ARE YOU PLAYING AT? IT CERTAINLY IS NOT CHUFFING SOLDIERS. THAT IS FOR SURE. REPLACE THE SAFETY CATCH. STAND UP. 'Getting up stood in front of him said.

'But Sergeant. He let his go first.' A lame excuse Sgt. Barnes mimicked.

'He let his go first...Coming closer to my eardrum, he yelled. LOOK LADDIE IN BATTLE. YOU DO NOT WAIT. SO THAT THE OTHER BLOKE CAN TAKE A POT SHOT AT YOU. YOU DO NOT SAY. HERE YOU SHOOT FIRST. IT IS KILL OR BE KILLED. Now get down and let me see you fire that rifle at the target in front of you, not at the moon. Wasting government property.'

During my dressing down, the odd bang had been ongoing. Scared shit of what Sgt. Barnes would do to me if I did not hit the target fell down into the slush again. Pulled the butt end of the rifle tight to my shoulder took up the aiming position. Then the sod next to me let off another round anticipating that pulled the trigger more by luck than judgment the bullet scored a magpie, quickly reloading shoved another round into the chamber.

'That's better 429. Now let off another; take aim and fire in your own time.'

Taking aim applied first pressure squeezed. BANG. The rifle butt slammed into my shoulder with a thud grunting in pain.

'Now 429. That shot was better. Pull the butt tight into your shoulder; you will not get such a wallop. In your own time. Carry on.'

He had no bleedin' sympathy; my shoulder might have been smashed to smithereens. Letting off all the rest, had a reasonable spread on the target. After the rifle shoot we visited the cookhouse, to clean out our rifles using boiling water then with a pull-through and a piece of 4x2 cloths oiled the barrel. Placing your thumb inside the back of the chamber presented the muzzle end of the rifle to L/Cpl. Gabe. To squint down to see if, there was any mud left in the barrel.

By this time, with many words of encouragement and bollockings, our basic training appeared to be heading in the right direction. Wilky had long since got over his nightly eye squeeze having accepting there was no way out and the rigors of training everyone endured. Doubling everywhere, we had become lean fit young men along with the weekly trip to the sheep shearer we were a smart platoon. Armed with rifles we drilled quick march slow march open order march close order march ground arms present arms saluting on the march trail arms, you name it we learnt it. Then grenades the exercise with mills bomb, launching this little pineapple at a bunkered target, which seemed about half a mile away. Do not think anyone hit the intended target but we did learn how to throw it correctly. Little Wilky became the best thrower landing it just short of the target. After that exercise another thirteen "Volunteered" for Guard duty. This time different souls, including Wilky, Gladys and Pilkington so during our time in basic training we all got a chance to. "VOLUNTEER" for guard duty. When Wilky arrived back early in the Morning I ventured to ask him.

'How did it go Wilky?' A sharp reply.

'Fook Off.'

It was our fifth week, having mastered the art of bulling and pressing. We all were keen soldiers fed up of being called piles of shite. With envy, looked at the smartness of the senior's mode of dress. Noticed that all NCO's BD tops were tailored. Single folds sewn into the waistband on either side across the back below shoulder height were three pressed creases and from the rear view the effect was very smart. John found a way to press these three creases into the BD. Soon everyone was doing the same. During inspection they were noticed. Those with creases received a bollicking for doing something. 'Not in regulations.' Those without asked. 'Why no creases?' There was no reply. They too got a bollocking and told to get them in. Apparently it was acceptable and it proved that we were now taking pride in our uniform.

In pairs, taught to handle the Light Machine Gun the "Bren Gun". Our first initiation of this weapon was in another hut, learn all its parts how to disassemble reassemble load it's 30 round magazines. Later in the week dressed in FSMO once again made a trip up Gittisham. This time half way up we marched into a field with a firing range of thousand-yard distance and given the opportunity to fire the Bren. Each member of the two-man team, mine was a member of hut thirty-nine were allowed to fire off fifteen rounds, five single shots to get to feel the gun then a burst of ten. In comparison to the rifle it was a magnificent gun, heavy but a delight to fire. Then it was back for pay parade less barrack room damages.

At mail call, received a surprise letter. After dinner had a chance to read it, it was a short note from my mate Derek; he had been made up to L/Cpl and posted to Brecon. Finishing off his brief note said we would meet up sometime, when I had finished basic training that seemed years away. Anyway, Gladys had also received a letter, let out a roar... 'Fooking bastard cow.' Moaning and groaning he raved on. Wilky shouted out.

'Wit's oop wit thee Gladys?' He yelled back.

'Fooking cow. She deeched mi.'

'Taught yers twer gitting married?' Now everyone's attention was drawn to the shouting match between Gladys and Wilky.

'I'll kill er. Win I git's 'ome.' Wilky replied.

'Te meet day yersel no gud deein thit.' From five weeks before Wilky was a totally changed character. Gladys screwed up the letter and threw it over his head shouting.

'Naybodi. Calls mi Gladys enymoor. I finished we er.' John shouted.

'Hoi. Gladys. Ter git fooking Dear John thit's tal.'

'Yer's a fooking Dear John. 'Gladys sighed and lay down on his bed clasping his hands behind his head. For the next day or so he moped about his Gladys. Soon got over it.

A session of Bayonet practice was a treat, imagining the sacks were Kingy, Sgt Barnes and the DIs. Yelling our heads off we charged at the dummies thrusting twisting with vengeance. Gladys went berserk and was forcibly hauled off one as he kept on repeatedly stabbing his beloved Girl Friend.

Bulling our boots one evening, John suggested that we go and collect the Platoon photograph and have one of us taken as well. Agreeing to his suggestion. We got ourselves togged up in our number ones. At the camp photographic "studio" a small room with one, chair a camera on a tripod, a stand with twin lights a briefcase against the wall, on either side of the window a set of patterned curtains with horizontal stripes. Rubbing his hands together, the Photographer greeted us.

'Hello Lads. Who is your platoon sergeant?'

'Sergeant Barnes.'

'Aah yes. I do have them developed. Let me see. There you are. One each.' John asked.

'Cud you tik one of uss tergither?'

'Of course. Stand over there in front of the window. Just pull the drapes across.' We obliged. Pointing to John. 'You in front and you behind. To show off your REME flashes. Stand facing that wall and turn your head to face the camera...As we positioned ourselves he got under his cape...Smile as if you are enjoying your stay here. Hold that..."Flash" same old patter...Once more Smile...hold it... "Flash". I will have them ready in two days time Okay. Now I will be obliged. If you will pay me. Two shillings and sixpence each. For the platoon Photos.' Back at the hut, everyone crowded around to see the platoons photograph, a good one. So most of them decided to buy. Maybe they had been waiting to see. If it was worth it.

Our drilling became even more intense. Although we thought, we were. "The bee's knees" at marching. Sgt. Barnes did not. When the Officer appeared he would watch with great interest, when he was about to leave, he made comments.

'Sergeant Barnes! The marching is poor. The rifle drill sloppy and the counting out numbers are not as it should be. You only have a week to get a grip of this bunch of?' Lost for words or as usual he did not want to swear, would salute and depart, leaving Sgt. Barnes fuming. We got it in the neck.

'RIGHT YOU SHOWER OF SHITE, START AGAIN. I WANT TO HEAR YOU SCREAM OUT THE NUMBERS BETWEEN THE DRILL STEPS. D.I's, GET A CHUFFING GRIP OF THIS BUNCH OF IDIOTS. WE HAVE A WEEK TO KNOCK THEM INTO SHAPE, BEFORE THEIR PASSING OUT PARADE. THE WAY THEY ARE PERFORMING. THEY WILL NOT MAKE THE SQUARE. EXTRA DRILL IS THE ANSWER THAT INCLUDES. SATURDAY AFTERNOON. A ROUTE MARCH. DRESSED IN BDS AND BATTLE DRESS ORDER. WE WILL GO AND SEE THE GLORIOUS SIGHTS OF DEVON AND IF, THERE IS NO IMPROVEMENT. IT WILL BE SUNDAY AS WELL.'

Music to our ears; our free weekend was drill, route march, more drill. That meant less bulling. Well that did not happen as we wanted. After OC's parade, we drilled, broke for lunch. Paraded, did more drill then marched out of the camp? It was dark when we arrived back and were ordered to bull our kit. Ready for Sunday morning's inspection. A very quick trip to the Naafi for replenishment. Sunday morning. That did happen. Our kit was thrown in all direction. All day Sunday we bulled. By Monday morning we were knackered. But still the repetitive BOOM. BOOM. BOOM did not cease. During our final week, we were to say the least run ragged. Drill, Rifle shoots, proficiency test, interviews by the Personnel Selection Officer. (PSO) Sat behind a desk a tall lean officer with blonde hair parted army style with a longish face and a long tapered nose, who asked.

'What. Do you want to do, in the Army soldier?' So told him.

'Get out of the Army.' He was very courtiest and kindly informed me.

'That is not possible. Two years is two years and, you could be posted somewhere on active service.' Shocked at his latest remark remarked.

'Sir. Do not want to go where there is any shooting. Don't like guns.' Hoping he, would take pity and give me an immediate discharge. No such luck!

'Now. Soldier. That is not the attitude we like to hear. I see from your records that you can shoot quite well. You would be useful in one of those postings...Stood there thinking. "Oh Shit. Why didn't I shoot the moon down? I'm getting nowhere here"...He continued...What would you like to do as a tradesman in the Royal Electrical and Mechanical Engineers Soldier? '

'Draughtsman Sir.' Now swelling up proud of my profession.

'No vacancies. What else?' This had me wildly thinking about resigning.

'Don't know Sir 'Aven't 'ad time to think about it.'

'What about Armourer? There are some training postings available.' Armourer! This bloke must be joking?

'No. Sir. As I said Sir. Not interested in guns.'

'Do you drive?'

'No Sir. Can ride a bike tho.' Thinking maybe transferred to the Post Office as a Telegram Boy?

'What have you done? Somewhere before?' Thinking hard about that question, before giving an answer.

'Well Sir, Did learn how to change a fuse and replace a pane of glass some years ago.'

'Aah. Ha. Now we are getting somewhere. Okay that is interesting. What about. Um. Serving overseas?'

'Don't mind Sir. So long as there's no fighting with bullets whizzing about.'

'I see. Well. I will think of something! Before you leave Honiton. You will be informed of your new posting. The best of luck Soldier. You are Dismissed.'

'Thank you. Sir.' Saluting and none the wiser about the interview, certainly not about the next two years in the Army, smartly left.

That evening during scoff time. All unsure of the outcome of our interviews with the PSO. Discussed them, Gladys back in the land of the living gave us his impromptu talk about his interview.

'I'm te be dreever.' So he said. Anyway, we had more bulling to do so we threw the remnants of the evening meal into the swill bin and got back to the hut. Kingy was not shouting as much as he used to, apart from BOOM -ing in the morning and light's out at night due to the fact that. The hut was orderly, spotless with all kit squared off and lined up in accordance with army regulations.

With the passing out parade on Friday. When we were not bulling, we all were practicing arms drill, silently counting numbers under our breath. John had picked up some American style drill movements, kicking the butt with the side of the boot, swinging, and twirling the rifle in front of him. All impressed by his feat of new rifle drill, until he dropped it. At that precise moment in walked Kingy saw the rifle lying on the floor, began ranting and raving at John. Ordered him.

'WITH YOUR RIFLE ABOVE YOUR HEAD. RUN AROUND BOTH HUTS TWENTY TIMES.' Kingy counted all twenty.

After that stint there was no more mucking about with rifles. A lot more bulling and further trips to the Naafi for more cleaning kit. The pair of us welcomed by, Dot and Mavis as old contemptibles. Dot suggested.

'Not long now soldiers?' I happily retorted.

'Nah. Just a few more days, then were out of this bleedin' shit 'ole.' Mavis spoke up.

'Tch, Tch, now then Soldier language. You're making me blush.' John retorted.

'I'll bet. It'll tek yooes ter lot te bloosh.' Dot piped up pouting her lips with expectations.

'Ooh. You're a sassy one then. Aren't you?' John quickly responded.

'An yooes.'

'Ooh. You gotta lot lip you 'ave. But your nice. I like you.' Drawled Mavis, she pouting her lips, pushing out her breast exposing a well-worn Naafi emblem. This mundane chat was going nowhere. Glancing at the watch.

'Cor blimey is that the time. It's bromide time.' This remark tickled their fancy they fell about giggling as they made out they were serving us. We took what we came for, paid and sat down. John said.

'Cud really makes te beetch squirm. Yer nor. but I'm maaried. Thinking, "Tough mate! But that's your mistake not mine". When we left Dot and Mavis, both choroused.

'Bye you two.' We never saw them again.

Thursday, Pay day our very own officer handed out our shrapnel, upon completion. He stood up and addressed us.

'Attention. B platoon. Tomorrow is your passing out parade. After which you will be posted to another training battalion. As I call out your last three and surname. Come to attention and shout SIR.'

With undivided attention we listened, then 429 Plant. Malvern. Electrics. Thinking. "Where the 'ell is Malvern and wots Electrics"?

With pay parade over, no time to laze about in this man's army. Midday scoff time. The mood was somewhat of a mystery, where was so and so? However, did discover John plus four others in our hut plus an equal number from from hut 39 had been posted to Malvern. None of us knew where it was? Gladys, promised to become a driver, instead became a 'welder.' Wilky, was to become an armourer. Poor little sod he always had difficulty lifting and manhandling a 303 rifle maybe he got it because he threw the grenade the best? Pilkington was going to be a Vehicle Mechanic we had discovered in civvy street he was a trainee Cook? Baffling, how did they sort out the appropriate trades. Late Thursday afternoon we began bulling all our kit, well into the night the iron was still red hot. Kingy permitted the lights to remain on, all had to be ready for the next day's passing out parade, kit and hut inspection. Every item of kit issued, had to be checked and accounted for.

After the usual mandatory very early morning call ablutions and scoff time. We paraded in our denims outside for roll call. Then it was kit check by the L/Cpl's. They with a list attached to a clipboard ticked off every identified item, they even checked the number of darning needles and the amount of cotton used in the housewife. In many cases that was plenty. Someone had lost their button stick, which amounted to sacrilege, apart from the bollicking had to buy a new one from the Naafi. Barrack damages often came into play. We broke for Naafi and returned to carry on the kit count. After dinner, it was dressing up time in our number ones ready for our passing out parade.

First, to leave the hut was Kingy he being a member of the Camp Band. We had never seen him dressed with his bleedin' side drum, we having always being engaged elsewhere doing other things, crunching his way out shouted.

'GOOD LUCK. THIS IS YOUR LAST PARADE. GOT TO ADMIT. YOU ARE A SMART LOT OF BASTARDS.' Wilky, uttered.

'Blooody 'ell. Wits up we im? Maybe he's glad to ge rid or us.' I looked at Wilky, smart as a pin nothing like the sniveling little lad we had first come in contact with many weeks before he had even taken up smoking, he was indeed a changed person, glancing around at the rest of them all pictures of what a soldier really looked like and, rearing to get on with the passing out parade. Sgt. Barnes entered and shouted.

'TAKE UP YOUR RIFLES. WITH YOUR BAYONETS IN YOUR FROG. FORM UP. OUTSIDE ON THE ROADWAY. IN SINGLE FILE.'

Outside, the three of them inspected us slight adjustments of the beret, belt centered or bayonet frog moved we must have all looked mirror images of each other. They being satisfied all were ship shape and Bristol fashion without a speck of dust or fluff to be seen, ordered us to form up into three ranks. In Open Order marched us down and along the top of the square into one of the side roads leading off the square where the band had already formed up waiting for our arrival. Marching past them wheeled and came to a halt in behind them. Sgt. Barnes ordered.

'FIX BAYONETS...pause all done...SLOPE ARMS...CLOSE ORDER MARCH...RIGHT DRESS. STAND STILL.'

That was when the butterflies crept into our stomachs. Flashing through ones brain. Would I remember the correct drill movement, drop the rifle to be shot on the spot for damaging government property? Possible errors. You could almost hear the silent counting that was going on, nobody wanted to fail it was eerie. On his square the BSM roared.

'SERGEANT BARNES. MARCH 'B' PLATOON ON.' Sgt. Barnes spoke.

'Now lads. When you march onto the square bags of smartness. Do not forget. What you have been taught and for Christ Sake. Do not panic.' His sincere words of encouragement, no longer bastards instead "His Lads". Swelled us bodily.

The Bandmaster yelled for the band to start playing. Two booms on the base drum, Sgt. Barnes roared.

'B. PTOON. BY THE EFT KWIK AARCH.' He was the one in control. The band at the same time struck up a lively tune and marched ahead of us we were off. All arms swung to the correct shoulder height, dressing kept. EFT. EFT, EFT WIOT EFT. Sgt. Barnes kept up the momentum. WIOT WEOL. EFT. EFT. EFT WIOT EFT.

We had something to be proud of we had made it and I am sure all of us were gloating in our inner self. As the band played on we marched onto the square; in the middle was a Dias. In between two support platoons already in position we marched into a wide gap ordered halt right turn right dress order arms and stand at ease. A single white line, had been drawn on the surface of the square where your toecaps should line up. 2nd. Lt Holmes arrived and marched to take his place in front of his 'Lost for words' smart platoon. As the band played on with a lively rendition of military tunes. The Inspecting Officer arrived on the square. The BSM yelled out 'PATOONS. ATTEN..ON.' All three platoons came together with a crash of boots. The Inspecting Officer mounted his Dias and then the fun began. From the BSMs mouth poured forth all the drill orders. We in turn responded en-masse. Apparently without a mishap.

The Inspecting officer got down from his Dias to come and inspect the three ranks. Here and there, he would stop and ask a question. After his entourage had finished he stood in front of. "B Platoon" Addressing us

'Congratulations. On a splendid turn out and display. God speed and Good luck at your chosen Training Battalion.' Thinking, "Chosen Training. What the soddin 'ell did he know about it? It was given".

With that all over he returned to his Dias, whilst we brimimg with self assurance and confidence were marched a couple of times across the square and back again doing rifle drill on the march, sloping, trailing, saluting etc. When that was finished the band struck up the REME Corps Hymn. We marched past the Dias for a final salute then off the square to the armory to hand in our rifle and bayonet and told to remove our yellow flashes. We did not have to change as we had heard. It was the time the. "Passing out Platoon". Got a slap up meal in the mess before going for a celebration piss up that Sgt. Barnes had organised a coach to take us into Sidmouth.

At the cookhouse. Recognised by the smartness of our dress BD's minus yellow flashes. The cooks gave us a choice. "Either those burnt fish cakes or, the other tray of burnt fishcakes". As far as they were concerned we were leaving their Ritz styled restaurant and served what they had "COCKED UP" at dinnertime and recycled for the evening meal served to everyone. Although. We. Did get a double helping of the white sauce with the green bit's floating about.

At 1800 hrs. We ambled down to the waiting coach parked on the other side of the barrier. Along with Sgt. Barnes Gabe and Smethers, including Kingy and the other one out of hut 39. Since our passing out parade all had completely changed their attitude towards us. As far as they were concerned their band of bastards that had arrived six weeks before. Had. Under their enforced guidance and instruction. Turned out to be the best Platoon they had ever had. Christ knows what the others were like?

The coach laboured its way up Gittisham Hill across the flat top where we had almost lost Jock in a snowstorm and down the other side of the hill where the coach pulled up on the roadway along the sea front. In an orderly fashion we crossed the road into a Pub or maybe a hotel on the corner of a street and ushered into a big room with a bar. There was a mad rush to be served first. With only about three bar staff the seniors were served first followed by us with our meager shillings. We soon bought pint after pint until we had had enough. There was much laughter when the DI's related about certain incidents that had occurred during our training. Of course my Tits were the source of much mirth. One pissed soldier from hut 39 threw himself on the floor and demonstrated the art of going through the sequence of Bren gun training that was loudly cheered and applauded. One of the Jocks got angry with Kingy. Sgt. Barnes stepped in informing all. What had happened was to break us and make us into a fine-fighting machine, which we all had more than proved. Jock and Kingy almost became friends. However, it all ended when ordered to finish our drinks get back into the coach, we had to be back in camp by 1930. Well before lights out. The return journey found many of us singing those drinking cider pissed out of their minds had to be helped back to the huts. Our final night in the confines of drafty Hut 37 there was no bulling and with the help of many pints; we slept the sleep of babes.

The next morning, low and behold Kingy came around shaking everyone awake saying.

'Come on it's time to get up, ready for OC's Parade.' What a gentleman?

OC's parade we did attend. The OC offered his warmest congratulation and thanked us for attending his camp. We were quite proud when we were marched off the square to spend the rest of the morning clearing out packing and returning bedding (for the use of). There was no Naafi break for us. That morning we could not care a shit. We had finished with that race. At 1100. We assembled outside the Admin Block dressed in FSMO with our packed UKs. We paraded for inspection. 2nd. Lt. Holmes called out our last three and name, handed each a 36 hour pass together with two rail warrants, one to our home town, the other. 'One way only.' To its named destination with instruction to where each soldier had to report at his next Training Battalion.

With the last chore completed we were dismissed to say our joyous farewells to the DI's. Including Kingy. Climbed up onto the army Lorry provided to be you might say. 'Our taxi.' The Lorry did a circuit of the square before turning down past the guardroom and the Camp exit. The Duty R.P raised the pole in our honour and just as quick lowered it back in place at the main road the Lorry was forced to halt. Whereas we cheered and shouted our farewells to Number 2 Training Battalion. With a jolt we were off again swaying around someone at the rear shouted out.

'UP YOURS. YOU BASTARDS.' Followed by loud cheers.

Arriving at Honiton Station we dispersed either to one side for London bound, the other those traveling North via Exeter. Much shouting was carried out across the tracks. Little Wilky doing most of the shouting. What a changed fellow? Until the Exeter bound train arrived and left. Then the London train chuffed and clanked its way in and stopped with a hiss. At last the promise of a real free weekend.

This time. We all got in the first carriage discarding our FSMO webbing and with our Uni's stacked outside in the corridor. We leisurely rested for the journey away from Honiton and for those from hut 37 knowing that we had finally rid ourselves of the dreaded Monster of Honiton L/Cpl. King. At Waterloo we all said our farewells, the two that were destined for Malvern agreed to meet at Paddington Station the following Monday.

Catching a 77 bus laden with kit was a bit of a pain as other travelers had filled up the luggage space under the stairs. So the nice Bus Conductor looking at me said.

'Full up! Catch the next one Soldier.' Cheeky bastard. Felt like telling him where he could f.....g shove his bus. I did get the next one and arrived home late afternoon. Out came the frying pan Mum was back on duty cooking for the troops.

I quickly changed into my civvies only to find that the family had been invited to a friends wedding therefore, with my impromptu return was cordially invited.

I had a good time and remained sober. On the Sunday went to Mass at St. Anne's, met Kenny Brian and Junior. Over a wet in the Beehive related my own version. Of Army Life. All about L/Cpl. King the monster of Honiton. That was not pleasing to their ears. Then home for a Sunday roast before preparing my Kit for my next adventure. Reporting to our new training Battalion at Malvern.

Friend of the families wedding

CHAPTER ELEVEN
BLACKMORE CAMP
MALVERN.

Monday morning up before six 'o'clock, with ablutions completed was down stairs making a pot of tea before Mum came down to take over her kitchen chores, making tea and toast that I ate before tying up my kitbag and putting on my webbing. Dressed in FSMO with kit bag over my shoulder said a quick. 'See you soon.' Left the house to walk to the Bus stop it was overcast but dry and unlike the first time, was full with anticipation of what to expect at the new camp. Nearing the bus stop spotted the familiar face of David Potter on his way to work waiting in the queue for the Bus and just had time to say hello before the bus arrived. Getting on he went upstairs to have a fag, whilst I, unable to sit down stood on the platform all the way to Waterloo Tube station. After a rather turbulent tube journey finally arrived at Paddington, where I had to force my way through the incoming tide of train commuters who did not care two hoots about a poor struggling National Serviceman trying to catch a train to an unknown destination.

Nevertheless, having found out the platform number the Malvern train was leaving from made my way to the barrier there to meet the three ex Honiton comrades in arms. Showing our travel warrants went half way along the platform and clambered up into a carriage, clumping along its narrow corridor found an empty compartment throwing our Uni's onto the floor removed our webbing in preparation for the long train journey heading west. About three hours later, it branched off heading north towards Worcester. Not long after leaving Worcester station, the train Guard poked his head through the door to advise us.

'Hoi you soldiers. Next stop is Malvern.'

As the train pulled into Malvern station, I looked out of the window and noticed it was much larger and very different from the pokey one at Honiton. Its wide platform was fully covered by the large canopy supported by metal post with cast ornate tops. The Lamp standards were the old-fashioned big square Gas light type. It must have been a bleedin' old place. However, that was not my concern more interested to see what the new camp had in store for me and looking forward to meeting John. Getting down onto the platform followed a few others heading for the exit going through an arched doorway entered an old booking hall, the Ticket Collector taking our warrants stated.

'You REME lads there's a truck waiting outside to take you to your camp.'

Outside a couple of Lorries were parked, their drivers were shouting out...'Engineers this truck.'...'REME over here.' Along with four others we clambered aboard I asked one of them. 'What camp you from?' A brief answer.

'Blandford.' The driver swinging up the tailboard secured it climbing up into the cab started the engine and with a grinding of gears drove off in bright sunlight down into Malvern turning right headed out along a main road. On our left the fields were as flat as a pancake; the huge hill on our right discovered later was the Malvern Hills. Slowing right down the driver turned left onto another long straight road. Driving past a big signboard with ROYAL ENGINEERS. About a mile further on the lorry came to a chicane; just around the bend was a signboard. REME. No. 9. Training Battalion. On the opposite side of the gateway stood a vacant sentry box. Driving between two stone pillars entered an avenue of trees and well-kept gardens to emerge into an open area of grass lawns. About a hundred yards ahead lay a group of buildings where the lorry came to a skidding halt. Switching off the driver got out came around the back let down the tailboard saying.

'That's It. End of road. Grab your kit and get down.'

An RP Cpl. emerging out of the Guardroom and in a courteous manner addressed us.

'You lot. Get yourselves in here and sign in.' His tone of voice surprised all of us. No bawling or shouting. Forming a file we entered through its doorway into a small room with a table and two chairs, the steel door behind was obviously the entrance to the cells. A L/Cpl sitting at the table shoved a book in our direction.

'One at a time sign in Number name rank and last camp, then fall in outside.'

We formed up in two ranks waiting for our next orders. The RP Cpl asked.

'All signed in then? Right. Let us get you to your spider. Pick up your Kit bags. Left turn. Quick march. Left, left, left, right left. Right wheel. Left, left, left, right left.' As we had been taught with a crunch of boots automatic synchronized marching. As we marched the RP. Cpl. kindly informed us. 'The Building on your left is the Admin Block. The one next to it with the middle walkway up to its entrance, that my friends is the Mess Hall. Behind that lies the cookhouse. Where I am sure some of you will do Fatigue duties....His comment. "Friends!" had me thinking, "Not bastards anymore"...The field on your right, is the sports field; the buildings in front of you are. On your right the MRS and on your left the Stores...Right wheel. Left, left, left right left...Onwards we marched towards the end of the road, a sharp word of command...Party halt. Fall out and follow me.'

We had come to a halt outside a row of buildings. "The Spiders'. Entering through an open green door into a long corridor, our studded boots created a staccato on the black composite floor, at the end the RP stood to one side.

'You lot. In there, find a vacant bed space. Remove your kit and stow it away in the cupboards provided. I'll be back later.' He left.

Struggling through the door entered into a long wide barrack room, its composite floors polished black and shining in the center was a big black stove, down either side were iron beds some already occupied by squaddies unpacking their kit, half way down on the right stood beckoning me was John approaching him he called out.

'Ee. Jaw. Yer al reet? I have kept ter bed space 'ere put ter kit down.' Shaking hands.

'How yer doing mate? Good thirty-six was it?'

'Ee. Eck. Twer greet, twern't long enuff thour' did not have time ter shite never meend ouit else.'

'How are yer missus and baby?' '

Yer. Twer alreet. Git some gouid grub fer change. How wert yours?'

'Oh not bad! As yer said, not long enough. Went to a wedding had a few beers had a good kip cleaned my kit that is all' Looking in disbelief at the cupboard. A partition divided it into two sections, one side was shelves and the other a long space for hanging BD's and Greatcoat, fixed to the door was a mirror! Unclipping my buckle removed the webbing dumped it on the bedsprings exclaimed.

'Ear John. This is posh. Ain't it? Much better than those bleedin' bed boxes at Honiton eh?'

'Yerr reet therr. And ter camp you'll see es reet bitter tanall. Fer me tis closer te Bolton. Wilt not take long te git 'oom ont leeve. Oonly took hoour toer get eer. T'others lads coom fra Blandford. Whirr ever thit is and a few more still ter cum fra Scotland.'

'How do you know that then?'

'RP. Teld us when he lef, when tothers haave arreeved he would cum back and tek us all to git were bedding fra stores.'

Unpacking my kit, it was creased up and in need of a good press, folded them neatly, squared them off before placing them on the shelves, enquired.

'Why did yer pick this bed space? Right close to that soddin' stove?'

'It twer reet in center of room outer draafts. Twer good place as any?' Thinking, "Yeah. So long as we don't have to clean the bleeder. Who was I kidding"?

'Ear John. As you come into the billet have you seen what's in all those rooms yet?'

'Oh. Tose. Nowt like Honiton. Wash rooms and piss 'oles are inside. Its gooin te be greet ere, cum on I'll show yer. '

In the corridor, situated either side were rooms the first two doors were labeled Sgt. Denning the other Cpl. Porter. The next door on the left revealed toilets washbasins and a big bath. John pushing me out with a big grin on his face dragged me into the next room. By its smell it was the blanco room. The room on the opposite side revealed an ironing board and iron they would be well used, the next room was empty. John murmured.

'Greet eh? Lot bettur tan Honiton.'

'Blimey. Yer can say that again. Won't have ter shove and push or fight to have a shave. Did yer notice? There's even bleedin' mirrors above the sinks but I'll bet there'll be fights over the bath you wait and see. I'm starving, when do we get any grub it's nearly twelve o'clock.'

'Didn't RP teld thee aboot mess tins?'

'Nope, only pointed mess out to us.'

'He told us twere same as Honiton.'

Finishing the tour collected our mess tins. Outside followed other squaddies dressed in denims heading towards the mess hall, there to join the end of a long queue. Slowly it moved up the long walkway towards the double door entrance. Just inside the queue split, to either the left or right, taking the right queue entered a mess hall immediately on our left were the serving tables with two cook's busy dishing out. Meat pie, potatoes and cabbage with a generous helping of brown gravy and for pudding prunes and custard. Food! You could enjoy eating. Unlike the shite, they dished up at Honiton. Throughout our stay, the meals were varied if you wanted more there was always second helpings, particularly on Fridays fish and chips were the menu of the day. At Blackmore camp, we never ever complained about food. Both left and right mess halls were the same with the exception of the right hand one, a blank wall separated the N.C.O's. section.

Back at the Billet, the spare beds just inside the double doors were strewn with discarded webbing and Uni's with no sign of their owners. A little while later the owners, noisily entered by their brogue they were the Scottish contingent. About half an hour later, the RP Cpl. entered someone shouted.

'NCO. Present.' All jumped to attention the RP ordered.

'Outside in three ranks.' We were marched to the bedding and crockery stores to collect our bedding etc, returning to the Billet we made up our beds, whilst he stood watching before we had finished the RP shouted.

'NCOs present... Brought everyone to attention...Stand at ease! This is Sergeant. Denning and Corporal Porter. They are in charge of this spider. When they issue you lot with an order. You will carry them out.' Then he left leaving the two NCO's surveying us.

Sgt. Denning wearing glasses appeared a bit of a weed, whilst Cpl. Porter was upright and swarthy. I noticed they did not wear boots and gaiters instead polished shoes. Splitting up they walked down each side of the spider viewing each bed space, whilst all remained silent and just watched what was going to happen returning to the entrance. Sgt. Denning addressed us.

'Welcome to Blackmore Camp. Your intake number is Nine/Elect/Seven. Remember that. Now amongst you, are a few back squadded recruits who are already familiar with camp routine! For those newcomers from Blandford and Honiton This Spider will be your home until you finish your course and pass out as Vehicle Electricians. Every day, including Saturday's OC's Parade. At precisely o' seven fifty hours. You will form up in three ranks outside and march to the muster parade on the square around by the Naafi shop. During morning, muster the officer of the day. Will inspect this Spider including all utility rooms,

148

ablutions, bed spaces all leave locker doors will remain open. On Friday night, every windowpane will be cleaned inside and out leaving no smears. Bathroom, urinals and the bath to be spotless. All floors to be zeboed and buffed including the potboiler. There is to be no dust or spillages otherwise all of you in this Spider. I mean all of you. Will be on a charge. Mealtime's lights out and reveille will be as they were at your previous camps. For recreation purposes there is an Army Kinema showing films every Thursday night. A small Naafi also a Naafi shop that you can purchase cleaning material. PLEASE. TAKE. NOTE. There are married personnel on this camp who also use the shop, so politeness is necessary. Understand...The Naafi shop is located around by the square and I suggest that you all get your money out to purchase Zebo and Brasso you will need it tonight...All those from Honiton, one pace forward the rest stand still... About a dozen of us took one pace forward...You Privates from Honiton listen up. Instead of bed boxes, there is a cupboard they are to be laid out exactly as this picture on the wall behind me. The lads from Blandford will help and assist you organize the layout within your lockers. Now weekend leave passes, for your information a thirty-six hour pass will be available on Saturday from twelve hundred hours until twenty three fifty nine hours Sunday night. After which. You will be posted AWOL. HOWEVER. NO PASSES WILL BE ISSUED TO YOU UNTIL SATURDAY APRIL NINTH. That is the weekend after you have started your Trade Training Course. Cpl. Porter takes over.

'Listen carefully. During the first two weeks, each Private will be assigned a general duty, either sweeping roads delivering coal, cookhouse fatigues and any other nominated duty. A list will be pinned to the notice board on this door behind me. Stating your last three name and assigned duty including the name of the Duty NCO you will report too. After muster parade, each Private will report to the stated NCO. '

Sgt. Denning then spoke.

'During your stay at this Camp. You will be taught the rudiments of becoming Tradesmen as Vehicle Electricians. Your first Trade Training lesson will begin on Monday. April third. Each Wednesday afternoon is dedicated to sports activities. Company Orders with information on the next day's work or, duties will be posted each evening on the bulletin board outside the Mess halls and everyone will read them. Now change into your working denims and continue sorting out your lockers. If anyone wants to ask any question knock on either of our doors.' They left us.

The rest of the afternoon was spent sorting out the locker layout. Some taking the opportunity to press or, Blanco their kit. With a trip to the Naafi shop, which was surprising although tiny was packed with stuff it also sold newspapers and did smell like one of the old corner shops, having checked my other cleaning items did require to replenish boot polish Zebo and brasso. The evening meal surprised all. They were not recycled but freshly prepared meals. Back in the spider there was nothing to do until Sgt. Denning entered and pinned two sheets of paper to the notice board on the door and said.

'Pay attention. These are the duty and cleaning rosters for the next two weeks. In addition to your own bed space area. You all have been assigned a specific job to do in the outer rooms and entrance passageway those will be carried out every day ready for Muster Inspection. That includes tomorrow morning. Everything black, especially the composite floors use Zebo before buffing. Clean windowpanes with brasso? I take it that everyone has purchased those two items. He left.

All interested in what their assigned duties entailed, quickly crowded around the two notices after reading mine was assigned to the Administration Block and cleaning the bath. John was assigned to sweeping roads and Blanco room, fortunately neither of us the potboiler. With only two buffers to buff, the Spiders long and wide composite floors presented a mammoth task it must have been at least sixty feet long and twenty feet wide between the outer walls that provided plenty of open space between the two rows of beds and ample space between them. Everyone had their bit to say, the solution; the floor was the last to be done. It was about nine thirty, when the centre of the floor was polished. It had taking over four hours to buff it up. To avoid scratches or, stud marks on its polished surface. Plimsolls replaced boots.

Tuesday, at 0600 hrs. With a kick on the bed, the voice of Sgt. Denning announced.

'Come on, time to get up.' That was it. No beating drum, Kingy and Honiton just an unfortunate memory.

On the way to breakfast, we were not the only ones wearing plimsolls again, the breakfast menu surprised us. Bacon, Eggs, Sausages, Fried bread. Of course with much better tasting tea. Back in the spider the rest of the chores were completed before boots and gaiters were put on. Very conscious of keeping the floors shining bright everyone tiptoed across the polished composite floor to line up outside in three ranks. Sgt. Denning and Cpl. Porter. Carried out some sort of inspection. Sgt. Denning questioned my attire.

'You. You are untidy. Why are you wearing oversized denims?' Immediately. I thought back to shoulder Tits. I truthfully replied.

'They were the ones issued. Sergeant. Did Swop em. But still too big.'

'Umm. Well. You cannot change them here. You will have to wear them. You're the untidy one of Nine Elect Seven!' Not amused by his comment refrained from answering.

They marched us to the parade ground. It was nothing like Honiton. A leveled out square patch of shingle representing a parade ground. Nevertheless, we understood that a new one was under construction alongside the Mess hall and cookhouse. Sgt. Denning marched us towards the rear and formed up behind the other Platoons. The usual commands were sung out. The OC welcomed 9/Elect/7 into his Battalion. After a short Parade, the Battalion dismissed and various Platoons marched off to their classrooms. Whereas we marched to the Guardroom.

Everyone was instructed where to report too. I had to report to Sgt. Denning in the Admin Block opposite the guardroom. The room was a hive of activity, with the noise of many typewriter keys being banged down by their masters, as carriages reached the end of the line with intermittent tings of a bell; they were zipped back to the next line. Such a familiar sound to me and I craved for the company of Eileen and Veronica. Oh. If only for the comfort and joy to be out of this man's army!

My duty. Fetch and carrying odd bits of paper from one desk to another and taking papers to other buildings, in addition in the afternoon was shown how to set up the Gestetner Machine using the wax template to produce copies of the typed Company Orders. When finished, convey them all over the camp to Notice Boards, Guardroom, OC's office, Officers Mess, Sergeants Mess. Stores, and various classrooms. Each day my duty finished well after 1700 hrs. However, each day I did sneak out a copy of Company Orders, to take back to the Spider so everyone could read it at their leisure.

On the Thursday John and I decided to visit the Kinema along with a few others we queued up outside in an alleyway, between the Kinema and another building the Naafi. When the doors opened a Placard inside announced the film showing that evening was Abbot and Costello in 'Meet the Ghost.' I think the cost was a shilling anyway going through the entrance viewed it was tiny with the rows of seats laid out on a steep incline as the entrance was about central and not wanting to climb up to the back. Moved into the centre row sitting down our feet was level with the collar of anyone sat in front. Taking stock of the inside, it seated about 80 odd with rows of seats above and below us, anyone seated down in the front rows would get a crick in the neck looking at the screen above them. Novel to say the least! However, by the time the film began it was well attended.

As the curtains were drawn, a Picture of a Bugler blowing his head off did a fanfare to the Army Kinema Corp. Then the film rolled first a couple of Disney Cartoons before the main picture. We howled with laughter at the antics of Lou Costello the stooge of Bud Abbott. There was no interval and no Ice cream. Nevertheless, the trailer for the next week was Abbott and Costello in 'Buck Privates' that was a film we were definitely going to see. (However, for me that nearly did not happen) At the finale a picture of the Union Jack was shown as the National Anthem was played that we stood at attention for before the doors were unlocked.

Immediately after Friday's evening meal in preparation for the OC's inspection the next morning bulling commenced. As far as we were concerned our kit was tip-top and only needed a wipe over with the duster. However, the Spider was our living quarters and cleanliness was necessary at all times. The duty roster was to inform all, that individual bed spaces were the responsibility of the person sleeping there included the eight small glass window panes the floor space up to the middle line of the spider. On either side of the Spider there were sixteen windows providing good daylight and did not include windows in outer rooms each had to be polished along with buffing the floors and entrance passage way.

Having got rid of the shackles and arduous Basic Training routine this was a different environment military discipline was paramount, we were there to learn a trade we strolled to the mess at meal times to eat good grub with the added use of the Telephone Kiosk opposite the guardroom, it was easy to communicate with home. From Saturday lunchtime the weekend was free with nothing to do, Sunday much the same, there was no rush carrying out ablutions, for breakfast there was no burnt offerings we had eggs, bacon, sausages etc. to eat.

Tuesday, second week of my Admin duty. Sgt. Denning entered the spider called out.

'429. Plant. Stand up.' Approaching me.

'Why. Is a copy of Company Orders. Lying about in the spider?' The hairs on the back of my neck stood up.

'Don't know Sergeant.' Quickly thinking, "I'll murder the bastard who left em out"?

'Is that so? Well I know. That. You. Are on a charge. On to-morrow muster. Join the Defaulters Parade.' Thinking, "Here we go again, more shite flung at me"?

Next morning the BSM marched four of us Defaulters into the tiny OC office. Each one of us was duly charged don't know about the others? But mine was four nights extra fatigues in the cookhouse. Washing up piles of tins after the evening meal.

After Thursdays pay parade, Sgt. Denning advised us about our forthcoming lessons. Stating that. Note Books would be provided, however gave a list of all other writing materials to be purchased from the Naafi: Pen and ink, pencils, ruler, coloured pencils, rubber. Again, it was more money to pay out in the Naafi. That same night rushing through my Cookhouse fatigues session, I joined the rest of the occupants of our Spider and visited the Kinema to see. 'Buck Privates.' That created a wonderful atmosphere of laughter. At the end of the film, the next week's trailer was another Abbott & Costello film. "Meet Frankenstein." We stood at attention for the National Anthem, and then they unlocked the doors. The consensus was. Next week we will be back at the Kinema.

Our General Duties finished on the second Saturday, as did my cookhouse fatigues. Apart from a trip to the Naafi shop to buy our requisites and a visit to the small Naafi lacking the presence of Mavis and Dot instead two old retired mistress's who provided the beers on Sunday. A real lay in with nothing to do Sunday night it was early to bed.

Monday morning. We were back at school. After Muster Parade Sgt. Denning marched us to a large Fabricated Classroom where he left us in the charge of a Civilian teacher. As I remember a tall fellow, with a strange resemblance to the Radio Actor Derek

Guyler of two famous Radio programme's. 'Itmah and Journey into Space.' He even wore the same type of glasses and spoke with a Scouse accent. He and L/Cpl Wood were the only two teachers I can recollect. After his brief introduction, he went around and handed out two notebooks to write up our studies. Then the lesson began. It was write, write, write pages of it all about the theory of electricity. By lunchtime, our hands were aching from constantly writing. It continued in the afternoon and thereon.

To summarize the long period of weeks we spent at Malvern, was in classrooms from Monday to Friday. The teachers were civilians with the exception of one Army teacher L/Cpl. Wood who taught us all about batteries. The first part of the course was the theory and principles of electricity, motors, generators, wiring circuits, instruments, and batteries. The second part the practical side. Wiring of generators, soldering different cables together, battery charging, instrumentation, working the 88 mm Ack-Ack gun and finally the electrics circuits of the Austin and Bedford vehicle motors. The third part was the final Trade-Training theory and practical exams. We all thought it was such an easy life attending lessons in between times we enjoyed the comradeship that developed between all members of our spider; the following relates to different incidents that I do remember only too well. Long gone were the rigors of Honiton other than adhering to discipline, doing as little bulling as possible that had flown out of the window. However!

On the Tuesday night, lazing about in the Spider in strides a Sgt. Nobody bothered to shout. "Stand up NCO present". Purposely he strode down one side then back up the other. Noticing this intruder all went quiet; some got up others did not. The Sgt. coming to a halt at the entrance, his very presence shone with authority. Like Sgt. Barnes, he was tall and big of statue with a stern face immaculately dressed and by the shape and cut of his BD. Had been in the Army a long time? Not saying anything he advanced to the nearest locker looked in, went to the next locker and carried on inspecting all until he had finished, then barked out.

'YOU ARE A SHAMBLES. GET ALL THESE LOCKERS. SQUARED OFF PROPERLY. I WILL BE BACK. IN FIFTEEN MINUTES TIME. TO INSPECT THEM. EACH AND EVERY ONE OF THEM. ' About turned marched out. John spoke up.

'Ee. Eck. Who de fooks thit?' Rather amused by this sudden interruption replied.

'Don't bleedin' ask me?'

'Whits he want? Lockers er te same as photo... John shouted out...Hoi. Anyone knows who te fook he is?'

A lot of shaking of head and No's came out of the woodwork. We were all baffled and surprised by this intrusion. Nevertheless, there was movement. Everyone looked in their lockers. Adjusting a few of my shirts and singlet's to make them neater smoothing out some creases the BD.s and greatcoat were in line on the hangers. John standing at the end of his bed muttered.

'Ee. Look oout. He's back... shouted... 'NCO PRESENT. STAND UP.'

Everybody as they were stood silent without movement. Entering the spider he roared.
'AT THE END OF YOUR BEDS. STAND AT ATTENTION. '

Everyone quickly moved to stand at his or her bed ends. Whilst on the opposite side the Sgt, studied the first locker's layout before springing into action. Everything came out to lay a heap on the floor including the top kit leaving a bare locker, the same thing happened at the next one and without looking did the rest as he rapidly advanced down the row of beds leaving devastation behind him until he came to the one opposite us. Addressing its owner.

'YOU. WHAT? ARE ALL THESE BOTTLES AND POTIONS. DOING IN THIS LOCKER?'
Ronald meekly replied.

'They're mine Sergeant.'

'NO. THEY ARE NOT. THEY BELONG. TO BOOTS THE CHEMIST. GET RID OF THEM.'
Emptying out the rest of the locker moved to the next one, having finished one side began
his tour of destruction down our side until all lockers were emptied and the contents lay in
heaps upon the floor.

'NOW. I WILL BE BACK AT TWENTYONE THIRTY. I WILL INSPECT EVERY LOCKER
AGAIN. AND THEY WILL. BE LAID UP IN THE CORRECT ORDER. IF NOT?' He left.
Observing my heap of kit exclaimed.

'Bleedin' 'ell. Were back at Honiton.' John began to laugh.

'Ee. Eck. Dist tha ears remarks aboot yonder bloke? Ee blooody 'ell Booit's Cheemist.'
Laughing at his comment regarding Ronald, of slight build about five feet eight in height
with thinning wispy hair, a small moustache and his complexion was not ruddy like ours,
maybe it was because of all the creams he applied. John called out.

'Heh. Ronald wit thee gooin te do wit mediceen chest?' Meekly he replied.

'Nothing. I need them all for my ailments.' I shouted.

'Bleedin' 'ell mate. Better you than me.' But Ronald did not take any notice.

What had happened. Was a whirlwind of destruction; it did not make sense, everyone
scratching heads trying to sort out the different items of kit and replace them squared off
in the lockers. 'Ear John. Who is this bleedin'' git of a Sergeant? He ain't got anything to
do with this spider. Go and ask Denning who he is?'

'Noo, Tay much te do. Git te put kit back inte locker afore ter bastard returns.'

I could not disagree, the pile of kit strewn around my feet was a shambles, all had to
be folded squared off in the lockers as per the photograph. That had many busy bodies
looking and pondering. By 2125. My kit was squared off back in the locker ready for the
inspection by this mysterious Sgt. Who we heard advancing down the outside corridor.

At precisely 2130 he entered. Went straight to the first locker without looking
everything came out including the top kit. Again his advance down the row was rapid
destruction at Ronald's locker he stopped. Seeing the array of bottles pills and potions
on the top shelve ALL neatly lined up military fashion. We watched as the Sgt. with arms
folded one upraised as his hand stroked his chin possibly thinking, "Now. How do I tackle
this one"? Picking up a bottle or jar of something walked around showed it to Ronald,
politely and deliberately halting his question, asked.

'Now. Then. Soldier. What. Is. This for?' Ronald peering at the label stated.

'Oh. That one! I get a rash after shaving. My Doctor has told me to apply this lotion.'
Ronald replied with conviction.

'Oh. Does he? Well. I had. Better put it back on the shelf then. Hadn't I?' The pair of
us engrossed by the proceedings watched.

'Yes. Thank you Sergeant.' Says Ronald a smile creeping into the corners of his lips.
Carefully, the Sgt. replaced it in line with the others. Nevertheless, ripped every other
item out leaving the cupboard bare except! Just about to turn away he lunged at 'Boots
the Chemist.' In a shower it all came out, crashing and smashing on the floor into a mish
mash of pills potions and creams. Roaring in Ronald's lug ole.

'THIS LADDIE. IS THE ARMY. IF. YOU WANT ANY PILLS OR POTIONS. FOR
AILMENTS. GET YOUR ARSE DOWN TO YOUR ARMY DOCTOR. CALLED THE MO.'

John and I. Trying to restrain laughter were almost piddling ourselves with mirth and
am sure; saw wax explode from Ronald's other ear. However, the Sgt. continued his tour
of destruction down our side until every locker was bare, again he bellowed out.

'NOW. YOU LOT OF 'ORRIBLE MELTS. CLEAN THIS FILTHY SPIDER UP. I WILL BE BACK TOMORROW NIGHT. AT NINETEENTHIRTY HOURS.' He stomped away up the corridor. Bemused and pissed off by this intruder we began cleaning up the mess he had left behind, even more so Ronald who had lost Boots the Chemist.

Wednesday evening, anticipating his return all stood at the end of our beds and sure enough on the dot, he returned. The whirlwind went into action leaving piles of kit on the floor, before leaving gave us another warning of his return at 2130 the following night. Thursday evening, waiting for his return we stood at the end of our beds the contents of our lockers stacked immaculately, in anticipation of his appearance we waited and waited nevertheless, the bastard never turned up and we had missed going to the Kinema to see "Abbott & Costello Meet Frankenstein". Later we found out the reason for the marauding Sgt's, 'Lax of Duty?' Whom John had nicknamed 'Frankenstein.' Was billeted two spiders down from us and had been demobed that Thursday. Possibly his parting gift to us was Destruction. However, Sgt Denning appeared and asked.

'For all those who want to go home this week-end stick your hands up...About half stuck up their hands...Okay before I come around and take your details, there are a few things you need to know so please pay attention. You all have been informed of the period permitted with a thirty-six hour pass. There are no rail warrants issued. Therefore, I suggest a cheap way to travel is. Hitchhike a lift home on your own and return by train on Sunday evening buy a single train ticket. After midnight there is a duty Lorry waiting at Malvern Station, to meet any late incoming trains to bring latecomers back to camp. So long as you make the o'eight, hundred hours Monday morning muster. It is overlooked. All those wanting to get a pass must apply by Thursday latest. Now I will come around and take your details. Passes will be issued to you on Saturday.' With all the names taken, he left. We thought, He was having us on trying to get everyone on a charge for being AWOL. However, next day in the mess hall spoke to a cockney, who informed me.

'No. He's right. He issues the passes. Listen mate you can catch the twenty-five past eleven train leaving Paddington it gets in Malvern at twenty to three. When you buy your ticket show your pass. Get a reduced fare it cost eleven bob?' That was about all I could afford and definitely was the way to travel. So adopted the hitch home-train back method.

Saturday morning was always the same. OC's parade. Then general duties, whatever the platoon had been designated. Sweeping roads, cutting grass with jack knives or daisy cutting and replanting in long straight lines. What the bleedin' 'ell for did not really know, as once replanted they all fell over. Naafi break was nothing like the Honiton race it was orderly and

Skiving Saturday morning   done with ease. After that continued with the duty skive, until 1200 hours. A race back to the spider change into number ones, signs out. The weekend trips home were ideal to bring back cakes, sweets, tins of goodies to share around to spread out our meager pay.

That first weekend I found hitching was a hassle nevertheless, well worth the effort. First a two mile march from camp to the nearest main trunk road, leading north to Worcester where John along with others parted company, whilst we traveled south towards Upton upon Severn. Walking constantly using the thumb before getting a lift to Cheltenham once on the main road to the Oxford roundabout, began thumbing any vehicles and if lucky it stopped, the driver would enquire.

'Where you heading for soldier?'

'London. Any chance of a lift Please?'

'Sorry only going to Oxford. Hop in drop you off on the way.'

Quick to learn, it did not matter how far the driver was going, it was get in go as far as possible. It might take six or seven lifts before arriving at a convenient London Underground Station. Catch a tube to Victoria, a bus to Vauxhall and walk home in time for an evening meal, go to the Beehive for a beer and a game of darts.

Sunday night, after a dance down the Club, left to catch the last train from Paddington provided you with those few extra hours of freedom. One can never forget the Paddington Station experience filled with hordes of squaddies and 'erks carrying small grips holding goodies, the very few wearing civvies with short back and sides stood out a mile. Not forgetting the ever presence of Red Caps who stood watching or strolled about in pairs as if they owned the bleedin' place just ready and waiting to book someone or break up scuffles, that did occur out of their sight. After purchasing your ticket at the platform barrier you would meet three or four others waiting for the barriers to be opened and then make a beeline for an empty carriage, pile in stand by the windows blocking any further entry to a full compartment, it usually worked. The purpose plenty of room to lie down and get some kip during the journey nevertheless, our only disturbance was the conductor checking tickets or announcing the next station.

'Reading, anyone for Reading.' and so forth. Didcot, Oxford, Moreton in the Marsh, Evesham, places where other squaddies and erks would get off. At Worcester you would be tidied up before getting off at Malvern, sleepily clamber aboard the waiting truck and whilst yawning like mad in the Guardroom, sign in then get to bed.

The following weekend, taking a different route via Moreton in the Marsh finished up in Oxford! Had a hell of a time getting out of there onto the road towards High Wycombe arriving home at nine'o' clock far too late to go out. Returning late back to camp in the Spider did not turn on the lights; lay down on my bed pulled the blankets over my head. Next morning, the Guard Sgt. shaking me pulled the blankets away.

'You. Time to get up and get sorted out.' Through bleary eyes peered at this Sgt. yawning muttered.

'Sorry Sergeant. Must have overslept.' Then he noticed I was still dressed in my BD and boots. Charged me on the spot. Four days cookhouse fatigues and a guard duty on the Friday night. Swift justice.

My cookhouse fatigues, meant cleaning masses of steel pans and Dixie's full of food remnants and grease a dirty job that had to pass the Cook Sgt's. Approval and top of that had to swab the floors if not to his satisfaction. You did it again. Having to do a guard duty on the Friday night excused me from bulling including Saturday morning O.C's. Nevertheless, was left in charge to finish cleaning up the spider ready for inspection. After doing the usual work party duty left with the rest of them homeward bound. Getting as far as Cheltenham thumbed a lorry that stopped. Climbing up into the cab thanked the driver a very chatty type of bloke. In second gear the Lorry lumbered along at a snail's pace together with his endless chatter and the monotonous drone of the engine after my previous nights guard duty, I fell asleep.

'C'mon. Soldier. get out. This is as far as I'm going today.'

Coming too, noticed we were parked outside a small café miles from anywhere. Getting out began walking to where I did not know? An hour later the noise of an engine had me thumbing, recognising the lorry and its driver with another squaddie sat beside him as he passed, I put two fingers up. He replied by tooting his horn. Learning from experiences to avoid tankers or the big Lorries, cars were the obvious choice and the route to take diagonally across country via the Oxford roundabout. High Wycombe, Uxbridge and then you knew you had cracked it.

Camp life was not too bad, the weather was good and enjoyed quite a bit of sunshine. Although the lessons were boring we were progressing, John and I had become the best of pals getting up to all sorts of pranks. On one occasion, whilst all were asleep gathered up all the boots in the middle of the spider including ours. mixed them all up. In the morning it was us that led the shouting ... 'Who mixed up the boots? I'll kill the bastard that done that.' Amongst other pranks were: tying together others boot laces, making apple pie beds and many others we carried out that all enjoyed. However, there was one event that nearly drove all of us mad. A Scotsman from Troon who played the bagpipes. William was well over six feet tall obviously nicknamed Big Bill Troon, every night sat on his bed he would practice on his chanter, everyone agreed. "He should take his fooking Chanter and 1play it in the Blanco room with the door shut". Taking the hint he did, then we got peace. John, who had commitments at home did not partake of a few beers so a group of us, three Scots. Jimmy, Georgie, and Bert. Jackie a Gordie and Jack a lad from Barrow on the odd occasion we had a couple of beers in the Naafi or, go to the Kinema on a Thursday.

Originally, during the War, the camp had been one of three American Army Hospitals within the vicinity and had facilities that only the Americans could afford during wartime. A second camp, the camp we had passed on our way in was occupied by the Royal Engineers, the third Blackmoor II was derelict and located about half a mile away. Our first visit there was after Saturday's OCs. The place was full of sheep, armed with our Jack knives ordered to cut the overgrowth full of nettles thistles gorse and weeds, down to lawn level. Here and there were areas of hacked grass previously done by other parties there did not seem any point in doing it; nobody was going live in those conditions? Nevertheless, without Naafi break we stayed until 1130. Then were marched back to be dismissed for a free weekend.

Jimmy Georgie Jackie kneeling Keith and I

Since we had arrived at Malvern, there were those who could not get home on the weekend, the ones I felt sorry for were the lads from Scotland. One night in the Naafi I asked Bert.

'What do you do on the week-ends?'

'Satuurday neet, gae te daances et Malvern's Winter Gardens. A dooty lorri taks war theer un brins oos baak at twenty two thirty. Sunday nae daying nutting.'

The next trip home I asked mum, if it was all right if I brought Bert home. Mum as usual had no objections as we being an army family had in the past all sorts of Servicemen stay. When I got back to camp suggesting it to Bert he accepted. Apologising to the other four who did not take offence. We put in our request, to Sgt. Denning, who asked.

'You going back to Scotland?'

'Nay. Geeing ome wee Plantee ter Lundun.' That was acceptable.

On Saturday, as Bert did not have a clue on how to get to London never mind finding our house. As a pair, we would try our hardest at getting lifts in whatever vehicle came our way. We walked to Cheltenham and on the London road a small car stopped to pick us up. Its driver was a Vicar who kindly gave us a lift as far as the Oxford roundabout. As regular as clockwork stuck up our thumbs but no joy. It seemed as if we would walk all the way. Thumbing a lorry, slowing down it stopped, the driver shouted.

'I'm going as far as Uxbridge. Any good?'

'Thanks. that'll do us.' It was a long low trailer; already sat on its bare boards were about a dozen squaddies, it was going to be an uncomfortable ride but at least we were mobile. The driver was rather considerate keeping a steady speed to avoid too much banging on bums. Nevertheless, stopped to pick up a few more eventually arriving at Uxbridge everyone got off rubbing their arses. It must have been the most uncomfortable ride, any of us had experienced.

Me , Dad, Bert & Mum.

We arrived home after seven, Bert was made very welcome. Yet again mum feeding the troops, out came the frying pan. A big plate of double egg, sausages and mountains of chips, was placed in front of Bert and I. Bert was togged out in civvies Before dad took us over the Nott for a few pints. Bert appreciated the hospitality and wrote a letter of thanks to mum and dad.

Monday morning, two squaddies Keith and Tony who had been back squadded joined our course. Now it may seem strange but some of the Squaddies did own cars and motorbikes and parked them close to the Spiders. One day on the way back from dinner, John and I were admiring a couple of the different motorbikes, when John saw a special one taking a closer look at it exclaimed.

'Ee. Eck. Ets a goood un bet tis poorwerful enoof t'enter TT.' He began manhandling it out. I exclaimed.

'Wot yer doing yer daft bugger. Can't mess about with that.'

'Ere. 'Eld me crocs, want tav' a go.' Taking hold of his crocs while he in shirtsleeve order still wearing plimsolls manhandles the bike in the right direction. Then begins to run with it along the road to bump start it, jumping on sidesaddle it did not go with me thinking he would stop, not him he runs further this time again he jumps on sidesaddle. Broom, Broom Bruuuuum it roared cocking his leg over he roars away. I thought. "He bleedin' mad. If the bloke finds out he'll go barmy". Shaking my head returned to the spider where Keith and Tony were moving in and soon found out both were from London and Tony was the owner of a SS Jaguar who gave Keith lifts both ways. About twenty minutes later John turns up full of Beams.

'Where the bleedin' 'ell you been? Did the bloke catch yer?'

'Nay. Bloooody goood rid ouit o' camp reet don ter cross roods an back clocked bloody seventy on her she a gooooer.'

'Yer bleedin' mad you are.'

However, I was more interested in cadging a lift home in Tony's Jaguar. That evening approached Tony and asked for a lift home he agreed saying.

'Look I drop Keith off at Hanger Lane Tube station and pick him up there on the way back, do same for you. As long as you pay some money for petrol, split it three ways about three bob each. Alright.'

'Done. Sounds good to me.' On Saturday, driving in style was at Hanger Lane by two thirty and home within an hour, Sunday night at 2300 Tony picked us up at Hanger Lane. Nevertheless, two weekends later meeting Keith at Hanger Lane we waited no sign of Tony not even by 0030 hours. Decided to start hitching a lift the odds of us hitching a lift in the early hours of the morning with hardly any traffic disaster! Drivers either did not see us or did not want to pick up two squaddies in the early hours of the morning. Only two Lorries stopped and by 0400 hrs, we had only got as far as the Oxford Roundabout and it was beginning to get light. Stranded! Until a milk tanker stopped, we climbed up into his cab, the driver said.

'I am going to Worcester where you two heading for?' We chorused.

'Malvern.'

'Well. I know where that is but can't take you there. Drop you off as close as I can.'

It was 0615 hrs when he stopped along a country road.

'Far as I can take you. It's about eight miles down that road. Best walk or if you're lucky thumb a tractor?' He joked.

We thanked him. Marching at a cracking pace we arrived at camp about 0750. The RP heard our side of the story.

'You two are lucky. I was going to book. YOU AWOL. Suggest you change into working clothes AT THE DOUBLE. ' Thinking, "At the double! We've just doubled eight

157

sodding miles to get here". We did make muster. Tony had returned by train his Jag had blown up or summat. My luxury trips home finished next time back to "Thumbing".

That Monday morning the first lesson was on Batteries with a new exercise book and a new tutor, L/Cpl. Wood. More writing and as his voice drawled on preaching the gospel about batteries having not slept a wink my eyes lids kept on dropping, shaking myself to keep awake his droning continued and my lids got heavier and heavier fighting to concentrate whilst trying to keep awake. To me his monotonous drone seemed to be far away or even next door eventually sleep overtook me. Someone shaking me vigorously shouting.

'YOU. WHAT'S YOUR NUMBER AND NAME?'

'Uh...yawned...429. Plant. Lance Corporal.' Yelling in my ear.

'YOU! ARE ON A CHARGE. ASLEEP ON DUTY. EXTRA DUTIES FOR YOU. OFFICES MESS KITCHENS. FIVE NIGHTS. PLUS A WEEKEND GUARD. NOW CONCENTRATE.' Thinking. "Aw. Soding 'ell" mumbled. 'Yes. Lance Corporal.'

Whilst the rest of the class were leering making 'orrible signs at me it was embarrassing. With droopy eyelids still fought hard to concentrate. At lunchtime. L/Cpl. Woods shouted.

'429. FOR THE NEXT FIVE DAYS. REPORT AT SIXTEEN THIRTY TO THE COOK SERGEANT AT THE OFFICERS MESS. HE WILL DETAIL WORK FOR YOU TO DO. AND I WILL PUT YOUR NAME DOWN AS. A VOLUNTEER FOR WEEKEND GUARD DUTY. DOUBLE AWAY.' Thinking, "Oh shit. Hoped he had forgotten about it". It seemed to me that charges were handed out without going through the formalities of appearing before the OC. Unless caught fighting, stealing, AWOL or there had been a drastic case of willful damage to Government Property. Like the Squaddie already in the detention cell waiting a Court Martial. The rumour was he desperately wanted a Discharge from the Army his reason being; his father a farmer had died at home and he had to run the farm or something being refused a compassionate discharge razored all his clothing into shreds.

In the Officers mess. I reported to the Cook Sgt who gave me the task of laying the tables up, plus other preparations for the evening meal no hardship just a pain. Nevertheless, with no leave was stuck in a hut at the main gate doing a weekend guard and unbelievably during the night it snowed all Guards were ordered to wear greatcoats. It wasn't a heavy snowfall moreover, it was the beginning of June? In the morning the tops of the Malvern Hills were covered in snow. "What a pretty sight".

My only consolation was the following weekend would get home for my sisters 21st. Birthday party. Margaret had invited Derek hopefully he would be there as it was always the case when I was on leave he was not. With the availability of the camp telephone there was no need for writing letters Saturday. I had a party to attend and was out like a scalded cat. Fortune was on my side, a lift all the way to Cheltenham. About a mile outside. Thumbing along the London road a car pulled up, winding down the window the driver said.

Me. Derek./Weekend Pass.

'I'm going to London any good?'

'Blimey mate. Thanks not arf that's where I live, What part you going to?'

'Hammersmith. Any good?'

'Yeah great do me fine. Thanks mate.

'Hop in then.' What luck no sooner in the passenger seat, we were off, and chatting like old pals. Nearing the Oxford roundabout spotted a Lance Jack with his thumb up thinking, "I know him"? Almost on top of him, recognised Derek about to drive past yelled to the driver.

'Ere that's my mate Derek. Can you give him a lift as well?' The driver looked quizzically at me asked.

'Who?'

'Ere. Look. Sorry about this not seen him for months. Bleedin' surprise that's what it is.' The driver did stop. Derek came running up opened the rear door got in the back unaware he called out.

'Thanks mate. I turning around.

'Glad of a lift Derek?' He exclaimed.

'Bleedin' 'ell Joe. How yer doing mate? ' Shaking hands introduced him to the driver still bemused by his latest pick up. However, by the tone of our conversation he soon understood that it was genuine. Derek offered the driver a cigarette, they both coughed away together; by the time we reached Hammersmith we were all pals. I asked.

'Thanks mate, do you want any money?' He refused Derek gave him another cigarette.

The party was a hoot. Margaret had also invited a few Jazz musicians, from the Jazz club they turned up in the early hours of the morning. One was Tommy Whittle the saxophonist, a base player and Alan Ganley the drummer. They had an impromptu jazz session, Derek and I both got drunk. What a terrific weekend!

Georgie, on Guard one night had made friends with another squaddie in the intake before us who lived in Worcester and owned a van. This bloke suggested he would take us

 on a Wednesday night to a dance hall he knew in Worcester. We were all for it. Obtaining a pass was not a problem. But two other obstacles had to be overcome. One the dance hall did not allow hob nail boots and secondly. Brogue styled shoes were not permitted to be worn with uniforms. We were stumped. However this squaddie suggested.

If we bypass the guardroom he would pick us up outside. That night we went over the fields into the lane and clambered into his van. We had a great time dancing and the same thing happened the following couple of weeks. However, one of the duty guards saw us leaving camp and reported us. So passes were stopped that was the end of our midweek trips to Worcester.

The following week after OC's parade. As a working party our intake was detailed to paint one of the disused spiders at the derelict camp each armed with a pot of paint and paintbrush; we were marched to the derelict camp and into the chosen spider. Ordered to paint all the walls, light green above and dark green below separated by a horizontal black line to be finished by 1200 hrs or, that would delay those leaving camp on a weekend pass.

Keith Me John Note my Braces

Well! We painted at a furious pace the top half first regardless of drips paint brushes were going up and down like fiddlers elbows. By 1100 hrs getting frantic we started on the bottom by 1200 hrs, we estimated that it would take another hour or so. However, the Jocks and others not going home volunteered to finish the job. Grateful to them requested Sgt. Dennings permission for eleven home seekers to leave that he did and we left the camp about 1330 hrs nevertheless will never forget that trip home.

Just outside Cheltenham thumbing anything that came along, a Rolls Bentley pulled up. Surprised ran to the car the driver, a middle-aged man speaking with a plumb in his mouth asked.

'Are you heading for London. Soldier?' Turning on the charm, manners pouring out of my mouth.

'Yes Sir. Would you mind giving me a lift? Please Sir?'

'Yes I can. Place your grip on the back seat come and sit in the front beside me, there's a good chap.' Thinking, "Blimey he's a bit of a Toff" Driving off he asked.

'Where in London are you heading for?'

'Vauxhall Sir I live with my parents I am just on a thirty-six hour weekend pass. That's all Sir.'

'Well. I am going to Knightsbridge. I can drop you off there is that acceptable to you.'

'Yes please Sir. That would be most acceptable. Thank you sir.' Thinking "I don't believe this? I cadging a lift in of all things 'A Rolls Bentley.' it's unheard of".

Sat in comfort with hardly any noise from the engine grinned at any squaddies with their thumbs up as we swished past they gawking at my luck. 'You lucky bleeder.' The ride was smooth silent and enjoyable. We chatted a lot about various subjects, apparently, he had been a Major in the army, but that was as far as he would say. At Knightsbridge, he dropped me off close to Harrods. Thanking him profusely, he wishing me luck we parted the best of pals. All I had to do was walk to Hyde Park Corner get a Number 2 bus to Vauxhall walk home. Despite leaving the camp late, arrived home well before five.

The first week in July was the week we completed the theory side of Trade Training. On the Wednesday afternoon sports session parading in our singlet's, shorts, socks and plimsolls, we were informed that our spider was to play football against number 8 spider-Thirty two aside and provided with a Rugby Ball ordered.

'No handling of the ball.' It became a hilarious game with masses of blokes chasing a rugby ball about, someone would kick it in the air and it would bounce in a different direction causing the ensuing mass to fall over each other in a heap. Six or seven blokes tried dribbling the ball hacking shit out of each other's legs nobody ever got near a goal. By the time the Sgt. Referee blew the final whistle all players were walking wounded and knackered. Thursday and Friday had been nominated as revision days however, because of the painting episode the Jocks and others who had not previously been able to take advantage of weekend leave were allowed a 72-hour pass home.

The following Monday, we began the practical side of the course. Provided with toolboxes were separated into two groups. One group concentrated on Electric motors and associated components the other concentrated on Batteries and motor wiring. That weekend Johnny Dankworth and his band were playing at the Malvern Winter Gardens so I stayed in camp to go to the dance. It was good but with boots and gaiters on was not allowed on the dance floor. Upon our return to camp walking back to the spider, the heavens opened up we got drenched. Very early next morning the Guard Sgt rudely awakened us shouting

'EVERYONE DRESS IN DENIMS. GET OUTSIDE IN THREES YOU'RE WANTED DOWN THE KINEMA IMMEDIATELY.' Whoever was on camp was being marched to the Kinema there we found the previous night's rain had flooded it out. The area in front of the stage was about five foot deep in water. Forming a chain used fire buckets to empty it out. We broke for lunch and then returned. By 1600, hours the last dregs were mopped up, we were all fed up with bleedin' water and the Kinema remained closed.

In mid July. A new RSM by the name of Dixie Dean arrived in the camp possibly to whip us into shape to mark the inaugural opening of a new parade ground. According to rumours, his bark was equal to the famed RSM Britain. Two weeks after his arrival after lessons on the Monday. All personnel had to draw rifle bayonets and march to the new square to form up under the eagle eye of Dixie Dean who put the Battalion through the usual rifle drill movements. It must have been twelve weeks since our Platoon had finished basic training and were not marching as synchronized as the later intakes it became a shambles. Sgt's. Cpl's, Themselves not being DI's and after months or in some cases years of being unaccustomed to parade ground drill, were shouting ranting and raving at the mass of squaddies under their charge. The RSM was doing his nut shouting out orders as he marched about using his pace stick in accordance to the drill book attempting to get everyone to march in step. All to no avail. Nobody was in step. In a fit of temper, he hurled his pace stick to the ground. Thinking, "He was going to jump up and down on it. " But he did not picking it up waving it about his head continued shouting orders, hurling obscenities at everyone. We must have done the Open and Close order movement a dozen times still not getting it right. The RSM was not going to be beaten ordered everyone to shout out. 'ONE. TWO THREE. ONE...ORDER ARMS.' He screamed and we screamed back at him... 'ONE. TWO THREE. ONE.'...Unfortunately, with all our aching arms one poor sod in front of me let his rifle go too far, in the process of grabbing it the tip of his bayonet tore a great weald in the back of the neck of the bloke in the front rank. 'OW' He screamed and the BSM screamed back.

'WHO SAID THAT? ONE STEP FORWARD. Nobody moved. SERGEANT'S FIND OUT WHO THE CULPRIT IS. PUT HIM ON A CHARGE.' The Sgt's scurried up and down the ranks found nobody on the ground lying dead or injured.

Nevertheless after the evening meal we continued in the evening sunlight doing the drill night after night until on Friday night the RSM gave up. Stomping off the square intending to take a short cut across the Battalion allotments stepped onto an upturned old wooden wheelbarrow, which under his weight gave way. Over he goes into a cabbage patch his pace stick flying through the air hit the glasshouse shattering a pane. Well! Those that witnessed this charade wet themselves on the spot. Retrieving his dignity and his pace stick firmly under his arm stomped through the cabbage patch in the direction of the Sgt's. Mess to drown his sorrows, whilst we continued parading for the next week.

Saturday the OC's parade was held on the new square. Duly christened with a lot of pomp and ceremony, including a visit from the REME Corp band. Dressed in Battle Order all performed well having got the orders correct for the bash the CO warmly congratulated us after the march past. We spent the next three hours, playing soldiers in the woods

Photo taken outside Spiders after OCs Parade. Bill Troon with Chanter far right.

surrounding the camp. "Search and Destroy". Do not know whom we were searching for but it did waste away the time skiving in the woods.

The end of the course was getting closer, weekend passes for us became non-existing it was also close to the time when no doubt we would all part company, being posted to other destination. We all wanted to stick together I do not know who suggested it but Parachute Training became a feature in our quest. The six of us put in chit has to see the OC. Requesting to be sent on a parachute course. We duly reported to his office. RSM Dean balling his head off marched us in. Our request was refused. His answer.

'No. After you have finished your Trade Training here. I hope that you will pass? You will all have different posting. Then if you still want to do it, apply through your new OC. Dismiss.'

The Friday evenings bulling never changed and it occupied the full evening. However, one person Ronald! Was always finished well before everyone else he did his fair share of the roster duties but for whatever reason never could put much effort into swinging the buffer. Nevertheless, his nightly bed routine was something John and I could not stand by 2100 hrs, already dressed in his pajamas sat up in bed nibbling cream crackers like a little rabbit, his moustache moved in unison with his nibbling. That Friday night we decided to teach him a lesson, gathering a few others charged down the spider swarming around his bed manhandling it lifted it shoulder high; his tin of cream crackers fell on the floor in the process was trampled into crumbs with Ronald hanging on and squawking like a chicken cried.

'Let me down. Let me down.' Forcibly carried him and his bed down the Spider other willing hands opened the inner and outer double doors, still protesting he was carried all the way across the walkway into the opposite spider. Dumping him down inside their entrance left him to get back under his own steam, we all retreating howling with laughter shortly after Ronald enveloped in his bedding re-entered.

Nevertheless, the other occupants also engaged in bulling took umbrage to the unsightly intrusion of a body and a bed in their Spider. They retaliated by throwing a bucket of water through our outer doorway all over our gleaming polished floor. So began the water fight, out came the fire buckets and stirrup pumps furiously manned as a stream of water was squirted into their spider. They retaliated by throwing full buckets of water it was then a case of one bucket for another into each Spider everywhere was awash. Stuck in between the showers Ronald! In his soaking wet pyjamas was like a drowned rat as he tried to dismantle his bed and carry it piece by piece to reassemble it. It had been a bleedin' good show and both occupants of the Spiders had enjoyed the mayhem it had caused. Nevertheless, all had to be mopped cleaned and buffed ready for OC's the following morning. Ronald. Never made any formal complaint and from then on remained out of bed until after lights out.

Nearing to the end of the course, one Friday night having finished dinner. Sgt. Denning entered the Spider and pinned a note on the Notice Board requesting everyones attention before he began his oration.

'Now you have finished the practical side of the course, on Monday you will sit your exams. Those that pass would be informed of their next posting. Those who fail would be back squadded to rejoin the part of the course they had failed on. On the notice Board is a list of future postings. Each of you can select three places they wish to be posted to. If you are lucky, you might get one. When you have decided, please inform me of you chosen three. Carry On bulling.'

The list stated a variety of different postings scattered in England and mainly Germany. The overseas postings, to Africa, Aden, Cyprus, Egypt, Hong Kong, Singapore, the West Indies and Bermuda. John confiding in me he was confident about passing the exams, yet dreading the possibility of leaving England. Assuring him he would get a posting closer to home did not convince him. However, he suggested if he got a posting overseas could he swop with me? That was okay by me. Later in the Naafi, the postings were the topic of our conversation. The six of us decided we should all stick together all wanting to see the world the further away the better so decided to volunteer for. Hong Kong, Singapore and Bermuda, the thought of failing and going through those lessons again was not a desire so, it was time for swotting.

Our last O.C's parade was held on the main square. The OC wished all in 9/Elect /7 the best in the exams. It was a very hot day some of us decided to go outside and lay on the grass to swot, it did not take long before everyone was outside one wanting to be comfortable laid out his blanket. A lot of tomfoolery began and swotting ceased forcefully I was grabbed by a gang of them, manhandled onto the blanket the sides were grabbed and was hurled up into the air coming back down unceremoniously was hurled up again, this happened a few time until coming down feet first straight through the blanket. A big ripping sound rent the air as the blanket was torn in two. Barrack room damages loomed. The owner unperturbed hands in his pockets stated.

'I'll sew it up. They won't notice when I hand it in.'

John arrived with his camera wanting to take a group photograph of 9/Elect /7 for prosperity yelled.

'All form up by the pipe.'

9/ELECT /7

Swotting for our three day exams

The following Monday the exams began. First part theory followed by the practical exams, finishing on the Wednesday evening. Thursday was crunch day. After dinner we were assembled in one of the large workshops and our results were read out. Only concerned with mine, listened if passed and where posted? '429 Plant J. P. Pass. Craftsman. Posting Singapore.'

Chuffed to blazes thought, 'Bleedin' 'ell Craftsman and Singapore". It was not until after the results had been read out everyone conferring where they were going too. Only two had failed and back squadded to practical. Bert, Georgie, Jimmy, Jack and Jackie had postings to Singapore. Therefore, we were all in the same boat. John a posting to Newcastle to a RA. Ack -Ack unit. Others had been posted to camps in England a few to Germany, Bill Troon to Paris! A couple to Cyprus and four to Kenya. I think all were quite happy. I phoned home that night and informed mum about the results and my posting. See you tomorrow night. That night 9/Elect /7 celebrated in Malvern and had a good piss up in The Red Lion pub half way up the hill.

Friday was packing up day, hand in bedding a quick visit to the MO to pass you fit and for those going overseas, a cocktail of jabs followed by our last fish and chip dinner. Back in the Spider Sgt. Denning handed out travel warrants and a week's embarkation leave pass to those going overseas he wishing all of us Good Luck. Dressed in our FSMO full of jubilance with Uni's slung over the shoulder, we left the Spider for the guardroom to sign out for the last time. Leaving as Trained Craftsmen climbed aboard the waiting Lorry to be driven out through the avenue of trees we had entered as Privates. I was sorry to leave Malvern, like Honiton it had its difficulties nevertheless; it had been great fun with a smashing load of blokes to share enjoyment and at times frustration.

At Malvern station, whilst standing on the platform thought back to the many night times we had arrived back early in the morning, the fact was the only time I had seen it in daylight was when I had first arrived and at that moment upon leaving. It was the same at Honiton upon arrival and leaving, how strange. Anyway, we all boarded the same train as far as Worcester where others heading North had to change to my mate John, it was goodbye. We had spent the first six months of army life together. Possibly the bond we had formed right from the start with a similar sense of humour that had kept us sane. To the others it was farewell but not Bert, Georgie, Jimmy, Jack and Jackie. In one week's time would meet them in Arborfield.

CHAPTER TWELVE
EMBARCATION

Something powerful had been pumped into me by the time the train had arrived at Evesham was sweating heavily; my arms and stomach ached, so decided to sleep. Stan Dakin shouting.

'Come on Mate wakey wakey, just left Slough. Paddington next stop. Wots matter with yer. You look fooking terrible?' Bemused as to where I was muttered.

'Wot. Where are we? Must have passed out?'

'Snoring yer bleedin' 'ead off, noisy bleeder.' Regaining my senses said.

'Sodding' 'ell. Don't ever volunteer for anything, how long we got?'

'Bout 'arf hour. Get yer kit on.' Sitting there stiff as a board my arms felt "Huge" pondered. "When we got into Paddington, it would be the rush hour! Aw sodding 'ell. Volunteer for Queen and country. Only to fight before you have even left the country. Oh well. There is only one-way, grin and bear it. When I get home, I will go straight to bed and sleep it off. Be okay in the morning"? As the train pulled into Paddington Station. Stan helped get my kit on before we said our farewells. Stan had a posting to somewhere in Scotland he asked.

'You are alright mate?' I hopefully said.

'I'll have to be. It ain't that far on the tube.'

'Nope. You'll be all right just think of me. I have to get to Leicester yet that is a drag?'

'Sod your luck mate. Anyway it's been great knowing yer. You take care; maybe see yer when we get demobed?'

With all my kit and not feeling too good, it was a struggle getting home particularly catching the number 2 bus at Victoria, which would take me within a quarter of a mile to walk no such luck. Eventually had to get on a 36 to Vauxhall, with a further mile to walk arriving home got out of me kit and went straight to bed.

The next day although still sore avoiding the thought of leaving home for a long period overseas tried to relax listened to music. That night went to the dance at St. Anne's. Had a few drinks in the Beehive and invited a few mates home for a piss up the following Saturday unfortunately Derek was in Norway on some army exercise. During the week, went to the Flicks up the West end and the Star Club. Had a few beers with Dad and Mike. The party was great we enjoyed ourselves. Sunday lunch mum cooked a smashing roast dinner leg of lamb with all the trimmings Jackie was the only one absent. After dinner, sorted out some small personal things before doing some bulling.

Very early Monday morning dressed in FSMO. Had the same feeling as when leaving to join the army. Not wanting to go. Bidding farewell to mum and dad who with both hands warmly clasped my hand, his parting words with a nod and smile said.

'Son. Keep your head down. Watch your back and good luck.' However, in his eyes I noticed something. Did he know something I was unaware of?

Catching the 77 bus, being so early there was not many on it the Conductor helped me put the Kitbag in the space under the stairs. With all my kit on sat perched on the edge of the three seater. Dinging the bell he casually asked.

'Going away Son?'

'Yer. Bleedin' Singapore.' To which he responded. 'Never bin there only got as far as Alexandria. Desert Rat yer know. But that was years ago. Anyway Good Luck. Any more fares Please?' He carried on his rounds nobody sat next to me.

Arriving at Waterloo in good time to catch the early train to Wokingham where outside joined others gathered around a waiting Lorry, slinging our kit onto the back scrambled up and soon were off to Arborfield.

At the gates of Poperinghe Camp we were confronted by huge blocks of concrete (Tank Traps) strategically placed in the road. The driver maneuvering around them stopped in front of the guardroom. The place was a hive of activity Double guards, RPs and Red Caps alike buzzing around. We did not have a clue what was going on. One RP ordered.

'All get down. Sign in at the guardroom.' Taking a good look at the Guardhouse thought, "Back to Honiton and drafty huts". Signing in the Cpl. questioned.

Poperinghe Guardhouse

'Number, rank, name?'

'23112429. Craftsman Plant.'

'Malvern last camp?'

'Yes. Nine Elcet Seven intake.' Any Jocks from Malvern, signed in yet?'

'Yes. Five came in early, allocated last hut far end you can join em.' I enquired.

'Okay! But what's going on here?'

'You'll find out later?' Outside picking up the Uni proceeded in the direction of the end hut three others joined me as we entered the hut. Bert greeted me.

'War ye bin?' 'Ye git los?'

'Nah. Wots going on here?'

'Dinna ken. Te guard wood nae say. Di ye ave a guid leeve?'

'Yeah sort of. Plenty of drinking and good food went to flicks once it was rubbish, can't even remember the name of the film so left and went to the Star Club listened to some jazz and on Saturday had a party, apart from that zilch.' Georgie interrupted.

'Gee'n collec' ye bedding' tek bunk doon yon end, war Jack is.'

'Where's bedding store then?'

'Doon neerr square near te guardhoose.' The hut was small and pokey struggling towards Jack he suggested.

'Ear. Take top bunk.' Slipping off the kit, slung it onto the top bunk, taking it apart slipped the belt back on.

Poperinghe was a transit depot with limited accommodation sleeping twelve per hut in double bunks. There were no lockers or boxes everything kept as it was or in the kitbag. The other three who had joined us, came from Barton Stacey camp. One a lanky person from the midlands a Welshman and the third from the Hull area. With hardly any room to swing, a cat there were still three bunks empty. At the bedding store, we signed for bedding issue plus a brown tin mug the store man stated.

'No plates. Use your mess tins.' Returning to the hut swept the webbing onto the floor kicking it under the bunks made up the bed. Georgie the ever-hungry one, using his knife and fork began beating a drum roll on his mess tins, a sure sign the call to dinner.

Dinner was not a patch on the food at Malvern, but edible and certainly better than Honiton. Rumours circulating in the mess hall indicated the IRA had raided the camp stolen numbers of weapons and ammunition; hence, the tank traps at the entrance. The Duty Sgt. of the day ordered. 'You have all to report to the MRS for a Medical. Then the Admin Block where you will be issued with passes to get in and out of the camp. Between the hours of eighteen hundred and Twenty-three Fifty-nine.'

Within the camp there appeared to be hardly any formality about moving in platoons. You were directed to be at a certain place at a certain time. We duly attended the medical, all were passed A.I. In addition received more booster jabs. Next the Admin block for passes the whole procedure took up the afternoon. Three newcomers had joined the hut one from Kent, one from Shropshire and one from Devon.

Georgie beating out a drum roll informed all it was teatime. In the mess, we decided to take in the sights of Reading. At 1800 hrs dressed in our number ones wearing black brogue shoes ready to trample on any girls feet at a dance if, we were lucky or raid a Pub. Showing our passes at the duty R.Ps. It was all very informal but worked. Outside the camp along with many others caught the bus into Reading. Getting off at the station headed for the first pub across the road. In the Public bar was a dartboard so it was a game of darts to start the evening off. With beer in hand sat down on a form took a swig. Next thing Bert was heaving me up possibly from the effect of the cocktail of drugs administered that afternoon had passed out. A sure sign not to drink much, maybe it had affected the others as after a few more beers we decided to return to camp. Outside it was still twilight a cool balmy night with hardly a breeze, during the week the weather was kind and did not rain.

The next morning outside the hut a roll call was made just to make certain we were still there. However were informed; in rotation would be chosen to do double picket guard duty and ordered to clean and tidy up our huts having finished there was nothing else to do. We escaped that night's duty instead went into Wokingham. Just as bad no dance hall open, but someone did mention a place called California that held a dance on a Wednesday evening.

On the Wednesday. Overseas kit was issued together with a White Sea kit bag. Olive Greens (OGs) tropicals, made out of light cotton material two sets of each. Jacket, trousers, shorts, green cellular underwear, light blue silk pajamas, woolen hose tops and puttees, single floppy jungle hat. Our 37-pattern webbing was exchanged for Olive Green 44- pattern lightweight webbing, with aluminum water battle. One set each of BD, denims, berets, belt, boots, gaiters, and two pairs of socks were kept to wear before changing into Tropical's. We spent most of the day trying them on. The puttees were long wide bandages that wrapped around your ankles, somebody made a joke.

'They are to stop a snake biting you.' That went down like a bomb, nobody had even thought of creepy crawlies, Tigers, Elephants or any other animals that made up the habitation of the Far East. The round shapeless cloth hats were tried on, causing much mirth amongst all. With the prospect of seeing the world wishing the days too quickly, go by. That evening leaving the camp, the Guards kindly pointed us in the right direction to California! Walking down the leafy lanes of Berkshire eventually found the Dance hall and was promptly turned away. No one in uniform was allowed in. We found a pub had a few beers and a game of darts.

Thursday another lazy day. After pay parade, there was nothing to do. Someone bought a local paper that covered the recent raid by the IRA. The rumors were right.

Nevertheless, it was Hazebrouck Camp not ours. We read the information with interest. Two local Constabulary Police Officers had spotted a van acting suspiciously, approaching it noting its occupants were agitated and spoke with Irish accents. Requesting to look into the back where they discovered many stolen weapons and ammunition. Everything was recovered.

Extract from local newspaper of IRA raid

Phoning home that evening. Mum told me Jackie wanted to speak to me. He had just arrived back and suggested. He would meet me at Reading the following night, to have a farewell beer or two. I suggested the pub opposite Reading station and was it Okay to bring along my mates? No problem.

Friday another day of doing nothing, but were informed four of us had been picked to do a Saturday/Sunday twenty-four hour guard. The rest if, they so required could apply for a 36-hour pass. That evening we were already in the Pub when Jackie arrived accompanied by Margaret and Lily. Bert, who was good looking had met both of them fancied Lily and it was not long before they started chatting together. Jackie in the Merchant Navy having just come back off a trip was flush with money and in his usual generous way bought all the rounds until 2100 hrs when they had to leave to catch the last train. I went with them across to the station to see them off Jackie gave me another tenner to buy more drinks for the lads. With a lump in my throat returned to the pub for more drinks before staggering back to camp.

Saturday. Mounted guard at 1200 hours. Provided with pickaxe handles and whistles. Ordered, if any IRA attacks blow your whistle then wait until assistance arrives. Nevertheless, with two of us on patrol it was not so tedious and whiled away the time.

Monday, we lazed about, after Naafi break were informed. Tuesday early morning reveille 0500. hrs. Prepare to leave the camp. Instructed to print on the bottom and sides of our Kit bags in broad capital letters number, name and rank. In addition ordered to write out our wills on any one of the three detachable pages at the rear of our AB64 Part I. Having completed the first chore all went outside into the sunlight laid on the grass verge to write out wills, selecting any one of the following:

(a) Leaving all your possessions to one person,
(b) To more than one person.
(c) Going on active service.

Collectively. We did not think the last two applied so wrote out instructions on (a). (Leaving all to mum was not much anyway; she could sell the bike, throw the rest away). Detaching the wills handed them to the Sgt. In readiness for the next morning separating our kit packed various items into the Uni for sea storage and into the sea kit bag for use on board the ship. That night, we went to Reading for a good piss up returned to camp all the worse for wear crashed out on our bunks.

Tuesday. Very early next morning using his pickaxe handle, the Guard banging hell out of the door woke up the sleeping bodies of the hut. His banging coincided with the banging in my head the verbal abuse issued to the Guard is not repeatable. It was just getting light time to get up and prepare to leave England. That morning was hazy to say the least. Early breakfast, provided with travel rations for the train journey with explicit instructions... 'Pack them in your white sea kit bag. Savvy? Hand in your bedding, collect your kit and get down to the parade ground, where trucks are waiting.' The instruction given was straightforward and simple. No. Good luck or kiss me arse or any other joyous quotation to help us on our way.

In the hut in a befuddled haze packed the brown paper bag full of Sarnnies into the top of the Uni. Tying up the securing rope gathering up bedding along with the others, struggled down to the Bedding store to hand it in. Collecting our kit bags headed for the square where others had already gathered in groups quietly waiting to climb aboard the line of Lorries. The rising sun was trying to penetrate through the early morning mist gave the feeling that it was going to be another fine day. A Sgt. bellowed out.

'Climb aboard with your kit. Snap to it.' Very quickly, the square emptied of squaddies and their kit. As the lorry drove off the square the last thing on view was a great big electric pylon sited almost on the square, why it was located there shall never know. As the truck maneuvered its way through the tank traps. We shouted out raucous drivel at the guard's. Next stop Reading station en-route to Liverpool docks and a troopship, a new experience for anyone traveling in her.

Troopships! It was the Royal Navy, who provided the original method of transporting military forces by ships to foreign lands that began during the reign of CHARLES II. The first convoy of troops to set sail was in 1662 when the Tangier Regiment sailed in Royal Navy Ships to occupy the Tangier Garrison, against any invasion by the Moors. As the British Empire expanded throughout the world, ships of the Royal Navy were used to, transport troops to the nearest available port in the country being occupied.

However. This method of transport had been used by many other conqueror, such as the Vikings, and Romans, whose ships were manned by oarsmen and using a large single sheet of canvas to be blown by winds across numerous seas. As time progressed, armies grew in numbers therefore to carry more men, the size and build of the ships increased, requiring more area of canvass. Until eventually, the age of steam arrived, when paddle wheels required boilers, to produce the steam that drove the paddles assisting the ships canvas, further progressed to the newfound method of ship propulsion. Propeller driven ships. The Royal Navy as did, the Merchant ships. Changed the design and requirements, of ships to the new screw propeller driven method.

The British Empire reached the four corners of the earth, requiring battalions of soldiers to build and maintain garrisons within those territories under the British flag. It was during the reign of Queen Victoria that the sub continent of India was colonised by British troops in their thousands together with the migration of families employed by the East India Company, they trading in the Far East became a massive trading company. During that period, the normal sea trip sailing via the Mediterranean Sea to Port Said, where the passengers would disembark, to travel overland down through Egypt to its southern port of Suez. That would take up to ninety days where they would board another ship to take them to ports in Arabia, India, Burma, or as far as China. It was not until a shorter route via the Suez Canal, a remarkable feat of engineering was finally completed and opened in1876. That created access for ships of all sizes to sail through its waterway, from Port Said to Suez. Many years later, thousands of Conscripts/National Servicemen, were to partake on the wonders of a sea voyages to worldly outpost of the dwindling British Empire via the Suez Canal, on different named troopships as follows:

Her Majesties Troopships: Andes, Aquitania, Athlone Castle, Asturias, Devonshire, Dilwara, Dorsetshire, Dunera. All the Empire ships: - Bura, Clyde, Fowey, Halladale, Ken, Orwell, Pride, Trooper, Wansbeck, Windrush (which sank in the Mediterranean on the 30th. Mar 1954 en-route from Kure Japan to Southampton) The County Ships: Lancashire, Oxfordshire, Somersetshire, or the Nevassa Samaria not to forget the Channel crossing troopship Vienna. Nevertheless. There were many others that are not mentioned.

Alternatively. Later another type of transport came into use. Aircraft handled by the Royal Air Force Transport Command. Flying out of Brize Norton or Blackbush, this provided for a limited number of passengers, but an even quicker way of getting to ones posting. Usually, the method employed was either fly out, return by troopship or, visa versa. However, our method of transport was a luxury cruise aboard. 'H.M.T.S Lancashire.'

CHAPTER THIRTEEN
A CRUISE LINER

At Reading station getting off the Lorry we were the first to arrive on the platform in a siding away from the main station where a train was waiting, the Sgt. ordered.

'You lot move along the platform and place your Uni's up against the railings. Do ensure your details are facing inwards towards the railway track.'

Doing as instructed with our six in places others began laying the bottom row on either side, as it grew I suddenly realised had packed my rations in my Uni seeking the attention of the sergeant asked.

'Er. Sergeant. By mistake, put my rations in the Uni. Can I get them?'

'Chuffing 'ell. There's always one that chooses to do it different from anyone else. Which one is yours Soldier?' Pointing at my Uni.

'That one. Middle bottom row Sergeant.'

'You. Bloody idiot! Go outside and see if you can open up the neck and get them out. Move your arse were about to start boarding. Otherwise. YOU will have to wait until you get to Liverpool?'

Having counted the number along to the last, one going outside located it tight up against the railings, it was impossible to untie the rope. As a few Porters started removing the top Uni's onto trolleys I gave up and returned to the platform to join the others as they boarded the train. Locating an empty compartment piled in and put our Sea Kitbags up onto the luggage rack settled down for a long trip.

At 0700hrs, the train chuffed out of Reading station. That journey was to take nearly all-day travelling via Bristol with a glimpse of the Clifton Bridge thrown in, onto Hereford to pick up more troops. During the journey, the other five had made light work of their own travel rations two flagstone size sarnies filled with corned beef and two hard-boiled eggs. "Did not want them anyway. Says who"?

About 1700 hours. The train arrived at Liverpool by that time I was ravished with hunger as it slowed to a crawl it crossed from one line to another and its wheels sounded like the scything of a bacon slicer, it went through a station that somebody mentioned was Lime Street station. Diverting away moved slowly in-between stationary wagons, from outside in the corridor someone shouted. 'Everyone there's a bloody great ship waiting for us.' In an effort to get a glimpse of this latest sight all spilled out into the corridor already crammed full of eager squaddies. Slowly the train came to a halt alongside the troopship. H.M.T.S. LANCASHIRE.

X marks our habitat below water line . (Posted @ Suez 1955)

Down on the quayside an R.E. Sgt. banging a stick against the side of the carriage came striding past urging everyone.

'COME ON. YOU LOT. YOU ARE LATE. GRAB YOUR SEA KIT BAGS AND GET OUT. SHARPISH. MOOOVE.'

Move we did. Berets and belts hastily clipped and adjusted kit bags retrieved from luggage racks, first out was Jackie opening the carriage door, exclaimed.

'Blooody 'ell mon. Tisa loong droop doon... Jumping down he called out... Awa, throw us doon wer kit bags. I'll catch umm.' Bert shouted.

'Aboot soodon' tim ye deen sommat useful.' Dropping each kit bag down Georgie was about to jump down from the carriage when striding towards us the R.E. Sgt. urged.

'COME ON YOU LOT. YOU ARE IDLE. STOP LAZING ABOUT. THE SHIP IS WAITING FOR YOU IDLE BUNCH OF BASTARDS. GET MOVING.'

Down on the cobbled quayside picking up our kitbags heard the whine and whirring of a dock cranes motor looking upwards saw a cargo net full of Uni's swinging across the ship's side too disappear. The rest of them roared with laughter, Jimmie yelled.

'Blooody 'ad it noo Planty.' Geordie laughing said.

'Ye gear we be in raags, be tim ye ger therre.' Jackie shouted.

'Ter rats on board wea be as fat as pigs.' Not amused ignored them. Crossing over the cobbled quayside towards a gangway. Everyone was gazing up at the vastness of this white painted ship with a wide blue stripe in-between two rows of portholes evidence of large rusty patches were everywhere. High above hanging motionless from their davit's was a line of white lifeboats beyond those a very tall yellow painted funnel with a trail of black smoke drifting upwards into the blue sky. Joining the rear of the REME contingent began our ascent up to a gap in the ship's rail, stumbling up the gangway Jimmie with a huge grin yelled back.

'Nae tuurnng back now ye ken.' At the top a ship's Officer and a R.E Sgt. gave out instructions where we had to go.

'To your LEFT. Half way down towards 'aft. Is a bulkhead doorway. Go through there and down the stairways. Just keep on going downwards. Keep moving up the front.'

On our left lounging against the ship's rail shirt-sleeved soldiers watched as we passed by, they must have been on board for some time. Whilst on our right the white painted steel walls had a row of closed cabin doors with portholes on the wooden deck between each door were large wooden boxes marked. "LIFE JACKETS". Coming to a large open area a big passageway gave access to the other side where more troops were leant against the ship's rail. Standing at a bulkhead doorway, a Sgt. bawled out.

'YOU LOT. THROUGH HERE. KEEP ON GOING DOWN THE STAIRWAY.'

Going through the doorway stepped onto a landing with a flight of steep stairs downwards, on our way we passed Deck numbers B, C, D, E, F, G, and H. Geordie behind me called out.

'Ye Ken. We'll be in te blooody ingine rroom soon.' Little did he know? The last double flight of ladders led down to a darkened deck space. At the foot of the stairway illuminated by the light from a bulb above his head another Sgt. pointing ordered.

'You six right over the back. When you doss down sleep head to feet. Counting out the six behind. You six behind down that side. When you doss down sleep head to feet.' So, he carried on.... Into the gloom, we followed Georgie in-between the bulkhead and rows of hammocks the semi dark gangway was illuminated by small lights spaced in-between the low rows of ceiling girders giving headroom of about six foot six inches from the deck, coming to a stop at the end Georgie remarked.

'Nae goo eeny father. Theese oor Buunks!' A row of twelve hammocks I noticed the ship side had a distinct inward curve. Geordie remarked.

'Heh! Ye ken warr we arrr?' I prompted.

'No. Go on tell us big head.' He hooted.

'Warr at. Te arse end of te boot.'

'How do you make that out?'

'Wooked on te ship's. An cun till from te sloop of te seeds ye ken.' Demonstrating his knowledge showed how the side sloped inwards and curved around... Te props arr behind us.' Jimmie cracked.

'Blooody 'ell mon. Nae dinna leeke arse end of anything.' Bert asked.

'What da wee da with our gear? Therre's nae bed boxes?' I suggested.

'Keep it in your kit bag.' Bert commented.

'Bedding's nae te guid either.' Neatly folded on top of the hammock was one blanket as cover.

'What do we do now? I'm starving.' Immediately brought a great peel of laughter as they chorused.

'Gee an find yur sooding Uni.' Taking no notice remarked.

'Bleedin' good this is. I was expecting a cabin to myself.' Geordie yelled.

'Whoo? De yu tink ye are. Ter OC?'

'Nah. I thought we were going on a cruise liner.' Some Taffy from within the gloom remarked.

'Hey did yu year that! Faking cruise liner. You're in the faking army mate. Fourth-class faking citizen. That's what you are.' Someone else yelled out.

'Were down in the fooking bilges. That's where we fooking are.' Another voice questioned.

'What the fooking 'ell are they?' Followed by a prompt answer.

'Where all the rats are.'

Discussing who was going to sleep where. Bert chose the top, Jimmie, the middle, me on the bottom, with Jackie aside of me above him was Jack, then Geordie. Slinging my kit bag onto the hammock a piece of stretched canvas laced to a steel frame, at either end a support chain was secured to the upright pole. Our activity was interrupted by the sound of machinery starting up. A loud whirling followed by a slow dull sploosh. sploosh. Jimmie exclaimed.

'Blooody 'ell! Warr mooving.' The ship shuddered as it began its voyage out to Singapore. I shouted.

'Ear. Were sailing.' Geordie exclaimed.

'Canna bee? We've only just arreeved.'

Somewhere in the bilge, a Tannoy bleeped and a loud voice hailed. 'The Lancashire. Is about to sail. Bound for Singapore.' I exclaimed.

'Wot did I tell yer. We are sailing! Let's get back up on deck.'

In a mad rush, everyone from the bilges chased their way up the steep stairways, by the time we eventually arrived on deck we were out of breath breathing like bleedin' galloping horses. The ship's rail was crammed full of other troops eager to watch the ship's departure from the quayside. Squeezing in amongst them watched as a tug nosed its way in between the quay and ship pushed it into the midstream of the brownish Mersey waters. The tugs having done their job headed back to shore; as the ship got under way, we sailed past the famous Royal Liver Building with the setting sun, glinting on its white clock face its hands pointed to ten past six we had not been on board more than half an hour. Most of the troops drifted away with the exception of a few as they watched the ship's bow waves far below with the strong sea breeze ruffling heads of shorn hair. It was boring. Jimmie suggested

'Awaa lits goo doon stairrs. Git ane ideas?' I vaguely remembered.

'The entrance is further back where that wide gangway is.'

Due to the motion of the ship, we none too steady on our feet swaying and bumping into each other made our way back to the wide gap and doorway down. At the bottom of the stairways the area was in a state of minor activity. Squaddies sat on hammocks or stood in small groups chatting. There was a mixture of different REME trades, Mechanics, Electricians, Recovery Mechanics, Armourer's, Welders to mention a few. In our dark corner we were the only ones from Malvern. However, my stomach was playing havoc inside of me grumbling and rumbling around aching for food I asked.

'Anyone got any food on them?' Jackie cracked.

'Awa man. Yours is in ye Uni doon in te hoold.' Bert asked.

'When de tay feed yee, un tis soodin' tub?' Geordie wandered off after a short while returning advised all.

'Ye ken. I've foond ter showers, n' ablootion room, joost paast ter stairway.'

At last, something of interest. To find out something you had to go and find it yourself. Georgie led us past the stairways to another doorway striding over the kick plate the red ceramic floor tiles was full of grooves, on one sloping bulkhead were a row of showers and washbasins opposite those was a row of toilets with canvas draw curtains. Our inspection curtailed by the bleep of the Tannoy announcing. 'Troop Deck 'H.' Meals are being served in the for 'ard mess.'

Eating irons, mess tins and tin mugs were hurriedly fished out of the sea kit bag to join the tail end of the hungry mob en route to the top deck. On deck making our way for 'ard, the sea was calm with a chilling breeze behind us the golden rays of the setting sun lit up the outline of the clouds nighttime was not far away.

We left that glorious sight and bumped our way along the wooden deck to join the rear of a queue leading to the entrance of a little hut, as we got close to it wafting up from below the warm air was tinged with the smell of fish. Going down two flights of stairs into the cramped space of the mess. Through the portholes on our left shafts of the diminishing sunlight provided a reasonable amount of daylight. Stuck out like oars and secured to the bulkheads and deck were long tables with seating forms, a narrow gangway separated more long tables and forms where several of the tables had Squaddies sat already eating. Jimmie, first in any queue for grub had taken a tray from a stack of steel trays remarked. 'Nae use te mess tins.'

Slipping the handle of the mess tins into the top of the trouser belt line taking a tray noticed it was molded into partitions for the food, following Jimmie towards a long open serving hatch; where a few Indians were dishing out food the first Indian prompted.

'Nex tray Sahib.' Offering the tray, he taking it lowered it below the serving top, placing food on it watched him pass it onto the next Indian, following its progress it was handed back with smoked haddock and mashed potatoes nothing else. By the hatch, was the tea urn filling up the brown tin mug with tea was aware of the upwards slope of the deck thought, "With the movement of the ship, walking backwards and forwards could be tricky". Sitting down beside Jimmie he already forcing the fish down his neck, taking a breather and a gulp of tea, growled.

'I dinae coome on te ship te eat blooody fesh' Ignoring him got stuck in; before anyone else started had finished and could easily have eaten a second helping. Bert twiddling his fork around in his mashed spuds stabbed the fish to make certain it was dead having made up his mind, he exploded with.

'I'm coomplainng te Captin aboot shitting meal, blooody disgrace! Fist te bunks doon yonder in te sooodin' Bilges. Noo wee's gee served fesh suppers. Tis nae Freeday ye ken.' Geordie muttered.

'Whets t'matter we ye Mon. Always blooody mooning ye are jest blooody eet't.' Through a mouthful of fish bones. Jimmie spluttered.

'Gee it to mi.' Bert retorted.

'Nope. I'll eet't.' At that very moment an RE Officer approached the table.

'Any Complaint's here?' Jimmie muttered.

'Gee on Bert noos yer chunce.'

'Nae sir! Verry neece Sir! Any secoond 'elpings Sir?' What a polite gentleman he was!

'Very good. Well. Wait until all have been served. Then go back to the Galley and ask.' Moving away, he continued his rounds. Geordie exclaimed.

'Yer skeeming bastard. Why dae ye no tell im te trooth? Tis blooody 'Orrible and cooild.' Breaking into laughter Bert retaliated. 'Ooze fer seconds then?'

Not going to be put off by Bert's comments; went for another helping washed down by a mug of tea that left me satisfied.

Leaving our empty trays on the table getting up began walking towards the exit when a tirade of shouting rent the air halting turned to see stood in a doorway was a cook, his big white Chefs hat hung down at an odd angle over his left ear dressed in his whites possessing a rather rotund belly, pointing his finger at a stack of dirty trays laid on the table shouted.

'Hoi. You lot. Get your dirty trays over here. Scrape your leftovers into the swill bin provided. I trust you have not left any. That meal has taken me all afternoon to cook.' Taken aback, we dutifully did what he said.

The swill bins were full too overflowing. So much for his bleedin' good cooking? Noisily we scraped the remnants from our trays, banged them down to inform him we were leaving his mess. Up on deck it was twilight, as the ship cut through the waves a stiff breeze was blowing against our backs as we bumped and swayed back along the deck.

Down in the bilge we sat or lay on our hammocks. The sound of others talking in the confined space was more of a hubbub than listening to individual voices. Lying there, aware of the gentle up and downward movement of the ship together with the repetitive dull sound of the sploosh of the propeller, sitting up looked around, on my left was the white painted curvature of the ships side that did not reflect any light obviously there were no portholes. On my right close to my face a big pair of Jackie's black boots in front of me was another row of hammocks with some Squaddies standing or others lying down beyond that to say the least it was gloomy. Behind me Bert was sorting something out of his Kitbag tucked in behind a long low girder where we had placed our kitbags. Wondering what we were supposed to do on this ship? I asked.

'Don't seem very much to do 'cept eat and sleep. Anyone got any ideas?' From above Jimmie retorted.

'Nae ask, war ter wee dee, nooting ye ken?' From even high up Geordie exclaimed.

'I cud mooder a peent raiht noo.' In the confines of the bilge a voice called out.

'Everyone gather around and listen up... a pause as the chattering ceased... C'mon. All of you move and gather at the stairway.'

En-masse all moved to see stood illuminated by the overhead light a R.E. Officer and Sgt, holding a clipboard and pencil. The Officer seeing he had everyone's attention, began his oration.

'Now. Listen up. Most important. Below decks. SMOKING IS FORBIDDEN...Next! Fire drill and abandon ship! Those two points I will come to in a moment. On 'A' Deck, there are some married families also WRAF and QARANC personnel. Their cabins are strictly out of bounds. ABSOLUTELY NO FRATERNISATION... Lights out at twenty hundred hours. Reveille o' seven hundred hours. Dress shirtsleeve order no berets or belts. Footwear. Plimsolls to be worn at all times. Meals three per day: breakfast, midday and evening will be served by sittings. A. B and C. This Deck 'H'. Will be served at the 'C 'sitting. Information will be given out over the Tannoy system and as appropriate take action on any orders issued. Cleanliness is of the utmost importance. Showers are provided and should be used at least once per day. For your information, ordinary soap will not lather; therefore, sea soap is available for purchase from the ship's shop. If you want to drink, water drink from the tap marked...Drinking Water Only. Any questions...silence... Every day commencing at ten hundred hours the Captain inspects the ship. All deck areas will be clean and tidy no clothing or any other loose material whatsoever will be on view so   pack everything away in sea your kit bags... A ship's daily notice is posted in the cabinet located on 'B' deck opposite the ship's shop; there is also a prize for guessing the number of sea miles travelled per day. The ships shop sells at duty free prices the following items. Chocolate, sweets, cards, reading and writing materials. Daily opening times eleven hundred until twelve hundred hours and fourteen hundred to fifteen hundred hours. Any question?...Located on 'C' Deck. The Naafi opens daily from nineteen hundred until twenty thirty hours. There is a daily beer allowance of two bottles per person also per week fifty free issues cigarettes will be provided.

Now. Most important. Two drills. Fire and abandon ship. Instructions will be given over the tannoy where the occupants of each deck must assemble. When they are announced there is to be no form of panic. Men will be detailed to carry out either of these two functions of drill. From time to time, you may be required to do some form of duty. Within reason, the rest of the time will be your own. Now. All return and stand by your hammocks. I will circulate amongst you and select willing bodies for fire piquet and lifeboat duty.' The mob disbursed to stand beside their hammocks. The Officer and Sgt. making their way over to our darkened corner ordered.

'You three. Fire piquet and lifeboat duties. Assemble at the foot of the companionway. I will inform you of your duties.' Volunteered! Geordie, Jackie and me. (I just cannot keep away from any bleedin' guard duties) Whilst they continued on their sortie to volunteer more, we headed to the companionway, muttered to Georgie.

'Sod it. Thought we could do what we liked? Who is going to raid us out here? The bleedin' IRA?'

Twelve bemused squaddies assembled by the companionway. On his clipboard, the Sgt. jotted down our Number Rank and Name. The Officer began his second oration.

'Fire piquet. Stags. Two hours on four hours off. Stand at your designated post in a companionway. Be alert and in case of fire yell. 'FIRE.' Wait until; someone asks you where it is? For this duty, you will be provided with a blue canvas bag with a strap. Hang it over your right shoulder. Whilst on your fire piquet duty. You will remain within the confines of this deck area. No visits to the Naafi etc.

For lifeboat drill. Tomorrow morning at eleven hundred hours, you all will report to the duty R.E. officer on B deck. For allocation of lifeboat station numbers and arms instructions. That is all. Take over Sergeant.'

That night. The three of us started our first fire piquet duty. Geordie was given his pouch, escorted by the Sgt somewhere to his post. Jackie was to relieve him and then it was my turn. We had been on board for several hours and spent most of the time down in the bilges when someone came down to inform all.

'If anyone wants to see the last sight of England. Better get up on Deck now.'

Once again, a mad scramble began to get the last glimpse of home. I had forgotten all about being restricted due to fire piquet. Arriving on deck we moved to the Left (Port) side railing. It was pitch black all you could hear from far below was the swishing of the waves against the ships side. Peering into the darkness we searched for some sign and it was a few minutes before Bert spotted a flash of light.

'Therre tis light yonder.'

'Can't see any bleedin' light flashing.'

'Therre tis agan.' All straining our eyes spotted a quick flash followed by another then another, someone called out.

'That's Land's End.' Silence descended upon the assembled company watching in the blackness a tiny light blink. It was Tuesday August 23. Not a day to remember too well slowly we dispersed back down to the bilges. Jackie was far from pleased when the duty Sgt. arrived and informed him.

'You're on stag duty now.' Soon after Georgie arrived, back moaning. Having been allocated the 2200 to 2400-fire watch there was still a further two hours to wait lying down on the bunk with the movement of the ship and the constant thud of the propeller succumbed to sleep. A shove in the back by a foot with a curt order woke me.

'Soldier. It is your stag duty time. Get up and follow me.'

Rubbing my eyes swung my legs off the bunk eased me out of the confined space. The red light provided a silhouette of bunks with squaddies snoring in unison or gabbling about their missed loves. Trying to motivate my legs to follow the retreating form of the Sgt., with the movement of the ship swaying badly almost fell into the opposite bunk occupied by a very sound sleeping form fortunately avoided the impending contact. Drunkenly, joined the Sgt. at the gangway he hissed.

'You took your time...adding...you been to the Naafi tonight?' Shitting myself in case he clapped me in Irons never to be heard of again replied.

'No Sergeant. Bin asleep.'

'Follow me.' Climbing the steps the studs of my boot made a squealing sound at the top he stopped turning around muttered.

'Craftsman Plant. Why are you wearing boots and gaiters?'

'Ere. Fell asleep Sergeant. Was about to change but you kicked me in the back. Told me to follow you.'

'That is a chuffing awful and stupid excuse. Make sure you are dressed appropriately for your next stag or I'll charge you.' Was his gruff reply.

Leading me up to the next deck along companion ways dimly lit by small red lights to the fire point station. Relieving Jackie of his canvas pouch smiling he handed it to me. A small blue flat envelope pouch slipping the strap over my shoulder the pouch lay snug against my arse there was nothing in it. What was it for? God alone knows. The Sgt. quietly reminded me of my duties.

'Stay alert and do not move from this fire point. If a fire breaks out. Shout. FIRE.'

The pair of them disappeared through a doorway that closed behind them leaving me prepared for any hint of fire a duty with a difference essentially I was the chief of the fire-watch station. Taking stock of my surroundings it was exceptionally warm and in the dim glow of the red light saw a gangway with doors at either end, in the middle from floor to the upper deck was a large square ducting surrounded by a small gangway possibly encasing the ship's funnel? Walking around it returned to my station that was it. Alone and conscious of solitude as I walked the sound of the studs of my boots squeaked against the metal deck and was sure the noise could be heard up on the ship's bridge, therefore to stretch my legs during that stag circumnavigated the ducting many times on tip toes (what an bleedin' idiot). Nevertheless, was so relieved and glad when the Sgt. appeared with another hapless bastard to relieve me of two hours of monotony that was indescribable. Removing the Blue envelope threw it at the hapless bastard who appeared, as he was still asleep nevertheless, he was wearing plimsolls so he was all right. A few words were passed and in company with the Sgt. retreated down to the bilges and bed. But could not sleep?

Lying awake for hours, listening to the steady rhythmic ease of the ship's propeller, ruump ruump ruump steaming Southwards away from England.

Someone, standing on the rim of the hammock using it as the last stepping-stone to the deck woke me. Possibly having slept two hours in total was knackered. The illumination from the red light was inadequate to see who the intruder was. Through parted eyelids visualised a pair of big feet pulling the blanket over my head tried to get back to sleep, but there were other movements going on. Squaddies waking up in an unfamiliar place trying to establish where they were and with many explosions of gas renting the air, squeaky loud and gor blimey anyway, it appeared pointless to lie there. Swung my legs off the bunk then realised was still wearing boots what a way to start a cruise? Sitting there contemplating my navel received an influence around the ear-ole, it was Jimmie swinging his legs out of his bunk caught me a wallop, I yelled.

'Aw sodding 'ell. Watch wot yer doing.' A grunt from above assured me that Jimmie was not all together with his senses. First task remove boots and to say the least, a relieve from their previously restriction peering at the pair of dark grey socks they appeared to get larger, standing up padded over to my sea Kit bag sorted out my plimsoll's padded back to sit down next to a dangling pair of lifeless legs. By then the bilge was a hive of motivation as squaddies erupted into action and began the day with ablutions, much to my concern found there was a queue for the urinals. Bert passing by happily remarked.

'Ye ken. Be up urrly te git te urrly morning pesh.' About to comment about his waking me up but thought it would be squandered on deaf ears. Eventually relieved returned to my bunk the inert pair of legs still dangled from the middle bunk shaking the legs said. 'C'mon. Wakey wakey...time to get up Jimmie.

'Aw. Gear awa.' Came a muffled reply. The glow of red lights had now been replaced by the inadequate daylight bulbs almost simultaneously the Tannoy came alive. A bugler deciding to liven up the proceedings played a few tinny notes of 'Wakey Wakey' the army's reveille. In our confined space loud enough to blast our eardrums including Jimmie's who let out a curdling cry of. 'Shoot. Te fook oop". Sitting bolt upright crashed his forehead against the upper bunk which in turn his other tirade of obscenities raised a howl of laughter from all.

It was time to begin the ablution rush; with washing gear was away to the washhouse to join the long queues. It was a toss-up, which you did first, the shorter the queue was the one you joined then to the other to have a shot. Having finished returned to the bunk space changed into denims and was ready to go to brekkers. All sat on bunks pissed off our combined opinion. There was no point in rushing around in the morning there were bags of time to take our ablutions, so the plan for the following day was no rush to get up. What seemed an eternity before the Tannoy eventually squeaked out the message. "C" sittings. Advance to the Mess deck.'

Like everyone else, it was a mad rush to get up the stairs to the top deck. Squinting in the daylight the sky was overcast; with a bit of a breeze and the grey /green sea had quite a swell. Joining the slow moving queue arrived at the servery. The tea trays were filled with English breakfast lots of toast and tea to wash it down. One good thing about the last sitting there was plenty of second helpings available. Full up and well satisfied under the eagle eye of the Chef cleaned our tin trays before leaving his mess hall. Obviously, he the Chef was satisfied that our previous night's misdemeanor had been noted and improvements carried out. Back on deck we headed for the ship's rail to watch the sea as it swelled up forming white crests on wave tops as droplets of water caught by the wind were blown away therefore, leaving white bubbly trails coursing down into the receding troughs. It was very boring and we soon got tired of watching the endless sea pass us by.

Back down in the bilges, it was a hive of activity everyone getting sorted out. The Tannoy announced.

'The Chief Chef. Is seeking volunteers for spud bashing duty. If anyone wishes to volunteer. Speak with the deck Sergeant.'

Our reply "NO WAY JOSE". Do not volunteer for anything we were already committed; anyway this for us was a luxury cruise.

We had finished clearing away our clothing and all was stowed away in our kitbags ready for the captain's inspection that happened sooner than later. A voice from afar called out. H deck. Stand by your bunks for captain's inspection.'

We all formed up three alongside the tiered bunks. Appearing at the end of our row of bunks the Captain followed by another officer and the deck Sgt., carried on around the back of us to re-appear on our left as he walked past we had a brief glance at his attire. A clean-shaven tall figure, wearing a white covered peak cap the peak emblazoned with gold leaf, just above was an anchor surrounded by a gold wreath the Merchant Navy emblem. His jacket had gold stuff on his epaulets four rings on each arm plus securing his jacket eight gold buttons and at shoulder height a row of his medal ribbons. Apart from that, he was a cut above the rest of his entourage. His inspection carried out in a zigzag manner was swift, everything appeared to be spot-on and that occurred every day. To put it bluntly a waste of time but under the circumstances, it whiled away minutes.

As ordered, along with about nine others the three of us 'Volunteers'. Attended the Sgt's, information parade. "On Abandon Ship Drill". Once he had checked our names. The Sgt. began his oratory.

'You Soldiers. Have been picked to ensure that. If, in the event the ship was to flounder? For those not accustomed to the word. Struggle to move, capsize and sink. In addition, if the signal is given. The clanging of bells and a hooter. ABANDON SHIP. Your duty is to quell any riot or, panic amongst the passengers and maintain an orderly queue for the lifeboats, if necessary shoot them. I say it in plural, as two Lifeboats will be under your command and your lifeboat station is in between two boats. When the signal is announced over the tannoy. You will. First attend the Armory to draw weapons and ammo from there you will run to your lifeboat station. Ensure you put on a Life Jacket and remain on guard throughout the evacuation of all passengers. That means. You will be the last person to leave the sinking ship! You may well ask about how many passengers are allowed on each lifeboat. Each passenger will be advised of which boat station and boat number that they have been assigned too. Therefore, there should be no. Cock. Ups. Understand? Now today, we will go through the motion of the drill and we will do it several times. So that you are familiar with. The location of the Armory and. Your designated lifeboat station furthermore, what is expected of you? As and when any practice drill is called out on the Tannoy. Any Question's?' Silence....

Yet again, could not believe my luck. Guard duty, albeit lifeboat stations. The Sgt. escorted us down two decks below where the armory was. Drawing arms and ammunitions returned to 'A' Deck to be allocated a Lifeboat station to guard until the "Abandon ship drill" was over. Three times, we did the exercise, finishing just before the midday meal however, that first run was just an instruction exercise. The rest of the day, I spent reading 'The Saint.' By Leslie Charteris a book that I had purchased from the ship's shop.

By the time, we had reached the Mediterranean the sun was beating down and it was quite pleasant sat on deck reading there were of course card schools that occupied many of the squaddies the legal tender free issue cigarettes in plentiful supply. It was a life of luxury apart from the daily interruptions, like meals the boat drill duty that happened regularly whenever the captain! Chose to upset our normal routine. The Tannoy would squeak and the sound of alarm bells would clang out "Lifeboat Stations". Then panic. Run like hell to the armory to collect arms and ammunition, bound up four flights of stairs to 'A' deck run to the boat station, heaving with exhaustion to don a clumsy lifejacket and stand on guard with rifle at the ready. Trying to catch your breath before other passengers, mainly families under my care would appear. They dragging small tots who did not want to play lifeboat drill it were then amusing to see the mothers dive into the lifeboat boxes take out the ungainly lifejacket and struggle to put them on. As they held a child by the hand to stop them running away then fit their kids with a lifejackets some were almost as big as the toddler. If, the ship did flounder and actually sink our duty was to shoot anyone who cared to panic whilst getting aboard one of the lifeboats. In that case. I would be the first one on the lifeboat.

The days of luxury were extremely boring; the sea was calm with plenty of sunshine beating down onto white exposed backs day-by-day gradually turning bright red. It was one evening after we had a shower in seawater with a cake of soap that did not lather. Went to the Naafi to purchase our ration. "Two bottles of beers". Sitting there chatting about what we were going to do in Singapore lazing about on white beaches meeting Chinese girls and having drinks a life of pleasure awaited us. Jack making a complete fool of himself suggested.

'Awar. We should vulonteer fer spud bashing dooties.' His suggestion opened up a can of worms and fuelled with two halves of beer a heated debate began. "Why should we volunteer"? The fact of the matter was finally put down to total boredom nevertheless, it would relieve us three of fire watch and boat drill duties. We had to do something different; it would only be for a couple of days. The next day on deck, six of us volunteered. The Sgt raising his eyebrows in mock disbelief said.

'You six? 'H' Deck! Uhmm, okay. Wait for further instructions.'

Halfway through the Med. Posted on Ship's orders. "All personnel change into Tropical Dress". Out came the badly creased OG's changing into them all looked untidy but the long long shorts created many a laugh.

 Monday Sept. 5th. the ship arrived at Port Said, dropping anchor the hum of machinery ceased she became very quite. Up on deck the sun was baking hot and with everyone leant against the ship's rail the ship had developed a permanent list to the starboard side. Gazing through a heat haze saw the shoreline of Port Said and a flotilla of small boats came racing across the waters towards our ship soon joined by others leaving other ships fed up of no sales. We were about to become besieged by the Egyptian Navy the infamous Bumboats. Riding the tidal wave they had created in their wake like flies,

 they arrived in their droves all attempting to be first to bump into the ship's side. Amid screams and shouts of Egyptian obscenities with much arm, waving and shaking of fist the boats jammed together en masse. Their crews three men to a boat, two operated the long oars whilst the third was a tiller man.

Bum Boat   *Passenger Ferries*

The boats flat and wide provided an excellent platform for all their wares to be laid out. The boatmen dressed in white flowing robes or long white shirt and baggy trousers wearing a fez or some form of turban wrapped around the heads, some of the larger boats were used to ferry passengers ashore. From our high vantage point we could see items of brassware, trinkets, pots, and plenty of other junk ready to be bartered for, but how could they sell it? High above them was their buyers shouting and jeering them on. 'Send em up. We ain't buying till we've seen them.'

With years of practice, one of the boatmen swinging a weighted rope like a lasso around his head let go of the end it came snaking skywards to land on the boat deck one of the squaddies secured it to the ships rail. It was their lifeline for any of the goodies to be hauled up in raffia baskets examined and if someone wanted an item, it was held aloft and the shouting began.

'This one. Sixpence?'

'No Jonnie more.' Then the bartering began, this went on until agreement was reached the money was put into the wicker basket and sent back down; no doubt some items were never paid for? One squaddie an 11th Hussar trooper had purchased a Fez that he wore with pride it being the same colour as the red band of ribbon around his beret. We discovered later they did not wear a cap badge they were called the "Cherry Pickers". He was the only one that had the guts to wear such a piece of headgear. However, there was a couple of Bumboats selling fruit some of it quite strange to our sight and to our palettes possibly unknown? Those unacceptable were hurled back down into the sea doing a dance on his poop deck the fruit Wallah was not a happy man. He and the others were most entertaining and it lasted for hours until the Tannoy called the first sitting and the rails became less packed.

About 1230, a motor boat nudged up against the landing platform loaded with about a dozen armed soldiers dressed in KD's and FSMO most wore a Tam 'o' Shanter headdress except a couple with berets. Carrying their Uni's they disembarked and came up the rigged ladder to arrive on deck on their way aft as they past us by amongst them noticed a young second Looie. Georgie recognised them as the Seaforth Highlanders. The others wearing Berets was a Sgt. and Cpl. in the RASC. When it was our lunch call we went down to collect our eating irons only to find they had been bedded down with us one of them was sitting on the end bunk busily cleaning his bayonet, not the pig stickers we knew more like a small Bowie knife curious asked him.

'What type of bayonet is that? '

'Stabbing bayonet.'

'Where yer bound for then?'

'Aden. Just getting a lift down there that's all.' Noticing his London accent asked.

'You come from London don't yer? Wot you doing in a Scots regiment?'

'Yeah live in Plumstead. Don't know how? Was a butcher in Civvy Street? Bin in nine months finished up in Egypt. Now on way to Aden. Advanced party or summat. Wots it like on this tub?'

'Oh you'll find out when we sail? S'pose that will be to-night we thought we might get off and get ashore but nope. Stuck on this soddin boat.'

'Well there ain't anything ashore except bleedin' sand more sand and bleedin' flies. Wouldn't let it bother yer. Where do come from in smoke?'

'Vauxhall. Near Oval.'

'Not a bad place been there a few times watching Surrey play matches.' Jackie' urged.

'C'mon Joe. Its nosh time.'

'Okay. I'm coming. See yer after lunch mate. Nice talking to a Londoner for a change.' Still cleaning his weapon, he mumbled.

'Well. I ain't bleedin' going any place?'

After dinner, sitting on deck for a lazy afternoons sunbathing we heard the Deck Sgt., calling out our names. Responding he said. 'You Six. Follow me.'

Puzzled, followed him towards the rear of the ship where sat on their haunches were several Indians, the Sgt. shouted at one of them. Getting up crossed the deck and opened up a tiny hatchway set in the wooden floor, climbing down disappeared into the depths below. The Sgt. said

'You three short arses. Down below... pointing at me...you go first.'

Approaching the hatchway saw the top rung of a ladder going down into a black void, turning around squeezed myself through the small opening climbed down into a dimly lit deck. The Indian stood by a big open door beckoned me over smiling in the pale light revealed a set of big white pearly teeth as he muttered.

'In Jonnie.' Going through the doorway immediately the coldness hit me shivered, peering in the gloom spotted big bags and sacks stored on top of each other behind me heard Jackie say.

'War ti fook arr war?' The pair of them stood beside me.

'Looks like a store room to me.' The Sgt. arrived alongside us.

'Right. You three. This is the vegetable locker and the cook wants vegetables moved up to his Galley. So it's your job to get them there.' Having noticed the size of the sacks thought, "Soddin 'ell we got to shift all that lot". Asked.

'Ear' Sergeant. How can we get this lot through that little hole up in the Deck? '

'Quite simple. One at a time up the ladder. You shove the other three topside will pull them out. The Indian knows what is wanted so; you three do as he says. C'mon we have not got all soding day. One of you take hold of a sack and move it out.'

Jack moved to the pile of sacks without any effort the Indian removed a triangular shaped raffia sack from the top placed it across Jack's shoulders, the Sgt. ordered.

'Right up the ladder with it. 'Next one. C'mon move.' The Indian placed a sack across my shoulders grabbing hold of its raffia ends moved out of the store across to the ladder stood waiting while Jack clinging to the ladder shouting.

'Git fooking held of the fooker. Puull it oout' as the sack was pulled out a shaft of light, illuminated Jack climbing down snarled. 'Waa fooker? Volunteered oos fir tis fooking job.'

Beginning the vertical assent with great difficulty managed to reach the top the triangular shape of the sack was awkward and heavy to push through the opening, hands pulling it out eased the weight a couple of heaves from me had it out. It was obvious, why the short arses were down below. Anyway, we humped shoved and pulled all of them through the opening until the job was completed. The Indian counting the numbers, with his arms spread out said.

'Finiss Jonnie Finiss.' Closed the door we climbed up out onto the upper deck to view a pile of sacks spread-eagled along a bulkhead wall. Although it had been cold down below we were streaked with sweat. The Sgt. ordered.

'Right. You idle bastards. Take all these sacks up for 'ard to the cook he will show you where he wants them stored. Spuds first then cabbages.' We made the trip for 'ard, each carrying a sack good job the sea was calm otherwise a sack or two might have finished over the side. Down through the mess hall behind the kitchens into another storeroom. The Cook, looking suspiciously at us asked. 'Did you lot volunteer for this then? ' Georgie blurted out.

'Yeah. Din nae why? '

'Well urry up. Get em down here as fast as you can. I ain't got all day' I've got mouths to feed.' When we had finished with the last sack. The Cook obviously a Scoucer, said.

'Well. That's good. You're not due down here until a week's time. So get some sunshine in. See you all then. Now Sod off.'

That night it was strange trying to get to sleep, there was no intermittent thrashing of the propeller or, gentle movement of the ship, but it was stifling hot. Early next morning the 6th. The ruump ruump began we were on the move. On our way to breckers noticed we had joined the convoy of ships entering the Suez Canal, which did not seem wide enough to accommodate big ships.

The Suez Canal Convoy

Behind us was the 'Delwara.' another Troopship, which had caught up with us. With Port Said behind us, the scenery was nothing but open desert, on the starboard side a roadway ran parallel to the canal now and again a couple of Army wagons would pass by, their drivers and escorts giving a hearty cheer and a wave towards the ship, before they

disappeared in clouds of dust. About half way on the Port, side passed a convoy of ships waiting in the Bitter Lakes. Talk about ships of the Desert? There was nothing else to see, it was back to reading and sunbathing until meal times, a visit to the Naafi for our beer ration then bed.

Bitter Lakes

Port Suez

Next morning leaving the canal at Port Suez. Entered the Red sea where another northbound bound convoy of ships were anchored waiting, whilst ahead of us other ships increasing speed passed the smaller cargo vessels. In the rising sun the sea appeared to turn a hue of red we went up for 'ard to get the benefit of the slight but warm breeze in the scorching sun looking down through the anchor holes watched a school of Dolphins weaving and diving through the bow waves fascinating to watch how they swam through the sea and the flying fish skipping out of the water to fly maybe ten yards before diving back in, caught sight of a sailfish leaping out of the sea in a graceful arc   After Captains Inspection, the deck Sgt. informed us.

'After our next Port of call Aden. You six will report to the chief cook to begin your two-week spud bashing duty until we dock at Singapore.' That statement came as a shock as we had only expected a couple of days of spud bashing not two whole bleedin' weeks. The day before we reached Aden the Tannoy clicked to announce. "All passengers could go ashore, with instruction on dress uniform. OG's long trousers, jacket with rolled up sleeves, belt, puttees and boots, white PT vests could be worn under the jacket. " Click.

Saturday morning the 10th the ship dropped anchor in Aden harbour. The Cockney

Seaforth Highlander departing very early just said 'Cheerio.' We had not seen much of them apart from when they were kipping down with us at night, most of the time they were being instructed by their Second Looie on deck doing some sort of training. With the Captains, inspection over having changed made our way up to the deck to join the queue along the rail waiting to depart the ship and gaze across the

Aden Harbour   water at the skyline surrounding Aden a range of craggy peaked mountains and in the middle was a flat concave shaped one. Was that the Crater? As we stared through the haze and dust at the quaysides and beyond at a row of two storied buildings the whole area appeared uninviting. Disembarked via the ship ladder down to

a platform at sea level we all managed to get on one of the flotilla of motorboats ferrying everyone across the open water bobbing and dipping our way across the open sea we came alongside a jetty, stepping onto *terra firma* then the fun began. Having spent two weeks getting used to the motion of the boat it was the reverse, talk about wobbly knees certainly a strange feeling as we walked along a wide and dusty hard packed mud road leading into Aden, with hardly

Aden main street

any cars about and turbaned Arabs rode the few motorbikes creating clouds of dust. Stopping at a group of shops, gazing through the window at trinkets hundreds of watches lighters, brass and other useless pieces of junk. Attracted and intrigued by one tiny lighter that was three quarters of an inch square with an intricate coloured design scrolled around it, that to me was a good buy going inside asked the fat Arab sat wearing a grubby cream suit with a fez on his head.

'How much?' Wobbling a podgy hand he said.

'Sterling. Two pounds.'

'Get off. Not worth that much.' Bert shoving me in the ribs retorted.

'Ye ken, its tinny nae wooth a tanner. Anywa, war de yer waant a leeter forr ye niver smookes?'

'Yeah. I know its tiny. I'll give it my dad when I get home; he only puffs at the Woodies now and again. Ear matey, give yer five bob for it.' The Arab shaking his head waved his podgy hands about. I retorted.

'Don't even bleedin' work.' Picking it up the fat Arab said.

'Good working you see.' Flicking up the cover thumbed its tiny wheel to produce a spark. See velly good? You want now?'

'Give yer half crown for it. That's all it's worth.' Rolling his eyes upwards shook his head I too shook my head turning about to leave when he urged.

'Okay. Okay Jonnie. Half crown sterling.'

'Done. I'll buy.' Out of my change gave him one half crown he inspecting it.

'Okay Jonnie. Okay.' Passed over the tiny lighter. Outside inspected my purchase; some quite rude comments were spoken about what I could do with it? Walking past some other shops that sold exactly the same sort of junk. Jack bought a wallet with a camel and pyramids etched on it, anyway there was nothing else to see. We bumped into Lofty who stated.

'Going up to the crater. Anyone want to go?'

'What's that?'

'It's an old volcano?' Quick as a flash Georgie commented.

'Ye Ken. Joe jist boort es oon volcaana.' This produced howls of laughter. Declining his suggestion, we wandered off down a side street. A row of hovels, large bare patches revealed layers of thin brickwork. There was nobody about, except a small herd of flea-ridden goats trying to eat dirt. We came into a wide-open area with not a blade of grass in sight; some Arab kids were kicking a misshapen ball about that was more like it. The ball was kicked our way so we started passing it to each other racing around this hard packed flat area sweating buckets trying to emulate the England and Scottish sides, whilst the kids were screaming in Arabic. Amid a shower of dirt and clouds of dust, a jeep arrived screeching to a halt three Red Caps jumped out and rounded us up. We were told the facts of life; 'Out of Bounds.' Marched back into the town center down to the quayside and put on the next ferryboat back so ended our trip ashore of at least two hours in Aden.

Back on board we lounged about on the empty deck; it was after dinner that the deck Sgt. came up to us questioned.

'Been ashore Lads? I am glad you are back on board, which means I will not have to search for you lot. Here are your times of duty down in the galley. You will be called at five thirty do your ablutions then at six o'clock report to the galley. The cook will serve you breakfast plus all other meals. So take your eating irons and mugs with you. The cook will show you the ropes and the best of british.' Jack was the first to say anything.

'Oot of fooking boonds and noo, blooody poonishment?'

By mid afternoon the first lot of squaddies arrived back on board, most had some form of a souvenir. Just after first mess call, the ship upped anchor and sailed out of the Gulf of Aden into the Arabian Sea. Having got used to a nice easy passage of sailing we were eating our evening meal when in an unfamiliar fashion the ship began to dip and yawl. Half way through our meal the Tannoy clicked.

'This is your captain speaking. The ship is heading into a monsoon storm. All personnel return to your bunks and lie down.' Click silence.

By that time the ship was really dipping; rolling from side to side then rising, it was like a roller coaster. Enjoying the ride finished our meal and swayed our way up to the deck towards the rail, ahead of us the sky was almost black the strong wind flattened what hair we had, steadily the yawing and dipping of the ship got worse whilst at the bottom of a trough the height of the waves were above us, slowly it rose upwards then we were way above them, before descending downwards into another trough it was all exciting stuff as each roller came towards us we cheered before deciding to get down to the bilges as we made a very unsteady way back aft the force of the wind on our backs almost blew us along. Some squaddies were still dotted along the ship's rail; amongst them was the Hussar with the Fez passing him we making comments... 'If he did not watch out he would lose it in the wind.' His response was soon decided he promptly threw up over the side and caught by the wind most of it landed on us. I yelled.

'Aw shite. Dirty bastard.'

At the top of the gangway, wafting up from down below was a distinctive odor of pewk that did not disperse as we made the rather unpleasant trek down to the lowest point in the ship where the dipping and yawing of the boat was not as severe as it was for those up on the higher decks. Lying on the bunk you would gently roll from one side to the other, now and again the sound of the propeller on its downward arc hit the water with a solid whack. Strange as it may seem but our conversation was about our favorite meals? Wanting a piss left them chatting arriving at the heads; about half of our deck was in there all quite happily spewing. The vomit was about six inches deep; it was revolting so headed back to my bunk and flopped down their conversation had not changed, it was then that a cough and a stream of spew descended downwards splashing on the deck, then another heave. Bert spluttered.

'Sorry cud nae elp ...huuuieugh.' Another stream came down that had someone else in the dimness heaving. Bert had started spewing sessions then the stench reaching my nostrils made me retch. That was it, was not going to stay down here had to get fresh air carefully avoiding the mess beside my bunk grabbed my blanket and headed for the top. On the way up pools of spew lay on the stairs and at every landing stage a few squaddies were noisily retching either clinging to the bulkheads or, lay dying in the corners it nearly had me going until reaching the top glad to gulp in fresh air.

It was blowing a hooley; the wind direction was coming from the starboard side. the open space between the port and starboard was awash; I was sure the ship wanted to turn turtle, drenched by the stinging rain was physically blown across it towards the leeward side, where sheltering out of the wind and rain quite a few squaddies were sat down on lifebelt boxes. Finding a spare one sat down and wrapped the damp blanket around my shoulders. Now I am not a sailor and hated getting sick, but with the constant motion my guts were playing havoc inside me in an effort not to throw up, took great gulps of air that appeared to work, deciding to lie down curled up on the box pulled the blanket over me. Waking up some hours later, it was dark the wind had died to a howl and the ship was still rolling and yawing but not as violent. One thing was certain was not going to venture down to the bilges until daylight, fell asleep until a voice woke me.

'Jonnie. Jonnie. Up. Up...Stood beside me was an Indian holding a hosepipe washing down the deck...moving away he urged. Up. Up. Jonnie.'

Blinking my eyes against the brightness of the morning sunrise, through the ships rail could see there was still a heavy swell with white horsetails streamed from the top of every wave but the ship was much steadier. Rousing me sat up looked around, further down some squaddies were sat on boxes or stood by the rail smoking. Cold and shivering I wrapped the blanket around my shoulders and made an unsteady way back towards the entrance the distinctive smell of carbolic entered my nostrils. Going down found all the stairways had been cleaned even down on our deck, the heads had been washed clean but the smell of vomit was evident in the enclosed space of the bilge nevertheless, the number of bodies lying on their bunks moaning was evidence of the state of all. Seasickness is not very pleasant. Over by our bunks, Georgie Jack and Jackie were waiting, Jack grunted.

'War ye bin?'

'Up top, slept up there all night...beginning to heave with the smell a mix of carbolic and vomit added. Got to get out of here.' Georgie reminded me.

'Woor late te start spud bashing'. Not very happy about spud bashing, certainly not at that particular time questioned.

'Wot about the others?'

'Nae leef em thae nae fit anyway ye ken. C'mon were exscuused mooster.'

Leaving them, made our way up and along to the galley reporting to the Scouse Cook who immediate gave us a bollocking.

'You're bloody late. Good job we had a storm last night! Breakfast is only boiled fish...The sheer thought of it had me about to retch...Urry up this way. I will show you what you have to do. Where's the other two?' I blurted out.

'Sick spewing.'

'Well you four will have to start on your own follow me.' He led the way through the galley area, where some Indians were busy cooking stuff; to me it certainly did not seem big enough to feed a thousand troops standing to one side Scousie, bawled out.

'You four in there.' Entering into a small room with a big wide oblong opening in the ships side, the deck was covered with slatted boards that led through to another tiny anteroom where stacked high on one side was a pile of sack's and two big steel dixie's lying on the deck. Scousie began to inform us on what we had to do.

'In that small room is a spud washing machine all those bags of spuds have to be washed peeled and de-eyed. First load them into the washing machine, turn on the tap then switch it on, wash and unload them in those two big Dixie's then with your knife, peel off the skin a de-eye em, when the dixie's are full take them into the galley. That is all there is to it, besides the carrots and other veg, you will have to do. But not this morning. Not many will be eating and it will be a waste. All peelings and other cuttings sling over the side. This place has to be cleaned spotless for Captain's inspection. Over there is a hosepipe, wash down the deck properly. When the others eventually show their faces, tell them what to do. I will be back before cap's inspection. I have meals to serve. Oh one other thing. You will eat your meals in here.' He left us.

Surveying the tiny room even with the larger than life porthole the smell of musty vegetables was overpowering and I certainly was not looking forward to spud bashing exclaimed. 'Soddin 'ell. Wot we let ourselves in for?'. Jackie urged.

'Awa. Let's git soome spuuds dun. Grab hoold of ter sacks poor em in yonder machine.'

Grabbing hold of one heaved it on my shoulder followed Jack into the anti- room, dropping his on the floor he turned on the tap as water gushed into the huge bowl I emptied the sack of spuds into the open top yelled.

'Right Switch on.' Jackie switched on. Nothing happened.

'Try again.' Nothing. Georgie standing behind me with a sack on his shoulder, shouted.

'Aw. Blooody turrn it oon wea ya.'

'I have done mon. It don't woork.' Georgie yelled.

'Joe goo fetch te cook.' I scurried away to inform the cook. 'The machines knackered and will not start.' Who yelled?

'Aw Jesus! You buggers busted it already?' He came running out of the galley, straight into the anti- room.

'You load of git's. Switch the bloody thing on with that switch there... Pointing to a trip switch as large as life on the bulkhead wall. Jackie slipped the trip switch, the machine started to whiz around with the spuds tumbling about...Next time. Switch on the sodding trip switch. Silly load of buggers.' He bellowed retreating to his galley.

We felt like a bunch of idiots having been trained as electricians had forgot the basic principle. "Check power supply". Nevertheless, now we had started it was time to move on. The spuds were swishing around getting dizzy and when Jack thought they were done switched off and pulled back a lever on the side letting all the spuds out through a flap in the front to tumble and roll about over the boards, avoiding a few shouted.

'You soding idiot. Now look wot you have bleedin' done?' Scrambling around retrieved the others threw them in a Dixie and as Jackie and I began de-eyeing and peeling them, Georgie tumbled in the next load and the machine was set in motion this time with rested a big Dixie beneath the flap ready to catch them. Georgie and Jack did the loading and washing and regardless of our frantic pealing we could not keep up with them; the pile of washed spuds grew larger and larger more hands were definitely needed and with my guts in turmoil had to leave them to dash to the heads with a dose of the trots. Fortunately, they were close by and just made it in time for a quick squirt after about twenty minutes of this too-ing and fro-ing and with a sore arse was able to continue with spud peeling. Meanwhile the Scouse cook was ranting and raving about.

'You four that volunteered for my best job are a lazy lot of bastards...Just then Bert and Jimmie arrived on the scene, both rather green around the gills. Therefore, Scousie let rip at them as well... Bloody hell. About bloody time. This is not a fooking luxury liner. I'm feeding masses of troops and I've employed two sick, one shiter and three has bins. AND IT'S NEAR EIGHT THIRTY. THE LOT OF YOU. GET YER FOOKING ARSES IN GEAR.' With that, he stomped away.

Taking the lead, Georgie, got them to de-eye and peel spuds. Slowly we began to get spud bashing organised, four sitting peeling, one loading, one operating the machine until Bert, decided to feed the fish again. Leaping up sprang at the large open porthole balanced on the tip of his plimsolled toes hangs his head out over the side retching violently to make out he is throwing up; he did not have anything more to throw up, apart from his plimsolls? Georgie ever thoughtful muttered.

'Tis al en ter meend ye ken. Thit's so es gits oot of spood bishing?' However, time marched on having peeled mountains of spuds delivered them to the galley for further treatment by the Indians. Thankfully, the cook said.

'Enough now clear up the mess.'

Turning on the hosepipe tap the water gushed out at an alarming speed at the end of a fire hose; we rolled up the ends of our shorts to half way up our thighs but still got thoroughly wet whilst hosing down. The Captain duly came around inspected what we thought," Was a well cleaned and tidy area". The cook got an ear bashing, then took it out on us. 'No breakfast for you fooking lot.' Not that anyone wanted it with dickie stomachs and the amount of spuds we had peeled; we had had our belly-full. Anyway, thanks to the sea, it became calmer and the ship stopped its antics and got onto an even keel. We had ridden the storm.

The spud bashing was not bad, being organised into the well-trained mob that we were gathered momentum and had most of the spuds cabbages, carrots and anything else he could throw at us well covered except the onions. That was a crying shame! The Cook warming to us was pleased and we got our rewards, whatever food we wanted steak and chips fish and chips eggs bacon sausages including a choice of fruit, you name it we chose it. Definitely not the swill others were

Colombo Ceylon

185

served in the mess hall. We dined in the confines of our tiny sweat hole in amongst the veg in addition did the fetch and carrying of all varied supplies for the different meals from the cold rooms aft and were quite happy being excused all duties including muster.

Five days later on Saturday the 7. The ship was due to dock in Colombo where all could go ashore for a few hours. Scouse said. 'If you can get all the spuds and other veg done for dinner before Captain's inspection. You can go ashore with the rest of them.' That was more than an invite we did the works, finished everything ready for the Inspection and must have been the last to go ashore however, we had to be back in the

galley by 1500 hours. Alighting from the ferryboat at Colombo harbour was a similar leggy experience nevertheless this time there was definitely no 'Out of Bounds.' playing football. Scouse had told us to get rickshaws up to the Naafi bar where everyone goes for a drink. Wandering around experienced the sights and many smells amongst the masses of Indians that flocked about the streets.

Ashore in Colombo   *Seeing the sights.*

Before hailing three rickshaws to ride in style up to the Naafi. Outside on the lawn was a large ring of squaddies, thinking it was a fight barged in to see not a fight but a turbaned Indian Fakir (snake charmer) sat crossed legged on the grass blowing some musical tunes on a long pipe. In front of him was a raffia basket with a snake swaying to the music by the shape of its flat hooded head indicated it was a 'cobra'. For some minutes intoxicated by the music the hood of the snake swayed from side to side until the snake charmer tired of puffing stopped whereas the snake fed up with swaying slithered out of its basket and swiftly snaked towards the nearest line of squaddies pandemonium broke out; squaddies were running in all direction including us. So we never made the beer and that was the end of our trip ashore. The boat sailed that evening on the final leg to Singapore.

The day before we arrived in Singapore during Captain Inspection he passed us with a clean bill of health and complimented us on the way; we had performed our duties during our time in the galley and in addition to that. Scouse said.

'You lot have done me proud. For your midday meal I will cook a meal you will not get where you're going? A large steak with chips and peas? Now you still have a lot of veg to prepare so I'll leave you to it.'

Having finished preparing the spuds and other vegetables for the midday meal, lazing around in the galley drinking tea when the Tannoy bleeped that stopped our idle chatter as the voice crackled. 'Attention! Immediately after the last sitting of the mid-day meal. All personnel disembarking at Singapore. Will assemble on 'B' deck for issue of universal kit bags from the hold. At the same time notification of immediate postings will be advised.' Click.

We cheered. Various suggestions about my "travel rations" became the topic of our conversation causing my stomach to churn over in anticipation for the worst thinking. "Nothing would be left to wear except the ragged remnants in my Uni. Cringing at the thought it would cost me an arm and a leg in barrack room damages. Aw. Soddin 'ell".

When the steak arrived, I was sure it was half a cow each. We sat around the little cabin and tucked in all aware of one thing we had done the right thing! Volunteering our services for cookhouse duties with all its humping, carrying, peeling of tons and tons of spuds we never de-eyed em we squared em, carrots and other vegetable cleaning up for Captain's Inspection not forgetting on several occasions several of the big Dixie's we unfortunately. 'Lost over the side'. Nevertheless, at the end of the day, we had come off better in many ways from the boring existence of the top deck, excused all duties lots of fun and freedom and fed fresh prepared meals from the galley with mugs of tea on call. After the sumptuous meal followed by lashings of ice cream we were so bloated out we could not move and definitely in need of a midday snooze down on our hammocks.

Our band of brothers stopped at the port side rail to watch the waves far below, the white crests of swirls and eddies against the deep blue of sea, after four long weeks at sea the constant swishing noise of the sea against the side of the ship was something we had become accustomed too but in the far distance the dark outline of the land could be seen against the contrast of the blue sky dotted with patches of white billowing clouds, which in some areas appeared to be in direct contact with a very mountainous land. Full up with the delicious meal; we had scoffed down and lost in the tranquility of motion as the ship carried us nearer and nearer to Singapore with drooping eyes the sweat oozed out of us the only cooling factor was the warm breeze, our moment of tranquility was cut short by the bark of the Duty Sgt.

'What are you lot staring at? Get down below to your midday meal.' Jackie responded.

'Alreedy eeten Sarge. War cook hoouse wallah's'.

'Aah. Scouse's team are you? Well that's all right then... joining us at the ship's rail stared out in the direction of the land...See that shore line over there that is Malaya, on the starboard side the land in the far distance is Sumatra Indonesia. We are now entering the Malacca Straits, which separates the two countries and will soon sail into what are called, the singapore roads. You will be there tomorrow morning in amongst all the singapore lil's. If you're lucky.' I asked.

'You been here before Sarge?'

'Well. Sort of. I go backwards and forwards on this old tub. She's due for the knackers' yard this is her last trip homeward bound then I'll get another ship.' We tore ourselves away from the sight of land to continue on our way down to the bilges to let the dinner go down before we returned to 'B' Deck.

By the time we got back up top along the full length of the deck laid one on top of the other tucked up against the ships rail were green universals. They had been sorted out in order of Regiment or Corps. Luck was on our side the REME. consignment was close to our gangway. Scanning the rows spotted mine tucked away on the bottom row it appeared intact. Dragging it out found the top was still securely tied up Bert coming alongside muttered.

'Ye stil uungry? G'wan opens it.' He laughed. Untying the securing rope eased the top open, folded back the green cover flap to reveal one intact brown paper bag. "Rations for the day". The relief on my face must have been very evident; the whole gang had watched the opening ceremony. Jackie enquired.

'Wot yer gaana do with it? Eet it?

'Sod off. It's a month old and 'ard as iron. Nah throw it over side fish food.' Quickly Jimmie responded.

'Blooody "ell. If te shark git's tha he'll break his teeeth.' Bert chipped in.

'One liss shaark ter eet yer arris thin.' I shouted.

'Right over the side with it.' Hurling it far out into the sea it landed with a sploosh, as the sandwiches disappeared a fountain of water nearly as high as the ship's deck came welling up from below, popping up again they floated away in the wake of the ship behind us. We were still laughing at the episode when the Sergeant. Came along with his clipboard calling out names in Alpha sort. The list of postings. Georgie, Jackie and Jimmie, were posted to camps in Singapore. Jack posted to a place called Jahore Bahru. Bert posted to Butterworth and me to Ipoh. 9/Elect/7 had been split up. When he had finished stating all the rest of the postings, he asked. 'Anyone want to exchange their postings?' What could we say? Not fancying Malaya but there would be no budging anyone changing postings. I ventured to ask him.

'Any chance of getting a posting to Sumatra?'

'No-way soldier. It is not British. Where you posted to?'

'Ipoh. Sarge.'

'Aah. Bandit country?' Ipoh it was but where the bleedin' 'ell was that? The Sgt. began his oration.

'Right. Gather around. Orders for tomorrow. 'The ship docks early in Singapore. Dress of the day. O.G's. Long trousers, Jacket sleeves rolled up, boots and puttees, beret, belt and bayonet frog. Pack the rest of your kit in both sea kit bag and Uni. After the ship, docks you will be advised when to disembark and taken by lorry to nee soon transit camp and provided with a midday meal. Those with Singapore postings will be taken by truck to their respective camps on the island. Those posted to Malaya, will be transported to Singapore railway station, to be entrained to Malaya. And the best of British to you bastards. The rest of the day is yours. To get smartened up, ready for disembarkation. Right dismiss.'

Everyone on deck picked up their Uni and began the long trek down to the bilge. Dragging the Uni across the deck towards our bunks, placed it alongside the sea kitbag between the steel girders of the bulkhead, as there was little time before we headed back to the galley sat on the bunk to polish my cap badge the boots could do later. Lying down on my bunk listened to the surrounding ongoing chatter and the constant, sploosh sploosh of the propeller driving us relentlessly forward, thinking. "I'm going to miss that bleedin' sound but, some lucky bastard will take over my bunk on his way back home, whoever he might be, was a lucky sod".

'Joe c'mon. Wake up. Tim fer Galli.' Bert standing on the edge of my bunk gave me a kick.

'Ugh. Must have fallen asleep.' Collecting my eating irons and tin mug followed the rest of the gang to the top deck. Where immediately our gazes were focused towards the shores of Malaya. The distant hills or, mountains we had first spotted were well behind us. Our first impression was just green jungle. Jackie muttered.

'Din't faancy tha' blooody place. Glad I'm ganning te Singapore.'

Arriving at the hatchway to the galley went down and into our tiny little space of solitude away from the rest of the ship. Scouse shouted.

'You're late. Get spuds done quickly.' Mechanically we set about the chores. Bert enquired.

'Who's te menu fa troops teneet Scouse.'

'Well. Thought I would give them a taste of home tonight. Shepherd's pie and bisto gravy with lashings of peas. There will not be much left of that to feed the fishes. Get the carrots peeled and chopped up; tins of peas have to be opened up. There are five boxes in the gangway. Chop chop. Here you lads you seen the coastline over there. That's Malaya.' Geordie responded.

'Te blooody reet, a waa git our postings.'

'Who's got Singapore?' Three lucky ones yelled

'Wallah.'

'Where you others going?' Bert said.

'Butterworth.'

'That ain't bad. Opposite Penang. That place is almost like Singapore.' I asked.

'Where's Ipoh then?'

'Ooh. Sodding 'ell. Dodgy! You ain't going there are you?'

'Yer. Where is it?'

'In middle of that mass of jungle over on the port side. Bandit country. Fook your didilly do. That's all I'm saying.' Jack asked.

'Wars. Jahore Bahru?'

'Now that ain't bad. It's on the other side of the causeway from Singapore. C'mon. Chop chop. No blooody time to play silly bastards. I got a hungry troopship to feed.' Shocked! Bandit Country. What the bleedin' hell did that mean? Geordie urged me.

'Awa mon. lud moor tattles in.'

'Sod off it all right for you. You got bleedin' Singapore.'

With the usual happy banter, gone for a while the thoughts of the pending postings. For the last time we sat down and de-eyed (squared) the spuds cutting away a lot of skin, throwing the peelings over the side cleaned up and hosed down the galley area, before the Indians arrived with the fresh and sweet tea they made, not like the liquid in the tea urn that everyone else was provided with. Scouse entered and asked.

'What do you want for your evening meal? having eaten Steak for dinner we were not certain on what to have. In the end, Scouse made up our minds for us...What about Shepherd's Pie Chips and peas?' Everyone agreed, a taste of home would be just right for our last meal on board...Right that's settled then I'll make a special. Give me an hour.' He left shouting out orders to his Indians. Twenty minutes later, about the same time as the first sitting in the mess, the Indians presented us with our whopping dinners. Half way wading through the meal. Scouse entered.

'Ear you are Lads. Couple of beers each. Just my way of saying thanks for your help. Not one of you grumbled about doing any of the galley jobs. Usually the mobs I get in here are forced to do it. The main thing. Has everyone enjoyed it?' Speaking for all answered.

'To bleedin' right. Better than lazing about doing bugger all, up top deck.'

'That's the ticket. Does anyone what any Rice pudding for after?'

'Aw. No thanks.' We were very bloated and I'm sure we had put on pounds in weight. Finishing our beers got ready to leave the galley. Scouse came back in shook us by the hand and wished us all good luck, his parting advice was.

'Watch out for all those singapore lil's in bugie street. Yer do not know what they will give yer?'

The beer had cheered us up, laughing at his suggestion left his galley en route to the top deck. Immediately went to the ships rail to look at the coast of Malaya. The blue haze had now vanished and the colour between sea and land was very evident, blue and green where the shape of tall Palm trees broke up the skyline, at sea level there was a hint of a white sandy beach high above and behind us the heat from the sun was on our backs. It all appeared idealistic. Leaving the rail we had cleaning to attend to.

The bilge area was empty; flopping down on our hammocks listened to the monotonous thumping of the propeller blades, aware of the foul smell of sweat mingled with the unforgettable stench of the latrines and washhouse, if there were any extractor fans they certainly were not working. I now began to think; I would be glad to get off this tub and breathe some fresh air into my lungs, easing myself out of my bunk sorted out my cleaning kit and boots. Sounding very loud in the empty bilge from his top hammock Geordie's voice announced.

'Ye ken. Tis oor last neet abooard this tub. War all splitting up temarra. Wat say wer hav a beer in ter Naafi.' That suggestion hit home to us. I suggested.

'Good Idea but I stink. After we have done our bulling and had a shower.'

'Ye right ye ken. Evreebody will be int ter neet. Geordie jumped down from his top hammock and began to sort out his boots and kit from his sea kit bag. Our little secluded area became a hive of activity. Spit and polish, clothes were sorted ready for the following morning's disembarkation. Sat there polishing my boots suddenly remembered John Parkinson's brown boots, burst out laughing. Bert asked.

'Wha ye so happy aboot?'

'I'm just remembering at Honiton. John Parkinson was issued with brown boots. He had to dye em black, wonder what he's doing now? He got a home posting to an Ack Ack unit in Newcastle.' Jackie interrupted.

'Loooky bugger. I shoood ave git ter one.' I retorted.

'Well you didn't. You're going to bleedin' Singapore.'

Having sorted out our kit, finished our ablutions ready dressed made our way up top and over to the port side to see what if, anything could be seen of land? It was pitch black apart from the bulkhead and lower porthole lights casting a glow onto the wake of the waves, there was nothing to see. At the Naafi joined the contingent of SAS dressed in their OG's. They always first in the queue. With our ration of two beers sat down at a table to watch others coming in. This being everybody's last night on board very quickly became filled to its capacity. We began to discuss, what we thought it would be like wherever we were going. It was plainly obvious that the happiest out of our bunch were. Geordie, Jackie and Jimmie, the least happy me. We had finished our two beers and tried for another one with success. Time flew by and it was closing time.

Having consumed three beers along with the other two Scouse had provided. Back down the bilges for the last night on board dressed only in our cellular OG shorts with plimsolls on our feet we wandered backwards and forwards to the latrines. The anticipation of arriving in Singapore was the talking point throughout the bilge, Scouse the Cook had told us to be up early and ready to see the sights when we docked. So did not cancel our usual early morning call by the fire picket. Thus avoiding the usual scramble with the rest of the squaddies in the bilge. Gradually the chatter ceased to be replaced by deep snoring.

Lying awake was unsure of what bandit country meant. When the RE Sgt. gave out the postings. After Craftsman Plant, something about Three Company R. A. S. C. IPOH. Listening to the sound of the propeller thinking about Malaya only knowing my brother Jackie had been there during the war fighting the Japs and much later. Johnny Hanson had been killed there; he too was a National Serviceman. During our passage through the Red Sea the second Looie had given a lecture to his small contingent of Seaforth Highlanders on "Ambush positions". Where they were going in Aden was a range of about one thousand yards. In Malaya just a matter of feet. What did all that mean? These thoughts whizzed about in my head. Trying to find answers to my present where abouts, certainly did not volunteer for Malaya.

CHAPTER FOURTEEN
SINGAPORE

After a few hours of unsettled sleep at five thirty one of the Fire Picket squaddies woke us, feeling exhausted I lay still until the other two had descended from their bunks. In the gloom of a red light we quietly got ready and by the time we were about to leave, the stinking atmosphere of the bilge that had been our home for the past four weeks was a hive of activity, struggling with our kitbags we ascended the stairways for the last time. The last flight up had us breathing hard before stepping onto the deck crossed to the Port side and made our way to about the middle of the ship and dumped our kit close to the rail ready to disembark. It was still dark with nothing to see gradually others joined us to line the ships rail. In the early morning light a couple of square sailed Junks sailed past, whilst one Chinaman manned the till a few others were sat on their haunches smoking, their exhaled blue clouds of smoke quickly dispersed in the slight breeze two of them pointing in our direction began laughing, "Here comes another boatload of British Bastards". they possibly would have repeated their comment when they passed the other troopship behind us, as we observed the sights of this new country the rising sun silhouetted the outline of palm trees.

The rapid rising sun cast its light onto the ship necessitated the wearing of sunglasses and illuminated towering palm trees with long spiky leaves sprouting out from the tops that overshadowed the undergrowth and white sandy shoreline below. Here and there, wisps of grey smoke drifted upwards from the shanty styled huts with funny thatched roofs, some fishing boats were moored against a wooden landing stage and gently bobbing up and down with the swell. A few natives dressed with only a coloured sheet wrapped around their waist their upper ebony coloured muscular torsos rippled as they pulled fishing nets out of the boats, further along other boats were beached on the white sand, on a road close to the shoreline a few cars and Lorries were speeding along. As the ship approached more conventional styled brick buildings the stretch of sandy beach ended so did the blueness of the sea below us that had changed to a muddy colour, floating on its surface were slicks of oil its rainbow colours glinting in the sunlight and as the tugs came out to berth the ship us, the sound of the ship foghorn sixty feet above blasted out loud enough to turn anyone in close proximity deaf. The ship shuddered and the sound of the engines stopped. At 0800 hours, the Lancashire docked in Singapore our cruise was over; we were alongside the *terra firma* of Singapore.

On the sunlit quayside below we watched two teams of barefooted-Chinese coolies run to the front and rear of the ship to grab hold of the ship's hawsers and slip them over the black steel bollards, some stripped to the waist or wearing a tattered singlet vest and black shorts tied around their foreheads was a strip of cloth. A line of Lorries laden with food and other supplies ready to be taken on board were parked alongside warehouses, their Chinese drivers dressed in similar garb as the other coolies, either lay on top of the heaps of food or sat on the running board of the cab, all were smoking. A group of Chinese policemen wearing black pillbox caps dressed in dark blue shorts white shirts black hose tops puttees and black boots, long black truncheons were strapped to their belts, standing away from them was their senior Officer wearing a Black Sam Brown belt and peaked hat with a pistol holder clipped to his belt and by his stance and colour obviously English. Also stood waiting were two other large separate groups of Chinese women dressed in pyjamas, some wore a large white bandana on their heads, whilst others wore big round whicker type hats.

Gone was the fresh cooling sea breeze instead the smell of burning wood filled the air and the humidity of the atmosphere became very oppressive, causing small rivulets of sweat to run down the front of my chest. The whirring sound of the ship's derrick caught our attention, as a hawser came down attached to its end was a square frame with a couple of wires dangling free, the coolies on the quayside started shouting as they grabbed hold and fitted the hawser to a gangway that was quickly lifted up towards the ship rail and secured. Immediately the two groups of Chinese women began their siege. Hordes of them scurried up the gangway onto the deck running past us, young ones old ones their slippers flip flopping against the wooden deck, all chatting excitedly in the new strange singsong tongue of the Chinese. Amused by this activity, Jackie shouted out.

'Awar. Still in te piejamas. Thur ear te give us a good time. Tat litlun's mine. I'm awar doon below.' Geordie retorted.

'Ye ken. Therre all wee and hae nae tit's.' Jack exclaimed.

'Herre comes tarmy!' Diverting our attention to the quayside, a convoy of lorries drove along the quayside stopping side by side facing the ship. Their drivers got out and stood in front of the Lorries. Observing their uniform, OG. Jacket, shorts, stocking tops, puttees, boots and beret, a Yellow tabs was visible at the top of their hose. I commented.

'They're bleedin' Boy scouts; look at those yellow tabs on their legs.' Jimmie retorted.

'Nay. Therre neet therre ter RASC.'

Watching all the activity going on it was getting hotter and more oppressive, the sweat was oozing out of every pore of our bodies if, we stayed any longer we would all melt away? The noisy singsong of the Chinese women announced their return to the deck, carrying rolled up canvas hammocks and bedding the bundles nearly as big as they were; they flip-flopped past us and like ferrets, scurried down the gangways across the quayside and out of sight. The Tannoy clicked to announce. 'All Troops prepare to disembark.'

Further along an Officer and Sgt. Began leading the troops down the gangway, at the bottom the Officer stood to one side whilst the Sgt. continued with the file of troops towards the waiting Lorries. Slowly we moved forward to stumble down the gangway and step onto the shores of Singapore. With legs like rubber, the weight of the kit bags became heavier as we stumbled to the next lorry, standing beside its driver the Sgt. yelled.

'Throw your kit bags onto the back and clamber aboard...recognising us, his tone of voice changed...Aah. Your scouse's party. You did a good job down there. Make sure you don't get any more cookhouse fatigues Eh?' Laughing loudly at his own joke. Little did he know? That we had enjoyed our stay down there. We climbed up the Lorries tailboard and moved up towards its cab and with enough troops aboard, the Sgt. shouted.

'Right enough bodies on that one. You lot behind. Next lorry.' The driver hoisted up the tailboard and secured it.

The lorry was uncovered and the steel roof of the cab was so hot, you could fry an egg on it. When all the Lorries were finally loaded as our driver was about to climb up I noticed his shoulder flash, Green with a Yellow Palm tree and Tiger (found out later the Singapore Flash). Someone behind enquired.

'How far is this Nee Soon Camp then?' Squinting his eyes against the blinding sun.

'About ten miles away t'others side of Island.' Geordie exclaimed.

'Singapore te big polace then! Dae wer gee troo Singapore?' The driver replied.

'No around the coast road then across country.'

Eventually, the convoy started up and left through the dock gates onto a main road where a couple of Red Caps kindly held up the traffic. Turning left the convoy picked up speed through a built up area. On either side were terraced buildings two-storied high with shops at street level, between each shop were round colonnades covered with Chinese letters. Hanging in between, the colonnades were rolled up horizontal bamboo type shades with English lettering. In amongst them spotted a bookshop called 'Wen Huey Book Co.' In front of each shop, two wide stone steps providing access from the road to the raised walkways, between the steps was a wide open deep concrete ditch. (Later we learnt they were monsoon ditches). Along the road, a few cars were parked with the odd Lorry delivering stores to one or two of the shops. In use were many old fashioned English upright bikes, some cyclist minding their own business and oblivious to us, were slowly

pedaling along as they puffed away on a cigarette. No doubt through the slits of their eyelids they were observing us. An old Chinaman, with a dirty old Tobie on his head, his open shirt flapped loosely about his skinny torso blackened by years in the sun, wearing a pair of black shorts his skinny legs were etched with wiry muscles, as he in bare feet pedaling his Tricycle taxi.

A typical street scene.

One or two street vendors some busily fanning charcoal braziers as they cooked some dishes in large round pans. We became aware of the aromas of different smells, charcoal, sweet fruit, Chinese cooking, Indian curries, new to our senses and no doubt, with the passage of time would become adapted to them?

Leaving the fringes of Singapore, the convoy drove through the countryside and along the road beside the beach and sea, the sun glinting on its surface like a mirror, which not less than an hour before we had been sailing through. On the other side up through dense long grass, groups of palm trees grew up like giant flower stems, in front of some bungalows were flat open grassland. A dirt track led to a large domed Temple. Every now and then well away from the road, a dirt track would lead to a small group of thatched roofed shacks. Nobody spoke, just trying to observe and take in this new experience of a very different world. Proceeding inland the convoy went through a place named Bukit Timah, then the road ran parallel to a railway track before crossing over, several miles further on passed some big lakes then a sign appeared. "Nee Soon Camp". Driving through its gates followed a long inclined road, where the convoy finally stopped near the top. A group of Sgt's shouted.

'Get down with your Kit. Spread yourself out along the grass embankment.'

Clambering down, scrambled up the grass verge and flopped down. As the last truck in the convoy drove by, with the sun beating down on the reclining bodies an eerie silence spread through their ranks until, a low whinnying sound could be heard coming from over the top of the hill. First, the silhouette of a soldier came into view, quickly followed by the outline of an armoured car and as it came closer, all eyes concentrated on this new attraction a six-wheeled armoured vehicle. The Soldier manning a pair of mounted machine guns, wearing headphones its wires attached to a small microphone strapped to his chest, in front below him was the head of the driver he too wore headphones and as he changed gears, the distinctive whine of its engine almost disappeared. As it trundled past its rear doors were wide open revealing more soldiers armed with rifles. Close behind was another armoured four-wheeled vehicle with a spare wheel fixed to its side, out of its turret poked a heavy gun barrel and a soldier in similar attire watched everything as below him in front was the driver. With the excitement over, so began the discussions "What were they"? Very quickly, information filtered back from another REME VM. (Vehicle Mechanic) One was a Saracen armoured personnel carrier and the other a Daimler Scout Car. It became somewhat of a mundane topic, as too the reason why they were in the camp, until they again reappeared over the hill to do another circuit. Someone decided to time them nevertheless, it was a mystery what were they doing here in Nee Soon transit camp? Further, down the road another convoy of Lorries arrived with the troops off the Delwara. Very quickly, information was passed up the line they were the South Wales Borderers. (SWASBIES) En-route to Malaya.

As the morning dragged on the sun got even hotter, yet the atmosphere was extremely humid. Having sat or laid there all morning we were soaked in sweat, the tightness of puttees around my ankles made my feet feel like they were about to burst open and no doubt, I was not the only one moaning about soddin Puttees. Yet again, the armoured vehicles reappeared, to do another round trip. Then a group of Sgt's. came marching down towards us. One was bawling his head off.

'EVERYONE GET THEIR EATING IRONS. MESS TINS, TIN MUGS. FORM UP ON THE ROAD. IN THREE RANKS.'

At last, glad that something was happening, opened up sea Kitbags fished out the eating utensils and formed up in Platoons on the roadway. The Sgt. obviously another cheerful bastard bawled out.

'THE ARMY. IS NOW GOING TO FEED AND WATER YOU. BEFORE YOU ARE SENT ON YOUR MERRY WAYS. ATTENSHOO.'

We were marched up the hill, as the APC & Scout Car rumbled past us to continue yet another circuit, what a boring job. Some ribald comments were uttered.

'Know what! They have lost the way to Malaya.' Another retorted.

'No. The stupid Red Caps. Have given them the wrong direction?' This banter broke up the strained atmosphere that had surrounded us since we landed. Upon reaching the brow of the hill, below us was a massive oblong hanger coming to a halt outside, dismissed to form up in single line before entering. "The mess hall". After our two weeks stint in the galley, we were back in amongst the troops queuing up. Quickly moving forward, Chinese cooks served us same old drill. 'Hold out mess tin.' Crash Bang Wallop. Baked beans, two sausages and mashed spuds. From another Dixie. Tapioca and jam pudding, as another Chinese cook ladled tea into your mug. It was like a conveyor belt. You left the line and found somewhere to sit, there must have been a over a thousand troops packed into that mess hall, the noise was deafening, the digging, scraping of metal against metal, slurping of the tea, that did not quench my thirst, requiring more liquid when a Sgt. came around with the usual question.

'Any complaints?' I asked.

'No Sarge, but could do with some more tea.' He strongly replied.

'Well. You. Will have to wait your chuffing turn. Won't you? Others have not been served yet. Stand up those going up country to Malaya? The three of us stood up. Right you three on your way out. Over the far end by the doorway pick up travelling rations.' He moved to the next table. I retorted.

'Bastard. Only wanted more tea.' Geordie retorted.

'I wanna pish.'

'Well do not ask that bastard. Otherwise he will say. Wait until everyone else wants one.' This brought a bit of a laugh around the table, but set everyone thinking, "They too wanted a piss". The back end of the queue came in sight, which started a mad stampede for seconds or, more drink thought, "Sod it. I'll die of thirst instead". Collecting up his eating utensils Georgie said.

'I'm awa for te pish.' The que for all of us. On our way out three of us stopped at a table piled high with white paper bags containing rations. Displaying a set of gold-filled teeth a smiling Chinese waiter, speaking in impeccable English asked.

'You go to Malaya Jonnie?'

'Yes.' Handed over a packet he said.

'Okay Jonnie. One packet each. Nice fresh sandwiches for your journey.' No way was this packet. Going to be lost.

Outside we joined a mob, milling around large tin water baths all trying to wash out Billycans in water swimming with the remnants of beans or mashed spuds. With that chore done, followed another mob of blokes heading for the latrines. A large corrugated tin box minus a roof. Everyone avoided one corner, where someone had thrown up, the stench was overpowering could not get out of there quick enough. Having been fed and watered, made our own way back to the slope. By then, above our heads menacing dark clouds had blocked out the sun nevertheless, the humidity was almost as if you were in a Turkish bath. Tidying away lay back down on the grassy slopes, as once again the whine of the APC returned somebody had clocked it. It had taken a half an hour for its journey.

A line of Lorries turned up and parked, then a couple of Sgt is armed with clipboards proceeded to call out names, amongst those: Geordies, Jackie's, Jimmies and Jack's. The Sgt's urging all,

'C'MON YOU IDLE SHOWER GET CHUFFING ABOARD THE LORRIES.'

Gathering up their kit bags. With hardly any time to waste us all shook hands, promising to meet up on the way home for demob. As they clambered aboard the wagons with a farewell wave were driven away. Two thirds of our band of volunteers from 9/Elect/7 had gone. Bert and I stood watching the last of the Lorries disappear out of sight. I said.

'Bleedin' 'ell Bert. Were next. Wots in store for us?' A glum reply.

'Nae fooking noo.'

The slope was less populated, big gaps between groups of troops were now evident and it was not long before it was our turn. A couple of Sgt's. Bawling out.

'LEAVE YOUR KIT BAGS WHERE THEY ARE. FORM UP ON THE ROAD. IN THREE RANKS.'

Once assembled we were marched to an armory, to be issued with a 303. MK. V. rifle. Knife bayonet with frog including ten rounds of ammunition, with a friendly warning, chucked in by the Ordnance soldier.

'Never let the rifle or ammo out of your sight. When you get to wherever you have been posted to. Hand in your weapon and ammo at the armory. If, you lose it whilst on Active Service. That is a court marshal offence. If found guilty. Shot at dawn. What is your rifle number? Calling out the rifle number, fear struck me. I should not be here, should be in Singapore...he demanded. Sign here.'

Leaving the armory pocketed the clips of ammunition and joined the platoon outside. Bert looked at me and me at him. Our grim looks said everything. The MK. V. was different to the standard 303. It was shorter, lighter the barrel muzzle was fitted with an anti-flash bell mouth and the rifle butt had a rubber shoulder pad. It did not make any difference; its purpose was the same, a killing machine. With rifles at the slope we marched back to find a line of Lorries waiting for us. The Sgt's bringing us to a halt ordered.

'FROM YOUR KITBAGS. TAKE OUT YOUR RIFLE SLINGS. ATTACH THEM TO THE RIFLES. REPLACE YOUR OLD BAYONET FROG. WITH YOUR NEW ONE. C'MON MOVE YOURSELVES. YOU GOT A TRAIN TO CATCH.'

Scrambling up the slope. Opened up the flap of the Uni, extracting the rifle sling swopping the bayonet frog on my belt put the old one along side my ration pack safely on top re-tied. Attached and adjusting the rifle sling slung it over my shoulder. Bert pulling the rifle up to his shoulder looked along the barrel exclaimed.

'Wa do ye do wit these?'

'Don't know, but I am sure some bastard will tell us very soon. What about this bayonet then?' Bert exclaimed.

'Te looks fookin vicious te mi!'

Ten minutes later, the same bastard arrived back and began bawling out.

'LISTEN UP. PICK UP ALL YOUR KIT AND GET ON BOARD THE TRUCKS.'

With the rifle slung over one shoulder, grabbed hold of the two kitbags and unceremoniously slid down the grassy slope, slinging both kitbags up onto the lorry floor, threw on the rifle. A Sgt stood a few feet away, bawled out.

'HEY. YOU SOLDIER. WHO GAVE YOU PERMISSION? TO LOOSE YOUR RIFLE? GRAB HOLD OF THE FOOKER. KEEP IT CLOSE TO YOU ALL THE TIME. YOU WILL NEED IT.' Retrieving it, clambered aboard and sheepishly joined Bert standing at the front.

'See I told you so. That bastard frightened the shit out of me bawling in my ear like that.' Bert just laughed.

The whine of the APC drove past us doing another lap of honour. Further down the road the Swasbies were already on the trucks and settled. Under the threatening skies of rain the convoy moved off, along the camp road the breeze against our sweat-wet tunics was chilly. Someone called out.

'Where's the blooody sun?' Leaving the camp took the same route, seeing the same views but as we entered the outskirts of Singapore there was a distinct air of despondency amongst all of us. Speeding past the dock gates came to a point in the road where a Red Cap stood insisting he hold up all the Singapore traffic. What an important job he had? Turning right the convoy entered Singapore Station. A grand majestic old Colonial styled building. That my brother Jackie had spoken about.

Singapore Station

'Go and see the railway station in Singapore. That's where the British Army surrendered to the Japanese during the second world war.' At that moment in time, that incident in history was far from my mind. Entering its forecourt the Lorries drew up in lines. The Red Cap having done his duty in restarting Singapore, walked along the back of the trucks, ordered. 'Collect your kit. Get down. Form up in three ranks.'

For what seemed ages we stood waiting for the next order. The humidity of the air was mixed with an array of aromas, burning charcoal, spices and curry. After the meager meal we had at midday, was beginning to get hungry and certainly could eat a curry. Five RE Sgt's. emerged from the station entrance, walking along the rows of soldiers began shouting.

'PICK UP YOUR KIT. IN SINGLE FILE. MOVE INTO THE STATION. '

Inside the vestibule it was much cooler; hanging from above the three large fans stirred the still air however, their slow rotating blades did not cause much of a down draft. It was practically deserted accept for four Chinese women sat on a wooden bench; the only sound was that of our boot studs, squealing upon the stone floor. As a railway terminus, it was tiny, with only two platforms covered by wooden overhangs, similar in design to those back in Blighty. At the far platform, a stationary train was butted up against a set of odd-looking red painted buffers fixed to the main concourse; its pistons extended about four feet. To brighten up the place flowering foliage had been planted between the two tracks.

Rear Carriage

The train's carriages with half moon shaped roof, looked like something out of a Western film, made of wood and painted in a livery of cream and milk chocolate brown, a big red stripe divided the two colours. The only entrance was at each end of the coach. In the far distance the methodically chuffing sound of the waiting engine could be heard as it puffed out black smoke.

The head of the column of troops began boarding the first coach, the Sgt. counting bodies moved the column along to the next one, at the third one he urged us to climb onto the open landing stage, surrounded by a wooden guardrail and in the middle was a small metal gate providing access to the next coach. Squeezing through the small doorway, we entered into a baking hot semi darkened carriage with rows of seats on either side. Making our way to the far end dumped our kitbags on the floor. The wooden slatted seats reminded me of the old London tram seats; on both sides, the wooden louvered windows were closed. Bert fanning himself attempted to open the window without success and then found two small catches to lower the window. However, it made no difference, the temperature inside was the same as outside. Hoisting up our kitbags onto the luggage racks above sat down with our rifles beside us, ready for the departure.

'Ear Bert yer know wot. We volunteered for this lot. Well at least Singapore. What did we get? Bleedin' Malaya.'

Ye ken. We've been 'ere nearly ten hoors un nae seen Singapore. Noo war aboot te leeve. Te others oor most likely swilling beer in te Naafi somewar.'

'Yer and we've got a sodding train journey to face. I wonder how long it will take.'

'All neet ye ken.'

Resigned to our fate, sat on the varnished seats that been polished to an immaculate sheen they were most uncomfortable and my backside was not used to such discomfort. With the carriage void of noise, everyone was just as gutted and could do nothing about it; soon the pungent sweaty atmosphere was filled with cigarette smoke. Going outside, was not an option. It was some time later the arrival of an RE Sgt. entered, passing by he counted bodies, at the far end, bawled out.

'ATTENTION...STAY WHERE YOU ARE...NOBODY LEAVES THE CARRIAGE...ANY INFANTRY IN THIS CARRIAGE?' No one responded...ALL CORPS THEN! Right, now we know where we are. This train will soon be departing for Malaya. Once it leaves the Island of Singapore. It will cross over, what is known as the Causeway onto the mainland of Malaya. Operational country. These trains like many others may come under fire from the CT's (Communist Terrorist). On the other hand, be subjected to mines and derailment. That means you will become engaged, raising his voice. YOU IN RETURN. WILL FIRE AT THE ENEMY. AS OF NOW. YOU. ARE ALL ON ACTIVE SERVICE. Guards will be mounted for two-hour stags. Two guards at the front. Two at the rear of each carriage. Rifles will be loaded with a magazine of ten rounds. Whilst on guard. One round will be loaded up the spout with safety catches on. During guard stags, there will be no talking or, smoking. Any Questions?' Silence was prevalent...Right Now Guards? Pointing directly at us. You and you. First stag front of carriage. Thinking, "Dear Mum. I want to come home". Selecting more unfortunates. 'You and you.' Front of carriage second-stag.' His monotonous tone of. 'You and you.' stuck in my brain, looking at Bert gazing out of the window, his brow furrowed with deep concentration, was shaking his head from side to side, a gesture of. "Oh no". Wondered, if he had shit himself? Nevertheless, was not going to ask such a bleedin' silly question?

The Sgt. returned and stood beside us. He was not that big about the same statue as L/Cpl Gabe. His tanned face gave him the appearance of being in his early thirties, with black eyebrows and a cultivated moustache. Three white chevron tapes adorned both arms, his shoulder flash a green square with a pair of white Kukris. It was only then I noticed a pistol holster was clipped to his belt. He appeared unconcerned as he announced.

'Attention. IF, we are engaged with firepower. The CT's normally aim for the windows. At any sound of rifle shots. Immediately fall flat on the carriage floor. Wait for my instructions. During the nighttime journey. I suggest that you sleep as best as you can on the floor. Derailment is another thing. It is more likely that the front coaches will endure the most of that form of attack. Again. You will act on my instructions. Savvy?'

As if we were under immediate attack, the silence erupted into wild conversation about what was likely to happen. Everyone began grabbing rifles, magazines were removed, the sound of bullets being fed into and dropped by nervous fingers added to the panic. Thinking back to being instructed on weapons at Honiton and it was the last time had fired a rifle. In our present situation we were about to be shot at exclaimed.

'Why can't they issue the CT's with pickaxe handles? Any guard duty going, I'm the bleeder that's picked.' Bert quipped.

'Ye ken. Ter go ferr ye shoorties. Nae so 'ard te hit and yon arse tis cloose t' floower.'

'Yer Wot about you then. You're on first guard same as me and look at size of you? You're a bleedin' easy target.'

'First seen of tet shoooting. Aim' drappen street te floower.' We were just loading in the last rounds, when the Sgt. re-entered I asked.

'When. Do we leave Sarge?'

'Hard nut are you? Want to see some action eh? Well. We are about to leave in five minute's time. The armoured train has left in front of us, to make sure that there are no mines on the track or the rails have not been tampered with.' Startled by his comment.

'Armoured train?'

'Yes. Armoured train. It travels about a mile ahead of the train. It is a four wheeled bogey engine, covered in armour plate steel including its chassis and floor plates. Inside two men drive the engine. Don't worry about it; they will go up before you.'

The information about the pending train journey were not words of reassurance? Ambushes, bullets whizzing around, armoured trains, derailments and we had not left Singapore. Did not fancy making this train trip in the first place nevertheless, it was too late. A long blast from the engines whistle set the train in motion and with a jerky start began the long journey into Bandit Country. What was it we use to say back in training? "Roll on death demobs too far away"? Well we were about to find out.

Gradually gathering speed the train left the built up area of Singapore and out into the countryside, a cool breeze rushed through the open window to freshen up the humid and sweaty smoke laden air. With the train wheels singing a Diddley–Dee -Diddley–Dah Diddley -Dee over the tracks, watched the countryside pass by. The colour of the sky still grey promising rain but dusk was about to descend. The train ran parallel with the road we had been driven along a short while before that crossed onto our left and into the trees. For a while the train ran beside an open lake until the note of the wheels changed as it rumbled onto the Causeway Bridge. The Sgt. came in from outside and called out.

'First guard front and rear stag duty.' Grabbing the rifle stood up alongside of Bert.

'Right you two engage your magazine. Slip one up the spout with safety catches on. – You. Point that bloody thing away from me.' The magazine clipped in easily, with a sharp bolt action slipped one up the spout, secured the safety catch. Satisfied with our drill he ordered.

'You. Take the left side. You the right side. Do not fall off. This mob in here is relying on you two! It will soon be their turn. Now no talking and conversing with the other two guards on the other carriage. And definitely no smoking.' I replied.

'Not one of my 'abit's. Sergeant.'

'No. I bet yours. Is shagging. Well there is no time for that. You two are lucky, as this stag is the shortest of em all. Guard duty starts at six in the evening and its well past six. If we are fired upon. Do not forget. You are a moving target. The chances of you being hit are slim. It will be pitch black out there. So identify where the flash came from before returning any shots. Any questions?' Bert asked.

'Dee we coom te inform ye if ter is gunshots?'

198

'No. You bloody idiot. Don't you think? We will hear them? I will be out alongside you in a flash. Don't you worry about that, now get outside.'

Reluctantly, we inched out through the doorway onto the little platform. In the near darkness could just about make out two shadowy figures on the opposite carriage. Moving to the left, Bert went right. Peering out into the disappearing light, as beneath our feet the rumbling sound of the train on the bridge continued over dark waters, ever getting closer and closer to the coastline of Malaya. The rumble of the wheels on the bridge ceased as the familiar staccato of wheels on *terra firma* of Malaya took over. We were in total darkness. Malaya. Bandit Country. Almost shitting myself my heart hit the pit of my stomach. "Oh soding 'ell".

CHAPTER FIFTEEN
MALAYA. BANDIT COUNTRY

Gripping my rifle at the port order, leant up against the carriage woodwork to sway in time with the motion of the train diddle-dee- dee-diddle- dee darring, on its merry way causing a chilly draft against my damp OG's, but at least my feet were cooling down. It was pitch black and my senses warned; we were very close to vegetation. The fleetingly glimmer of light cast from the carriage windows reflected upon the passing vegetation, masses of tangled foliage, giant leaves and what appeared to be tree trunks.

'You still there Bert? Silence......Bert?'

'War ye wan?' The rapid diddly-dee-darring of the wheels slowed as jerkingly the train-reduced speed, making me jumpy. "Christ trouble already"? Gripping my rifle tighter watched as the reflection of the carriage lights provided a hint of vegetation, into blackness before a single chink of light appeared, then many more chinks appeared and the vegetation became lighter as the train entered some town. Roadways, streetlights, people on bikes, cars and those trishaw things. We were back in civilization! Going through a station, on a large railway board printed in large English letters was 'Johore Bahru.' Beneath was a line of Chinese characters and below those some squiggly letters, possibly Malay. Immediately thought, "Christ that was the place, Jack had been posted? "

Not stopping, the train gradually increased its speed back into blackness, clattering over some points its carriages creaking and groaning in protest as the wheels rolled diddly darring along the rails. Very vigilant began to ponder. What was going on in Malaya? Back home there was little or nothing ever mentioned in the papers or, on the wireless about Malaya. Plenty about the Mau Mau in Kenya, Cyprus with its EOKA and the Arabs in the Aden Protectorate. But nothing about Malaya, what was it all about? At no time had we been briefed on it, only when Scouse the cook remarked. "Bandit country fook your diddly do". Even then did not understand and was still none the wiser. Shivering in the breeze of the moving train, realised it was sodding cold and more so had a lot to learn. The rest of our stag duty passed without incident about eight-o clock, the Sgt. emerged with another two idiots. 'Stag change. You two inside.'

The pair of us fought our way through the doorway, slumping down into our allotted seats, pleased to get out of the cold and back into the warmth of the carriage. In the dim light from the bulbs above, noticed the window had been shut tight. Sleeping squaddies were either slumped in their seats or lying on the floor with legs sprawled across the gangway, those still awake silently watched as the guards were changed. Stepping over the legs of those laying on the floor the Sgt. passed on his way further down the carriage. With a sigh of relief muttered.

'Thank Christ that bleedin' stags over, wot d'yer reckon then Bert?'

'Bugger all. Wit a wist of teem. Te start wee, I was shitting missel. but seeing as I cuid nae see anything oot there. Hoo te fook cuid pick mi oot? Even if the' war treeying. Yon leets from te carriage would be eesy targets ye ken.' Was his philosophical statement.

'Yeah, but on the other hand. The Bandits could rake the whole of the train with a hail of bullets. You know what the Sergeant said. They aim for the windows. Being a short arse, would get away with it. But you. Sod yer 'orrible luck.' With a hint of concern muttered.

'Din yee be such a blooody idiot. Let's gee ter whoor were geeing.'

Having spent just over two hours in Bandit country. We were now essentially 'Seasoned Soldiers.' What a load of shite. The Sgt. passing us stopped.

'You two. What you doing sitting down?'

'We just come off Guard. Sergeant.'

'Have you? What's the first thing you do with your rifles?' His question baffled me.

'Dunno Sergeant.'

'What is the matter with your rifles? Swiftly grabbed the rifle.... No. You bloody Idiot. What's that black thing stuck out underneath the bolt?'

'Magazine. Sergeant.'

'Right. Remove it. And without shooting anyone. Unload the one up the spout, then present the rifle for inspection.'

Removing the magazine, with a quick action of the bolt ejected the bullet with a clunk it hit the floor, retrieving it placed it in the same pocket with the magazine. Standing up presented the rifle muzzle in his direction. He squinted down the barrel, grunted. Leaning the rifle against the seat replaced the bullet in the magazine. Having inspected Bert's. He continued on his way muttering.

'Pair of bloody idiots.'

'Ear Bert. Guess what? Bleedin' ages since loaded a magazine. Bet he would have put us on a court marshal if we had left those magazines on. I'm bleedin' parched, could do with some tea.'

'Din he say sommat aboot a char wallah. Selling tee on ter train at sometime or, war it win we git te station?'

'Nah. He comes around. He'd better hurry or might die of thirst. You ask him when he gets back.' The Sgt. having sorted out the second stag came towards us. Bert was quick to ask him, about the tea wallah.

'He'll be around. He's got to serve all the rest and, if he has to step over sleeping beauties like this lot. It will take him all night. Where you two going anyway?'

'Ipoh!

'Butterworth! '

'Aah. Barring mines, derailment or ambush, normally all three at once and, I might add at any time. We should arrive in Ipoh late tomorrow afternoon. Butterworth! Late tomorrow night or, early hours of the morning. Therefore. You Jock will be on guard tomorrow night as well. Where was your last camp?' Bert answered.

'Malvern. Nea far fray Worcester. Then Arborfield fae transit.'

'Interesting, I was at Malvern years ago. Engineer's camp. Number one training battalion. Still that was a long time ago, when you lot was still in short pants. In this carriage, you lot are mainly REME and RASC and a couple of medics. Some of the Infantry are at the rear, the rest are up front. Some are getting off at our next stop Segamat, then Seremban and KL. A few of you at Ipoh and the rest at Butterworth.'

With the fact of him, being in Malvern, we had a little bit more in common. He seemed all right and it was worth continuing the conversation.

'Sarge. Wot's all this active service lark about then.'

'LARK! This is not a lark. It is a bloody war against communist terrorists. Commonly known as bandit's or CT's. It has being going on since 1948. It started in Ipoh where you're going. Then spread all over Malaya most of the action takes place in the Ulu. That is the name for jungle. But there are road patrols, Kampong Guards and such like duties. Anyway, you are neither infantry nor Armoured. So you won't be doing any jungle bashing.'

'How long yer bin out here Sergeant?'

'Since fifty three got another year to do, I might even sign on and do another Python.'

'Python! What's a Python?'

'Out here! A three year tour of duty.'

'Anyone get killed then?'

'Course they bloody have. It's a sodding war. Numbers on both sides, including civilians must be in the thousands.'

The train began to slow down, quickly he moved outside he was gone about two minutes then returned.

'It's okay. We will be arriving at Kluang in a few minutes, we won't be stopping.' He went back down the carriage and stopped to talk to someone dressed in K.D's. Recognized him as the RASC Sgt. on the Lancashire. Rattling across some points the train began slowing down to a crawl as it went through Kluang, rattling over some more points it began to pick up speed and not long after the Sgt. called out. 'Third guard stag duty get ready.' With the stag change over, the monotonous rhythm of the train lulled me into an uneasy sleep however, another disturbance jolted me awake this time a welcome one.

'Chai sahib...An old Indian char wallah, with a yoke spread across his shoulders, dangling from one end was a tray with glasses and from the other an antiquated tea urn...Velly good chai sahibs velly good.' Putting up two fingers muttered

'Two mate.'

'Velly good chai, dua panny each glaaas Sahib.' Pouring out the tea, handed them to us giving him the money he advanced to his next customers. It was a good time to eat our rations. The tea was sweet and very hot to hold much easier to sip than gulp but soon finished it off and placed the glass on the edge of the seat watched him still serving right down the far end, gradually my eye lids felt like lumps of sagging skin, well aware of our current situation sitting upright thought, "Just close my eyes and rest them".

Waking up with a start, the train was stationary. I was cold stiff and laid out flat on the wooden seat, my feet felt like balloons hearing shouting sat bolt upright. Bert was laid on the floor asleep.

'Bert. Bert. What is going on? With bleary eyes raised himself, responded.

'Dinna Ken.' Getting up I slid down the window, sticking my head out Bert joined me. We were in a station and dawn was breaking, on the platform troops were milling around with kitbags and equipment some Officers were talking to Sgt's.

'Where the bleedin' 'ell are we?'

'Dinna Ken.' Shivering in the damp morning air suggested.

'Could do with a cup of that tea. That last one along with the rations sent me to sleep. Bert gave an irritated response.

'Hey. Ye war snoring ye heed off. Ter Sergeant tell mi te poosh yon on te seat. I got doon on te floower te sleep. I cuid dae wit te pish.'

'So could I. Not been since Nee Soon, we'll have to wait until we leave this bleedin' station. Hardly drinking anything I've sweated it out. Hey, look there on your left, there's one of those Chico's selling stuff.' Bert whistled and shouted.

'Hoi yon oop err.' The Chico looked; waving at him, he took no notice. I yelled.

'C'mon were going soon.' Still he carried on serving then; coming towards us some other bleeder stopped him.

'C'mon hurry up. Tell yer wot Bert. We ain't going to get anything. We'll be off soon.' A voice behind startled the pair of us.

'Chai jonnie.' Turning around came face to face with an old Indian with a soiled white turban wrapped around his head, black as the ace of spades and skinny as a rake.

'Too bleedin' right. How much?'

'Two panny. Jonnie.'

'Okay. I want two. One for me mate here.'

'Tikai?' Squatting on his haunches with his knees close to his head, how he could sit like that was beyond me? His wiry hands turned on the urn tap a stream of tea filled the glass, I handing it to Bert. Outside the Chico called.

'Jonnie. Jonnie. You want buy.' Bert asked.

'War yer git?'

The char wallah, handed me a glass of tea, extended his palm.

'Tuan. Tu pannies. Jonnie.'

'All right mate. I ain't going to bleedin' run away. Bert I'll get yours...Showed him a tanner...I want two pence change mate.' Grinning said.

'Achaa Jonnie, Achaa. Tu pannies chang... From inside his white clothing, fished out a swag bag, which looked quite weighty undoing the string, took out two pennies handing them to me said...Tu pannies. Achaa Jonnie.' Lifting his yoke moved away to serve the others. Taking a sip of the piping hot tea, asked.

'What's he got Bert?'

'Fruit?' Moving to the window looked down at this little Indian chico, with sleek black hair greased and parted on one side wearing a little white shirt that hung over a pair of oversized OG shorts. (No doubt, half inched) His goodies, green bananas, some slices of reddish pink fruit and slices of pineapple lay out on a block of ice on top of a stool. I suggested.

'What about a fruit cocktail for breakfast Bert?'

'Och aye.' Reversing two fingers, pointed to the fruit.

'Two of each.'

'Okay. Jonnie. Two of each.' Taken aback by his command of English. A screech from the Engines whistle frightened the shit out of us; Bert nearly dropped his glass of tea. The chico having placed the items on a green leaf, handed them up.

'Six pennies Jonnie, six pennies. Grabbing hold of his offerings let Bert pay the chico his money, expecting the train to move sat down to eat the fruit. The pink and red slices were not unlike melons, not much juice but more substance, the bananas were very firm and tasty. Satisfied we sat drinking the remains of our tea whilst outside the rising sun illuminated the interior of the carriage and on the platform, the troops were in the process of leaving. Desperate to go for a jimmy riddle, with no sign of the train departing muttered.

'Wish they'd get a bleedin' move on.' Getting up looked out of the open window. About three carriages further up, a group of NCOs, were chatting and laughing amongst themselves, I exclaimed.

'Bleedin' 'ell. Their holding a mothers meeting up there.' The piercing screech of the train's whistle once again shattered the morning silence. With a shudder, we were moving.

Beating Bert to the bog. Well a tiny compartment you could hardly swing a cat in. In one corner, a tiny sink with a dripping tap the so called "toilet" a ceramic square stone bowl with a hole in the middle, on either side imprinted were reversed giant footprints muttered. 'Soddin' 'ell fire. Just a hole.' Standing on the footprints looked down onto the railway sleepers flashing past. Much relieved, had a quick wash of my sticky face and hands there was no paper so patted myself dry on my jacket sleeve. Opening the door was confronted by Bert in a contorted stance and behind him, another five all eager to get in.

Back in the seat slumped down to stare out at a wall of jungle, if you put your hand out you could touch its mass of vegetation. Observing the many different types of green vegetation, broad giant leaves hung down from a central stem, whilst another with large oval shaped leaves pointed skywards, rope like vines disappeared into the canopy of leaves above, stood out against the contrasting shades of green, were the greyish white coloured tree trunks, in places its denseness became areas of blackness. Then a small clearing would appear before re-entering a tunnel of vegetation cutting out the sunlight, creating semi darkness within the carriage, it seemed endless. The Sgt. was sitting on the other side looking out of the open window. Getting up crossed over and sat down to see more jungle, but did notice there was no other railway track. Puzzled asked.

'Ear Sergeant, There ain't another rail track?'

'That's right. There's only a single track both ways.'

'Well there were two tracks back in that station, so how come?'

'Bleedin' idiot. Because there are two platforms.'

'Wot happens when they meet half way or, wherever?'

'There's a section of rail track like a siding into which the down line train steams into. Waits there to let the other train go past. You will see it happen later on, anyway all you can see now is how close the Ulu is.'... Bert returned and sat down.

'Ear Bert. There's only one rail track for up and down trains. Wot dyer think of that?'

'After yon spill int yon bog cuid nae cares a shite.' The Sgt. interrupted.

'Oh. You have experienced its delights then?'

'Neely fel doon 'ole ye ken, nae paper not'ing.'

'Hey what do you lot expect. First class treatment. You're in Malaya now, not on the fooking Flying Scotsman. The Sgt. joked. Bert turned his head away muttering something under his breath. Attempting to change the subject

'Sergeant. Where was that last station anyway?'

'Seremban. In the state of Negri Sembilan. Were about half way now.'

'Who were those, that got off?'

'A mixture. Infantry and Corps, mostly replacements. Anyway, I have to do me rounds. Cannot sit chatting to you two idiots.' As he moved away, Bert muttered.

'Hoo dae he thinks is idiots. Nae bin on tae Fleeing Scootsmon. Un nae doot yon Baastaad as ither ye ken.' I laughed.

It was boring nothing to read or do, looking around the carriage there was ample room for all. Sat in the middle gazing out of an open window was the Sgt. and Cpl that joined the Lancashire in Port Said with the Seaforths? Noticed a few Medics but most of the blokes were RASC. One of them a bit of a loud mouth was the person who won hundreds of cigarettes playing cards? He had started another card school at the far end.

'Ear Bert. Wots that place you come from. Millborough?'

'Nay! Portobello. Nearr Musselburgh, Edinburgh.'

'Bleedin' long way from it nah. Ain't yer?'

'Och Aye. If I war at hame noo, I'd bae oot rowing on tae Forth. Ye ken.'

'You a rower then? Bet yer got blisters on yer hand. Eh?'

'Aye. Thit war years afore. Arden'd noo.'

'Wot eight's?'

'Nay. Pairs and ferrs.'

'Won anything?'

'Aye. A few wee cups and shields. I likes it tha's te main thing. Wat yu de?'

'Football.'

'Footba. Yon's a sissy's game, But I play's aw wee bit.'

'Naw it ain't. It's bleedin' hard in London. That's for sure.'

'Ye won yon medals then?'

'Yeah a few. With St. Anne's the club I played for on Saturday and Sunday league football. Played all over London, travel-Bleedin' miles for a game. Yer know where I live? Well, to get to matches have to catch a bus and tram. Had a trial for the London Fed of Boys Clubs. But the week before the trial, sodin' gashed open my knee. Ad a couple of stitches, so did not perform very well.'

'Nae hav yon problem. Sculling on Forth ootside ma doorr. Lucky I suppose.'

'Ear Bert. D'yer remember that football game we played at Malvern. Couple of dozen a side, with the rugger ball?'

'Aye. Whit a gam thit war Eh?' At the mere thought of it. We hooted with laughter.

'Bleedin' 'ell. That was no sissy's game. Jimmy broke his toe, he was like a bleedin' lunatic running around. Geordie socked thit bleedin' twat from, Elect Eight. That was. Get stuck in or, get killed in the rush. Can't remember how it finished up.'

'Tea wee Scoot Sgt. cuid nae controol it. He pished off. ' Bert roared with laughter.

'Yeah. When everyone saw him leave we all left.' Cor, we had some bleedin' good times back there. Didn't we?'

'Aye. Noo whar wee git?' The train slowed down and rattled over some points. Re-entering the carriage the Sgt. walking past us, stopped to speak with the other Sgt. who moved to the other side.

'Ere Bert summats going on?' In anticipation grabbed the rifle as the Sgt. came striding towards us.

'You two. Look out that side; you'll see the down train as we go past it. '

Relieved. Let go of the rifle, got up crossed over to see an area cleared of jungle growth. Positioned along the jungle fringes were several black telegraph poles with wires limply hanging between them. Below us was the second track. We passed a stationary square steel pyramid looking object with a few small lookout slits, assumed that was the armoured train. In a matter of seconds we were passing the stationary train, its engine

hissing out steam and slowly chuffing black smoke out of its stack. As both trains passed each other a crescendo of whistles sounded, passing the end of the train was back into the open space, crossed points back onto single track. The meeting over.

Armoured train taken at Ipoh Station

Passing Trains

Emerging out of the enveloping canopy, the train came into more open jungle. On one side, it was hilly, on the other side a gorge covered by a mass of tangled undergrowth, dotted with large ferns and other green vegetation. As the train snaked along this stretch of track, at one point you could see the engine chuffing out black smoke before it disappeared around a bend, the sound of its wheels changed as we crossed a bridge spanning an orange coloured river, its torrent of muddy water swirling on its endless journey. Like everything else, it appeared out of the jungle and disappeared back into jungle. Soon after that, the train went through another station called Kajang. Up to then we had passed through quite a number of small stations, which were nothing to write

home about however, Kajang seemed larger than the rest. The remainder of the journey into KL (Kuala Lumpur) was not very exciting, however as we approached KL Station. It was a weird but wonderful sight. Full of Eastern promise, spires, minaret towers, cupolas and arches, they were something to write home about. Slowly the train made its way into the covered station and ground to

K.L. Station approach.   a halt, our carriage stopped directly opposite the station board.
KUALA LUMPUR.   Painted below, Chinese characters and squiggly writing. At another platform stood an empty train. The activity on our side was in full swing, some of the occupants in our carriage, a few RASC Medics and REME guys were getting off. Swearing and blaspheming, as they manhandled their rifles and kitbags through the tiny doorway at the far end. Most of the cursing done by the loudmouth cardsharp. The platform was becoming congested with the detraining troops; it appeared a mass exodus from the train.

A char wallah came up and offered char. We obliged by taking it off him, paying the standard pennies in return. It was sweet; they sure knew how to make tea out there. He was followed by two little Chicos, their provisions on flat boards balanced on their heads, each carried a small fold up table that they unfolded and placed the board on top, one sold slices of fruit whilst the other peanuts, buying both the peanuts I would eat later.

After a stay of about an hour, the train finally left KL. The almost empty carriage was much quieter, little if any conversation was made. The countryside began to change from dense jungle clad areas, into what appeared to be a more civilized and working area with plenty of Palm trees, wooded copses, recognised a coconut plantation with trees lined up row after row. Yet another one appeared, which the Sgt. informed  was a rubber plantation. Pointing out the gouged out echelons V cuts in the bark, at the lowest point small cups were attached to catch the drips of pure white latex. We passed through small towns, large ones; we stopped at places called Tanjong Malim and Tapah. From there on, where the train ran alongside or crossed over a river noticed the colour of its water was almost orange. Here and there rising out of the ground strange looking hills with craggy walls of white stone pitted with what looked like caves, on top grew trees and other jungle vegetation giving it the appearance of a mop of hair.

In the mid afternoon, the hot sun warmed the air that gushed through the open windows that did nothing to cool us down. Ahead dark rain clouds were gathering as the endless soddin' rattle of the train wheels was telling on me, feeling very tired and was sure Bert did too? Could have dozed off but at the back of my mind the nagging thought, On Active Service was stopping me. Feeling very venerable could not wait to get off the train. It was late afternoon, when the Sgt. called out.

'All you lucky Bastards, who are getting off at Ipoh. Start getting your kit together. Load your magazines; shove one up the spout, safety catches on.' Thinking "Here we go, for Bert and me the parting of our ways. He still, had another three or four hours sitting on this bleedin' train. Sod his luck". At the far end, the KD clad Sgt. and Cpl. along with some other RASC blokes were preparing to get off. Getting up, lifted down my two kitbags from the racks, dropping them onto the seat, grabbing my rifle sat down beside Bert to clip on the magazine, shoved one up the spout slipped the safety on.

'Ear Bert. How we going to keep in touch?' Shrugging his shoulders replied.

'Dinna ken? Dinna war I'm geeing up yon? Eniwa wee'll met op on wey oome.' He answered without any justification. Just as dismally I exclaimed.

'That's soddin' eighteen months away. Christ. That's a bleedin' lifetime. Well! If we get out of this sodding hole and don't get shot?' So ended our conversation.

As the train clanked slowly into Ipoh, standing up we shook hands wished each other the best of luck. I was not a happy bunny. Slinging the rifle over my shoulder struggled out of the carriage to alight on the *terra firma* of Malaya.

My new home for God knows how long.

CHAPTER SIXTEEN
IPOH. PERAK. NORTH MALAYA.

Fed up! Dumped the two kit bags on the platform my rifle slipped off my shoulder, hitching it back up looked up and down the platform, by its size it appeared to be similar to that of Kuala Lumpur station, thinking, "Must be a quite a reasonably sized town"?

'HEH. YOU! REME WALLAH! WHICH CAMP ARE YOU GOING TOO?' Startled by the question looked back to see the RASC Sgt. he must have been well over six feet tall was lean and wiry, unlike the Corporal who was thickset about five foot ten he was dark of complexion and had a bristly moustache, both were well tanned as they stood in a group with a few other squaddies, so responded.

'Three Company. REME. Sergeant.'

'Sergeant Whitely to you. Three Company. That's our destination. You tag on with us. Pick up your kit and get outside.' They began to walk outside as I, lifting the Uni onto my shoulder grasping hold of the sea kitbag looked back towards the train and yelled at Bert leaning out the carriage window.

'See yer mate. ' He waved.

'Aye! Keep yon heed doon. Yer ken.' That was it. Four months of friendship gone.

Following behind the others walked through the dimness of the station booking hall and out into bright sunlight. Parked outside was a Lorry, its driver called out.

'Sergeant. Is your party for three company?'

'Yes. All of us. Plus the REME wallah.'

'Well Sergeant suggest you quickly get yourself and kit aboard. Its about to pelt down. Might just make camp before then.'

Amused by his statement looked at the black clouds rolling towards us thinking. "If it did pelt down? The wagon minus a canopy had no protection whatever. Without hesitation, very conveniently the Sgt. climbing into the drivers cab yelled at us.

'You lot. Load up and jump aboard. Sharpish.'

The Cpl. climbed aboard first and made his way up to the front, leaning on the cab roof began chatting to the Sgt. Once we were all aboard, the driver securing the tailboard hurriedly returned to his cab, revving up left the station entrance and drove around a big square grass area twice the size of a football pitch it was surrounded by colonial styled buildings. Turning off, carried on down a wide road lined on either side with shops and two-storied buildings of similar style to those in Singapore. On the way stopped at a few traffic lights, where some cars and a host of Chinese on bikes waited for the green light, thought, "This is novel, Home from Home." All the time the sunlight was fading as the dark clouds behind began blotting it out and by the time the lorry approached a long bridge over a river, it was almost dark. We had no sooner crossed the bridge than it started to rain, first a couple of splashes quickly followed by sheets of water cascading from the sky, within seconds

Home from Home

as if we were standing in a shower, our cotton OG's were saturated in warm water. Driving through the sheeting rain you could hardly see very much in front, everyone had their brollies up or were sheltering within the covered walkways in front of the shops, even the Chinese riding their bicycles had their brollies up, whilst we on the back of the Lorry were drenched to the skin. The shower lasted about five minutes before it abruptly stopped. From behind the clouds, out beamed the sun and it was baking hot!

Leaving the confines of the town, travelled along a main road lined with palm trees, slowing down the driver turned left into a side road towards an army camp. A big painted signboard stated. 15/19th The King's Royal Hussars. The driver slipping down through the gears, slowed the lorry down almost to a stop and took a sharp left, proceeding up a slight incline passing inbetween wooden billets and Nissan huts, until we came to another Camp, turning right stopped in front of the barrier pole. On the left side were three Nissan huts. In the doorway of the first one, stood the Guard Sgt. stepping out roared.

'NEW REPLACEMENTS EH. WELCOME TO THREE COMPANY ROYAL ARMY SERVICE CORP. IPOH. END OF THE LINE FOR YOU LOT. ALL GET DOWN WITH YOUR KIT AND REPORT INTO THE GUARDHOUSE.'

It was late Saturday afternoon on September 24. when the driver let down the tailboard. As Sgt. Whitely took off his kitbags, we dropped ours on the ground and got down. Sgt. Whitely leading the way into the guard house with rifles slung we formed a queue before entering inside, which to say the least was rather pokey and stifling hot ; sat behind a desk a Cpl. entered our details, behind him was a closed green door, the cells. When all formalities were completed, returned outside to find the lorry had gone. Stood beside our pile of kit bags was Sgt. Whitely, the Corporal the Guard Sgt. and another squaddie, the latter two wearing large groundsheets. The Sgt. bawled out

'Right! Before you are taken to your Basha, hand in your weapons at the armory, This Guard here will take you, then report back here.' The guard led the way around to the rear of the third Nissan hut then promptly left. Lent on the bottom half of a stable doorway the Armourer nonchalantly exclaimed.

'Before you hand over your rifle and bayonet. Unload the one up the spout, remove the magazines and replace the bullet. Read out the rifle number, then your number, name and rank.'

When it was my turn I, noticed within the interior racks upon racks of rifles, Sten guns and LMG is no doubt pistols as well. I was the last to return to collect my kit. There was no sign of Sgt. Whitely, the Guard Sgt. bawled out.

'All done. Right let us get you lot down to your Bashes. Gather up your Kit. It's about to rain.' No sooner had he said that when It began to pelt down again. Calling out two guards, they appeared in the doorway of the middle Nissan hut covered with groundsheets, fully equipped for the rain.

'You Perkins. Take the corporal and these three down to 'B' Platoon basha. Brown take this REME wallah down to the LAD basha. Now you lot listen to me. When you have left your kit in the Basha's. You will report to the QM stores to pick up your bedding etc. Get one of the blokes in the basha, to show you where it is. Off you go. Miserable looking lot of turds.'

As we collected our kit bags, the rain was sheeting down. A bedraggled five, set off en-route for our new abodes, being led across a big open space where huge puddles more like ponds had formed and on its surface dancing a merry plopping sound the intense rain was throwing water back up. As we were already soaking wet plodded our way through the ponds the only thing not wet on my person, was the hair under the beret. Upon reaching a narrow concrete path leading towards a long row of some sort of thatched huts, my escort enquired.

'Where you from mate?' Totally pissed off and soaking wet exclaimed.

' London! Rather be back there than soddin' well here.'

'Aw fook your 'orrible. This is my last guard duty. Going home in a week's time. Can't wait to get out of this fooking hole.'

His remark was far from what I wanted to hear. Drenched to the skin had to put up with this cheerful bastard. The RASC blokes in front peeled off into one of the huts and we carried on as my cheerful escort also carried on.

'The REME basha. Is down the far end, near the cookhouse. It's nearly nosh time so you'll be fed tonight that's for fooking sure.' Nosh! Had not eaten a cooked meal since Nee Soon, come to that was thirsty as hell and could do with a cuppa. Walking along the pathway passing between other thatched huts, entered a large thatched covered archway walking about half way through he stopped and cheerfully said.

'There you are mate. On your right and left, this is the Naafi and that sunshine through there in front on your left. Is the REME basha. Go through the first entrance and the best of fooking luck.'

With that he about turned and left me to carry on towards the hut. Emerging from out of the covered archway, with the Uni on my left shoulder partially obscured my vision observed in front on my right a small-corrugated shed of some sorts, to my left was the REME Basha. A short narrow path led down to an entrance, viewing that and the low overhang of the roof had to duck under the thatch, decided to drop the Uni down and carry it by its handle. Entering, dropped both kitbags on the floor. On either side rows of beds were separated by a small low cupboard in between were a few spare bare wired beds with bed boxes beneath them. Rumpled white sheets covered the occupied beds; some had half-clad brown bodies lying on top of them. Down the center of the hut, several six-inch diameter poles supported the thatched roof. Immediately on my right, a scrawny looking bloke with tight curly hair was busy writing a letter on his bed top, looking up abruptly enquired.

'You the new replacement VE? '

'Yes.' Thinking, " To this bloke I must look like a sack of wet clothing". Another abrupt question.

'Where you from?'

'Malvern. Nine /Elect /Seven.' He nastily retorted.

'No. Idiot. You're a bloody cockney!...Thumbed me to the other end... You. Down the other end of the basha. There are beds down there?' Carried on with his letter writing.

Rude bastard! Not even a bleedin' welcome Hi. Took an instant dislike to the sod. Puzzled at this invite and well aware was then being observed by enquiring eyes? Picked up the kitbags and struggled between the beds and poles towards the other end. Half way down, a bloke lying on his belly looking like a coconut mat, his back covered by a mass of black curly hair asked.

'How you doing mate?'

'Bleedin' wet and pissed off mate.' Carried on down towards the far end saw a spare bed, next to an occupied one, upon which lay a bloke reading a book. Heaving my two kitbags, on top of the steel wire springs was about to sit down when the bloke, speaking in a cockney accent said.

'Hoi! That bed's taken mate. Git anover.' This rude remark, did nothing to help me, first one bastard down the other end and now this bastard? ' I snapped back.

'Which one. Ain't taken then?' Lowering his book, he threw a lighted dog end onto the floor asked in a surprised manner.

'Hoi! You come from London?' I too could be rude.

'Yeah. Why? Wot's it to you.'

'Interested okay? Wot part?'

'Vauxhall!' Immediately, full of interest he sat up.

'Where abouts in Vauxhall?'

'Well. If it is all right with you mate. In the flats. next to the Grenada. Wandsworth Road.' His attitude totally changed?

'Bleedin' hell! Yer know the Tate Library. I live in Old South Lambeth road.'

'Get away! My Aunt lives down there in Hayford Terrace don't know the number; she lives in the second house right opposite the Crown Pub.'

'Soddin' 'ell! Ear. That beds Dens. He's on assignment up the Cameron's. Until he comes back, you take it. Wot a bleedin' shock he will 'ave? He lives in Wandsworth road as well...Shouting out...Ear Mick! Guess what? This bloke lives about five minutes' walk away from me.' The coconut mat shouted back.

'Fook his bloody luck.'

'Wots year name then?' Thinking. "He's bleedin' changed his tune".

'Joe Plant.'

'Mine's Al. Al Keene. You look a bit wet Joey. Like a bleedin' drowned rat.' He laughed, lighting up another fag offered.

'Smoke?'

'Nah. Don't use em.'

'Don't yer? I'll buy your free issue.' Bemused about his suggestion.

'Wot. Free issue?'

'While you're on active service mate. You get a tin of fifty each week. That mate. Is the only bleedin' good thing about it out here. Free issue gets nothing else.'

'Okay your on. I don't use em anyway.' Sitting on the bare springs, removed the beret and belt asked.

'How long you been out here?'

'About five soddin' months too long.'

'Where do I get bedding from? The Guard Sgt. said we had to collect it from the QM stores.' Not offering suggested.

'Bill Dineen, will be back in a minute, he'll take yer down there.' This was like an inquisition. How did I know him?

'Who's Bill Dineen?'

'He comes from bleedin' Peckham. Right prat he is. Talk of the prat. This is him now.'

Glancing back saw a bloke enter wearing a small white towel tied around his waist, slippers on his feet, holding his shaving and washing kit.

'Ear Bill. This bedraggled rat is Joey. Three guess's where he comes from?' Standing there looked at me...a pause...'London?...'Yeaah. Where abouts?... Peckham? Nah. Yer prat. Think again...New Cross? ...Nah. Yer sodin prat. Wots the matter with yer?'

'Not. From your sodding area?' A lighted dog end hit the floor to join the dozens of others lying around the support post, jubilantly he answered.

'Yeah. Lives in between Den and me.' This bloke Bill asked me.

'Is that right mate?... He offered his hand, we shook, he exclaimed...Well f...k me 'ole boots. Watcha mate! Wot are you VM?' Thinking this bloke Bill will most likely send me back down the other end answered?

'VE.' Instead spreading out his arms wide in a mock gesture of happiness exclaimed.

'Hey. You're my replacement. I'm going home soon ain't I Al?' Al laying back on his bed lit up another fag uttered.

'Sod off yer prat. Ear seeing he's your replacement. You take charge of him. Get his bleedin' bedding sorted out before nosh. Ear Joey, follow Pratty he'll get you sorted out.' Bill responded.

'Yer prat. Why din't you do it? instead of stinking in yer pit. Yer a lazy bastard.' Al retorted.

'He's your bleedin' replacement not mine! You Lec's are all the bleedin' same. Lazy lot of bastards.' Bill offered.

'C'mon Joey, Never mind that lazy bastard, he don't do f..k all. Just you follow me.' Dressed as he came in Bill walked out of the basha.

Bill Dineen

Grabbing my Beret hurried after him. Outside the rain had ceased however it was still overcast and it was very warm, with the heat of my body my OG's were beginning to dry out. Walking beside him he questioned.

'You just arrived by boat then?'

'Yep. The Lancashire docked two days ago then straight up here, Wotsit like here?'

'Oh! Its Okay. Bleedin' hot though. I'm due to go back in a couple of months. 'Q' told me I was getting a replacement. But I didn't think it would be that quick...He was full of chat as we walked past a large corrugated tin shed...Those are the showers. That is HQ's basha. Over there is the shit house. Be warned, do not sit on the thunder boxes, watch out fer crabs in there they jump six feet high. Do not have a shit after eight in the morning. That's when the shit Wallahs exchange the flowerpots, when they pull em out yer could be caught halfway through dropping a turd or, even worse If yer got the shits. Oh! And do not have a shit at night-time. Yer 'll be eaten alive by mossies or attacked by giant moths. If yer gets a dose visit the MRS. That's the long low building across the road, to get there. go out over the barbed wire its easier than going out through the main gate. The QM stores are in those Nissan huts...All this chat left me in a bit of a tizz wazz. Don't have a shit only at a certain time? The shits? What was a dose? ...We stopped outside a green door. Bill banging shouted. 'WAKEY WAKEY...A minute passed by, again he banged this time the door was opened by an Indian. C'mon. Yer lazy bastard. Yer been asleep again want bedding for me mate Joey here. Chop Chop. It's nosh time soon.'

'Beddin' Jonnie. No more to-night Jonnie all shut.' He grinned.

'Stop f.....g about and git it. Chop Chop. Get yer bleedin' finger out.' Bill banged on the door again... Lazy lot of bastards they are. Got to talk to em like that, but they're all right.'

The Indian returned with a mattress placed it on a table, going back into the stores returned with the rest of the bedding. Thrust a clipboard with a sheet of paper attached, and offered a pen.

'Jonnie! Pleese. You Sign here. Two sheets -one pillow -one pillowcase - one blanket- one mattress- one mossie net.' Signing for each item, he questioned.

'Any more Jonnie's ?'

'No. I'm the only REME.'

'Okay Jonnie yu finis.'

Picking up the mattress, slung it over my shoulder, collected the sheets blankets and the net. Bill intervened.

'No. No. No mate! It's easier to wrap the mossy net around the lot. Look this way...Unraveling the net, placed the bedding on top re-wrap the net around them...There carry em like that with yer mattress over yer shoulder.....he continued chatting as we made our way back to the Basha...Mossies don't 'arf bite out here. Little bastards draw blood. You taken yer paludrine tab today then?'

'Palu wot tablet. Wots that? Nobody said anything about tablets, had enough bleedin' injections to last a life time.'

'Oh blimey. You've 'ad it then.' Concerned about his implication thought, "What's he talking about? But soon found out back in the basha".

'Ear Al. Joey ain't taken his paludrine today.' Al, lying on his side reading a book turned to face us.

'Bleedin' 'ell! You're for it then. When those mossies find out they'll eat yer. Talking about eating its nosh time let's get over to the cookhouse. Joey. Leave yer bedding, grab hold of Dens crocks and don't forget yer eating irons. C'mon Pratty get changed.'

Untying the sea kitbag sorted out eating irons, slipped them in my top pocket picking up the crocs about to leave saw Bill, totally starker's engulfed in white powder wildly shaking a brown tin of talc over his private parts. Having finished powdering himself, slipped on a pair of blue PT shorts slipping into a pair of funny looking slippers, grabbing crockery and eating irons muttered. 'Chop Chop, I'm off.'

Tagging on behind Bill walked along a pathway, on our right surrounded by some form of split bamboo fencing was something of a garden, the only thing in there was a few young palm trees with limp leaves, behind that was a large wooden hut. At the end of the pathway walked onto an open concreted area, on the left was a large corrugated shed. Al leant up against the corrugated wall holding his crocs called out.

'Urry up Pratty, Joey join the end of the queue.' Thinking, "End of what queue he is the queue." Bill retorted

'Alright alright. Keep yer bleedin' shirt on?'

The three of us began "the formation of the queue". Looking around, was able to establish our whereabouts. The corrugated shed we were leaning against was the cookhouse, the two wooden huts opposite were the mess halls. A corrugated steel roofed canopy forming the shape of an 'H' joined the cookhouse and the mess halls together. Below which were placed, a long row of serving tables with a couple of Dixie's on them. A couple of cooks followed by two Indians came out of the cookhouse, all carrying more dishes of food to arrange them on the tables. Al suggested.

'Grubs not bad, there is a choice, soup salad or hot food, usually curry and rice. Do you like curry?'

'Yeah. Was weaned on it. 'Ad it every Monday night at home. '

'You'll like the curries they dish up here although they're far better down town. Later on, we'll take yer down town and try those. Eh Bill?'

'Too right. You'll like those in the Fed Mus?' Mystified by their chatter but aware of others joining our queue, they all very tanned wearing blue PT shorts and those funny slippers. Mick, the coconut mat in a broad scouse accent asked.

'Is that right. You're a cockney and live close to that bleedin' prat in front?'

'Yeah. Strange ain't it? Come all the way out here to find not one, but two that live almost on top of you.'

'Al! He's better looking than you.' Al retorted.

'Sod off yer scouse git. Don't know wot yer bleedin' talking about. Ear Joey. That Scouse git is Mick Bauer. He's run out of razor blades.' The pair of them started laughing like hyenas...Bill adding.

'He's the only bloke I know. That shaves twice before breakfast.' A further outburst of cackle as Mick responded.

'Yer tosser Dineen. At least. I can fooking shave.'

Famished, impatiently waited for the serving to begin. I needed something hot and substantial to ease the pangs of my hunger. Having finished laying out the dishes the cooks minus a white jacket, wearing check trousers, boots, with a forage cap and badge. appeared to are the only ones dressed properly, their two Indian helpers wearing OG shorts, stood barefooted armed with ladles ready to serve meals. Al blurted out.

'C'mon Pratti, start bleedin' serving were starving.' One of the cooks waving a ladle at Al shouted.

'If you say so. You cockney prat. Go on start then.'

Quickly, Al moved to the end table followed by Bill. The ongoing banter was not what I was expecting and it appeared to me this type of conversation was normal, everyone knew everybody and took the piss out of each other. As I moved along the table, the first dishes were a choice of sardines or pilchard salad, ignoring them chose a ladle full of tomato soup served by one of the Indians, holding out my plate the other Indian placed a big portion of rice on it then ladled two lots of meat curry over it, its aroma created saliva to flow in my mouth. Bill appeared out of the mess hall, with two mugs.

'Joey! Go inside. Al has a seat for you...Dipping the mugs into a large Dixie full of tea filled them up...C'mon 'urry up, follow me.'

Entering the mess hall, there were about twelve tables down each side each seating four, all the windows were wide open, hanging from the roof were two fans their blades lazily twirling around. About half way down Bill holding the mugs was stood at a table where Al and Mick were already seated, with both mugs indicated a spare seat.

'There Joey, sit on the outside.' Placing the mugs of tea on the table, he retorted.

'Hoi Pratty, there's your tea. It's your turn next.' Al responded.

'Sod off. I'm always getting your bleedin' tea yer prat.'

Placing my plates on the table went outside to help myself to tea, returning saw Al chatting with someone behind him.

'Ear Joey. This is Bill Beavis. He's Fred Cole's driver? Silly Prat reckons he's a Londoner but comes from bleedin' Watford. Gateway to the North.' Cheerfully this other Bill replied.

'Bleedin' right! It's a suburb of London. Watcha mate Bill's the name driving's my game. Just got here have yer?' Through a mouthful of curry. Bill spluttered.

'You prat. Wot a bleedin' silly question to ask. Yoove never clapped eyes on him before 'ave yer?' Al. interrupting.

'Well. Wot do yer expect from him? He comes from sodin Watford keep on telling him. He needs a passport to get south of the river thames. ' An indignant Beavis retorted.

'Bleedin' 'ell Al. Gives yer-bleedin' mouth a rest. I was only being polite yer might say.'

Al. retorted. 'Polite! You. Your bleedin' joking.'

Puzzled as to who Fred Cole was and not wanting to enter into the backchat, just listened, watched and observed. Al was just a little taller than me, slim in build with wavy

 blonde hair almost in the same style as mine semi crew. His most distinguishing facial feature was his sharp nose and overhung eyelids, like everyone else as brown as a berry. Bill Dineen was taller, with dark straight hair parted on one side sleeked back and groomed like Dennis Compton, stocky in built with a roundish face that had a permanent smile. He was quite a happy bloke, always ready for a laugh. Mick Bauer was the

Al & Me   complete opposite, dark almost Latin looking with thick black curly hair everywhere including his thick eyebrows, a real blue beard with a set of white flashing teeth, he spoke with a slow drawl of a scouser. Bill Beavis was possibly a little taller than Al. His long blonde hair parted on one side with the other swept back, his eyebrows were almost white. In the meantime, other tables had filled up increasing the hubbub in the mess hall. I noticed each table leg was placed in a tin of water, very curious why? But not daring to ask. The soup had gone down well and the curry was good and hot. Al finishing off his curry had beads of sweat trickling down his cheeks. Bill getting up said.

'I'm having another 'elping.' Quickly followed by Mick they left the table. Mick soon returned with his soup plate full not of curry but fruit, It did look appetizing he suggested.

'Here Joey, go and get some of this down you. Wash up your soup plate in the water bins outside.'

'Looks good I'll just do that.' About to get up, Al said.

'Ear Joey. You ain't said much 'ave yer?... wiping the sweat from his forehead added... bleedin' curries makes me sweat.'

'No. Too, busy eating. I was starving. This is the first meal I've had since Nee Soon camp. ' Bill returned with another plate of curry, sitting down urged.

'Bleedin' lovely. Chop Chop 'urry up get some more or it will all be gone.'

213

Leaving the table on the way out for some fruit, outside it was very overcast and had turned cold. Approaching one of the two big square water bins, seeing thousands of ants spread across the surface hesitated, someone joined me dipping in his soup plate swirled it around dripping wet went to the fruit Dixie. Copying this bloke, in went the plate a quick swirl then helped myself to the chopped fruit dish. Bananas, oranges, some pink stuff, pineapples, apples, pears. Returning back, sitting down remarked.

'This doesn't come from out of a can...Taking a mouthful muttered...Caw! This is delicious.' Mick answered.

'Yeah should be. The Indians make it fresh its real good stuff.' Al exclaimed.

'Bleedin' raining again. Bill. Go an get me some more tea.' Bill retorted.

'Piss off. Get it yerself. It's your bleedin' turn anyway.' Al getting up asked.

'You want one Joey?' Thinking, "That's nice he's polite".

'Yeah alright. If you're going out.' Bill commented.

'You. Prat Joey! Now yer done it. You will be getting his tea in future.' As he left. Al quietly murmured.

'We'll take turns.' Howls of laughter rang out Bill called after him.

'You and who's army?' Al returning placed the mug of tea in front of me.

'Your turn next Joey.'

'See! I told yer so. He has yer by the short 'n curlies...Chortled Bill...Ear. Beavis. Guess wot?' Beavis turning around questioned.

'Wot?'

'Al's. Just been and got Joey a mug of tea.' Beavis replied.

'Aw. Bleedin' 'ell. That won't last long. You don't know him mate? F...k yer hard luck.'

The noise of rain descending on the corrugated steel roof was deafening it practically stopped the chatter. Within three minutes it abruptly stopped, Bill suggested.

'Right let's make a dash for it.'

It seemed like everyone had the same idea. The scraping of chairs moving with some falling over, as a surge of bodies headed for the doorway. Plates were dipped and swirled in the bins of ant-laden water, followed by a mad dash back to the basha; behind us, others were running to miss the next downpour. Sitting down on the folded mattress; looked at the two inert kit bags on the floor. Al lying on his pit was lighting up another cigarette, sitting there not knowing what to do. 'Al wisecracked.

'Cheer up Joey. You've only got another eighteen months to do.' Cackle, cackle.

'Where dyer go for a piss?'

'Through that gap in the basha. See that corrugated tin shed. That's it.'

Looking through the gap, on the other side of the pathway saw the tin shed I had noticed on the way in. Heading towards it, discovered the urinal without a roof was open to all elements and reeked of urine. The piss holes! Were two steel pipes stuck out at an angle from the concrete floor with a cone shaped funnel. Much relieved upon returning, found three blokes around Al's bed. Besides Mick, two were sat on the bed witha very tall bloke stood chatting to Al, who throwing his lighted dog-end, hitting the support post causing a shower of hot ash to burst out, called out.

'Here he is. 'Joey, this is Harry, that's Gerry and Jock McCormack. Tell em how far away you live from me.' A pleased request.

'Well not far. About five minutes walk away. '

'Another blooody Cockney.' Gerry muttered, he sounding like another scouser. Shaking his head, Jock stated.

'Dye meen tae sae. I'm tae oonly Jock in the LAD.' Bill interrupted.

'Yeah and yer know what? He's my replacement.'

Waiting to sit down, the usual questions was asked. Where were you trained? Blah blah. A few more joined, Al did the intro's. Jim Mean, Towser, Jim Bowles, all Corporals, plus others, all were VM's. It appeared that Bill and I were the only VE's nevertheless, did notice regardless of the piss taking that went on, all got on very well together. Outside it was getting dark; Bill got off his bed and switched on a solitary light bulb that spread inadequate light around the area. As his latest dog-end hit the post, Al spoke up.

'Er. Joey. You'd better sort out your kit. Put it in that spare cupboard; take that bed-box under that bed over there.' My thoughts raced back to Malvern and the palaver we had there with that Sgt. and the cupboard asked.

'Is there any kit layout, in the cupboards or?'

'Nah. Just fold it up square as yer used too, so long as it's neat and tidy nobody inspects. Except the daily bed layout. Bill'll show you that one, won't yer Bill? Oh another thing. Wot don't fit in yer cupboard sling it in the bed box.' Bill interrupted.

'You goin down town to night Al?'

'Nah. Saving up, for when I go home to my Patti.'

My kit. Having been pushed into kitbags for the past four weeks, was creased to buggery and smelt mouldy. The clothing in the sea kit bag was not too bad; but all needed washing would sort that out later. Having folded and stowed most of it in the small cupboard, the remainder would go into the bed box. Pulling one out from underneath a spare bed, set it down lifting the lid up, a big black thing ran up one arm onto my shoulder, yelled so loud that it must have been heard up at the Guardhouse.

'CHRIST ALMIGHTY...The thing dropped onto the floor at top speed disappeared under Al's bed. My heart began thumping nineteen to the dozen... BLEEDIN' 'ELL. WOT WAS THAT?' BLEEDIN' FRIGHTENED THE SHIT OUT OF ME.' The pair of them burst out laughing.

'Ear Joey. Should 'ave seen your face...Al cackled...That was a sight for sore eyes.' Cackle, cackle. Bill politely in a matter of fact way, informed me.

'That. My dear fellow. Was a Malayan cockroach. Big, are they not? Always get into yer bed box or cupboard. Just tread on them.'

My heartbeats slowing down had me thinking, "These pair of bleeders, they could have warned me". Having finished putting kit away began to lay up my bed. One sheet over the mattress tucked it in followed by the other sheet and blanket. Carefully tucking in all the overlaps, did the pillowcase. Taking hold of the green mossy net, noticed Bill sat on the edge of his bed watching me, I asked.

'What do you do with this?'

'Don't know mate? But you had better start again. Ain't he Al?' Al lying on his bed, he too was watching retorted. 'You're a right prat Joey. Wot are yer? That ain't the way to make yer bed. You won't sleep under a blanket out here mate. Strip it all off start again. Blanket first, then sheets.' I retorted.

'Why didn't yer soding tell me. I was doing it wrong?'

'Why? Because we 'ave nothing better to do 'ave we Bill?' The pair of them began laughing. The bastards had watched everything without letting on. Stripping off the bed remade it as instructed and upon completion was sweating quite freely. Rivulets of sweat were running down my chest, still fully dressed sat down I was stinking with B.O, my feet felt like balloons. Two days before had bound them up with puttees, which by then had restricted the blood supply. It was time for a wash, grabbing soap and towel went to walk outside. Bill asked.

'Where you going Joey?'

'For a wash.'

'About time, you do smell clatty.' Outside in the warm air daylight was fading fast. Lights were on in the cookhouse and with a few more lights dotted about, made it easy to see where you were going. Entering through the opening of the washhouse Bill had pointed out to me. The interior was illuminated by a couple of light bulbs, on my right was a washing trough, a corrugated sheet wall separated three shower roses, there was nowhere to hang clothes, thought. "Sodding 'ell, where do you hang your clothes"? Returning to the basha, Al called out.

'Nice wash Joey?' A question followed by peals of laughter. The bastards! Were at it again. Bill cackled.

'Ear Joey. When you go for a shower. Yer don't wear anything, strip off in here and just wear a towel around yer waist that's all.' Thoroughly pissed off, thinking. "Bleedin' sods. Sod it. I'll leave it till tomorrow". From down the other end of the basha a very loud buzzing sound had everyone diving under their top sheet. Bill shouted.

'Wahey! One's coming this way, get under yer sheet Joey.'

Thinking, "Is this another prank of theirs"? The buzzing increased in volume. No. A big bleedin' flying object came buzzing up to our end. Not knowing what or, whatever it was ducked as it did a few dive bomb raids. Bill yelled out.

'Hurl a broom at it.' Whatever it was headed back up the other end, more yells and shouts rang out, boots were slung up into the air before it flew out. I exclaimed.

'Wot! The soding 'ell was that?' Emerging from under the cover of his sheet Bill answered.

'Shit beetle! If they hit you, they don't half hurt. Their covered in armour plating...Al, you sure you're not going out to catch the mid-night flicks?' Al didn't respond. Bill getting up, wandered down the other end of the Basha. Sitting there bemused about this latest activity. Shit Beetles! The hands on my watch showed it was a quarter past seven. I had not been in this soddin' camp more than three hours. Had been attacked by a Giant cockroach a Shit Beetle and then, heard another tiny sound around my head zzZZzz. zzZZzz. This. Waving my arm about to ward it off, silence. It had gone. zzZZzz zzZZzz. It was back again. Al, uttered a knowledgeable comment.

'It's only a Mossy, wait until it settles and then whack it.'

My feet were really aching so, unraveling the yards of green bandage loosened the trouser leg bottoms, untying laces kicked off the boots pulling off the socks as with a sense of urgency, blood gushed down into my feet. Standing up on the cool surface of the flagstone floor was sheer magic muttered.

'Aw! Bleedin' 'ell that's better.' Another dog-end hit the floor. Al asked.

'Got any books?'

'Yeah. I've got a couple of Saint Books you can read, bought on the boat they're in the cupboard.' Moving off his bed, Al sorted out the books, suggested.

'If I were you, go an 'ave a shower that will liven you up.' Lying back on his bed began to read the covers.

A shower that was the answer! Stripping off, aware of my nakedness quickly wrapped the towel around my waist walked out to the showers. There too wallow under its cool lukewarm spray, drying myself was a clean living being wound the towel around my waist. Much refreshed, returned to the basha. Bill, dressed in civvies long slacks, shirt, tie and shoes was combing his hair remarked.

'Ear Al. Can you smell an air of freshness down this end of the basha?'

'Yep! Only because I told the clatty sod to shower.' Another dog-end hit the floor. A call from down the other end of the basha...'C'mon Dineen. Were waiting for you.'... 'Alright keep yer shirt on. Just getting me money. Right you two, I'm off, Chop Chop see yer later, don't wait up fer me.' Along with a few others, left the basha almost empty, whilst I dressing like the others took the PT shorts out of the cupboard pulled them on walked back to the bed, unfortunately trod on one of the lighted dog-ends lying on the ground.

'Bleedin' 'ell.' Began hopping about that brought roars of laughter from Al.

'Silly prat. Yer not supposed to put em out with bare feet.' Angrily retorted.

'You should put them out first. Before yer throw em on the bleedin' floor.' Sitting down on the bed rubbed the sole of my foot.

'Ooh. Temper Temper...Do you play football Joey?'

'Yeah why?' My interest aroused.

'Who did yer play for back home?'

'St. Anne's in Vauxhall, played on Saturdays for the under eighteen's in the federation of boys clubs league and on Sunday, over eighteen's Sunday League. D'yer know em?'

'Yeah! They're a good team...interested he sat up...What position?'

'Right wing why?'

'Not another right winger? We got plenty of them even Bill plays there. You any good then?' A probing question.

'Well. S'pose so. Before joining up the season before last both St. Anne's teams won their leagues. Who did you play for?'

'Mawbey pub team. Sunday league. They're not bad either.'

'Ain't that the pub in Mawbey Street?'

'Yep.'

'Never been in that one. My local was the Beehive down near the Oval. My 'ole mans is the Nott Castle or Lord Morrison in wandsworth road. Sometimes he goes in the Crown to have a drink with me Uncle Alec.'

'Who. Alec Humbey? He drinks with my 'ole man. Maybe he knows your 'ole man.'

'I don't know? Sometimes he goes in the Wheatsheaf. Any chance of a game?'

'Don't know. The LAD play against the other RASC. Platoons. ABC Composite and HQ. There's six teams in all, plus a Company team that play against other regiments and corps, including local teams. Games are played on the Padangs in town. Usual kick off time, is at five 'o'clock in the evening. Less heat but it's still bleedin' hot. Maybe get a game in one of those matches....Another dog-end hit the floor. Thinking, "I. don't trust him and his bleedin' dog-ends" So while he was talking slipped on plimsolls... Joey. You don't need to wear them. The tailor sells flip-flops for a dollar fifty, everyone wears them. That's the next thing yer have to do. Get yer OG's tailored. When yer came in this afternoon. Yer looked like a sponge and so bleedin' miserable...he laughed again.... Did yer bring any civvies out?'

'Civvies. No, didn't know we had too, only a pair of brogues.'

'That's alright. The tailor will make yer a civvy shirt and trousers whatever yer want in double quick time...Looking at his watch I glanced at mine, it was nearly nine 'o' clock... Fancy mug of tea?' Surprised at his suggestion.

'Tea at this time of night? From the cookhouse?'

'No! C'mon, grab yer mug, I'll lend yer some dollars, until Thursdays pay parade.'

With tin mug, followed him out of the empty basha. It was still warm and had not rained since the mealtime. Walking through the covered archway, noticed a few blokes drinking in the Naafi. Al informed me.

'The Naafi shuts at nine, the basha on yer left is the games room; got a snooker table and dartboard that's all. The beers chemical called Anchor, pretty cheap though...We carried on towards another basha where a couple of blokes were stood with mugs in their hands...This is Whiskers place, he makes tea and banjo's, like bread rolls, usually filled with bananas, he's also the camp barber. The Indian barbers in town, take ages snipping one hair at a time, yer fall asleep. They even give you a massage after yer hair cut. Hey! Whiskers! Give us a mug of tea and a banana banjo. Want the same Joey?'

'Might as well.'

'Make that two Whiskers. Here's the mugs.'

'Make blaady mind up Sar. Whoo dis den, noo Chico? He gotta whit knees?' Replied the Indian, with a mass of curly black tangled hair and matching beard, his broad smile displayed a set of reddish tinted teeth, dressed in a long shirt that came down to knee level underneath which wore a long gingham tablecloth down to his bare feet.

'Whiskers! Less of yer bleedin' cheek and hurry up. He's always like that, tries to take the piss out of yer. Just tell him ter f..k off. ' Al advised.

Whiskers called out something to a young Indian lad who busied himself making these so-called banjos, watched as he peeled a greenish banana sliced it up and arranged it in this bread roll the size of half a loaf. Whiskers making the tea, spooned in tea leaves to each mug. From an old beaten up kettle poured in hot water followed by pouring condensed milk from a can into each one. With a spoon briskly stirred them before tapping the lips of the mugs, brought us the mugs of tea together with the banjoes, demanded.

'Borty cents each'. Al handing money to Whiskers suggested.

'Whiskers, Take it out of Joey's five-dollar.' Whiskers grinning, handed the change back to me and offered.

'Yoo want haircut ready for OC's Parade, two days time? Yoo com back tomorra.' Mystified. we left Whiskers and began walking back. Al added.

'He's right, you need a haircut. You'll be on OC's parade Monday morning. All new intakes have to go on that. Anyway, Where did yer get your hair cut back home?'

'Phil Bagley's. Opposite Brand's used to go every Saturday.'

'Bagley's! So did I. How is the Sod?'

'He's Okay! Well he was last time went for a trim before I went to Arborfield. Wots this OC's parade about? I am in the REME. Don't I have to report to whoever's in charge? '

'Yep, That's a must, the LAD (Light Aid Detachment) is attached to the RASC. We're a small unit, consisting of all the blokes in the basha apart from a couple on other duties like Den and Jacko up the Cameron's. Fred Cole is our Captain; his number two is Q. Threadgold, he also runs the company football team. Our workshops are on the opposite side of the road outside the camp. To-morrow, I'll get Bill to give you a tour.' Had me wondering. It's always Bill never him? Entering through the first doorway, on the first bed, reading a book was the bloke who directed me down the other end, he asked.

'Still serving Al?'

'Bleedin' right. He won't shut if there's a dollar to be made.'

Sitting down on our bed-box's, taking a sip of tea it was very sweet, milky and tasty, studied the Banjo before wading into it. Quietly asked.

'Who's that up there?'

'Him. Lance Corporal. Beasley. A right sodin prat! He's our welder and keeps all the list of guard duties and. He don't like Londoners. Snidey bastard. Keep out of his way.'

'Guard duties! We were told once we get to our next unit. We wouldn't have to do any.'

'Listen mate. That's a load of bollocks. Out here, you're on bleedin' active service. Besides working on bleedin' Lorries, armoured cars, motorbikes, we get all the shit as well. Doing guard duties on camp and at Kampongs, convoy duties, weekend duty roster. On top of that this LAD has a bleedin' big scammel recovery vehicle. We do recoveries as well. That's where Den is now up the Cameron's with Jacko, our recovery mechanic.'

Another dog-end hit the floor, noticed they were only half smoked and remained glowing for a long time, hence my burnt feet. Thinking what Al said about the LAD's complement, including me and the one on guard counted fifteen bodies in the basha. The persistent zzZZzz of mossies never seemed to give up attacking you, kept waving arms about at these unseen bleeders without making any contact. Popping the last morsel of the banjo into my mouth, finished off the tea. Sweating buckets felt exhausted tired and decided to get my head down.

'Al. How do yer put up this mossy net?'

'You getting tired then? It gets yer like that. All you do. Is put the end with the wooded slat over the top beam behind yer, pull out the net drape it all around the four corners of the bed. Then climb in.' He lit up yet another fag.

Doing what he said, extended the net and draped it around the bed forming a wide light green band of cloth that hung down well below the mattress, making it look like half a tent. Climbing in under the netting slipped in between the cool sheets, lay there thinking about Bert still on the train while I contemplating my luck at being posted to a unit like this one. With an added bonus of finding somebody that lived near me back home. Staring at the solitary light bulb through the minute mesh of the netting.

'Wakey Wakey! Rise and shine. Ear's a mug of tea for yer mate.' Someone shaking my foot woke me, it was daylight? Soaked in sweat, definitely no need for a blanket. Encased in the netting was unsure of where I was. With bleary eyes peered through the netting, saw the silhouette of someone holding two mugs.

'I'll put it on yer bed box, so don't spill it.' Unsure of who it was asked.

'Ta. Wot's the time mate?'

'Nearly eight 'o' clock. You slept well last night. When we came back you were snoring yer' bleedin' ead off...Ere Al. Wakey Wakey. Chop Chop.' Then recognised the voice of Bill. Al retorted.

'Yeah yer prat. Couldn't get ter sleep with your bleedin' snoring.' Levering myself up pulled the mossy net over my head.

'Don't remember falling asleep. Must have been knackered. What time was it then?' Al snapped back.

'Bleedin' nine thirty. Pratty.'

'Don't take any notice of him Joey. He snores just as bad don't yer. Al?'

'Not as much as you. Yer prat...Al added...Wot's fer breakfast?'

'Usual. Bacon, eggs, sausages fried bread. '

I heard a rustle then a match being struck. Thinking, "Surely. He's not smoking again"? Pulling the mossie net back over my head, through the opening of the doorway the bright sunlight lit up the interior of the basha. On the bed box was the mug of tea leaning over picked it up began to drink the nectar. Outside a couple of blokes holding crocs dressed in PT shorts and flip- flops were on their way to the cookhouse. Swinging my legs off the bed, pulled the sheet around me to watch the activity inside the basha, some beds were still covered by mossie nets hiding the inert figures of sleeping bodies, those awake were sat drinking tea. Taking note of the interior. The basha roof and side walls were made from long dried leaves laced together, on either side the sidewall panels were about four feet high with a gap of about a foot from the flag stoned floor, separated by each panel were three doorways. The upright supporting post and cross members, were lashed together by thick vines, the thatched roof overhung the walls by at least two foot, to allow rain to drip into the rain gullies surrounding the basha outside. A small patch of grass separated each of the six pathways into the basha. Focusing on the surroundings realised. This was to be my home for the next eighteen months. Mick approaching me towel around his waist flip-flops on his feet, a thick black stubble surrounding his chin carrying his washing kit, muttered.

'Morning Joey! You slept well?' Al requested.

'Ear Bill. Get us another mug of tea.'

'Sod off. It's your turn. I've just got em in yer prat.' Sitting down on the bed box sipped the tea, with the pangs of hunger gnawing away in my stomach thinking of what Bill had said about brekkers, asked.

'Wot time does breakfast finish.'

'On Sunday. Starts at seven thirty until eight thirty. A bit of a lie in yer might say...on workdays, its Seven until half past, every day dinner twelve till one, evening meal, five thirty until six. Oh yeah! Afternoon tea and cheese four thirty. Not bad Eh? Bill getting up off his bed-box, changed into shorts...Yer getting up for nosh then Al?'

'Suppose so.'

'Don't bleedin' hurt yersel. Yer a lazy bastard...Collecting his eating irons and crockery he urged ...C'mon Chop Chop.'

I did not need urging, getting up pulled on shorts slipping feet into plimsolls went to the cupboard to collect my eating irons and crocs, noticed they were crawling with black ants. Yelled,

'Ants. Wot the shite.' Al assured me.

'Mines the same. Little bleeders there're all right they clean yer plate, just dunk it in the water tank over by the cookhouse.' Walking along the pathway to the cookhouse, noticed on our left. A Badminton court, pondered today would be a day of discovery. Dunking our plates joined the queue. Laid out in trays were eggs bacon tomato sausages and fried bread, nobody was serving so helped myself to a plateful, joined the other two at a table to eat and listen to their conversation all about the Saturday football results back home, that really puzzled me and had to ask.

'Al. How do yer know about the football results out here so quick?'

'Tune into the twelve thirty BBC world broadcasting programme. If you want to listen to the wireless. You will have to pay some money into the kitty. We hire it from down town. Mick's the kitty holder, you see him. Talk of the devil, here's Bluebeard now.'

A clean-shaven but still blue bearded Mick sitting down beside me, exclaimed.

'Liverpool won again.'

'So did Chelsea! Joey wants to listen to the wireless.'

'Well show us your bloody money then. Fifty cents a week.'

Football dominated the conversation until, returning to the basha with more mugs of tea the mossy nets were raveled up and left hanging. Sat on the bed box there was nothing to do, others either laid on their beds to read books or write letters. The radio was on, the program record requests from a place called Surabaya, wherever that was. The music was not my type, nevertheless they played some hit's, of Frankie Laine, Dean Martin, Doris Day, to name a few.

'Ear Joey. Here's something to read.' Al passed over a magazine containing a month's issue of the Daily Mirror. Eight weeks old but something to read. Thumbing through knew most of what was in it? With regularity Al, threw his dog ends on the floor

About ten 'o' clock, at the far entrance to the Basha a little old Indian carrying a large dirty bundle, walked barefooted towards us midway stopped by a bed space. Wondering what he was doing in the Basha watched with interest. Squatting down on his haunches unraveled his rag bundle, revealing tins of boot polish, Brasso, Blanco and a range of brushes, took a pair of boots from under the bed and began cleaning them. Looking up, caught me watching him. Jerking his head up called out.

'Yoo Joey, I cleen buuts and wiibb yu pi me doollar. Okay?' Bill retorted.

'Pops. Yer a robbing bastard...Joey, this is Pops. He cleans all our webbing, boots and what have you. Keeps us smart for guards and OC's parade on Sat morning, Don't yer Pops? He charges us one dollar a week. Don't give him any more. He's a robbing bastard ain't yer Pops?'

'Yoo. faakum baastard Billie.'

'Hoi Pops! Less of the faakum swearing in this basha. Were all good un's in 'ere and its Sunday, our faakum day of worship?'

Pops, cleaning the boots took no notice. Replaced the boots with gleaming toes under the bed. Standing up, he was about four foot ten tall black as the ace of spades, with a wiry mop of graying black tousled hair a graying mustache like Hitler's, definitely in need of a shave. Wearing a dirty shirt that was miles to big for him, a pair of army issue P.T. shorts held up by an old army belt with shining brasses. Walking towards me stopped in front of me, waggling one finger and shaking his head at the same time, he said.

'Joey. Yoo pi mee nex pi-dia. one doollar...Smelling his curry laden breathes, did not have much choice...Yoo. Joey, on OC's Plade mollow. I cleen buut and wiibb now.' How did he know? Had not uttered a single bleedin' word.

'Well! Okay. Next pay day.' He ordered.

'Giv balt and baarge.' Getting up sorted out the beret and belt, whilst he took the boots from under the bed.

'Here's my belt and badge.' Thinking, "This is all right. Don't have to do any bulling".

'Ear Bill. Is this right we have servants?'

'Well. Sort of. Besides him, there's two others. Black Shadow and Lightning, they do all the other Basha's. They get more bleedin' money than we do. Robbing bastards. One good thing, it's worth the bleedin' dollar.'

'How did he know. I was on OC's then?'

'Clever bastards. Ain't they Al?'

'Bleedin' right. They know more than anyone else does in the camp. On their way past the Guardhouse notice board they read company orders. He probably knew you were coming here, before you got off the soddin' boat.' This caused an outburst of laughter.

'What about laundry? Does someone come and do that as well.'

'Of course. That's Chong's department, he's the dhobi wallah. Dirty washing is collected on Monday morning. If you want yer OG's or civvies cleaned and pressed, he charges yer for em. They come back all starched and as stiff as a board. 'Hoi! Get your shorts on.' Demands Al. Suspicion creeping in, demanded.

'What for?'

'That's the dress you wear for the OC's. Welcoming party tomorrow morning and the REME. Always go on parade the smartest. They. Might have to be taken up. We can help you out there. Can't we Bill?'

'Course we can. Chop Chop. C'mon Joey.'

'Nah. Can't be bothered.' Carried on watching Pops, slapping polish onto one of my boots. Bill impatiently said.

'C'mon. Joey. Chop Chop. Let's get yer shorts sorted out.'

Resigned to do what they were suggesting; getting up sorted out the crumpled and badly creased shorts. Ignoring the presence of Pop changed, doing up the waistband. They were very long, the leg ends were around my calf's standing there feeling a right fool. The pair of them erupted into howls of laughter,

'We said shorts, not long trousers they're far too long. You'll have to have them taken up, about two foot.'

'Two. Foot! How short they got to be?'

'I'll show yer mine...Bill getting up slipped into his shorts, the bottom hemline was half way up his thighs...That's how they should be. The tailor will do em for you.' The pair of them started cackling again. Al shaking his head, suggested.

'You can't go on OC's just like that. Have to wear hose and puttees. C'mon. Seeing as you've already got shorts on. We'll show yer how to dress properly. Put yer socks on then hose tops, last boots and puttees.'

Having never had to dress in shorts it was easy, standing up the hem of the shorts covered the hose tops. Howls of laughter,

'He looks like a bleedin' Boy Scout gone wrong. Al commented... You'll need blue flashes.' Bill laughed.

'No point. Won't be able to see em under his shorts.' Just then, Beasley came waltzing up. 'You! Are on OCs tomorrow morning. Its long trousers, boots, puttees and jacket. Not shorts!' He stated retracing his way up the basha. Al called out after him.

'Aw. Sod off Beasley yer prat. We're just having a laugh.'

'Ear. You two been taking the piss out of me again?' Al lighting up another fag remarked.

'Bleedin' right silly prat. You'd better get them along to the tailors, can't work in them that's for sure.' Frustrated with these two, demanded.

'Where's this bleedin' tailor hang out. Yer keep talking about is he on the camp?'

'Bill. Take this silly prat over to the tailors with his shorts. Show him where it is, while he's there. He can buy some bleedin' flip-flops instead of burning his feet.' Al laughed. Bill offered.

'Might as well. Give yer a tour of the camp. Okay Joey.'

'Hold on. Ain't going out dressed like this.' Quickly changed into PT shorts. So began my tour, passing Whiskers emporium three bodies lay asleep on string beds. Bill started quoting items of note....That big Basha is the sports stores...Walking around it into an open area of the car park, in front of us was the back end of the other camp with wooden huts.

'What camp is that?'

'15/19th Dancers camp.'

'Ain't they, The Lancers?'

'Yeah. Well you've 'eared of Old time Dancing and the Lancers ain't yer. Well it rhymes with dancers, don't it?' Crossing the car park area onto a road, that ran from on our right the Guardhouse and barrier, on our left at the far end was the barbed wire. Bill kept up a running commentary as we walked past rows of washing hanging on a multitude of lines...That's Chong's the dhobi wallah. That's his basha and the smallest one next to it, is the tailors. C'mon, walk the plank.' Leading the way over a wooden plank lying across a deep monsoon ditch and noticed had quite a few others made up concrete type ditches to convey the water down the slope from the 15/19th camp and into that the main one. Nearing the small basha, upon entering Bill shouted. Chop Chop Li. Got another customer for you.'

Following Bill in, saw a rather skinny bald headed Chinaman busy sewing, sat cross-legged on the top of a square table wearing a white singlet vest and black shorts, a measuring tape dangled from around his neck. Perched on the end of his flat nose were a pair of steel-rimmed glasses. Glancing over them, through slanted lids he eyed me up.

'Aah lu bling new min eh? Wit lu wan? Shirt, lowers mide.'

'Pair of Flip- Flops Please.' Nothing to do with clothing.

'Okay Jonnie, lil size.' Getting down, wandered across to some shelves took out a packet, coming back presented the palm of his hand.

'Won dolla fivty.' Bill asked.

'You finished my shirt Li?'

'Noo. Mr. Bill, pointed at the discarded garment lying on the table. Wook on shirt noow, one mooe diy Okay?' His other hand still out waiting for money. Bill prompted.

'Pay the man then.'

'Don't have any, didn't know was going to buy anything. '

'Hoi Li. Joey here new. No money. Open up slate, Okay.' Li, clicked his tongue. Handing over the flip-flops.

'Aah Okay, Mr. Joey lu pi liter.' From the tabletop picked up a little book, opening up flicked over pages full of Chinese writing. On a new page squiggles some Chinese, enquired.

'Lu LID?'

'LID? Oh. Yeah.. LAD.'

'Lu ere ling ling time?'

'Yeah bleedin' long long time.' Bill interrupted.

'Li, I go soon, RHE.' Li, tapping his book.

'Aah. Aah. Mr. Bill. Lu pi me beflore go.'

'You still got my shirt yer ole sod. Mr. Joey wants OG's tailored, okay bring em soon?'

'Okay. Mr. Joey. Bling en soo. Sama sama. See lu pi diy.'

Puzzled by his speech, clutching the packet of flip-flops headed back down onto the roadway...Bill continued with his tour.'See those three Basha's in a line behind the Guardroom? They are the HQ office, the OC's and Adjutants. That's where you will be tomorrow morning. All those Basha's over there along the back are, A, B and C Platoons, then the Naafi, ours and Composite is the one behind us and the big un, beside us is the HQ's Basha, where all the clerks sleep.'

'What's this Composite thing do?'

'That's stores and supplies. They issue out all food, ammunition and supplies from the stores down the road, they also issue POL (Petrol Oil and Lubricant), further over there. The bloke down there he's, Do alley. A nutter, walks about with an imaginary monkey.' Eager to see where I would be working prompted.

'Where's the LAD then?'

'Chop Chop. I'll show you where we spend all day. That wooden building opposite the guardhouse is the Sergeant's Mess...On our way out, Bill spoke to the Guard at the gate. Ear Brummie. This is Joey, my replacement just taking 'im up the LAD. Last stag are yer?'

'Yep. Only another hour.'

Leaving the camp turned left, pointing to a row of big open sheds covered by corrugated asbestos sheets Bill said

'That's our workshops.' Walking up crossed over and entered a large open parking area...Those three Nissan huts up there, are our offices. The first one, Capt Fred Coles, next to it, the stores and the last one is the Motor cycle shed, and behind that is our Battery shop.' Sweating buckets, muttered

'Bleedin' hot ain't it? Wots this big flat area with all the ruts and dips in it then?'

'Huh! Bleedin' Parade ground and lorry park for those lorries waiting to go in the bays for repair.'

'Blimey. It ain't very flat to be a parade ground is it? It slopes down towards the sheds.'

'This matey. Is where we all muster in the morning. C'mon let's get back. Chop Chop.'

Taking notice of the workshop, along its front was a deep monsoon ditch, at each of the eight bays laid across were thick flagstones to permit entry into the bays, four of the bays

View of main Camp from LAD

had Lorries parked in them. In the first bay stood three motorbikes behind them was a small caged office. Leaving the LAD. The familiar sound of the high-pitched whine of a Saracen engine came from inside the 15/19th camp asked.

'Wot do they do out here? '

'The cavalry. They patrol the roads, estates plantations and convoys. Further over there is the royal scots fusiliers camp also the sixth/tenth. gurkhas and the malay regiment camps are further out of town, as well as a big REME base workshop.'

'What's Ipoh like?'

'Not too bad. It's a garrison town, only draw arms and take them with you when you're going out of town riding shotgun. That can happen quite often, if there's a convoy going anywhere or up the Cameron's...At that time, those points of locations were of no consequence to me, passing the guardhouse, Bill suggested...Let's look at the Notice Board. See if your names listed? There you are. OC is at 09:00". Beasley was right, long trousers, puttees, jacket. Bleedin' 'ell. You're down for the rifle range at 10.00 hrs. Working dress, shorts, boots, belt and beret. How many came in with you then?'

'Five others. A sergeant, a corporal and three squaddies. What's this about rifle shooting?'

'See how good you are. Get some practice in. Yer never know out here.' His last remark had me wondering...Walking back along the road towards the cookhouse, pointing to a hut Bill said. Joey. If you have been down town with a prossie, that is the first place to visit. It's the PAC hut (Prevention against Cure) If, you get a dose and go on sick parade, you report to the MRS, that place I showed you across the road yesterday.' Thinking, "This is the second time he has mentioned 'dose' I will find out in my own time and will not ask these two bleeders". Returning to the basha, after about an hour out in the sun was red rosy and sweaty. Bob Watts, standing on his bed- box looked like a tailors dummy as Al adjusted his trouser bottoms, then the rear pleats of his jacket, jumping down, Bob put on his belt and beret, grabbed his rifle off his bed waddled stiffly up the basha, to start his guard duty. Al questioned.

'Bleedin' 'ell. Where you two bin, down town?'

'Nah yer soppy sod. We just went for an early morning stroll down petticoat lane. Didn't we Joey? He bought a pair of flip-flops.'

Placed on top of the bed-box, were two pairs of boots with polished toecaps, also the beret with a gleaming hat badge, on the top of the cupboard lay the green blanco-od top Kit. Pops had done his job. Putting the boots under the bed sat down to swop plimsolls for Flip Flops. Walked about, strange things to wear but not so sweaty.

'Guess wot Al? Joey's down for rifle practice already and in working dress.' Al. burst out laughing.

'Sod your 'orrible bleedin' luck. Going out dressed in those shorts. Hey. Grubs up, grab yer crocs.'

Menu/Corned beef salad or, Curry. Curry again. We spent about half an hour eating; then I paid a visit to Whiskers for a haircut. Outside his emporium he sat me down on a chair, draped a tablecloth over my shoulders armed with a comb and a pair of scissors Whiskers snipped away the bristles. To those passers by became the object of much amusement and ribald comments. "Hoi. Whitey get your hair cut.'/ 'Cut it all off Whiskers.' / 'Get yer knees brown". The operation took about twenty minutes, with a flourish and shake was relieved of the tablecloth, then charged one dollar. Another slate was opened. Rubbing the bristles, returned to find a basha full of sleeping bodies, lying down on the bed pondered about what had happened so far. Nothing much apart from constantly having the piss taken out of me, something to expect and accept.

About four in the afternoon, woke up hot red and drenched in sweat from my morning excursion out in the sun. My mouth was dry and furry physically feeling like a damp rag, glancing around. Al was reading his book, further down Bill was talking with Mick, others lay asleep, whilst outside the whirring sound of cricket's interrupted a soundless afternoon, sitting up exclaimed.

'Blimey just fell asleep!' Yawned.

'It gets yer like that. One-minute yer wide awake the next bleedin' asleep. Anyway, it's your turn for the tea. Take the mugs and fill em up.' Zip another dog end hit the post. A mug of tea, sounded a great idea swinging my legs off the bed, slipped on flip-flops. Bill shouted.

'Chop Chop, Joey, get the teas in.' It was definitely my turn? Collecting the mugs, ventured out into the blazing sun, one good factor it was a short walk to the cookhouse, returning with three full mugs of tea entered, Al greeted me with.

'Bleedin' 'ell Joey, wot took yer so long, did yer make it?'

'Bollocks!' Sitting down on my bed-box sipped the piping hot tea. Sweat, immediately oozed from pores I did not know I had running down my chest in rivulets. My back began to itch, with the plam of my hand rubbing my shoulder burst tiny water blisters feeling the wetness, thought, "I've been sun burnt before but blisters, never that bleedin' quick". A discarded dog-end hit the pole sending a shower of hot ash cascading onto the floor, watching the butt end rolling towards the center, when the sound of a slap on the floor close to Bills bed, spotted a green lizard, it lay prone on the floor, whispered.

'Bill! There's a lizard near your bed.'

'They're harmless they catch all the flies and mossies. He's been up to no good having a bit dirty little bugger. When he's finished he drops off her back. You watch I'll catch it for yer...Leaning over moved his hand very quickly towards the lizard...Gotcha!' He exclaimed. The lizard at speed ran across the floor, whilst twitching between Bill's fingers was a length of Lizard tail. He threw it at me...Never can catch them buggers, their tails grow again, but don't kill em.'

Looking up, in amongst the thatch spotted a couple of motionless lizards, maybe just waiting for a bus. Needing a shower and shave, thinking no sense in being coy got up and wrapping a towel around my waist left for the washhouse. Lathering up had a shave then showered, much refreshed returned. Bill lying on his bed was gazing at nothing Al, was still reading a book, changing into shorts sat down on the bed box out oozed the sweat; it seemed no point in having a shower.

'Bill. Nobody has told me what or, who were fighting out here. The only person that said anything was the sergeant on the train. What are we out here for?'

'CT's. Mate. The hidden enemy, thousands of them. Nobody knows where they are until; they strike. Maybe in a road ambush or on a train. That's why we have to carry rifles around you're on active service mate and will get a medal for it. They call it an emergency but it's an f.....g war.'

'Never heard of it back home. there was a lot about the Korean war in the papers and at the pictures on pathe newsreel but nothing about Malaya?' A match flared, Al lighting up another fag interrupted.

'Some bleedin' emergency. Don't you kid yerself; it's a soding war out here.'

'Wish ter bleedin' 'ell I was back home, did not volunteer for this. Well tell a lie, six of us mates volunteered for Hong Kong, Singapore and Bermuda. We got posted to Singapore. That's where we got split up. Three of em got Singapore; one down in a place called Jahore Bahru? One to Butterworth, and me to this bleedin' place.' Al responded.

'Serves yer right yer silly prat. Shouldn't have volunteered for anything.'

'Well. None of us wanted to get a home posting. We thought the best thing was get a posting overseas, more money.'

'You prat Joey. D'yer think. We bleedin' volunteered for Malaya then? No. bleedin' way. Wanted to stay in England quite happy there.' Bill interrupted.

'Your mates posted to Singapore, won't get a medal. What they all do down there Is try to get a trip across the Causeway. Stay overnight in a camp somewhere so they can get one. Jammy bastards. I think that's bleedin' wrong. If, they want a medal they should come up and do a bit of fighting. 'Al snapped back.

'Fighting! Wot Bleedin' fighting. Have you seen? Yer prat.' Mick interrupting called out from the middle of the Basha.

CT's training (internet).

'Hoi. You lot down there. Wot you lot on about fighting for. I leave that to the Infantry, that's what they're here for. We're tradesman out here to keep all the wagons going. The REME were in the Korean war the difference between that and this war is, they were fighting fookin' hordes of Chinese commies charging at you. Here a fooking army of CT's are deep in the jungle throughout fooking Malaya. The infantry have to go into the Ulu to find the bastards.' Gerry called out.

'The REME. Are always in the thick of it. They are the support unit's that keep the soding transport going. Without us the fooking army would come to a standstill.' Strolling down from the far end, Cpl. Bowles joined in the conversation.

'That is daft talking like that. What about the RASC? They drive the wagons.' Harry spoke up.

'Do not talk sodding wet, those sods run em off the road and we have to go out and rescue them.' Jock put in his pennyworth.

'Hey yer ken. Dinnay fergit. War ave tae dae therr fooking guards.'

Without realising it. Having asked a simple question had started an argument, adding fuel to the fire interrupted.

'Look. Only asked who we were fighting and how it started?' Quickly Bill answered.

'It started here in Ipoh, in June 48.' Mick shouted.

'No it bloody didn't. It was on a rubber plantation near Sungei Siput. Gang of fooking chink commies murdered the English owner. At the same time there was a second rubber plantation manager murdered further down the road. That's how it all fooking started.' Al interrupted retorted.

'No it wasn't. Ching Peng started it. That Chinese leader that the government are trying to start peace talks with to end this bleedin' war. Haven't you been listening to the soding wireless lately? Only last week they announced ole Tengku Abdul Rahman, wants to start peace talks with an amnesty. And what about that article in the straits times? Reporting that the Sultan of Jahore had made a statement about "Dire consequences" that would result if, the British left the country. Stick that up yer jacksy, read it.'

"Quote.

After denouncing those of his subjects who co-operated with the Communist Terrorists and who clambered for immediate independence, he declared. That if, Britain left Malaya the Communist would immediately take over, with a result that would be"Ninety-nine times worse than the Japanese occupation" It is all very well you, clamor for Merdeka (freedom) he declared. "But where are your warship's your planes, your armies to withstand and repel aggression from outside" After saying that he often wondered why the British people should continue to send their sons to be killed in Malaya, the Sultan Declared: "If I were British I would leave Malaya today. However, if the British go today, someone else will come tomorrow. Unquote.*

As the argument continued I listened with interest, but not understanding all the chatter that clearly was involving everyone who had slowly congregated down this end, all holding crockery and eating irons. It was obvious that the reason we were out here, was not for the good of our health and to obtain a nice suntan. I noticed Al kept on reading his book, then quietly collecting his crocs left the basha. As the argument continued after a while the rest of them realising Al had gone, run like scalded cats to catch him up. Throughout the meal the discussion continued whilst above us the long metal fan spindle oscillated madly as the blades whizzed round at an alarming speed, that did nothing to cool anyone involved, including the L/Cpl's and Cpl's. Back in Blighty the senior ranks would use their own mess however out here it seemed "not". Someone from the RASC squaddies joined the argument suggesting the REME should go out and do some convoy duties, instead of lazing about in the sheds. As Al got up to leave he shouted.

'Sod off. We have to keep you prats on the road; you do not even know how to soddin' well drive properly?' A loud boo-ing rent the air and then a voice piped up from amongst the RACS mob.

'Al! Who we playing Tuesday night?' His departing words were.

'Kinta Indians kick off five thirty.'

Very quickly learnt, it was just friendly rivalry there was no malice intended. Al's remark was just a jibe. We were all in the same boat and apparently, got on well together. As day turned into evening the activity in the basha turned to ablutions, getting ready to go down town. Bill asked.

'Coming to the flicks Al?'

'No saving up.' In a shower of sparks another fag end hit the floor. Bill invited.

'You coming Joey.'

'No ain't got any money and no civvies. Maybe next week?' After they had departed, there was only Al, me and Beasley up at the far end. Al got busy writing a letter. Thinking that is a good idea.

'Er. Al can you let me have a couple of sheets of writing paper?'

'Well! I can. But you can buy it from the Naafi, it opens at seven.'

'Not got any money to buy sod all. I've already got three slates going.'

'Here you are, a couple of sheets and an envelope, I suppose yer want a bleedin' stamp as well? Dyer want me to write it for you?' He quipped with a twinkle in his eye. Getting a pen from the cupboard began to write but was so tired, instead lay on the bed and dozed off. Bill's sharp words woke me.

'Hoi. Joey! Get out of yer pit. I've been over and got yer early morning char.'

Turning over peered through the mossie net, to observe the hunched back of Al. He muttered.

'Dineen. For Christ sake piss off.'

'Ear Al, got to be on our toes today, Joey is on OC's. Can't let the side down.' Al muttered.

'Sod off. Get me tea.'

'It's on yer locker, yer a lazy bastard.'

The glimmer of the light bulb glowing with the intensity of all its 40 watts was just about visible through the netting asked.

'What's the time Bill?'

'Nearly seven. Have a shower and wake yerself up yer noisy bleeder. Snoring like mad again last night.' Al sharply retorted.

'Yeah and I. Had to put yer to bleedin' bed again last night. Yer a lazy bastard Joey.'

I then remembered had just lain down to have a snooze, then it was Monday morning, wondering what time it was light enquired.

'Wot time does it get light out here?' Bill snapped back.

'If yer care to get up. You'll see the sun rise. Yer lazy bastard.'

Cold and clammy, sat up to drink the hot tea it was reviving, untangling myself from the mossie got up. The basha was a hive of activity, Beasley followed by Bowles passed by with their toiletries. Bill, already dressed in his working clothes, shorts, boots, socks rolled down on top of his boots. Was lying on his bed reading a letter. Al got out of bed, lit a fag and said.

'Right. I'm going for a shit, shave and shampoo, don't anyone stop me.' Instead just sat there, fag in hand drinking tea. Thinking, "This guy must be the weirdest bloke, I've ever come across". However, for me that morning had to meet the OC and then fire some bullets. Wrapping the towel around my waist with toiletries headed for the showers.

Outside, the cookhouse lights were on and the cooks were already laying out the breakfast dishes. Inside the showers many bodies with deep tanned torso's white backsides and tanned legs, obtained from many months exposed to the sun, were in different stages of personal hygiene. Showering, shaving, brushing teeth or, toweling down thought, "There is no ceremony here, follow their example". Someone shouted. 'Make way for a whitey.' - another. added. 'Get yer knees brown.' Taking no notice got straight into the stream of water they called a shower; the cold water certainly woke me up. Having finished ablutions headed back to the basha where beds had been squared off with top kits arranged; Bill and some others were finishing off laying up their kit. Beasley approaching said.

'Plant. As you are on O.Cs. Your excused 0800 muster. Then after that you're on target practice.'

As if, I did not know. I did not like this bastard; he was only an L/Cpl. and was asserting his authority. All the other senior ranks shared our mess and he was not amongst them that made me begin to wonder. Bill spoke up.

'Piss off yer prat. He's already read company orders.'

'You. Dineen will be on a charge.' Bill angrily retorted.

'Yer. Just you try it mate...Beasley just walked away...Joey he's a prat. Not worth the worry, he likes to know everything and tell everyone. Wot's going on or, wot they should be doing. He's only a f....g welder for Christ sakes and not very good at that.'

'That's all right saying that Bill, but he out ranks you and can put you on a charge.'

'Do not worry, were different out here we all have to muck in together. There's corporals and lance jacks all sleeping in the same basha. Since he was made up, he thinks he is God or summat; we do not take any shit from him the others don't pull rank so, why should he? You will soon find out we work as a team. Where is Al? It's time for brekkers.' Al came in as we were leaving. Chop Chop yer late.' Bill prompted.

'Save me a place. I'm coming now.'

Joining the tail enders, we moved forward as Al joined us, 'Q' jumping that raised a chorus's of boos. 'Get to the back of the queue.' Brekkers was not much. Scrambled eggs, a serving of hard-burnt fried bread with tea. It did not take long to eat. Back in the basha, Al prompted.

'Get yer bed space sorted out like ours. Whilst we are on Muster parade, the officer of the day will do a line inspection, when he enters be ready to shout REME LAD ready for inspection sir. Yer should know all about that, you being fresh out from Blighty.'

Alone in the basha, noticed all the beds and bed boxes were neatly lined up the same as back in Blighty. However on top of the bed, the plate and soup plate were reversed with the mug on top with the eating irons laid out table fashion, beneath the front foot of the bed lay the square folded black Uni, displaying number rank and name. Placed on either side, was a plimsolls with polished soles up and a best boot. The cupboard doors were left wide open with the top kits squared off on top. With the exception of the folded Uni, had everything in order by the time an RASC Officer accompanied by a Sgt. entered. Shouting out the norm, to which the Officer waved his swagger stick walking quickly through inspected the Basha without any comment. Gradually making their way down this end called out.

'New arrival are you?'

'Yes Sir. Arrived Saturday Sir.'

'Name Rank and Number?' - Bellowed it out.'

'Right. Your on OC's shortly.'

'Yes sir.'

'Get your kit bag sorted out before tomorrow's inspection Craftsman.' With that parting shot they left the Basha.

At precisely 0845, Beasley arrives. Disliking this bloke, what was he doing back in the basha? He bawled out.

'Plant .Your on OC's. Report to the sergeant majors office. I assume you know where that is?'

'Yes!'

'Yes. What?'

'Yes. Lance Corporal.'

'You Cockneys. Are all the same. Know-all's. Get ready and I'll march you up there and as you know your way you will be on time. Yer a little bag of shit.' Thinking "Bag of shit Eh? Well matey you are about the same height as me but scrawny with it and there ain't anything to describe you except maybe a sewer". Sure enough as if, I was a defaulter. He marched me up to the front of the Guardhouse where Sgt. Whitely and the Corporal, still dressed in KD's were moving about in a carefree manner. Beasley did not order, just quietly told me.

'Fall out and join the others.' Silently he crept away Beasley had shot his bolt. "Bleedin' Coward. He never said anything about my presence to Sgt. Whitely". Who shouted.

'You. REME Craftsman on OC's parade. Line up at the end and dress off.' Joining the line, noticed Beasley disappear towards the LAD. "What a jumped up shit he was, maybe his mum likes him. Poor cow". Doing the usual stamping of feet, dressing off next to a ginger haired bloke who was on the train. A couple of RPs was hovering about possibly making a mental note of the new intake. Nobody spoke until Sgt. Whitely ordered.

'Attention, Right Tur Quick March.' We were off to meet the OC. Right wheeled out of camp onto the main road, a few more strides right wheeled left wheeled onto the ochre coloured dust road, ordered to halt outside the O.C's Basha.

'Right Face. Stand Still.'

At precisely 0858. The CSM (Company Sgt/Major) appeared from out of the basha with his pace stick stuck underneath his arm, spoke up.

'Right. Let's be 'aving you lot then. Sergeant Whitely and Corporal McKay. One-step forward please. You two. Will enter the O.C's office first for your briefing. After that. You OR's (Ordinary Ranks) will be called. I want you all to be at your smartest... pointing his pace stick directly at me. That includes the REME contingent.'

This made me cringe, as all I had heard from Al and Bill we were the smartest bunch out. No way was I going to let the corps down. Then the shouting began. The Sgt. and Cpl. were doubled marched into the basha, after about three minutes emerging at the double, took up their positions. Like a conveyor belt we were doubled inside. The OC sat behind his desk, watched as the rabble in real long shorts doubled on the spot in front of him.

'HALT. LEFT TURN.' Brought us face to face with him.

The appearance of a tall man with a bristling moustache, his OG jacket was starched almost whitish green; his epaulets displayed his rank with a row of medal ribbons across his chest. On the corner of his table lay his swagger stick and officers cap. After the CSM had bellowed out our introductions, there was a pregnant pause before the O.C. rather timidly spoke.

'Now that you Drivers and 'Ahem.' the REME Craftsman. Have joined three company RASC. We expect you to carry out you duties without question. You are all on active service during this war. Bla Bla, he went on, making all of us feel shit scared of what we had to do....We must all pull our weight together. Dismiss. Carry on company sergeant major.'

A bellow from the CSM. Woke us up from our dreams about Blighty. Double marched out into the brilliant sunshine, ordered to halt stand still. Silence prevailed except for the lazy slap slap of the flags lanyard against the pole fanned by a cool breeze that you could not feel through the blazing sun and did nothing for our sweating bodies too enhance the mood of Malaya. Our mood of silent melancholy was rudely interrupted, as the CSM shouted orders.

'Sgt. Whitely. Take over the squad. Proceed to draw weapons and ammunition from the armoury and proceed by lorry, to the rifle range. Dismiss.'

In a cloud of ochre dust, the squad retreated to the Guardroom, brought to a halt by Sgt. Whitely who provided more instructions.

'When I give the order to dismiss. Double down to your Basha's. Change into working dress, double back to the armoury, collect arms and ammunition. You have five minutes to report back here. Dismiss.'

I was the last to draw weapons, the armourer issued out a 303 rifle and 10 rounds of ammo. Within a couple of minutes a three tonner pulled up; stood in the back were a number of other ranks. A Sgt. jumping down from the cab, ordered us.

'Climb aboard.' Sgt. Whitely and Cpl. McKay took up positions near the front. So they could converse with the other Sgt. Within minutes we were off on a jolly, the same route we had arrived but at the main tee junction, turned in the opposite direction.

After driving for about twenty minutes, we turned off the road down a dirt track leading into the jungle. Through overhanging foliage as the lorry bouncing and bucking, eased its way down along the rutted track, until finally it came into an open space. The rifle range.

We were ordered down, assembled into single line. Marched to the thousand-yard rifle range, allocated a firing position while our other travelers. The butt party was marched to the Butts at the far end of the range. Soon a red flag was hoisted, firing was about to commence. The Sgt. I/C firing party instructed us.

'Load the magazines on your rifles.' A white flag was waved at the far end, the Butt Party was ready. The Sgt. ordered.

'Take up your firing positions...Dropping down lay prostrate...When I issue the order FIRE. In your own time, take aim, fire five rounds and NO more.' Everyone murmured their agreement.

In amongst the grass in front, a slight movement attracted my attention. A little thing about an inch long similar to a worm was waving its head about, until it found another piece of grass. Latching onto that its rear swung round to attach onto another blade of grass, repeating this same motion watched intently totally engrossed by this distraction. Suddenly felt a boot jammed on the small of my back and the roar of the Sgt.

'SOLDIER! ARE YOU WITH THIS FOOKING FIRING PARTY OR. BACK IN THE UK. MAY. I ALSO REMIND YOU. THAT YOU'RE ON ACTIVE SERVICE. THAT MEANS YOU WILL PRACTICE WEAPON TRAINING. JUST IN CASE YOU ARE FIRED UPON. BY THOSE NASTY BASTARDS CALLED THE CT'S. YOU REME WALLAHS ARE A SHOWER OF SHIT. PAY ATTENTION, GET A GRIP OF YOURSELF AND YOUR RIFLE.'

Just about to tell him, I'd seen a funny thing in front of me, decided this was not the time to speak up. He was yelling at everyone else. 'NOW WE HAVE EVERYONE'S UNDIVIDED ATTENTION. WHEN I NEXT ORDER. TAKE AIM, FIRE IN YOUR OWN TIME... FIRE... I WANT YOU. TO TAKE AIM AT THE STATIC TARGETS. DOWN AT THE BUTT END OF THE RANGE. AND ONLY FIRE FIVE ROUNDS.'

Scrutinizing the grass, expected to see the thing, but it had disappeared. So concentrated on shooting. Checking the sight-reading adjusted it from five hundred to one thousand, pulled the rifle tight to shoulder, aimed at the bull on the static target and waited for the order ready to shoot any CT that came into view. Then with a shattering roar. 'FIRE.' Without thinking, pulled the trigger jerking the rifle. About one hundred yards in front, a spurt of dirt indicated a hit?

'YOU SHIT FACE. I TOLD YOU. TO AIM AT THE STATIC TARGETS AT THE BUTT END OF THE RANGE. NOT THE GROUND. AJUST YOUR SIGHTS. NEXT SHOT I WILL STAND BEHIND YOU AND WATCH INTENTLY.'

"Aw sodin' 'ell, not another Beasley. Will try my best this time and I'll show that bastard". Ejecting the spent cartridge, reloaded took aim and let loose another round. At the other end, the target was lowered. Coming back up a waggle from the marker indicated a magpie hit. A curt response from the Sgt.

'Hmm.' Your other shot was wasted.' And abruptly walked away to yell at someone else. Relieved of the pressure of not being watched, my last three shots produced a further two magpie's and a bull. At the other end the Butts Party, Were hauling down the static targets, in preparation for the snap shot firing exercise. The Sgt bellowed.

'WHEN YOUR SNAP TARGET APPEARS TAKE AIM AND FIRE.'

At the butt end, a small round white dot appeared. Letting off a round, got a wave from side to side indicating a miss that was not good. Finished firing had scored nil hits. No sodding good. By this time my back was burning. We were ordered to stand up and empty the breeches of our rifles, so that there were no stray bullets up there. Having done so the Sgt. addressed the firing party.

'WHAT A SHOWER OF SHIT. I HAVE NEVER WITNESSED ANYTHING LIKE IT BEFORE. YOU LOT. BARE IN MIND. THAT YOU ARE IN A BATTLE ZONE AND CAN BE FIRED UPON ANY TIME. THE CT's WANT TO TAKE YOUR ARSES FOR GRANTED. WHEN YOU ARE DRIVING YOUR WAGONS. EITHER IN CONVOY OR ON YOUR LONESOME. YOU. THE REME WALLAH. YOU WERE NOT BAD BUT. NO GOOD AT THE SNAP SHOOTING. THAT IS A MUST IN THIS FOOKING COUNTRY.... SERGEANT. WHITELY AND CORPORAL McKAY. I SUGGEST YOU GET ON THE NEXT SHOOTING PARTY. AS QUICKLY AS POSSIBLE. NOW JUST IN CASE ANY OF YOU FOOKING IDIOTS. HAVE LEFT ONE UP THE SPOUT. DISHCHARGE AND PRESENT ARMS FOR INSPECTION...The Sgt. walking along the rank, inspected each rifle. No incidents to report. He bellowed.

'RIGHT TURN. FALL OUT.'

Never knew his name, as he was going home to England the next week, lucky bastard. As we lined up to get aboard the Lorry noticed the back of the ginger haired lad. It was red raw from the rays of the sun. Thinking, "If his back is like that, mine will also be red raw. I'll have a shower before reporting into the LAD". The return journey did not take long. The Lorry took us all the way down to the cookhouse, where we got down to get boiling water from the cooks, to boil and oil our rifles then back to the armoury to hand them in. Walking back to the Basha my back was burning hot and definitely needing a shower. Entered the Basha. No such luck. Beasley was sat waiting on a bed.

CHAPTER SEVENTEEN
3 COY. R.E.M.E. LIGHT AID DETACHMENT (LAD)

3 Coy. R.EM.E. LAD. July 56.
28th. Commonwealth Ind' Inf. Bdge.
IPOH MALAYA 1955-57

'Now your back Plant. You have to report to our OC. Captain Cole. I'll take you up there.' Thought, "Blimey the bastards polite for a change"? Replied.

'I was going to have a shower.'

'No time for that. Get moving.' As we left the basha, he fell in behind me. With the effects of the sun, my back was burning and very itchy. Beasley could not care a monkey's toss. Marching out of the camp up the road towards the entrance of the LAD, he bawled.

'LEFT RIGHT. LEFT RIGHT. LEFT WHEEL. GET A GRIP OF YER SELF-CRAFTSMAN.' Responding to his orders, his bawling brought ribald shouts from onlookers in the workshop.

'HOI. BEASLEY. WHO THE FOOK DO YOU THINK YOU ARE? WE NEED SOME WELDING TO BE DONE.' /

'YER . TOSSER GET A LIFE FER FOOK SAKE.' /

'WOT A PRAT. TAKE NO NOTICE OF THAT SHITHEAD.'

Passing by the flagstaff, with the limp folds of the REME standard drooping from its dizzy heights. Directly ahead of me in the office doorway stood an Officer with his hands in his pockets. Before we even got near him, he called out.

'Beasley. Dismiss...there's welding to be done. Get on with your work.' I continued to march towards him then he spoke.

'Been expecting you. Plant isn't it? Come on in son.'

Retreating into his office, he sat down behind his desk, crunching in behind him. On my right sat at another desk was a senior NCO, he looked up as I entered. With stamping of feet and saluting blurted out.

'23112429 Craftsmen Plant. J. Sir.' Very proud that I had achieved promotion albeit a Trade one.

'Plant this is Q. Threadgold. Who is my number two? Under my direction, you take orders from him. Now. You are a replacement Vehicle Electrician from Malvern. So. Where do you hail from?' Standing up proud.

'London. Sir.'

'Well. Well. We have another of those. Eh. Q?' The Q stammered.

'Yes I s-s-suppose s-so. P.P.Plant. D-d-do you play f-football?' Thinking, "What a strange question".

'Yes Sir.'

'W-w-what position?'

'Right wing. Sir.'

'Oh.' I noticed a hesitation in his voice possibly the reason for this interrogation was quite simple. Apart from bleedin' Beasley, would I fit in with the rest of the mob? Captain Cole interrupted.

'Dineen. Is your senior VE. Q Call him up here. Let's have a chat.' Pondered. "Let's have a chat. Wot kind of army is this"? Q getting up from his table went outside roared.

'DINEEN UP HERE. IMMMEDIATELY.' Within a couple of minutes, Bill entered grinning minus belt and beret. He asked.

'Yes Q.' Captain Cole answered.

'No respect as usual Dineen.'

'Excuse me Sir. Can't salute Sir. No beret. Sir.' A good excuse.

'Look here Dineen. You are off back to Blighty soon. Take this young weed under your wing, teach him the RIGHT way. Not YOUR way. Isn't that right Q?'

'Y-Yes Sir.'

'Q. What are we going to do with all these cockneys? How many have we got now?'

'D-d don't know. Sir. They are a s-s-strange bunch t-t-to say the least.'

Whilst they chatted to themselves, I had time to take note of my two superiors. Capt. Fred Cole stockily built, sleek parted black hair wore glasses and a Clark Gable styled moustache. He appeared to me rather laid back in his attitude, whilst Q Threadgold, again his mousey coloured hair was sleek and parted typical army style, of good statue out of the two, although sat down he appeared taller. Possibly both in their forties wore a string of medal ribbons on their jacket. A resigned statement from Captain Cole stopped any further gazing...'Oh well. I suppose, we will sort them out. Dismiss the pair of you.' The Q ordered.

'Dineen! S-s-send up K-Keene. I want to see him n-n-now.'

Doing the usual saluting, stamping of feet to leave. Whereas, Bill just turned around and walked out. Well! He did not have a beret on. After the previous OC's interview was totally bemused by this OC's' interview walking beside Bill, enquired.

'After all the bullshit Beasley gave me. What the hell was that all about?'

'Ah. I have already told yer; take no notice of that prat Beasley. That Joey is Fred Cole, he is great and he wants everyone to work together. You mark my words this LAD is great. Wot with all the shit we get out here? We would do anything for Fred and Q. And they will do their utmost, to make sure we are all happy and contented.'

'Cheeky Sod. Called me a weed.' Bill laughed.

'Your names Plant ain't it? He didn't mean anything just joking...entering the workshops, as we approached the caged office. Bill yelled out...Al git yer arse up to the office. Q wants a word with yer. Chop Chop...he continued...Now Joey. First thing first... interrupting Al shouted...'What's he want?'...I don't bleedin' know he didn't say... Now where was I? Oh yeah you have to meet Stan Levine; he is in charge of workshops...Bill called out...Hoi Stan. This is Joey my replacement.'

Inside the caged office sat at a desk was a Sgt. of slight build, again sleeked black parted hair with sharp features. Turning around addressing me asked.

'What's your surname?'

'Plant Sergeant.' Even more bemused, at the attitude of everyone, was unsure how to take this change in discipline; obviously, there was great respect but a casual approach to the rank.

'Ear Stan, Fred said. I should show im the ropes. I'll take im up to the battery shop, introduce im to "Genny" and tell im how to work the charger.'

'Be quick about it, then report back here.'

Bill urging me out, headed across the square towards the end Nissan hut and around to its rear. Although two windows were wide open the stink of sulphuric acid was very evident, upon entering it was baking hot inside. On top of a long lead lined table, apart from a couple of glass jars about a dozen batteries were linked together to a bus bar system supported on a wooden frame, in comparison to the one at Malvern it was very primitive.

'These batteries are already charged. Grab hold of that hydrometer; check their S.G. (Specific Gravity) and voltage with the discharge tester. You do know how to do that?'

'Of Course! But how do you charge them up?'

'With Genny she's outside. Check those first then I'll show you how to work her, she's a soddin' obstinate cow we need a new one. C'mon...in between the two Nissan huts, tucked under a tarpaulin cover was a portable generator...To start the charging system, all yer must do is wank Ginny's crank handle until she fires up. As I said, she is an obstinate cow and needs to be handled with care. If she doesn't respond talk to her or, get Lance Corporal Moore ter git a grip of her, he's great with fixing Genny and Motorcycles.'

'Not met him yet.'

'Nah. He's up the Cameron's in the BMH (British Medical Hospital) has the shit's. You know. Dysentery'...'Who, do I go to, if Genny packs up?'...Ignoring my question he continued...Charging batteries, is the only thing we do in the battery shop, once you've set them up in the right sequence with the charging clips and cables. Start Genny, set the voltage and that's it. Joey. From that pool of water on top of the tarp' is an endless supply of pure water; use it for topping up the batteries. You can do that job as well, inside there's a glass bottle fill it up with water then top em up. Any other repairs on lorries are carried out in the workshops.'

Having had my first lesson on what to do with charging batteries; with the equipment not the same as at Malvern would just have to learn a different way.

'What type of electrical jobs come in for repair then?'

'Anything, it's our job to get them sorted out and back on the roads. C'mon, I'll take you to the stores, where we hold some of the spares.' Walking back to the middle Nissan hut entered through its rear door.

'Joey. This is Johnny, he's our storekeeper and guess wot, like me he's going home soon and that Chinese fella over there, is Wong. He's the LAD clerk...a grinning Chinaman, displaying a set of gold-filled teeth with his chin resting on his folded arms sprawled across the top of an ancient looking typewriter winked at me...Just come in to show Joey the electrical stores? All the stuff we want. You ain't got?'

'Aren't many I have matey? If yer want anything special. Wong ere, has to type out a requee and get em from the REME workshops out of town? Maybe get them same day or later, depends on what it is?' Replied the knowledgeable store man. Bill showed some light bulbs, a distribution box and other bits until Johnny putting on his belt and beret urged. 'Right it's chow time. Git out the pair of you got to lock up.'

'Okay keep yer shirt on. C'mon Joey, cookhouse calling, catch up with Al.' As we crossed the square towards the sheds other RASC Drivers were either walking alone or in pairs in the direction of the main camp. There was little or no semblance of marching as a squad. Returning to the Basha, from the bed tops removed the morning kit layout, with our crocs headed for the Cookhouse. The mid-day meal menu was either corned beef or tinned fish with salad, which never varied throughout my service in Three Company. Inside the mess hall, the REME occupied about four tables; there was not many RASC Wallahs present, due to the fact of driving duties. Dinner was scoffed and washed down with tea. In the basha, a towel was spread out on the bed to lie on to either read or sleep.

Someone shaking my boot woke me. Opening my heavy eyelids saw, Mick at the foot of the bed.

'Joey. Get back to work...moving away shaking Al's foot muttered...Wakey wakey.'

'Piss off. 'Mick replied unconcerned.

'It's up to you.'

Sitting up, looked around the basha, others were either still asleep or, sat on the edge of their beds bewildered about what time of day it was? I was soon to become quickly adjusted to this state of mind that occurred every day at lunchtime. Jolting me back to reality, Al suggested.

'Joey. If. You break any of Den's crock's, he will bleedin' annihilate you. Git yourself up the stores, get some crockery.'

'Where's the store then?'

'Evans is the guy you want to see, hold on he's just going past. EVIE! Got job for you?' Entering the basha, he asked.

'Hurry up what do you want prat?'

'Joey wants some crocs.'

'Not that new fooking REME raw recruit eh.'

'Yeah that's im. White knees there.'

'C'mon then, before I get any other interruptions. Empty your sea kit bag; you will not need that for years. Bring that and your tin mug along as well; I'll book all in at the same time.' Al interrupted.

'Evie you okay for tomorrow's match?'

'Yes. If I'm playing?'

'Right wing. Joey is playing as well. Better sort im out some boots and clobber at the same time...Mystified by all this cross chatting, looked at Al...Yeah you're playing at inside right. If you're as good as you say you are playing with St. Anne's. Now's the time to prove it and don't forget yer Uni. That's got to be painted.' Evans urged.

'Joey, grab yer bits and pieces. Let's get bloody moving.'

Grabbing all, hurried after Evans passing Whiskers Emporium caught him up as he unlocked the stores door. In exchange, he provided a full set of crocs and a cape adding 'Yer'll need that Poncho out here.' with a flourish of a pen the exchange completed.

'What size boots do you wear ?'

'Six!'

'Six! Bloody' 'ell. Don't know? Pick up your kit tomorrow; I might have sorted out a pair out by then.'

Returning to the Basha, placing the crocs on top of the cupboard, left the Poncho on the bed and picked up the Uni, was about to walk through the basha noticed still asleep on his bed was the inert form of Beasley. "Sod 'im." Left by our doorway.

Entering the LAD. Wondered what to do with the Uni? Near the cage, Bill was stood beside Sgt. Levine.

'Plant, leave your kitbag on the floor, come into the office and get assigned a toolbox... Inside the cage he ordered...Grab hold of one of those toolboxes with an "E" painted on it, take it outside and in an orderly manner. Lay out all the tools on the floor for an inventory check.'

As each item was called out, I placed it back into the box. After about twenty minutes all items had been identified as correct, signed the register as the proud owner of box number 17. Sgt. Levine proceeded to give a lecture on the responsibility of tool care.

'Plant. At the end of each work period return it to the office here, only take it off the premises if you are on convoy duty. At anytime a toolbox inspection will be called and any missing, cost will be deducted from your pay; my advice is, look after them ...adding... If you want any help, come and see me. Never mind about this prat Dineen.' Bill taunted.

'Come off it Stan. Where would you be without me?'

'For your info. Back in Blighty. Go and fix that generator on number 91RG52... it has just come in, its not charging. It has to be ready for tomorrow mornings Cameron's convoy.'

'So long as I am not going, I don't give a shit but it will be ready.'

'Take Plant here, across to the paint shop to get his kitbag painted, then he can help you.' Bill kicking the Uni urged.

'C'mon git, follow me.' Crossing towards a large caged area, in the first one Oxy and Acetylene cylinders were in racks but there was no sign of Beasley. The next cage was the paint shop Bill called out.

'Hoi Tony. Do Joey's kit bag for him, wants it back tonight. Joey give 'im yer details and come back for it knock off time.'

Back in the bay, a "QL" the type of Lorry unknown to me as the only lessons we had were on pre-war type engines located in a large open frame; however, that was in the past. Under Bills guidance, informing me of the procedures, began working on the generator system, - start the engine, check the ammeter, no charge, check the fuse box, located under the control panel all were working.

'Joey there're okay, so it means removing the generator. You can do that. located behind the exhaust pipe up the front of the engine; get a couple of spanners to remove it. C'mon Chop Chop. I'll watch you.'

Sitting down behind the front wheel, saw where the generator was located and the holding nuts from the toolbox took a couple of spanners, attempting to remove the Generator; every time my arms touched the hot exhaust pipe, they were burnt, exclaimed.

'Sodin' 'ell Bill, can't we wait until it cools down?'

'Nope get and do it. It has to go out, just bleedin' remove it.'...With the nuts undone, slipped off the fan belt and removed the generator...'that's it, Fetch it over to the workbench and I'll show you what the problem is. Most likely a common occurrence, just clean up the commutator. C'mon, you start on it, remove the housing pins, pull out the generator – hold it in the vice...doing as instructed... See, in-between those copper segments, they are full of carbon, that has to be removed, use a bit of a hacksaw blade, it's the right thickness.' Being taught on the job, proved invaluable throughout my time in the LAD. As I began to reassemble the generator, the others were knocking off Q was talking with Sgt. Levine. Captain Cole was stood outside his office hands in pockets watching Beavis lowering the standard. It was the end of a working day in the LAD. Urging me on Bill muttered. 'Urry up I want a mug of char. Get it back in place.'

Sitting back down behind the wheel maneuvered it into position by which time the exhaust pipe had cooled down, so it was easy to replace. Bill climbing up into the cab started the engine revving up, shouted.

'It's charging. Joey. Report to Stan sign the book. Fully charging.'

Sgt. Levine came out to check everything was working, and then signed off the worksheet.

'Plant your kitbag is in the office. You'll need that for tomorrow morning's basha inspection. Now piss off the pair of you.'

'C'mon Joey knock off time, there's nothing else to do, get yer Uni from the cage.'

Sweating freely covered in grease and grime with scorched arms, entered the cage. By the desk on the floor was the Uni squared off, painted black with my details in white but still wet. Placing the toolbox alongside the others, carefully picked up the Uni, as we left the workshops, enquired.

'Is that a normal workday?'

'Yep and when we get busy; we do not leave until the job is done. All sorts turn up here SAS, Malays anyone who has a problem with their wagon, apart from the 15/19th dancers; they have their own LAD down the bottom of the road. I' m the duty VE, but now you are here we can take turns, one day on one day off except on guard duty. The VM's have it cushy, as there is so many of them they have a roster. Ear what happened on weapon training this morning?'

'Yeah alright suppose! Got shouted at by the Sergeant for not paying attention. Spotted a funny little wormy thing waving about in the grass, about inch long almost black. Any idea wot it was?'

'Now then Joey! How the bleedin' 'ell should I know? I wasn't there. Did it 'ave a little flat end?'

'Don't know din't have a chance. That's when the Sergeant booted me up the arse.'

'Sounds like a leech, they wave about until they latch onto skin, bite then suck like mad, they become so bloated with gallons of yer blood yer arm falls off. Nasty bleeders they are.'

By the time we arrived back in the basha, the hint of a breeze was drifting through various open spaces making it quite cool inside. There was no sign of Al, until he entered armed with three mugs of tea shouted.

'Don't say anything Dineen.'

'Wot me! Nah. Would I say anything about it being your turn?'

'Prat!' Came back a short response.

Shoving the painted Uni under the bed sat down on the bed box to drink tea and sweat, a bit of chat went on between Al and Bill about nothing that I could grasp hold of before Bill said.

'C'mon, Chop Chop clatty sods shower time.' Al retorted.

'Wait yer bleedin' hurry. Ain't finished me fag yet.'

We occupied the three vacant showers, it was scrubbing time in the tepid water. Having finished, securing the wet towel around my waist padding to the entrance, slipped my feet into the new flip-flops. Stepping down onto the shiny wet surface of the pathway, immediately my feet went from under me, sprawling naked in a heap Al and Bill roared with laughter, whilst the occupants of HQ basha leaning out of windows joined in jeering. 'Get yer knees brown bleedin' REME Wallah?' Scrambling up, with face redder than my sunburn back, grabbed hold of the flip-flops towel and washing kit, ran naked into the basha to towel myself again, need not have bothered with the latest exertion was sweating buckets. Al and Bill entering chortled.

'Ear Joey, yer ain't arf got a white arse, eh Al?'

'And a bleedin' red back, what game was yer playing lying on the floor, rugby yer prat?'

Absolutely no sympathy from those two and it appeared to brighten up a dismal existence, regardless of any mishap to any unfortunate bastard whatever the circumstance, apart from death it made no difference everyone howled with laughter. Composing myself, so as not to add coals to the fire changed and was about to lie on the bed when Bill reminded me.

'Er Joey. Ain't you supposed to be seeing Li. about your tailoring jobbies. So he can take yer measurements, change into yer OG shorts and jacket; leave your spare pair with him. You'll get em back tomorrow, then swop em over. Pay im later.'

'Blimey. Forgotten all about that.' Changing left en-route to Li's. Entering into the gloomy depths of his emporium, he was still sat on the table stitching looking up recognised me.

'Aah Masta. Joey. Lu com bak. Lu wan o. gs chaang, I fix.' Presenting the garments to him. 'Li, need shorts and jacket tailored.'

'No ploblem, tik misures...Clambering down with a peculiar flat-footed gait shuffled towards me removing his tape from around his neck ordered...Do yap jicket...Buttoning up including the brass belt buckle, that he tugged...No ned. Off...Pulled back my shoulders, measured, returned to his table and began scribbling. Measured chest, waist, neck downwards, bending my arm into the rifle position took measurement, suggested...Lu luk gud n gurd eh?...Grinning like a Cheshire cat scribbled more Chinese characters into the book. Having finished with the jacket, he started on the shorts that did not take long...Luk, lik sholt sholts, sama sama Bill ?'

'Yeah. All right if you say so.'

'Wa longee lowlers?'

'Didn't bring em.'

'Tomollow sholts, jicket leady. Yu bling lowlers tomollow. Okay Masta. Joey! Lu pi liter.' It was done. Leaving him hurried back to the basha. Al was reading a book. Bill asked.

'All done then?'

'Yep but he wants me long-on's tomorrow.'

'Wear 'em with yer boots on, take those shorts as well.' Changing back into PT shorts, sat down on the bed.

'Er how much does he charge? Didn't bother to ask im.' Al flicked another dog-end hitting the post in a shower of red ash, interrupted.

'Bleedin' 'ell Joey. Yer done it nah.'

'Wot der yer mean?'

'You Prat. Should have told him how much you were going to pay him, ain't that right Bill?' Bill, lying on bed staring out of the doorway made a uninterested comment

'Yup. Tough shit. It'll cost yer nah?'

Not knowing whether to believe either of them. Would have to wait and see what Li did charge? Just then, the lookout up the other end shouted. 'Here they come.' The ensuing panic of grabbing eating irons and crocs, had the LAD charging out of the basha racing across to the cookhouse. First in the queue again.

The evening meal consisted of Tomato soup, Tinned Fish salad or, curry. Sitting down alongside Al, about to tuck into the curry. I noticed at one of the table legs, a line of tiny black ants crawling up the side of the water-filled tin. "That was the answer. They drowned"! Having finished the curry went for some fresh fruit salad, upon returning found an intense argument had developed about the weekend's football back in Blighty. Listening to the banter that was going around, shouts about Liverpool, Manchester, Sheffield. Glasgow and all parts of the country, the loudest one shouting was Al, all about Chelsea. The din increased in intensity until, Al getting up nonchalantly walked out nevertheless, the banter continued.

With another mug of tea, returned to the basha to sit down and produce more sweat while watching Harry preparing to go on guard. At five to six Harry the tallest in the basha, walked stiffed legged until he got to the doorway, keeping his legs straight he somehow, managed to do a limbo dance under the roof overhang. With Beasley i/c roster, there was always one REME person on guard throughout the week and weekend. The guard duty times, were the same as back in Blighty. Outside daylight was fading, a rainstorm was brewing. Al, lying on his bed was fast asleep snoring, a disgarded book lay wide-open on his chest. Bill, reading a book muttered.

'Joey. Turn on the light and let's see what I'm reading. Urry up I'm just getting to the good part?'

Easing myself across the bed reached out to flick the light switch on the post. At that precise second, a thunderous clap overhead quickly followed by a zip of lighting, frightened the living daylights out of me and so began the storm. As the rain thundered down it was deafening you could not hear yourselves speak. It even woke Al up; taking no notice he lit up a fag. After about ten minutes, the storm abated and the temperature had really dropped, the amount of rainwater that had lashed down gurgled along the outside gullies, as they transported gallons of water away into larger monsoon ditches elsewhere. It became strangely quiet the only sound left of the rainstorm, was the steady plopping of rainwater dripping off the attap roof into the gullies. Bored and fed up, sat on the bed box to listen to the radio. Later, getting ready to get into bed draped the mossie net around the bed. About eight thirty Al gets up.

'Der yer want a mug of tea and a nanjo from Whiskers.'

'Might as well.' Bill was sound asleep, so did not bother to wake him. Passing the Naafi, plenty of OR's, were swilling beer.

'Al. Why don't yer go into Naafi and have a drink?'

'Nah saving up fer me wedding to Patti when I get back home.'

'Blimey! Is the wedding to be held as soon as yer get back then?'

'A couple of months, then that's it.' Al called out his orders...Tea Whiskers and a cheese an onion banjo. Wot der fancy Joey?'

'Wot else has he got?' Whiskers replied, advising of his very short menu.

'Tamata, chaase, onnion or mixure, Banana, what you pleese'

'Umm, cheese and tomato please.'

'Te, Caffe, Coco, Ovitiin, velly guud make you sleep sleep. He added.

'Er Tea.' Whiskers turned around and spoke possibly Malay to the little Chico sat in the background, immediately he jumped up and started preparing the Banjo's whilst Whiskers busied himself making the Tea, speaking to me said.

'Yoo, Nis fello.' Al retorted.

'Git off yer randy bastard. He isn't like that. Keep to yer Chicos and 'urry up.'

Two mugs of tea and two massive Banjo's, like two halves of a cob loaf stuffed full of what we had ordered were handed over, Whiskers demanded.

'Biffty cents one. '

'Whiskers! Yer a robbing bastard put it on slate. Put Joey's on as well, we'll pay end of month.'

'Eh yu Joey com gen, Yoo not like 'im baastard. 'Al, about to take a bite out of his Banjo retorted.

'Ah. Piss of yer prat.'

'Yoo play futbal gens Kinta Indians tomollow nite?'

'Yer. What about it?'

'Yoo No blooody goood. Geet beet tu nutting.' Walking away Al replied.

'Ger-off, you still don't know wot yer bleedin' talking about.'

Joining him, took a bite out of the banjo. We had just sat down when Bill woke up, whether it was the smell of the Banjo's or the tea, glancing over towards us murmured.

'Yer pair of sods! Why didn't yer wake me up, I fancy a banana Banjo...stifling a huge yawn his hair in disarray, swung his legs off the bed...Aw, I don't know have to walk up there don't I? ' Al taunted.

'Git going yer lazy Git, he will be shut soon.'

'Who. Whiskers? He'd sell is mother in the middle of the night, scheming bastard.'

Tuesday morning, with a shove of the bed, Bill's voice woke me.

'Wakey Wakey 'ands off cocks on socks, 'ere's yer tea yer lazy git...Hoi Al! Git up yer lazy git it was your turn this morning.'

'Sod off, did it last night.'

'Yer a prat, always got an excuse not to get the tea, watch 'im Joey.'

Lifting the mossy net over my head, shivered in the morning chill moving my legs over the edge of the bed sat up and dragged the rumpled sheet around my shoulders, leaning over grabbed hold of the mug of tea, drinking the nectar it was sweet and refreshing to a parched mouth. Further up the basha, there was plenty of coughing going on but not much movement. Mick in a daze walked past holding his mug, croaked.

'Morning Joey.'

'Morning Mick.' Outside it was still dark, within two minutes Mick returned completely awake, sipping his tea asked.

'Is that right, you are playing football tonight Joey?'

'So Al says.' Al interrupted.

'That's right, I know the team he plays for back in London, and they are a reasonable side. If he plays for them then he ain't bad, but he ain't good, if yer see wot I mean. Anyway he's REME.'

'Well if you say so, what position? '

'Right wing.'

'Heh. That's Evies place.'

'I know that. I talked with Q about it. Joey's 'aving a trial that's all.' Surprised! Mick still sipping tea asked.

'What against Kinta Indians?' Al suggested.

'So! He'll be alright; you keep an eye on him.'

'Here Bill. Listen to him. How can I keep me eye on him, I'm Centre half have enough problem keeping an eye on Al.'

'Sod off Mick, go and drink yer tea.'

So ended the conversation. It was nearing seven and almost light outside. Getting up walking to the locker trod on a lighted dog end, yelled.

'Aw, soding 'ell put the bleeder's out?' Al laughed.

Full of anger slipped on flip-flops. (All the time whilst in the Basha, never wore flip-flops but did on occasions, suffer from the burnt feet until a year later when Al finally left.) Anyway, with ablutions done grabbing crocs quickly walked to the cookhouse, selected some food about to sit down and eat the relish. Bill enquired.

'Where yer bin? We've missed yer.'

'Went and ad a shower 'n shave, is that all right?' He replied.

'Yer don't do that until after brekkers. Ready for muster at eight.'

'Wot about the inspection then.'

'Wot inspection? Ear Al. Wot inspection he ask?' Al questioned.

'Yer going sick already?' Bill added.

'Short arms eh. Dirty git.' They having finished got up and disappeared back to the basha, not caring for the brekkers got up disposed of the burnt offering and returned to the basha, Al urged.

'Urry up Joey, musters at 0800 git yer bed and kit laid out and get up to the LAD.'

On the LAD parade ground, in line of order all Platoons were assembled. At precisely 0800 hrs, the CSM roared into life.

'PARADE...SHUNS. PARADE...STAND AT EASE. PARADE...SHUNS. PARADE...STAND AT EASE.' The CSM, with his pace stick pointed at some individual roared. SARGEANT CUMMINS! THAT MAN IN B PLATOON. TAKE HIS NAME HE'S IDLE ON PARADE'

'YES. SERGEANT MAJOR.' Then as the OC drifted onto the square, escorted by the Adjutant and another Officer, the CSM roared.

'PARADE,,,SHUNS.' With a quick salute of greetings and salutations. The CSM issued the order

'PARADE...OPEN ORDER...MARCH.' Crash bang wallop...RIGHT DRESS...shuffle shuffle... STAND STILL.' Feebly the O.C. asked.

'Company Sergeant Major. Any Sick Parade Today?'

'YES SIR. TWO WITH THE BLIGHT AND ONE WITH SO CALLED MALARIA.'

'Right Sergeant Major Proceed.'

The CSM, requested each Platoon in turn to report the count of heads 'A' Platoon 'B' platoon etc. etc. REME LAD. 'Q' bellowed out the number on parade. Having seen the shambles stood before him the OC stated. 'Carry on Sergeant Major.'

'YES SIR. Three bags full sir. PARADE...CLO..OSE ORDER MARCH...PLATOON SARGENTS. TAKE OVER.'

The OC disappeared as each Sgt. in accordance with regulations, took charge of their individual platoon. A lot of shouting went on Sergeant. Levine came alive and with all his five foot six bawled out.

'REME PLATOON STAND AT EASE. PLATOON ATTENSHU. RIOT TURN... QWIK MARCH LEF WEEOL FORWARD MARCH...We had gone about five paces down the square, when he shouted... PLATOON HALT. PLATOON TO YUR DUTIES...DISMISS.'

A sharp turn to the right a stamp of boots, muster parade was over. We peeled away, removed belts and beret ready for work. Totally amazed at all the bullshit. It must have taken all of six minutes. After all, we were on Active Service. Bill ordered.

'Joey get up to the battery shop, check the charged batteries and start up the Genny we have more batteries to go on charge.'

Wandering off across the square, many Lorries were leaving en-route to whereever they had to go. Walking alongside the Nissan Hut the pungent smell of sulphuric acid caught the nostrils, opening the door entered into its dominant smell. Having completed the check had to start Ginny. She was a right cow! Must have sweated off six pounds in weight whilst all the time thought, "Am I to spend the rest of my time, starting this sodding beast up"? When eventually she coughed into life, my right arm was aching and was lucky not to have broken a wrist with her kick back. I heard the sound of footsteps coming along the back way from the stores, then Bill called out.

'Joey where are yer? Chop Chop can't hide from me...Appearing behind me exclaimed...About bleedin' time yer got her going!'

'Sod off, she's fair wore me out. Need a rest.'

'No time for that. It's Naafi Break. Urry up or yer will be killed in the rush. Leave her. get yer arse around the front sharpish.'

Not hesitating, accepted his invitation left Genny chugging away on her own, followed him around to the front of the Nissan huts where a Little Chinaman, dressed in a pristine white shirt, trousers and white shoes with a white Tobie on his head, was serving goodies from his tricycle. A bike, an improvised long low aluminum sidecar with its lid fully open within its depts he kept all his wares. Approaching the so-called queue, those who had purchased some of his wares, were already seated in the shade of the Nissan huts eating and chatting away between themselves. Bill shouted out.

'Wot yer got t'day Wang, nothing special yer silly ole bastard?' With a huge gold-filled toothy smile, he replied.

'Miming masta Bill. Sama sama.'

'Why don't you put on a curry or summat special? Instead of same 'ole bleedin' things, Egg 'n bleedin' Tomato, Cheese 'n bleedin' Tomato bridge rolls. They have never changed, ever since I bin 'ear. Give us, two egg 'n tomatoes and a Fanta.' Thinking his tirade was directed at me, just to let me know there was no alternatives. A smiling Wang replied.

'Masta Bill. Lu pi noo. Baastar.' Whilst Gerry / Harry added words of encouragement.

'Bleedin' pay the sod g'on.' / 'Yer never pay anything yer tight fisted git. G'on pay the man.'

'Hoi you lot. Always pays me bills maybe late but always pays me bills.' Having taken his rolls and Fanta retreated to the limited shade of a Nissan hut. Ordered the same as Bill. Wang said.

'Sexty cents.'

'I can't pay! Next payday Okay.' Getting used to this pay racket business. Wang asked.

'Lu Lectian Sama Sama Bill?' Puzzled by his Chinese singsong muttered.

'Yer Wot's matter with that?'

'Bluudy Sama Sama. Nam Joey. 'Lu go wite n buk.' In his little book scribbled some figures down. Handed over two bridge rolls and a Fanta went to sit alongside Bill, unfortunately the shade had shifted somewhat and I sat down in the shade of the blazing sun. Wang having no more customers left pushing his tri-cycle amidst a motion of cheers, to which he put two fingers up in our direction.

The Naafi break lasted about fifteen minutes. Sgt. Levine returned to work, without hesitation we all followed. Beginning to understand the code of conduct and discipline shown by all. Naafi breaks were just a break, not to lounge around for hours on end there was work to be done and that was the purpose of our being out there. The rest of the morning I spent in the Battery shop tending to the charging of batteries, whilst outside along side the Battery hut, Bill and Al had water fights with two Fire Extinguishers from the Battery shop, until Bill charged in soaking wet.

'Knock off. Chop Chop. On the way down grab yer beret n' belt.' The normal lunchtime routine followed.

Mick, shaking my boot, rising from a deep sleep shook my head. Al thickly spoke.

'Joey! Knock off at four fifteen, get down to the stores and get yer football kit. Q's given the Okay. Bill's playing as well.'

That afternoon at four fifteen, As he and Al left Bill shouted.

'Joey! I'm off.'

Ahead of me Mick and Jock were just leaving. Collecting my beret and belt, was just about to leave the sheds when Sgt. Levine shouted out.

'Hoi Plant! Where you going?' Startled by the question answered.

'Playing football Sergeant. Q said it was alright.'

'Bloody. Hell! Won't get any jobs done, another bleedin' footballer. G'wan piss off.' Catching up with Mick and Jock, asked.

'How many of the LAD play in the matches?'

'Maybe seven, depends on where they are when he's here Den always plays, but as you know their up the Cameron's. It is not that the RASC don't have the players, they are not always available and I must add we are the best. You mark my words.' We arrived at the sports store. Evans greeted us.

'Urry up otherwise, I 'm going to be late fer Kick-off.' Evans handing over neatly stacked kits, they signing departed leaving me to be kitted out in a blue and white shirt numbered ten, white shorts and socks, shin guards and a pair of boots size six. Evie jibbed.

'There y'are, size six! You sure this is not a baby team you're in?' Entering the basha Al yelled.

'Where the bleedin' 'ell you been? You only had to draw kit, its a quarter to five. Bleedin' urry up Bus leaves in fifteen minutes.' Aware he was not in the mood to listen, took a gulp of tepid tea, off to the showers a quick sluice down, returning to the basha, Al, Bill, Mick and Jock were all sat togged up waiting. Ribald shouts urged me to get fooking kitted up. They departed yelling meet them at the car park near the guardhouse.

Waiting in the parking lot was a Lorry converted into a school bus. Amidst cheers or, jeers from all the team already seated climbed the small ladder, bench seats were on both sides and down the middle, noted four of the spectators were armed with rifles and Sten guns, thinking, "Are we playing this game in the Jungle"? Took the next spare seat on the end and with a bellow from Cpl. "Nobby" Clark. The driver, not caring about the ruts and dips, moved off over the uneven ground. Two spectators, holding a Dixie full of orange juice with lumps of ice (our half time refreshment) that was slopping all over the place. shouted. 'Daft bastard. Wots the matter with you slow down'. Not taking a bit of notice the driver, finally drove onto the road briefly stopping outside the guardhouse, reported where he was going and were on our way towards Ipoh Town, went right through town across a bridge with a river flowing beneath it, thinking, "That must be the river Ipoh". Onwards and outwards, presented different sights sounds and smells until the lorry slowed right down. Hogging the middle of the road in front was a long procession of Indians. The noise they were making was deafening, ringing bells beating gongs, the constant clash of symbols and sounds of Indian flutes. The driver had to crawl along behind them until they turned off the road, as we passed saw the form of a shrouded figure covered in garlands being carried by many mourners, all holding up the sides of the makeshift coffin or whatever, whilst in front and behind it the noisy orchestra played on. Simple but, very memorable and a different culture. Behind us, driving the jeep was Bill Beavis with 'Q' sat beside him they had caught us up.

Arriving late at the football field. Not in the jungle! The other team, Kinta Indians was already lined up in their positions. Alighting from the bus, leaving our four guards leaning out over the sides the referee shouted out.

'Other captain quickly over here.' Al sauntered over; winning the toss possibly out of spite chose the opposite end. Making the barefooted Indians change ends not a boot amongst them. At a quarter to six, we kicked off. The game was fast and furious; having never played against a team of barefooted players, they were very quick. Playing my usual hard game trying to impress the right people nevertheless, at halftime it was still a draw and I flaked out on the grass. Jock came over and advised.

'Hey Joey, slow doon ye dayin okay, hae a drink.' Gratefully swallowed a pint in one gulp. As we lined up for the second half. Al said.

'Joey. You watch that left back, he's a bit of a bastard.' As the game progressed, was wary about kicking shit out of their shins need not have bothered; they were as hard as nails, moreover, when a corner was awarded felt the pain handed out by their left back. Evans crossed over the ball, the left back and I jumped for it on the way down he landed right on my ankle. "Bleedin' 'ell he's broken it". Laying in agony, received sympathy from Al, who shouted.

'I told yer to watch im.' 'Q' advanced with the magic sponge, administered the medicine all he said was.

'G-g-get s-s-stuck i-in P-Plant.'

Limping about wore off the pain. Midway through the second half, Mick passed the ball to me controlling it, passed it ahead of Al who banged the ball past their keeper. One nil, the final whistle was blown we won. Trying to impress. I'd run my arse ragged, having

243

not played a game for nine months, walked off the field knackered with wet shorts and shirt clinging to my body, my legs feeling like solid pieces of lead wearily climbed aboard the bus and slumped down. Someone passed a ladle of orange juice, with deep gulps drank, that evaporated before it hit my stomach followed very quickly by another. Must have been totally dehydrated. With everyone on board, we were off on the return journey. Wearing the soaking wet strip, the cold draught from the speeding bus began to freeze me up; it was almost dark when we arrived back at camp. Stumbling down the steps staggered back to the basha, flopped down on the bed exhausted.

Wednesday morning. Bill shouting.

'Hoi you. Wakey wakey, morning parade soon, 'ere's yer tea.'

Coming too, still in football kit including my boots, my head was at the foot of the bed and an indescribable taste was in my mouth, had a headache and ached all over. Someone had draped the mossy net over me. Al inquired.

'Yer alright Joey?'

'Aw, 'ell wot time is it? Need some food.' He mimicked.

"Wot time is it"? He's all right! Last night yer crashed out and missed supper. Gerry put yer ter bed and it's time for muster. Get showered yer dirty git.'

I was still none the wiser about what happened the previous night, struggling to get my mossy off, swung my legs off the bed focused on the mug of tea with both hands lunged at it, swallowing some of its contents to revive myself out of a dark sleep of twelve hours. Stripping off left it in a heap on the floor. The shower was cold and breathtaking, having finished, ate whatever was on offer in the cookhouse. That single game of football was one hell of an experience. Fortunately, was picked to play in all other matches during my time in Three Company.

That Wednesday "A" Platoon. Left the camp in convoy enroute somewhere down South, leaving their two bashers vacant. "B & C" Platoons were fully occupied carrying out more transporting duties. That evening, returned to Li's tailor emporium who handed over my tailored OG's.

'Joey! Lookee, he produced a beige coloured lightweight cloth. Fingering it he said. Gud matewial. Fo lu I mik vite shilt n' lowlers civys. Okay.' Liking the colour asked

'How much?'

'Shilt. Tu Dolla! Lowlers. Fiv dolla !'

'Yeaaah. Okay when ready? '

'Lu wan wik-en? Leddy flidiy Okay.'

'Okay. pay later?' Need not have bothered saying that he was busy writing my latest order in his slate book.

Later that evening, Beasley came down and sat on the end of the bed to inform me.

'Plant. Tomorrow morning. You've been picked for Kampong guard. You will be called at o' fourthirty hours hours, Get dressed in long trousers, jacket, boots, puttees, webbing ammo pouches, and small pack containing, mess tins, eating irons, mug, water bottle. Get a breakfast in the cookhouse, and then proceed to the armory draw weapons and ammo.' He, having decided he did not like me, started throwing more shit in my direction.

'Eh! C'mon mate, I've just arrived the other day, wot about the other geezers?'

'I'm not yer mate! Address me as Lance Corporal. Besides they've done their turn many times. Just waiting for a replacement. That's you Plant. Now it's your chance to make glory.'

'Nah yer got the wrong fella. Al scored not me.'

'Well that's bye the bye. You're not playing football. Your names on the Guard Commander's Kampong list. When the guard shakes you. You will be up and ready bright an early.' With a smile on his face returned up his end of the basha.

'Ere Bill wot the bleedin' 'ell is a Kampong Guard?'

'Aw soddin' 'ell mate. They are unmentionable eh Al?' Thinking, "Here we go another wind up between the two of them". Al kindly responded .

'I eared wot Beasley was saying, go and tell 'im to stuff 'imself.' Carried on reading.

'Bill! Wot is a Kampong?'

'Dyer know wot a stalag camp in Germany was during the war? They were to keep POW's in, well out 'ere, it's very similar. Not to keep em in but, to keep the commie bastards out.'

'Where are these Kampongs then?'

'There located all over the place, normally alongside a roadway easy to get to.'

'How many yer done then?'

'Bleedin' hundreds.' Al retorted.

'Dineen. Yer a lying git.' When was the last one yer did?' Al now full of interest, he was eager to argue with anyone about anything.

'That's not the point. Joey asked how many I had done and truthfully answered his question.'

'Don't give me that bullshit Dineen; the last time you did one was months ago.' Bill retorted.

'Yer well I'm excused ain't I. I'm going home soon.'

'Wots this bleedin' hundreds then? If there's sixteen in the basha? That means yer git one every two to three days. How long yer been out ere?'

'Too sodding long, sight longer than you yer prat.'

'Ger'off. Yer done about ten at most you're a lying git Dineen.' In a shower of red-hot ash another dog-end hit the post, he said.

'Ere Joey. You don't' smoke der yer?'

'No. You've already asked me.' Al offered.

'Right, I'll ave yer free issue then.' Bill was ready for an argument.

'Joey. Don't take that, charge him for em.'

'How much for fifty free issue then?'

'50 cents that's go-ing rate.'

'Nah sod off yer tight bleeder...I Yelled out...Anyone want my free issue?' From the depths of the basha, only one response. 'Seventy-five cents.' Thinking,"That ain't much". Al quickly intervened.

'I'll give yer a dollar no more.'

'Done.' Thinking, "That will pay for Pops charge".

'Hoi. Bill yer still haven't told me wot goes on at these Kampongs?'

CHAPTER EIGHTEEN
KAMPONGS MORE BLEEDIN' GUARDS.

'Aw bleedin' 'ell! Wot do you want to know about it for? It all happened way back in 1950 or there abouts. All I know is, after Gurney was killed up Frasers Hill the guy that took over was General Briggs. It was his idea to stop the CT's intimidating and demanding money, food and recruiting new members from the Chinese squatters, living close to the jungle and move them into these Kampongs. They were built like cages, surrounded by barbed wire fencing with one gateway, they had their own water supply, houses, schools and other bleedin' things. like I said small POW camps. The squatters were allowed to grow vegetables and keep chickens, pigs so they were self-sufficient. They even had their own Police station manned by the Malay Home Guard; their duty was to guard the gates, letting only the workers in and out. At that time Three Company were based in KL and were involved with transporting all the squatters, with all their bit's and bobs, cats, rats, pigs, chickens. You'll see wot I mean tomorrow?'

On the evening news, the announcer stated the following report.

A statement was released today in Kuala Lumpur. Tengu Abdul Rahman had received a communiqué from the leader of the Communist Terrorist Chin Peng. The letter stated. He was willing to send an emissary, to negotiate with a Delegation of the Malaya Government on the restoration of peace in Malaya. The letters received were postdated Saturday Twenty-fourth September and posted in Kilian Intan a village a few miles inside the Malay Thailand border.

Listening to this Al said.

'Ere Joey. Ole Ching Peng heard they were sending you out to sort em out.' To which Bill retorted.

'Nah. The state he arrived in, would stink 'im out.' Caused howls of laughter.

'Aw piss off the pair of yer. Is that the normal news on the radio?' Bill responded.

'Yup. Possibly an everyday occurrence just listen to wots said, gives yer an update of wots going on in Malaya, not much about England and the rest of the world.'

Frightening the shit out of me, one of the guards shaking my shoulder, quietly murmured.

'Hoi.! Get yerself up its four thirty.' Stirring myself sat up lifting the enclosing mossy net, got up to switch on the light resulted in grunts and groans from the sleeping occupants, dreaming about Blighty and what they were missing with girl friends. Tough! Having completed ablutions, eaten at the cookhouse with bed and kit laid up, grabbed my small pack switched off the light and set off for the armory. The bleary-eyed Armourer, checked his list handed over a Sten gun, a pouch carrying sten magazines, yawning said. 'Here y'ar signs here.' Armed to the teeth, made my way around to the guardroom where the guard Sgt. logged me as present for duty.

'Go outside and wait alongside the Pig in the parking lot.' In the darkness, the glow of a few lighted cigarettes indicated where this Pig was, one of the smokers spoke.

'How do mate?' Thinking, "What a statement to make at this ungodly hour. How Do"? Honestly replied.

'Well. No bleedin' better for seeing you.' A dismal response.

'Well it all happens to us some time.'

'Right bleedin' time to get out of bed. You done this before?'

'No mate. First time, got clobbered being the newest arrival.'

'Same as me. Always get copped for soddin' guards.'

The arrival of a Sgt. and duty driver stopped any further conversation. The Sgt. called out. 'All. Happy to be up?' Chorus ...'No Sergeant. '

'Good! When I call out your name answer Yes. Drivers...Norton...'Yes.'...Smith...'Yes.'... In addition. Craftsman Plant. REME.'...'Yes.'

'All present and correct. All drawn weapons? ... Chorus. 'Yes. Sergeant.'... All got safety catches on? Don't want any mishaps do we lads?' .... Chorus. 'No. Sergeant.'

'All got eating utensils mess tins and mugs?'.... Chorus. 'Yes. Sergeant.'...Right. Clip on a Magazine. Safety catches on.' In the dark, a lot of fumbling and clicking went on.

'Those who have not been on these parties before be warned. If we come under attack or ambush, use the slide ports on either side of the Pig to let off your rounds. At all times. Keep your safety catches on, understood?' Chorus...'Yes Sergeant.'

'Now get in and let's get going.'

A small bulb at the far end illuminated the interior of the Pig. Behind us, the rear door was clanged shut. It took a little while to adjust to the dim light inside. The few boxes on the floor acted as seats. The engine stuttered into life and the Pig rolled forward, bumping its way out of the parking lot stopped, some talking was heard. I asked a silly question.

'Er. Can anyone tell me, why we are in a Pig?' From within the dimness a gruff voice replied.

'It's a fooking armoured coffin, that's what it is!'

As the Pig began its journey, it was quite claustrophobic in the back, with nothing to see even if you stood up and peered out of the tiny slits, you could see sod all. All being new to this exciting experience, little or nothing was said. We must have traveled for an hour before the Pig stopped; more words were spoken, moving forward it stopped again. As the rear doors were opened, a blaze of light illuminated a couple of armed Malay Policemen closing two barbed wire gates, constructed out of poles lashed together to make a square frame criss crossed with barbed wire. As the Policeemn began pad-locking it, the Sgt. appearing ordered.

'C'mon get your arses out. You two take hold of those compo boxes, take them into the guardhouse.' I recognised one of the Drivers, as the Ginger haired bloke on the rifle shoot, leaving them to it got down into the pool of light from floodlights high up on poles.

'You! Close the rear doors after them.' The doors closed with a solid thud, the Pig revving up moved away, reversing around returning approached the gates, kindly reopened by the Police; it went through them on its return journey the noise of its engine fading into the blackness. The gates were locked and the silence of a Malay night came back to life. Noisy croaking frog's, the endless noise of clicking, grinding, whirring wings, plus any other noise those insects could muster up. The Sgt. ushered us into the guardhouse a small basha. In one corner supported on short poles was a wooden platform, where four sleeping Policemen were laid snoring their bleedin' heads off. Furniture: a small table and one chair. Standing beside the doorway, the Sgt. ordered.

'You two put the ration boxes down beside the table along with your small packs. Remove your magazines, then listen up? During the hours of daylight between 0600 am and 1800pm. We will take over guard duty from the Malay Police. Stags will be two hours on, four off. During your stag mount, before you let anyone in or out. You will check and search everything, boxes, bags, bike pumps, frames, bulky trouser pockets, funny hats etc. etc. Anything that is liable to contain food, money, hand grenades, small arms. Any questions so far?' No response....Right Plant! You are doing first stag, 0600 until 0800. Smith. 0800 until 1000, and Norton, 1000 until 1200. Plant: 1200 until 1400, Smith: 1400 until 1600. Final stag you Norton. Any questions?' Smith murmured.

'Sergeant. How are we going to blooody understand what they are saying?'

'Good point Smith. Do not concern yourselves; you won't be on your own. A Malay Soldier will be with you. He will act as an interpreter, they will be arriving soon. Any more Questions?' I asked.

'Yes Sergeant. What about food?'

'Aah food! Those boxes Smith and Norton kindly brought in, contain compo rations for the day. We will cook our meals here. Anyone good at cooking? No? Right Plant! Since you asked the question and will be fully rested by 1100 hours, you are duty cook.'

'Me Sergeant?' Musing. "Sod my luck. The only thing I have cooked is some eggs and bacon at home and then remembered when Derek and I were on a camping holiday on the Isle of Wight. Successfully blew up the cooking stove". What an hilarious week that was. By the Friday, along with his mates we had run out of money and seven of us slept in a two-man Bivouac tent".

A bit of commotion outside, had the three of us looking out the window. The arrival of another Pig. My watch hands pointed to a quarter to six. Once inside. A Malay Sgt. opened up the steel doors, shouted something like. "Bagoose" Out jumped three heavily armed Malay Soldiers. All grinning they entered, one carrying beside his rifle a Bren gun. They chorused...'Hi Johnnie.' Checking their weapons rattled the bolts to ensure they were in working order. It all looked quite serious to me? Their arrival stirred up the sleeping bodies on the wooden bed. With stifled yawns stretching and farting in unison, amidst the smell in the air was a hint of tea, unbeknown to us the Malay Police had been brewing up; one came around with a big steel bucket. ' Te Jonnie Te.'

'Bleedin' right mate.' Fishing out my tin mug, he filled it up. 'Ta Mate.' The sickly sweet tea was too hot to drink, only sip. The Sgt. ordered.

'Plant! First stag Chop Chop.'

'Ain't finished me tea yet Sergeant.'

'Yes. You bloody well have. Pick up your sten load the magazine and get out on guard.' Grumbling about being thirsty put down the tea. Took hold of the Sten, slipped the magazine into the barrel safety catch on. Following my other sidekick, a Malay soldier. Went out towards the Gate, walking alongside the Sgt. he said.

'Plant. Do what the Malay does. It's not hard to follow. The gates are normally opened at 0700 hrs, for the early morning rush of workers. Just keep your eyes trained on the roadway and the jungle opposite the gates. Anything suspicious, indicate to the Malay. And for Christ sake do not panic.'

There was no formal guard mounting ceremony; we just relieved the two Malay Policemen with a curt nod. 'Okay Jonnie.' That was it. In a nonchalant manner with his Sten gun resting on his shoulder, the Sgt. stood beside me looking up and down the road.

'You a cockney Plant?'

'Yes Sergeant.' At a time like this? What's he asking me that for?

'What part?'

'Vauxhall South London Sergeant.' Thinking, "Right then the best place on earth".

'That's near the Oval isn't it?'

'Yes Sergeant. Rather be there than in this bleedin' ole.' He assured me.

'It isn't all that bad. Once you get used to the routine out here.' Warming to his interest, asked.

'How long you been out here then Sergeant?'

'Well I originally came out in late 49. Three Company was based down in KL. Then, we were moved up here. That is when I decided to stay out here for another Python. However, that time is up and I've had enough. So I'm going home soon. Nevertheless, you get on with your duty. I've got tea to drink.' Thinking "That's bloody good. The Sod never gave me the chance to drink mine".

I was on one side of the gateway with the Malay soldier opposite, he nodded at me.

'Okay. Jonnie.'

'Yeah Okay. You alright?"

'Yu nu hah?'

"Yeah first time.'

'Jonnie! Yu lik plinty Gig Gig?'

'Yeah! Plenty Gig Gig?' Thinking, "What the Bleedin' "ell does he mean"?

'Heh. Jonnie. Yu lik?' Grinning, he made a gesture with his fist moving his arm like a piston, laughed immediately thought. "Oh shit. What he means is f......g". mumbled. 'Nah bad for your eyes.' Nevertheless, he kept on laughing pointing at me and making the gesture. That was my first introduction of having a conversation with a Malay. A conversation was not, going to repeat back in the basha to be ridiculed further by those two bastards. However, now understood what Gig Gig meant.

It was still dark and we were stuck in this large pool of light, easy targets for any bandit's that would like to take a pot shot at us or, attempt to raid the Kampong. At least there was reinforcements back up of the Malay Policemen. Nervously looked across the roadway at a black void. There was no movement in either direction of the roadway that disappeared into darkness. The first signs of movement came from behind us. Out of the gloom, moving from side to side two cycle headlamps came into the light too reveal the riders as a couple of Chinese in singlets, long black trousers wearing flip-flops. The Malay Guard shouted something, possibly "stop" They halted a few feet away. The Malay soldier spoke... 'Jonnie yu sarch.'...Unsure of what to look for approached them, no bicycle pumps, no boxes but under both saddles were small bundles of cloth and two vicious looking hooked knives. Very aware of the strong smell that hung about their persons, not sweat but a sweet rubbery smell. Pointing at the knives demanded... 'Wots this?' Making a motion with my hand to remove them, the Malay soldier shouted...'No Johnnie No.'... 'They are knives. Cannot have them. Sergeant! These two are trying to get out with knives of some sort.'

The Sgt. appeared in the doorway, looking over.

'No Plant. They are their tools, they are okay Let em out. Their Rubber Tappers off to start their day's work.' Shaking his head went back in.

Unlocking the padlock, the Malay soldier pulled open his side of the gate. None the wiser waved them on, as they passed by laughing and jabbering away in Chinese. Nodding their heads still laughing and chatting no doubt, about the stupid bastard English soldier they peddled away into the darkness. Still unsure of what we were supposed to search for, turned and was startled by the face of a very young Chinese girl who had silently arrived during my recent encounter? Standing astride her bike with one foot still on the pedal dressed in the normal fashion, black pyjamas. Approaching her noticed on the back carrier, one of those weird

Kampong Gates

looking knives and secured by some vines a small package wrapped in a chequered cloth, she too had that strange smell about her as she smiled I pointing to it. 'Open it!' She said something in Chinese, lifting her foot off the pedal leant her slight body against the bike frame, untying the vines opened up one flap of the cloth revealed cooked rice, shouted.

'Sergeant! Found food here.' Outcome the Sgt. striding up looked.

'Silly bugger. That is her food for the day. She's a Rubber Tapper, let her go.'

'Well you did say food.'

'Food! Yes, fooking dried rice and stuff like that, not small fooking cooked dinners. You will find they will try to smuggle it out in small dried quantities hidden in their bike

pumps or, anywhere else you would not think looking suspicious. So keep looking.'
"Thinking, about the young Chinese girl and where she could hide it".

'Er Sergeant. Wot about body searches?

'Plant. Keep your hands to yerself and your mind on the job.'

'Well Sergeant. Wots that pong they stink of?'

'Get use to it, it is the smell of latex the sap of the rubber trees.'

With a second embarrassing episode over, carried on looking with just an eye-search for anything that looked suspicious. The rest of the Tappers all smelling the same, were allowed out to go about their daily work. In the background the sound of a cockerel pronouncing it time to get up disturbing the morning stillness, as the sun rose above the jungle treetops, the floodlights went out with a ping. The morning commuter escape parties, continued for some time and with the "search and let go sequence" ongoing until about 0745 when it appeared. All inmates were out and about their work; it was soon time for my stag duty to finish. Much relieved, returned to the guardhouse. Removing the magazine from the sten, with another four hours to wait settled down to drink the brew of tea Newton handed me. The morning was extremely boring, there was absolutely nothing to do except sit at the table or lay on this big wooden bed recently vacated by the Police. The Malay soldiers just sat on their haunches cradling their weapons. The temperature inside the basha was rapidly increasing, hot and sweaty the tight puttees around my ankles were making my feet feel like balloons. At least I could look forward to being the duty cook. Says who? Staring out of the open window space watched Smith pacing up and down. Nothing seemed to be going on, a couple of Chinese trucks went whizzing by and an occasional Rubber Tapper rode by on his bicycle. The crickets kept up their endless scratching, whilst the croaking frogs had given up maybe they wanted some throat sweets. Sod 'em! Noisy bleeders. 'What you thinking about Plant? The Sgt. Startled me with his question.

'Er nothing Sergeant. Just frogs.'

'Noisy buggers ain't they?' The Sergeant seemed quite friendly and ventured to ask.

'Sergeant. Wot's the story behind these Kampongs? Understand there's 'hundreds of em, is that true?'

'Your right there, in June nineteen-fifty, as soon as they had these purpose built so called New Villages. The squatters had to be relocated lock, stock and barrel, even their livestock, they did not like that and hundreds objected but the Infantry just made 'em do it. At that time apart from a detachment up the Cameron's, three company was in KL and it was our job to collect all squatters from the jungle fringes, pile them into wagons and transport them. We spent more time doing that than convoy work.'

'Blimey did they move em all in one go? There must have been hundreds of em to be moved?'

'No—oo! It was Gurneys plan to resettle the squatters to stop them supporting the CT's gangs, located somewhere in the Ulu, they used to intimidate and force the squatters to provide them with money and food. That is when General Briggs arrived in nineteen-fifty. Ole' Brigg's idea was to build these self-supporting villages. Over the following two years, Kampongs were built all over the place, from Jahore Bahru up as far as the Siam border. All had platoons of the Police to protect them just like this one here. They seem to be working. Although it is an extra duty to carry out during the daytime, normally the Infantry do these guards. This one is called Rimba Panjang; Anyway, I could not care a shit. I'm going home. C'mon Norton it is your stag duty. Time to relieve Smith.' Norton looked like he was just about to fall asleep, but getting the message got up. With slight interest, watched the formalities take place there wasn't any. Smith hurriedly returned to the basha, moaning about the heat.

'Blooody glad, that's orr. Blooody hot standing out there. Any tea about?'

'Yep if yer like to make some.'

'Blooody 'ell mate. Your duty cook not me.'

'Well! It's easy to make, just get some water in yer mess tin, light the white block on that little cooker, heat the water put tea in and dried milk that's all.' The Sgt. entering ordered.

'Plant. You're the cook. Brew up.' Doing the necessary, discovered Ginger Smith came from Leeds; he played football and wanted to play. A mutual friendship developed between us, suggested would speak with Al to see if Ginger could be fitted in with a game. Outside the sun beat down relentlessly, whilst inside we sweated our lives away with the heat from the cooker, the temperature was unbearable; our OG's looked like sweat rags, the Sgt. broke up our conversation by suggesting.

'Plant. It's about time you started cooking. Open up the compo boxes, then you can eat before you go back on stag.'

Faced with the task of cooking up a meal. removed tins from the open compo box marked, Sausages, Bacon, Beans, Irish stew. Packets of hard tack biscuit's, dried fruit and sheets of toilet paper, sachets of curry powder, salt, pepper, Bourneville chocolate, two tiny metal objects.

'Ear Smithy! Make yerself useful, open up one of the tins of sausages and beans and pour em into one of my mess tins.'

'What! Okay got nowt else to do. Where's opener?'

'Think it's one of those little metal things.'

'What the hell do you do with this? Holding it next to the tin...can't open it with this blooody thing.' The Sgt. noticing our ignorance, came over picking up the piece of metal, demonstrated how to use it.

'Smith! See that little hinged hook open it, put it over the rim of the can, puncture the lid then move it round the can with a sawing action. Quite simple. Who likes curry?' I responded.

'I do.'

'Open up the Irish stew and throw the curry powder in with it. Use my mess tins hurry up I'm hungry.' Thinking. "What a Bleedin' novel suggestion! A choice of meals. Bacon, bangers and beans or. Curry". Smithy muttered.

'Don't like curry.' The Sgt. interrupted.

'Don't like curry! After a while out here you will be eating curry and like it. Makes you sweat and puts' airs on your chest, it makes yer randy you wait and see.' Smithy responded.

'Doubt it. Blooody sweating like a blooody pig noo and don't need anything to make me randy.' Interrupting the pair of them said.

'That's all right, I'm bleedin' duty cook. Can do curry separate just mix your beans in with the bacon and bangers. I will cook em all together. Open the cans up empty them into the mess tins.' Smithy emptied the beans into a couple of mess tin. Whilst he did that I opened the other box took out the other metal stove, set it up ready for the curry. Lighting the naphtha blocks their heat increased the temperature of the already hot interior, making us sweat more buckets. When the meal was cooked it was shared out leaving sufficient for Norton. We ate our fill the Sgt. smacking his lips in the direction of Smithy who was not impressed. Another lesson learnt. "Cooking".

Armed with the Sten relieved Norton. whilst the Malay soldier sucking his teeth watched the jungle fringes opposite, waiting for some CT to charge out turning to watch our change over asked me.

'Yu Jonnie nu?' Lying replied.

'No been out her bleedin' years.' End of conversation and the end of his stag, out came their Sgt. accompanied by the soldier on stag with me earlier, he grinned.

'Hey Jonnie yu Gig Gig?'

'Naw, get with it mate.' Fanning his hand in front of his face, he replied.

'Heh Jonnie hot hot?'

'Yer bleedin' hot. Yer can say that again.'

The mid-day sun beat down out of a cloudless sky, stood there my feet felt like large balloons, the jacket and trousers sticking to my sweaty skin were drying on me this was no picnic. A lone Chinese truck raced by that was the transport situation. To break up the monotony from somewhere inside the Kampong a little Chinese fellow came waddling towards us, suspended across his shoulders was a yoke hung from either end were two square silver-coloured kerosene cans covered by some green leaves. By the masses of creases on his mahogany coloured face, he was ancient. Picking up one of the long rods by the gate, having been informed to use when making holes in sacks to see what poured out. Rice! Stopping the Chinese gentleman, much to the disapproval of the Malay soldier who called out...'No Jonnie No Tada Bagoose.' Or summat like that.

He fanned his hand in front of his nose, thinking he was saying it was hot; nevertheless, I carried on with my search. Moving one of the leaves revealed some green liquid should never have done that! The bleedin' smell that wafted out took my breath away, only then understood what the Malay was explaining. This Chinese gentleman was the shit Wallah and always-on merit, without being searched allowed to pass through. Nobody had told me! We both scattered away from the lingering smell letting the Chinese man through' Crossing the road he disappeared into the jungle soon to return with clean tins, both swinging freely on the end of his yoke. Passing me by he gave me a toothless smile with a happy thought. that he had fooled some young English Bastard. By the time Ginger relieved me was dying for a piss, scurried back into the basha.

'Sarge! Where is the toilets?'

'Little hut around side of basha.' Found this little hut, well it was more like a sentry box with a deep hole in the ground. "The toilet". Desperate, quickly started pee-ing down this hole the noise coming up was indescribable, like a thousand flies whirring around amongst the shit down the bottom, standing well back aimed at the hole. Quickly retreated, complained to the Sgt. who just laughed 'Get on with it.'

For the rest of the afternoon lying on the wooden bed, listened to the grunting of pigs and the shrill laughter of children playing somewhere in the Kampong, I was sweating and listless on several occasions dozed off. Just before 1800 hrs, the Pig arrived at the gate in the light of day was able to have a good look at it. It was a converted three tonner covered in armour plate, the front was shaped like a pig's snout, and several slits were in the sides and front. It did indeed look like a pig. Clearing up, left the remnants of our compo rations for the Malay Policemen, who arrived to take over for their night-time guard. Our duty finished and the first of another three, each time with different Sgt's, the first one never saw again.

Armoured Personnel Carrier. 'PIG'

The inside of the Pig was like an oven. After about an hour arrived back in camp, it was dark. Handing in our weapons and ammo straight down to the cookhouse to receive a breakfast meal of bangers, bacon, beans, as an extra, a couple of fried eggs, well rubber eggs. Returning to the basha Ignored the ribald comments from, Al and Bill. 'How many commies did you lot shoot?' Concentrated on removing the puttee bound ankles, the rush of blood made me feel giddy. Spending time in the shower paddled my feet back to their normal size, shaved ready for next mornings muster.

Being on Kampong duty missed the Thursday Pay parade. After Muster, Sgt. Levine told me to report to Captain Cole to collect my pay. In his office presented myself, saluting called out.

'429 Craftsman Plant. Reporting for my pay. Sir.' Captain Cole questioned.

'Where were you yesterday? You missed pay parade?'

'Kampong guard duty Sir. All day Sir.

'Um that was a bit quick. Q what is going on? We running out of bodies?'

'N-n-no S-sir j-just the w-w-way L-Lance C-Corporal B-b-Beasley arranges the r-r-roster.'

'Oh well! How did you find it son?'

'Boring Sir. Not much to do out there Sir.'

'Well. Now you know what it's all about, better give you some pay then.'

'Yes Sir. Please Sir.' Eager to be solvent and pay back all the slate money I owed Li, Wing, Wang, Wong and Whiskers plus Al.

'Q. Cash box please.' Q. Taking out a cash box from a drawer, passed it to Capt Cole who with a key unlocking the box took out a wad of money, expertly thumbed through the notes separating a few passed them over.

'There you are Plant. One weeks pay that includes trade and active service pay.' Check it, should be fifty dollars in total.

Counting. Ten, five red coloured Malay dollars. 'Pay and playbook correct Sir.'

'Right return back to the workshops. Oh, do you have your OG's jacket and shorts dobied for OC's parade tomorrow?' Truthfully replied.

'No Sir. Nobody said anything to me Sir.'

'Well report to Sgt. Levine, tell him you need to get your OG's dobied for tomorrow. That is all dismiss.' Q. asked.

'P.-p-Plant how's you're a.a.ankle?'

'Ankle! Oh. It's alright now Sir. Was a bit sore but it's fine.' Capt Cole asked.

'What's all this then, Plant?' Then explained about the football incident.

'Um in the wars already are you. Do not be carried away with all this active service pay now. Spend it wisely.'

'Yes sir.' Uncertain of what he meant. Flush with money, how much? Would ask Bill. On my way put the wad of dollars in the back pocket of my shorts, reported to Sgt. Levine...'Capt Cole told me to inform you. Got to have my OG's dobied for tomorrows parade.'

'Yes! Get your other pair of shorts and jacket; take them to the laundry basha next to the tailors. Tell Chong, you want them dobied, must be back today for OC's tomorrow. Tell him Sgt Levine sent you. Then report back to me.'

Returning to the basha, collected my Dobie and headed for Chong's. Outside his basha, sat on her haunches was a Chinese girl doing washing. I enquired. 'Chong?'

'Basha.' In their basha the atmosphere was like a Turkish bath, on a long table were several stacks of O.G's; with Chinese girls in the process of ironing. A Chinaman, most likely Chong was leaning over a cauldron stirring boiling water. Hearing me enters, Chong shouted. 'Wah?'

'Sergeant Levine sent me. OG has to have em dobied by tonight, for OC's tomorrow.'

'Yu Joey. Nu LEME. Wallah?'

'Yer wot about it?'

'Yu staat chit?' Not surprised, was getting use to this. "You don't pay. You put it on slate lark".

'Yes if you like.'

'All Dobie finnis, yu pay Okay?'

'Yer Okay. Done tonight?'

'Okay Joey...entered some Chinese scribble in a book...Okay finnis tonigh bling to LEME basha. Okay.'

'Yer. Okay.' Everything was Okay, so Okayed out of his basha wondering how he knew my name? Returned to the workshops.

Sgt. Levine called out.

'Joey in bay five, the tail light of the QL needs fixing, get on with it. If you want any help see Bill he is working on the scout car.' Full of importance, picked up the workbox and was about to leave the cage, when Levine asked.

'You taken your Paludrine tablet yet?'

'Er no. What's that?'

'You taken any since you arrived.'

'No. Don't know anything about them? Well Dineen did mention sommat but, what are they?'

'Anti Malaria tablets to be taken one a day. If you catch Malaria and your blood sample contains no evidence of the drug, you will be on a fizzer. Here you are take one, you can get them from this jar, make sure you take one every day. Get some tap water to swill it down.'

He handed over a small white tablet, dropping it into the palm of my out stretched hand. Looking at this tiny white pill thought, "A pill a day keeps the mossies away". Leaving the toolbox on the ground, went to the tap turning it on popped the tablet into mouth and took a swig of warm water swallowed. Christ the soddin' taste was foul; the tablet was still in my mouth, guzzled at the stream of water swallowing until the tablet had disappeared into the depths of my gullet. But what a bleedin' vile taste; furthermore, from that moment on, had to take one of these sodin' things every day shivered at the mere and unpleasant thought of it. Retrieving the toolbox went to bay five to start work on my first solo assignment. A faulty taillight, clambered up into the cab, behind the steering wheel was the instrument panel. Expecting to see a switch marked taillights, there was none. This panel was different to the one we had trained on, there were a few switches and knobs, a speedometer, an amp charging dial, two small red and yellow-coloured bulbs, recognising both, as red: charging, yellow: oil warning. On the large black switch, noticed capital letters H, S, T. Head, Side and Tail, turning the switch to the T jumping down from the cab, at the rear all lights were on, back in the cab switched off There appeared to be no problem. Decided to get Bill to check it, climbing up the side of the Scout Car peering down through the top opening, saw the top half of him under the dashboard. 'Heh Bill got a minute.'

Bill, Lawson, & Me.

'Wot's up Joey?'

'Levine has given me a job on a QL. Tail lights not working. But they are, can't see any problem.'

'Okay Dokey just a minute. Right got that out...Grinning he emerged covered in sweat...Dun arf sweat in these bleedin' things. C'mon which QL is it?'

'That one, bay five.'

'Switch on the rear lights and I'll watch...Yep they're working. Try the brake lights, depress the brake pedal.' Sorting out the brake pedal depressed it, no response from Bill. Urry Up he called. Depressed the other pedal. Yep they're working nothing wrong with them. Coming along side of the cab. Must have got it wrong, no problem with them. Go and check with Stan.'

Having only been given the job fifteen minutes before, having checked and double-checked with Bill with apprehension approached the cage, where Q was talking to Levine thinking. "Christ this is going to be difficult". Q looked at me, Sgt. Levine asked. 'Yes Plant.'

'Nothing wrong with taillights. Sergeant. I've checked them and so has Dineen, including the brake lights.'

'Well the driver has said one is not working. Let's check his sheet...Flipping through sheets of papers attached to a clipboard, hesitated...No, written here, is taillight.' Handing the board to Q, who read and nodded his head in agreement.

'W-w-who is the d-d -driver. '

'Meluish. B. Platoon.'

'R-r-right P-P-Plant go along to "B" P-p-platoon and a-ask for M-m-Meluish to report here now. I-it's that first Nissan hut p-p-past the e-e-end bay.' Headed in the direction of the first Nissan hut, where a couple of blokes were standing outside. Enquired.

'Anybody called Meluish here.'

'Ask the Corporal inside.' Sat at a desk recognised him as Nobby Clark, one of the players in the team.

'Hi Joey what der yer want?'

'Driver Meluish. Q, wants to see him.'...

'Got over yer exhaustion, you were running around like a maniac. Not bad though! MUSCLES...Get out here on the double somebody here to see you. C'mon stop skiving.' From within the inner sanctum, emerged a weedy looking character brown as a berry not an ounce of fat on him with his sinewy muscles very pronounced.

'Wot der want?' he gawped.

'Q, Threadgold, wants you now, its about yer wagon.'

'Well double off then' ...Nobby uttered ...must be important if Q, wants you.'

On the way back to the cage, he did not say anything thinking, "Wot a sad sack he is". Approaching the cage Q, turning round called out.

'D-d-Driver, Y-y-your w-w worksheet says "taillight not w-w-working" whets wrong with it? We have checked it and it is w-working perfectly w-well?'

'No Q. Not taillight. Its convoy light that ain't working.' Q took hold of the scribble board, flicked through the sheets stopped. Presenting the board to Meluish. 'This is y-y-yours isn't it?'

'Yes Q. It's mine but.'

'You b-b-bloody idiot, wasting our time I-in f-future write w-what is w-wrong with the d-damn thing not w-what you think. G-go and report to Corporal C-Clark tell him your p-p-problem. P-p-Plant go and check the c-convoy light. B-b-bloody RASC. D-d-drivers don't know t-their arse f-f-from their e-e -elbow.'

That was the end of the matter but not for me. Where the bleedin' 'ell was the convoy light? Needing assistance, told Bill what had gone on.

'Muscle! Bleedin' twat always gets it wrong. It's attached to the bottom of the lorry above the back axle, you'll see a big white painted spot on the back axle, it's just above that. Probably a bulb has gone you can do that.'

Finding it, got a replacement bulb from the stores. With that job done reported back to Levine, he scratched off, ordered. 'Drive it out of the bays, back over to B Platoon.'

'Don't drive Sergeant.'

'Oh. Don't you? Well we will have to teach you then. Go and fetch Muscles, he can sign it off as well.' Just about to leave the sheds when Bill shouted.

'Joey Naafi up. C'mon, get it. Chop Chop.' Ignoring him reported to Nobby.

'Corporal can you tell Muscles, to collect his wagon and sign it off.'

'He'll do that after his Naafi break.'

Approaching the Naafi on wheels. Wang shouted.

'Lu Joey ow mi muny.'

'Wotcha got?' Holding out his hand demanded.

'Muny lu play up. Play day yesday.'

'How much yer sod.' Opening his little book turned over some pages.

'Yu play won dolar benty cen. Okay.'

From my back pocket, took out the wad of notes pealed out one five-dollar note and gave it him, demanding.

'Wotcha got in yer wagon?' Bill interrupting.

'Same as always. Bleedin' bridge rolls, tomatoes and cheese or egg mayonnaise. Wang. Why don't yer get summat different?'

'Yu Willi no gud. Yu wastard.' Wang answered him back pushing his white Toby further back on his head. Bill started laughing.

'Sod off. Don't know wot yer talking about.' Mick called out.

'Dineen. Leave the poor little sod alone. Ain't done you no harm.'

'Nope, that's right, but good for a laugh ain't yer Wang?' Wang laughing replied.

'Yu wastard Willi.'

'Er Wang. Yer going to serve me or not?'

'Yu wastard tu Joey al Lectrian wastards.' Grinning showed all his gold teeth. However, he opened up the top of his mobile canteen. 'Two egg rolls 'un take it out of that.'

'Joey . Yu gud wastard. Yu pay on tim. No lik Willi wastard.' Bill called out.

'Don't you start on me? I pay yer don't I?'

Wang taking no notice, handing me the rolls and my change closed the lid mounted his bike. Bill getting up gave him a friendly shove, quickly with his feet pedaling away almost raced downhill across the square, en route to 'B' platoon Nissan hut.

The rest of the day, I had little or nothing to do but help Bill to complete his job. In the afternoon, there were no more jobs for us; instead we spent the rest of the time sweeping out bays, clearing out the monsoon ditch and tidying up the workshop ready for OC's next morning. Nevertheless, there was something else to be carried out down at the basha. "Interior Economy".

With the exception of Gerry who was on Guard. Everyone went outside to clean up the surrounding area of the basha, sweeping out monsoon ditches de-weeding the little stretches of dirt, surrounding the patches of grass that was more a form of creeping plant. I discovered when you waved your hand over its leaves; they closed up tight before reopening, fascinating! This Friday evening procedure was part of OC's inspection next morning.

Interior Economy

Having completed that chore, returned back inside for a mug of tea. Chong entering the basha made his way up to Gerry, laid some Dobie on his bed.

'Ta about bloody time Chong. You make me late for Guard Duty.' Jibed Gerry.

'Yu Okay. Plentee tim. Lookee Joey.' Gerry pointed.

'Down that end.' Chong spotting me approached with that funny Chinese waddle. Separately laid out the dobied OG's on top of the bed.

'Okay Joey. Yu lookee smar on OC plade Okay?'

What a difference from the crumpled pair handed to him earlier. They were pristine, full of starch, creased pockets pressed square as were the flaps, the shorts legs together creased flat as boards, impressed.

'How much?'

'Wun Dolar. Lu Joey, alwass dobi Mondays. Yu OG's, vilt shilts, weddy fo mi, colec and dobi like sama sama Blilli, Al, Okay... Chong nodding like mad advised me. Lu pay Chong ater. Okay?'

'Yer Okay.' Gave him a dollar note, he scratched summat in his little book possibly paid; he drifted away from us up towards Gerry.

'Bleedin' 'ell, more money to pay out. Ear Bill how much do it cost yer a week? It's a dollar fer this a dollar for that, do we pay for sheets and pillow cases as well?'

'Nope, Army pays for them. After Monday basha inspection, Chong comes around leaves clean set, that's all there is to it. Collects dirty ones in afternoon. Yer only pay for civvies and OG's, otherwise you'll Dobie em yerself. Anyway, it's only a dollar a set, ain't much and yer do not 'ave to worry about 'em. Ear. Don't you have to collect yer civvies from Li to night? That's more dollars yer got to pay out. Chop Chop off yer go. Don't forget pay him.'

Had completely forgotten about civvies. Taking some dollars trotted off to Li's. They were ready.

'Joey play seben dolar, Okay?'

No need for a fitting, if he could do the OG's and get them right he could do the same for civvies, anyway two days is not a long time to get things made. Back home, it might take you six weeks for a fitted shirt and trousers. Handing over the money, left with the civvies over my arm. Entering the basha Bill lying on his bed said.

'C'mon give us a fashion show. Summat to look at eh Al? '

'Yep. C'mon Joey might as well 'ave a laugh.'

Having not worn civvies for the past six weeks was eager to try them on. Quickly changing they fitted just right.

'Well. Wot dyer reckon, all right eh. When we going down town?' Al commented.

'They're all right, all yer need now is a tie can't go out in civvies without a tie and shoes of course.'

'Got shoes, but no tie or socks '

'Yer prat. Could have bought them from Li. Buy em tomorrow.'

Pleased with my new purchase, hung them in the cupboard, leaving the clean set of OG's to unfold tomorrow. Settled down to write a few lines home, Bill provided the address of the camp having finished addressing the envelope stuck on a stamp, felt that tiredness overcoming me and was ready for bed asked.

'Where's the post box?'

'Don't be a prat all yer life Joey. There ain't no GPO out here. Just give it to Mick he'll deal with it.'

It was Friday night, with not much going on, settled in bed beneath the mossie gazing at the solitary light bulb reflected about the previous Friday night on board, having a few beers knowing that we would all be split up. Nevertheless, for me that first week in the LAD had been a revelation. The people around me were all friendly and pondered if; at another camp would I have encountered the likes of Al and Bill. Both South Londoners and being very familiar with Al's locality only five minutes' walk away, whereas with Bill's Peckham, during my early school days had played football on the Rye. In addition, there were two other Londoners Den and Jacko yet to be acquainted with. Recollecting that week, had rifle practice, played a game of football, done a Kampong guard, some bleedin' weeding and to-morrow an introduction to the O.C's parade.

A violent shove on the iron bed woke me.

'C'mon git up yer lazy bastard. OC's this morning ere's yer tea. Chop Chop.' Bill's melodic voice drifted through the mossy net. Fighting my way out from under its folds, took hold of the mug on the floor as Bill ranted at Al.

'C'mon Al, wakey wakey. Yer lazy git. It was your bleedin' turn this morning.'

'Sod off.' Came the muffled voice of Al. I watched as with the rustle of his mossy withdrew it from the bottom of his bed, swinging his legs out reached across for his fags, as he lit one up with a puff of blue smoke he was back in the land of the living.

'Why don't yer give it up?'

'You can sod off as well. Yer prat.' Muttered Al. taking another draw on his fag then a swig of tea.

'C'mon chop chop lets be 'aving yer.' Bill urged. Maybe he did not go to sleep last night. Still dark outside, in the background could hear the noisy sounds of some bodies talking loudly in the showers. Draining the tea swung my legs over the side of the bed, straight onto a burning dog end.

'Oh. Sodding 'ell. Can't you aim em anywhere else?' Al laughing was definitely back in this world, cackled.

'Ain't my bleedin' fault it hit the post and rolled in your direction.'

Hobbling over to the cupboard grabbing the towel, tied it around my waist picking up toiletries hurried to the showers to join Bill already showering. The water was cold so I did not stay long, had a shave before returning to the basha, pulling on shorts collected eating utensils enroute to the cookhouse. There was an atmosphere of urgency about everything, even the queue moved quickly. Joining Bill and Al at the table there was no chatter as they stuffed their breakfast down their throats, so quickly ate mine as they left was joined at the table by a couple of the other VM's. Towse uttered.

'Morning Joey. First O.C for you. 'Urry up don't want to be late.' He was a big bloke, thick as two planks, broad in the shoulder and twice as tall as I was, after having been out there a least a year was nut brown in colour but possibly, it was the natural pigment of his skin but there again he was fair of hair.

'I know. Everyone seems to be in a 'urry.

'Well, you'll find out soon enough, Get moving.'

Back in the basha it was a hive of industry beds being made, Al using a broom swept up the mountain of dog ends around the post. Cpl. Mean called out. 'Twenty minutes, let's have everything squared off and lined up. Then up to the LAD. C'mon move yourselves, Chop Chop.'

From down the other end, a long piece of string was produced; Towse carried it all the way down towards our end pulling it taunt. Now came the bullshit, everything was lined up against the string, adjusted correctly then the other side. Noticed Al and Bill dressed upwards, grey socks were pulled fully up, dark blue hose tops covered them blue flashes fitted, hose tops turned down, Boy Scout fashion, last thing boots and puttees, standing up slipped on shorts then jacket top, both helped each other to apply the shoulder flash, they never sat down. Pulling my jacket on Bill urged.

'Chop chop Joey. Stop farting around. Where yer flashes? '

'Ain't got any.' Bill called out.

'Gerry! Let Joey borrow yer leg un shoulder flashes mate.'

'Cum and get em.' In my starched shorts walkied stiffly down to Gerry, took the sets and retreated back. Al snapped.

'Urry up. Give em here. Passing them to him, he fitted them to the press studs sewed onto the jacket. There you are, make sure you get new sets for next week.' Cpl. Mean called out

'Five minutes everyone, up the LAD Now.'

That was Al's cue, on went his belt and beret stiffly walked out of the basha. As he adjusted his beret. Bill urged.

'C'mon Joey. This is your first un, bit of a bleedin' lark this is, you'll see.'

My watch hands pointed to 0745. Quarter of an hour to go. Properly dressed felt very smart, however hampered by the starch in the O.G's walked or marched stiffly up to the LAD, where a few of them were standing about. Al as usual had a fag lit up, very soon all the LAD was in force including Sgt. Levine. Q. arrived on the scene, sparkling in his starched uniform, ordered.

Waiting for OC's

'G-g-get lined up in thru-threes. P- Pl-Plant s-short arse. L-last in the r-rear rank' we maneuvered into position. Unfortunately next to me stood the prat Beasley. 'Open order March.' A crunch of boots. 'Right dress.' Q inspected each rank looking for something out of order, there was nothing? Finally, the rear rank he stopped.

'F-f-first one. P- Pl-Plant. Where d-did you g-get the f-flashes?'

'Gerry let me 'ave his, he was on guard last night.' He muttered.

'G-good cannot let the s-side down.' By this time the RASC. Platoons were being organised on the rutted surface of the square. The CSM shouting out his orders as the Platoon Sgt's responding accordingly.

'R-Right Sergeant Levine. It's t-time. M.m March t-them onto the p-parade.'

'LAD Close order March...Bang...Left turn...screech bang...By the left quick, March. Right wheel Left wheel. Halt. Right Dress. With Beasley stood next to me I raised my arm and gave him a good shove, he turned to me and was quickly bellowed at by Sgt Levine 'Beasley Eyes right dress off.' Shuffle shuffle. Arms down,we were in line with the rest of the other RASC. Platoons stretched out across the square. With us at the end and me last man in the front rank. Q, advancing along the line with his hankie he dusted off any dust that had formed on our boots. Thought, "This is weird. What bullshit? After the nonchalant way the LAD had acted throughout the week". Captain Cole arrived smart as a button adorned with his Sam Brown and medal ribbons, with a few salutes flung about he took up his place in front of his LAD platoon with Q behind him then Sgt's Levine.

Then the pomp and ceremony began. The O.C. Marched on parade with his entourage of supporting Officers The CSM barked out

'THREE COMPANY...PARADE...ATTEN... TUA.'

Crash bang wallop 'PARADE...READY FOR YOUR INSPECTION. SAR.'

The usual call out by the platoon Sgt's. "A" platoon numbers etc. Then Sgt. Levine called out.

'REME LAD. ALL PRESENT AND CORRECT ONE ABSENT GUARD DUTY.'

And so, the O.C began his inspection. First the RACS platoons to hear charges been fired about for sloppily dress attire. Then it was our turn. More salutes were flung up, as the imposing figure of the OC. Who then could see was well over six feet tall, dressed in his OG's regulation long shorts beige Boy Scout socks and yellow flashes wearing brown shoes brogues (I might add) sporting his Sam Brown and whipping stick. Alongside him Capt Cole, just as impressive and behind followed the CSM and Q, so began our inspection or, scrutiny down the front line he stopped at me.

'New arrival aren't you?'

'Yes Sir.'

'How you finding it out here?'

'Hot. Sir.'

'Good Craftsman. Very Good turnout for first parade keep it up. Eh Captain Cole?' Turning to Fred who acknowledged the compliment with a broad smile. It appeared, there was not any love lost between them. They disappeared around behind me and completed the three ranks. Apparently all was in order. More salutations and then back into position. The OC returned to his position in the front and with a slight stamping and about turning faced his charges.

'Company Sergeant Major. Dismiss the Parade.' He squawked out, saluted and with that retreated.

'SAR.' More salutations then.

'SENIOR OFFICERS ON PARADE DISMISS. Capt. Cole, Q and the other Officers did the usual right turn and marched off.

'PAR..AADE. STAND AT EASE. PLATOON SERGEANT'S TAKE COMMAND. TO YOUR DUTIES DISMISS.'

This was followed by bawling and shouting, as the individual platoons were brought to attention and marched off in order. HQ, B, C & Composite marched out through the LAD entrance we us in tow, back towards the main camp where the others formed up in the parking area whereas the LAD platoon carried on down the road to the cookhouse. Halted. Dismissed, back to the basha to change into work clothes. Returning to the workshops, just in time for Naafi break. As Bill was duty VE. If he wanted any help would be available however, there was no work for us, so we skived about in the battery shop, until it was knocking off time.

CHAPTER NINETEEN
A SURPRISE EVENT.

After dinner returned the shoulder and Hose top flashes back to Gerry who was lying on his bed, the lids of his eyes visibly drooping. Thanking him for the loan and repeated what Q had said. He replied.

'Listen Joey. We don't get picked up for anything, we are the so called 'inferior lot' here, so we prove them wrong by being the best at everything and they don't like it. We know its bullshit, but we have Captain Cole, Q, Threadgold and a good bunch of Sergeants. In fact were all good muckers you wait and see, very soon you'll understand.'

'Well thanks for the tip. Anyway, what does the red flash with its yellow star mean?' Loudly yawning replied.

'That my friend, (yawn) represents all the Federal States of Malaya, there are eleven states...yawn... and each point a different state...yawn...noting his constant yawning, left him to sleep off his guard duty, whilst I lying on my bed watched a bleedin large Hornet with a massive sting in its tail burrow a hole in the upright post by the doorway whilst in the background radio Surabaya's record requests, lulled me into sleep. Someone shouting.

'KEENE. TELEGRAM FOR YOU.' Woke everyone up. In a state of drowsiness pondered. "Telegram out here can't be? This is going to be interesting". With a serious look on his face, Al answered.

'Hoi down ere.'

As the Duty Clerk approached, Al rolled off his bed onto his feet.

'Ere you are Al. It came through ten minutes ago. If you want to send a reply, come up to the Admin basha tell me what you want sent back. Alright.'

Taking the telegram Al thumbed open the flap, taking out the folded piece of paper with a big grin announced.

'Bleedin' 'ell, I'm an uncle again, my sister Audrey has given birth to a little girl named Kim.' Bill said.

'Ear Al, Congrats. that is bleedin' good news ain't it? How many is that she's ad?'

'Second one, the other's a little boy called Lee. He's about a year old now.' Bill yelled.

'Ere guess, wot? Al's a daddy agin. Whey hey! Bleedin' drinks all round to-night. There were shouts of congratulations. 'Mine's a pint.' etc etc. The news was greatly appreciated and I added mine.

'Congrats Al. When did she 'ave it then?' Rereading the telegram, replied.

'Thirtieth. That's yesterday Friday. Hoi Bill. Wot did yer invite every bleeder out fer a drink fer? I'm saving up can't afford it' Bill suggested.

'Yer just bleedin' tight fisted, ain't anything to do with saving up lets 'ave booze up.'

As he left the basha, a jubilant Al called out. 'Naw. Can't afford buying beer for all you lot of sods.'

Being Saturday, and the proud owner of new civvies was eager to go down into Ipoh to visit one of the three cinemas, aptly named the Odeon, Ruby and the Rex or, stay in camp and have a few celebration beers in the Naafi. Nevertheless, all afternoon right through teatime, Bill and I had nagged Al about. "A drink in the Naafi" It was getting dark outside when Bill and I with the intention of going down town, having showered and shaved returning to the Basha, Bill suggested.

'Look Al. Seeing Joey has civvies. We can 'ave just one in the Naafi. Then go down town show 'im the delights of Ipoh. Then catch a midnight movie, wot der say?' Al sat on his bed box smoking a fag, a happy grin on his face was unconvinced until I suggested.

'Look. I wanna go out, not worn civvies for bleedin' months. I'll buy the round then we can go out. Alright?' Al with a faraway look on his face looked at me before he said.

'Right we'll go to the Naafi. Joey's buying a round.' Bill retorted.

'Thank bleedin' Christ. Wot took yer so long to make yer soddin' mind up. Gotta wet babies 'ead 'aven't we Joey?' Bill winked.

'Yep best thing out.' Thinking, "Never have wet a baby's head furthermore, didn't know anyone who had given birth to a baby, certainly not in my circle of friends nevertheless, it will be good to 'ave a beer at last".

'Sod it! Right yer pair of prats, bin soddin' moaning all afternoon about a bleedin' drink. Let's see the colour of yer money. Joey getcher dollars out. Let's get across to the Naafi. You an all Bill git your money out...That was the signal from Al to get moving, picking up his tin of fags and a box of matches thinking, "He's going to ave one beer and forty fags"... C'mon you pair of prats.' He urged as he led the way three others joined us, Jock, Mick and Gerry.

The Naafi, was nothing to write home about, just a larger version of a Basha apart from the fact that it had one blank attap wall with a serving hatch let into to it, a juke box, holding about forty records, spread out were a number of wicker tables with four matching easy chairs. Hurrying to a table Al sat down, shouted.

'Joey's round.' To which Gerry quickly responded.

'Heh. Al, it's your sister that's had the baby not Joey's.'

'Nah, he offered din he. I'll buy the next round.' I asked.

'Wot's it to be?' - 'Anchors! There's nothing else.'

Approaching the open serving hatch, framed within it was the face of a bald headed Chinaman with a moon shaped face looking at me though slits of eyes he spoke.

'Lu Joey newy? Wat wan?'

'Six Anchors please.'

'Okay. Joey? Quickly placed six pint bottles on the counter top then six-pint glasses, expertly flipping off the crown stoppers remarked. Tu dolar fortee.'

'Forty cents a bottle, that's cheap 'ave some more of that.' Handing over three dollars, took two bottles and glasses back to the table, doing a shuttle for the other picked up my change of the counter carried the rest back. In the traditional way sloping the glass poured. "Carefully does it". Need not have bothered it was a pint of froth. Bill laughed.

'It's all bleedin' chemical Joey, don't matter how yer pour it out. Anyway 'appy birthday Al, or to your sisters nipper.' With a mouthful of froth coughed and spluttered.

'God damn it, that's foul.' Mick questioned.

'Not used to the hard stuff eh Joey?'

'Sodin' 'ell. Bitter yes but this is piss.' Jock spoke up... 'Ye wit te temorra. Dinna tak te meny. Yer ken.' More of the LAD joined us. We were still drinking at closing time. Nobody went out that night and I became one of the lads.

Sunday morning. My head was splitting my tongue felt like sandpaper and about four sizes too big. Al was groaning, so was Bill, so happily joined in. Mick walked past with his crocs and a frog in his throat, croaked.

'Joey! It's all your fooking fault.' Croaking back.

'It was Als.'

'Gawd 'elp me.' moaned Bill.

'I'll elp yer wif a boot up yer arse. Shut up...Moaned Al...urry up git the tea in.'

Somehow, untangled myself from the mossie net, just as Jock arrived at the bottom of the bed.

'Heh Joey, yi geeing te mass? ye say yer war last neet.'

'Oh Bleedin' 'ell did I? Can't stomach that this morning. No fit state, next week.'

'Aye jus us wil ye ken.' He departed to the cookhouse. Bill exhaled from underneath his mossie net

'Joey! You're Bleedin' going. You say a prayer for Al and I yer prat.'

Could not remember during the previous night saying anything about religion? Shifting my legs out from under the mossy net and over my head, eased myself off the bed, stood up, the basha started revolving, "Bleedin' 'ell what was in that beer"? Moving, nay swayed toward the lockers to collect mugs and staggered to and from the cookhouse with three mugs of tea, placed them close to the two suffering bodies. Bill Uttered.

'Gordon Bennet.' I replied.

'Thought you lot could 'andle that Anchor stuff?' Bills muffled reply.

'Yer. Only about two, that's the most, then its whahey.' Al moaned.

'I'll tel yer, it ain't same as back home, it's lethal.' Bill responded.

'Tel yer wot, you'll still feel pissed after dinner.

Sunday Afternoon

Neither Jock nor Gerry (also a Catholic) went to Mass that Sunday. Which was a blessing in disguise; it took me all day to get rid of the effects, even after three showers, it made no difference. That evening Al gave up his saving routine. We visited the Naafi for a couple. Well it was dirt-cheap and something to enjoy as well as the toasted Tomatoes sandwich, they made with plenty of pepper, costing pittance. The jukebox had a few Benny Goodman records and some other Jazz EPs. So for background music, kept on putting ten cents in, much to the annoyance of others. So what?

Monday it was back at work. Beasley. Without my permission and in retribution for my shove, had volunteered me for a guard duty. Tuesday night another new experience. A brief stop at the armory to draw a rifle and ten rounds of ammo, followed by the normal routine, mug of tea, shower, meal, then prepare for guard duty. The dress, OG's starched and pressed Jacket sleeves rolled down, long trousers, puttees, lead weights slipped down the trouser legs.

First Guard Duty

what the procedure was and were dismissed into the guardhouse to be allocated what patrols we had to carry out. Given first Stag patrol at the LAD. A Cpl. marched me and the Composite guard out of camp to our respective posts. Halting us outside the LAD, he dismissed me to patrol around the LAD perimeter to make sure nobody would pinch a lorry. Although very familiar with the surroundings, as daylight fell into darkness it was creepy, afraid of encountering snakes a Tiger or, other creepy crawlies. Was about to get a slurp of water from the tap noticed a tiny white light coming straight towards me, the hairs on the back of my head stiffened, with rifle and bayonet pointing at the oncoming light I challenged! On it came, an insect floating past its fluorescent arse or head careering through on its nighttime jaunt. An innocent little insect that had put the fear of god in me, later discovered it as 'a Firefly.' As time progressed, there was plenty of activity going on in the 15/19th dancer's area, the whinnying of the Saracens going backwards and forwards. At 2158, on the road outside the Cpl. halted the change of guard, ordered me to fall in. We continued down to relieve the Composite Guard before marching the pair of us back to the Guardroom. Our rest room was the middle Nissan hut with eight bare bedsteads. Placed on the end of one was a large flat cooking tin, our evening supper containing a congealed mess of cold eggs, bacon, beans and hard fried bread. A Billy full of tepid tea. That mess was a most unwelcome sight for anyone starving. At 2357, we were assembled to carry out our second stag, a case of creeping around to surprise anyone about, challenge them if warranted shoot. If you did? You were put on a charge for wasting ammunition and Court Marshaled.

Thursday my first official payday. Back in Blighty, it was regimented and that was expected. About 1055 Sgt. Levine called out 'Pay Parade.' Whereupon bodies swarmed out from in or under trucks covered in grease or grime unlike us pair skiving in the battery shop. With berets and belts on, we congregated outside Captain Coles Office. No dressing into three ranks for us. The lean-to shed for Capt Cole's jeep, provided ample shade from the searing sun either, sit in his jeep or lounge against the uprights. From inside the office Q called out. Your last three, name and rank. 'Sir.' then the real formality. Entering the office came smartly to attention, slung up a salute received your pay, checked it and uttered the words. "Pay and pay book correct sir". Sling up another salute, right turn, crash and retreat out of the office. To lounge about until within a short period, Pay Parade was concluded and officially dismissed by 1115. Quite amazed by the so-called lack of pomp and ceremony, being on active service served its purpose. After dinner it was payout time, clearing slates for the following week. If you did not? There was no slate available.

Friday, after dinner Bill and I were in the pit, trying to remove a QL's starter motor, when the Scamell towing a QL swung out on a Gib, came screaming around the square, with a hiss of brakes stopped short of careering through the shed. Bill nodding in its direction.

'He's a nutter, the way he drives that bleedin' Scammel.'

'Who you talking about?'

'Jacko. Mad bastard.' Glancing over from our vantage point saw two pairs of legs in long trousers land on the ground followed by two clunks as doors were slammed, following the progress of the legs emerged two tall figures, Sten guns resting on their shoulders, one was slightly shorter than the other. From further down one of the bays Al shouted.

'Hoi Joey! Den's back. You'll ave to find another bed...then called out...Hoi. Den! Got a surprise fer you down here.' The shortest one waved his Sten at Al before they entered the office. Al came and sat on the edge of the pit lighting up another fag said.

'Joey. Wot we will do is drag one of the spare beds down to our end, Den will not mind. He's all right, ain't he Bill?' Sgt. Levine shouted.

'Hoi Al. You haven't any time for skiving, get back to work.'

'Just cadging a light Stan.'

'Bloody likely story. Those two buggers don't smoke.' Al got up and walked away.

'As Al says Den's alright, he's a Lance Jack nothing like Beasley, jumped up shit. Ow! Watch wot yer f....g doing with that soddin' spanner yer prat.'

'Sorry it slipped.' Bill nursing a finger moaned.

'I'll bleedin' smack yer one, if yer do it again.'

I watched as the two newcomers left the LAD enroute to hand in their weapons. Being rather inquisitive about Jacko asked Bill about his statement, him being a "mad bastard".

'Who Jacko. He's all right just bleedin drives that Scamell at breakneck speed all of thirty-eight miles an hour towing anything, says he can't stop incase CT's take a pot shot at him. He goes so fast they couldn't bleedin' hit him. Yer know wot, he is the only one in the LAD who has done Pokey. Him and three others, his mates in the RASC got pissed up one weekend, went AWOL down town had all the MPs out looking for em, never found em silly lot of sods. The three of em waltzed back into to camp and were found sitting in the Naafi drinking Beer. They all got banged up. On OCs Jacko and Russell got twenty one days and the other two Hutton and Robertson were sent down to Kinrara Jail. For being AWOL on Active Service, Load of bollocks if you ask me? Talk of the devil here they come now.' At the far end, Al was waiting for them and guiding them towards us. Bill clambering out of the pit said.

'Watcha mates ave a good time up there?' Al interrupted.

'Den. That young prat down there is Joey, arrived couple of weeks ago. Guess where he comes from.'

'I dunno yer prat. Timbuktu?'

'Nah. Bleedin' Wandsworth Road not far from you.'

'Bleedin' 'ell. Did yer miss the 77 bus to get out here? Den cackled...This is Jacko, he comes from Wembley or Harrow or somewhere, he's a Northerner has a passport an all.' Jacko defending himself responded.

'Bleedin' Southerners, yer all bleedin' same load of bastards, cocksure of yersel you lot. Ear Joey you don't want to get in with these bunch of prats. You come with me I'll see yer alright, eh Den?' Den laughed.

'More like the opposite with you yer prat. Eh?...changing the subject asked. Where abouts do yer live in Wandsworth Road?'

'The flats next to the Grenada.'

'Aah. I know em, live in the flats up on the Union Road Estate.'

'Blimey. I used to work in Auto's opposite those.'

'You did? Dyer knows a guy by the name of Big Dougie?'

'Well sort of, he was chief engineer there. Forgotten all about them now.'

'He used to go in same pub as me, small world, ain't it?'

'Say that again, wot with you and Al, living so close soddin' surprising.'

'Right I'm for a shower, get me kit and collect bedding, do usual, c'mon Jacko.' Al interrupted.

'Ere Den. Joey's got your bed space. I said he could 'ave it until you got back, we'll do a shove around when we finishes here, ain't long to go now.'

'Yeah Okay, keep together down that end.' He shouted as they returned to the Scamell, operating the Jib, let down the QL parked ready to be worked upon, collecting their kit reported to Sgt. Levine. Al shouted.

'Hoi Den get teas in, it's your turn.'

'Sod off. Its your turn yer prat.' Pondered . "Where have I heard that remark before"? Anyway, Bill had managed to get the starter motor out, placed it on the workbench to repair it.

'Now then Joey, basically its same as the Gernerator, you sort that out and I'll watch.' Constantly advising what to do, having finished reassembling it, fitted it back in place. By that time it was well past knocking off time, everyone else had left the sheds. Bill climbed up into the cab started up the engine that cranked in immediately...Joey go and tell Stan it's fixed.' Informing Stan, he came out and shouted.

'Dineen. Drive it down to the parking lot, report to HQ Basha, job done.'

'Righty Oh. Chop Chop Joey; fetch our belts and berets I'll drive yer down.' Joining him in the cab, he drove out of the LAD stopped at the guardhouse, then continued into the parking area stopping switched off...That's it. Job done, let's get some char, Chop Chop. Oh by the way your duty VE this weekend Joey.'

'Am I?

'Yeah but do not worry, there will not be anything to do, It's seldom you are called out, most of the jobs are mechanical.'

As we walked to the Basha, evidence of "Interior Economy" Was being carried out at other Basha's but not ours. Bill muttered.

'We're in luck; they've done it for us.' Entering the basha, found Den and Al lounging about on their beds. Bill asked.

'Where is our char then?' Den quipped.

'Get it yersef lazy sods. Where yer bin anyway? Skiving to miss Interior then?'

'Just finished job on a HQ wagon that's why were late back.' Al answered

'More like skiving, so yer don't ave ter get tea in.' I reminded Bill.

'Bill ain't yer got to report to HQ Basha, about wagon being fixed.'

'Oops. I'll do that. You get the teas in. Chop Chop.' Al promptly suggested.

'Heh that's a great idea. While you're over there get us refills.'

'Sodding cheek, give us yer mugs.' Armed with four mugs headed for the cookhouse, fortunately an Indian was pouring fresh tea into a Dixie. With four mugs burning my fingers had to hurry and dump them onto a bed box, spilling some Bill shouted.

'Watch out silly prat, will not send you again.' Al suggested.

'Nope, for spilling the tea he can do it all next week.' Den interrupted.

'Now I'm back, there's four of us so we'll 'ave a proper roster.' Joey you can do it all next week.'

'That ain't fair. Where the roster then?'

'You are! Now' for the serious stuff bed shuffling. Al and I, have decided to move the cupboards and beds so after we have drunk this. Will move four cupboards, against this back wall. Bill your cupboard and Joeys will be in between ours, the beds will be turned heads to the wall same as yours Bill.'

'Soddin' 'ell Den that means I'll 'ave further too walk.'

'Extra walking! Yer a prat Dineen. What are yer? Look, it'll give more room down this end, you wait and see.' Noticing the absence of Jacko, questioned.

'Where's Jacko sleep then? Thought, he might be down this end. '

'Him! Nah he's a Northerner, he's stuck up the other end with that mob. Grabbing his crocs Den mentioned. C'mon Grubs up.' The scramble was on, however Jacko, leaving from the other end of the basha, taking a short cut was jumping over the fence that surrounding the so-called garden. Den shouted after him.

Bob Watts, Harry, Jacko ,Gerry

'That's cheating. Git ter back of the queue.' Jacko yelled back

'Piss off, nothing says you can't.' Booing and catcalls were directed at him.

After dinner, the move got under way. Beds were moved, cupboards shoved up against the wall, placed on top were two empty one creating more bed space for each person. While this activity was going on, the others were making observations; very soon, it looked like Pickford's removal men had arrived. Transforming the entire layout, with one exception Mick's bed and cupboard with the radio on top. That night the four of us ended up in the Naafi. Talking with Den, found out he worked in a garage somewhere around North Clapham, knowing he knew Big Dougie, asked if he knew Eileen, he didn't nevertheless, Al came alive and said he knew her, she lived in South Lambeth Road, he knew more about her than I did, what a small world it is. It was decided to make a trip into Ipoh, to show me the hotspots.

Saturday afternoon, visited Li's to buy a tie and white pair of socks. Having not worn civvies for the past three months was eager to take in the sights of Ipoh. That evening on our way out passing Gerry he reminded me.

'Don't forget tomorrow morning Jock and I are taking you along to Mass, you missed last Sundays now you have got civvies you will look the part in church, alright.'

'Yeah Ok what time do we leave Camp?'

'About nine thirty walk around the back way.'

Leaving the basha, at the guardhouse we obtained late passes until 0200 hours. Chose a couple of waiting tri-shaws to take us into town. Den and Al set off in front with Bill and I lagging behind, careering down a flat road one side was in total darkness, the other had a sporadic line of streetlights constantly being attacked by swarms of insects and moths. Their glare illuminated giant palm leaves and in the gloom behind the outline of a bungalow could be seen. The still warm air was filled with the fragrant sweet smell of flowers and in the quietness, a cacophony of croaking frogs drowned out everything else whilst overhead the Bats shrieked as they swooped around, at that moment Bill chose to mentioned a fact.

Tri Shaw Wallah

'Joey on your left, you won't see it but there's the football pitch we play on...urged the tri-shaw Wallah...Hoi. 'Urry up pedal faster, beat them bastards in front.'

'Okay Jonnie. 'Pedaling like fury the tri Shaw wallah drew level and was about to overtake when Den urged his trishaw wallah.

'C'mon faster.' The race was on, gradually they drew ahead we careered around a few bends, then sped down another straight sloping road at a tee junction. Turning sharp left just about made it without tipping over. Bill shouted.

'Steady on twat. This is Anderson Road the main drag.'

The well-lit road was very wide, gone was the fragrance smell of flowers instead the smell of burning charcoal tinged by the odd smell of sewers. The structure of the buildings were exactly like those seen in Singapore, deep monsoon ditches with flagstone bridged walkways leading up onto a raised pavement and the shops. Just in front of us, their trishaw came to a halt. Bill called out.

'Okay Jonnie whoa.' The trishaw Wallah applying his brake came to a slow halt with a rusty screech. Bill paid the grinning toothless Trishaw Wallah Fifty cents. Standing there was very skeptical as to what these three buggers would get me into.

The Ruby Cinema

'Right Joey. We'll start here. Den suggested This'ere on the corner is the Ruby Picture house. Over there is the little café, we have breakfast after seeing the mid might movie. Behind the back of those buildings is what is called Kampong Java, where all the prossies 'ang out. Bill interrupting.

'You don't want to go their matey. Pick up nasty things; besides being picked up by the Red Caps, they're always on the prowl. What's on at the Ruby?' Al uninterested replied.

'Rubbish. Ear Den. Walk up to the Odeon see wot's on there? On the way can show 'im where the Indian barbers is, he needs a haircut don't yer Joey?

Along the covered pavement, shops were open; at the end of the block was the Indian Barbers emporium. Inside the Indians were snipping away at some heads of hair. Bill informed me.

Jubilee Park far right.

'Cost yer a Dollar fer 'aircut and for a massage two dollars...Good ain't they Al? '

'There're Okay. You should know. Always down there getting yerself ponced up.' Leaving that block crossed over a main street....... This is Brewster Road.' Passing an open doorway, above it was a red neon sign. "Jubilee Park". Bill asked.

'Joey dyer fancy a dance?'

'Nah not with you prat. Wot yer on about.'

'That place is the local dance hop. Free to get in, but yer ave to pay for a dance. Don't open until ten.' Very curious asked.

'Why dyer have to pay for a dance then?' Den interrupting.

'The birds in there are called Taxi Dancers. Buy three tickets for a dollar, one ticket per dance and if you fancy dancing with a nice slim bodied Chinese girl, full of Eastern promise. Buy another three.' Bill invited.

'Take yer in there one night, introduce yer to Lu Lu. '

'Sod off, ain't paying for a soddin dance.' Taken aback but intrigued, the thought of a dance.

We came across an impressive looking building covered in beige coloured tiles, emblazoned on the top, was a red neon sign. "ODEON" its exterior was the same as their cinemas back home. Entering its vestibule, in the center was a round bar that served beer and other goodies. The picture showing was not to anyone's fancy, so we left there. Back passing the Jubilee Park turned into a side street, there was another picture house. "The Grand". That was small and unimpressive it looked more like a fleapit. Den muttered.

Grand Cinema

'Not very good in there, pictures not good either. C'mon show yer Chinatown where all the Chinks live.'

We had not been gone very far down the street. When three Red Caps stopped us. the Sgt. enquired.

'You Lot. Where you going?' Den replied.

'Just strolling down this road that's all.'

'Well the four of you can stroll back the other way. This area is Out of Bounds during nighttime. Do you want to get a knife stuck in you or, maybe you four are looking to start trouble with the Chinese. What Camp you from?' Den responded.

'Three Company REME LAD Sergeant.'

'Well. Let us Escort you out of this area back to Brewster Road. Then you can go the other way. Otherwise, I will book you all for being out of bounds. Now you don't want that. Do you soldiers?' Den answered.

'Sorry Sergeant didn't thing about it. Only going to the Flicks.' Just past the Grand, they left us to return to China Town. I exclaimed.

'Bleedin' alright ain't it. First night out in town and you, bleeders want to get me in trouble. Bill replied.

'Don't you worry you little 'ead Joey. Well look after yer. Wont We Den?'

'Piss off Dineen.' Den responded. Left me thinking, "So far that's, somewhere Prossie 'ang out, three Picture House's, a Café, a Barbers, a Dance Hall. Once again, out of Bounds. Not much to write home about here". Al suggested.

'Fancy a nice hot curry Joey? Burn yer 'ead off it will.' Before we go for a curry. Let us see what is on at the REX. Den questioned.

'You into curries Joey?'

'Bleedin' weaned on em. Mum and dad were out in India. My brother was born there.' Proud of the fact, knew about Curries.

'Well that's all right, we'll order a hot one for you.'

By that time, we had walked back down another side street and rejoined Anderson Road; it appeared to be some sort of market area, with many Chinese stalls. The air was heavy with the smell of ripe fruit, cooking and burning charcoal. The stalls lit by kerosene pressure lamps hung from poles, radiating a stark white light down onto their goods on sale. Some of the stalls sold different dishes of food. Noodles, fish, chicken, vegetables, Christ knows what else, all being cooked beside the stall in an inverted domed dish heated

by a charcoal fire. The ingredients thrown in, creating different dishes were mouth watering to say the least. Amongst them were fruit stalls selling rather large green looking gooseberries, Pineapples, Papaya, Bananas, Coconuts and other fruit did not recognise. Some of the stalls sold skinless sliced Pineapple and slices of Papaya, both laid out on blocks of ice to keep them cool. Banana fritters cooked in deep

Fed Mus and beyond the REX. batter. It was fascinating just to see it.

The road was a hive of activity; there was a mixture of Chinese, Malays and Indians all in different attire. The Chinese mainly dressed in white trousers or shorts with white shirts, the women mainly in pyjamas, the Indians wore black trousers and coloured shirts did not see too many women dressed in saris. However, the Malays, dressed in black trousers and white shirts with a funny hat on the heads, their women wore some form of a sarong with a scarf over their heads. In some of the side street there were beggars hunched in odd places with a funny smell lingering around them. The traffic was mainly trishaws with a few taxis that spent most of their time honking their horn as slowly they inched their way through the throng of people. Amongst those dressed in civvies were other squaddies and a few RSF's dressed in their OG's, black Glen Gharries with a red and white squared band around its rim. Overseeing all were the ever presence of Red Caps sat in their jeeps watchful of signs of trouble. As we progressed down the road from above I heard a lot of cheeping, looking up was amazed to see perched on the overhanging telegraph wires between the poles, all the way down the road, masses of starlings. Passing by the Federal Muslim curry house, on the walkway within the depths of the overhang, was a charcoal burner with the biggest cooking dish I had ever seen full of steaming grey coloured curry gravy, it aromatic smell was overpowering. The Indian stirring it must have known the other three pretty well as he Salaamed and touched his forelock to each of us, muttered.

'Aacha sahib. Pointing upstairs. Velly guud carry tonite sahib.' Bill acknowledging his call answered.

'Yep we'll be back. Want nice and hot one fer me mate Joey ear.'

Outside the REX Cinema we joined hordes of Chinese with their woman friends some dressed in those Chinese Cheongsams, very fetching as you squeezed past them the aroma of sweet scent surrounded them. All were queuing up for tickets to the midnight movie. "Three Bridges at Toko Ree". The very film had taken Joyce to see on my last night of freedom although missed a lot through snogging. However, that night, would see the film without any interruptions. Having booked our seats, the strong aroma of curry was tickling our nostril enticing us to have some. At the entrance went past the Indian and up the stairway to the eating area. The room's decor was very sparse; with about twelve empty tables covered with plastic tablecloths except in the far corner, there were only two other civilians sat at a table eating, as it was nearly ten o'clock suppose others had already eaten and gone. Two barefooted-Indian waiters dressed in long white shirts a blue and white tablecloth wrapped around their midriff stood waiting with serving trays. We sat down at one of the tables; a waiter came over and stood beside the table Al. speaking to me began advising me of what their menu consisted of.

'Joey. Seeing, as you know all about curries. Wot yer fancy from their limited menu of three dishes. The cheapest is the gravy, that was the one downstairs on the boil, only fifty cents with a bowl of rice or. There is mutton curry or, the dearest the Chicken Biriani, at a dollar fifty. It is all-good. I am 'aving the Biriani. I noticed the waiter nod and smiled. Wot dyer fancy then Joey?' Bill interrupted.

'Curry gravy and rice for me, that's mine sorted out.' Al retorted.

'Dineen, Wait yer bleedin' turn yer prat. Let Joey choose.' I thought for a minute about the Biriani but at a dollar-fifty said.

'I will try the gravy with the rice, see wot it's like, can always try another dish next time.' Al asked.

'Wot you 'aving Den?'

'Me. Haven't had a good curry or weeks, the curry and rice. Al ordered.

'Hoi matey. Four curry gravies and boiled rice 'urry up. Anyone want a beer, fanta or water?' Cold water was the order. Den queried.

'Er. Al thought you were goin' to 'ave a Biriani?'

'Nah. Just want a curry; it's cheaper saving up, besides it's quicker.'

The waiter arrived with four glasses of water with ice floating on the top, unceremoniously set them down on the table. The other waiter arrived carrying a tray at shoulder height, placing it on the table set out four bowls of rice and four bowls of curry gravy the colour of deep grey with spots of yellow oil floating about. Al invited.

'There're Joey. Wot dyer reckon?' All eyes focused on me. Stirring the curry around the yellow spots of oil dispersed within the juice. Spooning the gravy over the rice grains, which instantly changed from pure white to a light gray. Taking a mouthful savored its taste, it was good but spice wise not that hot, swallowed. The three of them not eating watched me then I began to feel the heat well up from my stomach, the flavor of hot chili burst into a tingle in my throat onto my tongue and lips.

'Soddin 'ell.' Grabbed a glass of water taking a gulp that did not quell the heat of the curry. Den laughed.

'Told yer Joey. It's the best curry you'll ever taste that's for sure.' It hit's yer stomach, and then comes back at yer... adding... you just wait for the sweating.'

As they tucked into their curries, the sweat gradually oozed out around my nose and eye area, they all in the same predicament mopping their noses and eyes. Nevertheless, that meal all for fifty cents was delicious.

At 1100, we entered the REX. Its interior was the same as back home, if you have been in one picture house you been in them all. Except here Chinese filled the seats.

The films started at 1115. Therefore, by the time it had finished it was getting on for 0115. It was then time for an English breakfast. Big fat chips, egg, bacon, tomatoes and plenty of HP sauce. With iced coffee served in a half pint glass with lumps of ice floating on the top plus two straws. All that cost a dollar fifty. We hired a taxi back to camp, signed in. My first night in Ipoh Town a memorable one; that would follow the same weekly pattern of events throughout my stay.

CHAPTER TWENTY
THE WIND OF CHANGES.

Sunday morning. After brekkers, showered, dressed in civvies the three of us left camp via the rear barbed wire fence, walked around the road hugging the 15/19th Hussars Camp, crossed over towards the Garrison Church, just a large wooden hut built on top of a hump overlooking the Heli Pad. Inside handful of service personnel were already seated amongst the few rows of seats, walking up the aisle, near the front we genuflectedand sat down to await the arrival of the Priest. *Me &Jock*

About 0955, a Captain in the Royal Army Chaplains Corps entered. Quickly passing through his congregation carrying his small case containing the Sacraments, laid it on the small table like altar retreating behind it changed into his robes. Two of his civilian congregation got up to act as servers. The mass began and was conducted at a rapid pace midway through, the noisy landing of a helicopter outside drowned the rest of the mass. The Priest blessed everybody before briskly walked up the aisle, stood in the doorway, and thanked all for turning up. Noticing a new face amongst his flock, politely asked.

'Hello Gerry and Jock. Who's this with you. What is your Christian name? (Unsure of how to address him, as Captain or Father settled for Father) 'Joey. Father.'

'Joey. Eh. I hope you enjoy your stay out here see you in two weeks time. God Bless you all.'

Curious about the short time taken for Mass to be said questioned the pair of them, Gerry answered.

'He is the only Priest between Taiping and Tapah; he's got a busy schedule and says all masses.'

'Wot about his comment see you in two weeks?'

'Well he only visits this communal church every second week. On the odd Sundays we go to the Catholic church in Town, so if that prat Beasley has not got you down for a weekend Guard, well take you there.'

'Don't like that sod. But sounds alright.' Gerry responded.

'Not many do, jumped up shit.'

That Sunday, was the first of many visits to that little church including one memorable occasion. Upon entering, it was full of uniformed RSF's. Draped over the alter was the Flag of St Andrew. About halfway down found some seats genuflected moved in abut to sit down when Jock hissed 'C'mon. Git oot...confused we left. Outside laughing explained...Ye ken. Cud ah bin mordered bin therr, its a Church of Scotland Service".

On alternate Sundays, a long walk down Jalan Abdul Jalil road alongside the girl's convent through a back lane that led to the Catholic Church. A large colonial constructed building inside it was big and spacious, I was surprised to see it was packed full of mixed worshippers. Even with all the windows open and the overhead fans, whizzing around it was stifling hot. On the altar, the Chinese Priest spoke in Latin and Mandarin however, was able to follow the passage of the mass. After mass, we went to the Odeon Cinema located behind the church to order an iced coffee before returning to camp for the mid-day meal.

Monday morning. Along with the other five new RASC arrivals, plus another few from other camps, had to attend the Education Centre opposite the Composite depot. It was just a wooden hut with many wide-open windows and a few desks and seats. An Education Corps S/Sgt provided the class of about ten with books about Malaya then proceeded to give us a lecture on the history and geography of the countries origin. it was a very boring morning. During that week, Jacko and Beasley were notified they were homeward bound. With the pending departure of Beasley. To me, that was a welcome relief. No more Kampong duties, but was wrong still had to do them and on one later occasion was to have my first experience with a snake. Well the inmates managed to catch the intruder in their makeshift pigsties. The Python had helped himself to a pig and was sleeping it **off**. Whilst at the guardhouse, a group of the villagers arrived carrying a long bamboo pole, entwined and secured to it was a very large Python that had eaten one of their Pigs.

Pig in a Python

What they did with it I shall never know nevertheless, I do know that Chinese make a meal out of snakes.

Captain Cole notified Den, he was to take over Jacko's Recovery Mechs job and in turn, he enlisted Al and me as part of his recovery team. The arrival back of Bunny Moore,

after his bout of dysentery came as a surprise to all. He was very tall and thin as a rake but well tanned and looked the picture of true health. I found him to be very amenable and quite a laugh. Corporal Kershaw was promoted to Sgt. and relocated in the Sgt's basha. Jock, departed for a parachute-training course at the jungle training school in Jahore Bahru.

Bunny ripping the baize

The following Wednesday Den approached me. 'Joey. Stan told me you don't drive, so I have to teach you, after dinner we will drive the Bin wagon to a place, the other side of town, where you can learn off the roads.'

Being attached to an LAD, we were expected to test drive the Lorries we had fixed therefore, it was almost mandatory that everyone learnt how to drive. The Bin wagon was an old World War II three ton Bedford 'OY.' Mainly used for convoy work, as a "stores on wheels". Settled in the cab, Den set off for this special driving place on the outskirts of the town. Turning off the main highway onto a dirt track, roaring with laughter we bumped and jolted about before we came to a vast open area. "A Public Works Department Communal Rubbish Tip". In the distance coolies were burning piles of rubbish producing clouds of smoke, a few trucks were tipping more waste into piles, carrion eaters fought for morsels of scraps. Den brought the Lorry to a skidding halt that caused clouds of dust to blow away in front of us, switching off the engine he said.

'Here you are Joey, it's all yours get into the driving seat.'

Anxiously getting out went around the front to clamber up into the driver's seat. In between us was an extremely long gear lever.

'Right 'ere you go. Gears first. Take hold of the top. Don't forget every time you change gear, you double the clutch.'

'Double the clutch. What's that?'

'Bleedin' prat, don't you know anything?'

'No. Not about soddin' driving trucks.'

'Well you wouldn't being an Electrician. Those three peddles at yer feet, are brake, clutch and accelerator. When you change gear, you have to depress that clutch pedal once to disengage the gear, twice to engage another gear. Never mind about reverse at this stage. Start again. Depress the clutch; push the lever over and down into first. That's it. Now second, depress the clutch, lift yer foot off, pull the gear stick out, across, depress the clutch, push down into second. That's it.' After completing this about half a dozen times. Now start up the engine.'

'Wot already?' Now anxious about driving.

'C'mon. We 'ain't got all bleedin' afternoon.' Pressing the starter button, the engine coughed and with a sickening lurch jolted forward. He yelled.

'Yer silly bugger, you left it in gear.' I yelled back.

'You didn't tell me to take it out.'

'Temper Temper. Now start again this time, put the gear lever in neutral. Yer know where that is don't yer?'

Taking no notice set the gear stick into the neutral position, started the motor, depressing the accelerator pedal right down, caused the engine to race the noise of the screaming engine was unbearable, could not hear Den shouting, shoving me gestured lift foot of the pedal, the screaming subsided as the engine died to a modest tick over, he shouted.

'Wot the bleedin' 'ell yer doing? Not so hard on the accelerator pedal, put her into first gear, ease out the clutch, gently depress the accelerator pedal until you can feel the engine pull.'

Doing as he instructed, the engine pulled so took my foot off the pedal, the engine cut out. Holding his head in his hands, he shouted. 'You Prat release the hand brake before you drive off.'

'Yer didn't say anything about bleedin' 'and brake did yer?'

'Let's try again.'

This time proceeded through the start procedure and at last, got the monster moving at a slow pace along this dirt track. Den murmured.

'Increase yer speed.' A side-glance in his direction noticed he was holding onto the side of the door ready to spring out. That provided me with no confidence. Shaking in my boots from even attempting to drive this bleedin' monster. He murmured.

'Second gear.' With a grinding of gears that was sure could be heard back at camp, somehow managed it. In leaps and bounds we jerked along like a kangaroo into a reasonable speed. He murmured,

'Third gear.' We completed about three circuits of the dirt track, before he said.

'Right that's enough, pull up, I'll take over.' As he walked past me. He laughed.

'Not bad that Eh Joey? Dare not let you on the road that's for sure. Maybe in two years time when yer get home your driving along the Wandsworth road, I'll make sure I'm nowhere in sight.' He laughed.

'Sod off.' Wringing with sweat my shorts a wet rag like I'd peed myself. On the way back. Den muttered.

'After that experience? I need a cup of char to calm my nerves.' Driving along he explained certain movements, so by the time we got back to camp my mind was full of do' and don'ts. Glancing at my watch it was nearing four o'clock. Had been driving for over two hours, learning of how not to drive. The first person to greet us was Captain Cole.

'How did he do Lee?'

'Bleedin' 'Orrible sir. Need a new gear box in the wagon?'

'Um. As bad as that eh? Plant. You will have to pay for that. Can't go around damaging Government property now can we? Take him out again Lee. Make sure he selects the right gears next time.'

That was it, my first lesson and I had to pay for a bleedin' gearbox? Den never mentioned anything until during our evening meal. In a raised voice. Highlighted my expertise as a budding driver. The RASC. Drivers, jeered and catcalled, at the misfortunes of a REME Wallah.

Not every day there was a mail call some received others did not however, it was accepted by all, apart from the more intimate sections that snippets of news was freely given. Late in the afternoon after work sat in the basha drinking tea, Mick entered with the mail call. Two for someone, three for someone else, two for Keene and a rolled up parcel. Three for Dineen one for Den, nothing for me. Al threw over the rolled up parcel

'Ear. Joey, read that.'

'It's yours.'

'It's all right it's only the Daily Mirror. Let me 'ave it back.'

Reading the Daily Mirror.

Tearing off the outer wrapping, unrolled copies of the Daily Mirror, grateful for the opportunity to at least read something. As everyone became absorbed with reading the basha became quiet. Sitting there itchy and covered in grease before reading the paper, decided to have a shower. Returning cleansed, the mood of the basha had changed the conversations were about news from back home. Sitting on a bed box, dripping sweat thinking, it was all too frustrating. "This must be the worst soddin' place on the earth. There was not anything to do, except work, do guards, play football, watch a film in town, eat, sleep and sweat yer balls off. Al interrupted my thoughts.

'Ear Joey. That last letter I wrote to Patti, told her about you and where you came from. In this letter she said her 'Ole man, used to own the pub at the end of Wilcox road, dyer know it?'

'That's the bombed out one, all boarded up. It was hit by a bomb during the war, never been open since.'

'That's the one, next to the stonemasonry works.'

'Well, it don't serve beer any more, it's either the Lord Morrison or the Nott. My ole man uses both, more so the Nott.'

'Shut up will yer. Ain't finished reading. Go and get us a mug of tea. Den, Bill, Joey's getting the teas in.' As another dog end hit the post, Bill urged.

'Urry up, get me mug I'm thirsty.' From behind his letter, Den stated.

'About bleedin' time. Urry up.' Getting up trod on a burning dog end yelled.

'You prat Al. Will you put your bleedin' dog ends out?' Al burst out laughing.

'Serve's yer right. Watch where yer walking.' Collecting the mugs, leaving the basha angrily retorted.

'Sod this for a game of soldiers. You lot wait, when I get some mail. You can get the bleedin' teas in.'

The tea Dixie was almost empty; tipping it on its side filled the mugs up, upon reentering received no response at all.

A couple of days later. Jock arrived back of from his jungle Parachute course. Proudly showing off his blue wings, I asked him.

'What it was like?'

'Blooody dingeross, Ye ken.' I ventured to ask.

'Always fancied doing it. Months ago. Back in Blighty while doing trade training, me and my mates volunteered for it. How did you get to get on the course then?'

'Aye, an ef yor thinking of daeing it, dinna wiste yor teem. Naer courses, ferr ages. The Rhodesian and New Zealand SAS, are booked ferr six moonths.' His comment made me question, how would I get in touch with the others, did not have a clue which camp any of them had been posted to?

This seemed impossible. Anyway if it was booked up there was no point. Nevertheless, it would be many months, before any of us would meet again, which prompted me to create a "DAYS to DO". Calendar. beginning 1st October. Everyone had one and diligently they crossed off the days, as they passed into the setting sun. Using the exercise book given out at the Education Lesson began lining up the dates, working out the total days until demob being 1956 was a leap year added up to 492. A Bleedin' lifetime in this hole?

However, the following Saturday Beasley had "volunteered" me for a 24 hour guard duty. Allocated Main gate. First stag, 1200 until 1400 hours. It was blazing hot and there was a lot of traffic coming in and going out. Whilst operating the barrier, it was going up and down like a bleedin' seesaw, until finally about 1330 the flow of traffic eased off and was able to relax a bit. At 1400 hrs. the change of Guard procedure was acted out. Retiring to the rest room, the heat inside the Nissan hut fair knocked me over, choosing one of the spare beds sat on the springs and proceeded to sweat buckets. Later returned to the basha, to collect eating irons, crocs and a blanket, whilst on weekend guard that was one item you were permitted to have. At 1800 I began the second stag and there was plenty of activity for those leaving camp for a night down town, including Den Al and Bill, who invited me out for a curry. Bastatds! Located immediately behind me, the Sgt's mess became very boisterous. At 1930 saw a couple of the guards returning from the cookhouse with our evening meal. At 2000 changing guards, retired to eat the cold English breakfast swilled down by a mug of equally cold tea. At 1200, the mid night stag and beginning of the steady arrival of a stream of latecomers, some drunk included a couple thrown into the cells to cool off. Finally, the last few to book in were the late night movie viewers and as the voices of Den Al and Bill faded into the dark interior of the camp, it became quiet. Finally relieved by the other Guard returned to a cold Nissan hut, to sleep on a spring bed covered by a solitary blanket for four uncomfortable hours, as the temperature dropped lower, was shaken awake at 0545 cold and shivering given a mug of tea, before my last two hour stag. Finally at midday the next Guard Mount took over and I returned to the basha very knackered, to sleep all afternoon. 24-hour guards are not recommended.

A new point of attraction, was the resurfacing of the LAD Square. However, not to the delight of Al who during that period had to work on an old Tilley wagon out on the square. The gang of Coolies all Tamil women had to work around him and what he did not say was no bodies business. What a tedious job the Coolies made of it? When the ruts and potholes were filled, they just walked over them or, stamped their feet to flatten them before they began

Al not a happy bunny resurfacing. Over a wide area, a couple of Tamil men poured black tarry liquid, then the covering shingle was applied by a dozen Tamil women balancing flat wicker baskets full of shingle on their heads. In line they ambled over from a lorry load of shingle and with a twirling action of the basket sprayed the shingle over the tarred area, before ambling back to a lorry for refills. The whole operation took about three weeks. The exit next to the sheds was rebuilt over a monsoon ditch from the Parade ground down onto the roadway, they poured concrete smoothing it out and while it was wet someone had a bright idea to space out stones, forming the letters L. A. D.

The resurfacing was a great improvement to the parade ground and was duly christened on the following Saturday with the OC's Parade. Marching and stamping of many army boots, raised clouds of white dust to cover boots with a fine white powder much to 'Q's dislike. All lined up Q proceeded along our line, with his handkerchief flicked the dust off our boots to reveal shiny toecaps. Thinking, "That's extreme. But we were the REME". Nevertheless, the resurfacing did have its faults. It was the monsoon season and the daily heavy downpours of rain, washed down the loose shingle into the monsoon ditch along the front of the sheds, it lay in piles along the bottom. The only way to clear it was with a long handled scoop, made up in the welding shop and became a bit of a hazardous job, as you had to get down into the ditch where a snake might have dropped within its depths.   Another area snakes might drop into was the inspection pits. A morning inspection could reveal such a serpent. On one occasion, Gerry spotted something tiny in a corner of the pit, suggested to me.

'Let's get it.'

'Wot for? We should kill it.'

'No, we'll have a laugh with someone; it's not a python. Find a match box, we'll put it in there.'

'Then wot?'

'We'll give it to Towser he like snakes?' Armed with a matchbox and screwdriver, we got down into the pit a closer inspection stopped Gerry.

'Hold on. That's a bootlace?'

'No it ain't, it's wriggling about.' Slipping the screwdriver under the serpent lifted it out with both ends hanging loose, he exclaimed.

'Not a bootlace yer prat. A bleedin' deadly Bootlace snake.' Immediately I dropped the screwdriver and retreated away.

'C'mon Joey. We've got to get rid of it.' From a safe distance I replied.

'Well you get rid of it.'

'Don't be daft, its only about five inches long it's a baby one, normally they only grow to twelve inches long. You're scared? You hold the box.' That did it with trepidation, managed to get it into the matchbox and slid the top over. Gerry muttered.

'It's not going to get out of there. We'll keep it, see what happens in a couple of days time. Put it up on one of the cross beams.' About a week later

we retrieved it, gingerly slid off the cover, found it curled up dead. But there were other incidents involving snakes that did occur in camp. The Duty Officer on Guard, killed a Cobra outside the Guardroom and as a warning, draped it over the notice board.

Outside Whiskers Barbers shop

Whiskers.' Stood behind.

On another occasion the QMS found a Python curled up on top of a pile of blankets, he obtained a pistol from the armory and shot it through the neck.

The next day, during the midday news. An announcement was made on the radio. Mick shouted out. 'Hoi you lot did yer hear that? The Aussie infantry are joining in the fight; their advance party is arriving soon, coming up here in the North somewhere.'

In our sleepy state, it did not register, but whilst enjoying the afternoon tea with chunks of cheese, it became a talking point. The consensus was, it was only the Australian Infantry. We were not going to get involved with any of the Australians.

However, another new VM arrived, by the name of Des Britland, Des had been transferred from Korea, possibly a replacement for Lim the Chinese fitter who along with Wong the Chinese clerk, were transferred to the local REME base workshop. About a week or so later two more VM's arrived, Brian Hayward a lad from Streatham, not far from Vauxhall and Vic Martin from Hastings also a Recovery Mech John Anstis, from High Wycombe, (Jacko's replacement) Although at that time there was not that much work going on, our ranks were swelling; the accommodation in the Basha was tight. Brian, Vic, and John, being Southerners took up bed spaces close to us, whilst the others found bed spaces up the Northern end.

Thursday morning pay parade. Sgt. Levine ordered us to assemble outside Capt. Coles Office. Sgt. Levine and Sgt. Kershaw ordered us into three ranks. Discipline kicked in with mutterings of. "Wots all this in aid of?"

Fred emerged from his inner sanctum wearing his peaked hat, accompanied by 'Q.' Sgt. Levine barked out.

'Platoon Attention.' Bringing us to attention. Capt Cole, (God Bless Him. After all, it was blazing hot.) Ordered.

'Sergeant Levine stand them at ease please.'

'PLATOON Stand at ease.'

'Look you shower of, I do not know what's. Mainly bloody cockneys. Eh. Q? I have some news to announce to you. Three Company RASC. Including we, the REME LAD. We will no longer be part of the North Malaya Division. Instead going to become part of the Twenty-eight. Independent Commonwealth Infantry Brigade. The original Twenty-eight. Infantry Brigade was formed during the Korean War. Now that may seem a little indifferent to what you normally are doing. However, I can inform you. That a contingent of the Royal Australian Army Service Corps number 126 Transport Platoon. will shortly be joining this unit. They have their own Officers, Sergeant's and OR's. Their OC. is Captain Goodall. Therefore, I am instructing you, at all times to abide by the normal military procedure when being addressed by or, talking to their officers. Exactly when they will be arriving I cannot say, but it will be before Christmas that is for sure. To this LAD. It means more Lorries to fix, their vehicles are American GMC Two and a half ton six by six wheeled Lorries, including a Water Tanker and I believe a few Harley Davidson motorcycles, which will be as and when necessary repaired by us. As time progresses Company orders, will provide more details. Right let us get on with paying you chaps, cannot have you lazing about. Sergeant Levine seeing that we will become very busy, I think week-end jungle training won't go amiss.' Retreated into his office to begin the pay parade.

The rumours were confirmed, the talk was all about these Aussies coming to join us. Al stated his opinion.

'Bleedin' Aussies can't play cricket.'

CHAPTER TWENTY-ONE
28TH. COMMONWEALTH. IND. INFANTRY BRIGADE.

It was about that time, the head of the Malayan Legislative Council. Tengku Abdul Rahman and Ching Peng Leader of the CT's, was engaged in secret communications on the possibility of a cease-fire. Due to this, the activities of the CT's had been curtailed. However, there had been no statement made about where or when the intended talks were being held.

On the first Saturday in October. Having finished work our usual routine was to eat in the mess before relaxing in the afternoon. However, at the cookhouse, we found a long queue of unfamiliar figures dressed in K.D's wearing the famous Australian Slouch Hats. The Aussies had joined us. Being at the rear end of the queue was not to our liking. The bloke in front a tall lanky fella, who by the colour of his arms and face was more than tanned, he appeared much older than any of us, possibly in his late thirties and judging by his fellow comrades, they too about the same age, they certainly were Regulars. The first person to open up the conversation was Al.

'Ear mate. Where you lot from?'

'Awsstralia! Where the blaady hell do you think?'

'Wot unit are you then?'

'One Two Six. Transport Platoon Royal Awstralian Army Service Corps, who you lot then?'

'REME.'

'RAEME?'

'RAEME! Nope. REME. Get the name right mate.'

'RAEME is the Royal Australian Electrical Mechanical Engineers, how do you say it?'

'REME without the A. Were better than your lot.' Al spoiling for an argument.

'No Blaady way mate!' A sharp response.

'Well where are they then? With you lot then?'

'Nope were on our own.' (Having already been informed by Fred, Al continues).

'We have to look after your Bleedin' Lorries then?'

'Blaady right mate. We aren't, not our job, we just drive the buggers.'

'What are they QLs?'

'Not blaady likely. QL's. Are those the blaady Larries your blokes transported us down from Penang in?'

'Yeah, so you ain't come up from Singapore then?'

'Nope. Got off the troopship Georgic at Penang.'

'Wot do you lot drive then and where are they?'

'American type Studebakers, Bloody old war surplus bangers.

'Ear Digger, wots yer name?'

'Darkie's, my name! An yours?'

'Al. This 'ere is Joey, Den, and Bill, and the mob behind are all REME. So, we'll get to see a lot of you Diggers in the workshops. That is, when you want your lorries fixed?' As we moved forward, Darkie asked.

'Wots the Tucker like Al?'

'Tucker? Oh, grub. Load of crap, but you get used to it.' Nevertheless, the Aussies in front by their age statue and looks, some of them must have been in the Second World War. Surveying the dishes of food lay before them, voiced their opinion at the two cooks wielding spatulas looking very scared, as one huge Aussie bloke who looked like two versions of Desperate Dan put together, shouted.

'Do you call this Tucker? Not fit for blaady lizards.' This was followed by further unrepeatable scorn, as they made their way into the other mess hall with raucous shouts. Busily tucking into his curry Mick quipped.

'Blooody funny bunch of bastards, those Aussies, bet their going to cause trouble. Joey! If that big bastard plays football, don't upset him he'll make mince meat out of you.'

'Bollocks. I'll run through his legs beat him anytime.' That brought a lot of jeering. However, above our normal level of banter, with all the windows wide open the rowdiness of complaining in their mess hall drowned out ours. The Aussies soon made known their presence and certainly not shy in coming forward with their complaints. Banging on the tables and shouting. 'Not eating this Tucker. Its blaady lizard shit.' The English Officer of the Day, having been around our tables with the usual question, when he left our mess hall to visit theirs our chattering stopped so we could hear what was going on. He asked.

'Any Complaints here?' The big fella bawled out.

'The blaady tucker you lot serve up. Is not fit for blaady lizards.' Blaady dung that's what it is.'

Then they all joined in. The Officer beat a hasty retreat. Very soon their OC. Captain Goodall and Platoon leader 2nd. Lt. Hall arriving, took the matter in hand, speaking to them, which seemed it resolve their moans for the time being. As it was a normal weekend for us, we were going into town to see a movie. On our way out passing by the Naafi, it was bulging with Aussies, there must have been the whole platoon of sixty or so in there swilling beer, shouting and carrying on much the same as we would. Nevertheless, down in town witnessed a very funny sight. That of an RSF running along Brewster Road being chased by three Red Caps, Nothing unusual about that, however he haring along the road showing a bare hairy arse, the RSF minus his trousers that were swinging freely over his arm, still wearing his Jacket, boots and puttees, with Glen Gharrie stuck on his head. We cracked up. Never did find out if he got away.

Sunday night the Naafi again was packed to the gunnels with Aussies.

Monday morning Muster had assembled, leaving a wide space of at least the distance of two platoons. Sgt. Levine had marched us almost to the middle of the large square. Just before 0800 hrs we watched as the Aussies, led by their three officers all dressed in KDs. Long trousers, jackets and slouch hats, dangling from their bayonet frogs were 18 inch Bayonets. The two platoons with rifles at the slope marched into the void space, their Sgt in a deep growl of a voice, ordered them through the usual arms drill, stood them at ease. The Duty Officer arrived, took over the Muster Parade normal routine, checking platoon numbers, sick parade etc., before dismissing the parade. The topic of conversation was the Aussies attending muster with rifles and bayonets that was not even done on OCs? That evening we ventured into the Naafi, occupied by Aussies swigging beer straight from the bottle, there was not a glass to be seen. Sitting at one of the vacant tables, we did notice they never bought a round, it was a case of. "If I want a drink I will buy my own, you buy yours". Same with their fags. Quite strange, unlike us buying a round or handing the freebies out.

By the middle of that week, the Aussies were taken back to Penang to collect their wagons. A day later, a convoy of 10 wheeled American GMC' wagons, along with Harley Davison M/C', caused clouds of white dust as they drove into the square and parked up in line. All were wearing OGs plus their slouch hats. After about a week, we found out the results of their complaining about our 'Tucker'. The Aussies had been granted an extra sum of seven shillings a day for. 'Steak Money.' What a bleedin' cheek? We did not get it moreover, they were on a far higher pay than we were. Nevertheless, they continued to eat our 'Tucker' in the mess and spent their extra money, on Anchor Beer in the Naafi. So much for us complaining about equal rights. We did not get it. Forget it. We are British. Nevertheless, it was not long before one GMC arrived in the workshops, towed in by the Scammel. Jacko, in his usual style sauntered into Stan Levine together with the Aussie driver Bluey, advised.

'Bloody brakes failed fished it out of a ditch GMC's are rubbish.' Left Stan to consult with the Driver.

The departure of Jacko and Beasley was celebrated over the Naafi, much Anchor was drunk. One evening the four of us, were drinking beer in the Naafi Al was puffing away at a fag, Bill was talking to Den, whilst I remembered what Capt. Cole had remarked about, Jungle training during pay parade, intrigued as to what it was all about, raised the question.

'Er. Den. Wot is this Jungle training lark Fred was on about? Some place called Lumutt?' Looking at me before answering he nudged Bill, who for once stopped chatting and listened.

'Lumutt and week-end Jungle Training go together. That is where we go. It's on the coast about fifty miles away, all the way through Bandit country.' Bill quickly responded.

'Joey. You're not included. Can't have two elect's away at same time. Can we Den?'

'No. tough shit. Anyway, you wouldn't like it. Sun, sandy white beaches, dip in the sea, palm trees, sleeping under the stars.' Disgruntled I replied.

'You're talking a load of bullshit. That ain't no jungle training, anyway ain't seen any white beaches since I been here.' Al ignoring the ashtray on the table casually flicked his dog end on the floor retorted.

'Not likely too either.' Immediately thinking, "Here we go again a wind up, why can't these bleeders answer a simple question".

'Come on. You're all taking the piss. Heh. Den! See if I can go on this jungle training lark?'

'Well. If Fred suggested it, he must know something big is coming our way. I'll see how many want to go. Can't all go that's for sure, new one's maybe get their feet wet. I'll have a word with Stan.' It was left to Den to organise the trip.

Saturday after OC Parade. Nine of us armed to the teeth, left camp in a QL borrowed from the RASC and Bin wagon. Den and Al were driving the QL with five of the others riding in the back, whilst Bill and I were driving the Bin wagon that was full of bedding, tables, compo rations and personal kit. Travelling in a southwesterly direction towards the coast into the area known as the Ding Dings. We eventually left the main road and drove through part jungle and bush before turning off along a sandy winding track in between tall palm trees. Arriving late in the afternoon, we stopped opposite an offshore Island. (Pankor) Clambering down sorted out the weapons, rations, table and chairs beddings and kit, having taken our own mattress and bedding the five seasoned ones? Set up their bedding up in the back of the QL, leaving the four new ones to camp on the ground, underneath a canopy draped from one side of the QL as cover. I decided to set up my bedding in between the front wheels of the Bin wagon hung the mossie net over the axle. With everything sorted, was able to take a good look at the surrounding area. As the lapping sea washed against the small stretch of white sand up to the jungle fringes dotted with high Palm trees and as the setting sun slowly disappeared behind the offshore Island, it presented an almost dark silhouette of its hilly shape, standing there in the cool sea breeze. I was lost in the magic of an idyllic moment until, Den I/C party called out.

'Joey. You start a fire, get some driftwood and use yer parang to dig a pit in the sand.'

Now. This was the life. In the fading light far away from camp, happy as a sand boy beachcombing for driftwood, began collecting dried palm leaves to start off the fire, before wandering about the beach to find bits of wood, taking them back dumped them into a pile, by which time it was dark. With the parang began digging a pit throwing the sand to one side, as I dug the sound of whirring surrounded me. An angry voice yelled out.

'YOU BLEEDIN' PRAT JOEY. STOP DIGGING .' Wondered what was going on. About five bodies ran past me, Kerplash! Sploosh in they went, thinking they were going for a swim, yelled after them.

'WOTS IT LIKE IN THE WATER?' 'The sound of whirring about my head increased that had me waving the parang about. The voice of Mick yelled back.

'YOU YER PRAT, THAT'S A NEST YOU DUG UP! Then Bill yelled.

'THERE'S MILLIONS OF THEM FLYING ABOUT.' Still wildly waving the parang about, yelled back.

'WHAT THE BLEEDIN' HELL ARE THEY?' Someone switched on the headlights of a lorry to reveal in its beams, me in among the middle of a mass of swirling insects just like white snow, as I rapidly retreated up the short stretch of beach towards the Lorry, the voice of Den yelling at me.

'YOU BLEEDIN' PRAT JOEY. THER'RE BLEEDIN' SAND FLIES. YOU PRAT.'

By the safety of the QL turned to see caught in the beam of light, a group of heads submerged up to their necks in the sea some wearing jungle hats. Obviously, they were taking an early shower! Someone else dug a pit further away to cook our rations, one duty I was never to get again. After eating, had a few beers before settling for a night under the stars. My cosy bedding just about fitted in between the two front wheels and was as snug as a bug in a rug. During the night a storm broke, from out at sea the wind howled in with driving rain, to avoid the onslaught of a mini typhoon there was much shouting as the others scrambled up into wagons. I fully sheltered behind the front wheel, listening to the force of the howling wind for about ten minutes, and then it was gone. The next morning the corners and edges of my mattress were sodden very quickly; the beach became littered with drying mattresses and mossie nets hanging from palm trees. That day we swam, by removing the inner tube out of the spare wheel the non-swimmers were able to get into deep water, to paddle around in the tepid sea. The short days outing was over all too quickly, clearing up heading back to camp, all glowing red after a day by the seaside.

Lumutt Beach   *Compo Rations*   *The other side of Beach*   *Ducking Non -Swimmers*

For some reason or other I had to return to the basha to get something, upon entering found a squaddie sat on a bed with his kit on the floor, he did not look too happy so thinking back too when I first entered the basha the reception I received from pratty Beasley I enquired.

'Can I help yer mate?' to which he replied

'Is this the REME basha?' Quickly noting his cockney accent replied.

'Yes, you joining us? Where der yer come from in London then?'

'New Cross. Know it?'

'Soddin"ell. You'd better sleep down the other end of the basha with us lot, were all from Vauxhall. You join us down there mate there's a spare bed alongside Bills, he's from Peckham. You might know him. My names Joey Plant.'

'Mines George. George Greenaway.'

'Right. George. When they've finished work yer'll meet the others. You got to report to Capt Cole?'

'That's 'im, forgot his name?'

'I'll help with yer gear, then take you up the LAD to meet Fred.' Observing he was about the same height as Al, his blonde hair almost bleached white. With my wanted item, we left the basha with George relating his misfortune.

'I've been out here six weeks at the REME Workshops. Last week they said I had been posted down here.'

'You must be Beasley's replacement. He's not long gone, he was a right prat. Ear when you get into the Office. I bet you. Q will ask if you play football, you wait and see?'

We arrived at the office, poking my head through the doorway.

'Captain Cole. There's a Craftsman Greenaway here the new welder. He's from London. New Cross Sir. Not far from us. Sir.'

'Oh my Goodness. Not another one? Well send him in Plant.' Passing George, muttered.

George

'In you go, don't forget what I said.' Amid a crunch and stamping of boots, left him to it. Informing Al, Den and Bill of our new arrival too swell the cockney blood in our basha. They could not believe it either. George reported to Sgt. Levine, who came out shouted. 'Keene 'Q' wants you up in the office now.'

Leaving the cage Sgt. Levine and George crossed over the grass space to the welding shop to spend some time in there, during which time Al returned.

'That bloke George. Wot's his name plays football so 'Q' says. He wants me to organise a football game with HQ Company.   I am going down to see Evie and get it arranged, I'll be back shortly. Tell Stan I'm off on Q's orders.' Upon returning, Sgt. Levine must have spotted Al walking towards the main Camp asked.

'Where's Al going?' Den answered.

'Q' ordered him to speak with Evie about a football match with HQ.' Stan turned to George and asked.

'Greenaway. By any chance. Do you play football? '

'Yes Sergeant.'

'Oh my God? Right return to the basha get your kit sorted out and change into working dress then report back.' George about to leave nodded at me.

'Ere Mate you were right. Q wots his name, did ask about football.'

Not long after George had left, after Al had seen Q he came back and informed us.

'I've just been down to see Evie and arranged a match.' When George reported dressed for work. Den introduced him to Al.

'Nice to meet yer George. What position do you play?'

'Inside right why?'

'Well you got to play a game of football for the LAD, and seeing you come from New Cross, I'll bet you're a Millwall fan?'

'Wrong. Charlton's my team. Anyway, who told you I came from New Cross?'

'Fred did. He asked where it was? And I told him about four miles away from us lot. He just shook his head. Laughing said. It was a Cockney LAD he had under him.'

'Like Joey said. First thing 'Q' asked me if I played football?' Den interrupting.

'C'mon yer bunch of housewife's, git yer eating irons and let's get some grub.' Joey you take George down to the bedding store.' Over dinner Bill and George shared stories about Peckham and New Cross and what or who they knew.

Tuesday evening. The match against "HQ". Our team consisted of six from the Company team, plus George, Brummie in goal, Sgt. Kershaw Gerry and Des. Kitted out, both teams boarded the QL Bus for the trip down to our pitch. Being less than a mile away there was no need for escorts. As the match was a trial for George, Al switched me to left half, alongside Mick and Gerry. 'Q' gave us a pep talk, about tactics and how to get a grip of the match, even Captain Cole turned up to cheer us on. The game started, it was supposed to be a friendly but with mixed spectators on the sidelines, along with quite a few Malays from the bungalows opposite, inter- rivalry took hold. We were an opposing force and Al's shots at goal, were saved on more than one occasion by the Company goalkeeper, he determined not to let Al beat him. George performed well and by half time everyone

Half Tme.

was knackered. The second half began; the opposing winger was Evie, of stocky build and weighed twice my weight. In the first half he being quite a dribbler had beaten me a few times but I was determined that would not happen again, being quicker and faster if he did chased him to retrieve the ball, which frustrated him. With about twenty minutes to go Al scored from a through ball by George, five minutes later Jock crossed the ball over and Al headed the ball past the Keeper. Two minutes later Den, made a massive clearance that Al brought down the ball turned and thumped it past the keeper. It finished three nil. Jubilant! Minus a knackered George, many Anchors were downed in the Naafi.

By that time, the Bin Wagon had been registered as 'Beyond Local Repair.' (BLR'd) Its replacement, a one tonner general-purpose welding truck. With not much welding to do George was put in charge of it. The mail call revealed nothing for me having sent one letter to mum just to let her know my address in Malaya that she must have received by then. Lying there whilst others were reading, listening to the news the constant news bulletins, came thick and fast. Operations so and so that was going on. CT's had been identified, searches by the Security Forces were in progress, unlike the rest in the basha, they appeared unconcerned about the events Yes, we had been trained but not for Jungle warfare. I began to form a picture at home of mum chewing her nails worrying her head off about me in Malaya left me thinking, "Oh, shit. How I wished was back home, instead of being out here in the stinking heat nevertheless, I did receive two letters on the next mail call one from Mum and my sister Margaret, this was my time to shut off the world around me and concentrate on what was an occurring back home. Even Al obliged, by getting the tea? Oh, it was heaven lying on the bed, reading those letters repeatedly;, a kick on the bed by Bill brought me back to reality and stopped any further reading,

'Git yer arse in gear, read 'em when yer get back yer lazy git. You've already read 'em a thousand times. C'mon.' Followed the ensuing rush for the evening meal and I'm sure all the time there, we were never second it appeared to be a competition; we had lookouts everywhere watching for the cooks to start laying up the meal.

Before going to the Naafi, nearly everyone became engrossed in writing letters at 1800 hrs. The news announcer gave a resume of incidents during the first two weeks of October.'

Gangs of Terrorist in Jahore wrecked a number of Lorries and other equipment in attacks on estates and plantations, destroying rubber trees and clashing on several occasions with the local security forces. On October thirteenth. A British Officer a Captain

in the Royal Welsh Fusiliers and two other ranks, were killed and another soldier seriously wounded in an ambush near Seremban.

On October seventeenth, it was announced in Kuala Lumpur that preliminary talks had taken place between members of the Malayan Government and Ching Peng, Leader of the Communist Forces. Their first meeting, to be held in connection with the Amnesty terms announced in August. The meeting took place at an undisclosed venue.

In Singapore on October nineteenth. It was announced by, The Far East Land Forces H.Q. As reinforcements. The second. Battalion. Royal Australian Regiment and a New Zealand SAS Squadron would join the 28th. Commonwealth Independent Infantry Brigade.

On October twentieth in another incident, terrorists seriously wounded Mr. C. G. Stanley, the British manager of a rubber estate near Labis in Jahore. A follow up by Security Forces is in progress.

The news was not very encouraging, but perhaps the winds of peace might change the situation, however it appeared amnesty or no amnesty, things seemed to have warmed up again on a larger scale. Having already done a weekend guard plus a few Kampong guards. The report about the Royal Welsh Fusiliers was the first bulletin I had heard mention British troops had been killed. But too our small group they appeared unconcerned nevertheless, I was a newcomer and most likely would hear and learn more about the fighting in Malaya as time passed by. It was four weeks since my arrival when Bill said.

'Because I'm going home, 'I've nominated you for convoy duty as Electrician and shotgun rider, Towsers going as the Mechanic. Convoy's going to Tapah tomorrow.'

'Why not you?'

'Nope. We take it in turns. It's your turn to draw arms and ammo, your toolbox. I'll sort out a couple of electrical spare parts. You're riding shotgun in the cab of the last wagon. If ambushed, shoot the first commie yer sees... say's Bill.... Nothing to it or, if yer like me run like 'ell.' Anxiously asked.

'Wot happens if a wagon breaks down?'

'If it's electrical! While you sort it out the driver takes your rifle and covers you. At least there will be two of you.'

'Wot about the others in the convoy?'

'Oh them. They just carry on don't they Al?'

'Sod your luck.' He did not care a shit.

The next morning, in normal working dress plus jacket ammo pouches and water bottle along with Towser drew weapons. Five QL's loaded with stores were lined up in the main parking area, it did not seem much of a convoy. Going to the last Lorry, the driver a lanky lad from Birmingham, very slow in his mannerisms and later found out. Not one for talking. The convoy set off along the road leading south. A 15/19th Saracen and Daimler joined us as escorts. This duty was a good opportunity to see the countryside with its narrow roads, close verges; tall trees intermingled with coconut palms and jungle. A river almost the colour of copper flowed along the left side of the road, frequently the jungle encroached right up to the edge of the road, its denseness blotting out the sun before emerging into bright sunlight. Driving into a stretch of clear vegetation, in the distance a group of hills came into view. Brummie casually mentioned.

'That's the Cameron Highlands in front, as the crow flies thirty-seven miles away by road almost seventy.'

The convoy kept up a steady speed, passing by some funny looking piles of chalky hills possibly the same ones seen from the train. Brummie murmured.

'Those are the Gunong Rapat caves.' Several time we crossed over wooden bridges spanning a river, going through villages that did not seem to have many inhabitants, until at Gopeng there were signs of habitation, we drove another few miles along the jungle roads and I began wondering where the camp was, asked.

'Where is this camp then? In a slow drawl Brummie answered.

'The Malay Regiment camp is just outside Kampar.'

At least that name was something I recognised as the place the train had stopped. Finally, we drove into this camp similar to our own with rows of Bashas laid out in military order. We were directed to the stores, there met by a squad of Malay soldiers, quickly they unloaded the supplies and very soon we were on our return journey. Arriving just after midday, handed in our weapons had dinner then back to work. Overall, the experience was nothing to write home about.

I was working under a QL, when Capt Cole accompanied by Q and Beavis entered the sheds called out.

'Corporal Towse! Where's Sgt Levine?'

'Working on the Scammel with Lance Corporal Lee. Sir.' They strolled past towards the Scammel, heard them chatting amongst themselves before they all walked back to the office, Den walking towards the caged office called out.

'Al, Bill, Joey, Harry, motorcycle bay sharpish.' As usual, Al raised the question

'Wot's all this about Den?'

'Keep yer bleedin' hair on? I'm about to tell you. The 15/19th. Dancers are holding a Gymkhana and there is a competition for the entry of the best Unit Jeep. Fred has entered his jeep. Now you know what state that is in? He's asked, what could we do with it? Beavis suggested. Get a new one Fred told him to shut up. I didn't really have an answer, mechanically it is in good nick, could do with a lick of paint but, all I could suggest was to strip it down and rebuild it. Fred thought about it and then said. If, we had to do that without interfering with our normal repair jobs get on with it; get some of you blokes to work on it. Harry asked

'How long we got?'

'Two weeks, Gymkhana's on Sunday thirteenth November.'

'Blooody 'ell that's not long? Impossible.' Sgt. Levine approaching us said.

'If you lot, are going to work on Fred's Jeep, it's only going to be when you have no work or, you're waiting on replacement spares.' Den questioned.

'Ear Stan. We know that, but you 'eared wot I told Fred, what do you think?

'Uhm. Well. Two weeks, is very tight but if, you start right away maybe possible, when others are free they can also help, instead of loafing around ... he went quiet for a moment...Al. Your wagon is waiting spare isn't it?'.

The LAD waiting for Knock off time

'Yep, nothing else to do at the moment.'

'Bill what about you?'

'Nope, got problems with ignition system.'

'Harry!'

'Nearly ready. Just got to do a test run?'

'Joey.' Your charging batteries, you can start with Al.'

Thinking "Blimey, first time he's addressed me like that must be accepted"...Right these bikes are waiting spares; move them out, sweep out the bay. Get started.'

The motorbikes and their bits were moved into a corner, we had just about finished sweeping all the grime and dust into the monsoon ditch when Beavis drove the jeep into the bay. Getting out exclaimed.

'Ear y'are Al, yer can start work on it.'

'Yer bleedin' prat Beavis. You're enjoying this, as if we ain't got enough work to do, we have to do all your dirty bleedin' work while you sit around skiving. I bet you put Fred up to this?'

'No. I did not! Anyway told im, need a new Land Rover. You lot are the VMs, so I'll sit and watch what you do.'

'Piss off Prat'...adding...well make yourself useful. Remove the canopy and all your bits of shit.' Cheerfully he replied.

'That's easy piece of piss. Won't take long.' Al retorted.

'C'mon Joey, leave him to it.'

'Aw c'mon Al. Give us a hand...Oh, shit! Just remembered... got to take Fred home, so I can't start on it.'

'Beavis you stupid prat. Wot are yer? Fancy forgetting your job; just have to start tomorrow then.' Al did not forget the subject. During the evening meal Beavis became the brunt of Al's jesting.

Next morning after muster work began on the Jeep. We did help Bill to get the bits and pieces out of the way, the canopy, bonnet, and all the attached pieces came off. Den i/c working party ordered.

'Joey with that lot off you can remove all the lights and electric fittings, and then you can take out the wiring loom. By the end of the day, just the chassis of the jeep stood on four blocks. The demolition of this Jeep caused great interest by the passing Aussies they making ribald comments. Al always up for answering back did not let them get away with it, and so began the start of a good alliance between them and us.

To cut a long story short, when we were not working on our other jobs, we were busy with the jeep however, by the second week everything was reassembled. Bill and I worked together to rewire the Jeep, at some time or another all the mechanics worked on it. The body had been cleaned repainted Olive Green, red paint was used on certain parts. I got the job of painting the flashes and lettering on and around the jeep including the Jerry can. Upon completion, the engine was switched on without a hitch; tappets were adjusted and all worked perfectly. Saturday afternoon by 1600 hrs, the Jeep, ready for the competition the following day looked as if it was brand new.

The Finished Jeep

Sunday morning, Beavis left very early to take Captain Cole to the Gymkhana an all-day event. For us another normal day of lazing about waiting for Beavis to return. He arrived back in the Basha well after dark. Mick attracting our attention, questioned.

'Ear Beavis how did you get on, Come in first did you?' He being right down the far end quietly muttered.

'Nah second. But the Jeep was the best one there, got top marks.' All ears were then wide open as Mick asked.

'Who came first then?'

'Gurkhas Land Rover. It was bleedin' brand new. As I said to Fred. We should have got one.' Interrupting Al called out.

'Hoi. Beavis! If it was the best one there? How come you got second place then?' Beavis gave an inaudible reply. Al shouted.

'DIN'T EAR YER. WOT D'YER SAY.' Beavis raising his voice shouted.

'FORGOT ME TOOL KIT, LEFT IT IN THE SHEDS. THAT IS WHAT I LOST MARKS FOR.'

'LOST MARKS, FOR NOT HAVING YER TOOL KIT? BLEEDIN' 'ELL, WOT A BLEEDIN' PRAT. WOT ARE YER BEAVIS?' Den yelled.

'BEAVIS, YOU'RE A PRAT.' Then everyone started to hurl abuse at him. He quickly disappeared out of the basha. However, that was not the end of it. Next day immediately after Muster Fred, hands deep in his pockets followed by a sheepish looking Beavis, entered the sheds and gathered the jeep party together.

'You lads did a bloody fine job. Congratulations to all of you. I even got a nod of approval from the Lieutenant Colonel of the 15/19th. For a bloody good show. However, this person beside me. Beavis did not do you proud. Fancy leaving his tool kit behind? However, next Friday evening, I wish to invite all of you to my residence for an evening meal, dress in your civvies. That will be my thank you. Right back to work.'

Friday night, at a rapid pace Interior Economy was completed. We hired taxis to Fred's house, where he and Mrs. Cole welcomed us. Treated us to a sit down supper of fish and chips with beer thrown in. It was a very good evening out.

Two weeks later, after the usual Saturday curry on our way to the Odeon, going past the Jubilee Park, Bill suggested.

'Right tonight after flicks, we'll introduce Joey to the dance hall. You fancy a dance don't yer?'

'No I don't. Not really.'

'Well we'll go in anyway. Shows you the taxi dancers in there, yer might even fancy one never know?' I was to be baptized.

After the film, we walked the short distance back entered the dimly lit interior. The Chinese doorman believe or not dressed in a white Tuxedo and black bowtie, very pleased to see new customers welcomed us warmly, through a set of gold teeth suggested.

'Tacket, tree for one doolar. Welly gud taxi dancees, you lik?' Bill breezing passed him answered.

'Nah. Just looking around.'

It was free to get in, so we walked into a rather dimmed smoke filled emporium, smelling very heavy of cheap perfume. At the far end on a stage, a small Chinese band sounding much too tinny, similar to a small jazz band from the 1930's were jamming it up. The small dance floor, was crowded with couples jigging about, when the music stopped the lights were turned up, revealing many squaddies coupled up with Chinese birds dressed in long silk Cheongsams, with splits from the bottom hemline nearly up to their waist revealing quiet an expanse of white leg in some instances a show of lacy knickers. A few elderly European couples possibly Planters, returned to their table placed around the edge of the floor. As the band struck up and played another tune. I spotted Ginger Smith and his mate Pyatt. Both the worse for drink clinging onto two Chinese Taxi Dancing as they stumbled around the floor. Near the doorway stood a group of Taxi Dancers. Al and Den were watching what was going on. Nudging Bill indicated the ones by the doorway said.

'Ear Bill, ain't they tiny?'

'Not arf, slim as 'ell, tiny little waists, no bleedin' tits though just fried eggs, try em out see for yersel. They won't mind?'

'Silly prat just can't go up and try em.'

'No! Yer prat yer got to dance with them! Get a dollar's worth then you'll see. C'mon I fancy a quick couple of dances, then were off.'

Dance Ticket.

He moved towards the Chinese door attendant, much intrigued by his description followed and bought three tickets; Al called out.

'You pair of silly prats.'

 Bill. Eagerly sorted out two Chinese girls, each one gratefully took a single ticket from us thinking. "Bleedin' 'ell this is novel. Wonder what the girls back at St. Anne's would think of this malarkey. Not much I guess"? The Chinese bird Bill had chosen for me looked like a doll. Wearing a green long Cheongsam emblazoned with
dragons all over it. She was about four foot six aged about fourteen, with her face thickly powdered with red rouge plastered on her cheeks and tiny lips, her hair was tightly pulled back to emphasize high cheek bones with slits of eyes, thinking. "What if she's a CT spy"? Taking hold of her, slipped one hand around a tiny waist doubt if it was more than fifteen inches? She, pressing herself against me was flat chested and stank of some cheap perfume. As we glided around passing Al and Den a few times, who were killing themselves laughing. When the dance ended, she invited.

'Lu wan nu wance?' Not fancying asking another suggested.

'Might as well.'

'Lu giv nu takets?'

'Oh. Okay here.' She grabbed both, I was booked for two.

'Welly good, we wance. Yu nis fella.'

'Yer so me Mum keeps telling me.' What an experience? By the time the three dances were over sweating buckets reeking of her cheap perfume, a smirking Al remarked.

'Ear Joey, yer made a nice couple dancing out there. You in love now?'

'Silly bleeder just had three dances, that's all couldn't fancy any of em.' Bill laughing aloud said.

'Told yer, nothing to em. Nothing like the girls at the Peckham Co-op. Every time I have a dance in the Joob, its always the same.

"Lu play takets pleese. Wik stip, Chop Chop." Had us all in fits of laughter as we left there for our next visit. English breakfast, then taxi back.

Sgt. Levine striding down from Freds Office, shouted out.

'Joey want a word with you now! Wondering what I had done called back.

'Coming Stan.'

Meeting half way down he said. 'Tomorrow morning. There's a convoy going up the Cameron's, you're the duty VE so you will ride as Shotgun in the last lorry with a driver from 'B' Coy. Take your tool box and get Bill to give you some spares, he will know what you should take. It's leaving after Muster so draw a rifle and ammo and be ready to go. 'Immediately was a bit concerned, but having already gone as far as Tapah without any incidents, the trip up to the Cameron everyone seems to have done

'Okay. I'll check with Bill.' After I had explained all that to him, he just said.

'You'll like it up there a sight bleedin cooler than down here. About half way up watch out for the Saki Women, you might see 'em they are half naked.' Very interested in his suggested was more than keen to go.

In convoy to the Cameron's.

'Well I'll watch out for them that's for sure.'

The Convoy consisted of four GMC's, and four QL's loaded with stores, plus a ten-ton Hippo Lorry loaded with Artillery shells. At Tapah, we joined onto the rear of a row of civilian cars and Lorries, our escorts the 15/19th. Hussars stationed at the front middle and rear of the convoy. It was my first trip up. As we progressed upwards, the winding road was flanked by jungle, a break in the terrain overlooked a valley with a bluish hue to it, I knew the driver Andy who's Lorry I had worked on before he informed me.

'That's the blue valley, where they grow Tea.'

'Ear you seen any of these half-naked women then? Bill Dineen was telling me about.'

'I've seen em a couple of times there're Malayan Aborigines live in the jungle use Blow pipes to kill Monkeys and wild pigs and all that. When we get close to em, I'll point them out if you are lucky you only get a fleeting glimpse of em that's all. Back in camp I have some phots that I'll show yer later.'

Malayan Aborigines

'Thanks. Appreciate that.' Full of anticipation began observing everything. (However did not see any half-naked women when we got to Tanah Rata, the gradient flattened out, it was then I felt the drop in temperature and by the time we had arrived in the LAD compound at the top, it was misty. The LAD consisted of a few Nissan huts, a small workshop and a parade ground. We did not stay long enough to see much, the British Medical Hospital, a row of shops and a Golf course, but thought it looked a delightful place. We had a bite to eat, before leaving on the downward journey of the afternoon convoy. Passing through Tanah Rata you could again feel the heat of the afternoon sun. Travelling was monotonous, turning corner, losing sight of the trucks in front, we had not gone that far when we heard the sound of shots further down, Andy shouted.

'Bloody 'ell that's the last thing we need fooking Ambush.' For me nearly shitting myself, it was rifle at the ready. After the initial burst did not remember hearing any more shots being fired. When we reached Tapah, there was a bit of a pow wow going on with the 15/19th. No doubt discussing the incident. We headed back to Ipoh. It was only when we had stopped in the square, we discovered one of the Aussie drivers had been lucky, a bullet hole through the metal casing behind his head, was clear evidence the Aussies had received their first taste of potential danger.

Since the Aussies had arrived, the LAD had become very busy with different wagons needing repair. Late one morning the Pig was driven into the LAD. The driver spoke to Sgt. Levine, who shouted.

'Joey! Pig's petrol gauge needs urgent fixing; it's got to go out.'

The Pig was driven out of the LAD before returning to slowly reverse up to the water tap. Wondering why? Asked Pyatt the driver who came from Southend.

to wash it out, just taken a dead Commie bastard full of bullet holes, down to the Police Station. Got shot up in a rubber plantation down near Gopeng. Fooking stinks in there. The Police Sgt. Said he would give me a couple of photo's of them when he gets 'em developed, give yer one if you like getting one for Smithy as well.'

Dead CT.

'Well if yer can spare one Okay.' As he got on with washing out the spilt blood with buckets of water, aware of the stench and the claret coloured water I sorted out his Petrol problem only a sticky float in his petrol tank, finished the job. "The Pig was indeed an armoured Coffin".

A broadcast on the news that evening announced. *Two European planters, Mr. E. King. and Mr. J. Hall was seriously wounded when Terrorist attacked a Rubber estate in the Rengam area of Jahore, A follow up by Security forces is in progress.'*

With interest listened to the announcement, which appeared to be the same as all the others. Hit and Run tactics by the CT's. Four days later another bulletin. Did catch everyone's attention.

On Sunday November twentieth. A large scale attack by over 100-armed Communist terrorist on a New Village of Kea Farm, in the Cameron Highlands took place. In an exchange of fire one Policeman was killed, a villager murdered before the Terrorist escaped with a number of weapons, a large quantity of ammunition and food.

To combat the recent intensified attacks in the south and central areas. The first Battalion the Hampshire Regiment and first Battalion North Rhodesian Regiment, a Squadron of the Special Air Service. Have been relocated, increasing the existing force in the areas, by 1300 troops. Following the recent attack in the Cameron Highlands. General Bourne announced that after December First . Full-scale operations against the Terrorist would resume.

Mick shouted out. 'There go the blooody peace talks?'

Left me wondering, if the previous skirmish by CT's, whilst coming down from the Cameron's was anything to do with this latest attack, but over 100 that was quite a force. Anyway, Cpl. John Mean, who played for Ipswich Town was getting packed up ready to leave our basha, on the 23rd. it was another Piss-up over the Naafi. With his going, Bunny Moore was made up to Corporal. On our way back to the Basha, reading Company Orders to see who was posted for Guard Duty? Reading a paragraph.

"Effective immediately. Everyday Working Dress! Shorts, Puttees, Hose Tops with flashes, OG Jackets will be worn when driving outside camp limits".

This caused a lot of disapproval to us and prompted a lively discussion amongst the LAD. The consensus was 'No Way'. How could we work in our best OG's? In addition, be expected to keep them clean, from the muck and grease we encountered every day. They were reserved specifically for OC's. Parade. We complained to Sgt. Levine. Who took the matter up with Q then Fred. However, too no avail, we had to obey Company Orders. This did not go down well with us, taking great care; we sat on sheets of newspaper or pieces of cardboard to avoid getting any grease on our number ones, and obviously slowed down our working pace. By lunch break we were saturated, the hose tops were sweat sodden and dirty still complaining.

'You'll have to lump It.' answered Sgt. Levine. Nevertheless, our own thoughts were different. If the Aussies could complain about the "Tucker" as they called it. We must be able to do something about our working dress. Den suggested we carry on at a very slow pace, he prophesized. 'You wait it will happen.' On the Saturday, we turned up for OC's, in our normal working dress washed and pressed but shabby with oil stains, Bill and I wore shorts that had little holes in them from acid burns. Before we went on parade, The Q did an inspection and did not approve. Looking at us, he questioned.

'D.D.Dineen. P. Plant. Why are y.y.you wearing t.t.those s.s.shorts?' To which Bill truthfully replied.

'Can't 'elp it Q. Acid burns. Been wearing best shorts as per company orders. Q.' shaking his head he knew we were trying to prove a point, just walked away. We went on Parade like that and I am sure out of earshot the OC did have words with Capt Cole.

After a week and a half at our slow pace, all eight bays were full with three lines of Lorries parked outside waiting repairs. During dinner break, Nobby Hill our clerk informed us.

Bluey still waiting

'Capt Jardine–Wallace was in Fred's Office this morning complaining to Fred, about the number of Aussie wagons off the road. Fred told him. It was the fault of the mode of dress and he would try to sort something out. He had words with Q and told him to get Sgt. Levine to get a grip.' Den the instigator of the go-slow muttered.

'See I told you all something is about to explode.'

Immediately after dinner break. 'Q' came striding down along with Stan Levine, holding his work sheet clipboard came around to each Lorry asking us.

'What's the hold up? How long will it take?'

'As soon as I've finished.' However, Den intervened and spoke of what we all thought.

'Q. We can't work, dressed in this bleedin' clobber; more time is wasted caring about our clothes than the wagons.' Sgt. Levine was quick to add and back us up.

'That's the main problem, I keep on telling them to hurry up, but they all walk around as if their treading on glass. I can't do much about it.' Q pondered for a moment and then reported to Fred. Whilst we stood around doing nothing. Within minutes, he is back out and striding down towards the Admin Offices. We watched from the sheds as his diminishing figure entered the OC's Basha. Five minutes later, he came out striding briskly back towards the LAD entered the sheds, gathered us around before speaking.

'G.g. go down c. c.hanges into y.y.your F-f-f-f ....g n-normal working d-dress. They are a b-b-bloody s-s-shower. Tonight's C-c-company O-o-orders will confirm. W-what I w-want to see. In the n-n-next t-two days is a-all L-lorries off t-the F-f- f...g s-s-square D-d-do you hear. See to it Levine.' With that tirade off he stomps to report to Fred.

Company Orders, did confirm the Change. *"For REME personnel only".* With an added sting in the tail. *When out Test driving or on recovery work the wearing of Boiler suits will be worn these will be issued shortly".*

'Wot Bleedin' Boiler Suits?' Was the question? Two days later, we were issued with them, Very heavy (certainly not lightweight) white thick twill Boiler suits. Miles too big for any of the short arsed people. I think they were Navy Boiler compartment issue. However, we were delighted with our success. Many photographs were taken as evidence of the stupidity, of change in working dress at work and in such a climate. The following Saturday we turned out for OC's all spick and span with a beaming Q.

Normal work dress.

Number Ones

Ridiculous issue

On the following Wednesday evening the week after the fiasco about boiler suits. After work, we and all the other Platoons had to parade on the big car park inside camp. The RASC OC Turned up, the CSM just ordered all.

'Stand at ease.' It was an informal parade of sorts. The CO In a squeaky voice began his oratory.

'As we have all joined forces in the fight against the Communist Terrorist. You are all now part of the Twenty-eighth Commonwealth Infantry Brigade. Unfortunately, I have received from the Medical Officer in charge of the Medical Reception Centre. A damming report of the increase of venereal disease within three company during the last month. This is not acceptable. We all know you are all far away from home in difficult circumstance and times. In addition, it is a disgrace to catch such a disease. Fraternisation with the local female forms must be avoided at all cost. Kampong Java the local place of iniquity is strictly out of bounds... then recited the riot act...Take a hold of yourself. I... it faded out as a burst of boos jeering much muttering and laughter from all the personnel gathered, the OC taking umbrage promptly stomped away. Leaving the CSM to quell the laughter and dismiss the Parade. It was aimed at the Aussies, as they had only been there a couple of months. Nevertheless, we got on very well with the Aussies and found there were a few of them who had emigrated from England, two of them from North London, Hammersmith and Ealing, another from Warrington, he really looked like an Aussie. None of them could find work in Australia so joined up. All of the Aussies had nicknames, the big bloke who looked like two versions of Desperate Dan was called Maxie Payne, his sidekick the same size as me and twice as broad, was called Shufftie. Why do not know? Maybe he shuffled along beside Maxie. There was Darkie, Junior, Whitey, Bluey, Blackie, Shorty, Snazzy and dozens more. Their main interest was cricket, Alan being a good cricketer would rile them up about Test Matches. It was all good rivalry and it soon caught on with the rest of the REME wallahs. At the far end of the LAD parade ground, the Aussies took over the vacant 'A' Platoon Nissan hut. Parking their Lorries along the far side of the square with 'B' and 'C' Platoon parking theirs down the middle. The Aussies having noted the stones we placed in the concrete at the entrance. Outside their hut, they had a concrete square laid in the shape of Australia. Each of the five States painted in a different colour with flagstaff and the Australian Flag in the centre. Nevertheless, they had watched with interest how we dismantled and rebuilt the Jeep, which indicated to them our capabilities as a knowledgeable working unit.

Australia

The Scammel team towed in a GMC; it had broken down not far from Town. Fred, Q, Sgt. Levine, Harry and Bluey the driver, gathered around the stricken GMC. A lot of scratching of heads and discussions took place, before the cause was identified and left to Harry to sort it out. The problem was resolved and the repaired GMC was sent out. To cut a long story short, repairs to any GMC become a big problem. They were ex-war surplus, left in mothballs for years before being shipped to Malaya. They had arrived spray painted olive green inside and out including under the bonnet, everything was green. The major problem was lack of spares that was something if, working on a GMC we all experienced. I was given a job to sort out a problem with one of their headlights. Easy, just replace the light bulb. Wrong, they were all sealed units, which included the beam and side light. With the other one working, it was decided to send it out anyway. It was soon discovered you did not repair an item. 'Take it out, Replace with a brand new one but from where? Not so easy, all spares had to be requisitioned that meant a long wait. The more miles they did, the more faults occurred, they became regular customers. As a mixture of English and American Lorries being repaired in the bays or, lined up on the square GMC's awaiting spares became a familiar sight.

Discussing a GMC.

In the mail, received a box from my brother Michael opening it up; found some packets of spangles plus an imitation 'Bottle of Guinness' with a note. 'Don't drink it all at once.' He was up to his tricks again it cheered me up. The following Saturday night, we went to see 'The Seven Year Itch.' at the Odeon. In their foyer bar on one of the shelves, noticed a small bottle of Guinness that looked very lonely and most inviting, making a mental note, I said aloud.

'Next time were in here I'll have that Guinness.' Of course, Bill was the first to comment.

'Ear Joey I didn't know you were Irish that's a navvies drink, put airs on your chest.' To which that received an accolade of jeers

Two weeks later, we returned to the Odeon to see. 'Love is such a splendid thing.' That was my time to order the Guinness, when the barman poured it out it was like treacle, something not to be relished, but with all the goading had to force it down, it was ghastly stuff must have been there since before WWII started.

For the Christmas festivities, Three Coy RASC planned a knock out football competition, the final to be played on Boxing Day. A competition for the best-decorated Basha /also a Company Concert to be held in the mess Christmas afternoon. Anyone who sang, played an instrument or made a fool out of himself should put their name forward. Prizes for Football. A shield and $50 and for the best-decorated basher. Twenty-four bottles of Anchor. Forget the Concert; we had to beat the RASC. We decorated the basha with cut up strips of crepe paper, from the jungle took large branches of Palm trees to hang our Christmas cards on. It was during that foray that Den Bill and Jock found a Japanese 4 inch Mortar weapon. That was placed alongside our Flagstaff, a great Trophy and souvenir.

All platoons had a football team, even the Aussies who played Australian Rules, but they did field a team. Whoever organised the competition? Made sure the LAD team played all the Platoon football teams. Our first game was against the Aussies, we trounced them, and subsequently we beat them all to be in the final against Composite Platoon, who had not played anyone? The week before Christmas, I was on guard so, at least that was something that would not occur over Christmas.

That Christmas was the first that any of us had spent away from home, therefore it was inevitable that we would enjoy what we could. It was also fortunate that Christmas day fell on a Sunday, essentially a free weekend. Under no illusions, Fred made sure; all bays were empty of wagons needing repair. On the Saturday OC's parade, The OC. with reluctance announced.

'The winners of the Best Basha Competition, was jointly won, by the REME and Composite Platoon. Well Done!' That was bit of a farce compared with ours, theirs was hardly decorated, but we shared the prize.

Harry. Waiting Inspection

Winners in the Basha Competion

Collecting half the Prize.

Christmas Eve, as per our normal weekend a trip into town had a curry then see the mid-night movie. There was nothing worth seeing at the Ruby and Odeon and on our way to the REX, opposite the Ruby met up with Mick Gerry and Jock. Mick stated.

'Nothing worth seeing anywhere tonight.' Den responded.

'Agree with you about those two, but maybe go down the REX we'll take a look at that one.' Gerry commented.

'We had a look at that, but we didn't fancy it. Bill interrupting suggested.

'While we make up our minds, fancy a beer then.'

'Sounds a good idea let's all go.' Next to our brekkers café, there was a really small bar, entering through its saloon bar styled swing doors we were ordering Tiger beers, when Bunny, Harry. Des, Bowles and Towser joined us, and soon after followed by the rest of them then the beers did flow. It was the beginning of our Christmas. Someone suggested we go to the Jubilee Park for a Knees-up. The challenge was taken up; it was going to be a raucous night for sure. We paid our bills, hailed a couple of passing Tri-shaw Wallahs. Six climbed into one, two was manageable! Six no-way. Our combined weight tipped the scared Trishaw Wallah two feet off the ground; desperately holding his handle bars cried out.

'No. No. Jonnie No. Tada Bagoos.'

Untangling our bodies, walked the short distance to the Jubilee. It was packed with Aussies and assorted squaddies from all the regiments. Without tickets, we fell about dancing; the Aussies started a fight with the RSF's. Pandemonium broke out, shrieks from the Taxi Dancers, the band disappeared, laughter, shouting, flying fists, clubbing, chairs being smashed likewise tables it was all happening. The Local Police arrived; big Sikhs wielding long clubs waded into the mass of slugging bodies on the dance floor, soon to be followed by the MPs wielding short ones. The Aussies went out through the door, followed by myself Towser, Jock and Harry, swept along with the tide. On the rampage they went one way, we went the other, and Towser was a big strong chap grabbing me I resisted. He threw me into a waiting taxi shouting.

'C'mon Joey, taxi back to camp. Three Company bloody 'urry.' Back in the guardhouse he held me up, while we signed in then back to the basha to crash out. The next morning, Q, woke me, holding a mug of Rum laced tea.

'H- Happy C-c-Christmas P-P-Plant, drink this it will s-s-sober you up.' God what a wake up. Fred, Sgt.'s Levine, Kershaw and Williams, were administering Rum tea, to all the others. Den was retching up over the wall, Al was groaning and Bill was moaning. 'What a bleedin' night.' Fred shouted out.

'Anyone for more Tea? Your breakfast is ready.' That had Al jumping out of bed to throw up on the opposite side to Den. I felt bad, no doubt as everyone else? About half an hour later, the Basha began to stir that was 'signs of life were emerging.' The rum tea had rekindled my spirits; do not know about sobering me up. However, got up went for a shower; it was going to be a long day.

In the mess, the tables had been rearranged into two long lines, with the chairs at each place setting at the table with two free bottles of beer per person. The dinner was Roast Turkey with all the trimmings, served by all the senior Officers and NCO's. It was great. After dinner, we went straight into the Naafi to spend our winnings. The beer flowed; the table was awash with bottles not bothering to go to the concert we stayed there. With all the singing and partying going on it was not long before Sgt. Williams plus a lot of Aussie's joined us. We had a whale of a time, whilst we sang different songs; Bunny played his harmonica with the only tune he could play. Harry did his mime of Three Blind Mice. Late in the evening at throwing out time; we staggered back the twenty yards to our basha with the remains of our beers. There to drink the dregs and get our heads down.

Christmas afternoon

Christmas evening in the Naafi

Harry's Three Blind Mice.

The next morning Boxing Day. With sore heads, it was the day of the football final against Composite Platoon. Still pissed we turned up including our supporters, who had made hats out of the REME magazine.

The game started, it was a doddle we beat them 9-1. Much to the annoyance of their OC, who handed over a shield to Al? Nevertheless, to the delight and joy of Fred and 'Q.' we collected our beer prize, returned to the Basha. However the smell from the latrine was disgusting it was awash with urine, the funnels were full of pewk and the Latrine Wallah ' Wanky Wanky ' was not on duty, he was nicknamed that due to the state of his arms that had been badly broken by the Japanese during the war, how he held a brush is a mystery. Anyway, we got buckets from the cookhouse and washed it all away, then it did smell sweet and we were able to drink our prize of beer well into the evening, even Bob Watts who was on Guard ventured in to tell us. 'The Guard Commander said you have to be quite.' "Quite" He was told, exactly where he could go! But not without a drink.

Don't give it to the REME.   *9- 1 Triumph.*   *Our band of Supporters .*   *Celebrating our winnings.*

Monday morning muster parade, the smell of sour beer oozed out of everyone's sweaty pores. We certainly had a good Christmas without anyone being slung in the Guard House. However, there were quite a few Aussies including RASC Wallahs on Defaulters Parade, sporting black eyes, thick lips bumps and bruises from the fracas they caused down the Jubilee

After the Christmas celebration, we were back repairing Lorries. Nevertheless, there was a change in the hierarchy before the New Year. The OC. RASC suddenly left Three Company and was replaced by Capt Goodall. RAASC. Therefore, we were under Aussie Rules until another replacement came along, which never did happen. The change we thought, was due to the imposing rules aimed at the Aussies? Thay did not care about discipline or, apparently VD.

New Years eve, we went into town for a curry and watch the mid-night movie. On the second was on guard so, it was soldiering as usual. However, during the week Den found out that there was a Chinese Nude show on at the CAPITOL on the other side of town. Not one of our usual venues, he suggested we all go. Al still on his saving lark asked.

'How much is it?'

'About Three dollars. Get a Taxi to the Railway Station, have a drink in the upstairs Bar, then take in the show.' Bill eagerly stated.

'Cor! That sounds good. See a bit of Chinese titty. Chop Chop.' To which Al sarcastically responded.

'Dirty bastard! That's all you think about Dineen you're a silly prat.' Nevertheless Den as I, was eager to see the show. All agreed we'll go to the afternoon show on Sunday.'

Sunday, outside camp we hired a taxi to the Railway Station. On the way passed hordes of Chinese milling about outside the CAPITOL. Arriving at the station, we went upstairs, stood at the bar to order our drinks. A smartly dressed waiter ushered us away towards a table then took our orders, returning with our drinks placed them on the table plus several small bowls of peanuts, pouring out the drinks left the bill on the table. To us, this was. "Up market stuff ". We had found a new place to visit. Even the European clientele were swigging G & T's. We drank up, paid the bill and left to walk the short distance to the CAPITOL joining the throng paid for our tickets.

Inside it was just like a normal picture house, with the light full on we occupied seats near the front. At 1530. The Chinese announcer came on, prattled off in Chinese about the acts to follow before, speaking in English stated.

'Stwickwy Noo Fotigwifs.' Whatever that meant? The lights dimmed the curtains came apart for the show to begin. By the sound of the band, it must have been the same group as those at the Jubilee. On came the Tumbling acts, Chinese Dancers, Jugglers, Singers all painted up like dolls, their shrill sing song voices enough to drive you potty. We sat through all that for a good hour or so, but no Nudes. Words were muttered at Den. On came the last act. A group of Chinese dancing girls in multi-coloured Cheongsams. The music started, they pranced about much to the glee of, Oooohs, Aaaghs and sighs of their Chinese audience. Gradually they removed an item of clothing, this made us sit up and pay more attention, still gyrating to the music they all stripped down to their knickers and bras, before the lead dancer began her strip tease. Off came her Cheongsam to reveal only a sequined encrusted knickers and bra, with a crash of cymbals she whipped off her bra. Blimey! It was evident, she did have a pair. Still gyrating in time with the tinny music advanced to the center of the stage, with thumbs inserted into the waistband of her knickers turned with her back to the audience continued gyrating her backside before she spun around to her front, then very slowly peeled down her knickers. Well the front row of Chinese onlookers were in for a treat. Just at the final showing, there was a flash as a camera bulb exploded. Immediately the culprit ran out, pandemonium set in, amid the shouting thought, "There's going to be a lynching". The curtains were very quickly closed. We got out of there sharpish; outside we ran away from a baying crowd, further down the road we hailed a taxi back to the safe side of town, to partake of a curry, Den said.

'Didn't see much.' Al quickly hastened to add.

'Neither did I, when the flash went off I was lighting up a fag.' Full of glee I remarked.

'Serves yer right, shouldn't have been bleedin' smoking.' However, Bill with a glazed look in his eyes exclaimed.

'Cor Blimey! Didn't she have a pair?'

Nevertheless, by chance we had found a new venue to visit, the Station Bar with free peanuts. On several occasions we went there to sit out on the veranda have one drink then return into town. The last visit we made, were refused entry not because we were rowdy or anything, it was all down to the Clientele who objected to our presence. The Ipoh Station Hotel was the watering hole of (as we called them) the 'Tin Planters and Rubber Miners.' The very people we were out there defending.

It was about mid January, having glanced through the two-month-old edition of the Mirror, interested to see if there was anything about Malaya, which there was not. It seemed strange to me even before being called up, there was nothing relating to Malaya, Korea, Kenya, Cyprus and the French fighting in Vietnam was always reported. Whilst in Malaya thousands of troops were engaged in combing through dense steaming jungles for weeks on end searching for the 'willow the wisp CT's.' Being in a support Corps, although just as involved we were much more fortunate than the Infantry spending weeks in the jungle. Fed up reading, lying on the bed contemplating about what was really going on out here when Mick came around with the mail call, received three letters from Mum, Margaret and a mysterious one in a yellow coloured envelope. Leaving it to one side, read the other two. Mum's letter informed; Derek had paid her a visit and gave her the enclosed note with his Army camp address in Brecon. Certainly would have to drop him a line. Margaret's letter, gave worrying news mum was not too well and had been told by the doctor to rest in bed. Being concerned about mum's health, this news did not help. Opening the third letter was a complete surprise! Having forgotten all about Cecilia, her letter had me puzzled as to how she got my address? She wrote about the jazz clubs, her work etc.etc. Ending. She loved me madly, missed me terribly and wanted me to write to her. Re-reading her letter brought back memories of our Saturday night jiving and snogging sessions made me think, "Must have been bleedin' mad to give her up". My thoughts were interrupted by Al.

'Who's that from yer fancy bit?'

'Nope. Some girl used to go out with; somehow, she's found out my address. '

'Silly prat. Yer ain't put her in the pudden' club have yer?'

'Al! Don't you be such a prat all yer life, have not seen her for fifteen bleedin' months'

'Wot' she writing to you for then?'

'Don't ask me? She says she loves me madly.'

'How'd she find out where yer were then?'

'How the soddin' 'ell do I know? Nosey parker. Bleedin' letter only arrived today; you concentrate on your Patti?' Lighting up another fag threw his other dog end onto the floor replied. 'Don't you worry about my Patti; I'm a drug to her. Ear why don't you write to my sister Annette? I'm sure; she'll send you a letter.'

Giving up. Was in no mood to argue, had other things on my mind. A roar from the other end of the Basha.

'They're on their way.'

After the evening meal and before we went to the Naafi, I settled down to scribbling letters to Mum, Margaret and Derek so he could spread the word around the club about my whereabouts. Over the following weeks, received letters from Margaret's friends Lily and Sylvia and did reply but not to Cecelia, still a concern until pondering. "It would be polite to reply". Composed a letter about Malaya, living conditions, new friends and questioned 'how she got my address?' Handed it to Mick for posting.

CHAPTER TWENTY-TWO
AN EXISTENCE.

During the week after work, our existence in camp was utterly boring, nothing to do laze about read letters books or, the local papers, write letters, argue, listen to records that individuals had bought down town. Mick as often as he could play his record of Porgy and  Bess, Bob Watts and I jazz, others with vocals records. There was a snooker table in the so-called Games room of the Naafi, but you could never get on it to play. When they opened the Naafi, have a couple of beers before they shut followed by a nightcap of a Banjo and mug of tea from Whiskers. The day's oppressive heat always made you tired and everyone was asleep before lights out.

Saturday Siesta Time.

One mail call, I received a letter from Cecilia informing me she had phoned mum for my address, also enclosed was a photo of her stood outside the hut where eighteen months before we had spent time snogging. Lying on the bed gazing at the snap, thinking of what Derek had said about 'relationships.' "Once you're in the Army they don't work out"? However, the receipt of her second letter and the comments about her undying love, made me wonder if it would have been like that?

Early in February on the radio, a News bulletin announced that a letter had been received from Ching Peng declaring that the Amnesty was over. Mick shouted out.

'It's all back to square one with the Commies.'

However, a strange event was to happen. Whilst working in the sheds Al was called to Fred's office, returning collected his Beret and belt, spoke to Levine then left the LAD. Bill eager to know what was going on called out to him.

'Hoi Al. Where you going?' To which Al, putting up two fingers carried on.

Sometime later Al returning to the LAD went straight up to Fred's office; he stayed there for sometime before coming back to the sheds to speak with Levine then carried on working on the Lorry. I was working at one of the benches and was interested to know what it was all about; obviously, Bill eager to find out what was going on shouted from under a Lorry.

'C'mon Al, spill the beans, wot was that all about?' Al replied.

'Nothing that would interest you yer prat... then he yelled...Ear Joey fancy a trip down to Seremban?' I was then part of their conversation and replied.

'Seremban! That's way down south. What for? You getting posted?'

'Nope. Yer prat. You're as bad as pratty Dineen.' An inquisitive Bill butted in.

'C'mon Al. Chop Chop. Spill the beans.'

'Look. If you must know I had to go and see that Aussie Captain Goodall. He told me I've been picked to play cricket for the Combined Service Team. He is playing along with other Officers from different Regiments but I refused, did not want to go on my own. He said. You are playing, take someone with you. That's why I went and spoke with Fred. I told him, but he already knew. He suggested I take Joey.' Startled I replied.

'Wot dyer mean, I don't play cricket, not my game.'

'No yer prat. You're not playing. You're going as my escort. Bill listening to all this conversation suggested.

'Ear Al. I'll go with yer, fancy a trip down there. I'll be yer escort.'

'Sod off Dineen. Fred said Joey.' This was more interesting enthusiastically asked.

'When is all this 'appening then?'

'Leaving Monday, Be away three days. Games next Tuesday and Wednesday come back Thursday.'

'Well Okay. How come you're in the team?'

'Somehow. Goodall found out that I played wicket keeper for the Surrey Colts, that's all I know?'

Monday, we checked in bedding, collected rations. Dressed in long trousers and Jackets with a spare set in our small packs plus toiletries, departed to the Guardroom where Capt. Goodall along with 2nd. Lt. Hall were waiting by his Jeep and driver.

'You two, draw arms, book out get into the back of the Jeep. Get moving.' At the station we boarded the train, we had been allotted sleeper but not with Goodall's party of fellow Aussies Officers already on the train. We arrived early in the morning at Seremban and transported to the Ghurka camp where we were to stay. After handing in our arms, were provided with bedding to sleep in the REME Basha. It was empty of bodies, so left our bedding on two empty beds. We were all driven down to the Main Padang (Sports Field) in the pavilion. Capt. Goodall provided an itinery for the two days play. The game was to start at 1130. Al was kitted out with whites and wicket keepers gloves Capt Goodall said to me.

'Plant you're familiar with cricket. You are the scorer! That includes changing the numbers on the scoreboard.'

I was handed the scorebook, therefore was lumbered for the whole match between a scratch team from the North against a similar side from the South who went in to bat first. I sat on the Pavilion verandah, entering the runs in the scorebook. Every run that was scored I changed the numbered plates on the large scoreboard, to me it seemed surreal and strange, here we were in the middle of a bleedin' war and for all intense and purposes, it was just like a Village cricket match back home. A Buffet lunch was served for lunch and by the end of day's play; the South team were all out having scored over 100 runs. Returning back to camp Al and I were fed in the OR's mess with Chicken curry cooked by the Ghurka Cooks, one of the best curries I had ever tasted and spent the evening chatting with the other REME wallahs.

The next day, the opening batsmen were Goodall and Al. He was quite good, the pair of them, knocked up over 50, before Al was bowled out with a score of mid 30's. Like the previous day, a buffet lunch was served in the Pavilion and then play was resumed, late in the afternoon they declared winning by a comfortable score. After the match, Capt Goodall instructed us to gather our kit up and prepare for the return journey that night. On the train back, Capt. Goodall invited us to join in with other Officers and were handed Tiger beer. Their chat was all about cricket, to me it was boring but Al was in his element. We eventually left their company to get some sleep, however not in sleepers it was seats due to the fact we came back a day earlier. On our way through one of the coaches, spotted an Indian women breast-feeding. Must have been staring at her she gave a cold look as if to say 'Go away.' We arrived in Ipoh just after daybreak.

A chance to head off north, on a short weekend's trip in the direction of Penang Island, came about when Q had organised a football match against another LAD team located at Butterworth. A place that I recalled Bert had been posted too. Leaving after the Saturdays OC's parade. The football team bristling with arms, piled into the back of the one tonner. The area North of Ipoh was where most of the Tin mining took place, it had been cleared of a lot of vegetation and laid open with clumps of Jungle areas to drive through, the road and the surrounding area was declared Black. About half way just before

A quick Fanta

the road leading off to Taiping, we stopped at a roadside café; ordered Fanta's orange drinks and were in there for about twenty minutes or so before leaving for Butterworth.

We had not long left the vicinity, when we heard a dull thud from behind. Taking no notice, carried on a long straight road passing through a few small towns and eventually arrived around about midday at Butterworth. The Camp we were heading for was about two miles the other side of Butterworth the terminal for the ferry crossing to Penang. Driving into the camp parked up, checked in weapons and was shown to the LAD Basher. Conveniently located on the beach in the shade of  palm trees, what an ideal spot for a camp. Entering their basha, did meet up with Bert we had a long chat about his posting to another Aussie Infantry Camp but as he put it. 'Not much work to do'. The football game began in the late afternoon and was played on the sandy beach pitch outside their basha. Cannot remember the score, but we all had a few beers in their Naafi, before bedding down for the night.

Next day we took the ferry, across to Penang into George Town to see what it was all about, the same as in Ipoh but there were other attractions on the Island that we did not have time to explore. Maybe another time? After farewells to Bert. 'See you on the boat home.'

Bert's Basha   *On the Beach opposite Penang*

Left for Ipoh. Half way, was about to stop at the little Café, discovered it was closed; a grenade had been thrown in there the previous day? So ended our weekend jaunt.

On the news, the announcer mentioned the loss of a RAF Valetta aircraft that crashed in the vicinity of Ipoh whilst on a supply drop. A search is in progress. It is feared there are no survivors.

Another event, that Jock was involved with was a Rifle shooting competition, he was away for a week in Singapore and returned with Cups which he had one in the shoot off, in the Malaya Rifle Championship. The event led to another night in the Naafi. Furthermore another new arrival a VE by the name of Taffy Morgan who was an addition to us VEs.

It was during February, one of the RASC Cpl's died; do not know how? That was never discussed. His name was Cpl Quinn and he was the

Jock's Cups.

Corporal together with Sgt. Whitely, along with the other three Drivers that had sailed with us on the Lancashire. The next day he was buried in Taiping Military Cemetery. That night on the badminton court, they sold off all his personnel possessions for his wife back in Blighty. I remember. A penny piece was sold for a shilling.

Towards the end of February, an announcement on the radio stated. *"The Royal Air Force carried out a bombing raid on a CT camp discovered near Kluang. During the follow up by ground force troops. Thirteen Communist Terrorist had been found dead".*

A few days later, another announcement stated.

"A RAF Valletta. On a supply drop crashed into hills in the Cameron Highlands. It is feared there are no survivors".

The Hippo ten-ton Lorry arrived at the workshops with a failed charging system. Sgt. Kershaw allocated the job to me and with all the bays full, it was parked alongside the Battery shop. That meant me working in the sun all the time. I soon discovered that to get access to the Generator all the flanged diesel pipe work had to be removed. Rivulets of sweat constantly ran down my face and under my chin, forcing me to wipe it away with hands covered in diesel, whilst repairing the generator in the sheds was pleased to get out of the sun. In the afternoon, I was able to fix it back into position and reassemble all the pipe work before starting the engine up to find it was charging okay. By that time, it was late in the afternoon and my back was burning. Two days later, my face developed a red rash with white pimples. It was a sick parade job. Up too that time my previously so-called illnesses had been a dose of ringworm a mild case of Teenia, foot rot, leg ulcers, treated with Tiger Balm a fever of some sought and many times suffered prickly heat, its cure to stand starker's in the pouring rain that relieved it. But nothing as bad as this. At the MRS, the Doctors diagnosed weeping Teenia. Therefore, they painted half my face with Gentian Violet and ordered. 'Do not sweat? Report back in a week's time.' Leaving the MRS with an Excused Shaving chit! Reported in the LAD for work looking like the man from mars. Much to the amusement of Al Den Bill and George.

'Keep well away. Ring your bell you leper.'

The first week was very unpleasant. On each Muster Parade CSM Brown demanded.

'Where's your excused shaving chit?'

Doing the correct military two-step produced the "CHIT" he looking at it said.

'You. Shave tomorrow.' As he marched a way I stuck two fingers up. Absolutely no sympathy? In the following weeks my condition got worse, even did a Guard Duty. To avoid the wrath of the CSM tried clipping my straggly beard with a pair of nail scissors. One morning Gerry joined me on sick parade. He was diagnosed with weeping Teenia in his crotch, but he was lucky no white spots. At least with him, the application of Gentian Violet did not show. Several times the MO changed my medication, with different potions and creams. Baffled they concocted a special cream; a mixture of Whittle's and something else, it was pink and smelt vile. He advised apply three times a day stressing. Avoid Sweating?' For Christ sake! How could you not sweat? It did nothing for the infection and every morning without fail, received a bollocking from CSM Brown.

'Craftsman. You're dirty and unshaven. Get a grip of yourself. Let me see your excused shaving chit.' With the correct military two-step removed the chit from my rear pocket of my shorts and presented it. He did not even look at it. He was the biggest shit you can imagine. Fed up looking like something from Mars, Having informed Mum of my condition. In return received her parcel enclosed was a tin of Johnston's Baby Powder. 'Apply that.' Mystified at its purpose after showering shook the tin vigorously around my chin, with so much powder on my face looked like a Baker, quick comments flowed forth from the other three, from Al.

'You look a right Piccadilly ponce.' From Den.

'Joey! You can't take your handbag on parade. From Bill a suggestive one

'When are we going to get married? However, it was all in jest, although fed up with it had to laugh. Nevertheless, for the following week on muster still received a bollicking, as gradually after almost seven weeks the condition dried up. All due to the powder drying out the affected area. The irony of the episode was when I did present myself clean shaven not a word was spoken by the Idiot. CSM Brown.

Wang, the Naafi Wallah duly arrived everyday selling bridge rolls with the same fillings. All sat eating our purchase's, when Gerry turned up with a large green leaf in his hand; calmly sitting down opening the leaf began to eat the contents. The eating of Bridge rolls ceased, as many pairs of eyes recognised a handful of Chinese Mee Foon disappearing into Gerry's mouth. Bill about to gorge a Bridge roll, cried out.

'Hoi! Where yer get that from?' Gerry with a contented look on his face replied.

'Down behind the Ed. Center, there's an Indian wallah that cooks em. Bloody cheap and all...as Gerry fed handfuls of the noodles into his mouth all watched aghast, in between a mouthful he stated...Mmm. You lot should try it.' Bill eagerly asked.

'What else does he do?'

'I don't know, go and find out.'

Next morning, our Naafi break was spent at this new found food emporium. Very delighted at what was on offer. Chinese dishes and a curry, mugs of tea, big banjos. All according to the owner. 'Velly Cheep.' We tucked into our orders, before returning to the LAD. These short Naafi breaks were to last exactly three days. On the third day, all dirty and grimy were enjoying our savory meals, when in walks four MPs. In charge was. 'Fatso.' The Aussie Staff Sgt. who looked the spitting image of Ernest Borgnine the film star in "From Here to Eternity". He roared.

'YOU LOT. ARE ALL OUT OF BOUNDS. LEAVE EVERYTHING WHERE IT IS. FORM UP OUTSIDE.'

Not understanding why it was O. o. B. leaving half-eaten meals and mugs of tea gathered our Berets and belts and trooped outside. They formed us up into threes and marched us to their Guardhouse (that incidentally was back to back with the Food Emporium) all seventeen were lined up along the front of their two Nissan Huts. In turn, each one of us was marched into their Hut and charged O.o.B. When all that malarkey was finished, on the road outside ordered to form up in three ranks and under a four-manned MP escort were marched back to the LAD. Outside Fred's office, the bellowing of 'Fatso' brought us to a smart halt. Fred, wondering what all the stamping of boots and shouting was about? Came out of his office followed by Q. Fred demanded.

'Staff Sergeant. What the hell's going on here?' Ole S/Sgt. Fatso bellowed out.

'SAR. ALL THE OFFENDERS STANDING BEFORE YOU HAVE BEEN CAUGHT OUT OF BOUNDS. ALL ON MORNING MUSTER. DEFAULTERS PARADE SAR. CAPT GOODALL. OFFICER COMMANDING THREE COMPANY ROYAL AUSTRALIAN ARMY SERVICE CORP. HAS BEEN INFORMED BY TELEPHONE MESSAGE SAR. I WILL LEAVE THIS MATTER IN YOUR HANDS. THANK YOU SAR.' Salutations followed. Then four of them marched off.

Now the inquisition, Fred demanding.

'You shower of buggers! What the hell's going on?' Bunny Moore, with some aplomb explained the situation.

'Just having a bite to eat at that cafe behind the MPs lockup. How could it be out of bounds. It is inside the Garrison Sir? It's not as it is a den of iniquity is it and they made us leave our meals behind as well.' Fred baffled, looked hard at Bunny and the assembled shower before stating.

'No time for jesting Moore! Dismiss. All of you get back to work.' As we fell out, Fred retreated into his office. Very soon with his hat on and his swagger stick tucked under his arm hands in pockets he took a stroll down to the main camp to have a pow wow. That night Company Orders stated.

The Food Emporium located at the rear of the Military Police Huts is deemed. Out Of Bounds. Specifically to ALL REME LAD PERSONNEL.

All charges were dropped. The following day, Wang with a big smile displaying his set of gold teeth was a happy man again; nevertheless, he took a lot of barracking from us. And I bet the MP's used it every day.

Early in March, Bill was homeward bound, during the run up to his leaving date; he had knocked it into our heads.

'Hoi you lot of skivers. I am leaving this god forsaken 'ole of a place. Bound for the sunny outdoor life and sanity of Peckham Rye. When I'm gone you lot will miss me, you'll see?' The weekend before he left, we had a good piss up. The following morning it was sore heads. Possibly, the night of Bill's Piss up, Bill Speakman VC, arrived in our Naafi. At the time, he was attached to the RSF's. Why he picked our Naafi God alone knows? Maybe he knew Bill was leaving. Nevertheless, after that on various occasions he was to spend many nights in there "asleep". As the week progressed Bill did nothing, Al got fed up with his.

'Hours to do. Chop Chop.' Constantly retorted.

'Can't wait to see the back end of you. Yer silly prat Dineen? Wot are yer?'
'Now then Al. Don't be so jealous, your turn will come. Chop Chop.'   One thing. The banter would cease, but I think Bill was sorry to go?

A new civilian swimming pool was opened, on the other side of Town. Somehow, Q obtained permission, for us to use it. We went there a few times after work apart from a few Chinese, it was always empty so. We had the pool to ourselves until someone complained, that was the end of that.

Annie Vic Den and me   *Me diving off the board.*

We were warned about Anzac Day April 25th. A Day of Remembrance for Australia and New Zealand. The Aussies in the camp were to have the day off. They held a service in the Naafi before they began their drinking spree. At lunchtime, having finished in the Naafi taking the piano from the Corporals Mess, loaded it onto the back of a GMC. I think it was Big Maxi 'Desperate Dan' that done it on his own, then they ripped up a small Palm tree from the makeshift garden and threw that on the back. They left the camp in two GMC's, we watched them going past the LAD the one in front had the piano and Palm tree and underneath the limp leaves was a pianist jingling the ivories to the tune of 'Waltzing Matilda'. All singing their heads off enroute down town. Do not think the Piano was ever returned. Nevertheless, we understood they did have a good binge up.

A trip to Lumutt had been arranged to coincide with Easter. Half of the LAD left camp after work on the Friday, so we would have at least one full day on the beach with Bills departure I had been upgraded to sleep in the back of the QL with Den and Al. The rest to sleep on the floor underneath the Lorries canvass sheeting. On Saturday, we swam and lazed about with a few beers before retiring for the night. During the night, shrieks and yells rent the air, having everyone up very alert with rifles at the ready, until the voice of Vic shouting. 'Snakes in the tent.' From the safety of our elevated perch we watched as illuminated by the moonlight; many white bums were seen haring in all directions over the beach. Without leaving his vantage point, Den managed to turn on the headlamps to provide some light to the surrounding area, it also revealed the tall frame

Harry's Snake.

of Harry slowly advancing out of the dark towards the tented area in the darkness to his rear, voices could be heard saying,' Did yer see it? It was a big one.' However, Harry killed it. Excitement over.

The following Saturday morning we were at the Station, to say our farewell to Jock, normally they occurred after Thursdays Pay Parade nevertheless, for some reason it did not happen to Jock. After the OC's Parade dressed in best OGs. We piled into the back of a QL to make the trip to the station, Fred and 'Q' were there to wish him Bon Voyage.

Jocks Departure.

Furthermore, at the end of the month Bill Beavis departed from our Basha homeward bound, the usual Piss-ups were held in the Naafi. Beavis's replacement was a Brummie Lad, by the name of Ernie totally the opposite slow and spent most of his time sleeping, Al nicknamed him Dozy.

Company Orders stated. All personnel were to engage in rifle shooting practice on the jungle range, located beneath the Gunog Rapat Caves overlooked by the 1/6th. Ghurka's camp. A rota system had the LAD scheduled for a shoot after Saturdays OCs. Issued with Mk 5 rifles and ammo, plus targets in the shape of men. With Fred and Q in the jeep, followed by us in the one tonner and a QL. We set off for the jungle range. Leaving the

main road drove into the jungle along a well used winding dirt track for about a mile, where a cleared stretch of land was laid out at 25 and 50-yard distances. There were no butts, the target area just an area of banked earth against the base of the cliff. High above monkeys swung about, chattering angrily at being disturbed.

Gunog Rapat Caves   After setting up the targets, parties of four

Twenty five yard range.

took turns to let off five rounds, after that shoot was completed moved back to the 50-yard distance repeating the exercise, even Fred and Q using Pistols, let off rounds. Upon completing, the shoot returned to Camp.

These sessions happened every fortnight, with different types of arms. To make it more interesting, the targets were hidden within the undergrowth. On one occasion armed with sten guns, I was stood next to Nobby Hill; suddenly his Sten went off spewing about 10 rounds into the ground creating a neat round hole between his boots Nobby waving the sten about exclaimed.

'But Sergeant! It just went off.' Responding sharply Q loudly shouted.

'B-B-BLOODY I-IDIOT H-H-HILLS S-STOP WAVING THE F-F-F......G G-GUN AROUND.'

Nobody seemed to know, why these shooting sessions took place nevertheless, we became proficient shots so much so that Fred suggested.

'Next shoot, bring lots of empty beer bottles.'

Armed with loads of beer bottles from the Naafi. Fred raising the level of his voice ordered. 'First squad. Place them upside down in the earth. Now you clever buggers. See if you can hit them.'

Much to Fred's appraisal each Squad took pot shots until there were no bottles left. Cannot remember the number of visits made before they were stopped, must have been six or so, after each shoot having to boil out and oiled the barrels they had become a pain.

Football was our only recreation. Matches were played within the local league. The RSF had a very good team; the 15/19th was good as were the REME Workshops, the Ghurkas and the Malays Regt. were the only other Military teams in the league. The other teams in the league were the Police, Public Works Department and other Indian and Chinese sides. In most of our matches we did well and had the chance to play on the main Ipoh Padang against the Ghurkas who really appreciated football, turned out as ever, smartly dressed in starched football togs. We beat them but there was another type of Military football competition. Six a Side. Twenty minutes each way and played on the

normal size pitch. In the heat it was fast and grueling; Three Company's five a side team consisted of three REME and three RASC. Al was captain along with Mick Me, Smithy, Pearson in Goal and Jock Donaldson. Most of our games were played locally but two other games played, one against the 4th. Malay Regt. at Tapah who we beat to put us in the

Five a side final at Taiping   final against RASC 2nd. Supply Depot at Taiping. Travelling to Taiping black clouds threatened rain. Ten minutes after the start the downpour the pitch was awash with huge puddles everywhere and the weighty ball became immersed in water with two players hacking away at it trying to retrieve it, it was more like Water Polo. By half time, it was one-one Deciding to play on. A quick turn around was made. By the end, we conceded another goal to lose. 2-1 Small Cups were handed out to the winners. The losers, received a German drinking steins. (which I still have). Yet, there was one game Al, was challenged, by the Indian Store man, to play against his Kampong team on their pitch way outside the Towns boundaries.

LADTrophies won.

Having obtained permission, along with supporters all carrying weapons set off. The store man, on his bike was waiting beside the roadway to guide us to his Kampong. Three Lorries turned onto a jungle track, travelling some way into the jungle before we came to their Kampong. A huge open area, surrounded by Basha's on stilts. The pitch far from flat with ruts and dips had already been marked out with broken white lines. The game began and the villagers whooped and shouted their appreciation we convincinly won. It was the gratitude of this Kampong, which gained our attention. An Army team agreeing to play football against them. Talk about 'Hearts and Minds'

Whilst in the Naafi, discussing another trip to Penang. It was generally thought that in twenty-five years time, it would be a good idea to return to Malaya to see how it had developed. To cut a long story short, six of us Den, Al, George, Des, Annie and I got permission for a seventy-two hour pass to Penang staying at Minden Barracks. Den hired from an Ipoh Car Dealer an American Ford with bench seats. Leaving immediately after work on Friday. Dressed in civvies, drew arms and set off. Making good time, then trouble. Clouds of steam erupted from under the bonnet. We stopped by the roadside to check the radiator, obviously that had blown and needed filling up. Seeking the help of a Malay family living close by who gave us an old gallon tin can of water, we gave them a few dollars for their trouble. A few more miles further on the radiator was steaming; the three in the front seat were sprayed with hot water onto our legs. Stopping again, carried out an inspection found cracks in the engine block; in the middle of nowhere we were stranded and it was twilight. We pushed the car for what seemed miles, into a closed garage at Bengan Surai, miles away from Butterworth. Being hungry, decided to sort out a curry house. Strolling into their market place, quickly noticed the surrounding attitude was very hostile, certainly was not friendly. Foregoing the meal retraced our steps back to the garage. Throughout the night took turns keeping watch. The next

In the Garage

morning, decided to abandon the trip and head back to camp. Luck was on our side, right opposite the garage was a railway station. Buying tickets waited for the down train to Singapore. Back in Ipoh. Den demanded our money back and explained where his car was parked in Bengan Surai. That was an episode to forget.

Waiting at the Station

It was about this time that a news bulletin was broadcast over the Radio stating.

In an area on the outskirts of Kuala Lumpur. Yeong Kwo Secretary- General of the Malayan Communist Party, who was responsible for the MCP.s Political offensive. Was shot dead by a patrol of the Rifle Brigade.

The last week in April, Gerry and I were summoned to Fred's office. Whilst donning Beret and belts. Gerry muttered

'What this all for? What have we done?'

'Don't ask me? Soon find out though'   Fred sat with his arms resting on the table 'Q' was scribbling on some forms.

'You two are going up the Cameron's on Saturday's convoy. You will be there a four days on Rest and Recuperation...Thinking. "What the hell for"?... Take your big pack and civvies with you. When you get up there, report to Sergeant Williams in the LAD he knows what to do?' Have a good rest. Dismiss.' That was it. No real explanation.

Being passengers, sat in one of the Lorries going up the Cameron's. It was strange looking out from the back instead of riding in the cab, but still very vigilant cradled our rifles, I said to Gerry.

'Wot did reckon about this R and R Fred was on about?'

'Don't bloody care. A few days fresh air up here in the Cameron's do us a power of good. Maybe chat up some Alex Nurses up here at the BMH.   Bunny Moore said he fancied one of them, but same time as he returned to the LAD she was going home. Anyway, anyone of 'em can Mother me back to health. That's for sure.' Hopefully he added.

'Gerraway. You will not get a look in. You're on R and R. Not going into Hospital. You're not sick.' At the top, the lorry drove into the LAD dropping us off, where Sgt. Williams greeted us.

'Been expecting you two. Hurry up Jump in the Jeep and I'll drive you there.' Driving past the BMH. Puzzled, looked at Gerry who opened his arms wide and shook his head. Taking another turning leading up to a big house overlooking the BHM. This was strange, as we thought we would be in the BMH. Puzzled I asked.

'Where we going Sergeant? '

'That big house in front of you. It's an old Lutheran Mission House...driving up to its main doorway he stopped....There you are. I'll pick you up for your return journey. Make the most of your R&R.' He drove off, leaving us bewildered. Coming out of the entrance was a very tall Monk dressed in long white robe wrapped round his waist was a large row of Rosary Beads with the Cross hanging free, he greeted us.

'Welcome to the Roman Catholic Mission House. Please come inside and follow me.'

We went up a flight of oak stairs along a long corridor to a room at the far end. Opening the door, he let us enter.

'Choose one of the beds, change into your civvies and when you're ready, come down into the main room down stairs on your right.' He closed the door behind him. Gerry exclaimed.

'What the hell's going on?'

'I don't know? I thought we were heading for the BMH. This is a strange setup that's for sure.'

Neither of us had a clue what it was all about. Changing into our civvies took stock of the room. Four beds and by the boots underneath, two were already occupied. A small washbasin with running water a small chest of drawers and a cupboard. The beds sheets were crisp and white with blankets just like home. We left that to go down stairs entering a large room, where about twenty or so other lads all in civvies were seated or gathered in small groups. The room was spacious and the far Bay windows overlooked the valley below, the outlook of the other large window gave a grand view of the hills behind a number of tables were laid up with cutlery I counted six places.

The Monk was talking to a group and noticed we had entered said.

'Ah Good Now you are all here let me brief you on what is expected of you all. You all have the run of this house; you can walk in and out as you please, there are some good walks around the Cameron's. Meal times have been set the same as your normal Army times, so please do not be late back. We shall say prayers and I am sure, during your stay, they will not intrude, but it would be nice if we all did it together. Now you are all from different Regiments and Corps from different areas of Malaya and have been singled out because of a bullet, gunshot wounds received or, illness of some sort... (I did notice one young lad was full of the shakes...) To spend a few days rest up in the Cameron's. If anyone wishes to read, there is plenty of reading material available, but the main point of you being here is to Rest and Recuperate. Dinner will be served in about half an hour's time. God Bless you all.'

That was it freedom for about four days. We were billeted in rooms, about four or six to a room, good bedding and excellent meals with fresh veg grown by the Brothers. The two young lads in our room one was from the Lincolns and the other from the Hampshire Regiment but they did not say much. Services were held but they were not intrusive. It turned out to be a delightful place with its cool temperatures just like England on a summer's day. However, I still pondered on what was happening in Malaya, with all these young lads about the same age, all National Servicemen some with harrowing tales to tell about how they received their injuries fighting in the Jungles. Whereas there was Gerry and I just with Teenia. These young lads so to speak, were just the tip of the iceberg maybe I would be able to find out more and understand what it all really did mean. We did enjoy our short stay, before four days later travelled back down on the afternoon convoy.

The LAD Recovery team was constantly on call to recover various Lorries or, armoured cars that had broken down or run off the road. On one occasion the call out was to recover a 15/19[th.] Daimler that had broken down. Changing into the regulation white boiler suits, a wonderful target for any CTs who might want to take a pot shot at us. With Den, Al and Annie in the cab whilst I being shotgun cover, was on top armed with rifle settled down beside the base of the crane. About half way to Tapah, located the Daimler parked underneath an avenue of overhanging jungle, with no one to explain the reason it had stopped? Den starting up the engine, slipped it into gear it did not move forward or in reverse, further investigation revealed its brakes were locked solid. It was a job for the workshops, releasing the break pressure, extending the Gib and hooked the Daimler up for the trip back. We had travelled less than two-hundred yards, when the rear tyres began to skid along the road surface blue smoke billowing out behind it, banging on the cab roof shouted.

'Stop its wheels are locked, it's skidding along the road smoking like mad.'

Stopping. I stayed on watch, whilst they checked the rear wheels. An on the spot repair was necessary; to release both locked brake pads before setting off again. We had not travelled very far, when the same thing occurred again. It became a frustrating trip back stopping, pouring water onto the brake shoes to cool them down. We had a good six miles to go when our water supply run out so. Decided to continue as slow as possible, until the road ran alongside a brownish coloured river. Den pulled over, handed me a Gerry can to fill up, with me paddling about in its shallows the other three formed a bucket chain and began pouring water onto the brakes shoes. On our final leg, we had a few more stops. At 1830, we drove it into the 15/19th LAD, unhooking it left it close to their workshops. Informed their  Guardhouse, of its whereabouts and problem. Having missed our evening meal, the cooks provide us with a breakfast meal the same as the Duty Guard.

On another incident, to pick up an Australian Artillery Howitzer, which had come to grief on the road? Taking a bend too fast they had managed to sheer the wheel nuts off the axle holding bolts. With the Howitzer sprawled across the road only supported by one wheel. This presented a problem; the Gib could not extend out sufficiently to bodily lift and suspend the Howitzer. Furthermore, with only one wheel could not tow it. The only

solution was to hook the howitzer onto the Scammel towing eye and wrap the Gib cable around the free end of the axle lifting it free off the road. At speed, the howitzer behind us weaved it own path so reducing speed took us some time to reach 12 Inf. REME Workshops for them to fix. Another job was loading any Beyond Local Repair (BLR), vehicles onto the flats (Railway rolling stock) that included armoured cars and Lorries, to be transported by rail to Singapore for repair at REME Base workshops.

One of the GMC's engines was labeled BLR. This type of job was destined for the local Infantry Workshop. However, Fred and Q knew better, knowing there was no spares in the LAD or, in the local Infantry Workshops, decided by scavenging parts off the other BLR

GMC the very one I had hit. (See next chapter). We could repair it having seen the work we did on Fred's Jeep, the Aussies let us get on with it. Using the Scamell it was a case of removing one engine to replace with the other. Work began mostly mechanical, except for the wiring that I did at the start and upon completion of the job. Within a week, the

engine started up and was returned that earn't us the respect of, Capt Goodall and Lt. 'Breathless' Hall. Why he was nicknamed 'Breathless' we never knew. Nevertheless, it was common knowledge when he was the Guard Commander, he would sneak up on anyone on Stag duty if, the Guard did not to challenge him he would book him. I became one of his victims whilst guarding the Stores stag area. Spotted him moving around the rear of the store, when he came around the corner challenged him. Charging at me grab me around the throat. Swinging the butt of the rifle downwards whacked him on the shin, He gasped. 'Well done. You're very alert.' Then limped off. You had to be alert on his Guard Commands.

Friday the 22nd June my birthday, a good night was enjoyed in the Naafi. With thick heads for OC's next morning. That night whilst in town Den suggested.

'Seeing as we all come from Vauxhall and Al's due home soon. What about the three of us together having a Photo taken at Lai Wah's before going to the flicks.' We agreed. Lai Wah was the military photographer and I had

Al Den & Me   bought my camera from him. We trotted in and he was only too pleased to do the necessary. We had the photo taken then went to the REX to book in for the midnight movie "Rebel without a Cause". Having done that had a curry; every time we went into town, our routine never changed. The following week we collected the Phots.

Company Orders stated. Each platoon was to go down to Lumutt for a two weeks Jungle Training. (R&R). However, HQ and Composite Platoons, as they were still required, could send a few with each of the other three Platoons. A, B and C. However not the LAD. We understood why, but took it up with Fred & 'Q', they suggested. As we had done before on a weekend, operate a Rota system. Within the next two or three weeks Al Gerry and Harry were due to leave the LAD. All wanting to visit Lumutt for the last time. Arriving at Lumutt, we returned to our old site set up our meager campsite. Further, along the beach the Aussies had pitched their camp a conglomerations of Tents including none other than old Moonface the Chinese Naafi barman serving. We did visit the Aussies and 2nd. Lt. Breathless welcomed and invited us to have a few beers in their Naafi that night. Accepting, had a raucous time, it was a good job it was a clear moonlight night as we staggering back along a sandy winding path. Late on the Sunday afternoon having swum, sunbathed and fed well on compo rations. We returned to camp and that was to be my very last visit to Lumutt.

A week later stopping to read company orders, posted in big letters were the names of Alan Gerry Harry and Des to leave camp homeward bound, with a date two weeks later on the Thursday. Al expressed much jubilation.

'Whoopee! That's the best news I've had since I got here. I'm on my way back to Old South Lambeth Road. Ear you two are both lucky Sods. You got to stay in this soding place for bleedin' months.' Den. quickly responding suggested.

'Al. You're a Prat Don't be surprised if they decide not to send you home. You're an asset to the LAD. Ha Ha!' Disconsolate with his news, thinking "Why not me"? Hastily added.

'Says who? Sod Off. He cans bleedin' well go. Get rid of all the bleedin' fags I tred on.'

Upon entering the Basha, there was a shout from the far end then in the middle and at our end from the four named Bastards. Chanting. 'We are going home. We are going home.' Al collecting the mugs was about to leave the Basha in mock amazement I said

'Hoi Al. That's my job, I always get em. Wots up with you then sick?'

'That's all right Joey. I've been saving them up. Going home mate.' He laughed.

'Sod off yer Prat. Yer hardly ever get them in. As Bill would say. You're a lazy Bastard.' Den making a better suggestion shouted after his retreating figure.

'Yer that's right. Well if you've been saving em up. Now's yer chance. Do it until you leave.' He never did! Many times we told him to shut up. All he did was laugh and shout.

'Your turn will come you prats.'

Saturday, the week before their departure, we had a good piss up. Sunday everyone was shattered. As Al, had been the most arch rival of the Aussies he certainly got up their noses when he riled them about Cricket and as England had so far, beaten Australia 2-1 in the Test series with still the 5th to be played. It was odds on they would beat the Aussies to retain the Ashes. Nevertheless, the Aussies provided their own parting salutes. 'Al it's about time we got rid of you. You are the biggest Pommie bastard out. / 'Blaady Pommie, Never mind Cricket, don't know your arse from your elbow. Piss off back to Pommie Land.' Plus a load of others.

The Thursday arrived, whilst we were saying our farewells, Al said.

'Joey, when I get home, I'll go and see your mum, tell her you're Okay.'

Many letters, later Mum did write, to say herself and Dad had met Al's Mum and Dad in the Crown. However, the same day they left the News announcer on the radio stated.

Colonel Nasser President of Egypt. Has Nationalised the Anglo—French Controlled Suez Canal Company.

That did spark a lot of interest. Mick our local earpiece shouted out the news.

'Heh you lot, now that Nasser has taken over the Suez. I bet that will stop those blooody four getting home, you wait and see Al will be back here next week.' A despondent George replied.

'Bleedin' hope not. Just got rid of him.' Den interrupting.

'Don't be daft. He is an asset. Exactly what I said to him when he was leaving. Send him to sort out Nasser, he will win easily. Silly prat.' Happy at the thought of Al going to Egypt yelled.

'Well that's a bleedin' good idea. Don't want to get me feet burnt again.'

After their departure, much Mickey taking was spent on the future fate of Al however; there were fewer arguments and less discussions, he being the biggest instigator of all of them. One thing we did miss was the monthly edition of the Mirror. Consequently had no idea what had happened back in Blighty. Apart from the BBC World News. At the end of August it did announce. *British and French Forces have sailed for Egypt.* Mick, listening to the news called out. 'Quiet listens to this news, British and French troops are heading for Egypt. It's, about bloody time some other buggers, got involved with a war.'

However, on the Local Radio News announcement. *An offer had been made by Tenku Abdul Rahman. Promising that the Malayan Government, would provide terrorist with a subsistence allowance of 100 Malayan dollars each per month if, they agreed to return to China.* No one in the basha thought that offer would work and the CT's would carry on with their war, in the end it was proved right the war trundled on until 1960.

CHAPTER TWENTY THREE
DUTY CALLS.

Our workload never ceased. It was case of. Get moving, there is another job waiting and on occasions we helped out working on the mechanical repairs with the VM's. Sometime in August there was an article published in the Straits Times, showing photos of six-wanted top terrorist operating in and around Ipoh, each one with significant sums of rewards in Malayan Dollars on their heads. This was soon endorsed, when another newspaper article printed a gang of terrorist had been located in the Gunong Rapat caves. RSF Troops, 15/19th Hussars, Gurhka's and Malay Police including the RAF. were involved in flushing them out. Whilst working in one of the bays attracted by the noise of a four-engine plane, watched a Lincoln bomber with its bomb doors wide-open flying at low level in the direction of Gunog Rapat. After about a minute saw a stick of bombs drop from the plane, quickly followed by a series of muffled explosions and clouds of debris evolving skywards. Whoever was under them must have been killed. However, a couple of days later a Platoon of disheveled SAS drove into the LAD. Both their Lorries needed repairing, I never found out if they had anything to do with the above incident. Although a vacant Basha had been provided for them to sleep in, whether they used it or not I do not know, furthermore they did not eat in the Mess instead cooked their compo rations outside on the grass verge, creating quite a mess. That evening in the Naafi, it was more than rowdy. Early next morning without a sound, they had gone leaving the remnants of their stay behind.

During the period I was in the LAD, accidents did happen. The main cause was the GMC Lorries they were unpredictable. We knew they had been mothballed in Australia after the war, mechanically they appeared sound but failures in their servo system caused many brake failures. I was one of a few who failed to stop a GMC, due to that. One had ignition problems, climbing into the cab let off the hand brake to roll it into an open bay, madly pumping the brake pedal nothing happened; it careered straight into a workbench sending it flying out into open space. Much to the displeasure of Capt Cole, who just happened to be standing nearby?

'You again Plant?' On another occasion, the exact same thing happened to Bob Watts unfortunately, it did not stop and the top of the GMC canopy crashed through the roof removing a big section of the corrugated Asbestos coming to rest in the monsoon ditch. Nobby Clarke decided to have a go on a Harley motorbike, having completed one lap of the square drove into a vacant bay, its brakes failed, the bike finished up in the pit Nobby jumped off and finished up nursing a badly bruised shoulder.

Aussie Despath Rider.

I was working on the magneto system on a Matchless Motorcycle, after completing the job it was only in order I give it a test run. Having never rode a motorbike before and seeing the Parade and Car park area completely void of any Lorries, except one parked on the far side. (Mentioned in the previous chapter). Kick started the engine, put it in gear unsteadily drove away it was a great feeling, whilst concentrating on changing gear with the foot change looked down. Crash! Hit the only lorry on the square, one very large GMC. Getting up found the impact had cracked the headlamp glass. Reluctant to ride it again pushed it across the car park towards the Workshops, only to see not one but a host of laughing VM's. What I was called was no-bodies business. Sgt. Levine standing with his hands on hips shouted.

'PLANT YOU NEED BIKE LESSONS.' I never did learn.

I was in the end bay of the workshops, busy dismantling the headlamp of a Harley Davidson, when the familiar noise of a Helicopter taking off from the Heli-pad increased, glancing up watched as it soared away. Suddenly there was a terrific bang, for a few seconds the Helicopter hung motionless in the air; dropping hit the ground with a woomf. Up sprinted the Aussie Dispatch  Rider minus his jacket and helmet, pushing me out of the way kicked started his bike into life roared out of the LAD racing up the road. Sometime later, he arrived back racing across the parade ground with the headlamp freely swinging over the front wheel, skidding to a stop beside me excitedly shouted.

 'Blaady hell mite! That was a blaady close call, just as I arrived two lacky baastards in the chopper were climin aat, one was holding his wrist and the other had blaad pouring aat of his forehead, even the blaady pilot survived. I got there before those baastard crooks the MPs arrived. I heard one of them say he was blaady Lt. General Festing and his son. They took 'em to the MRS in the meetwagon. The choppers a right blaady mess and the plice is swarming with those crooks. I've taken Phots, when I get them developed, I'll give you one. Okay mite.'

'Thanks mate, now can I get on repairing your bleedin' bike.'

'Too rite you pommie baastard. You do that.' Off he trots to his company office to pass on his news. What puzzled me, where was his camera? Nevertheless, a couple of weeks later, true to his word he gave me some photos of the crashed chopper.

Another incident was when Captain Cole actually congratulated me! Smithy drove his QL into the LAD with a malfunctioning starter button. Given the job to sort out, was in the cab alongside Smithy who was explaining what was wrong I pressing the starter button, sparks flew out causing it to weld solid before bursting into flames. White smoke filled the cabin engulfing both of us. Smithy jumped out leaving me to grab the hand fire extinguisher, with tears streaming down my cheeks coughing with the acrid smoke, aimed it at where I thought the starter butter was, somehow put the flames out. Coughing my lungs up, literally fell out of the cab onto the feet of Fred, he demanded.

'What's going on Plant?' Kneeling up, in between wheeze's and coughs taking great gulps of air, explained what had happened expecting a bollocking, he responded.

'Well done. Quick thinking, Carry on, get it fixed. ' He strolled off.

A chance came about, to experience a bit of Jungle Bashing. Fred knew some Infantry Officer, who suggested some of the LAD might like to experience what it was like in the Jungle. About eight of us volunteered. Duly armed departed the camp for a march into the Jungle somewhere south of Gunog Rapat we disembarked from the one tonner. Before we attempted to go into the Ulu orders were given out on what to expect if, we did run into any CT's. Accordingly, the likelihood was voiced as nil. Then we set off in single file following some partially hidden tracks through virgin and secondary jungle, the latter being the worst tangle of all. It was extremely heavy going moving through the entanglement of vegetation and quickly became sodden wet. We slogged it for about a mile, before our leader decided to return to the truck and back to the sanity of our own environment. Over a period of six hours, the whole experience was well worth the effort and I certainly did not envy any of the Infantry, who spent weeks in there hunting CT's. I was quite happy repairing Lorries.

An experience worth trying. But leave it to the Infantry.

One day, about mid afternoon, I was in the hut topping up batteries when Sgt. Levine arrived at the doorway, stated.

'Joey leave that. There's a bit of a flap on. You and Bob Watts are on convoy duty up the Cameron's. Get changed into into long trousers and jacket, draw weapons, collect your toolbox and report to 'B' platoon offices. On the double. Sharpish.' Very surprised at this as normally convoys went up first thing in the morning

'What's up then. Stan?'

'Don't ask. Just get moving.'

Bob and I duly armed and ready, reported to 'B' Platoon offices, Nobby Clarke informed us.

'Joey you're with Driver Scrimmons in the last QL. Bob you're in last but one with Scouse Bonner?' I asked.

'What's the big flap then?'

'The convoy's taking a load of Four Malay Infantry guys up to Tanah Rata, where they will take over from the Gurhka's. When the Gurhka's come out of the Ulu. They will be transported back down to Tapah Railway station. Where they will entrain down to Singapore. That's all I know. Hurry up were about to get going.'

Scrimmons, was a weedy character and had not been out there that long. Placing my toolbox in the well of the cab, told him.

'I'm riding shotgun with you.'

'I know Clarky informed me.'

The convoy along with our 15/19th armoured escort began the journey towards the Malay Regiments camp at Kampar. When we arrive, they were all lined up fully kitted out and armed ready for a trip into the Ulu. Within ten minutes, the convoy was heading up towards the Cameron's. There were no incidents on the way up, by the time, we reached Tanah Rata it was twilight. The Malays climbed down, formed up then disappeared into the semi-darkness. The convoy moved on, to turn around then return to Tanah Rata. where it stopped Scrimmons said to me.

'You can drive back down. Can't you?' Promptly I replied.

'No Mate! That's your job, mines fixing breakdowns.'

Waiting in the darkness, it was bloody cold there was hardly any talking now and again a glow from someone's lighted cigarette end showed their presence. It must have been a couple of hours later; the dark figures of the Gurhka's emerged out of the Ulu. Quickly they climbed aboard and the convoy began the downwards decent in darkness. Having only been up and down a few times during daylight. It sure was bleedin' scary as the headlights illuminated the lorry in front until it disappeared around a bend and then picked it out again, before it rounded another bend. The Gurhka's in the back must have been most uncomfortable; I heard coughs as quite a few of them threw up. That was one hell of a journey down. Just as it was getting light the convoy arrived at Tapah Railway station. Very disheveled, they disembarked to wait the arrival of the down train to

Singapore. Apparently their purpose, as reinforcements for the riots in Singapore that had been going on for a couple of weeks. I thought, "It was bloody mad. Why didn't they send the Malay Regiment instead"? The convoy headed back to Ipoh to arrive back in camp at lunchtime with no incidents to report.

The LAD was to see the departure of Captain Fred Cole, Q, John Threadgold and Sgt. Stan Levine. Their replacements, Captain Chris Collier, S/Sgt. Miller and Sgt. Watham. After such a good working relationship with our seniors, we accepted these changes with caution. What would these changes bring, more Bullshit? Cpl. Bunny Moore was to leave and Den was made up to Corporal, Mick to L/Cpl. The day Fred held his last pay parade; to us it was just a normal payday. However, Fred came out and addressed us, thanking us for our support during the time he was in Command, adding that he hoped we would all give support to our new OC Bla bla.   As a parting gesture, he shook hands with all before continuing with the formalities of Pay Parade. That was a sad day for us. All three were well respected. In retrospect the change did not affect us all that much, to begin with there was a bit more bullshit, but that soon died a natural death. I think Ole' Fred, briefed Captain Collier, on our way of working within the LAD.

Nearing the end of October, during pay parade Capt Collier having given me my pay asked.

'Plant in the next few months, you are due to leave the LAD. How would you like to sign on?' Thinking, "Fancy asking me that daft question".

'Haven't really thought about it Sir. More intent on getting back home.'

'Well you think about it, we need you in the LAD.'

'Yes Sir. Thank you Sir. But No Sir.' That was the last I heard about it.

The period after that incident went by slowly and I was getting itchy feet for Blighty. On the weekends the three of us, went into Town to have a curry and visit the flicks, Football was still the only recreation we really enjoyed, the games played were still hard and full of rivalry, gradually as some of the better players departed home, the football team was not doing so well.

In mid November, I was to say Cheerio to Smithy and Pyatt two RASC wallahs, who

were on the boat and had joined Three Company the same day. Having finished marking off the third page of my 'Days to Do Calendar' Made it 33 days to Christmas Day, which made me ponder even more about my own limited time in Malaya, would I soon get good news of my RHE date, to be at home for Christmas.

Still Days Too Many Days to Do

During November, another news bulletin announced that.

Lau Lee. Ching Pang's right hand man had been shot dead in an ambush at Tankak Jahore. That must have been a blow for Ching Peng.

Yet a further News bulletin announced the Crash of another RAF Valetta Supply aircraft making a steep turn crashed in the Cameron Highlands. An air search is in progress it is feared all on board were killed.

After hearing that news thought that is the third one this year. Yet twelve days later a further announcement was made regarding one of the RASC Dispatchers' on the plane having survived the crash he had already left the crash site, sustained by rations off the plane. Malay Soldiers found him. Now that is what I call Luck.

However, Christmas did come about and in comparison to our previous one Christmas festivities; as it occurred on a weekday it was a quiet event. Whether it was lack of interest by the Aussies or, whatever there was no competitions being organised.

Beginning the day with the traditional Rum laced tea followed by dinner, in the afternoon a few beers in the Naafi completed our festivities.

Boxing Day we were back at work Two days after Christmas, Vic brought in a copy of the Straits Times.

'Hey you lot! Have a read this. On Christmas day, some REME Sergeant

Xmas No. two

Chomping on a chicken

was shot in a bleedin' White Area. He was a recovery call out when about 30 CT's' ambushed them. Throwing the paper at Brian. Here read it.' A couple of others have to read it before I had a chance to read the snippet. This was news! An ambush particularly in a White Area. It was brief and to the point, apart from the named S/Sgt. Harris there were seven Malay Soldiers of the sixth Malay Regt, including one officer killed. A patrol of Gurhka's found the carnage. Amongst the casualties was a young 15-year-old boy, who turned out to be S/Sgt. Harris's son, he was unharmed but had witnessed the whole ambush near a river crossing on the Bentong Mentekab road. The newspaper reported that the area would possibly revert to 'Black. After reading that thought, "Bloody hell, they seem to be on the march again, when am I getting out of this stinking hole"?

Wednesday 16th Jan. by this time, totally pissed off with the whole episode of ever being sent home, was under a QL working on a defunct Generator. Staff Miller striding down to the sheds, shouted 'Joey.'... 'Under 'ere Staff.'... A pair of brogue shoes and long beige socks appeared in vision... Joey! Get your arse across to the Admin office sharpish; clean yourself up before you go. That's an order.' Struggling with the nuts asked... Can't it wait Staff, until I get this out...? That's up to you, get moving, might be some good news? ' Thinking, "Good News! At last, perhaps a ship to take me home, Sod the generator it can wait". With a quick wash under the tap, collected my beret and belt and hurried down to the Admin basha. Inside CSM Brown was talking to the admin clerk L/Cpl. Pearson. He left with a curt. 'Pearson deal with this REME Wallah?' Pearson was all right and asked.

'How about you going home Joey? We've received your movement papers.'

'Yer wot? Say that again. You really mean it. Bleedin ell, finally when do I leave, wot's name of ship, I am sailing on?'

'Not a ship. You're lucky, flying home from Singers. How about that? Is that okay with you?' Thinking, "Blimey, no long haul by sea for me, air ticket home, can't be bad".

'When do I leave?'

'A week tomorrow. Next Thursday twenty-fourth, catch the train down to Singapore; report in at Nee Soon, where you will be kitted out for Blighty. The Admin bunch down there will fill you in with all the other details.'

'Anyone else traveling down with me?'

'No just you, but understand there are three RSF's on the same train, that's all. It will be on to-nights company orders. Good luck mate, been nice playing football with you. Oh, another thing report to the MRS for a Cholera Jab, you'll need it. By the way, have you got a civvy jacket or anything like that?'

'No. Shirt, trousers, ties, socks and shoes, nothing else. Why?'

'Well you had better get a jacket; Indians do not allow British troops to fly over India in uniforms. Soding daft if you ask me? Better see Li, he'll fit you out in no time.'

'More Bleedin' money to pay out.'

'Pay him next Thursday before you leave.'

'I'll add it to my slate; anyway thanks its best news I've had.' Cock 'o' hoop, with more than a spring in my heels, walking smartly into the LAD yelled.

'Ear you lot, Sod yer 'orrible luck. At bleedin' last I'm flying home next week.' Towser shouted back.

'About time yer little bugger glad yer going.'

'Thanks mate.' Feeling very chuffed with myself, carried on to the offices to report my good news to Staff, entering Nobby Hill was sat with his hands behind his head gazing at his typewriter waiting for it to work, gave a big wink and smiled, he already knew.

'Staff. I'm R.H.E. next Thursday. '

'Yes, I have been informed, so you had better start preparations for your homeward trip. But no skiving still got work to do. Good news anyway lucky bugger.' Retreating out of the office, about to continue working on the QL, standing beside it as usual doing nothing. Were Den and Vic, Den asked.

'What's this mate, you pissing of home then?' Vic interrupted.

'When you leaving?'

'Bleedin' great ennit? Flying all the way from Singers. Well I'm leaving this poxy place next Thursday, heading down to Nee Soon, then I don't know but knowing my luck could be bleedin' weeks, I'm due to be demobed in two weeks time?' From under a lorry, Bob Watts shouted. 'When's yer piss up then?'

'After Pay parade. Tomorrow night. It's a good time as any, ain't getting pissed the night before that's for sure.' By this time, most of the lads had gathered around, wishing me bon voyage along with all the other comments that you would not think very appropriate. Sgt. Watham arrived.

'It isn't knocking off time. Get back to work.'

After lunch, visited Li still sat on the table, his needle and cotton flashing in and out of a garment, glancing up said.

'Lu Joee spec velly soon, Lu go Wa H E yes?'

'Bloody 'ell, how do you know Li?'

'Haa. Mestar Joee, looky Chinee wospers wound cam, Lu wan coat yes.' Resigned to his knowledge of my pending departure asked.

'What material yer got for blazer, got to be warm you know its bleedin' cold in Blighty.'

'Okay. Me looky.' Clambered down from the table padded around to the rear, returned with four rolls of material flinging them on the table. 'Looky, lu fel velly good material.' The colours a dark brown, a light green and two different shades of blue. Forgetting the other colours selected the blues, feeling the darker of the two, a light woven material medium weight, but liked the colour.

'How much for jacket?'-

'Benty five dolla.'

'Sod off, too many dollars. Heh look I'm not that big, bet you charge Sama Sama for Corporal Lee and he's much bigger than me.' Emphasizing an exaggerated height. He studied my physic

'Benty dolla Okay?'

'Nah fifteen, me always good customer?' Breaking into a torrid of Chinese, shook his head with his hands up muttered.

'Ighteen.'

'Be ready next Tuesday or no deal?' He beamed flashing some of his gold teeth.

'Lu buy! Weddy oosday Okay? How lu pay?

'Thursday's pay day, promise Okay?

'No, lu leaf ursday, lu go Singapore. Li no get paid. Lu pay coat oosday, or no coat.' Not wanting to argue with him agreed, left him entering more Chinese characters on my tab. I did not owe him anything so must have been on a good wicket, for him to accept my latest order. Still baffled by the way news spreads so quickly. Returned to the basha just in time to see Bowles, waking everyone up. Thank Christ at last was getting out of there. Grabbing the beret and belt left for the LAD. It must have been the very first time had beaten everyone back and was busy at work when they all staggered back. That evening before we went over the Naafi to celebrate I crossed off that day. Noting the day I was to leave 3 Coy, was a month after Christmas day, nevertheless on the calendar added more to the final days.

SIGNING OFF

The following days passed slowly by. Saturday, went into town bought a brown canvass holdall, an ornate painted tin chest and a few locks, to pack my bits and pieces in. Records, cigarettes and personal items, they would be sent by sea so it would be months, before they were delivered. Saturday night, we had a few drinks in the Naafi, headed down town to have a last curry and see a midnight movie. "The Lady-Killers".

Monday, basically had finished working on Lorries, instead I painted my home address on the tin chest. Taffy took over doing all the jobs, all I got from him was.

'Joey you're a f......g skiver, I'll be glad when you piss off.' Told him where to get off. It was the same in the mess, including the chi-ackintggg from all the Aussies I had known from the time they had arrived. Most of the old RASC. Wallahs had already been shipped home, so was not that well acquainted with the new ones. That night it was announced on a radio bulletin.

"Jan. 20th. Chan Choi a Communist Party Branch Secretary and his mistress, were shot dead near Ipoh".

It was possibly the last news bulletin, to hear and even more pleased was getting out of it.

Tuesday, visited Li, picked up my Blazer and paid him in full. He gratefully received the money, struck me off his tab book shaking my hand said with a big grin over his face.

'Luk Luk. Bi Bi Mr. Joee.'

'Yeah Bye Bye Li. Won't be coming back.'

Nice New Blazer

However, my last days were full of nothing, apart from getting rid of the tin box and moping around the Bays until Thursday arrived. After breakfast, when all had left for the LAD, set about getting my final bits and pieces packed in my sea kit bag. OGs, webbing, boots and other equipment, my civvies packed in the holdall, handed in my bedding and crocs. Returning to the Basha made sure there was nothing left. Taking a final look around the basha with their kit all laid out neat and tidy on the beds. A place that had been my home for the past eighteen months. My empty bedsprings, a reminder of all the sweaty guards done, now vacant and waiting for the next poor bastard to take over. Finally, ready to leave at the other end, heard a familiar sound entering the basha the whirring of a shit beetle, that brought back happy memories nevertheless, hastened my departure grabbing hold of my kit left.

Attending my last pay parade, said my goodbyes to the entire mob. Taffy Morgan muttered. 'Going to miss you yer English Bugger'...there were other well words spoken from the Aussies. Bluey wished me luck and said...'Joey when you get back to Blighty, if you bump into Al, you tell him from me he don't know a blaady thing about Cricket.'...Den and George. Muttered see you back in London sometime in the future. Den added.

'Give us yer phone number; I'll ring yer when I get back, maybe meet up with Pratty as well.' Gave him the telephone number.

At 1130, hrs, outside the Guardhouse having signed for a rifle and ammunition, slung my kit into the back of the duty Lorry climbed up into the cab to ride shotgun for the last time down to Ipoh Station.

At the station three R.S.F's with sea kitbags and grips were already stood waiting on the platform, they were all about twenty about the same height as me but was drawn to one of them with snow-white hair, it certainly was not fair that had me wondering what happened during their time spent jungle bashing. Joining them enquired.

'You going back to Blighty?' A curt reply stated.

'Nae Scootland yer ken.' That was appropriate for those three. Anyway, was not part of their party only a tagger on, wondering if Bert would be on the train?

The escort buggy entered and careered past without stopping, about five minutes later the train arrived and came to a grinding halt. The transport Sergeant in charge checked us.

'Right you four get yourselves aboard the train.' I enquired.

'Sergeant is there any REME guys from Butterworth on.'

'No. A few Aussies and a handful of Lincolns.'

The journey was uneventful, fortunately was not picked for guard duty and got a reasonable but uncomfortable night's kip. At Singapore station, a QL was waiting to take us to Nee Soon. The four of us booked in, handed in our weapons taken to our sleeping quarters, which to say at least was rather "Novel". A square tin shack made out of corrugated steel, the four walls were hinged at the top and held open at the bottom, by long steel rods just like large windows. During the day they were supposed to keep one cool, they did not; you just sweated your balls off all day. Provided with bedding crocs, and fitted out with BD's. There was nothing to do, except stay in these sweatboxes, have our meals in the massive canteen and laze about. On occasions a Cpl. came around to see, if we were still alive he stated.

'If you leave camp. Do not go into Singapore, only visit Nee Soon Village.'

I did go into Nee Soon, but it was the same as any other place in Malaya not worth the effort. We had been told that out flight out was on Sunday the 27th. Then were informed it had been delayed. More frustration.

Monday afternoon, the Cpl. entering the sweatbox announced.

'You four are very lucky. Due to the Suez problem, the Army is flying you out by a civilian aircraft. Tomorrow morning I have booked an early morning call for 0500 hours. Dress in your civvies, hand in your bedding and then take all your kit to the Mess hall for breakfast when finished, leave your crocs in the Mess hall. Outside transport will wait to take you to the Guardhouse to sign out, then on to Changi that's all you lucky bastards.'

At last, the best bit of news yet. Having never flown before, was very apprehensive about flying a new experience and extremely pleased to be flying in style.

PART THREE

AFTER.

Flight home : BA706 Super Constellation. reg no. GANUX Pilot: Captain Sutcliffe.
Left Singapore. 29th. Jan. 1957 took off at local time 0851.- gmt 0121.
Arr.Calcutta 0826 dep. 0916.
Arr. Karachi 1536. dep. 1649 Crew & Pilot change: Capt Moss.
Arr. Basra 2309 dep 0108.
Arr. Istanbul 0744 dep. 0910 Crew & Pilot change: Capt Rowbottom.
Arr. Zurich 1530 dep. 1604.
Arr. London Heathrow. 1830.
All stops made, were for refueling, changing crew and lasted for about an hour.

CHAPTER TWENTY-FOUR
RETURN HOME ENGLAND (RHE)
January 1957.

That night I doubt very much if the four of us really slept, the number of fags the other three smoked was unreal, maybe they were trying to get rid of their duty frees. At the stated time we were duly called. Dressed in civvies we handed in our bedding, collecting our chattels went to the mess hall to be served a good breakfast. As instructed, left our crocs behind but as a souvenir slipped my mug in between the folds of my BD in my sea Kit Bag (Now safely on display in the British Army Museum). Outside we clambered aboard the waiting QL, moving up behind the drivers cab sat down on our sea kitbags. At the guardhouse signed out at 0600 hours, the Lorry left Nee Soon for the long drive into Singapore.

The three Jocks soon lit up their cigarettes one offered me one, thanking him refused. In the darkness, they conversed amongst themselves whilst I glad to be wearing a warm blazer against the cold breeze created by the speeding Lorry, mulled over the past couple of hectic weeks since Christmas. Until approaching the built up outskirts of Singapore we all got up to lean on top of the drivers cab, to catch a last fleeting glimpse of the various Chinese roadside hawkers moving about in the glare from their bright kerosene lamps. Most of whom were dressed in a white singlet shorts and flip-flops, puffing away at a fag as they stoked up their charcoal burners ready to serve up chow mien or whatever was on their early morning menu. Every now and again, the sound of tinny Chinese music would become loud then faded as the QL sped past on almost empty roads. The cold morning air was tinged with the smell of charcoal and the Far East. It was still dark when we arrived at Changi airport stopping in front of the entrance clambered down from the back of the QL with our chattels, the driver replacing the tailboard said.

'All I can say is you're lucky buggers. I still have six months to do. Good luck anyway.'

All grinning like Cheshire cats did not make any comment, as I led the way into the airport. It was not that big and at that time of the morning there was hardly anyone about. There was nobody at the information desk, so waited until a Chinese girl dressed in a white blouse and black skirt arrived, yawning she asked.

'Gentlemen. Where are you going? Show me your ticket...showing our travel warrants...Aah! Please to report to the B.O.A.C. desk down to your right and on the other side of the hall. They will take care of you.'

Approaching that desk, another Chinese ticket girl checked our one-way only flight tickets, our travel warrants and in a sing song Chinese/English way informed us.

'Gentlemen. Your flight number is BA 706 and is due to take off at eight forty-five. Pleese to make way through customs into the departure room. You will be informed over tannoy when to board the plane. Keep your personal cabin bag. I will take possession of all your kitbags.'

There was nobody at the customs desk, so we had to hang about until a Chinese Customs Officer appeared on the scene. Looking curiously at us all dressed in civvies requested.

'Passports Please'. To which I replied.

'Ain't got one. But this is my travel warrant.'...handing it to him he checked it before demanding...'Where you from?...Ipoh Malaya... You all Army...Yes. Show me your flight ticket...What is the purpose of your flight sir?' In my case full of importance replied.

'Ain't got one. But this is my travel warrant.'...handing it to him he checked it before demanding...'Where you from?...Ipoh Malaya... You all Army...Yes. Show me your flight ticket...What is the purpose of your flight sir?' In my case full of importance replied.

'Going 'ome to Blighty mate...to which he asked...Anything to declare?' Did not know what he was talking about and possibly neither did the others so answered... No...Okay your papers are in order...addressing the Jocks... Are you three the same? They chorused. 'Aye'...Okay. Go along this corridor to the departure lounge on your left. '

The departure room was empty; obviously, we were the first to arrive. We sat there with nothing to do but wait in the coolness of the early morning as the dawn began to break the fans suspended from the ceiling were switched on to whirr around creating a down draft. Soon the arrival of the early morning cleaners and general helpers began to appear; some other civilian passengers began to arrive with their chattels and spread themselves out amongst the vacant seats. A small kiosk opened up where you could change currency so sorting out the remnants of my service pay of Malay dollars changed them into English pound notes and few lumps of shrapnel, not much but it would have to suffice when I got back to Blighty. At about 0830 an announcer called out the departure of our flight number. Immediately feeling a great knot in the pit of my stomach gripped hold of the holdall, followed others to join the queue at the exit where another Chinese women attendant checking our tickets stated.

'Please to follow other passengers to that plane in front of you.' Pointing to an airplane on the tarmac parked broadside towards us. My first impression was "Blimey a big un". Following other civilian passengers, crossed the open space all the time taking more notice of the planes size parked on three sets of landing wheels, one in front under the cockpit and one under each wing, although could only see one of the wings it had two massive engines. Its silver fuselage was very long and sleek ending at a boom tail with three tailfins; the entrance door was just to the rear of the wing where passengers already climbing the stairway disappeared inside. Approaching the foot of the stairway was greeted by two gorgeous stewardess's dressed in dark blue skirts, white blouses and on their heads wore a forage style cap, both had tantalising figures (English of course). With the exception of Mrs. Cole they were the first white women I had come across since leaving Blighty, with beaming smiles said.

'Good morning sir. Welcome aboard.' Ascending the stairs at the top paused to take a last look back, saying aloud.

'Goodbye Singers. Never did see yer. I'm going home.'

Entering its interior, on either side was a row of two separate orange coloured seats. The gangway in between them led to a blank partition with a doorway at the far end, suppose that was the pilot and crews quarters. The inside curvature was padded and light grey in colour, at ceiling level was a rectangular box the same width as the gangway with rows of lights illuminating the length of the gangway. Another stewardess separated the four of us sending the three Jocks to the rear and me towards the front to a seat overlooking the wing with a porthole style window and draw curtains. Pushing my holdall under the seat sat down in the armchair type seat, which for those with greasy hair had a long cotton headrest. When all the passengers were in their seats, from the rear heard the sound of a crump as the aircraft door was shut tight. Pulling the draw curtain aside let in the sunlight to see the airport building surrounded by palm trees, there was nothing of interest to see so working out the seat belt clip buckled up. The seat beside me along with the two opposite were vacant furthermore remained vacant throughout the journey. A stewardess making her way down the aisle presented a tray full of barley sugars, requested.

'Excuse me sir. During takeoff please suck a sweet.' Not aware of what for took two. After about fifteen minutes the tannoy bleeped, a stewardess intoned.

'Ladies and gentlemen. Would you please fasten your seat belts for takeoff? Please extinguish all cigarettes. No smoking during takeoff. Thank you.'

This was the moment when the knots in my stomach tightened; glancing out of the window gazed at the two enormous engines, the tips of their lifeless blades painted yellow. Suddenly, the outer engine spat into life coughing out a plume of black smoke, at first with a jolting movement its propeller slowly turned until spinning easily gathered momentum to whizz around creating the illusion of a yellow circle. Fascinated, watched as the wing began to vibrate then with a cough and a cloud of black smoke the inner engine span into life. With both rotating at speed, the wing was vibrating so badly it seemed as if it was about to fall off, gradually the propeller speed increased alarmingly before throttling back. Then the back rear edges of the wing folded down, must have been what they called flaps. After about five minutes of this trial and error stuff, the plane eased forward and rumbled its way around to the runway and with a squeal of brakes; it came to a halt. For a short period remained stationary then with a deafening roar the engines were revved up to full throttle and with a lurch the plane launched itself down the runway, as it thundered along its forward momentum pushed me further back into the seat gripping the seams of my trousers as she gently left the ground and became airborne. My ears became blocked holding my nose and blowing did nothing, doing what the stewardess had instructed 'suck a sweet' unwrapped the cellophane popped one into my mouth, within a few swallows my ears cleared. As the plane climbed above the noise of the engines I heard a whirring sound below then a big clunk as the wheels were housed, in a giant arc the plane banking left providing an aerial view of Singapore below with Changi airport runway and buildings and soon the surrounding sea dotted with many islands ships and junks. Flying over Jahore the tip of Malaya, presented a picture of one mass of green jungle before flying out over the coastline of Malacca and over the sea we had sailed through en-route to Singapore, captivated by the sight was startled by a stewardess's voice saying. 'Sir. You can now unfasten your safety belt and move about.'

Unclipping, ventured across the other seats to look out of the window, far below etched out by its white sandy shoreline was the coast of Malaya and one mass of green jungle thinking, "Somewhere in that green hell many Infantry lads are sweating their balls off chasing invisible CT's whilst the lads in the LAD lazed about in the sheds. I sat there for sometime before that sight soon disappeared from view. Looking out at a clear blue sky reflecting upon what had I actually seen of Singapore? Nothing, the rest of the time was Malaya with no leave apart from a couple of weekend jungle training bashes and a few days up the Cameron's. What a bleedin' waste of my time, but what of my future after demob? My old job, it would be good to see John and Harry again then could tell him some stories. Returning to my seat, with nothing except sea to see below watched as the stewardess's moved amongst the few passengers. With the constant drone of the engines, the flight became boring; the only thing to read was a booklet in the pocket of the seat in front, which revealed pages of maps with routes marked by a red strip where the planes flew from one airport to another. Far below a long stretch of Islands came into view and from the map in the booklet; identified them as the Andaman's.

During the flight, the stewardess provided free soft drinks and later brought meals around on a tray similar to the troopships but made out of plastic or bakelite, not a lot but good grub. The flight attendant came along pushing a cabinet and asked if I would like a drink of orange or something else. I did not have very much money so declined the offer and settled for the freebies. She was one of the two English girls who welcomed us aboard at Singers. I had watched her going backwards and forwards obviously she became the focus of my attention, as she leaned over to place the drink on the little table could not miss the aroma of the expensive perfume around her. She was very attractive with wavy mousey hair a pleasant smile as she conversed with me, noticed had a smudge of lipstick on one of her teeth she asked. 'Have a good stay in Singapore Sir?' Thinking. "Sir! What a pleasant sound, must be the civilian clothes a bit early not demobed yet but who cares a shit. I was glad of the question putting on the charm entered into a conversation with her.

'No. Actually, for the past eighteen months I have been in Malaya. Did not see anything of Singapore. What is it like there? Can you tell me?'

'I don't really know that much about it, we only fly in and out but sometimes stay at Raffles overnight, therefore do not see it ourselves but it's supposed to be a nice place. Look when I finished serving theses drinks, I will come back and have a talk with you.'

'Yes. That would be very nice. Thank you.' Thinking. "Whoopee! Maybe when we get to London might take her out"?

About an hour later, she did come back and we had a brief chat about Singapore. I ask you Singapore? Never seen the bleedin' place but did find out that the plane having flown all the way from Darwin in Australia only landed there. She was quite pleasant, about twenty-four her name was Amanda but she did inform me that they were leaving the plane at Karachi, change of crews or summat thinking. "Bang goes my invite?"

Daylight turned to dusk and the colour of the sky was deep red then faded into darkness, outside it looked very cold you could hear the popping sound from the engines exhaust ports as they spat out tiny spurts of blue flame. The plane began to descend to land at Calcutta the fasten seat Belts came on. The tannoy bleeped and the stewardess advised us to.

'Ladies and gentlemen. Would you please return to your seats? Fasten your seat belts for landing. Extinguish all cigarettes. No smoking during Landing. We will be staying in Calcutta for approximately one hour for refueling. During which time please remain in your seats. Thank you.'

As we rapidly descended, heard a whine and a large clunk as the wheels came down. We landed with a couple of bumps before slowing down and finally coming to a stop, as it was dark there was nothing to see. An hour later with the same procedure we took off. Amanda brought another meal and later provided me with a Blanket. 'There you are Soldier. Keep you warm during the nighttime.'

'Oh. Thank you. I am getting cold and will need that.' I responded but wondered how she knew I was a soldier? I had never told her. During the night it was freezing although wrapped in a blanket sat up was uncomfortable and did not sleep very well. In the morning, we were provided with a breakfast and with nothing to do fell asleep again. I was woken up by the other stewardess and told.

'Sir. Please stay on board this is change of crew stop. We had already landed at Karachi, it was early afternoon and the sun was high in the sky looking out of the window saw a few Indians manhandling hoses as fuel was pumped in from fuel tankers on the ground, in the distance a few buildings surrounded by a masses of palm trees. I never saw Amanda to thank her for the blanket but she, could have kept me warm that was for sure. Following the same drill, the plane took off for our next stop Basra. With new stewardess's on board we were fed dinner I slept in the early hours of the morning, we landed at Basra again for refueling and took off for Istanbul, where we were allowed to get off. Spent two hours in a desolate lounge. On board, there was another change of crew, throughout the day totally bored did nothing but look out of the window wishing the time away, fed meals and again slept wrapped in the blanket. It was daylight when the stewardess woke me the lovely sight came into view mountains and trees covered in snow. As we flew into Zurich on the descent noticed along the landing strip where the landing lights were the heat from them had melted the surrounding snow. I was fearful of the plane skidding off the runway and when the Fasten Seat Belts warning came on, I was already securely strapped in and doubt whether Houdini could have got out. We landed with a couple of bumps before reducing speed and stopped. We were allowed off, but with all that snow lying about did not fancy the cold. "Not on your Nellie". Stayed on board wrapped in a blanket and well strapped in for the take off.

We took off on the last leg home. As we sped closer to England the drone of the engines never ceased, agitated at the thought in four days time would be demobed. Free of the shackles that had taken two years of my life, having met and lived with some great comrades in arms throughout basic and trade training and during the past eighteen months serving in the sweat hole of Malaya. Realised it was the camaraderie that kept us all going. Taking all the bullshit that we all had to put up with. My thoughts went back to those mates in the LAD basha. "Bleedin' 'ell what time was it there now"? Several times, they had told us to adjust the time, the hands on the watch pointed to quarter to five. Laughing loudly thought back to two years previously, "Sgt. Barnes called them Mickey Mouse watches". In my jacket pocket was the last letter from Cecilia, taking it out re-read it however, there was something odd about her wording that was strange? Nevertheless soon all would be revealed.

January 30th. Finally, we touched down at London airport; it was dark as the plane taxied towards the building with a squeal of brakes came to a final halt. In the light shining from the various windows watched as with an exhausted twirl, the yellow ring of the outer engine became a yellow tip. I was home, my Mickey Mouse watch hands pointed to 6.30 p.m. I watched as the other yellow ring stopped twirling and joined its partner. Sitting there it dawned on me, just over two days before I was sweating me balls off in Singapore and now I was shivering with the cold, didn't make any sodding sense. Joining the rest of the passengers queued up for the exit where a stewardess uttered.

'Thank you sir. For flying B.O.A.C. Enjoy your stay in London sir?'

'Thank you.' Thinking, "Enjoy your stay? Mines going to be a bleedin' long one that's for sure". Nevertheless, that evening had to report to Aldershot. At the doorway, a blast of cold air hit me going down the stairway stepped onto English soil and practically ran into the building to retrieve the sea Kitbag. The three R.S.F's collected theirs and disappeared to their final destination Scootland. While like a frozen turd shivering, teeth chattering and pissed off hung about waiting in the baggage reclaim area. About two hours later, a porter asked.

'Excuse me mate. Is this you're kitbag?' Looking at the label.

'No not Dean Plant.' He retorted.

'Well it must be yours. That's last piece of luggage off that flight I'll watch you open it up and check.' Undoing the rope opened the neck and saw my beret cap badge exclaimed.

'Bloody ' 'ell mate it is mine. More than relieved to get it back asked. Ear mate where can I catch a bus into London?' Scratching his head replied.

'Seeing its yours take it, go outside the main entrance catch a 140 bus for Yeading, get off there and get a 97 to Ealing Broadway station.'

'Well thanks for that.' Leaving the reclaim section followed the way out signs through customs, there was nobody there not that I had anything to declare. Outside I caught the stated bus and after travelling halfway across the outskirts of London, at Ealing Broadway bought a ticket to Waterloo. It was 1030 when the tube arrived at Charring Cross where I had to change onto the Northern line. Frozen to the marrow suddenly decided. "Sod it. I'm going home. My excuse, missed the train"? Getting out went up the exit into the main station area walked across into the station and towards a telephone kiosk, sorting out pennies dialed home, impatiently waited until it was picked up heard Dad say.

'Reliance...' immediately Pressed button B, chink. 'It's me Joe. Get some beers in please, I'm at Charring Cross station, I'll be home soon.'

Dad's voice, crackled over the line. 'Joe! Is that you Son?'

'Yes Dad! I'm home. Get the beers in.' Slammed down the receiver. Outside in the forecourt hailed a taxi, throwing my kitbag and grip into the back called to the cabbie.

'Grenada wandsworth road. Step on it mate?' The cabbie, chatted all the way there; he was ex army and warmed to my tale of woe. I noticed at Lambeth Bridge he flipped up the flag on his meter. When we stopped opposite the Grenada, getting out with my kit bag and holdall, slamming the cab door shut asked.

'How much do I owe yer mate?' The cabbie said.

'Just give us 'arf the fare. 'Alf a crown all right, that will do I am on me way 'ome anyway.'

'Ta mate. Really appreciate that... It was just as well, did not have that much cash and was sure Dad would have coughed up. Sorting out some shrapnel passed it through his window...Ta and the best of luck young 'un...Thanks mate cheerio.' As he drove off, the freezing cold air brushed against my face. As I smelt the smell of London, looked towards the Pub its neon sign spelling out 'NOTTINGHAM CASTLE.' across to the Grenada foyer that was full of lights and void of patrons still inside watching the flicks. Definitely home.

Knocking on the door, Mum opened it. Anyway after greetings were over, was forcibly dragged into the front room sat down in front of the fire, the steady roar of the gas jets set the coke glowing red, definitely in need of that to thaw out. Mum re-entered threw a blanket over my shoulders went out and returned with a cup of tea. Noticed how tired and drawn she looked, wiping away her tears enquired. 'Why didn't you let us know, you were coming home?'

'I did, at Charring Cross but they lost me sea kit bag with my BD in it. Took 'em hours to find it.' The sound of the front door banged closed.

'Here's your father back with the beer.' Getting up crossed towards the door, dad entered.

'Hello son welcome back, this is a surprise.' Handshakes. 'Why didn't you let us know you were coming home?'

'Well just before leaving sent a letter from camp, suppose you haven't received it yet?'

'No not yet. When you got to report back or are you demobed already? Your due out soon, isn't that right?'

'No. Not demobed Dad. Had to report back to Aldershot tonight, but I missed the train didn't I?'

'What? You're AWOL?'

'Well sort of.'

'Silly bugger, you can be on a charge twenty-eight days more. Well we'll have you up crack of dawn and on your way.'

'Bleedin' 'ell Dad, I've been away for bleedin' eighteen months and your having a go at me already, I've done my bit of soldiering I'll be on my way tomorrow. They've messed me about, everyone due home left over six weeks ago. I was lucky to get a civvy airplane back, much quicker anyway. Yes I'll be demobed in three days time.' By that time, Dad had poured out the beers and handed me one.

'Cheers son. Watch your language. It's very good to see you back home safe and sound.' We drunk the beer another was poured out, it was question time and relating what had gone on out there. Mum told dad to phone Margaret who was staying at Lily's that night. We had another beer by which time I had thawed out. Margaret arrived home by taxi, more greetings, soon after Michael, surprised at my being home even more greetings, more beer, then packed off to a warm bed with hot water bottles.

Early next morning Dad woke me with a cup of tea.

'C'mon son get up you have to get back to camp.' The house was freezing cold, quickly sorted out my uniform, dressed went into the bathroom, before going downstairs to finish of dressing, boots, gaiters and BD top with neatly sewn above my left breast pocket. My inch of bravery medal ribbon.

'When did you get that?'

'Awarded out there, the medal is upstairs in the holdall. I'll show you it later.' With belt and beret in place, Dad handed some money over.

'Get a cab up to Waterloo, it's quicker that way.'

'Thanks don't really need that, can catch a bus.'

'No get a cab.' Picking up the half-empty kit bag. 'Cheers Dad, see you in three days time when I am finally out of the bleedin' army. He just grinned...Say Bye to mum for me.'

Leaving the warmth of the house, it was still dark and freezing cold. The roads were not busy and not many people about; the early morning rush had not even begun. By the time had walked as far as Wilcox road, a lone taxi was cruising towards me flagging it, he did a U-turn. 'Waterloo mate and hurry.' Throwing in the kitbag got in; well fell into the seat as he accelerated away he enquired.

'What camp you going to then?'

'Aldershot getting demobed. About bleedin' time too, done my bit.'

'Where yer bin then?'

'Malaya. Got back yesterday.'

'Where's that then?

'Don't yer read the papers? There's a war going on out there.'

'Never 'eared of it mate. Nuffin in newspapers, Korea yerse, but that's bin over fer years. Where's this place Malaya then?'

'Ever heard of Singapore mate?'

'Yerse! It's out Far East somewhere... Oh, there was a Bob Hope film called. "The Road to Singapore" or summat. Saw that I did. Never 'eared of Malaya tho.' Thinking. "You prat no point in talking to you then". Nevertheless, he prattled on about what had happened over in England that went right over my head, in response grunted a few times or said. 'Is that right.' When we arrived at Waterloo, paid him the fare and was going to give him a tip but he refused.

'Nah mate you keep it. I don't pick up many squaddies. Anyway, yerse's bin out fighting a war somewhere, you have a beer on me.'

'Ta mate I'll do that.' Slammed the door shut thinking. "Cheeky sod! I'm paying for me own bleedin' beer". Having bought a ticket just missed a train however, this time was en-route to get demobed. Had to wait half an hour for the next one, went and had a cup of tea. Clambering aboard the train noticed the state of the trains had not changed. At Aldershot station, asked the porter

'Where's (cannot remember the name). Camp?'

'Get the bus to? Where ever?' Arriving at the guardhouse reported in. Instantly recognised the R.P. Cpl. from Malvern, he questioned.

'You Plant?'

'Yes corporal. 23112429 Craftsmen Plant reporting in.'

'You were supposed to report in last night. You're AWOL.'

'Well did try to get here, but they lost my kit at the airport.' He now standing up retorted.

'That's no excuse. You should have found a way to get down here.'   My heart now thumping thinking, "Aw shit. He's going to put me on a charge just like Dad said Twenty-eight days detention AWOL". Ventured.

'Er. Corporal. Weren't you at Malvern?'

'Yes! What about it?'

'You're Corporal Kirk aren't you?'

'Yes. Were you there as well? What intake?'

'Nine Elect Seven. March until July. 55.'

'Blimey, that's long time ago. Not long after you lot left they moved the camp down to Borden. Where you just come from then?'

'Malaya. Three Company REME LAD. Twenty-eighth. Commonwealth Infantry Brigade. Stationed at Ipoh with the Aussies...added...Never got any leave.'

'Oh. What was it like out there?'

'Bleedin' 'orrible, lot of commie bastards and stinking hot.'

'Where did you stay last night?'

'At home. London. As I said, they lost me kit at the airport. Eventually they handed it to me but it was so late, I'd missed the last train so went straight home and this morning got the early morning train.' Changing his tune asked.

'When you due for demob?'

'Next monday the third.'

'Nope. You are late. Some of the others due out same day, got demobed early today. Just sign in here and get yourself down to hut number twenty, then collect bedding. You'll be here for about three weeks being processed.'

'What! Three weeks? I'm due for demob on the third. Not in three weeks time.'

'Well! That's what it takes to complete documentation. You should have been back a month ago.' Not wanting to push my luck signed in, with instructions where to go left the guardhouse. Finding the hut entered, there were some double bunks spaced out, a group of blokes either standing lounging about or laying on their beds. Pissed off, kicked the door shut behind me went towards the farthest spare bed slung my kit on it. Asked the bloke lying on his pit.

'This ain't anyone's is it?'

'No mate take it. Where you come from?'

'Just arrived back from Malaya. Where you come from?'

'Us lot. Just come back from Egypt. Sent out during the five-day war. Glad to be back home.' I was amongst veterans like me so there was no point in swinging the lead amongst these blokes, enquired.

'Where's the Q M store?' He gave me directions so left heading to the bedding stores. Signed for bedding carted them back made up my bed and sat down.

'What's the form here then, do we have to do anything parades or something?'

'No mate, just lounge about wait for your demob papers. Dinners usual time down at the cookhouse, evening meals are at five, there's the camp Naafi or you can go into Aldershot, apart from that nothing.' Thinking. "Christ this is going to be a total waste of my time and want to be out by the third. But that wasn't going to happen".

The accommodation was drafty, freezing cold and caught a cold from someone else; everyone was choking with colds or with the smoke that hung about from the freebies.

Had a medical, coughed enough times at the doctor spraying germs over him; he was not impressed. Instead was pronounced A1. By the weekend, my cough had subsided and some of us went into Aldershot for a few drinks at one of the pubs. There were many Para's about who had also just come back from Egypt so the place was heaving with drunks. I could not wait to get out, but the time really dragged on, what a waste of bleedin' manpower.

Thursday 14th. Finally. Demob day arrived lined up for my final pay parade received money, my discharge papers, a rail warrant to Waterloo. Instructions to report to a TA place in South Wimbledon. What for did not know. Finally, out of the Army having served two years and overtime more than had bargained for.

Along with a few others, we were given a free trip in a QL down to the station. In the train compartment, there were a couple of blokes, who had been in the same intake at Honiton. One had been in Cyprus; the other had been out in Kenya. We chin-wagged but never got into

Demob Papers

any meaningful conversation. Now a free man began to surmise what I was going to do. My first thought, meeting Derek have a few weeks off lazing about, report to this TA place and get rid of the kit. Once back in work would meet up with Al and maybe meet Cecilia again.

Back home Mum greeted me with open arms, surprised to see me still in uniform. That did not last. Quickly upstairs changed into civvies, only then did I feel a real free man. Whilst changing Mum had cooked me a big plate of double egg and chips. That was the best meal I had eaten since leaving home nineteen months before. Dad arrived home from his morning shift; it was not long before we were heading over to the Nott for a few pints and a man talk. He filling me in with the problems that Mum had endured along with other matters, which made me think more about my prolonged absence away from home. That night slept the sleep of a free man with a long lay-in. While Dad was at work without him twittering on about the noise played my jazz records, Mum did not take a blind bit of notice, she was very happy bringing me endless cups of tea.

That evening after a smashing fish and chip meal, suitably dressed with overcoat and scarf instead of walking, caught a couple of buses to Derek's. Knocking on the door, his mother very surprised to see me invited me in.

'Hello stranger. Long time no see. Derek out but come on in for a cup of tea.'

Over a cup of tea answered all the questions she asked, having drunk the tea suggested.

'If Derek arrives back early tell him to meet me at the Club or Beehive. I'll see you later Mrs. Beamish. Oh and thanks for the tea.' Catching a bus back to the club, walked in through the door there in the little hallway sat George, the guardian of the club still controlling who was allowed in, his small table almost barring the entrance. looking up.

'Hello stranger! Long time no see. Your nice and brown been on your holidays?'

'No. Not been on my holidays, but its freezing back here.'

'Yes I suppose so; someone told me you were out in Hong Kong. Must have been hot out there? Did you like it?'

'No. And it wasn't Hong Kong. Ain't paid any subs can I get in?'

'Well all right, seeing I know you. You seen Derek lately?'

'Not really. Ain't seen him for eighteen months or more. I'm looking for him now spose he's not 'ere then?'

'No. Wouldn't be asking you if he was here would I? He owes his subs?'

Behind someone else coming in distracted his attention. Not wanting to continue with this mundane conversation. Squeezed through the gap, entered the hall to the sound of music. As usual pairs of girls were dancing together, a couple of boys were playing table tennis. Leaving my coat in the cloakroom returned into the hall looking around did not see many familiar faces apart from Bill who was dancing with an unknown girl? At the far end stood by the stage spotted Kevan, avoiding the dancers heading towards him with hand extended he called.

'Hey Joe. Where you bin then? Ain't seen yer down the club for a few weeks. 'Ome on leave are yer? A quick shake of the hands followed by a favorite...When yer going back?'

'No. I've just got demobed; I'm a free man done my bit that's for sure.'

'You're looking brown. Where yer bin Cyprus on yer hols? Heard there's a bit of problem out there. Did yer do any fighting?' I quickly retorted,

'Not Cyprus. Bleedin' Malaya.' These questions were pissing me off, first it was Hong Kong now Cyprus. Then casually he asks.

'Where's Malaya?'

'Wot dyer mean where's Malaya? It's out Far East, there's a war going on out there.'

'War! Wot war?' Giving up asked.

'Is Brian and Kenny here?'

'Nope. They're both in Kate. Ain't seen them for some time, tell a lie. Brian was in 'ere the other weekend with his girl friend Sylvia.' Just then, Joyce entered walking straight over kissed me.

'Hello stranger, nice to see you back Derek said you were out in Singapore, have a good time? Yer looking browned off.' She giggled. Grinning thought. Not browned off. Pissed off. Nobody had missed me but there again with time memories do fade.

As there was not much going on, had a few dances with Joyce before inviting her out for a drink over the Beehive, she accepted collecting our coats left. The Beehive had not changed and whilst drinking Joyce spoke of the events that had occurred at St. Anne's. Invites to a few eighteenth birthday parties, dances trips out and other things, however she had not seen much of Derek as he was seeing a girl called Maureen. As Joyce prattled on, slowly began to realise that all had changed; it was not going to be the same ever again. By the time we were thrown out, was quite inebriated and walked or rather staggered her home she holding me up. Outside her front door, we began to snog for the past two years Joyce was the first girl had physically been close to and got a wee bit too amorous to which she retorted. "NO". Was not getting anywhere anyway; needing a pee asked.

'Joyce. Where's yer bog?' Giggling said.

'You be quite, do not wake up my parents.' Opening the front door, she guided me along a dark passageway and out through a side door, whispered.

'It's at the rear of the house.'

In the darkness staggered towards the rear and found it, hopefully hitting the target. Staggering back tripped over something, fell headlong through the frozen washing hanging on the line and in the process ripped a sheet in two. Having unraveled myself found the back door, bumped along the passageway to where Joyce was waiting at the open front door, in a low voice she asked.

'What was all that noise out there? I heard a crash. You'll wake up the household; you'd better go now before my dad gets up.'

'Oh. Nothing kicked something out there; think it was a cat.' I lied. Having destroyed her mother's washing, thought it was a very good time to leave, gave her a good night peck she whispered in my ear.

'We haven't got a cat, Good night see you again soon.'

'Okay. See you later.' That was the last time was to see Joyce. Staggering home laughing at the incident, thinking how ironic the last time we went out together was the night before I went in the army and Joyce was the one, I never wrote too. Mind you did not have her address a good excuse I suppose. At home, let myself in to find Michael had just arrived in, we had a few more beers unable to stand up he put me to bed.

A blazing hangover was on the cards; around midday having recovered my senses, washed and shaved whilst mum cooked a fry up for lunch. Then Derek arrived, so she cooked him a meal as well. Much fed we went over the Nott for a few drinks and catch up on our past. After he was demobed he did get his old job back and was then going steady with a girl called Maureen who lived in the flats in Union Road, which appeared to be a strange co-incidence, did Den know her? Nevertheless could tell from his attitude that he was smitten with her. Derek reiterated what Joyce had told me. When I related my amorous ways with Joyce the previous night and the climatic end, he howled with laughter. We arranged to continue the drinking session that night.

Just like old times, we met down the Beehive swilled beer, played bar billiards, darts and swilled more beer in that order. He talked about Maureen and her family was in the process of immigrating to New Zealand and he had already received the papers and was going that summer. It was something in his infrequent letters to me; he had mentioned and asked.

'How about you come with me?'

'Hang on mate, I've just been away nearly two bleedin' years and would like to see a bit of civvy life, get a job with some money. Maybe later but not that bleedin' quick.'

'Oh well can't change your mind can see your point of view, maybe later.' We walked or staggered down to the Oval agreeing to meet the next morning at mass.

Next morning woke with another hangover but went to St. Anne's, possibly to meet up with some of the old pals however like me much the worse for wear, it was only Derek. After mass, we visited the Beehive for the hair of the dog. As we conversed, it was becoming very clear after being away for such a long period, it brought changes that could not be recaptured or rekindled. With Derek going out with his girl and me not wishing to interfere with his arrangements, left me going back to the club hoping to get a game of football, but no such luck. New young blood had secured positions in the team, there was no place for any old has bin's as they say. Out on a limb, thought much about what or how I could get back to the social life I so much enjoyed before going in the army. A period that had certainly turned my life upside down. That Sunday mum cooked a family welcome home roast lamb dinner. Kay, Eddie her husband, also Lily sat down to eat, so it was a full house with wine and a few beers that I really appreciated.

After a week of kicking my heels. On the Friday night with nothing to do decided to call Cecilia. In the bedroom reread her last letter before plucking up courage to make the phone call.

'Wanstead 1234? Hello.' recognising her mother's voice replied.

'Hello. Could I speak to Cecilia, its Joe?'

'Joe? Joe who?'

'Er. Joe Plant is Cecilia in?' A pregnant pause while she registered who Joe Plant was?

Er. Sorry Cecilia is out now, suggest you call back tomorrow she will be in then, is that all right?'

Er. Yes. Uhm all right I will call back tomorrow. Thank you.' Replaced the receiver could not be puzzled about the timing; after all it was early on a Friday night decided to go down the Club.

Saturday round about lunchtime I called Cecilia.

'Wanstead 1234? Hello.'

'Hello. Is Cecilia in now? May I speak to her please?'

'Who is this calling? Oh. You called last night. Hold on. Cecilia it is for you. It's that fellow Joe?' Clunk! Down went the handset silence then.

'Hello.'

'Heh. Cecilia it's me Joe. Just got back from Malaya. Thought I would give you a ring and thank you for writing to me, how you doing?'

'Oh Joe! Your back, bet your nice and brown with all that sunshine. When did you get back?'

'A month ago, but just got demobed last Thursday.' Nevertheless, as our conversation progressed gave her details of what was going on out there and asked what she was doing? She had changed jobs and was going out with a bloke called Steve.

'Sorry Joe, have to get ready to go out, pleased you got back safely and it's been nice chatting with you.' Getting her message replied.

'Oh. Okay thanks for writing to me, really appreciated that you have a good time. Cheerio.' Clunk. That was the last time of contact with her. Another possibility gone so had no fear of getting deeply involved anymore. Once again, all had changed; Margaret was courting a bloke by the name of Pat, an ex R.A.F. NS, Lily was going out with someone else. Derek and I had met Junior, who was going out with Anne a girl he had met at the Flamingo Jazz Club. Therefore, it left me at a loose end.

I had been home two weeks and my discharge book stated a date to report to the T.A. Unit on Thursday 7th March. With all the kit in the Uni walked to Stockwell and caught the tube to South Wimbledon. Found out that the TA place was within walking distance about a quarter of a mile away. Reporting in handed over my kit, when signing the release documents the Stores Sgt. said.

'The Commanding Officer wants to see you his office. It's at the end of the corridor on your right.'

'What for?'

'Just do it Laddie!' Although out of the bleedin' army was still getting ordered about. Knocking on his door entered to see a rather old Major with grey parted hair and a matching walrus moustache; I think he was a remnant of the First World War retorted

'You want to see me. Plants my name.'

'Ah yes. Come on in sit down, there's a good chap. Been expecting you. I see from your records, you have seen active service in Malaya. Not very pleasant what? How long have you been in England?'

'About five weeks.'

'Uhm. Not very long Eh?' I being very receptive retorted.

'No.'

'Look I would like you to sign on in the territorial army at this depot.' Taken aback by his request. Quickly replied.

'No. No thank you. I've done my bit can I go now?'

'Don't be too hasty, think about it you're still in the TA on the reserve list for a period of three years and could be recalled to do training. This TA unit is a Royal Artillery unit with Ack-Ack guns.'

'Being polite, told him where he could shove it. Nevertheless, he persisted.

'Look Plant. Your report from Malaya stated you were a good Vehicle Electrician. In addition, have a good reputation playing football. How would you like to play for our team?' Quickly thinking, "Maybe he was short of players and was looking for the likes of me to fit into his team that would mean signing papers? Moreover, was not going to be influenced by that. This was my cue".

'I know nothing about guns, only engines, spent all my time repairing them on active service. Besides I'm already playing for another team?' Twiddling a pencil, he pondered over my last statement firmly replied.

'Plant! When and if? We do call you back you will have to report here.'

Thank Christ that was the end of the interview. Unfortunately, according to him was still in the bleedin' army. Having done that chore needed to start work, money was running out and needed that too. En-route back home stopped at my old firm and was in for a big surprise? Upon entering the admin office there was no Eileen, Veronica or, Pauline but a young girl banging away at a typewriter. Harry sat at his disheveled desk, looking up exclaimed.

'Blimey where you come from? Missed you, come back for your job then Joe?' Walking over shook hands.

'Well, been on active service for the last eighteen months in the Malaya war. Nice to be back home though. '

'Yeah. Can see you're browned off. Plenty Gig Gig out there Eh? Especially in Singapore. Eh? Bring back any of those Chinese girls in yer kitbag to surprise your mum eh Joe?' His jokes were never ending.

'Nah. Do not be bleedin' daft Harry. Never was in Singapore, anyway got better sense than that. Where are all the girls then?'

'Well they've left that is. Eileen and Veronica got married, Pauline do not know. Things are not too good Joe, but John will tell you all about that. Want a cuppa?' Noticed his tie still bore signs of dinner stains, replied.

'No. Ta anyway, better go and see John he still in the D.O.?'

'No he's up in Mr. Marlow's office.'

'Okay. Have a talk with him.' Leaving the office took the stairs up to the directors office wondering what all the changes meant, surprised about the girls disappointed about Eileen. Knocking on the door the voice of John's boomed out

'Come in. '

Opening the door, immediately smelt tobacco smoke poked my head around it saw John sat at a desk engulfed in pipe smoke. No change there! Dropping his pipe onto an ashtray, he got up.

'Well I never! Look at what the cats brought in? Offered his hand, Joe! Sit down.'

Noticed his Drawing board was located next to the window puzzled at this, walked forward shaking his hand said.

'Hi John want me job back. Where's Mr. Marlow?'

'Oh you wouldn't know, but he took ill and died about six months ago. I took over his job. Where have you been the last two years? Been so long forgotten all about you.' Thinking, "Christ how could you forget me"! He listened intently as I explained all about my service life and had come back to start work. Then the bombshell.

'Sorry mate. Cannot help you were just hanging on, it might be that the firm will have to wrap up. It is all down to the Suez crisis. You heard about that didn't you?'

'Yeah we did. Anyway what does that have to do with my job, according to the Labour you've got to take me back on when I'd finished me national service.'

'Well! Er yeesss. Only if there is a job for you. But, am afraid there isn't. With the prevailing circumstances nearly all the service engineers have gone, only got a couple down in the workshop one of them is Ron...pointing to his Drawing board...as and when any drawing is required I do it. So I'm afraid work has dried up and with the current oil shortage the future does not look too bright.' Shocked at his announcement asked.

'Ain't there anything you could give me until the work starts coming in?'

'I'm afraid not, Harry will be out of a job soon he's looking around himself. Look Joe I am sorry. But the best thing I can do is give you a good reference.'

This was baffling. Finally out of the army with no job. What the sodin' 'ell had happened? Definitely in the shit, responded.

'What good with that be? I haven't been near a drawing board for two years.'

'Well! I have heard that a couple of the big companies working on coal-fired power stations are looking for Draughtsman, it might be worth your while writing to them. See what happens.'

'Who are they?'

'Foster Wheeler and the other one is Babcock and Wilcox. Both are up in London somewhere. The other thing you should do is sign on at the Labour. You will get some money until you get a job. Tell them about this interview and what I have suggested, they might have something going anyway.'

Rather dismayed left John with his "Good Luck"ringing in my ears on the way out, quickly visited Harry all he said was.

'Grim ain't it? See you around sometime. '

Walking home, miserable and mystified all because of a bleedin' oil crisis. Everything appeared to be negative, out of work, skint, whereas everyone else appeared happy and contented with their own way of life, seriously felt like going back and signing on! Now that! Would be like signing ones death warrant and certainly was not that bleedin' stupid. No! Something will turn up. Back home opened the door must have looked like as if the weight of the world was on my shoulders. Mum noticed something was up.

'How did you get on then? Got rid of your kit?'

'Yes and me job. On my way home decided to go back to Auto's ready to start work, saw John he said there was no job for me. Go back to the Labour and find another job was his words.'

'Cup of tea?'

'Please. May as well drown myself in tea.' Mum busied herself making tea asked.

'Well son what you going to do then?'

'Don't know Mum. Get myself a job somewhere. Problem is have not been near a drawing board for two years. Who's going to take me on? What's the time?'

'Nearly half past twelve, here's your tea drink that make you feel better.'

Sitting drinking the tea listened to a very lively tune on the wireless, its rhythm had my feet tapping to its beat the announcer said. 'That listeners was the new sound of "Bill Haley and his Comets" with their version of "Rock around the Clock". That sound livened me up not all was doom and gloom, at least there was music. 'Any idea what time the Labour exchange closes mum?'

'No. But am sure it will be open until five. You going to pay them a visit?'

'Got too. No money, no job might as well go they'll probably give me a job sweeping the roads. I'll go on my bike.'

'Do you think that's wise; you haven't used it for so long. It's still in the pram shed.'

'Be Okay.' Getting up sorted out the pram-shed door key; left the house, unlocking the door pulled it open, there was my trusty steed rather dirty with a rusted chain all in need of a bleedin' good clean, shaking my head shut the door went back and told mum.

'I'll walk, see you later.'

It was a cold but reasonably bright day. Arriving there found they were closed for dinner and would open again at two. With half an hour to wait went across the road to the pub and had a pint. Sharp at two was waiting for them to open the door. Ushered into an office. One of their "Thin tie Civil Service mob" interviewed me, he was not impressed when told had been on active service, fighting for Queen and Country. As far as he was concerned, was just another dodger looking for handouts signing out of work forms and looking for benefits in kind, when finished. Gruffly he asked.

'What kind of work you looking for?' Just as gruffly, answered.

'Draughtsman! In a drawing office.'

'Well let me see. What vacancies we have?' Extracting a sheave of papers from his wire paper tray with his training cast an expert eye over each page, turning over page upon page, then spoke.

'I am afraid. Nothing like it in this list. Did you have a trade in the army or, were you infantry?'

'REME! Vehicle electrician and shooting bleedin' bullets.'

'What kind of job was that?'

'Keeping the electrics working on Lorries and other vehicles and shooting bullets out of rifles to kill commies.' Not responding to my quip.

'Oh garage work...again scrutinizing his pages...No nothing there. What about the building trade there is plenty of vacancies there? However, you should go back to your old firm. By law they are obliged to take you back. Part of the agreement as laid down in the National Service Act of 1948.'

Maybe he was quite familiar with all the other bleeders like me, passing through his office who had been forced into doing anything in the army but their own trade? Getting really pissed off with this prat's attitude. Who could not give a shit about me, retorted?

'I did that this morning. Otherwise would not be paying you a visit. They are closing down. Ain't got nothing. They told me to see you lot.' Leering at me, responded.

'Well! We do not have anything you want. Now you have signed on come back next week might have something in your line then.' Interview finished. Getting up bleedin' angry about my current predicament, felt like dotting him one instead left slamming the door behind me. Back home, related all to mum and dad, his comment was.

'You'll get nothing you're looking for out of that shower. Your best bet is to do it yourself. Write away to some firms, go to the Tate Library and look in the newspapers. Some firms do advertise their vacancies that's for sure. '

'Well yeah, suppose so. I'll do it Monday too late now. Anyway I'm seeing Derek tonight so will commiserate with him.'

Dad enquired. 'How did he get on when he came out?'

'He didn't have a problem! Did you know he's applied to immigrate to New Zealand?'

'No. What does he want to do that for?'

'I don't know, says he likes the idea, he wrote to me about it ages ago wanted me to do it as well, if things don't improve might just think of joining him...A look of concern appeared on mum's face...quickly thinking, "Should not have said that"...Aw don't worry mum it won't come to that you'll see. Look mum at the moment I can't pay you anything to the household but when I get a job is that alright.' As usual, mum had the answer.

'Joe. You have been away long time without contributing so a few more weeks won't make that much difference will it?'

'No spose not but thanks, things will get better when I fully employed.'

That night Derek and I got plastered. Next-days forecast another hangover.

Monday. Up early to visit the Tate library, there was plenty of vacancies in the newspapers but not for draughtsman, those advertised were outside London. Maybe tomorrow? Leaving the library glanced across the road to where Al lived. It was about time to reunite my acquaintance with Al and then changed my mind; no doubt, he was out working. Therefore, decided to call later. The following days revealed nothing, but remembered what John had said about those two firms. The librarian was very helpful in finding their addresses. Back indoors, Mum provided the writing paper so settled down to compose two letters, then posted them.

Friday evening. As Derek was out with his girl decided to visit Al, knocking on their front door got no reply, tried again with louder bangs just about to bang the knocker again when a young girl about ten opened the door.

'Is Alan in please?'

'Yes.' She just stared at me.

'Can I see him please?'

'Yes.' Shutting the door, heard the receding sound of her running footsteps inside, as I stood waiting for what seemed ages then a voice from below hailed.

'Who is it?' Leaning over the rails looked down at Al, partially dressed in a boiler suit the top half down around his waist tied by the sleeves thus exposing a couple of pullovers he was wearing, maybe he was still feeling the cold?

'Al. It's me Joey. Come to see how yer are mate?'

'Joey! Bleedin' 'ell. Why didn't yer tell Alexis it was you she knows all about you? We don't use the door upstairs, come down this way... retreating down the steps shook hands with Al...C'mon in. When did yer get back? Shut the door behind you. Come into the kitchen and meet Lil.' Following him down a small hallway into a kitchen.

'Lil. This is Joey. He's back from Malaya.' Normal formalities.

'I'm pleased to meet you. I've heard so much about you from Alan'

'Hello Mrs. Keene. Only the good bit's I hope'

'Those and the rest of the not so good ones. Like a cup of tea?'

'Er yes please if it's no trouble.' Al interrupting

'Lil bring it into the other room by the fire, he looks like a frozen turd. C'mon Joey follow me into the sitting room.' Thinking, "He hasn't changed". The sitting room was warmed by a blazing fire Al sat down in an easy chair close to it, another two easy chairs were occupied his younger sister and brother watching a television in the corner. 'Alexis, Andrew this is Joey. Andrew move out of that chair let Joey sit down close to the fire he's frozen.'

Andrew reluctantly moved and sat down on a pouf, all Alexis did was stared at me. Al lit up a fag we chatted about the blokes in the LAD, understanding what had happened and laughed about past times. Chirping away in the background was a Budgie was sure it was trying to join in our conversation. Al had no problems with working back in his old firm. His mum brought in mugs of tea.

'Ear Joey, fancy a pint? When Patti gets here we'll go over to the Crown and have a beer or two; I know that she'll like you.' He said with confidence....but Alexis still kept staring at me that found very embarrassing.

It must have been nearly seven when the door opened, in walked a blonde bombshell in a green coat her ash blonde hair was pulled back into a roll at the back of her head, briefly glancing at me; she approached the table up against the wall behind the door. Undoing the coat buttons too reveal a light blue work coat from which she began taking change from the pockets and placing them on the table. Al said.

'Annette. This is my mate Joey I told you about.' Standing up offered my hand, taking it; she winced at my grip immediately apologized. 'I'm Sorry. Nice to meet you.'

'It's nice to meet you.' she replied but with no conviction in her tone. However, did notice her blue eyes, high cheek boned features and a tiny pair of pink lips. I was smitten. Leaving the room, she re-entered minus her overcoat underneath the wrappings of her work coat she had a good figure, at the table she began counting the money. Al enquired.

'How much did yer make in tips today then?' A sharp reply.

'None of you business.'

'Ear Joey. Annette's a hairdresser, every night counts up all her tips must be worth a bleedin' fortune by now.' A knock on the door interrupted any further discussion he got up.

'That'll be Patti, I'll bring her in and you can meet her.' About to meet his famous Patti stood up, but could not keep my eyes off Annette the beautiful ash blonde-haired girl. Al re-entering said.

'Joey! This is Patti. Were getting married in June.' So, what he had predicted was true.

'Nice to meet you Joey. At last, after all I have heard about you Alan was always talking about you, I practically know you. You glad to be home then?'

'Blimey not half, would have willing come back with Al.'

'Patti don't take your coat off, Joey's buying the beers over the Crown. I'll have a quick wash.' Immediately thought. "Hold on. He asked me out for a beer." Patti enquired.

'You coming over Annette?'

'No thank you.'

Pat! was a nice pleasant girl about my age, good looking full of laughter and by the way she conversed with me, very easy to get on with. Al returned and the three of us left the house, disappointedly without Annette. We spent the night in there until chucking out time. We talked about Malaya, about their forthcoming wedding. During the evening, my uncle Alec came in, welcomed me back and bought us a round adding.

'Joe. You visit your aunt she would like that.'

'I will Uncle. As soon as I got a job.' That night was the first night Al and Pat had been out for a very long time obviously at his invitation still saving up. Al asked.

'Want a game of football?'

'Yes, who for?'

'Meet me tomorrow about one' o'clock in the Malbey, I'll see if we can fit you in the team.'

Saturday lunchtime, in the Malbey at one of the tables Al and his mates were sat with pints of beer, all ex either Army or Air force National Servicemen. So was accepted as one of them. Standing watching as they played a hand of Solo a game I had played years before. As it progressed the captain of the football team Henry Informed me about the Pub team and where they played on Sunday's. To me very familiar places nevertheless, not in the same league as St. Anne's so no possibility of playing against them? And he promised would soon get a game.

As the Labour Exchange money was not good, strapped for cash and could not afford too many boozy sessions as Derek was essentially tied up seeing his girl friend, just as well our trips to the Beehive were not that frequent. However, some nights Michael bought me a few down his local. Hoping Al would have some news about me playing football knocked on their door, Lil opening it.

'Hello Joe. Alan's away working, I've just made some tea come in and have a cup.' Not having anything to do accepted and was ushered into their kitchen and greeted with a pleasant surprise. Sat at the table was Annette and their dad Cecil.

'Cecil this is Alan's mate Joey, just back from Malaya.'

'Hello heard about you. What work do you do?'

'Nothing. Ain't got a job.'

'Another bleedin' lay-about. Lil I'm going out to the shed.' A rather brash introduction, thinking. "His remark was uncalled for and stupid." However, Lil offered an excuse.

'Don't take any notice of him; he always goes out to his workshop outside, sit down at the table.' Placing a cup of tea in front of me as she washed and dried up continued chatting to me, when finished gave me another full cup pouring herself a tea left the room leaving me alone with Annette who lit up a fag before asking.

'Not got a job then?'

'Nope. Firms going bust or summat. What do you do?'

'Hairdresser, in a top class hairdressing salon in Wardour street.'

'Really. Know the West-end quite well; go to some of the jazz clubs.'

'I'm afraid that kind of music is not my cup of tea, ballads singing and the musical film scores.' With all the tea drinking needing the toilet, asked.

'Where's your toilet please.'

'Just at the top of the stairs, the door right in front of you.'

Excusing myself made for it. Closing the door, a very large dog began barking its head off at a small window at head height, frightening the shit out of me. Hurriedly finishing got out passing the side entrance door it attacked that too. Thank Christ it was closed tight otherwise it would had had me arse. Running back down the steps into the kitchen, a grinning Annette apologised. 'You've met Rex then? Sorry, I forgot to tell you about him he does that all the time.' We seemed to chat for hours until her dad came back in, poking his head through the doorway said.

'You still here, ain't yer got a home to go to?' Annette replied.

'Shut up Dad.' Noting his suggestion decided to leave she saw me to the door.

A few days later a letter arrived from one of the firms, requesting me to attend an interview the following Monday. Highly delighted but apprehensive at my chances decided to get out my old night school drawings and swot up. Contacted John and asked him for a reference, he told me to collect it that afternoon. Upon arriving at the Admin office found Harry had already left the firm for another job.

Monday turned out to be a smashing day, the sun was shining and spring was in the air. At South Kensington tube station asked for directions to Ixworth Place. Down Pelham Street, it is at the rear of the Michelin building, it was within walking distance. Turning into Ixworth place stood out on the pavement noticed a Sgt. in the Commissionaire Corp. Immediately thought; if this firm employs someone of his stature, thay must be big. The nameplate on the entrance stated Foster Wheeler Ltd. The Commissionaire asked.

'Can I be of assistance sir?'

'Come for an interview with the chief draughtsman.'

'Report into the receptionist inside up the flight of stairs on your left.' At the main desk told the receptionist?

'Come for an interview with Mr. Davidson the chief draughtsman.'

'Thank you please takes a seat.' The receptionist made a phone call.

After a few minutes a young girl came down asked. 'Mr. Plant?'

Standing up. 'Yes.'

'Please follow me.' She escorted me up flights of stairs to the second floor through a big drawing office, with row upon row of drawing boards occupied by draughtsmen in white coats. In comparison to the two drawing boards at Auto's, this was quite a disturbing revelation. The girl led me into yet another drawing office where a few young girls were working at some of the boards and as I passed by showed much interest. The experience of walking through a real Drawing Office blew my mind, after two years of nothing, with heart bumping away inside me, was I ready? My escort left me at the door of a big office saying.

'Mr. Davidson this is a Mr. Plant to see you.'

'Mr. Plant. Come on in please sit down. Thank you for attending.' Recognising his accent as Geordie, could understand him perfectly well. Mr. Davidson was a big stocky fellow with a cropped head of graying hair, began by asking.

'Well Mr. Plant what is your work experience?' Having related all about my past employment and two years of N.S. he said. 'So you have not worked in a drawing office for two years?...Immediately thought, "Here we Go"...That's correct sir....What good will you be to me?...At this point my heart sank. I had to think of something quick. Producing John's letter handed it to him...I have a reference from my original employer...Oh you went to the trouble of obtaining a reference then?' To me, this appeared not the usual practice, however he, putting on a pair of horn rimmed glasses, opened the letter now and then, raised a bushy eyebrow and in quite an unusual fashion shrug of his shoulders, removing his glasses before he could say anything, I interrupted.

'All I can add to the letter is. Drafting is the only job I've ever done and wanted to do since leaving technical college.' This last statement prompted him to ask several questions about the type of education, before asking.

'Mr. Plant, what certificates did you get and did you attend night school? '

'School leaving certificate and did attended night school but had to leave it half way through the course to join the army. But am prepared to rejoin next autumn!'

Once again picking up the letter, he studied it. Removing his glasses remained silent, and then with a shrug of shoulders spoke.

'Your academic and previous working period is of mechanical background, in view of your current circumstances I am going to take a risk. If, I was to offer you a job, when could you start?' Both hands tightly gripping the blazer sleeves promptly answered.

'To-morrow sir.'

'No. What about next Monday nine 'o'clock. However, please understand that your employment will only be based on a month's trial. Regarding your salary that will be six pound fifty shillings per week subject to normal deductions. There will be overtime, paid at time and a half. Is that acceptable to you?' Thinking. "Blimey. Six pound fifty shillings a week that's a fortune in comparison with the three pounds two years ago".

'Yes. Thank you sir. That would be acceptable.' Standing up he asked.

'Mr. Plant. What's your first name John?'

'No sir. Joe.' Extended his hand we shook.

'Right Joe. I will confirm what we have agreed in writing. I take it; you do own your own drawing instruments, set squares? As we do not provide any, apart from pencils etc.

'Yes. I do own a set bought when first started work.'

'Good. See you Monday nine' o'clock sharp.'

Walking back through the two drawing office's, a very happy man. At last. I had a job and a creditable wage. Now all I had to do was wait for his letter before going back to the Labour to sign off. They were no bleedin' good anyway.

Thursday, two letters fluttered through the letterbox, one addressed to Mr. Plant and the other a Brown envelope O.M.H.S. addressed to 23112429 Cfn. Plant. Immediately thought. "Oh. Shit it's the TA. Have to report back for training"? Discarding that opened up the other one. It was confirmation from Foster Wheeler, the start date wage, etc. etc. That lifted my spirit, then opened the other one. Unexpected. It was my final army payment a Postal Order for £20.19s.3p. (Overtime pay). Thinking, "Bleedin' 'ell I'm rich, got a job and solvent again. On my way to the Labour Exchange, decided to change it at the Post Office. At the Labour exchange in gratitude for his efforts or lack of, told the. "Thin tie, Civil Service bloke". What he could do and stuck two figures up. Saturday lunchtime met Al. at the Malbey, told him my good news.

'That's bleedin' good. It's your round anyway.' Henry asked.

'Can you play tomorrow? The games at Mitcham Common meet at the pub at twelve.'

'Yes. That's great thank you.' I having bought the round Al suggested.

'Ear, you come around the Crown on Tuesday night. We're having drink to celebrate Patti's twenty first birthday.' Delighted to accept might meet his sister again.

On the Sunday. Played a good game. The future was looking very rosy.

The Malbey Team

Monday, well before time arrived at Ixworth Place, had to wait in reception until sent for. Mr. Davidson welcomed me and introduced me to a Mr. Brown. (Ex N.S. Army Officer) my new Section Leader of the Pulverized Fuel Section. Similar questions were asked, as well as my service time (which raised his eyebrows) before he introduced me to other draughtsman in his section. Most of whom had done their National Service; one of them was Pete Burridge ex RAF. Who had only been demobed about two months before? Once again; being accepted into the brotherhood as one of them. The D.O. I had walked through to get to Mr. Davidson was a separate entity, they were designing Oil Refineries. Whereas The D.O. I was working in contained about sixty drawing boards with several different sections dealing with; various design areas of a Power Station. The girls at the other drawing boards were tracers, all pretty and young, one was about to immigrate to Canada.

I was allocated a drawing board. My first drawing assignment was to redraw a Mechanical Coal Feeder and to my concern, was a complicated piece of machinery, with many different parts separately drawn on other drawings that had to integrated within the drawing to illustrate a final General Arrangement incurring plenty of detail, printing and a completion date of one month. I was being tested out but did not mind.

That first day brought me to my senses. What I had drawn at Auto's was nothing compared to what was expected of me. It took me all day to figure it and its associated parts out and wondered if, being away from a drawing board for two years. Would I be capable and more so accepted? However as the days went by Pete and the others helped me a great deal.

Tuesday night. Did meet Alan and Pat in the Crown and had a couple of drinks before Lil, Cecil and Annette arrived for a celebration drink. Cecil, to say the least was very direct and really did not know which way to take him. Anyway, things went fine and started chatting to Annette. The evening finished back at their house for a coffee. Plucking up courage asked Annette out for a drink the following Friday, the very day would receive my first civvy wage packet and together with the army back pay would be flush with money. To my surprise, she accepted.

Friday night, smartly dressed called on Annette, we walked to the "Canton". A rather IN pub for those days. We spent the evening there, she drinking Babycham's me with pints. Escorting her home, suggested we did the same thing the following Friday she agreed, we repeated the outing. There was no kissing or cuddling. The following weekend, was Easter so asked, would she like to see a film on the Thursday at the Brixton Astoria, again she accepted. We caught a bus into Brixton, the film showing was "Brothers in Law" and the cinema was packed. After it had finished, as it was a warm night we walked home, suggested we might stop for a drink at a Pub. (The one opposite the Labour Exchange). We tried, but with the Sunday licensing laws no drinks after ten, we walked the rest of the way to her home, kissing her goodnight she responded. It was the beginning of our courtship.

To cut a long story short. During 1957 I was accepted at work and spent the next thirteen years at Foster Wheeler before moving on. Saturday June 22nd. my 21st birthday, we had a wow of a party. The following Friday the 28th. Derek left for New Zealand. Very disappointed to lose such a good mate. The next day the 29th. Alan married Pat. In September, returned to night school to continue my studies. During the year up the west end a chance meeting with George occurred, whilst both of us were out with our girlfriends, however never saw him again and likewise with Den he did get in touch with me and arranged to meet up with Al in the Malbey. To talk over old times, Den had signed on again that was the last we saw of him.

The following year 1958, The Mawbey Pub football team did well winning the league. On 20 September, Margaret married Pat. That was the day I proposed to Annette and she accepted. On September 5th. 1959. Annette & I were married and are still happily married. During that period we have sired three children, two girls and a boy and now blessed with seven grandchildren.

Annette & Me.

In retrospect, looking back on my days as a National Serviceman, which interrupted and took me away from my once easy and enjoyable way of life nevertheless, did provide me with a chance to see other places and cultures of life that possibly would not have even thought of venturing out to see. It did not do me any harm, instead it certainly was informative, meeting new comrades, packed with excitement and incidents, good and bad and like many others National Servicemen it did have an effect on my life and changed it quite dramatically. I would never have met Alan out in Malaya, met and married his beautiful sister Annette, lost my job and found a better one. Now years later have learnt much more about the so-called "Emergency." An undeclared and forgotten War, which lasted twelve long and brutal bloody years, incurring the loss of life of some 2,220 Commonwealth Servicemen, a high majority of which were National Servicemen who buried in Malaya would never again tread the shores of England, as we that were so fortunate and grateful to do so.

CHAPTER TWENTY-FIVE
MALAYSIA REVISITED.

May 1981. My employer asked if, I would consider a six months assignment to Jakarta and Singapore. Having spent periods on assignments in several other different countries, discussed the subject with my wife Annette and agreed to the conditions. Therefore, along with another work colleague Andy boarded a flight at Heathrow to Singapore, immediately transferring onto an Indonesian Airways flight to Jakarta the capital of Indonesia. Our accommodation in a Hotel was for two days until we were joined by two additional colleagues and were settled into a company bungalow, to be looked after by a House servant, cook, a cleaner and a driver, who drove us to and from our place of work. The first Saturday afternoon was spent getting acclimatized to the extreme heat and with easy access to the roof of the bungalow we spent some time up there sunbathing, although very overcast it was extremely hot and humid as I recalled when first in Malaya some twenty-six years before and felt the same experience of being exposed to the sun. Andy stated when he was exposed to the sun he went brown, he was in for a shock as later that evening turned out to be the colour of a lobster and took a few days to get over his sun burn and embarrassment.

The following day we were taken to our place of work and shown what our task was I was put in charge of the team and very quickly set the wheels in motion, capitalizing on the knowledge of all the team reorganised the working procedures that were being followed by the Indonesian Nationals.   Within weeks our efforts changed the scenario and had gained valuable time.   As a team got on very well together and it was to be a strange but fascinating period of working with Indonesian Nationals, who appeared to employ six Nationals to one ex pat. As time went by, encountered a Typhoon that had water cascading through the roof drenching the girls and all the paper work, subsequently they dried out the paperwork laid out over the floor with steam irons (Hilarious), felt earthquake tremors. Mastering the job within a matter of months had progressed it so much that the six-month assignment had been reduced, therefore before returning to England Andy and I were scheduled to go to Singapore, as it happened Andy went to Battan Island south of Singapore. However being in that environment recalled something in the distant past whilst sat in the Naafi in Ipoh drinking beer, someone had mentioned about hoping to return back some twenty-five years later, that very thought set me wondering about going back to mainland Malaya and to Ipoh. It was too good an opportunity to miss, having already suggested to Annette she should fly out and we would have a holiday in Singapore, it was agreed that Annette together with Alan and Pat (Patti) would all meet in Singapore, then catch a plane to Penang and spend a fortnight there, before returning to Singapore see the sights before leaving for Blighty. I arranged their flights through our London office, whilst in Jakarta I arranged the hotels in Penang and Singapore, however upon leaving Jakarta flew into Changi airport and was surprised at the enormity of Singapore's skyscrapers and ultra-modern way of life, possibly in the older parts and outskirts had remained the same but obviously drastic rebuilding changes had changed the City.

After a period of six months away, we all met at Changi airport where we transferred onto an internal flight to Penang. It was during the flight having got permission from the stewardess's who provided glasses, opened a bottle of champagne I had purchased in Singapore. When the cork went off with a loud bang it caused much concern amongst the other passengers, the stewardess had to reassure them and calmed them all down. The flight did not take long before we landed at Penang airport.

PENANG . 1981.

To accommodate all the luggage had to hire two taxi's for the drive out to Ferringi Beach Hotel, arriving in the early evening. much too late to see anything, but settle in have a meal, a few drinks and make plans to hire a driver to take us back to Taiping , Ipoh and finally a trip back up to the Cameron's. It soon became common knowledge by the Servants, that Al and I were National Servicemen during the Emergency, revisiting their country, word got back to the Malayan hotel owners, who welcomed us and bent over backwards to accommodate us, the warmth and gratitude shown was unexpected but gratefully accepted. When they learnt of our plans they placed at our disposal, a car and a driver named David, they even arranged our accommodation in Ipoh and in the Cameron Highlands. We spent three days at the Hotel to recuperate from their long haul flight. During those three days were taken by car to see the sights of Penang a place briefly visited by Al and me, so many years before but not seen. The only way to describe our ventures within this story is by a series of photographs that in many cases relate back to passages within the previous chapters and trust the reader, may even recall similar sights of their involvement during their time spent in Malaya many years before. (But not at the Ferringi Beach Hotel)

Left view from Veranda

Ferringi Beach Hotel

Right view from Veranda

Relaxing poolside

Malay dress

Treated as special guest
Candelabras on our table
not on any of the others.

Floating around.

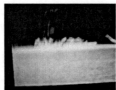
Tenku Abdul Rahmans
Beach Bungalow

Caught the big one.

Patti caught one too

Swimming off the Boat

Annette
My Pearl of the Orient.

Miles of White sandy beaches

Snake Temple

Many Buddhist Temples

Longest reclining Buda.

Batu Maung Chinese Fishing Village

Dragon Temple

Funicular Railway

Penang Hill Stop. Penang Hill

Penang Hill

George Town Time for a Fag

Penang Ferry

Passing Ferry Boat

TAIPING 81

In Georgetown we crossed on the ferry onto mainland Malaya, through Butterworth down to Taiping, where our stay was to be short . David our driver suggested we visit his Aunt the owner of a Chinese Café where we had a superb Chinese meal before taking to the road again enroute to Ipoh.

Welcome Taiping.

David's Aunts Kitchen

Time for a Chinese meal

IPOH 81

Our scheduled visit to Ipoh was to be a two day stop over just to revisit our old haunts on the south side of the river Ipoh. As we drove in the first sight was the Central Pedang and the Railway station, then on to the RUBY Cinema. We were to stay in a small Hotel owned by the Ferringi Hotel; it was comfortable and adequate for our purposes, of walking about in the main streets of Ipoh as we knew them. It would have been quite a surprise for Annette and Patti if we had taken them to the Jubilee Park for a dance, unfortunately that had all gone. As was the Federal Muslim Curry house. Ipoh had changed but not to the extent that we had expected.

Old and New Malaya

Gateway entrance to IPOH

Central Padang

Ruby Cinema

Site of Jubilee

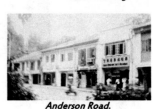
Anderson Road.

Chinatown Market

Back of the Odeon

Jalan Abdul Jahlil

Our Football Pitch

Bungalow Opposite

Site of 15.19th Lancers & (R) our LAD

Outside Sgt's Mess

Looking back from LAD

Site of Heli Crash & old Naafi building.

Outside the MRS

Back of Camp/Latrines on left

Girls Convent Lane

R.C Church

En Route to Tapah Cameron's In Distance

Leaving Ipoh en route to the Cameron's could visually see them in the distance and stopped at a café at Tapah before taking the winding road up to the Cameron's.

Café at Tapah

Road up to Cameron's

TANAH RATA

CAMERON HIGHLANDS 81

As we drove up the winding road, the weather was fine, half way up there was no sign of the Saki Village instead a café with quite a few cars parked. Up onwards and upward into Tanah Rata again feeling the change in temperature, before we reached the Cameron's. Visible signs of changes were evident, a few new hotels and shops. We were staying at the Smokehouse hotel, a place Gerry and I had only seen from the outside in 1956 when were at the RC Mission House, then it was an Officers Only establishment. We were welcomed, shown to our rooms endowed with Four Posters Beds, the height of luxury. Back in the lounge downstairs, a Colonial English Tariff was presented. Cucumber Sandwiches, Scones and Blue Valley Tea. Our stay was very comfortable, yet cold at night. During the day we found the old LAD although occupied by locals and a visit to the Roman Catholic Mission house proved useful, but could not understand a word spoken as the Brother was FRENCH and he could not understand me. Visited a waterfall and took a walk around the Golf Course. The Cameron's was a delightful place to stay but we had to leave. On our way down stopped to taste the Durian fruit extremely sweet very tasty and smelt like foul stale garlic. We bought one but David insisted it travel in the boot Why do not know?

Smokehouse Hotel

Officers Only (not in 81)

Tea & Cucumber sandwiches

Four Posters.

LAD Parade Ground

LAD Sheds

R.C/R & R Missionary House.

Old BMH

Waterfalls

On the way down

Blue Valley

Tasting the Durian Fruit

FAREWELL PENANG 81

We made haste back to Penang for our final but brief stay. During which time the staff had really warmed to us and joined us in discussing what had happened during and since the Emergency. Strange as it may seem they being much younger were born well after its end, and they showed their appreciation for the part the British played in ridding their country of Communist Rule. In our brief but memorable stay in Malaya, even after twenty-five years we had seen some changes at the places we had visited and were convinced that more changes would take place in the future, maybe in another twenty-five years, we would return and not recognise anything.

The Management and staff turned out to see us off and presented Al and I with a small Plaque to remember them by.

If ever you want to return to Malaysia and wish to stay in Penang, can recommend a very hospitable and welcome at the Ferringi Bay Beach Hotel.

Last Supper

Fond Farewells.

The Plaque

A Friend.
Strengthens the heart...
Repairs the hurts...
Encourages the discovery...
Dissolves the pain...
Banishes the loneliness...
Understands the anxieties...
Increases the Joy...
Deepens the spirit...
Frees the soul...

SINGAPORE 81

Our flight to Singapore did not take long and upon reflection would like to have travelled down by train, but time was short and flying was the quickest route. Both Al and I had never seen Singapore having only had a brief stay upon arrival and departures at Nee Soon. There was nowhere, we could say we were to revisit, and went along with the other tourist, visiting various places of interest. The Gold Street full of shops selling Gold with armed guards everywhere. The Railway station, Raffles Hotel the Britannia Club where all servicemen went to have a beer and a swim in its pool. There was no Old World, Happy World, New World or Bugie Street, again only names we had heard about. However, we did find an old Café off the central boulevard reminiscent of years gone by, where we had a Tiger beer, much to Al's displeasure or, amusement. 'Just Froth.'

After all those years, something that had not changed, we could not get away from it. Just another mishap was when he left his false teeth in the Sheridan Hotel, overnight the ever clever Chinese decided to have them gold plated. Silly prat, do not think he was amused.

We took the cable car to Sentossa Island but it was during a monsoon downpour and was unable to see much of its attractions. We can only say Singapore was somewhere all those twenty-five years before we never did get to see, and cannot provide a good impression of them then and now, except the extreme humidity that was still very high. However, Malaya had been granted their Independence in 1957 and by a treaty signed in 1963: between Malaya, Singapore, Brunei, Sabah, Sarawak, had formed the country of Malaysia. Nevertheless Malaya was the place we shall never forget and gratefully the People of the Malayan Peninsula will never forget us, as they had proved during our brief and memorable stay.

Sky Scrapers

Sheridan Hotel

Singapore Center

Raffles Corner

Britannia Club

Select your own meal 50c

Still Frothy Beer

Monsoon Ditches

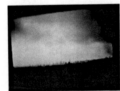
Overcast Sky

The Station Out and In Lines

Farewell Singapore

ooOoo

NB this is a story about the comraderie that was formed by many during their term of office as Conscripted National Servicemen. They did not want to do it, but I am sure that they like me had some great times apart from the shit that was dished out! I sincerely trust that the chapters within my story do relate to similar incidents albeit under different cercumstances that occurred to thousands of others during their 'Term Of Office' For all of us. It was a period of you had to do it. No if's or buts, and for many that did enjoy that way of life did re-enlist Good Luck to them. Nevertheless, I can hosestly say that I now look back with pride that I became one of the millions of young Conscipts who did survive to tell the tale.